W9-BFL-775

Women's Movements in the Global Era

Women's Movements in the Global Era

The Power of Local Feminisms

Amrita Basu
EDITOR

WESTVIEW
PRESS

Westview Press was founded in 1975 in Boulder, Colorado, by notable publisher and intellectual Fred Praeger. Westview Press continues to publish scholarly titles and high-quality undergraduate- and graduate-level textbooks in core social science disciplines. With books developed, written, and edited with the needs of serious nonfiction readers, professors, and students in mind, Westview Press honors its long history of publishing books that matter.

Copyright © 2017 by Westview Press
Published by Westview Press,
An imprint of Perseus Books
A Hachette Book Group company
2465 Central Avenue
Boulder, CO 80301
www.westviewpress.com

All rights reserved. Printed in the United States of America. No part of this book may be reproduced in any manner whatsoever without written permission except in the case of brief quotations embodied in critical articles and reviews.
Every effort has been made to secure required permissions for all text, images, maps, and other art reprinted in this volume.

Westview Press books are available at special discounts for bulk purchases in the United States by corporations, institutions, and other organizations. For more information, please contact the Special Markets Department at 2300 Chestnut Street, Suite 200, Philadelphia, PA 19103, or call (800) 810-4145, ext. 5000, or e-mail special. markets@perseusbooks.com.

Library of Congress Cataloging-in-Publication Data
Names: Basu, Amrita, 1953- editor.
Title: Women's movements in the global era : the power of local feminisms / Amrita Basu, editor.
Description: Second edition. | Boulder, CO : Westview Press, [2017] | Includes bibliographical references and index.
Identifiers: LCCN 2016035715 (print) | LCCN 2016045451 (ebook) | ISBN 9780813350127 (hardcover) | ISBN 9780813350639 (ebook)
Subjects: LCSH: Feminism--History--21st century.
Classification: LCC HQ1155 .W686 2017 (print) | LCC HQ1155 (ebook) | DDC 305.4209--dc23
LC record available at https://lccn.loc.gov/2016035715
PB ISBN: 978-0-8133-5012-7
EBOOK ISBN: 978-0-8133-5063-9

10 9 8 7 6 5 4 3 2 1

For my mother,
Rasil Basu

Contents

Acknowledgments

This second edition of *Women's Movements in a Global Era* includes both substantially revised and new chapters. I am grateful to all the authors for their excellent contributions and for their willingness to engage in this collaborative project. Sadly, Ana Alice Alcantara Costa passed away in 2014. Her dear friend and collaborator Cecilia Sardenberg honors her vital influence on an earlier version of this chapter and feminist scholarship and activism by identifying her as co-author of the chapter on Brazil. Elaine Salo wrote the chapter on South Africa while battling a grave illness but did not live to see the book in print. We mourn her loss and are honored to include her contribution.

Katharine Moore at Westview Press has been enthusiastic, efficient and encouraging. Three Amherst College students, Ayoung Kim, Jessica Maposa and Ashley Perry, have assisted with the manuscript. My greatest debt is to Kate Hartford, who served as a developmental editor for the book. Having worked for many years with the Ford Foundation in Beijing, Kate is enormously knowledgeable about many of the issues this book addresses. She is also a fine editor. Kate sent the authors detailed and constructive feedback on their chapters and helped keep the project on track. This book is far better for her efforts.

My mother inspired my interest in feminism and began my practical feminist training while working at the UN Secretariat's branch on women's rights. I accompanied her to the first world conference on women in Mexico City in 1975 and to women's conferences in many other parts of the world thereafter. I learned from her about the energizing, unwieldy process of organizing global women's conferences and about the power of local feminisms. This book is for her with loving appreciation.

Abbreviations and Glossary

31DWM: 31st December Women's Movement
ACFODE: Action for Development
ACWF: All-China Women's Federation
ACT: American College Testing
ADFM: Association Démocratique des Femmes du Maroc or Democratic Association of Moroccan Women
adivasi: tribal
AFSPA: Armed Forces Special Powers Act
AFTURD: l'Association des Femmes Tunisiennes pour la Recherche sur le Développement or Association of Tunisian Women for Research on Development
AIDS: Acquired Immune Deficiency Syndrome
AIDWA: All India Democratic Women's Association
AIWC: All India Women's Conference
amanat: treasure
AMB: Articulation of Brazilian Women
AMNLAE: Luisa Amanda Espinoza Association of Nicaraguan Women
ANC: African National Congress
ANCWL: African National Congress Women's League
Anjoman Rahai Zan: Association for Woman's Emancipation
ANNA: "No to Violence" Association
APVVU: Andhra Pradesh Vyavsaya Vrithodala Union
APWA: All Pakistan Women's Association
Arab Spring: Uprisings against corrupt dictatorships in Tunisia, Egypt, Libya, Algeria, and Bahrain
ARD: Alliance for Rural Democracy
ATFD: l'Association Tunisienne des Femmes Démocrates or Association of Tunisian Democratic Women
autonomas: enjoys autonomy
awami: people's
AWID: Association for Women in Development
BCM: Black Consciousness Movement

BEWC: Black European Women's Council
bint: daughter of
BJP: Bharatiya Janata Party
BLM: Black Lives Matter
BPFA: Beijing Platform for Action
BPO: Business Process Outsourcing
BWL: Bantu Women's League
CACA: Christian Apostolic Churches Alliance
CARE: Cooperative for Assistance and Relief Everywhere
CBWM: Committee of the Bulgarian Women's Movement
CCP: Chinese Communist Party
CCT: Conditional Cash Transfer
CDD: Catholics for the Right to Choose
CEDAW: Convention on the Elimination of All Forms of Discrimination Against Women
CEDLAS: Centro de Estudios Distributivos Laborales y Sociales or Center for Distributive, Labor and Social Studies
CEE: Central and Eastern European
CEHAT: Centre for Enquiry into Health and Allied Themes
CEPALSTAT: The database of ECLAC—the Economic Commission for Latin America and the Caribbean
CEWIGO: Center for Women in Governance
chaddi: underwear/panty
Chipko movement: literally hug; a movement to protect the trees from deforestation in North India
CID: Crime Investigation Department
CIDDEF: Centre d'Information et Documentation sur les Droits de l'Enfant et de la Femme or Center for Information and Documentation on the Rights of Women and Children
CIS: Commonwealth of Independent States
CLADEM: Comité de América Latina y El Caribe para la Defensa de los Derechos de la Mujer or Committee for Latin America and the Caribbean for the Defense of Women's Rights
CLRA: Communal Land Rights Act
CNDM: Conselho Nacional dos Direitos da Mulher or National Council for Women's Rights
CoE: Council of Europe
COO: Chief Operating Officer
CONTRALESA: Council for Traditional Leaders
COSATU: Congress of South Africa Trade Unions
COSEF: Conseil Sénégalais des Femmes or Senegalese Council of Women
CPI: Communist Party of India
CPSU: Communist Party of the Soviet Union
CREDIF: Centre de Recherche, d'Etudes, de Documentation et d'Information sur la Femme or Center of Research on Documentation and Information about Women

CSD: Campaign of Survival and Dignity
CSOs: civil society organizations
CSP: Code de Statut Personnel or Code of Personal Law
CSWU: Communist Czechoslovak Women's Union
CTOP: Choice of Termination of Pregnancy Act
cuidadanos y cuidadanas: male and female citizens
Dalit: Scheduled Caste or untouchable
damini: lightning
DEAM: Delegacias Especializadas de Atendimento à Mulher or Police Stations for Battered Women
dilaasa: crisis center for domestic violence victims
diyeh: blood money or compensation rate
dowry: price parents must pay groom's family for daughter's marriage
dupattas: lightweight scarves
EC: European Commission
ECC: End Conscription Campaign
ECOWAS: Economic Community of West African States
EEC: European Economic Community
encuentros: gatherings for sharing ideas, or encounters
ENEM: Exame Nacional do Ensino Médio or National High School Exam
EOTF: Equal Opportunities for All Trust Fund
ESF: European Structural Fund
Etehad Melli Zanan: National Unity of Women
EU: European Union
EWL: European Women's Lobby
FAOW: Forum Against Oppression of Women
farayand-mehvar: process-centered
FAS: Femme Africa Solidarité or African Women's Solidarity
FCRA: Foreign Contribution Regulation Act
FEDSAW: Federation of South African Women
feminista: feminist
feministómetro: feminist yardstick
femocrat: feminist bureaucrat
FIDH: International Federation of Human Rights
fiqh: Islamic jurisprudence
FIS: Front Islamique du Salut or Islamic Salvation Front
FMC: Cuban Women's Federation
FMLA: Family and Medical Leave Act
FOWODE: Forum for Women in Democracy
FPL: Family Protection Law
FRA: Forest Rights Act 2006
FUNCW: Fourth United Nations Conference on Women
GDP: Gross Domestic Product
GEAR: Growth, Employment and Redistribution Strategy
GM: Green Movement

GONGO: a governmental nongovernmental organization
GUPW: General Union of Palestinian Women
GWU: Garment Workers' Union
hadith: sayings attributed to the Prophet Mohammad
Hamgarayi Zanan: Convergence of Women
heiba: respect
himaya: guidance and protection
HIV: Human Immunodeficiency Virus
HIVOS: Humanistisch Instituut voor Ontwikkelingssamenwerking or Human-
    ist Institute for Cooperation
HRCP: Human Rights Commission of Pakistan
hudud: punishments
I CNPM: I Conferência Nacional de Políticas para Mulheres, or First National
    Conference on Policies for Women
I PNPM: I Plano Nacional de Políticas para Mulheres, or First National Plan
    of Public Policies for Women
IACHR: Inter-American Commission on Human Rights
IBGE: Brazilian Institute of Geography and Statistics
IBOPE: Instituto Brasileiro de Opinião Pública e Estatística or Brazilian Insti-
    tute of Public Opinion and Statistics
ICCPR: International Covenant on Civil and Political Rights
ICPD: International Conference on Population and Development
ICT: Information and Communication Technologies
IDRC: International Development Research Centre
II: international institutions
ijtihad: reasoning
ILO: International Labor Organization
IMCAW: Inter-Ministerial Committee for the Advancement of Women's Status
INSP: Islamic National Salvation Party
intifada: Palestinian uprising
INAMUJER: National Women's Institute
INGO: international nongovernmental organization
institucionalizadas: those who sought change through formal institutions
IPC: Indian Penal Code
IR: Islamic Republic
IREX: International Research and Exchanges Board
Islamist: supporter of Islamic revivalism
IWD: International Women's Day
IWF: Independent Women's Forum
JACWR: Joint Action Committee on Women's Reservation
jagruti: awareness
jalsa: a gathering
Jamiát Bidari Zan: Society for Awakening of Woman
Kanoon Shahrvandi Zanan: Women's Citizenship Center
KGB: Komitet Gosudarstvennoy Bezopasnosti or State Security Committee

kgotla: traditional ruling council
Khwendo Tolana: Sister's Group
LCWRI: Lawyers Collective Women's Rights Initiative
LGBT: lesbian, gay, bisexual, and transgender
Madaran-e Azadar: Mourning Mothers, or Mothers of Laleh Park
Madaran-i Kampaign: Mothers of the Campaign
madrassahs: religious institutions
Majlis: Parliament
Mardan baraye Barabari: Men for Equality
MARS: Mahila Atma Raksha Samiti or Women's Self Defense Association
MAS: Movement for Socialism
MDGs: Millennium Development Goals
Melli-Mazhabi: national-Islamic groups
MENA: Middle East and North Africa
militantes: party cadre
MFI: Monetary Financial Institutions
MIFTAH: Palestinian Initiative for the Promotion of Global Dialogue and Democracy
MINMUJER: Ministry of Woman's Popular Power and Gender Equality
MoEF: Ministry of Environment, Forest and Climate Change
MOLLI: Moscow Organization of Lesbian Literature and Art
motalebeh-mehvar: demand-centered
Movimiento de Integración y Liberación Honosexual: Law to Establish Measures Against Discrimination
MPLA: People's Movement for the Liberation of Angola or Movimento Popular de Libertação de Angola
MSM: men having sex with men
MST: The Landless People Movement
Mujeres Creando: Women Creating
Mujeres y Asamblea Constituyente: Women and Constituent Assembly
mutá: temporary marriage
MYW: Maendeleo ya Wanawake
NALSA: National Legal Services Authority
naw-andishan dini: new Islamic intellectuals
NBCC: National Building Construction Corporations
NCA: National Constituent Assembly
NCW: National Commission for Women
NCWA: Native and Coloured Women's Association
NCWD: National Council for Women and Development
NCWI: National Council of Women in India
NEIM: Nucleus of Interdisciplinary Women's Studies
NEWW: Network East West Women
NFIW: National Federation of Indian Women
NGOs: non-governmental organizations
NMEW: National Mission for Empowerment of Women
nirbhaya: fearless

NIS: Newly Independent States
#NiUnaMenos: Not One Less
Novib: Netherlands Organisation for International Assistance
NOW: National Organization for Women
NPA: National Plan of Action
NRM: National Resistance Movement
nüxingzhuyi: feminine-ism
nüquanzhuyi: women's right/power-ism
NWC: National Women's Coalition
NYWF: New York Women's Foundation
OSC: One-Stop Centre or Nirbhaya Centre
OST: Socialist Organization of Workers
Oxfam: Oxford Committee for Famine Relief
PA: Palestinian Authority
PAGFB: Persons Assigned Gender Female at Birth
PAISM: Programa de Assistência Integral à Saúde da Mulher or Program of
    Integral Assistance to Women's Health
PFWAC: Palestinian Federation of Women Action Committees
pitsos: traditional ruling council
PJD: Justice and Development Party (Morocco)
PLO: Palestine Liberation Organization
PO: Protection Officers
pouya: dynamic (reasoning)
PR: proportional representation
PR: Rewmi Party
PRC: People's Republic of China
PS: Socialist Party
PSU: United Socialist Party
PT: Partido dos Trabalhadores or Workers' Party
PWDVA: Protection of Women from Domestic Violence
qisas: retaliation
RACCW: Russian Association of Crisis Centers for Women
Rahat: ensures socio-legal support for victims and survivors
rajol: male, or a politically experienced and knowledgeable person
RDP: Reconstruction and Development Program
RSS: Rashtriya Swayam Sewak Sangh
RWM: Rural Women's Movement
saathin: friend
SADF: South African Defence Force
sati: widow immolation
Sazandegi: era of construction under Hasemi Rafsanjani
SEDLAC: Socio-Economic Database for Latin America and the Caribbean
SENASP: Secretaria Nacional de Segurança Pública or National Secretariat of
    Public Security
SERNAM: National Women's Service

SESM: Sociological Study of Women
SEWA: Self-Employed Women's Association
Sex Alone: the term qualifying the constitutional prohibition of gender discrimination
SEZ: Special Economic Zone
shalwar kameez: tunic and baggy trousers
shehadah: courts
SHG: self-help group
sighe: temporary marriage
SMART: Specific, Measurable, Achievable, Reliable, and Time-bound
SMS: Short Message Service
sunnati: traditionalist (jurisprudence)
SWC: Soviet Women's Committee
TAC: Treatment Action Campaign
Taghyir Baraye-Barabary: Change for Equality
Tahirih Qurratu'l-Ayn: also known as Fatemeh Zarrin-Taj
TCB: Traditional Courts Bill
thub: traditional peasant woman's dress
TISS: Tata Institute of Social Sciences
"Todos somos feministas!": "We are all feminists!"
TUC: Trades Union Congress
UAF: l'Union d'Action Feminine or Union of Feminist Action
UFBA: Federal University of Bahia
UGTT: Union Générale Tunisienne du Travail or the Tunisian General Labor Union
UK: United Kingdom
ukhot: a sister
ulema: clerics
UN: United Nations
UNAIDS: Joint United Nations Programme on HIV/AIDS
UNCRPD: United Nations Convention on Rights of Persons with Disabilities
UNESCO: United Nations Educational, Scientific and Cultural Organization
UNIFEM: United Nations Development Fund for Women (now UN Women)
UPA: United Progressive Alliance
URD: Union for Democratic Renewal
URW: Union of Russian Women
USAID: United States Agency for International Development
US-NIS Consortium: United States and New Independent States Consortium
US: United States
USSR: Union of Soviet Socialist Republics
UWESO: Uganda Women's Effort to Save Orphans
UWONET: Uganda Women's Network
UWOPA: Uganda Women Parliamentary Association
UWT: Umoja wa Wanawake wa Tanzania, or Union of Women of Tanzania
VAWA: Violence Against Women Act

velayet-e motlaqe faqih: absolute guardianship
VHP: Vishwa Hindu Parishad
WAF: Women's Action Forum
WAMA: Wanawake na Maendeleo
WAVE: Women Against Violence Europe
WB: Women's Budget
WCALC: Women's Center for Legal Aid and Counseling
WCSW: Women's Committee for Social Work
WDG: Women's Democracy Group
WDN-U: Women's Democracy Network—Uganda Chapter
WAF: Women's Action Forum
WF: Women's Federation
WFM: Young Women for Minorities
WFS: Women's Feature Service
WIA: Women's Indian Association
WIDE: Women in Development Europe
WIDF: Women's International Democratic Federation
WILPF: Women's International League for Peace and Freedom
WLP: Women's Learning Partnership for Rights, Development, and Peace
WLUML: Women Living under Muslim Laws
WNC: Women's National Coalition
WOR: Women of Russia
WPA: World Plan of Action
WSF: World Social Forum
WWII: World War II
YFA: Young Feminist Activism
YWCA: Young Women's Christian Association
Zanan: Women (magazine)
Zanan-e Emruz: Today's Women (magazine)
Zan-e Ruz: Woman of the Day (magazine)
Zinda Laash: Living Corpse

Introduction

AMRITA BASU

Women's movements are among the oldest, strongest, and most globally interconnected social movements.[1] They have engaged in nationalist, democratic, and anti-authoritarian protests as well as autonomous struggles against gender inequality. They have challenged and changed dominant discourses, laws, political institutions, and family structures through consciousness raising and direct action. They have created and energized regional and global networks as well as national government agencies that promote women's interests.

And yet, despite the strengths of women's movements, gender inequality is systemic, severe and pervasive throughout the world. Many feminist demands remain unfulfilled; many achievements have been reversed.[2] In recent years, the religious right and xenophobic nationalists have increasingly opposed women's rights and freedoms. Wars and militarization have increased women's vulnerability and weakened women's movements. The spread of neoliberalism, which transfers control over economic resources from the public to the private sector, has deepened structural inequalities while decreasing states' responsibilities to address them.

This revised edition of *Women's Movements in the Global Era* charts the trajectories of women's movements, with particular attention to the more than two decades since the UN's 1995 women's conference in Beijing. It tracks the roles of women's movements, amidst the growth of organized assaults on women's rights, as well as popular struggles—from Occupy to the Arab Spring to Black Lives Matter. This edition contains six new chapters by leading scholars of women and gender studies, on individual countries and several major regions of the world, to illuminate both national and supra-national patterns. There are chapters on nine countries (Pakistan, China, India, South Africa, Palestine, Iran, Brazil, Russia, and the United States) and four major regions (Africa, Europe, Latin America, and the Maghreb, which comprises Morocco, Algeria, and Tunisia).

As politically savvy, strategic actors, women's movements thrive in the most diverse and fraught political environments. At the same time, the strength of women's movements varies enormously across nations. At one end of the spectrum is the Russian women's movement, which, Lisa McIntosh Sundstrom argues, barely exists. At the other end is the Brazilian women's movement, which Cecilia Sardenberg and Ana Alice Costa describe as strong and flourishing. Capturing a theme that describes many other settings, Benita Roth, drawing on Jo Reger, describes US feminism as both everywhere and nowhere: while in recent decades feminist *ideas* have become pervasive, many women's *movements* have apparently disappeared. What explains this? How should we characterize the strengths and weaknesses of women's movements, and what explains differences in their cross-national character, size, and power?

In the years since the publication of the first edition of *Women's Movements in the Global Era* and its predecessor, *The Challenge of Local Feminisms,* many important works have appeared on women's activism, feminism and women's movements. This revised edition of the book makes several distinctive contributions. First, unlike many studies that focus on transnational or global movements, this book examines women's movements primarily within their national and regional contexts. Whereas the extent of global influences on national and regional women's movements varies widely through time and space, national conditions are always significant. Of particular importance are structures of national power, what Raka Ray describes as political fields, which include the state, political parties, and social movements (Ray, 1999).

Second, unlike studies that focus on a single issue across countries, the chapters in this volume consider a range of issues that women's movements have addressed. To provide bases for comparison, the authors were asked to explore whether and to what extent women's movements have addressed a core set of questions—sexual violence, political representation, reproductive rights, and poverty and class inequality. They also explore whether and how women's movements have addressed Lesbian, Gay, Bisexual and Transgender (LGBT) rights because of the importance of this issue and the convergence of feminist and LGBT struggles.[3]

Third, this volume analyzes women's movements in diverse rather than similar political, economic, and social settings.[4] Women's movements have emerged and grown under divergent conditions, and it is illuminating to compare the challenges that they confront in different locales. In particular, the close examination of feminist struggles in the global South emphatically challenges myths and misconceptions that feminists are most active in the global North, that global flows of information and ideas are primarily North to South, and that international influences always have a positive impact on women's movements in the global South. As several chapters in this book demonstrate, the opposition that women's movements encounter does not generally emanate from "traditional" cultural and religious values but from organized political forces, some of which are transnational.

Fourth, the chapters in this volume address women's movements that span the scales of political life and work with diverse populations. There has been extensive scholarship on state feminism, in which *femocrats* (feminist bureaucrats) play crucial roles. There is also a rich literature on community organizations and grassroots movements. This book includes accounts of feminists who work within and outside the state, nationally and locally, and among the poor, middle classes and elites. Capturing the diversity in women's identities and conditions across multiple lines of stratification necessitates examining a range of organizations that have challenged gender inequality and the multiple forms that feminist struggles have assumed. How feminist activists have negotiated the local, national, and transnational arenas is another key theme of the book.

There are risks in adopting the approach I describe. One is to unduly privilege the state and national boundaries. To address this issue, chapters on Latin America, Europe, Africa, and the Maghreb explore cross-border activism and the cross-fertilization of ideas among women in each region. Many of the chapters critically assess the relationship between feminism and nationalism and weigh the costs and benefits for women's movements of working with and within the state. Islah Jad describes the challenges that the Palestinian women's movement faces in working with a divided, quasi-state with limited authority that endures continued subjection to the Israeli Occupation.

Another risk is that description may overwhelm the theoretical analysis that can yield fruitful comparative insights. However, all of the chapters address a core set of comparative themes concerning how women's movements achieve a productive balance between alliance and autonomy in several spheres. This entails, first, attaining strong foundations within the national context while forging productive links with transnational forces. Secondly, as several chapters show, women's movements have been most successful when they have engaged the state through contestation and collaboration, without abdicating their own identities, constituencies, and concerns. Third, women's movements have been best served by joining other social movements and groups within civil society while maintaining their own objectives and identities.

This introductory chapter is organized in five sections. In the first section I provide a definition of feminism and its relationship to women's movements. The second, and longest, section, explores the different forms that transnationalism has assumed, including the United Nations (UN) international women's conferences, transnational and regional advocacy organizations, and internationally funded non-governmental organizations (NGOs). It assesses the different implications of transnational influences on women's movements in the global North and South and authoritarian and democratic settings. The third section shifts attention from the international and regional to the national level and discusses the domestic conditions under which women's movements emerge, emphasizing their connection to nationalist and democratic struggles. Section four describes women's movements' negotiations with the state, particularly around political representation and economic justice in the neo-liberal era. Section five explores two burning issues that women's movements have addressed: violence against women and sexual orientation. The conclusion reflects on the challenges women's movements confront going forward.

I. Feminism and Women's Movements

Many women who engage in struggles to achieve gender equality do not describe themselves as feminists. Often they are reacting to the perceived roots of the term. In some settings, feminism is associated with Westernization, as Nayereh Tohidi notes in the case of Iran. Women's rights activists in Central and Eastern Europe, as Silke Roth argues, had an ambivalent relationship to both socialist state feminism as well as to Western feminism, which did not adequately address the concerns of women in postsocialist societies. However, some gender equality activists, as in Morocco and Tunisia, have long described themselves as feminists, and other activists who in the past avoided the feminist label embrace it today. Such is the case in Russia, Sundstrom suggests. Aili Mari Tripp comments that young African feminists have increasingly redefined feminism in African terms. Wang Zheng states that the younger generation of Chinese feminists has rejected the ambiguous term *nüxingzhuyi* (feminine-ism) and openly embraced *nüquanzhuyi* (women's right/power-ism).

Not all feminist interventions take the form of self-identified women's movements. I use the term *women's movement* to describe organized social movements to challenge gender inequality and the term *feminism* to describe struggles that have the same goals but need not be organized women's movements. Feminism, unlike women's movements, can occur in a variety of arenas and assume a variety of forms. Feminism connotes both ideas and their enactments, but does not specify who will enact these ideas or what forms these enactments will take. It includes women's ordinary day-to-day activities that defy proscriptions of ruling clerics and transgress patriarchal norms and boundaries. For example, Tohidi notes that many Iranian women do not describe themselves as feminists and lack ties to feminist networks, but have strengthened women's movements through their acts of defiance. She speaks of the power of women's presence as they challenge, resist, and circumvent state repression in their daily lives. Feminist discourses influence the character of speech, thought, and expression in the home and the workplace, among individuals and groups, in everyday life, and, episodically, in politics, culture, and the arts. Feminists have made cultural interventions through magazines, bookstores, coffeehouses, clubs, novels, poetry, plays, and performances. They have created new epistemologies and subjects of research.

These expressions of feminism have a cumulative impact on society, the polity, and the economy that is powerful, if difficult to measure. But the significance of feminism rests not solely on its impact on societal structures and institutions, but also on the opportunities that it creates for women's self-expression. The performative dimensions of feminism often draw on earlier repertoires of protest. For example, Tripp describes how in many parts of Africa, women used to strip in public to curse and shame male abuse of authority. In the contemporary context, women have organized collective naked protests in Kenya, Nigeria, and Uganda. Embodied protest has far-reaching implications for women and for society as a whole. Farida Shaheed argues that the most effective political actors in Pakistan, including the religious right and armed extremists, have employed expressive means of occupying the public sphere. She believes that the survival of the women's movement depends on including vibrant, expressive dimensions.

The authors in this book use the term women's movements to describe movements of women that have sought to challenge gender inequality. However, to appreciate the diversity and dynamism of these movements, they include in their definition not only autonomous women's groups but also other social movements in which women have made feminist demands. Women have been active in many social movements that are neither wholly composed of women nor primarily committed to addressing gender inequality. To exclude women's activism in movements for decolonization, democracy, human rights, and economic inequality risks narrowing our definition of women's movements and confining attention to liberal, middle-class movements.

Following Maxine Molyneux (1985), one might differentiate between women's practical and strategic interests. She suggests that strategic interests, commonly identified as feminist, emerge from and contest women's experiences of structural gender subordination. Practical interests, by contrast, emerge from women's immediate and perceived needs. Elisabeth Jay Friedman fruitfully employs this distinction to describe the greater commitment of leftist governments in Latin America to addressing women's practical interests, concerning economic inequality, than their strategic interests, concerning bodily autonomy and identity recognition.

However, the distinction between the two is not always clear. Elaine Salo points out that racism and misogyny were so tightly intertwined under South Africa's apartheid state that black women's struggles against bus boycotts, rent strikes, land occupation, and pass laws were both strategic and practical. Furthermore, movements are dynamic entities. What may begin as a struggle to achieve women's practical interests can turn into a struggle to defend women's strategic interests, and vice versa. Sardenberg and Costa argue that women's strategic interests in Brazil are contextually defined; they vary by time and place, and by female activists' social locations.

A key feature of women's movements in the contemporary era is their focus on coalition building and intersectionality (a recognition of multiple and overlapping inequalities). The two are closely related since women's movements must often ally with other social justice movements, including peace, environmental and human rights movements, to address the breadth of women's interests. These alliances can be informal and are sometimes barely visible. Benita Roth argues that not only has an understanding of intersectional oppressions become part of US feminisms, it has also been incorporated into the DNA of other social movements. By way of example she cites Black Lives Matter (BLM), which was founded in 2013 by three black women who were social justice activists, to fight police violence against African Americans. Benita Roth considers BLM a good example of how the feminist concept of intersectionality has permeated other social movements.

II. Transnational Influences

Some of the most significant influences on women's movements over the past decades have been global institutions, discourses and actors. Transnational advocacy networks, international funding for NGOs, and global discourses concerning women's rights, have dramatically expanded. The growth of market forces and communication technologies has fueled the growth of transnational networks.

Observers sometimes refer to global influences on women's movements without carefully differentiating those influences. I use the term international to refer to nations and transnational to entities that operate between and beyond borders. Transnational networks differ in important respects from international organizations. Whereas international organizations are typically composed of representatives from multiple national member organizations, transnational networks are coalitions of loosely affiliated, decentralized coordinating bodies, whether government-connected or not.

Three distinct types of international and transnational influence have had the greatest impact: UN international women's conferences and treaties that seek to promote gender equality; transnational and regional networks and advocacy groups; and international funding for NGOs. All three of these transnational and international influences have generated new discourses, particularly by introducing or increasing a focus on women's rights or, more specifically, women's *human* rights. All of these global influences have contributed to institutionalizing women's movements by strengthening NGOs and collaboration between the state and women's movements.

The UN International Women's Conferences

The UN is the source and site of vital transnational linkages among women's movements. It has produced international agreements on gender equality that most national governments have endorsed. The most important of these is the Convention on the Elimination of All Forms of Discrimination Against Women (CEDAW), which the UN General Assembly adopted in 1979 and implemented two years later. CEDAW is an international bill of rights for women that addresses discrimination in areas such as education, employment, marriage and family relations, health care, politics, finance and law. Countries that have ratified CEDAW are legally bound to implement its provisions and submit national reports to CEDAW every four years on measures they have taken to comply with their treaty obligations.

Four UN world conferences on women—in Mexico City (1975), Copenhagen (1980), Nairobi (1985), and Beijing (1995)—provided key sites for interactions among national governments, between NGOs and governments, and among women's movements cross-nationally. These UN conferences strengthened and were strengthened by national women's movements in several ways.

The first involved preparing for the UN global women's conferences. Feminist groups organized meetings throughout their respective countries to learn about women's conditions across regional and class lines and formed linkages with local women's groups and other social movement organizations. Sardenberg and Costa describe preparations for the Beijing conference as contributing to the growth of the Brazilian women's movement. Shaheed notes that because governments lacked relevant expertise, they often relied on women's organizations to prepare draft plans and final reports for the conferences. The skills that feminists developed through these processes enabled them to lobby more effectively for better laws and policies.

Second, the UN conferences enabled women activists from around the world to meet and collaborate, forming relationships that lasted long after the conferences ended. They also increased the visibility and legitimacy of nationally based women's organizations, especially in authoritarian settings like China. The Chinese women's movement, writes Wang Zheng, was the driving force behind China's decision to host the Beijing women's conference. The opportunities that conference provided to network with international and diasporic groups strengthened the Chinese women's movement.

The third important impact of the UN women's conferences was in getting member nations to arrive at a common set of goals to promote gender equality. Thanks to lobbying by feminist organizations, the UN conference on Human Rights in Vienna in 1993 took important steps to protect and promote women's rights. Twelve years later, the Beijing women's conference extended and expanded these initiatives. The UN conferences offered unparalleled opportunities for women's movements to share experiences, gain legitimacy, and influence their national governments. Jean H. Quataert and Benita Roth summarize the conferences' contributions aptly:

> They strengthened local women's movements' collective hands and encouraged, through preparatory processes, the makings of links on the ground among actors interested in women's rights even across borders. They facilitated exchanges among women where western hegemonies of understandings about women's rights, inclusive alliances, and development agendas were challenged. They also forced states, democratic and nondemocratic alike, to grapple with plans for actions on women's and human rights that emerged from the meetings. (Quataeret and Roth 2012)

The most impressive and ambitious outcome of the Beijing women's conference was the Platform for Action. It covered twelve major areas: poverty, education and training, health, violence, armed conflict, economy, power and decision-making, institutional mechanisms, human rights, media, environment, and the girl child. It asked states to ensure that women held at least 30 percent of elected positions. It called on governments and NGOs to engage in gender mainstreaming, namely, ensuring that gender perspectives and the goal of gender equality were integrated into the design, implementation, monitoring, and evaluation of legislation, policies, and programs. UN Women, formed in 2010 by the General Assembly, took responsibility for implementing these goals by working with national governments, intergovernmental agencies and civil society organizations.

In March 2015 the UN Commission on the Status of Women undertook a review of governments' progress in implementing the Beijing
Declaration and Platform for Action, twenty years after its adoption. It
reported on some positive developments, including a global rise in
women's life expectancy, more laws to address violence against women,
increased girls' enrollment in primary and secondary education, a
growth in women's labor force participation, and women's increased
access to contraception in most regions of the world. Citing a study by
Laurel Weldon and Mala Htun on seventy countries over four decades,
the report acknowledged that feminist organizations have played decisive roles in countries which have made the most progress in adopting
gender equality policies and attaining women's rights (Weldon and
Htun 2012).

However, overall, the failures and setbacks were more striking. UN
Women stated in its report:

> Twenty years ago we were buoyed up by the unified determination
> and conviction of the Beijing Declaration and Platform for Action.
> …Twenty years on, it is a hard truth that many of the same barriers
> and constraints that were recognized by the Beijing signatories are
> still in force globally.
>
> In recent years, progress on gender equality has been held back
> by forces in the global political and economic landscapes that have
> been particularly hard to mitigate or combat. Persistent conflicts,
> the global financial and economic crises, volatile food and energy
> prices, and climate change have intensified inequalities and vulner-
> ability, and have had specific and almost universally negative im-
> pacts on women and girls. ("UN Women Summary Report: The
> Beijing Declaration and Platform for Action Turns 20," 2015)

The Report's findings are sobering: women are more likely than
men to live in poverty and to have fewer opportunities for decent work,
assets, and formal credit. Due to pervasive occupational segregation,
women are overrepresented in low-paid jobs, have less access to social
protection, and are paid on average less than men for work of equal
value. Women's employment outcomes are further limited by the dis-
proportionate share of unpaid care work they perform. Women are
more seriously affected than men by climate change. All regions have
unacceptably high rates of violence against women; according to recent

global estimates, 35 percent of women worldwide have experienced physical and/or sexual intimate partner violence or non-partner sexual violence in their lifetimes. Women remain significantly underrepresented at the highest levels of political office as well as across public and private sectors. Discrimination against women embedded in the legal system remains pervasive, particularly in family law.

UN member nations decided not to hold a Fifth World Conference on Women in 2015 as a twenty-year follow up to the 1995 Beijing Conference. Some opposed another global conference on the grounds that the gains women had achieved might be reversed, given the increased strength of conservative anti-feminist groups. In 2015, a group of countries describing themselves as "Friends of the Family" formed a delegation at the UN to challenge women's rights for supposedly threatening the family.[5] Some opponents of another global conference felt that governments should devote themselves to implementing the Platform for Action before adopting new goals. Some feminists worried that government representatives and bureaucratized NGOs would dominate a fifth world conference and exclude more radical perspectives.

Opposition to a fifth world conference on women is a sad commentary on the global political climate for feminism today. Concerns about the bureaucratization of feminism that follows upon its institutionalization, in part as a result of UN mandates, are well founded. However, some observers believe that the response should be to create more inclusive processes rather than giving up on UN conferences (Sandler and Goetz, 2015) A fifth global women's conference would have enabled feminists to put collective pressure on governments to implement the Platform for Action and to devise strategies for confronting right-wing attacks on women and sexual minorities.

Many seasoned feminists who participated in the UN conferences and no longer view the UN as a platform for progressive struggles consider the World Social Forum (WSF), a venue of anti-neoliberal activists, a more desirable, radical alternative (Wilson, 2007). At the 2002 WSF in Brazil, feminists launched the Campaign against Fundamentalisms, a network of Latin American Southern Cone feminist organizations to challenge neoliberalism and religious fundamentalism. Feminists from the global South organized packed sessions on Feminist Dialogues in Mumbai in 2004 and Porto Alegre in 2005 that explored how feminists could address gender inequality within the global social justice movement. Thanks to the efforts of Tunisian feminists, women's rights figured prominently in the WSF in Tunis in 2014. Impressive as these achievements are, the WSFs are not a substitute for UN women's conferences since they cannot devise programs that carry treaty obligations. More broadly, the UN remains an important site for pressuring the state, which retains the ability to deny or support many feminist demands.

Transnational and Regional Networks

Transnational networks are broad based coalitions that engage in research, lobbying, advocacy, and direct action to achieve gender equality and women's empowerment. These networks are a product of globalization and have addressed the inequalities it generates with respect to climate change, unemployment and low wages. They have also engaged in struggles to promote women's health, reproductive rights and family law reform.

Transnational networks take many forms. Some include governmental and non-governmental actors, foundations, the media, and regional and international agencies (Keck and Sikkink 1998, 9). Other more activist-oriented networks exclude government representatives. This latter group includes Development Alternatives with Women for a New Era (DAWN), Women in Development Europe (WIDE), the Association for Women's Rights in Development (AWID), and the Women, Environment, and Development Organization, all of which have addressed the impact of neoliberalism and globalization on women (Moghadam 2005). Although movement activists may participate in transnational networks, the networks themselves are not movements but broadly affiliated groups.

Regional feminist networks have taken up UN mandates and worked with transnational groups, but their character and concerns are deeply influenced by regional political and economic forces. Some regional networks have explicitly or implicitly contested national borders.

Regional networks have been especially robust in Latin America. For Latin American feminists and women's organizations that joined other human rights groups in democratic struggles against military dictatorships in the 1970s, a rights-based approach has been relatively uncontroversial. Such an approach considers certain rights universal rather than culturally specific, a claim that feminists in other regions of the world have contested. Sonia Alvarez argues that "the peculiarities of the regional and national political contexts in which feminisms un-folded also impelled local movement actors to build trans-border con-nections from the bottom up" (Alvarez, 2000, 30–31). Since 1981, Latin American and Caribbean feminists have organized *encuentros,* gather-ings for sharing ideas, developing strategies, and fostering closer links among women's movements in the region. They have also brought to-gether indigenous women, lesbians, and Afro–Latin American and Af-ro-Caribbean women who experience marginalization within national and regional contexts. *Encuentros* have taken place in Argentina, Bra-zil, Chile, Colombia, Costa Rica, the Dominican Republic, El Salvador, Mexico, and Peru. Participants in the *encuentros* have fiercely debated contentious issues and insisted on inclusion despite differences (Fried-man 2015).

Regional networks in Africa have sprung up in the aftermath of civil wars and ethnic conflicts since the mid-1980s. They are a product of both international influences and the cross-fertilization of ideas among national women's movements that are committed to peace, security, personal law reform, and economic justice. Women have mobilized for peace in con-flict-ridden nations like Nigeria, Burundi, South Sudan, Somalia, and the Eastern Congo as well as through regional networks. Liberian women's peace organizations have been particularly active, and worked with Afri-ca-wide peace organizations like Femmes Africa Solidarité.

In Europe, alongside a number of regional networks that address women's rights and development, the European Union (EU) has strengthened ties among women's movements and led the twenty-eight EU member states to adopt more gender-equitable laws and policies. Silke Roth argues that the EU played a significant role in strengthening feminist demands. She suggests that gender equality legislation was an unintended side effect: initially France, the only founding member with equal-pay legislation, demanded that the other member states fol-low its lead. Over the years, gender equality policies expanded beyond pay equity. Prospects of joining the EU led—for example—Polish, Czech and Irish feminists to lobby their governments for gender equal-ity legislation, and for the creation of official bodies and funding to support their activities. Silke Roth describes EU policies as a hybrid of liberal and social-democratic approaches that reflect the policies of dif-ferent member states.

In the Maghreb, as Valentine Moghadam describes, regional net-works, like the Collectif 95 Maghreb-Egalité, created by feminists in

Algeria, Morocco, and Tunisia in the early 1990s, have sought to advance women's rights. The Collectif worked with women's groups across the region to fight for egalitarian family codes and women's full and equal citizenship. The Collectif also forged ties with other transnational feminist networks: first with Women Living Under Muslim Laws (WLUML), formed in 1984 in opposition to Islamic fundamentalism and discriminatory family laws; and later with the Women's Learning Partnership for Rights, Development, and Peace (WLP), established in 2000 with many network partners. A WLP conference facilitated networking between Moroccan and Iranian feminists. In 2009, Iranian feminists collaborated with the WLUML in the Stop Stoning Forever Campaign.

The strongest networks of Asian feminists have emerged in countries that share conflictual histories and contested borders. In 1989 Kamala Bhasin, at the time an officer with a UN agency, organized the first gathering of South Asian feminists in a small village in Bangladesh. Suspicion and recrimination among women who had experienced wars, militarization, and ethnic violence gave way to strong affective ties and a shared political commitment to denationalizing identities and strengthening cross-border ties and perspectives (Chhachhi and Abeysekera, 2015). Several regional gatherings and South Asian Feminist Declarations in 1989 and 2006 followed. In 1998 Sangat was formed, a network of South Asian gender activists and trainers. Sangat has broadened its focus from gender inequality to address justice, peace, and democracy throughout the region.

Several authors comment on the open, inclusive character of regional networks. Tripp notes that women's movements have demonstrated an extraordinary capacity for building coalitions across ethnic, class, religious, and other cleavages in nations riven by civil war and violence. Moghadam argues that although critics have long faulted women's movements in the Maghreb for being westernized, elitist, and intolerantly secular, in fact these broad networks include both men and women, both religious and secular women, and both younger and older activists.

International Funding for NGOs

A third form of transnationalism occurs through international funding for nationally based NGOs that engage in education, advocacy, service provision, income generation, research and documentation, and, sometimes, protest activities. The impact of NGOs on women's movements has generated heated debate. Some critics claim that NGOs, driven by donor funding and agendas, dissipate feminist activism. Others who may share some of these questions nonetheless consider certain NGOs crucial to sustaining feminist struggles, believe women's movements can avoid donor dependence, and worry about increased government restrictions on funding for women's rights NGOs.

One influential critique concerns the very conditions associated with the growth of NGOs (Alvarez 2000). International funding for NGOs has grown alongside neoliberalism as states have transferred tasks they once performed onto civil society actors (Fraser 2009 and Silke Roth in this volume). As a result, Silke Roth argues, women's movements became NGO-ized in East Germany and other Eastern European countries in the wake of the state's retreat from social welfare in the 1980s. This raises the question of the extent to which NGOs can and should take up responsibilities that states are better equipped to handle.

Another critique is that women's NGOs have contributed to the demobilization of women's movements. As one observer notes,

> Part of the problem is that the science of delivery has been strangling the art of social transformation. Driven by the need to measure results, donors have helped to nurture a cadre of contracted civil society organisations, who are excellent at "accounts-ability" but less good at disruptive change. (Sriskandarajah, 2015)

Islah Jad questions a tendency to use the terms *social movement* and *NGO* interchangeably in Palestine. She argues that the grassroots women's organizations that emerged during the first Intifada in 1987 mobilized women across the class spectrum. International funding transformed women's organizations into NGOs that collaborated closely with the Palestinian Authority and failed to challenge the Occupation. In the process they left a political vacuum that Islamist forces have filled.

The kind of funding NGOs receive and the freedom they have to determine how to use their resources often constrain the activities of progressive grass roots organizations. Most donors are located in the global North and fund large, professionalized civil-society organizations that have the capacity to deliver tangible outputs. In South Africa, Salo argues, professionalized, urban NGOs have failed to work with poor rural women. The most restrictive funding in Africa, Tripp notes, is from corporations that do not fund programs that address the structural underpinnings of gender inequality. However, even multilateral and bilateral donors provide relatively little funding for grassroots organizations. Moreover, women's organizations generally do not receive multi-year and unrestricted core funding that they can use to strengthen their organizational capacities (AWID 2011).

NGOs have become increasingly bureaucratized and de-politicized. Sundstrom suggests that Western funding in the 1990s was partly responsible for the emergence of women's NGOs that addressed violence against women and formed crisis centers in Russia. International funding enabled these activists to achieve autonomy from the state and critique its policies. But if foreign funding played a valuable role in the short run, it deterred NGOs from mobilizing domestic resources to achieve long-term viability and establish their own agendas.

Until around 2000, Shaheed notes, women's organizations in Pakistan received foreign funding for programs of their choosing. Thereafter, donors began tying funding to their own agendas, using a bidding process and boxing ideas into Specific, Measurable, Achievable, Relevant, and Time-Bound (SMART) outputs. This increased competition among women's organizations and impeded the creation of broad-based coalitions. It also shifted activists' attention to specialized activities and measurable outcomes, limiting the scope for independent, innovative activism aimed at achieving broad social-change goals.

However, Shaheed cautions that blanket, sweeping criticisms of NGO-ization in Pakistan and elsewhere can reflect and provoke broader opposition to feminism and human rights. Movements that reject international funding are deprived of resources that are essential to sustaining and expanding their activities. She notes that in both Pakistan and Bangladesh, many feminist NGOs that have accepted international funds have resisted donor-driven agendas. Shaheed's observation is especially valuable because she was a founding member of the leading feminist organization in Pakistan, the Women's Action Forum (WAF), which has always refused funding from all government and international sources as a matter of principle. Shaheed argues that although WAF's financial autonomy enabled it to launch a radical movement against the Zia dictatorship in the late 1970s, it has been hampered by a lack of resources and effective fund-raising strategy.

Many feminist NGOs must choose the lesser of two evils. Sundstrom argues that independent activists in Russia can either join or create NGOs whose funding is meager, unreliable, and constrained, or join state-supported organizations which are more stable but completely dependent on the government. In Iran, where foreign-funded NGOs also operate under severe constraints, Tohidi notes that women's organizations are either hindered by a lack of resources or by being branded foreign agents and thus subject to government repression.

Indeed, foreign-funded NGOs' ability to achieve autonomy from the state has declined as many governments have restricted the funding and activities of progressive, social change-oriented NGOs. A report by the Carnegie Endowment for International Peace identifies fifty countries that place restrictions on overseas funding of NGOs ("Foreign Funding of NGOs: Donors Keep Out," 2014). In Russia, for example, a law enacted in 2012 limits NGOs' ability to receive foreign funding by requiring them to declare themselves "foreign agents" or face fines and eventual dissolution. A decade after the Beijing women's conference in 1995, the Chinese government restricted international funding and engaged in increased monitoring and control over NGOs. In 2016 it passed a law constraining the work of over seven thousand NGOs; women's rights NGOs figure prominently among them.

Poulomi Pal points out that foreign funding does not provide women's rights NGOs much autonomy, given increased government regulation of NGO activities in India. The Indian government canceled the registrations of thousands of foreign-funded NGOs, supposedly for failing to file tax returns in 2015. It also temporarily put the Ford Foundation, one of the largest donors to Indian women's organizations, under watch and froze its bank accounts.

The extent to which women's movements can function autonomously is deeply influenced by global geo-political inequalities. Among the countries described in this volume, the US women's movement has historically been least influenced by international forces. Benita Roth points out that with the exception of a few individuals and organizations, the US women's movement has not been very active in transnational organizing. On the one hand, this has been costly to American women; the US has not joined other countries in promoting women's rights through such measures as ratifying CEDAW and adopting gender quotas. On the other hand, given the wealth and power of the US, its women's NGOs have not needed international funding and have thus avoided donor dependence.

III. The National Context

Women's movements have arisen alongside other social movements— for independence, democracy, and socialism—for several reasons. First, like other national social movements, women's movements emerge following the creation of modern states. As Charles Tilly (1995) argues, states constitute both the citizens who are claimants and the objects of their claims. The state's authoritative control over resources, power, and violence makes it the target of national social movements. Second, women often become politically active as old regimes collapse and existing power structures erode, thereby temporarily loosening patriarchal control within the family and broader society. Women achieved significant political gains in Europe and the US following the first and second world wars and in large parts of Asia, Africa, and the Middle East during and following decolonization. Third, the close links between women's movements and other social movements reflect the intersectional nature of women's interests in fighting to achieve freedom both for the nation and as women.

Women were extremely active in anticolonial nationalist movements in many of the countries discussed in this book. In most of these instances, they challenged traditional gender roles both explicitly and by virtue of their activism. In Cameroon and Nigeria, Tripp notes, women became active in nationalist struggles to advance their own gender-specific and other agendas, including those related to taxation and market prices. Nationalist leaders in Guinea and Mali recruited women into independence movements by appealing to women's concerns. But while women achieved certain political rights in the aftermath of independence, most countries failed to address deep-rooted patriarchal practices in the postcolonial era.

The Palestinian women's movement, Jad argues, has been inextricably linked to the Palestinian movement for independence. However, although Palestine has yet to establish statehood, the women's movement has declined. The Israeli Occupation threatens Palestine's existence and stifles citizenship rights in the West Bank and Gaza. At the same time, the Palestinian Authority has depoliticized civil society and demobilized the women's movement. Palestinian feminists face the nearly impossible challenge of mobilizing against Israeli Occupation while seeking rights from what is not a full-fledged state.

State repression, particularly when it transcends the political domain and permeates civil society, has often been a catalyst to women's activism. Women played critical roles in movements against authoritarian regimes in Latin America. They have been at the forefront of struggles against state repression in post-Khomeini Iran. Women's rights activists were deeply engaged in the Arab Spring protests in 2010–2011. In Africa, women's activism was essential to the collapse of military dictatorships. In Kenya, for example, women were at the forefront of the democracy movement in 1992; more recently, women participated in Côte d'Ivoire's democracy movement in 2011.

Women's groups have been active in drafting constitutions in newly formed multiparty democracies. Thanks to feminist pressures, the Polish constitution includes an article decreeing equal rights for women and men. In South Africa, the Women's National Coalition waged a successful struggle to ensure that the constitution guarantees equality and freedom from discrimination for all, regardless of race, gender, religion, sexual orientation, and disability. The post-2000 constitutions adopted in twenty-two of the twenty-nine African countries that recognize customary law include provisions that allow statutory law to trump customary law. After the collapse of the Ben Ali government in Tunisia in January 2011, feminist groups mobilized to ensure a democratic transition that supported women's rights. In Morocco, women's rights organizations persuaded the government to ratify CEDAW's Optional Protocol, which permits the CEDAW Committee to receive and consider communications from feminist groups.

However, democratization has also given rise to the emergence of conservative civil society organizations that the state is either unwilling or unable to contain. Diane Mulligan and Jude Howell note that

> Civil society is a double-edged sword for feminists. It can provide a site for organizing around feminist issues, for articulating counter-hegemonic discourses, for experimenting with alternative life styles and for envisioning other less sexist and more just worlds.... Yet it can also be an arena where gendered behavior, norms and practices are acted out and reproduced. (Mulligan and Howell 2005, 6)

Burgeoning civil societies have given rise to conservative, misogynist groups that claim to speak in the name of "traditional" religious and ethnic values. Such is the case in India, Palestine, Iran, and South Africa, among other countries in this volume. Jad notes that the growing power of Islamists in Palestine has weakened the secular women's movement and its attempts to strengthen secular over religious law. In South Africa, Salo argues, rural women have been subject to extensive discrimination, particularly with respect to land ownership and inheritance. Jacob Zuma's presidency has strengthened chiefs who exercise enormous power over traditional courts and communal land and oppose women's inheritance rights. In India, reactionary forces have grown within both civil society and the state. Hindu nationalist organizations have policed women's sexuality, resulting in attacks on interfaith couples and assaults on women who frequent bars. Since the BJP came to power in 2014, Pal argues, it has lent support to these organizations, crushing citizens' democratic rights and restricting space for dissent.

The Catholic Church became the major opponent of reproductive rights once democracy was achieved in Latin America, as well as in Eastern and Central Europe. Thus, despite state support, women's movements have been unsuccessful in securing the right to legal first-trimester abortions in Poland, Russia, and Latin America. Friedman argues that while leftist governments in Venezuela, Bolivia, Argentina, and Chile have addressed socioeconomic inequality and increased women's representation in decision-making bodies, they have been less willing to confront the Church on sexuality and abortion. In Brazil, Sardenberg and Costa describe how the Church has supported legislation prohibiting distribution of the "morning-after pill" through the public health system in several cities. The growth of Christian fundamentalism in Latin America has further threatened the rights of women and LGBT groups. In the US, the religious right has crusaded against abortion and attacked abortion clinics. Right-wing Republicans, Benita Roth points out, have sought to defund Planned Parenthood and influenced many state legislatures to limit a woman's right to choose. A 2014 Supreme Court decision established the right of employers to make their religious beliefs grounds for limiting their employees' access to reproductive services.

Women's movements have responded to these conservative forces in a variety of ways. They have tried to influence policies by putting pressure on executive branch agencies and through organized mass demonstrations and petition campaigns. They have forged alliances within civil society, sometimes with religiously observant women who share some of their objectives. They have sought to legitimate their claims by using international instruments. These attempts have sometimes been successful; at other times they have provoked an even more conservative backlash.

IV. Women's Movements and the State

Women's movements have often directed their demands at the state because of its power over so many feminist goals: increasing women's political representation, instituting laws that punish violence against women, curtailing discrimination based on gender and sexual orientation, ensuring equal pay, making abortion accessible, expanding social welfare, and providing services like shelters for battered women.

However, when and to what extent women's movements confront the state and their success in achieving state concessions varies. Women who have contributed to the creation of new regimes have leverage in getting them to address gender inequality. In the aftermath of anticolonial struggles, we witnessed women's movements securing states' prohibition of gender discrimination, as in India, and of discrimination against women and LGBT groups, as in South Africa. Women's movements are also likely to confront the state when there are glaring gaps between official pronouncements and actual policies. Examples include states that recognize only some women's citizenship rights, acknowledge the rights of racial or religious minorities but not those of women, accept and then retract women's rights, and violate international conventions and constitutional guarantees prohibiting gender discrimination.

Given the extent to which women's movements have made demands on the state, they are strikingly ambivalent about working with it. There are good reasons for this caution. The first is that the terms of collaboration are generally set by the state rather than by feminists, and activists often fear that the strength and radicalism of women's movements will be depleted by institutionalization. For example, excessive reliance on the state to enact public measures supporting gender equality in Poland and Russia during the communist era impeded the development of autonomous women's movements. Similarly, Silke Roth notes that Northern European social-democratic welfare states, which emphasized gender equality and integrated women into political institutions, weakened independent women's movements. By contrast, in liberal democratic states, which pursued more conservative social and economic policies, women's movements were stronger and more sovereign.

A second reason for feminists' ambivalence is that working within the state highlights and exacerbates stratification within women's movements. Educated, urban, elite women are more likely to be drawn into women's policy machineries and run for office than poorer, less educated, minority women. In the US, as Benita Roth argues, the neoliberal, minimal welfare state has promoted liberal feminism, which has favored the interests of middle-class over poor women and hindered cross-class coalitions and alliances.

Related to this issue is a debate among feminists involving the extent to which the state's institutionalization of feminist demands has diluted, narrowed, and undermined the goals of women's movements. The chapters in this book suggest that the answer to this question depends on the character of the state and its relationship to women's movements both historically and in the current period. The most productive relationships between feminists and the state exist when women's movements and other social movements play important roles in bringing sympathetic governments to power and continuing to pressure them to improve women's conditions.

Another key question concerns the character of state feminism and its relationship to women's movements, both of which have changed significantly. What was termed state feminism in the past and was associated with authoritarian, modernizing regimes in Africa and the Middle East, depended on the goodwill of political leaders. Moghadam describes two important older models of state feminism, Tunisia under Habib Bourguiba (1956–1987) and Egypt under Gamal Abdel Nasser (1956–1970), who circumscribed women's rights much more than Bourguiba. In Africa, Tripp argues, the state-affiliated women's organizations that most African countries created from 1975 to 1985 were designed to generate support for ruling parties. As single parties lost their grip and multiparty competition grew in the 1990s, autonomous women's groups displaced these state- and party-affiliated women's organizations.

In the contemporary period, we see several different patterns of state feminism. One pattern, which Jad describes, is for the state to appoint femocrats—because of their patronage ties and not their feminist commitments—to pursue the state's agenda. Another pattern, which Salo describes, is a declining role for progressive femocrats in South Africa in the years after Jacob Zuma came to power. She argues that the African National Congress Women's League (ANCWL) jettisoned feminism and became wholly aligned with President Zuma's personal agenda. A third pattern, which Wang Zheng identifies, is for state-affiliated women's organizations to work surreptitiously to support feminist goals that exceed state dictates. She argues that Western feminists mistakenly fault the All-China Democratic Women's Federation (ACDWF), which is officially linked to the Chinese Communist Party (CCP), for submissively toeing the party line. In fact, she argues, the ACDWF has maneuvered behind the scenes to achieve feminist goals. Feminist NGOs have relied heavily on the ACDWF's funding, organizational networks, institutional legitimacy, and administrative reach. One of their most important joint achievements was the passage of China's first law against domestic violence in December 2015, after two decades of persistent feminist struggle.

The most effective forms of state feminism entail close and open links between femocrats and strong and independent women's organizations. According to Sardenberg and Costa, this is the case in Brazil, where state feminism emerged because of pressure by women's movements from below. The election to national office of the progressive Workers' Party (Partido dos Trabalhadores, or PT), which was committed to participatory forms of governance, provided further support for feminist demands. Sardenberg and Costa recognize, however, that many rights, including sexual and reproductive rights, have yet to be achieved in Brazil. Friedman makes a similar argument about Latin America more broadly and anticipates that feminist and LGBT rights are likely to experience a setback amidst the ascendency of the political Right, which has strong ties to the Catholic Church. Further damage stems from austerity measures that disproportionately affect poor women and transgender people.

Political Representation

One of the most important gains that women have made since the mid-1990s is increased political representation in national legislatures. As Dahlerup notes, "The quota system shifts the burden of recruitment from individual women to those who control the recruitment process" (Dahlerup ed., 2006). Women parliamentarians worldwide grew from

13 percent of all parliamentarians in 1998 to 21 percent in 2013. Thirty-seven countries achieved the UN mandate of having women constitute at least 30 percent in their lower houses of parliament. In the past decade alone, women's legislative representation has increased by at least five percent, with especially marked increases in Arab states. Much of this increase is due to the implementation of gender quotas by approximately 128 countries.

Quotas are not confined to any particular region of the world but they are more or less likely in certain political contexts. They are uncommon in former communist countries. Sundstrom suggests that women's political representation in post-communist Russia declined following the abolition of Soviet-era legislative quotas. Governments have introduced constitutional quotas after attaining political independence, as in in Pakistan and Bangladesh. Governments in countries that have experienced democracy movements, like Algeria, Tunisia and Morocco in the aftermath of the Arab Spring, have introduced quotas in response to feminist demands. Regional influences play a significant role. For example, after Argentina revised its electoral laws in 1991 to require that all political parties nominate at least 30 percent women to run for office, other Latin American countries followed suit.

International factors, like the UN Women's Conferences and CEDAW, have encouraged some governments to adopt quotas. Countries that have experienced civil war and extreme conflict, like Nepal, Afghanistan, Liberia, and Rwanda, introduced quotas as a result of international influences, notably UN Security Council Resolution 1325 (adopted in 2000), which promotes women's participation in decision making on peace and security issues.

However, international pressures cannot ensure quotas' success. Countries with strong women's movements are sometimes resistant to quotas (Hughes et al, 2015). One possible explanation is that strong women's movements may be unenthusiastic about quotas. There is some evidence for this in the Indian context. Although on balance the Indian women's movement supports quotas, it is not without ambivalence. Indian feminists have worried that quotas could create a ceiling rather than a floor, and that male politicians would field pliable wives and daughters as proxies. Further, feminists have criticized quotas for treating women as a homogeneous group and ignoring the deterrents to the candidacies of poor, low-caste women. Low-caste parties have similarly opposed women's quotas on grounds that they would be filled primarily by upper-caste women. As a result of this combination of opposition and ambivalence, reservations for women as yet exist only in the *panchayats*, local elected bodies. A bill mandating 33 percent reserved seats in state and national legislatures still awaits parliamentary approval. The higher the political office, the greater the challenges women confront. Thus, women in Russia, Brazil, the US, and India have achieved greater electoral success in local than in national elections.

Countries that adopt quotas do not always implement them, fully or at all. When, as is often the case, only small political parties adopt voluntary party quotas, this has relatively little impact on women's political representation. Voluntary quotas have been much more successful when adopted by dominant parties, for example the ANC in South Africa. Some countries have adopted party quotas for elections decided by proportional representation drawn from a party's list of candidates, but do not specify the list's rank ordering. Parties may place women candidates at the bottom of the list, putting them at a severe disadvantage. In many countries there are no sanctions for noncompliance with party quotas and little financial support for female candidates' election campaigns. In this respect, constitutional or legal quotas that regulate the activities of all political parties and are more effective than voluntary party quotas.

In general, quotas have reduced but not removed the innumerable barriers impeding women's electoral success. Furthermore, some countries with legislative quotas for women otherwise have poor records on women's rights. Although women's increased political representation is valuable in and of itself, clearly it is insufficient to address the structural bases of gender inequality. And women's movements have been much less successful in addressing poverty and class inequality because states, political parties, and the most powerful international actors are generally less receptive to these demands.

Economic Justice and Neo-liberalism

In the past, welfare states in the global North and South adopted social welfare policies that provided a safety net for women in poverty. Most states today fail to do so. Reconfigured states (Banaszak *et al.* 2003, 6–7) have downloaded power and responsibilities to lower rungs of the state, uploaded power and responsibility to higher branches of the state, laterally delegated responsibility to non-elected state bodies, and off-loaded responsibilities to non-state actors. Encroachment on states' authority by institutions like the International Monetary Fund, World Trade Organization, and World Bank and many bilateral and multi-lateral treaties have reduced national states' accountability to women's movements. By off-loading responsibilities, states have shifted social welfare responsibilities to NGOs that cannot or do not seek to address the macro-level causes of poverty and inequality.

In some countries and regions, women have engaged in mass resistance against austerity measures. Silke Roth describes coalitions that have emerged in Turkey and the UK to protest public sector cuts. Sundstrom analyzes widespread protests in Russia, that began in 2002 and grew during the financial crisis of 2008–2010, to oppose employers' failures to pay government-provided parental leave benefits.

With the exception of a minority of countries in which left-of-center governments occupy power, most governments are unsympathetic or hostile to demands for economic justice. As Wang Zheng notes, although urban female workers in China bore the brunt of economic reforms, and were the last to be hired and the first to be fired, Chinese feminists could not rival the state's power to privatize public assets and regulate labor relations. The same could be said of other countries in which even the strongest women's movements cannot change states' macroeconomic policies.

Still, most women's movements have not prioritized questions of poverty and inequality. Rights-based approaches that women's movements have fruitfully employed to address violence against women are primarily concerned with civil rights and liberties—even though some proponents of the women's human rights approach have sought to address economic rights. A chasm has sometimes emerged between middle-class feminist organizations that focus on social and political issues, and labor unions, peasant organizations, and social justice movements that focus on poverty and class inequality. Benita Roth argues that in the US, while liberal feminists have addressed equal pay largely for the middle-class, women-of-color organizations have addressed problems of black and Hispanic women on welfare. In other contexts, like Iran and Palestine, the climate of political repression has narrowed the agendas of women's movements to confronting overt physical violence rather than systemic or structural violence.

V. Burning Issues

Violence Against Women

From the "Stop Stoning Forever Campaign" opposing the stoning of women who are accused of adultery in Iran, to the One in Nine Campaign against rape in South Africa, to protests against femicide in Brazil, violence against women has been a central concern of women's movements. Feminists have expanded definitions of rape and sexual harassment and revealed the entanglement of violence against women with other forms of domination and power. Women's movements have proposed multiple levels of intervention, from legislation and public policies to assistance for individual women. They have advocated the creation of shelters, family courts, walk-in assistance, and counseling centers for battered women. They have engaged psychologists, social workers, lawyers, and doctors to work with survivors. They have developed education and job-creation programs so that women do not have to return to abusive situations. Movements combating violence against women have scored some important achievements among the police, judges, medical professionals, and other government officials and professionals who interact with survivors. An indication of movement effectiveness is the increasing involvement of municipal governments in founding and supporting crisis centers that NGOs have formed. European Union members and candidate states have adopted a variety of policies to address gender violence (Montoya 2013).

International forces, from the UN women's conferences to international treaties to internationally funded NGOs, to transnational advocacy networks, have encouraged women's movements to confront sexual violence. In Pakistan, Shaheed observes, activists only started using the internationally recognized term violence against women in the early 1990s, when they engaged with global forces. In Russia, Sundstrom notes, many of the terms concerning violence against women are of English origin.

However, the extent to which transnational forces initiate movements concerning violence against women varies. They have been important in situations in which the state is repressive and the possibilities for women's activism are constrained. They have been less influential in countries that have strong civil societies and somewhat responsive states (Basu, 2000). In India, for example, the women's movement has been organizing campaigns since the 1970s against the rape of women in police custody and "dowry deaths," that is, the murder of newly married women following their being tortured and abused by their husbands and in laws on grounds that the dowry at the time of marriage was insufficient. Men who murder their wives often remarry and receive another dowry from the families of their new wives.

Struggles addressing violence against women have deepened and grown when the state has vacillated in its commitments and demonstrated biases in addressing violence against women. In both Brazil and South Africa, women's movements have allied with LGBT groups to confront the state's shortcomings and address gender violence in a more inclusive manner. As Pal shows, in 2012 the Indian government, under pressure from women's groups and other civil society organizations, established a committee to address reforms of laws and public policies relating to rape, trafficking, and sexual harassment. The committee strengthened women's organizations by involving them in the consultative process. Feminists and LGBT groups demanded, among other things, that laws should define sexual harassment and rape more broadly, decriminalize homosexuality, criminalize marital rape, redefine the age of consent, consider violence against *dalit* (Scheduled Caste or untouchable) and tribal women aggravated sexual assault, employ gender-neutral terms to refer to victims/survivors, and hold senior public officials and members of the armed forces accountable for rape. They achieved some of these demands.

South Africa offers a particularly important instance of how the movement to stop violence against women has evolved and grown. Salo shows how the One in Nine Campaign (named to emphasize that only one out of nine rape survivors reports the attack to the police) emerged to support a woman who charged Jacob Zuma, then deputy president of South Africa, with rape. After a court acquitted Zuma in 2006, the campaign extended its support to other women who had filed rape charges in the courts. Over the next few years, it protested homophobic rapes and murders targeting black lesbians. A catalyst for the sustained struggle was the fact that the South African Parliament enacted a law in 2007 that criminalizes marital rape, expands the definition of sexual assault to include all forms of non-consensual sex, and includes men and children as potential victims of sexual assault.

However, the depressing reality is that, despite sustained activism by the women's movements and LGBT activists, India and South Africa still suffer among the highest rates of sexual violence in the world. Salo notes that sexual violence against women living in urban informal settlements and the rural periphery is especially extensive. Government measures have not addressed major underlying causes: the cultural and material bases of gender oppression; links among gender violence, poverty, and class inequality; and the growth of conservative, patriarchal ethnic and religious nationalisms.

Sexual Rights

Our authors were asked to address the conditions and struggles of sexual minorities because the oppression of LGBT groups, as of the poor and racial and ethnic minorities, is central to a broadly conceived feminist agenda. Furthermore, there are many similarities between the conditions under which feminist and LGBT struggles succeed or fail.

As is true of women's rights, there is enormous cross-national variation in the rights of LGBT communities. Many states have pursued homophobic policies. Homosexuality is illegal in seventy-three countries, including Iran, Pakistan, India, Morocco, Tunisia, Algeria, and thirty-four African countries. The Palestinian Authority has not passed legislation on homosexuality but male homosexuality is illegal in Gaza under an old British criminal ordinance code. Homosexuality is subject to the death penalty in Iran and Pakistan. Even in the absence of clear laws on the subject, the Chinese state has engaged in harsh treatment of homosexuals. In India, the Delhi High Court in 2009, struck down Section 377 of the Penal Code, a colonial law that deems certain sexual acts "unnatural" and punishable by law, but four years later the Supreme Court overturned the High Court judgment. Although homosexuality was decriminalized in Russia in 1993, there are no laws prohibiting discrimination on the basis of sexual orientation. The city of Moscow banned gay rights parades in 2011, and a national law bans *gay propaganda.*

By contrast, LGBT groups have achieved important legal gains in the US, Latin America and Europe. Same-sex marriage is now legal in the US, Canada, New Zealand, Argentina, Uruguay South Africa, and many EU member nations. As Friedman describes, Argentina has been a regional and global leader with respect to LGBT rights. It legalized same-sex marriage in 2010 and soon after passed a progressive gender identity law. Venezuela has promoted equality regardless of sexual orientation in banking, housing, policing, and employment. The new

Bolivian constitution is progressive on transgender rights but does not recognize same-sex unions. The Chilean government has legally recognized same-sex unions, but executive attempts to prevent discrimination against LGBT groups have not won legislative approval.

Like women's movements, LGBT activism has been greatest when states are sympathetic to their demands and/or vulnerable to their opposition, and when activists have formed alliances with other social movements, or organized within a broader human rights framework. The South African constitution provides far-reaching protections to gays and lesbians, including legalizing same-sex relations and banning anti-gay discrimination, and has thereby catalyzed the growth of activist organizations like the Treatment Action Campaign (TAC), which has been at the forefront of AIDS activism. TAC has advocated better access to health care for gay and straight men and women. Its allies include the Social Justice Coalition, the Anti Eviction Campaign and the Congress of South African Trade Unions. Groups like the Human Rights Campaign have lobbied for marriage equality in the US. In Latin America, Friedman argues, LGBT activists have, like feminists, been most successful where they have been able to use constitutional reform openings and the executive branch has supported their demands. By contrast, when states have repressed LGBT groups, activists have organized in an underground, defensive manner. Such is the case in Russia, Tunisia, and China.

The very gains of LGBT movements, as of women's movements, have often increased homophobic hate crimes. Relatively few countries have adopted laws prohibiting incitement to hatred based on sexual orientation. The June 2016 massacre of forty-nine people in a gay bar in Florida raised public awareness of homophobic violence. An article in the *New York Times* revealed that there are far more hate crimes against the LGBT community than against any ethnic or racial minority in the US (Park and Mykhyalyshyn 2016).

In most of the world, LGBT groups continue to face discrimination in employment, housing, education, health care, religious practice, and adoption of children. Like feminists, LGBT activists have debated the extent to which they should intensify struggles to expand their legal rights. Some activists worry that legal struggles divert energies from grassroots movements and the attempt to change cultural values and economic structures. The question surfaced in the US after the Supreme Court decision to legalize same-sex marriage; some prominent

LGBT activists cautioned that the decision should be seen not as an end in itself but a step towards eradicating systemic biases against the most vulnerable LGBT groups, including trans communities, people of color, immigrants and sex workers. For these groups, as for many women's movements, one important priority is to forge alliances with other oppressed groups and another is to address substantive rather than simply legal inequalities (Vaid, 2013).

Conclusion

The chapters in this volume chart the immense challenges women's movements confront, their response to these challenges and the tasks ahead. A crucial question is how women's movements can address the multiple inequalities that women, especially subaltern women, experience. Women's identities are determined by myriad social cleavages and for poor women from racial, ethnic, and religious minorities, the compounding of inequalities mitigates against single-issue campaigns and claiming singular identities. As a result, there are few issues that concern all women across social divides. One important exception is sexual violence which affects all women. Not surprisingly, most women's movements and many transnational and regional networks have addressed this issue. Most governments are at least in principle committed to stopping violence against women and international organizations, particularly the UN, have taken a lead in doing so. However even violence against women has different consequences for women from different social backgrounds and calls for intersectional approaches.

A bigger challenge concerns the efforts and effectiveness of women's movements in addressing poverty and class inequality, which is often overlaid with racial and ethnic inequality. Rights-based liberal feminism can be quite radical in highly repressive contexts, as Tohidi observes, but is ill-equipped to address structural inequalities, particularly in the current neo-liberal era.

For women's movements to effectively address homophobia, minority rights, and race and class inequalities necessitates forming sustained alliances with movements of other oppressed groups. Women's movements have often grown out of broader political struggles: the civil rights and antiwar movements in the US; nationalist movements in Palestine, South Africa, and India; and movements against authoritarianism in Latin America. Links between the women's movement and other popular democratic struggles have broadened the social base of women's movements. The chapters in this book record the productive linkages women's movements have increasingly forged with AIDS activists, health, labor, human rights and civil liberties groups. Indeed, women's movements are more committed to inclusivity and coalitional politics than most other social movements.

Another challenge is generational. Pal, writing on India, and Shaheed, on Pakistan, call for older feminists to listen to younger women and to appreciate their distinctive modes of activism and demands. Drawing younger women into women's movements requires greater use of social media, which played a key role in the Arab Spring, the World Social Forums, the Occupy movement and Black Lives Matter. In Pakistan, an Open Forum on WhatsApp preceded the highly successful WAF national convention, which was held in 2016 after a ten-year hiatus and brought together different generations of feminists. In Europe, Silke Roth notes, "interactive communication repertoires" have given rise to new forms of online activism and transformed women's networks. Tohidi describes how new communication technology in Iran has enabled Iranian feminists to interact with diasporic and other transnational groups. Sundstrom states that feminists relied on social networking sites to stage recent pro-choice demonstrations in Russia. Some of the most exciting developments in this regard have occurred in China, where young feminists have found the Internet a powerful medium for organizing. As Wang Zheng shows, they have used the Internet to make visible commonly unseen violations of women's rights, and WeChat to challenge heterosexual normativity and to forge links with women worker organizations.

Women's movements face formidable challenges that emanate from the global political and economic environment. As external challenges have become more daunting, they sometimes widen class, ideological, and other differences within women's movements. Some issues like the growth of militarization, the religious right and economic austerity, are simply too daunting for women's movements or any social movements to change. It is a credit to women's movements that they have tackled these issues at all.

The chapters in this book identify the dynamism of women's movements in enduring, evolving, and adapting to changing circumstances. Activists who were principally committed to a single set of issues and a single set of strategies have broadened their agendas and adopted new modes of organizing. Secular feminists have formed alliances with religious groups. Feminists have forged alliances with LGBT activists. Many activists who were exclusively concerned with gender inequality have increasingly addressed racism and indigenous rights. Movements have altered their strategies of working with the state and international donors in response to changing political conditions. While cognizant of enormous challenges, the authors in this volume illuminate the resilience and power of feminism and women's movements then, now, and in the years to come.

Notes

1. I am grateful to Elisabeth Jay Friedman, Kate Hartford, and Mark Kesselman for detailed and very helpful comments on a previous draft of this chapter.

2. I use the term "feminist" to describe ideas, discourses and practices supporting gender equality and discuss the concept and its relationship to women's movements below.

3. Although I use the short hand term LGBT for convenience, it does not capture the varied forms of gender and sexual self-identification within and across nations.

4. The Comparative State Feminism series, for example, focuses on women's movements in democratic, advanced industrial societies in order to develop testable hypotheses about their achievements.

5. Friends of the Family includes: Belarus, Egypt, Indonesia, Iran, Kuwait, Libya, Malaysia, Nigeria, Pakistan, Qatar, Russia, Saudi Arabia, Somalia, Turkmenistan, Yemen, and Zimbabwe.

AFRICA

1

Women's Movements in Africa

AILI MARI TRIPP

Introduction

Contemporary women's movements in Africa can trace their antecedents to women's mobilization within movements for independence and in the women's organizations established early in the one-party era. Today's movements emerged during struggles for democratization and in the context of peace movements during civil war. The new political space that opened up with democratization in the 1990s and in postwar contexts after 1990, but especially after 2000, has allowed for new forms of autonomous women's mobilization. Women's activism was also inspired by changing international norms regarding women's rights, highlighted in the 1985 UN Conference on Women in Nairobi and the 1995 UN Conference on Women in Beijing. It was further buoyed by foreign donors' new interest in supporting women's mobilization, even if these funding trends were not always sustained.

As a result of such influences, the women's organizations that emerged after the 1990s were characterized by their independence from national states and ruling parties. The organizations that formed in this period selected their own leaders and had their own sources of funding, which allowed them to chart their own agendas independent of the state and dominant party and enabled them to engage in greater policy advocacy, a marked shift from earlier mobilizations.

This chapter provides a historically framed overview of the development of contemporary African women's movements. It first looks at the roots of contemporary women's mobilization in sub-Saharan Africa in the struggles for independence and during the years of one-party rule (1960s through 1980s). It shows women occupying important roles in democratization movements from the early 1990s on, gains that influenced later mobilization. It examines how the decline of conflict in at least sixteen countries opened up new possibilities for mobilization, when women had been engaged in peace movements during war. The chapter explores the factors leading to the rise of autonomous women's movements after the 1990s and their impact on women's rights reforms. It describes the key issues that have engaged women activists and the characteristics of women's mobilization, illustrating the more general points with a closer look at Uganda as a case study.

History of Mobilization

Although African women's movements today have new agendas, strategies, and forms of leadership, they sometimes draw on older forms of protest and on experiences of women's mobilization that were used prior to colonialism and during the struggle for independence as well as during the single-party era that ran roughly from 1960 to the early 1990s. For example, women in precolonial African societies drew on forms of action based in local cultural norms to achieve strong social impact. In Cameroon they used *anlu*, or naked protests, to shame misbehaving and abusive men. Later under British colonial rule, Cameroon women drew on their tradition of *anlu* to ridicule and shame colonial male authorities in the late 1950s (Diduk 1989). Tapping into cultural symbolism of life and death, tactics of stripping were historically used as a curse against male abuse of authority, but in the modern context they have been used against repressive police and governmental authority in colonial and postcolonial Africa. Collective naked protests, for example, were used by women in prodemocracy movements in Kenya in the 1990s, the anti-oil company and environmental movements in the Delta region of Nigeria in the early 2000s, and the land struggles in northern Uganda's Amuru district in 2015.

Women have also drawn on traditions of protest that emerged during the independence struggles and wars of liberation. Women fought in large numbers in the Algerian war of independence in the 1950s. They participated as combatants, porters, and spies, but also in supporting roles as nurses, cooks, and launderers. In Kenya's Mau Mau movement, women provided fighters with supplies and in some cases fought alongside men (Kanogo 1987; Likimani 1985; Presley 1991;

Santilli 1977). Women also fought in the later armed liberation struggles in Mozambique, Guinea Bissau, Zimbabwe, and Eritrea. Women were in the leadership of the independence movement in Tanganyika during the same period: Bibi Titi rallied women, in particular, to the cause of independence, and was regarded as one of the two leading figures (along with Julius Nyerere) in that movement (Geiger 1997; Meena 1992). Women formed a women's section of the Tanganyika African National Union to demand independence, and Bibi Titi headed up this section.

Women traders had particular grievances against colonial rule and were among the most vocal advocates of independence. They rioted and protested colonial tax policies in several Igbo provinces in Nigeria in 1929, Pare District in Tanganyika (Tanzania) in the 1940s, and Bujumbura (Burundi) in the 1950s (Hunt 1989; Ifeka-Moller 1973; Leith-Ross 1965; O'Barr 1976; Van Allen 1972, 1976). In the 1940s, the Nigerian Abeokuta Women's Union, which represented over 100,000 women, organized demonstrations and tax boycotts and even sent a representative to London to present their demands to suspend female taxes. They were able to get female taxation suspended and in 1948 a woman gained a seat on the transition council that was the precursor to the parliament after independence (Parpart 1988:213).

Women's particular concerns were sometimes, but not always, articulated or addressed by nationalist movements, even when women were important participants. In some cases, as in Algeria, they were actively sidelined after independence, much to the disappointment of women activists. In other cases, such as Mozambique, women's rights issues were articulated by the liberation movement leadership, but were postponed, to be taken up after liberation. In Guinea and Mali, women's demands were seen as integral to the process of independence, and leaders of the struggle made concerted efforts to recruit women into the movement by appealing to women's concerns. Finally, in some contexts such as in Cameroon and Nigeria, women got involved in nationalist movements to advance their own gender-specific and other agendas, such as those related to taxation and market prices. For example, at least 1,000 of the 6,000 recorded petitions from Cameroon sent to the United Nations Trusteeship Council came from women nationalists. These petitions were one of the first forays of African women into advocacy within the international arena (Terretta 2007).

Post-Independence Mobilization, 1960–1990

During the first thirty years after independence, one-party systems like Tanganyika African Union and Kenya African National Union dominated the political scene in Africa. After the 1970s several governments were also led by military rulers such as Jerry Rawlings in Ghana (1979, 1981–2001), President Shehu Shagari (1979–1983) and Major General Mohammadu Buhari (1984–1985) in Nigeria, and Idi Amin in Uganda (1971–79). During this period, often the ruling party and the state controlled women's mobilization through patronage politics. The leaders of the women's organizations were often relatives of those in power and benefited from their positions in the form of salaries, cars, trips abroad, and other such perks.

Women's organizations were depoliticized, tending to focus on religious, domestic, cultural, and social welfare concerns, or on income-generating activities, including handicrafts. Domestic concerns involved cooking, hygiene, and how to manage a household. Some organizations were engaged in agricultural production and microcredit. Many adopted a "developmental" approach while attempting to keep women depoliticized. They focused on bringing women into development through agricultural production and informal sector activities and through microcredit and input schemes (Ngugi circa 2001). There were some legislative reforms in this period that carried benefits for women, but only if supported or initiated by the ruling party, and if posing no challenge to its priorities. Women's organizations carried out "gender sensitization" or "conscientization" (consciousness raising), but in general eschewed political advocacy, particularly if that would put them at odds with the party or government (Geisler 1995:546). At the local level their primary political role was ensuring votes for the party in power, populating political rallies in support of party leaders, and providing food and entertainment for visiting dignitaries. In some countries, like Zambia, the Women's League included among its activities a focus on women's morality and preventing women from having affairs. A similar program was adopted by the Union des Femmes du Niger (UFN), the women's wing of Parti Progressiste Nigérien (PPN), the leading party of the pre-independence period and the only legal party in the first Republic (1960–74). They demanded that women be educated and allowed entry into judicial, social, and political careers, and be supported as wives and mothers: this was a way to liberate women and uphold them as wives and mothers, and a way to stamp out and prevent urban sexual immorality and prostitution (Cooper 1995).

Some of the organizations during the first decades of independence were women's wings of the ruling party. Others were mass organizations that fulfilled essentially the same functions. For example, Development of Women (Maendeleo ya Wanawake or MYW), the largest membership organization in Kenya during one-party rule, limited its concerns to those of child rearing, care of the household, literacy, and handicrafts, with a primary goal of supporting the ruling party, Kenya African National Union (Wipper 1975:100). As noted above, these organizations generally operated along patronage lines and their leaders came from the families of men high in government. Ghanaian first lady Nana Ageman Rawlings chaired the 31st December Women's Movement in Ghana (31DWM); Nigerian first lady Maryam Babangida was president of the Better Life for Rural Women in Nigeria; and Sophia Kawawa, wife of Tanzania's former prime minister Rachidi Kawawa, was chairperson of the Union of Women of Tanzania (Umoja wa Wanawake wa Tanzania, also known as UWT). The tradition continued into the multiparty era as first ladies were associated with their own nongovernmental organizations (NGOs): In Tanzania, Wanawake na Maendeleo Foundation (WAMA) was run by Salma Kikwete and Anna Mkapa was the chief patron of the Equal Opportunities for All Trust Fund (EOTF). Uganda's first lady Janet Museveni was a patron of the popular Uganda Women's Effort to Save Orphans (UWESO). Not surprisingly these types of NGOs have been used for explicitly political purposes. For example, the Zambian former president's wife, Vera Chiluba, used her Hope Foundation to attack the political opposition.

It is worth noting, in addition to the party-related associations, there were some Christian organizations, such as the Young Women's Christian Association (YWCA), Girl Guides, and Mothers' Union, which were formed during the colonial era. There were also a handful of professional organizations, but the dominant organizations were the party-led unions and leagues.

Generally, the ruling party or government or both controlled the leadership of the party-affiliated women's organizations as well as their financing and agendas. This basically kept them from challenging the status quo. Some policy measures were adopted from time to time as a result of pressure from these organizations, but for the most part, they did not tackle the difficult issues such as marital rape, land rights, inheritance, and so on. For example, the National Council of Women's Societies in Nigeria lobbied the Government in 1986 to amend its discriminatory family planning policies that targeted only women and not polygamous men. It also got the state Commission for Women upgraded into a full-fledged Ministry of Women Affairs and Social Development, but it did little beyond these types of measures. The close ties between the Ghanaian government/ruling party and the 31DWM, which absorbed many of the independent women's organizations, limited the extent to which the women's organizations could press for change (Dei 1994; Mikell 1984).

Many governments relied on governmental women's policy agencies rather than on women's organizations to shape policy affecting women. In Ghana, for example, the National Council on Women and Development (NCWD) was formed through a parliamentary act (NRCD 322) in 1975 as an advisory body to the government on all issues affecting the full participation of women in national development, particularly in the areas of income generation, education, and vocational training. They also sought to eradicate prejudices against women. Their target groups included rural women, the urban poor, school dropouts, and working women. Under the Jerry Rawlings government in Ghana (1981–2000), the NCWD was able to get the inheritance laws reformed and degrading widowhood rites banned. However, the relationship between women's groups and the regime was "maintained at the expense of the women's struggle....In so doing women's issues have been shelved; or at best, they have received very casual attention" (Tsikata 1989:89).

Thus, state-affiliated women's organizations became a mechanism through which the ruling party and government depoliticized women. Although they claimed to represent the interests of all women within their countries' borders, particularly rural women, the organizations were primarily a means of generating votes and support for the party and for dancing, singing, and cooking for visiting officials. Women were further marginalized by being relegated to party women's wings, rather than integrated in a meaningful way into the party machinery, which would have afforded them more input into the party policies and candidate selection processes.

Between 1975 and 1985 most African countries established women's policy agencies or "national machineries," as they are referred to in Africa, to coordinate gender policy. Many were formed after a 1975 UN

Resolution called on member states to establish such machineries to promote women in development. Some countries formed these as ministries; others established women's bureaus or departments. These machineries were also created to serve as a link between the government and the domestic women's organizations and international institutions. However, they were often under-resourced and lacked the capacity to engage women's organizations effectively. Their commitment to women's concerns came into question in countries like Zambia and Ghana because of their weak ties to the women's movement, their weak leadership role in advancing legislative reforms, and the use of their leadership appointments for patronage purposes (Mama 2005; Phiri 2006; Tsikata 1989). In Uganda, Idi Amin created the National Council of Women in Uganda in 1978 and situated it inside the Prime Minister's office, while at the same time banning all other women's organizations. In many countries tensions arose between the women's movements and the national machineries, and women's NGOs often accused the women's policy agencies of trying to usurp the role of their organizations and of competing with women's NGOs for funding (Tripp 2000).

As single parties lost their grip and multiparty competition took hold in the 1990s, these institutional artifacts of the post-independence decades—mass unions, leagues, women's wings of parties, and state-related umbrella organizations—decreased in influence. They were sidelined by independent organizations that rose in importance, partly because donors began to redirect funding toward independent NGOs. Some of the state-related organizations strove to become independent, but generally their history weighed against them.

Changes in Women's Mobilization Starting in the 1990s

After the 1990s, new forms of mobilization proliferated around issues such as violence against women, environmental protection, land rights, inheritance rights, poverty and debt, reproductive rights, female education, peace, and many other concerns. Some of these movements gained international prominence, like the Greenbelt Movement in Kenya, led by the late Nobel laureate Wangari Maathai, which became an important force for political change. The peace movement during the Liberian wars (1989–96, 1999–2003) gave visibility to activist Leymah Gbowee, who won the Nobel Peace Prize in 2011 as a result of the efforts of her organization, the Women of Liberia Mass Action for Peace,

TABLE 1.1 Founding of Contemporary Women's Advocacy
Organizations in Africa

Year Founded	Organizations Founded (%)
before 1990	5%
1990 - 1999	24
2000 - 2005	40
2006 - 2011	30

Source: *Data provided by Angelika Arutyunova, Verónica Vidal of AWID, 2013.*

in bringing about peace in that country.[1] But these are only a few bet-
ter-known examples of the flourishing organizational growth that began
in the 1990s. Table 1.1 shows that the number of associations founded
increased rapidly after 1990, and burgeoned especially rapidly in the
first half-decade of this century. The increase continued, though more
slowly, after 2006, according to data from the 2011 Association of
Women in Development provided to this author.

Women's Mobilization and the Opening of Political Space

The new forms of mobilization resulted from the opening of political
space, which affected even the most repressive governments. Pressed
by civil societies and by donors, governments began to take halting
steps to liberalize, often shifting to multipartyism and electoral democracy with the aim of continuing to maintain control through more democratic means. The political opening, however incomplete, afforded
women greater possibilities for mobilization. Moreover, women activists themselves were heavily involved in political liberalization processes and were often on the front lines of pressing for change. In Mali,
President Moussa Traoré shot at 2,000 demonstrating women and children when they marched in front of the Ministry of Defense in 1991.
The killing of women and children so incensed the public that Traoré
was forced to make major concessions to the opposition before his fall
in a military coup, which set in motion the political transition process.
In Kenya, women were at the forefront of the democracy movement.
In 1992 a group of women who had gone on a hunger strike in Uhuru
Park in support of political prisoners found themselves in a violent

confrontation with police. In this incident, older women stripped themselves naked to level one of the strongest curses possible against the military police who tried to break them. More recently, in March 2011 in Côte d'Ivoire, 15,000 women held a protest to demand the resignation of President Laurent Gbagbo, who had refused to cede power after losing an election to Alassane Ouattara. The protestors included 500 women who marched naked to inflict a devastating curse on the government. The naked women held brooms and leaves in their hands while others wore black, drawing on powerful female symbolism that emphasized their role as generators of life who have the power to figuratively negate life. Gbagbo's troops opened fire on the women protesters, killing seven women and wounding 100. Gbagbo was eventually forced out of power, but only after his troops killed over 3,000 people and displaced a million.

In the 1990s we saw countries shifting from military to civilian rule and from single-party to multiparty states. We saw political opening, even if limited, with greater freedom of speech and freedom of association, and more openness to advocacy. Some countries later experienced a reversal in democratization, as has been the case with each wave of democracy historically. Some countries became hybrid regimes, neither fully democratic nor fully authoritarian, where democratic reforms were inconsistently protected and repression was unpredictable. But there has been at least some opening in most countries, allowing for women activists to mobilize. Where the lack of political opening did not allow for an autonomous civil society to flourish, as for example in Angola and Eritrea, considerably fewer improvements in women's status were evident.

Women's Mobilization and the Decline of Conflict

In many of the war-torn countries, women's movements started out as peace movements. Women have mobilized for peace in the context of conflicts like those in northern Nigeria, South Sudan, eastern Congo, and Somalia. The end of conflict also had an impact on women's mobilization, as long-standing conflicts or intense wars declined in over sixteen countries in Africa in the 1990s and 2000s. Civil wars had particular effects on women's status because their end required a reordering of the polity, unlike proxy wars or interstate wars. This allowed for women's rights activists to press for reforms in the context of peace talks, the rewriting of constitutions, truth and reconciliation commissions, the creation of electoral commissions, and the establishment of other such institutions. The new international and donor discourses on women's rights after the mid-1990s combined with political opening helped foster new women's activism, which sped up processes of women's rights reform (See Tripp 2015 for an elaboration of these trends).

Countries affected by major conflict had experienced serious disruptions in gender relations, forcing women to play greater roles in their households and communities, and at the national level. Men and boys fled or hid to avoid conscription into militias, or they participated willingly or unwillingly in the fighting. This meant that women had to provide for their households in new ways. The involvement of some women in the fighting also challenged gendered expectations in various countries. After the war, women claimed top positions in business, politics, education, and many other sectors where they had previously not been leaders.

During the years of war in Liberia (1989–96, 1999–2003), women peace activists worked at the grassroots level and went individually to request that the various militias to lay down their arms. They organized workshops with the warlords to encourage them to stop fighting. They negotiated behind the scenes with various militia leaders to persuade them to come to an agreement. They took their pleas for peace to presidents in the region, politicians, party leaders, churches and mosques, as well as other key players. They organized women from the refugee camps to hold a sit-in at the 2003 Comprehensive Peace talks in Accra, Ghana, to press for peace, using the international media, and communicating with UN agencies, the African Union, external powers involved in the peace talks, and others. They negotiated in those same Accra peace talks to get their demands met. They also mobilized regionally with sisters from Sierra Leone, Côte d'Ivoire, and Guinea through organizations like the Mano River Women Peace Network. Liberian women's peace organizations worked with Africa-wide peacemaking organizations like Femmes Africa Solidarité.

This mobilization during the conflict was a precursor to mobilization after the war ended. A decline in hostilities did not always translate into a decline in violence for women, who often experienced continued and even heightened violence after the war in their homes and communities. The legislative and constitutional reforms regarding land, violence against women, and women's representation (minimum quotas) were considerably more pronounced after major conflicts because of the gender disruptions that occurred. Thus it was no coincidence that the first woman elected president in Africa was in post-conflict Liberia. Rwanda, recovering after the orchestrated genocide in 1994 that killed 800,000 people, emerged as the country with the highest rates of legislative representation for women in the world after 2003. Because of the role of women's movements and coalitions, post-conflict countries had considerably more extensive legislative and constitutional changes than countries that had not experienced conflict (Tripp 2015).

Historically there have been certain conditions under which war has shaken up existing power arrangements in a way that makes women's rights reforms more likely. The presence of active women's movements is an essential ingredient in ensuring that women's rights are advanced, along with the diffusion of international norms regarding women's rights. We saw these same patterns in parts of Europe and the US after World War I, after which women gained the right to vote. We have seen them in Africa after the 1990s and especially after 2000, with the end of major conflicts. These changes in Africa had not occurred after earlier conflicts when women's movements were not actively pressing their agenda.

International Pressures for Reform

Several things had changed by the 1990s to make women's rights mobilization and reforms more likely in Africa in the context of political reform and a decline in civil conflict. Changes in international global norms influenced gender regimes. Interest in women's rights spread across Africa, promoted by the South African Development Community, Economic Community of West African States (ECOWAS), and the African Union, in addition to UN agencies and other multilateral and bilateral donors. Many African women's organizations attended the United Nations conferences in Nairobi in 1985 and in Beijing in 1995, which lent momentum to women's mobilization in Africa. There was also diffusion of influences among women's organizations across the continent, particularly among women's rights activists within countries enduring conflict, and a diffusion of ideas around legislative and constitutional reforms pertaining to the adoption of quotas, rights of land ownership and inheritance, violence against women, gender budgeting, peacebuilding, and many other such issues.

Tackling Challenging Cultural Impediments

One of the innovations in post-2000 constitutions, particularly in post-conflict countries, was the provision that the constitution or statutory law would override customary law in the case of a conflict between the two. Customary law has been particularly challenging for women's rights advocates in the areas of marriage, divorce, and inheritance, and family law more generally. Gradually we are seeing changes in these areas of law. Countries where customary law or sharia law traditions are strong have encountered the greatest resistance in reforming family law to accommodate women's rights. But even among the 29 countries that recognize customary law in Africa, in 22 of them, constitutional provisions have been introduced that allow statutory law to override customary law should there be a conflict when it comes to women's rights, e.g. in Chad, Ethiopia, and Somalia. Moreover, personal law is invalid if it violates constitutional provisions on non-discrimination or equality in 5 out of 12 countries, including Sudan and Nigeria.[2]

Cultural practices that are considered harmful to women have been another area of contestation. Sometimes these involve the maltreatment of widows or young women. For example, Ghana, Benin, and Togo still have a form of ritual servitude called *trokosi,* in which families or clans use young virgin girls to pay for services or as part of religious atonement for transgressions by family members. The girls work without pay—or consent—as slaves of priests, elders, and owners of a shrine. Gradually such cultural practices that are harmful to girls and women are being challenged and abandoned. As an example of inroads against one of the most widespread practices harming girls and young women, today at least 24 African countries out of the 29 where female genital cutting persists have banned the practice, most of them since 2000. The latest to ban the practice include Gambia and Nigeria.

Some cultural practices have proven to be less problematic than others. While family law reform has been especially challenging in predominantly Muslim countries, the adoption of parliamentary quotas has not been as controversial. Many of these countries—Tanzania, Senegal, Sudan, Algeria, and Tunisia among them—have been pressured by women's movements to adopt quotas for women in the national legislatures. Today, Muslim countries in Africa, including North Africa, have on average only slightly lower rates of female legislative representation (20 percent) than non-Muslim countries (22 percent).

Senegal is a case in point. Because of weak general ... women politicians, the Senegalese women's movement pre... quotas. Women's organizations and women party leaders, with th... port of the UN and other donors, sought gender parity for the Sen... lese legislature beginning in the mid-1990s, in efforts that lasted near... two decades. The Senegalese Council of Women (*Conseil sénégalais des femmes*, or COSEF) spearheaded the parity campaign. COSEF was formed in 1994 to advocate for women's increased political partici-pation. It was made up of women's associations, political parties, and NGOs. COSEF pressed the political parties to adopt quotas, and the parties pledged their commitment to do so. But after the 1998 elections it was evident that their moral commitment was insufficient, and COSEF decided it needed a legal means to bring about parity.

Fortunately, Abdoulaye Wade, who became president of Senegal in 2000, had made campaign promises regarding gender parity, and COSEF seized the moment to advance the issue. Again in Durban in 2002, when a group of African activists under the NGO Femmes Africa Solidarité (FAS) asked him to support the 30 percent quota of women representatives within the African Union, President Wade offered to advocate for a 50 percent quota, which is what the AU adopted (COSEF 2011). In 2004, still under Wade, Senegal signed the African Union Protocol to the African Charter on Human and Peoples' Rights on the Rights of Women in Africa (commonly known as the Maputo Protocol), which includes a provision about gender equality. Senegal also added the Maputo Protocol to its constitution.

In 2005, non-governmental organizations like COSEF, together with the Monitoring Committee for the Implementation of Gender, launched the campaign "Let's consolidate democracy with gender par-ity!" This marked a turning point in the struggle for parity (Sane 2010). Early on, COSEF and its allies gained support from parties like the Union for Democratic Renewal (URD), the Socialist Party (PS), the And-Jëf/African Party for Democracy and Socialism, and the Rewmi Party (PR). COSEF worked with women from those parties. On March 23, 2007, almost a thousand women from all parties dressed in white and marched from the Independence Square, the symbol of national freedom, to the Palace of the Republic, the seat of political power, chanting the word "parity!" The "white march" was organized by the Ministry of Women under the direction of Minister Aida Mbodj, along with COSEF. The head of state was quick to respond to the women's

r the march he proposed bill No. 23/2007,
It amended the Electoral Code to provide
ntation party list composed of alternating
ne gender parity law was finally adopted in
ervatory on Gender Parity, established by
ed the implementation of the parity law in
\3).

,..u, COSEF and the Ministry of Women's Af-
...uren, and Female Entrepreneurship, supported by the UN, launched a public awareness campaign in fourteen regions of Senegal and trained about three hundred women candidates on the electoral lists.[3] Thus while the impetus for the gender parity law came from women's organizations within Senegal, external actors like UN Women played an important role in supporting the domestic actors, providing both financial and technical support. As a result of the parity law and the well-aimed support, the number of female parliamentary representatives nearly doubled with the 2012 elections, jumping from 23 percent to 43 percent of the seats.

Characteristics of New Women's Movements

Autonomy

The new women's organizations which emerged after the 1990s were largely autonomous of ruling parties and the government. As a result, they set their own agendas, controlled their own finances, and selected their own leaders. They were diverse in their objectives and forms of mobilization, in contrast to the women's unions and leagues that were tied to the ruling party during the one-party era and that sought to encompass all women's interests. Moreover, they took on more advocacy causes because of their autonomy. Their independence also made it easier for them to build coalitions across ethnic, religious, and other differences. A few countries, Eritrea and Angola among them, still lack associational autonomy. The case of Angola can serve to illustrate what the absence of autonomy means.

Even though Angola has multiple parties, there are few truly independent NGOs. Most are tied at some level to the dominant party, the People's Movement for the Liberation of Angola (Movimento Popular de Libertação de Angola or MPLA), which is able to rule through patronage, repression, and intimidation. The ruling elites maintain their power through their access to oil and diamond wealth and as a result are able to buy off potential opponents. Through the state they also threaten opponents with loss of opportunities such as jobs, passports, bank loans, or university enrollment; at times they also use physical intimidation, imprisonment, and worse. One sees pockets of resistance in the cultural scene, but the country's policies have mainly served to create a quiescent population that does not challenge the status quo. Angolan women's organizations, almost all of them at the national level, are tied to the ruling party. Even organizations that seem independent are associated in one way or another with the ruling party and government, which means that women's organizations can only take up issues that are in accordance with the priorities of the ruling party. Although there are women in leadership positions in Angola and women constitute 37 percent of all legislators, there is little advocacy outside of the parameters set by the MPLA (Tripp 2015).

In those countries where one finds a strong and autonomous women's movement, women's rights have advanced more vigorously and a wider range of issues has been addressed. Having women in parliament or other positions of power and having a strong women's parliamentary caucus is important, but it is not enough, as the Angolan case shows. Organizations need to be autonomous in order to realize major women's rights reforms. This is borne out in the case of COSEF, which worked closely with the Ministry of Women and other governmental bodies, yet maintained its independence and hence its leverage.

Organizational Agendas

Autonomous organizations have been much bolder in challenging societal taboos. They have been more political and sometimes more confrontational in challenging government policy. Issues like domestic violence against women, marital rape, and sexual harassment only began to be addressed with the rise of independent women's organizations, as did inheritance and land laws and customary practices like female genital cutting. A few examples help illustrate the controversial issues autonomous organizations can tackle.

- In Morocco, every year thousands of children are abandoned and single mothers suffer severe discrimination as a result of social stigma, while the penal code criminalizes extramarital relations. The plight of single mothers in Morocco began to receive national attention starting with the formation of Solidarité Féminine in the mid-1980s, and the Institution Nationale de Solidarité avec les Femmes en Détresse (INSAF) in 1999. INSAF, for example, is involved in preventing the abandonment of children born outside of marriage. It supports the accommodation of and reintegration of single mothers into society and works toward the eradication of underage girls in domestic work. It also works as part of networks and national coalitions to defend the rights of women and children.

- In Sierra Leone, a large percentage of maternal deaths stem from complications of unsafe abortions. Women's organizations were able to get the Safe Abortion Act passed in 2015, allowing abortions during the first twelve weeks of pregnancy. After the twelfth week abortion is permitted only in cases of rape, incest, lack of a viable fetus, or risk to the health of the mother.

- In Tunisia, Article 226 of the penal code rules against outrages to public decency, a catch-all law often used to target the country's LGBT community. But the country has an active LGBT movement. It includes organizations like *Shams—pour la dépénalisation de l'homosexualité en Tunisie* (Sun—For the Decriminalization of Homosexuality) and *Chouf* (See), whose members use audiovisual and multimedia tools to promote human rights and gender equality. They seek to redefine feminism to give voice to all Tunisian LGBT women.

The rise of African feminism in the post-2000 period was another development tied to the expansion of women's rights agendas. Feminism here is regarded as a goal or target for social change, not a movement per se. Mobilization around this goal of social change can take place in many different arenas—within women's movements, but also within governments and many other societal institutions (Ferree 2006).

Up until the 2000s, feminism was often seen as a Western ideology of individual women fighting against men, with men as the main enemy of women. This was a stereotypical perception of feminism that was often promoted by politicians and the media in Africa. After the 2000s, African feminists became more vocal in redefining feminism in African terms and their views gained greater acceptance, particularly among younger activists.

Organizers of the first African Feminist Forum, held in Ghana in 2006, adopted a Charter of Feminist Principles that articulated some of the new thinking about feminism on the continent:

We define and name ourselves publicly as Feminists because we celebrate our feminist identities and politics. We recognize that the work of fighting for women's rights is deeply political, and the process of naming is political too. Choosing to name ourselves Feminist places us in a clear ideological position. By naming ourselves as Feminists we politicise the struggle for women's rights, we question the legitimacy of the structures that keep women subjugated, and we develop tools for transformatory analysis and action. We have multiple and varied identities as African Feminists. We are African women—we live here in Africa and even when we live elsewhere, our focus is on the lives of African women on the continent. Our feminist identity is not qualified with *"Ifs," "Buts,"* or *"Howevers."* We are Feminists. Full stop.[4]

This was a remarkable document in that it was a conscious break with the earlier ambivalence and defensiveness regarding feminism. There was a recognition of the plurality of feminist perspectives and that these differences were part of the strength of the women's movement. At the same time the feminist forum pointed to a consensus on the need to address issues like "poverty, illiteracy, health and reproductive rights, political participation, and peace."

Heterogeneity of Organizations

As the foregoing examples suggest, the new organizations which emerged after the 1990s were heterogeneous compared with the organizations of the single-party era. Today, the organizational landscape includes formal NGOs working on environmental issues, reproductive rights, and female leadership, health, and education; and single-issue groups that focus on female genital mutilation, land rights, HIV/AIDS, and women's sports. Some organizations advocate for particular groups of women like the disabled, widows, single mothers, and second wives in polygamous marriages, who often experience fewer rights and privileges in marriage than first wives. There are professional associations for university women and for women judges, lawyers, media workers, engineers, doctors, and other such groups. There are development-oriented organizations that promote women's credit and finance, trade, entrepreneurship, farming, and informal sector activities. At the local level one still finds the organizations that promote savings, farming, income-generating projects, handicrafts, sports, cultural events, and other such concerns.

Women's organizations come together around particular policy advocacy coalitions to advance causes with a specific focus on women, such as the adoption of legislative quotas, but also around issues which affect marginalized people more generally, such as debt, land, poverty, and climate change. Women's movements often act in concert with other civil society actors, parliamentarians, women's ministry officials, and UN agencies. One of the key areas of concern has been politics, where there have been major efforts to increase women's representation at all levels. Women's organizations in many countries—Tanzania, Uganda, Kenya, Cameroon, and Mali, for example—are the most highly organized and strongest sector within civil society, which is why they are often represented in the leadership of key civil society networks. Finally, there are regional networks of women activists, including the Africa Regional Sexual and Gender-based Violence Network, Forum for African Women Educationalists, and the Women Peace and Security Network Africa, as well as international networks in which African women are active, like MUSAWA (which means "equality" in Arabic), Women Living Under Muslim Laws (WLUML), Global Alliance against Traffic in Women (GAATW), and Development Alternatives with Women for a New Era (DAWN).

Women's organizations in Africa, according to a 2013 global survey by the Association for Women's Rights in Development (AWID), have focused their activities on the following, in rank order: women's economic empowerment, women's leadership, access to education, reproductive rights and health, gender-based violence, economic and social and cultural rights, democracy and governance, political participation, microfinance, and sexual rights. They serve a wide range of populations, listing, in order of the frequency with which they were mentioned: rural women and peasants, women with HIV, grassroots women, community leaders, women human rights defenders at risk, women with disabilities, women in post-conflict contexts, indigenous women, women in politics, and businesswomen. They employed diverse approaches, as well. Asked to identify the top five strategies prioritized by their organization, about two-thirds mentioned training and capacity building and/or women's empowerment programs; approximately half, advocacy, campaigning, and lobbying and/or awareness raising; about one-third, leadership development; and around one-quarter, communication and information, microfinance, sexuality education, and/or organizing meetings to analyze and strategize.

Independence of Funding

The same AWID study also found that women's rights' organizations in Africa found sources of funding independent of the state, which allowed them a measure of autonomy in delinking from state patronage networks. Several types of donors support women's rights activities in Africa. In the AWID study, women's organizations self-reported their major sources of funding, which included women's funds (37%) and self-generated funds (27%), followed by significantly less funding from international NGOs (8%), national governments (7%), local governments (6%), bilateral donors (6%), religious institutions (4%), multilateral donors like the UN (3%), foundations (1%), and local NGOs (1%) like Oxfam, Novib, HIVOS, and CARE.

Women's funds have become especially active in Africa in recent years. Focused specifically on women's needs, they often are more attuned to the specific concerns and needs of women's organizations than other, more generalized donors. The US-based Global Fund for Women works in twenty-seven African countries, making grants of US$13,000 on average. The UK- and Ghana-based African Women's Development Fund, the Netherlands-based Mama Cash, the Mediterranean Women's Fund, and the Kenya-based Action Fund for Women's Rights are similar organizations. Nationally based women's funds include organizations such as the Fonds pour les femmes Congolaises, Women's Fund Tanzania, Ghana Women's Fund, Nigeria Women Trust Fund, Pitseng Trust Women's Fund (South Africa), and the Women's Trust (Zimbabwe). These organizations fund a wide range of initiatives: women's literacy classes, programs combating violence against women, training sessions for women's leadership, and technical support in each country, with tools and information on sustainable agricultural practices.

Aside from its leadership role in setting the international agenda regarding women's rights, the United Nations has also created a

TABLE 1.2 Comparison of Women's Organizational Priorities, Donor Funding, and Gender Gap in Africa

	Organization Priority	Donor Funding	Gender Gap
Women's leadership and empowerment	51%	22%	15%
Women's economic empowerment	55	23	66
Access to education	35	22	85
Reproductive rights and health (contraception, abortion, maternal health)	28	23	97

Source: *World Economic Forum, Global Gender Index, https://www.weforum.org. Data provided by Angelika Arutyunova, Verónica Vidal of AWID, 2013.*

multi-donor fund supported by the governments of Spain, Norway, and Mexico to fast-track women's economic and political empowerment. The goal is to strengthen partnerships between civil society and governments as well as to provide long-term funding to women's rights organizations. The primary bilateral support to women's organizations comes from Spain, followed by Norway, EU institutions overall, Germany, Denmark, the UK, and the Netherlands.

Foundations tend to focus on specific concerns and regions. The Bill & Melinda Gates Foundation focuses on gender data gaps. The Ford Foundation supports women's rights and reproductive health in Africa; the Rockefeller Foundation, women's education; Carnegie Corporation, university education; the John D. and Catherine T. MacArthur Foundation, girls' secondary education in East Africa and Nigeria.

With the growing global interest in corporate social responsibility, major corporations such as Coca-Cola, Exxon, Chevron, and Intel have in recent years become interested in supporting projects benefiting women and girls. A recent study conducted by AWID, Mama Cash, and the Dutch foreign ministry found that, among 170 corporate initiatives, a total of US$14.6 billion had been pledged for women and girls around the world from 2005 to 2020. About half those resources are to go to sub-Saharan Africa.[5] The downside? As we have seen, government funding may discourage women's mobilization around more controver-

TABLE 1.3 Profile of Women's Advocacy Associations

	Africa	Outside of Africa
Median income of organization	$12,136	$65,134 overall $20,000 Latin America $24,000 South/Southeast Asia
Received donor funding	82%	82%
Receive core support	23%	31%
Have multiyear grants	15%	25%
Give grants to other organizations or individuals	25%	13%
Have lost donors in past 10 years	25%	19%

Source: *AWID 2011 Global Survey: Where Is the Money for Women's Rights.*

sial issues; the new corporate funding focuses on economic empowerment, entrepreneurship, and women's health and girls' education, but very little of it targets human rights or peace or other structural issues underpinning women's rights.

Diversification of funding helps, but the picture even so is far from rosy. There is a mismatch between the priorities identified by women's organizations and those of donors. As Table 1.2 shows, the disconnect is greatest in the areas where the gender gap, according to the World Economic Forum, is the greatest: in the area of women's political and economic empowerment (See Table 1.2). Relative to other parts of the world, African women's organizations receive the least external support in terms of core funding (AWID 2011).

Women's organizations also face numerous challenges because the types of funding they can obtain focus too heavily on short-term projects or on narrowly defined advocacy to produce easily measurable outcomes (vaccinations administered, women who learned to read, leadership training workshops held, etc.). The long, painstaking, and unpredictable work of changing and implementing legislation, policy, and culture is not so attractive to donors, because its success is contingent on so many other social actors and factors. Yet this is often where women's rights activists need the most support. Thus, activists still point to the need for donors to think more long-term, and to focus on networks, movements, and processes of transformation to bring about structural changes that will have longer-term and lasting impact.

Building Unity Across Difference

One of the most striking characteristics of women's mobilization in Africa has been its capacity for building coalitions and unity across difference, particularly in the context of conflict. In the past two decades women in sub-Saharan Africa have been increasingly engaged in peace movements, grassroots peace building activities, and peace negotiations. In virtually all peace negotiations, women assiduously worked across ethnic, clan, religious, and other differences—in part because they were excluded from official representation in formal peace negotiations. In countries like Liberia, Burundi, Democratic Republic of Congo, and Somalia, where the male negotiators (often warlords) sat at opposite ends of the table fighting over positions of power, representatives of women's organizations sat together and worked across difference. Unity was their starting point rather than their end point. In Somalia, women from all clans came together, calling themselves the sixth clan, in order to gain recognition in the peace process, because only a feuding clan could get representation in the talks. During Liberia's war, women joined across the Muslim-Christian divide and across ethnic and class differences to forge a united front in pressing for an end to the conflict. This type of coalition-building between Christians and Muslims has been significant in Nigeria as well, in protests against Boko Haram kidnappings and activities.

Women's peacemaking and peacebuilding initiatives have taken a variety of forms. Women in countries as diverse as Mali, Mozambique, and Uganda organized rallies and boycotts urging small arms confiscation; they led reconciliation ceremonies, and negotiated with rebels to release abducted children and child soldiers. Women peace activists have played a role in preventing the resumption of conflict by monitoring and advocating against the sale of small arms and participating in campaigns to prevent the sale of diamonds to fund armed conflict.

Rather than seeing peace as something that had to be achieved to carry out reconstruction, women activists in post-conflict countries often regarded the process of reconstruction itself as *the way* to peace. Because of their involvement in more quotidian concerns, the working out of problems of access to water, food distribution, garbage disposal, and town cleanliness *was* the process through which peace was built in a country like Liberia. Peace was built piecemeal through the rebuilding of society. This is a radically different notion of peacemaking and departs fundamentally from the way peace negotiations are generally framed.

A Case Study: Uganda

The movement emerged at a time of change in international gender norms, and UN agencies and bilateral donors played a role in fostering women's rights reforms in Uganda as elsewhere. As the war was winding to its end, many women activists went on their own to the 1985 UN Conference on Women in Nairobi. They returned energized to change the status of women in Uganda, which they felt had fallen behind that of other countries. The first independent women's NGOs began to emerge. Some of the early demands of the movement included political power, an end to violence against women, microcredit, education for women, (including higher education), and broad legal reform.

Local-level gender disruptions had taken place as a result of the war. Women began to demand more access to resources and economic opportunities and began to push for more control within their communities both during and after the war. In the early 1990s, for example, as I describe in my book *Women and Politics in Uganda* (2000), there were a series of local-level conflicts in which women sought to control resources and were being challenged by local male leaders in doing so. For example, women fought to start and run a health clinic in Wakitaka, Jinja, against the wishes of the male local council leaders who felt that women should not take such initiatives. They sought to protect market space in Kiyembe market in the national capital, Kampala, which was being claimed by male vendors. They struggled to control the funds of the traditional birth attendants' organization in Kamuli, which were being claimed by a man. They also sought to control the terms of a World Bank infrastructure project in Kampala which would displace numerous residents. Residents of these communities depicted all of these struggles as new ones that had emerged as a result of women's new-found voice. In her study of survivors of sexual violence from the 1981–1986 war in Luwero, Liebling also found that the war had changed women's sense of themselves, and that they had come to express themselves as autonomous and capable rather than vulnerable and dependent (Liebling-Kalifani 2004).

Ugandan women assumed new leadership roles in local councils and also in religious, political, business, civil society, and market institutions, both at the local and national level. New networks emerged to address problems of women's access to land, peace in northern Uganda, education, and other concerns. Women also led coalitions concerned with land rights, hunger, debt, corruption, and poverty more generally. The older model of having an overarching women's organization to represent all women is no longer popular. The variety of Ugandan women's organizations today reflects the diversity in the movement, which includes women who are differentiated by religion and location, but also women who have diverse interests and occupations, including second wives, sex workers, and women athletes.

Women's organizations were initially supportive of the NRM because Museveni appointed women to key ministerial posts and introduced an electoral quota for women. (This support diminished over time as Museveni remained in power over 30 years, tried to manipulate the women holding reserved legislative seats, and withheld support for key demands pertaining to land rights.) Ugandan women became one of the most important organized forces in the country. This was evident during the 1993 constitutional reform process, when women's organizations submitted more memoranda to the Constitutional Commission than did any other sector of society (Bainomugisha 1999:93).

With each election, women's coalitions issue a Women's Manifesto, articulating the key demands of women's organizations for the political parties. The 2016–2021 Women's Manifesto was the product of consultations by the Women's Democracy Group (WDG) in fifty districts. The Women's Democracy Group, a coalition of women's civil-society organizations (CSOs) in Uganda, was established in 2009 with an aim of strengthening women's leadership and influencing gender responsiveness in democratic governance. It is made up of five leading national women's associations: the Uganda Women's Network (UWONET, which acts as the coordinator), Action for Development (ACFODE), Center for Women in Governance (CEWIGO), Forum for Women in Democracy (FOWODE), and Women's Democracy Network–Uganda Chapter (WDN–U). In drafting the manifesto, the coalition consulted a wide range of CSOs, political party officials, local government representatives and administrators, academics, donors, and other key opinion leaders from religious, traditional, business, and other institutions as well the women's leagues of six major political parties in Uganda. The coalition identified women's health, land and property rights, education, economic empowerment, and political empowerment as the key areas of concern.

As a result of pressure from women's movements, the presence of women in leadership positions in all three branches of the national government has dramatically improved. The number of women in Parliament increased from 0.8 percent in 1980 to 18 percent in 1989 and 35 percent in 2015. The number of women running for parliamentary positions more than tripled from 1996 (135 candidates) to 2011 (443). Rebecca Kadaga became the first woman to serve as speaker of the Ugandan Parliament in 2011. Speciosa Kazibwe served as vice president for almost ten years from 1994 to 2003, and has been the longest serving female vice president in Africa. In 1988 there was one woman out of 33 in the cabinet; this increased to eight in 1989. Today women hold one-third of the cabinet positions. Women are often placed in "softer" ministries, as ministers of Gender, Labour and Social Affairs, Education and Sports, Tourism and Wildlife; but they have also been appointed as ministers of Defense, Internal Affairs, Trade and Industry, and Justice and Constitutional Affairs.

The expansion in female leadership extended to the judiciary as well. Of today's eight Supreme Court justices, three are women. Out of forty-six High Court judges, twenty are women. A 2012 study showed that about one-third of the justices on the court of appeals and one-third of the chief magistrates are women, while 47 percent of those in Magistrate Grade 1 are women (Global Network of Women Peacebuilders 2012).

Not only did the women's movement influence the number of women in leadership positions; it also effected policy changes. In Uganda, legal reforms were spearheaded by the women's movement together with the Uganda Women Parliamentary Association (UWOPA), which has allowed women to work across party lines (Wang 2013). In 2006–2011 they were instrumental in passing a steady stream of legislation affecting women with respect to land, refugee rights, maternity leave, employment, sexual harassment, equal opportunities, defilement or rape of girls under 18, disability rights, trafficking, domestic violence, female genital cutting, and many other concerns. The International Criminal Court Act (2010) criminalized sexual exploitation of women during conflict. A law passed in 2006 established the Equal Opportunities Commission, which had been mandated by the 1995 constitution to oversee the implementation of policies regarding women's rights. In 2010, Parliament ratified the Maputo Protocol (the African Union's treaty regarding women's rights), overcoming powerful opposition by the Roman Catholic Church and the Uganda Joint Christian Council. There are still important gaps in legislation, particularly with respect to marriage, divorce, and land inheritance, but the legislature has continued to pass laws benefiting women. The first National Gender Policy was passed in 1997 and the second Uganda Gender Policy was launched a decade later in 2007. It sought to bring a gender perspective to all levels of planning, resource allocation, and implementation of development programs. The priority areas include improved livelihoods, promotion and protection of rights, participation in decision-making and governance, and recognition and promotion of gender in macro-economic management. A National Action Plan was also passed in response to the United Nations Security Council Resolution 1325 requirement that countries develop policies in peacemaking and conflict resolution that address the concerns of women and girls and incorporate women into decision making processes.

The courts have also played a role in promoting women's rights. For example, in 2007, a constitutional court struck down key provisions of the Divorce Act, the Penal Code, and the Succession Act that limited women's right to inherit property. It also issued a ruling that decriminalized adultery for women (it had not been criminalized for men).

Uganda still has a long way to go before women enjoy equal rights with men. However, considerable progress has been made since the early 1990s. The reasons for the gains by the women's movement are similar to the overall patterns one finds in Africa. Uganda experienced a major conflict, which eroded traditional gender relations in a way that forced women to play more public and important roles in their households, communities, and ultimately in the nation. The end of conflict made it possible for the government to take steps to open political space. Although Uganda remained a hybrid regime which was neither fully authoritarian nor democratic, enough space opened up for women's organizations to mobilize.

Unlike in the past, when most women's mobilization occurred under an overarching umbrella organization tied to the ruling party and state, today Ugandan women's mobilization is autonomous, heterogeneous, mostly independent of party agendas, and has its own leadership and sources of funding. This has provided the organizations with sufficient autonomy to determine their own policy agendas and exert pressure on the country's leadership to move ahead with further reforms. At times the government has taken regressive steps, dragged its feet, and undermined women's demands. But the overall patterns suggest that there has been considerable progress for women, which came as a result of pressure from women's organizations.

Conclusions

The 1990s marked the introduction of multipartyism and the decline of the one-party state and military rule in Africa. It saw an increase in associational freedom, freedom of the press, and political rights. The 2000s saw the end of major conflicts in Africa and a decline in the numbers of conflicts starting or reigniting. Both these trends, coupled with the changing international norms regarding women's rights after the mid-1990s, helped give rise to autonomous women's organizations and coalitions as well as women's movements, which advocated for women's rights reforms. With access to their own resources and donor funds, they began to challenge the chokehold that clientelism and state patronage had on women's mobilization in the post-colonial period. Associational autonomy allowed women to select their own leaders, raise their own funds, and set their own agendas. It also made it possible for women to forge new alliances across ethnic, religious, clan, racial, and other divides. It meant that women's organizations could expand their agendas, engage in advocacy, and take up political concerns rather than simply "developmental" issues that focused on income-generating and welfare concerns. They could now more easily challenge the laws, structures, and practices that constrained them. It allowed women activists to broaden their demands and many for the first time took on issues like domestic violence, female genital cutting, and rape that had been considered taboo in the past. By the early 2010s, issues of LGBT rights, abortion, and other controversial issues were gaining traction, even if haltingly.

Until the 1990s, even governments that were generally disposed in favor of women's advancement saw the concerns of women's rights advocates as a sideshow to the broader project of development rather than part of it. But in the 1990s we began to see substantial changes in Africa in gender policy with the adoption of quotas for legislative bodies, the adoption of gender mainstreaming practices in the development of national budgets, the closing of the gender gap in education at all levels, some improvements in health measures affecting women, and the increased availability of microcredit and finance to women. Governments began to adopt policies that addressed violence against women, sexual harassment in the workplace, family law that discriminated against women, and many other concerns women brought to the table.

Fierce cultural and political challenges remain. The weakness of civil and political liberties and the constant threat that political space will close in the many semi-authoritarian and authoritarian African states impose serious constraints on women's mobilization. Nevertheless, women are in movement in Africa and they have set in motion important and unprecedented societal transformations that are influencing international debates on women's rights.

Notes

1. Co-awarded, together with President Ellen Johnson-Sirleaf.

2. See http://wbl.worldbank.org/data/exploretopics/accessing-institutions. Accessed April 20, 2016.

3. See http://www.unwomen.org/en/news/stories/2012/7/following-elections-proportion-of-senegal-s-female-parliamentarians-almost-doubles. Accessed April 20, 2016.

4. See http://awdf.org/wp-content/uploads/Charter_of_Feminist_Principles_for_African_Feminists.pdf. Accessed April 21, 2016.

5. See http://www.awid.org/news-and-analysis/womens-rights-organisations-alarmed-attempt-dilute-funding-call.

2

A History of Feminist Moments

The South African Women's Movement, 1950–2014

ELAINE SALO

Introduction

The South African Constitution is celebrated internationally for providing women and sexual minorities with an impressive array of rights and freedom from discrimination. These rights have expanded social and economic opportunities for women and the LGBT communities. Women and LGBT communities have entered erstwhile white- and male-only spaces, such as the military, corporate governance, the judiciary, and the presidency. Constitutional rights have legalized abortions and have enabled lesbian and gay people to marry, parent children, and become legitimate heirs to their partners' estates.

Other gendered gains are reflected in South Africa's rank as seventeenth globally in closing the gender gap[1] between men and women with regard to share of resources and opportunities. In addition, South Africa is widely celebrated, after Rwanda, as having one of the highest numbers of women represented in state institutions. Women hold 40 percent of parliamentary seats in the current government and are well represented in the private corporate sector. Females are more represented than males throughout the educational system, with the exception of postgraduate education, where men dominate.

These shorthand numeric measures reflect the recent historic gains for women and LGBT minorities, which result from their participation in ordinary South Africans' struggle against the legalized racist system in the twentieth century. Most of these gendered gains are the result of women's protests as an explicitly gendered collective against the apartheid state, in alliance with a broad democratic movement that gained uneven momentum after 1950 and reached a climax in the early 1990s.

Contemporary gains are juxtaposed with current gendered conflicts: women's quotidian struggles against gender-based violence, their claims for substantive sexual and reproductive rights, and widespread homophobia. These struggles are imbricated with extreme socioeconomic inequality, and the contradictions between women's constitutional rights and traditional chiefs' claims to authority over rural women.

Borrowing from the ideas of Ernesto Laclau and Chantal Mouffe (2014), I argue here that the progress of gendered rights in South Africa can be understood as a series of feminist *moments*, marked by a conjuncture between the dominant consciousness of black men's claims to substantive citizenship, and women's legitimate gendered claims to equal citizenship status. Such conjunctural moments are marked by a transformation in gendered power relations, so that women gain equal status to men in legal, socioeconomic, and cultural arenas and make significant gains in the struggle for gender equality. During a conjunctural feminist moment, women's collective gendered claims to rights are recognized as legitimate, just outcomes of their participation in the broader struggle for democracy. The character and content of these rights claims are informed by the specific histories of democratic struggle and the cultural expressions of gender.

Chandra Mohanty (1991) has argued that the gendered meanings of the category *woman* are not constituted *a priori*; rather they are informed by gendered histories that are grounded within specific geopolitical contexts. Similarly Naila Kabeer (1998) and Lila Abu Lughod (2013) have maintained that women's gendered experiences are culturally diverse.

The history of women's protests in South Africa is marked by two significant feminist moments, when normative power relations between men and women were contested and women won gender gains. These moments were marked by women's mass protests for full citizenship rights, formulated in the two Women's Charters in the 1950s and in the 1990s (see also Hassim 2014). Feminist moments in the post-apartheid era, in contrast, are brief, characterized by temporary alliances that advance the realization of women's and LGBTI communities' formal citizenship rights in everyday life. These protests during the apartheid and democratic eras revealed the complex intersections between the women's movement, women's intersectional identities, and the opportunities and constraints set by the broader political context.

In this chapter I map out a brief history of South African women's movements and describe their struggle for substantive gendered citizenship. I argue that the significant gendered gains made are due to the women's movements' contribution to the national struggle against apartheid, and to the ongoing struggle for the realization of gender rights in the post-apartheid era. The character of the South African women's movement is inextricably shaped by two historical periods. Between 1950 and 1994, the form of the women's movement and its strategies for claiming gender rights were imbricated with the national democratic struggle and the overarching claims for black South Africans' democratic rights. In the post-apartheid era, the women's movement is characterized by the demand to make gendered constitutional rights and freedoms real, in a context of resurgent black nationalist patriarchy and extreme socioeconomic inequality and constraint.

Twenty-one years after the official onset of democracy in South Africa, we witness the country's contradictory progress in ensuring women's and other sexual minorities' gender rights. On one hand, the country has successfully reduced the national rates of maternal mortality, and has launched one of the most successful national programs providing sex education and Anti-Retroviral Treatments (ARTs) to combat HIV/AIDS. On the other hand, women living in the urban informal settlements and the rural periphery experience high rates of maternal and infant mortality and shoulder the burden of economic poverty, and rates of sexual violence targeting women remain unacceptably high throughout the country. The ruling African Nationalist Congress (ANC) supports women's and sexual minorities' constitutional rights, but also upholds customary authorities' absolute authority over rural women.

Women's rights and activism have to be situated within the post-apartheid context of great socioeconomic inequality juxtaposed with a liberal constitution that enshrines South Africans' citizenship rights. Constitutional rights mark the legal recognition of women as full citizens and legal persons. They also marked the high point of women's collective agency in the apartheid era. The constitutional ratification of these gendered rights also points to the complex relationship between the anti-apartheid movement on the one hand, and the women's movement, feminists, and LGBT activists on the other.

South African women both black and white have played a significant role in shaping the struggle for substantive democracy and to end apartheid. The shape and form of the women's movement during the anti-apartheid struggle and the extent and character of women's agency inform the makeup of local feminisms, and must be located in the context of the broader set of political, racial, and socioeconomic divides that characterize South African society.

But Is This Feminism?

The question of whether women's mobilization in South Africa constitutes feminism invariably arises. I define feminism as a *temporal moment*, when women have won the space to assert their collective gendered identity and transform existing gendered power relations either partially or wholly. When and how women are able to do so is always informed by local histories of gender relations (Kemp, et al. 1995; Mohanty, Basu 2010; Salo 2010, Beuno-Hansen 2015).

Postcolonial feminist theorists[2] have challenged hegemonic definitions of feminism that emanate mainly from the West. The theoretical concepts that arise from struggles in a specific context such as Britain, for example, do not assist us in understanding why women's resistance movements arise and take on a specific form in Nigeria or Egypt or the Caribbean. Mohanty (1991) has argued that meanings of gender and womanhood are multiply informed by *located* histories, the diverse cultural meanings of femininity, and by women's *lived* material realities. In addition, women mobilize on the basis of those intersectional identities that have been politicized through struggles set within a specific domain of power relations, and are expressed in particular cultural idioms (Van Allen 1972; Beuno Hansen 2015).

South African women have mobilized on the basis of their gendered identities, as these have been historically informed by racial, socioeconomic, and geopolitical differences and inequalities. Rural women prioritize access to land, safe water, and health services, while urban women consider personal safety in the public sphere crucial. At the same time, transnational connections between feminists in global governance forums such as the United Nations and international nongovernmental organizations also inform the issues around which women have mobilized in the national context.

Ann McClintock (1995) claims that "all nationalisms are gendered and all nationalisms are dangerous." She points to nationalisms' ability to instantiate women into deeply entrenched, prescribed feminine roles of biological and cultural nurturance and reproduction, thereby underwriting patriarchal leadership. McClintock's point about nationalism is only partially helpful for analyzing nationalist struggles in the global South. On the one hand, she provides us with the analytical tools necessary to understand the entrenched gendered binaries of nationalisms that inform the oppression of subject peoples. Her perspective is helpful to analysis of gender dynamics in fascist Chile, British colonial rule in Kenya, or Afrikaner rule in apartheid South Africa.

McClintock's analysis is less helpful, however, in our analyses of nationalist struggles by subject men and women, for democratic rights, waged through struggles for national self-determination against colonialism or racial and ethnic domination. Subject women's subjectivities are simultaneously imbricated with gendered tensions as well as the solidarities they experience in relation to subjugated men. Feminist struggles against gender inequality in such contexts *are* more complex because they must account for gender struggles that reflect the multiple axes of subjugated women's intersectional identities.

I argue that the character of the South African women's movement, the nature of local feminism, and women's gendered victories and challenges must be understood in the context of the anti-apartheid struggle and the battle to realize constitutional gender rights in the post-apartheid democratic era.

White Nationalism, Segregation, and Apartheid

South African women's struggles throughout the twentieth century, and the gendered roles and identities that they elected to mobilize as vehicles of resistance, have to be placed within the context of white racial domination and Afrikaner nationalism.

The first democratic elections in 1994 marked the first official act of citizenship for the majority of black[3] South Africans. Prior to this event, modern South African nationalism was officially defined by white racial exclusivity and the black majority was denied full citizenship in the modern nation. Women's protests in general and the character of the anti-apartheid women's movement in particular must be embedded in the framework of white nationalism and black economic and social dispossession,[4] which was increasingly exacerbated by a suite of discriminatory laws beginning with the onset of South African independence in 1910. It is necessary therefore to provide a brief history of these two processes below.

South African white[5] nationalism drew on dominant Eurocentric notions of ethnic nationalism that defined citizenship and belonging as the exclusive right of those who shared a common ancestry, a common faith, and a common language, culture, and territory. The modernist ideology of racism and sexism informed white, Afrikaner nationalism as it naturalized the belief that blacks were less civilized than whites as a whole; further, that white men in particular were entitled to the national wealth of socio-economic and physical resources. White women were considered the embodied boundaries of the race, and were often the instruments to facilitate racial exclusion. They were regarded as the embodiment of racial purity and the nurturers of the new generation (Hofmeyr 1987; McClintock 1995). Consequently white women's sexual relations with black men were a cultural and legislated taboo. The majority of white women did not identify with or participate in black people's struggle against racism. White women's claims for the franchise were embedded in their moral campaign against alcohol and were located in their attempts to combat white poverty in the 1930s, and their access to suffrage was acquired on the back of black male disenfranchisement in the 1940s.

The ideology of white supremacy, instituted through colonialism and nurtured during the segregationist period of the South African Union after 1910, reached its apogee during the apartheid era between the 1950s and 1990s. Black displacement and exclusion from the fruits of the national economy sharpened after the Afrikaner Nationalist Party was elected in 1948 and began instituting apartheid legislation. The state sought to institute a slew of repressive racist legislation between the 1950s and late 1980s (Wilson and Ramphele 1989; Salo 2004).

Forced removals of blacks had occurred since the early twentieth century, enabled by a suite of legislation centered around the pass laws and land ownership (Wolpe 1972; Legassick 1974). The Population Registration Act (1950), the Group Areas Act (1950), and the Bantustan[6] Act (1970) increased such forced removals and racial and ethnic categorization and separation across the country. White nationalism and the racist dispossession of black wealth, and of African ownership of land and live-stock in particular, neatly served the need for a cheap, exploitable male labor force in the mining and agricultural industries (Wolpe 1972; Legas-sick 1974). Increasingly, land for cultivating and animal husbandry was constrained as people displaced by forced removals were resettled in the reserves. The gendered and generational effects of the pass laws and forced removals ensured that mainly women, children, and the elderly were concentrated in the reserves, while male labor continued to oscil-late between white-owned mines, manufacture and agriculture, and re-serve households. These laws reshaped the black geopolitical landscape into gendered spaces, as African men remained in urban spaces as work-ers, while the majority of African women were confined to the rural re-serves (Bernstein 1975; Murray 1981; Wilson and Ramphele 1989). The apartheid state had effectively instituted the slow extermination of Afri-can households through a suite of racist legislation and politicized the private domain of the black household and women's reproductive roles.

The legislated process of separate development also instituted a hi-erarchy of deprivation with regards to public education, health, social security, water and sanitation services, and leisure amenities. The white population enjoyed the lion's share of the state budget spent on these services, while far less was spent on services for Indians and coloureds. The smallest budget was spent on services for the African population, particularly in the reserves. Laws such as the Immorality Act (1950) and the Mixed Marriages Act (1949) criminalized sex and marriage across race, and homosexuality was banned under the sodomy laws (1957). The apartheid legislation progressively impoverished the black population as a whole and the African population in particular. By 1986 whites, who constituted 15 percent of the population, enjoyed 65 percent of the in-come. In contrast the 73 percent of the population who were Africans received only 25 percent (Wilson and Ramphele 1989).[7] In 1985 the infant mortality rate (IMR)[8] for Africans in urban areas was 124 per thousand live births, and in rural areas, 135. In contrast, the rate for whites in urban and rural areas was 12 (Wilson and Ramphele 1989).

South African Women's
Anti-apartheid Struggle, 1900–1994

For most of the twentieth century, African women's gendered struggles were primarily against a racist patriarchal state and secondarily against an indigenous patriarchy that sought to instantiate their status as minors through the retention of customary laws. The pass laws politicized African women's roles within the household, and threatened their right to share the labor of social reproduction with men. Consequently women's resistance to the white state was expressed through their identities as wives and mothers.

Women's earliest organized campaigns date back to 1908 in East London, when they protested against high rents and the threat of arrests (Kemp et al. 1995). Between 1912 and 1913, women began more sophisticated campaigns against the pass laws in Waaihoek, in the Orange Free State. Black women formed their autonomous organization, the Native and Coloured Women's Association (NCWA), in 1912 to raise support for women activists jailed for anti-pass protests (Ginwala 1990). The NCWA planned the campaigns that targeted the state's attempts to extend the pass laws to African women, requiring them to purchase permits that would allow them to move outside the designated black areas. Another organization, the Bantu Women's League (BWL), led by Charlotte Maxeke, was formed shortly after the NCWA, as an affiliate of the men's ANC. The BWL (later the National Council of African Women) was less militant than the NCWA and focused mainly on welfare issues. Nevertheless the BWL supported the NCWA anti-pass campaigns in the Free State.

Women used multiple strategies in their protests: petitions to the Ministry for Native Affairs to desist from extending the permit requirements to women; refusing to carry passes; and marching to protest arrests. The campaign spread to other towns in the Orange Free State and involved hundreds of women. Newly formed men's political organizations such as the ANC and the African Political Organization supported the women's campaign and encouraged them to defy the law. Ultimately the proposed legislation requiring women to purchase permits was withdrawn. The NCWA and the BWL campaigns proved successful and warded off further attempts to extend the pass laws to African women until the 1950s.

By the late 1920s the fledgling textile industry was employing small numbers of urban working-class women of all races. These jobs were generally low status and poorly paid. Trade unionist Solly Sachs led the formation of the first nonracial women's trade union, the Transvaal Garment Workers' Union (GWU) (Marks and Trapido 2014). The GWU led two strikes in the early 1930s for better wages.

Ultimately the increasing racial segregation of
made unionization of women across race differ
tain. However, the trade union and communist m
working-class women, and ultimately provided
ship for the mass nonracial women's organization
South African Women (FEDSAW).

Trade unionists such as Lilian Ngoyi and Ray A
leadership skills that they had acquired in helping   ...ια FED-
SAW in 1954. The first conjunctural feminist moment occurred in
the 1950s, as FEDSAW mobilized women in a context of worsening
racist repression. FEDSAW provided ordinary South African women
with a collective voice to challenge the renewed threat to extend the
pass laws to African women, and to resist impending apartheid legislation. The pass laws threatened the African household and extended
the state's intrusion into the most intimate spaces of black family life
as it sought to confine the majority of African women and their dependents permanently to the rural Bantustans (Wolpe 1972; Murray
1981).

Until the 1950s African women resisted their forced removal from
urban South Africa. Racist apartheid legislation implemented after
1950 reduced African women and men to dehumanized labor units in a
white political economy. The minority of African women allowed to remain in urban areas would serve only to carry the burden of white and
middle-class households' reproduction. African children were parented
vicariously and unevenly, and were often confined to rural reserves.
Women would resist such policies through mass organization (Mashinini, 1989; Kemp et al. 1995).

FEDSAW drafted the Women's Charter, calling for the full enfranchisement of all, and for the recognition of women's equal rights to
property, equal remuneration, and the end to women's minor status
under customary law. FEDSAW, together with the African National
Congress Women's League (ANCWL), organized a series of mass campaigns to resist apartheid laws and publicize their demands. The campaign culminated in twenty thousand women marching to the Union
Buildings, the seat of government, in Pretoria on August 9, 1956, to
present their demands to the state. The Strijdom government suppressed the women's campaigns and banned or jailed their leaders,[9] in
an attempt to destroy mass resistance to apartheid, from the mid-1950s
to the mid-1970s.

men's resistance movements were effectively shut down until 1970s, when the Black Consciousness Movement (BCM) gained momentum. The Black Consciousness ideology promoted black self-reliance. It was mainly male-led, and the unequal gender relations within the movement were never questioned. Asha Moodley, a BCM member, recalls, "The concept of gender was always on the periphery of one's consciousness" (Kemp et al. 1995:138). Women such as Mamphela Ramphele participated as equals in the BCM, and had to sustain the movement as male leaders such as Steve Biko and Peter Jones were murdered, banned, or forced into exile.

The Black Women's Federation (BWF) was formed in 1975 as an affiliate to BCM, to address women's concerns about the effects of apartheid on their communities. Fatima Meer was elected as its first president. The BWF was sustained for two brief years before its leaders, Fatima Meer and Winnie Mandela, were banned. Such actions confirmed that the apartheid state was the primary enemy, that patriarchy was differentiated, and that black men did not share in white men's patriarchal dividends.

Black women were resolute that the struggle against racism was primary. Their gendered demands emerged unevenly, and were first expressed in the FEDSAW Women's Charter. These gendered demands would emerge more powerfully through the struggles and debates of the women's organizations in the 1980s. They shaped the feminist agenda as a claim for a democracy in which racial and gender equality would be ensured and where all would have access to the national wealth. However, the struggle for racial equality in solidarity with male democrats would exist in uneasy tension with the claims for gender equality. These nascent tensions would play themselves out in the post-apartheid era, in the form of women's demands for bodily safety, sexual autonomy, and reproductive rights.

During the early 1980s women reestablished grassroots organizations that would resist the state by engaging local issues such as housing shortages, poor educational and health services, the pass laws, and the army's occupation of townships. These regional organizations included the Federation of Transvaal Women, the United Women's Congress in the Western Cape, the Natal Organization of Women, Rape Crisis, and organized women workers such as the Clothing Workers Union. During the 1980s, individual women also claimed their right to their own and their dependents' survival as they moved en masse from the reserves to urban areas, where they established informal settlements such as Crossroads, KTC in Cape Town and swelled the population of Alexandra in Johannesburg. The state unleashed a brutal campaign of removals against these women. The forced removals campaign was overwhelmed by the tide of migration and organized protest (Cole 1987). The pass laws were finally repealed in 1986, as the white state attempted to reform apartheid.

The Black Sash, which consisted mainly of white middle-class women, supported black women's organizations as allies in their protests. The Black Sash drew on a greater net of material and professional resources to provide legal support to women jailed for contravening the pass laws and maintained a database of forced removals, resettlements, and pass law contraventions (Spink 1991).

White women's identities as mothers became politicized as their sons were conscripted into the South African Defence Force (SADF) to advance the illegal occupation of Namibia and Angola. Black women whose children were jailed or killed during the school uprisings, together with some white women and disaffected white conscripts, formed the End Conscription Campaign (ECC). The ECC organized protests against the SADF's presence in townships and white men's enforced conscription (Conway 2012). The black religious women's organizations such as the Manyanos (women's prayer organizations) and the Anglican Mothers' Union, and the interfaith multiracial organization Women for Peace, tended to be apolitical and did not participate overtly in political protests until the late 1980s when mass public protests became the norm (Kemp et al. 1995).

Throughout the 1970s and 1980s, black women dismissed the relevance of Western feminism to their struggles. Lewis and Hendricks argued that "prescriptive, Western-centric, middle class and white orientation [created] an unease with the feminist label" (Lewis and Hendricks 1994:64). Radical and liberal feminisms' tendencies to speak about an undifferentiated patriarchy without regard to black men's subjugation to an Afrikaner nationalist state, or black women's multiple experiences informed by the intersections of race, class, and location, effectively marginalized black women's forms of resistance.

Western feminism could not account for women's participation in socioeconomic protests such as bus boycotts, rent strikes, land occupation, or pass law protests, while insisting that these factors informed sexual and reproductive rights. Concepts such as practical gender needs and strategic gender needs (Molyneux 1998) could not adequately account for the ways in which particularly black women's specific social and political location *vis-à-vis* a racist patriarchal state required them to engage in a broad range of issues that affected women and required contestation on a number of fronts. For example, health services provided black women with sterilization and long-term contraceptives with alacrity, but could not ensure a reduction in rates of cervical cancer or black maternal mortality rates (Wilson and Ramphele 1989); apartheid welfare and educational institutions instructed them on how to be good wives and mothers (Gaitskell 2010), but pass laws robbed them of any semblance of uninterrupted parenting or a united family life under one roof. These quotidian gendered experiences of subjugation emerged as interrelated and fluid, and were incrementally transformed into feminist issues as black women's multiply located identities were politicized. Black women, often in alliance with a minority of progressive white women allies, identified and addressed the sources of their racial and gender inequality in the most strategic ways they could. The white state's subjugation of black men reflected a differentiation of patriarchal power. Consequently black women considered black men's subjugated racial status as part of their struggle too. Still, women's attempts to address their wholly gendered subjugation, such as their minor statuses under customary law as well as gender-based violence, created tensions with black men.

The Rural Women's Movement (RWM) and the National Women's Coalition (NWC) marked the second feminist conjunctural moment in the 1990s. In both cases women were able to articulate gender demands as rights, as the tightly interconnected set of structural socioeconomic and political factors upholding men's power had become partially dislodged.

The RWM addressed the specific inequalities that rural women faced in the remote rural Bantustans where they lived under the customary authority of male chiefs. Here they were dependent upon migrant men's remittances and relied upon the chiefs' provision of access to land for survival. They were excluded from the traditional ruling councils (*pitsos* and *kgotlas*) and were unable to represent themselves in decisions affecting them directly. The RWM, assisted by the Transvaal Rural Action Committee and the Black Sash, succeeded in winning women's right to represent themselves at the traditional councils (Kemp et al. 1995).

The Women's National Coalition (WNC) was formed in response to the anti-apartheid Malibongwe Women's Conference call in 1990 for the formation of an independent national women's organization. Frene Ginwala, the first WNC convener, acknowledged the tension between the national liberation struggle and the specific call to address women's gendered oppression:

> The African Nationalist Congress' overall priority is national libera-tion…but we have progressed by moving to integrate into it an un-derstanding of gender oppression and a commitment to the emancipation of women….[Unless] we empower women…we can-not liberate ourselves. (Beale 1990:13)

Ginwala's support for a national women's organization independent of the ANC Women's League, her parent organization, reflected her recog-nition that women had to build a collective power base outside the most powerful national liberation organizations. In 1992, the WNC was launched as a loose coalition of more than ninety women's organizations across race, class, religious, and political affiliation and from every geo-graphic region. Member organizations included the women affiliated with diverse political parties such as the Pan Africanist Congress, the ANC, the Congress of South African Trade Unions (COSATU), the white Nationalist Party, the Democratic Party, the Zulu nationalist Inkatha Freedom Party, as well as women from religious groups such as the Christian Women's Manyanos and the Union of Jewish Women. The di-verse collective of women's organizations, representing millions of women, gave the WNC immense legitimacy and power. Ginwala and others worked hard to maintain a balance of power among the WNC's membership, which was racially and politically diverse and often frac-tious. The WNC's greatest success was compiling and adopting the *Wom-en's Charter for Effective Equality* campaign. The Charter reflected its members' demands for participation in the national negotiations and for gender equality to be reflected substantively in the new constitution. The Charter incorporated rural women's demands that women be equally represented in civil and customary law (article 2); as well as women's equal participation in development, with access to safe water, sanitation, land, safe transportation, and effective communication (article 5). The WNC marked another feminist unitary moment, as women de-fined gendered demands for the national negotiations agenda that

would inform the future democratic South Africa. The WNC instanti-
ated women's collective gendered demands, formulated across the differences of race, class, ethnicity, religious affiliation, and geographic
location. That unitary moment enabled many constitutional gains for
women's agenda from the early 1990s to the first five years of the Mandela administration. Political parties who participated in the NWC
agreed on the principle of women's political representation but differed
on the quota of places to be reserved for women. Conservative political
parties such as the Nationalist Party and the Inkatha Freedom Party
wanted minimal representation of women, while the ANC wanted
more substantive women's representation at the negotiations table and
in the new democratic state.

The onset of the democratic era marked a historic shift in women's
gendered struggles and the beginning of a new set of demands for gender equality—a struggle for the substantive realization of constitutional
gender rights in quotidian realities, and the push for women's equal
socioeconomic rights. That struggle would begin in the corridors of
government and be taken up, albeit unevenly, in civil society. The new
character of the gender struggle would be marked by feminist moments
of brief duration, defined by the development agenda that each presidential administration prioritized and reflected in fluid alliances and
short, targeted campaigns.

The Post-apartheid Women's Movement:
State Femocrats, Feminist Alliances, and Rural Patriarchs

The post-apartheid Constitution framed the vision of gender equality
in the newfound democracy, but the substantive realization of this
right had to be propelled by other means. Women's gendered gains
have been shaped by the state leadership's commitment to gender
equality and the collaborative opportunities that such leadership creates through its developmental agenda. The post-apartheid era is
marked by the different development agendas that the three presidential administrations, led by Nelson Mandela, Thabo Mbeki, and Jacob
Zuma, have promoted. The gender concerns in the post-apartheid era
have been determined by the extent to which each administration's
development agenda was gender sensitive, as well as the public response to the quotidian implications of women's and the LGBT communities' rights.

Presidential Administrations in the Democratic Era

The Mandela administration's early years (1994–1996) were devoted to the difficult task of redressing racial and gender disparities. The Reconstruction and Development Program (RDP) provided the blueprint for national development and aimed to ameliorate the huge racial and geographic disparities in housing, access to land, clean water, social security, healthcare, and public works. The RDP was developed in a consultative conference with the ANC, the trade unions, business, parastatals, and various civil society organizations. Gender was poorly conceived in the RDP, which only recognized the need to "ensure a[n] equal role for women in every aspect of our economy and society" (RDP, 1994 section 1.4.6).

The state claimed its membership in the international community as it ratified and signed a suite of international human rights protocols. These included the Convention on the Elimination of All Forms of Discrimination against Women (CEDAW), the Beijing Platform for Action (BPFA), the Rome Statutes, and the African Charter on Human and Peoples' Rights. South Africa's ratification of these protocols promoted the local gender-sensitive legal and policy environment.

A new state bureaucracy was set in place that in the wake of the NWC included an extensive gender machinery to ensure women's participation in governance. The South African commitment to the CEDAW protocols supported the gender machinery and informed the gender mainstreaming processes in the state (Hassim 2007). In addition, the expanded social security net provided a crucial support for poor women, adolescent mothers, children, and the disabled (Patel 2008). However, the AIDS pandemic was taking hold. In 1996 HIV/AIDS was present in approximately 3% of the population, and its threat to the newly democratic state would continue to reverberate.

The Mbeki administration (1999–2008) inaugurated a more conservative neoliberal economic development agenda to instill global confidence in the economy and to stem capital outflow. Trade liberalization was introduced, the financial system was consolidated, and expenditure on state-owned corporations and the civil service was curtailed. Gross domestic product (GDP) growth remained steady at 3.1 percent, and the effects of the 2007 global recession were held off until 2009 (Gelb 2010; OECD 2015). However, state expenditure linked to the RDP program continued as the primary means to address poverty and income inequality. Women headed households and adolescent mothers benefited from the expanded social security net and the expanded public housing provision (Patel 2008).

The impact of the HIV/AIDS pandemic also became clear as the seroprevalence rate increased to approximately 11 percent in 2002, mostly among women aged between 15 years and 29 years (HSRC 2002). President Mbeki questioned the causal relationship between HIV and AIDS, and undermined public faith in prevention programs and anti-retroviral drugs that delayed the onset of AIDS (Robins 2004). Between 2004 and 2008, the Treatment Action Campaign (TAC) led an international and local campaign against the state's AIDS denialism. Eventually the president retracted, but by then, 300,000 AIDS deaths were attributed to the state's intransigence (Robins 2004).

The Mbeki administration had a mixed legacy. It had ensured that the country's economic status and state institutions were robust and highly regarded internationally, and it promoted equal race and gender representation in the labor force. However, socioeconomic inequality was entrenched, reflected in a Gini coefficient[10] of 0.63 in 2009. The poorest sectors of the population, mainly women, were concentrated in the informal settlements and the rural areas. The effects of HIV/AIDS continue to be severe in these contexts. The Mbeki administration failed to effectively address the needs of vulnerable people, particularly women, youth, and people living with HIV/AIDS.

The Zuma presidency (2009–2018) was elected in controversial circumstances after the ANC ended Mbeki's rule prematurely in 2008. Zuma's reputation was sullied by allegations of rape in 2007 (explored to a greater extent later in the chapter). Zuma also redefined the process of appointing public servants, prioritizing party loyalty over public service. Consequently, effective public administration was undermined. The Mbeki administration had appointed a skilled bureaucracy to ensure effective service delivery; in contrast Zuma required public servants' unquestioned loyalty to him, to control opponents in the ruling party. Public faith in state institutions was eroded as the gap between policy intent and delivery widened (Kondlo 2014; Munusamy 2016). Media reports suggested that the Zuma presidency's tendency to centralize decision making regarding public finance and the treasury have instituted a culture of corruption. President Zuma's abuse of public monies to renovate his private residency has ignited a furious debate about corruption, and consumed public servants' efforts to defend him (Munusamy 2016).

The character of presidential leadership in the three post-apartheid-era administrations has determined the extent to which women's and LGBT communities' gendered constitutional rights are realized. The successive administrations' commitment to gender rights has also determined femocrats'[11] efficacy in government, and shaped feminist strategies to ensure that women's and LGBT communities' constitutional rights are realized.

Femocrats and Gender-Sensitive Legislation

Women's gendered gains in the new state during the Mandela administration were substantive and created the framework to realize women's constitutional rights. Feminists and women's rights activists from the anti-apartheid movement were recruited to the state. These femocrats helped formulate and promote gender-sensitive legislation.

A suite of legislation was ratified that entrenched women's, LGBT, gender, and sexual rights and recognized women's status as legal persons. These laws included the Domestic Violence Act, the Child Maintenance Act, the Sexual Offences Act, the Customary Law on Marriages Act, and the Choice on Termination of Pregnancy Act (CTOP). Laws that accounted for discrimination against women's bodily security, reproductive rights, and legal personhood were repealed. Discriminatory legislation such as the Immorality Act, the Mixed Marriages Act, and the Sodomy Act were all repealed. In addition, labor legislation was reformulated to take account of sexual discrimination and harassment in the workplace (Kemp et al. 1995; Salo 2010).

Femocrats assisted in conceiving and institutionalizing the state gender machinery, consisting of the Office on the Status of Women (now reconstituted as the Women's Ministry), and the autonomous Commission on Gender Equality. Femocrats' transnational alliances, as well as South Africa's ratification of international protocols such as CEDAW and the BPFA, helped inform the establishment of the state gender machinery.

Women constituted 27 percent of members of parliament in 1994, but only 7 percent of the Mandela cabinet posts. The proportion of women cabinet ministers has increased in successive administrations. They constituted 45 percent of the Mbeki cabinet, including South Africa's first woman Deputy State President, Phumzile Hlambo-Ngcuka[12]; and constitute 42 percent of the Zuma cabinet. Women's presence in the state may have increased under the Mbeki and Zuma administrations, but spelled the end of gender sensitive legislation as femocrats were pushed out of the state. Women's rights organizations had lost key allies in the state and had to find more innovative ways to promote the gender agenda in civil society.

Women ministers have diversified the gendered makeup of the current Zuma administration. However, they have not supported the sexual and economic rights of poor women, who live under customary law in the old Bantustans or in the vast urban informal settlements. The majority of women cabinet ministers are members of the ANCWL, which has jettisoned the gender agenda (Hassim 2014). The organization has been reduced to a platform for reinforcing women's loyalty to the ruling ANC, and to promote president Zuma's personal agenda.

Individual femocrats—such as Pregs Govender and Nozizwe Madlala Routledge, who were gender rights advocates—were marginalized during the Mbeki presidency. Others such as Phumzile Hlambo Ngcuka were recruited by the UN. Currently, women cabinet ministers are caught up in the defense of the president's reputation and capacity to lead. Their commitment to the substantive realization of gender justice has been sidetracked.

Post-apartheid Professionalism, Alliances, and Campaigns

By the late 1990s, women's rights activists realized that the gender-sensitive legislation and women's presence in the state, while important, had proved insufficient to improve the lives of the majority of South African women and sexual minorities. Feminists interested in emancipatory politics grasped that transformation in women's gendered rights could not be entirely entrusted to the state, even one run by an erstwhile liberation movement in a new democracy (Hassim 2005).

The women's movement within civil society has had to regroup and redefine itself in relation to the new formulation of old gender challenges. First, the legal recognition of women's gendered and sexual rights in the Constitution had to be realized in their everyday lives. Second, the incomplete battle for rural women's socioeconomic rights under customary law had to be taken up (Salo 2010).

The unitary character of the women's movement, expressed in the WNC, was a necessary, key historical moment to ensure women's full participation in the democratic transition and to ratify their gendered rights in the new constitution. Since then, the women's movement has diversified, variously expressed through NGOs addressing different aspects of the gender rights struggle such as socioeconomic rights, lesbian women's rights, providing shelter from domestic violence, and rape. The movement has also become more fluid, and regained its localized character. The unitary character of the women's movement is now expressed as a temporary alliance of organizations and individual feminists based in the NGO or academic sectors, addressing specific time-bound campaigns aimed at the realization of women's constitutional rights. These campaigns are targeted at multiple levels in the state and civil society (Gouws 2014).

The contemporary diverse women's and LGBT rights movements post-apartheid reflect the triumphs of past gendered struggles. Such variation also presents two major challenges: first, how to build a strong feminist alliance across the divides of urban and rural differences and sexual orientations, incorporating the numerous NGOs and civil society organizations; and second, how to engage the democratic state in furthering women's claims for substantive gender rights, particularly socioeconomic rights and the right to bodily integrity and safety. These new challenges occur in a shifting landscape marked by extreme economic inequality and the reassertion of men's dominance, reflected in the high levels of gender-based violence. The population in the rural areas is feminized because men have migrated to urban areas over the centuries. Rural women's socioeconomic rights are crucial to alleviate poverty in these areas.

In the face of these new challenges, the women's movement has been characterized by a brief series of feminist alliances rather than a sustained feminist moment born from collective activism alongside men.

The NGO sector utilizes donor funding to organize ordinary women in strategic campaigns that allow for women to participate in policy debates as a mass collective over short periods of time. The character of the women's movement has changed as NGOs have been professionalized and supported by international aid. Donors' priorities do constrain NGOs' local agendas, despite consultation with donor representatives. NGOs require trained professionals to navigate donor-driven agendas and administration, while meeting ordinary women's diverse needs. In the gender-based violence sector, individual women seek a wide spectrum of services including counseling, health, shelter, and assistance in negotiating the criminal justice system and litigation. Most NGOs providing services in education, litigation, and psychological counseling for survivors of gender-based violence were founded in the mid-1990s, and tend to be based in the urban areas (Salo 2010).[13] Their clients are mainly black working-class women who are living in urban townships and informal settlements, or who are homeless and living on the city streets. NGO services in rural areas are few.

The socioeconomic divides between the NGO staff and their clientele provoke class-inflected tensions with their less educated, poorer constituencies. These tensions place further stress on professionals as they navigate potential distrust to ensure support for well-intended agendas. NGO employees also have to secure donor funding to sustain their work (Salo 2010). Little time is left to engage the state and society except in short intensive campaigns to claim women's substantive rights.

NGOs, together with individual feminists based in the academy or at research centers, combine human and material resources as they form temporary alliances in single-issue campaigns. The alliances are short-lived, the membership is fluid, and the campaigns they engage in are time-bound and targeted. Most importantly, the campaigns give voice and some agency to otherwise invisible gendered constituencies such as black lesbians, allowing them to influence policy formulation and implementation. The alliances intervene at different geopolitical levels; each involves a specific targeted process of engagement with as well as protests against identified state institutions, such as the Department of Justice or the Department of Cooperative and Local Government (Gouws 2014).

Some alliances, such as the One in Nine Campaign, the Shukumisa Campaign, and the Campaign for Rural Democracy, operate at the national level to call attention to the state's failure to implement gender-sensitive policies or support women's constitutional rights. Campaigns such as the TAC and the Triangle Project anti-homophobic campaign address local judiciaries and communities about sexual diversity and hate crimes. These campaigns are embedded within and based on constitutional rights and the robust policy frameworks set in place by the first cohort of femocrats in the state. I address each of these campaigns later in the chapter.

Women's Economic Participation

Feminist activism in population, social development, and financial policies in the Mandela and Mbeki administrations brought about important gendered changes. The skewed racial economy still mainly benefited white South Africans as the effects of the racist apartheid economy continued in the democratic era. Femocrats mobilized the opportunities afforded them by the RDP and the international WB campaigns. The RDP and the Women's Budget were implemented briefly between 1994 and 1996 to redirect state expenditure to social spending that benefited poor women. Social security and welfare spending increased by 7% between 2003 and 2010 partly due to the WB activism and the feminization of poverty (Hassim 2010).

The RDP prioritized the socio-economic needs of poor communities and equality for women. The WB was briefly implemented as an aspect of the Mandela developmental agenda. Individual women helped formulate gender-sensitive legislation and challenged the state's budgetary priorities. Since 1996, Statistics South Africa[14] has disaggregated all statistical data by gender to assess the effects of the socially responsive budget on women. The WB, which focuses on the gendered outcomes of budgetary decisions, required state departments to mainstream gender. Gender mainstreaming raised state awareness about how men and women are differentially excluded or incorporated into development programs. Femocrats such as Pregs Govender used gender mainstreaming to show how state expenditure on arms removed essential resources from women's health needs, in particular women living with HIV/AIDS (Salo 2010).

The Ministry of Finance initially supported the WB, but removed resources when the state embraced a neoliberal macroeconomic plan and instituted an economic structural adjustment program called the Growth, Employment and Redistribution Strategy (GEAR) in 1996 (Govender 2007). The GEAR policy created a difficult environment to realize women's socioeconomic rights. It required a reduction in state employment and social spending, particularly in the care sector. These cuts affected women disproportionately—state sector employees in health and education tend to be mainly women, and women tend to be the main beneficiaries of social security (Hassim 2010; Salo 2010). The domestic textile and leather manufacturing sectors, which relied upon female labor, contracted because they were less competitive in the global market. Factories shut down and workers were retrenched as GEAR legislation was implemented. Approximately 350,000 women lost their jobs in the textile industry and had to rely upon social security for economic support (Salo 2004). Between 1998 and 2009, the size of children's social security grants was cut, even as access was extended; the size of the civil servant workforce, mainly women, was slashed and remuneration reduced. Civil servants initiated a strike in 2007, to no avail.

Mbeki's AIDS denialism prevented the rollout of anti-retroviral drugs in the public health system, affecting the majority of HIV positive people, most of whom were women. The seroprevalence rate for pregnant women increased to 24.5% in 2001 (Robins 2004). The provision of ARVs proceeded only after TAC initiated national and international campaigns. Currently South Africa has the largest state-run ARV program in the world. Women's and queer communities' right to health is entangled with socioeconomic rights in the old Bantustans. However, feminist activists face intractable opposition to ensure rural women's legal agency under customary laws.

Legal Plurality, Custom, and the Alliance for Rural Democracy

The South African Constitution recognizes the legitimacy of customary law. However, the gendered rights and freedoms of women and sexual minorities take precedence over such law. Tensions between civil and customary law provide opportunity for democratizing the latter. However, a more conservative defensive approach entrenches a reified, inflexible interpretation of customary law that subjects rural women to male authority.

Approximately 1.7 million people, most of them women and their dependents, live in rural areas ruled by traditional leaders. They are often the *de facto* heads of extended households, and rely upon migrant men's remittances. Women's rights to inherit property, to own land, and to operate as independent financial agents are crucial for their own and their dependents' survival. Their claims to equal rights are rendered vulnerable, as the ruling ANC relies upon the Council for Traditional Leaders (CONTRALESA) to deliver rural political support for the party during elections. Conservative interpretations of customary law by CONTRALESA, with the associated definition of women as perpetual minors, have strengthened during the Zuma presidency (Judge

2012). The chiefs have enjoyed a resurgence of authority, expressed in terms of inviolable cultural difference. Despite the RWM's victory in the late 1980s, rural women face considerable challenges. They rely on chiefs and male relatives to represent them in the courts, they are denied access to land, widows are denied inheritance of property, and child brides are kidnapped, bedeviling the substantive reality of equal citizenship.

On proposed legislation such as the Traditional Courts Bill (TCB) and the Communal Land Rights Act (CLRA), the Zuma administration has consulted only CONTRALESA, thereby strengthening CONTRALESA's claim as the only official interpreters of customary law, and entrenching its patriarchal authority. The state's limited consultation also forestalled the participation of customary law specialists and of women in the formulation of the proposed legislation.

Proposed laws empowering the traditional leaders' control over land and entrenching inflexible constructs of cultural identity, such as the CLRA and the TCB, threaten to reinforce rural women's inequality. The TCB would not allow women to represent themselves in traditional courts, thereby reversing the victories of the Rural Women's Movement in the 1980s. The TCB would also entrench homophobia because traditional leaders oppose same-sex relationships (Judge 2012). The Alliance for Rural Democracy (ARD), consisting of more than thirty human and gender rights organizations based in the academy and civil society (Alliance for Rural Democracy, Feb. 3, 2014), was formed to challenge these bills. The ARD held educational workshops informing rural women about the gendered effects of the Traditional Courts Bill, and arranged for rural women to participate in public hearings on the bill across the country. The ARD also utilized a multimedia campaign to publicize the TCB and the threat it posed to women's equal rights.

The ARD campaign ensured that the diverse intersectional identities of rural women became visible. The TCB was rejected in 2014, renewing the call to improve rural women's rights.

Gender-based Violence and Women's Right to Physical Security

Gender-based violence is widespread and presents a difficult obstacle to women's substantive democratic rights (Gqola 2015). Public health

studies in the Eastern Cape and Kwa Zulu Natal provinces found that
27.6 percent of men interviewed had committed rape, while 37 percent
of men interviewed in Gauteng province, the wealthiest province, admitted to rape (Jewkes et al. 2009). Intimate partner femicide was the
leading cause of female homicide in 2013 (Abrahams et al. 2004).

Between 1994 and 2009, femocrats in the state worked to promote
the promulgation of laws such as the Domestic Violence Act and the
Sexual Offences Act. These sets of laws assisted women in seeking justice for gender-based violence and sexual assault. Many NGOs were
founded in the gender-based violence sector between 1995 and 1997 to
assist survivors of sexual assault and domestic violence.

The state provided some relief to sexual assault survivors in response to the public outcry. In 2005, the Justice, Police, and Health
Departments collaborated to provide integrated emergency services to
rape survivors through the Thutuzela Care Centers. These centers
were conveniently located in offices near or in police stations and provided victims of sexual assault with counseling and medical services to
ameliorate the effects of rape. Dedicated sexual offenses courts were
established in 1993 to ensure that sexual assault cases were dealt with
more efficiently. Seventy-four sex offenses courts were in operation by
the end of 2005. The Minister of Justice Bridgette Mabandla shut down
the courts and curtailed the number of Thuthuzela Centers, citing financial austerity. The new Justice Minister Jeff Radebe reopened the
courts in 2012, and by 2014 approximately 298 courts were operational
(Watson 2014). The provision of integrated emergency one-stop services and the sexual offenses courts, laudable though these are, represent small victories in comparison to the entrenched normative culture
of gender-based violence and its power in South Africa. This intractable
problem is reflected in the Zuma rape trial and has been key in shaping
the post-apartheid women's movement.

The Zuma Rape Trial and the One in Nine Campaign

The rape charges against the then-deputy president Jacob Zuma and
his trial in 2006 formed the moment that redefined the character of the
women's movement into a fluid series of alliances between NGOs, ordinary feminists, and citizen-based organizations. The debates that ensued—particularly between supporters of the female complainant on
one hand and the accused, Jacob Zuma, on the other—also reflected

the deep, fractious argument about women's sexual rights and men's assumed cultural entitlement to sex.

The One in Nine Campaign was the first of the alliances formed against gender-based violence, named after the statistic that only one out of nine rape survivors reports the rape to the police. The alliance initially supported the woman who charged Zuma of rape. The campaign supported the complainant and protested rape inside and outside the court. They also engaged Zuma supporters in furious public debates focused on women's rights to sexual independence and to Zulu cultural identity. Jacob Zuma was acquitted of rape on the grounds of insufficient evidence.[15] Thereafter, the One in Nine Campaign extended its support to other women who brought official charges of rape to the courts. It also focused on secondary victimization in the judicial process.

The One in Nine Campaign's alliance-building model was used to great effect in three successive campaigns: the protests against homophobic rapes and murders targeting black lesbian women between 2006 and 2008, the Shukumisa Campaign[16] to publicize the economic cost of gender-based violence, and the ARD (Salo 2010; Hassim 2014).

Black Lesbians and the Anti-homophobia Campaign

The South African Constitution ratifies the human rights of the LGBT community. However, homophobia is deeply embedded in the society, fueled by the dominant heterosexual gender ideology and ignorance about sexuality. Between 2006 and 2008 six "out" lesbians and one gay man were murdered across the country. LGBT organizations, such as Triangle Project in Cape Town and the Gay and Lesbian Center in Durban, suspected that they were the victims of homophobic attacks because they were unjustly blamed for the spread of HIV (Judge 2012).

Zoliswa Nkonyana, one of the victims, was open about her positive HIV status and her sexual preference. She was attacked by a gang of four men, urged on by a woman who called her a "tom boy, who wanted to be raped" (ibid.:5).[17] Zoliswa's murderers were identified and arrested. The trial was postponed numerous times, until the TAC and Triangle Project alliance together with feminist activists and ordinary citizens held public protests and drew attention to the justice system's failures. The protests drew international attention to the trial, and it was given priority in the courts.

The LGBT NGO Triangle Project also provided professional testimony in the trial about the effects of homophobia in promoting hate crimes. In 2012, six years after the murder, four men were subsequently tried and sentenced to long prison terms (ibid.). The protests assisted in ensuring that the trial was resolved, and educated legal professionals and the public about homophobia.

The Sexual Offences Act and the Shukumisa Campaign

The Shukumisa Campaign was formed in 2008 through an alliance of forty-seven women's organizations ("About Shukumisa" n.d.). The alliance targeted the national implementation of the Sexual Offences Act (SOA), which expanded the definition of sexual assault. The expanded Sexual Offences Act redefined sexual assault to include all forms of non-consensual sex, beyond forced heterosexual penetration. The Act also included men and children as potential victims of sexual assault.

The Act became law in 2007, but six years later the processes required for its implementation still had to be determined. The Shukumisa Campaign rallied its partners at the national and local levels to push for the SOA's implementation and to draw attention to the extent socioeconmic cost of gender-based violence, and of sexual offenses in particular. Organizations such as Rape Crisis Cape Town and Tshwaranang Legal Advocacy Centre engaged the national and provincial state on policy implementation in consultative meetings with the Department of Justice. Organizations such as Women on Farms addressed the legal and psycho-social needs of rape survivors in rural areas by providing legal aid and psychological services to communities in the Western Cape.

The campaign influenced the national parliament to prioritize the SOA policy framework and to ensure its implementation.

Conclusion

The South African women's movement has been shaped and constrained by the struggle for democracy during the apartheid era and for the realization of constitutional rights in the democratic era. Women's ability as a collective to challenge, erode, and transform unequal gender power relations is best understood as a history of discrete feminist moments. Feminist moments in the anti-apartheid struggle were characterized by women's claims for citizenship that were recognized as democratic demands. In the post-apartheid era, these feminist moments are characterized by brief, temporal alliances marked by women's and LGBT communities' demands for their constitutional gender rights to be realized in their everyday lives.

South African feminists and gender activists have learned that gender-sensitive policy formulation and implementation are inadequate to ensure gender equality in women's and sexual minorities' ordinary lives. Ordinary South Africans have to inculcate gender equality as a norm in quotidian activities. South Africans continue to accept a gender ideology that reinforces binary heterosexuality with a discrete sexual division of labor and the assumption of women's status as inferior to men. The task of addressing and undoing this ideology in everyday life will remain the pressing challenge for the South African women's movement in the future.

Notes

1. The Gender Gap Index measures the extent to which the gap between men and women has been closed in four key areas, namely economic participation and opportunity, access to basic and higher education, political power and representation, and health and survival. Gender gap scores can be interpreted as the percentage of the equality gap that has been closed. The highest possible score is 1 (complete equality); and the lowest possible score is 0 (complete inequality). South Africa's gender Gap score is 0.759 (World Economic Forum 2015).

2. Examples include Reddock (1985), Karam (1998), and Mama (2001).

3. I use the South African designations of race throughout. Black refers to all who were of African, mixed race (coloured), or South or East Asian descent. Apartheid laws were differentially applied to people classified as Indian, coloured, and African (apartheid racial categories) in a hierarchy of oppression, and as a means to divide and rule the black majority. In order to indicate the differential application of laws, I use the apartheid racial designations to indicate the targeted population more accurately.

4. Black economic and social dispossession began with the onset of European colonialism. However, the history of such dispossession during the twentieth century is relevant to my analysis of women's movements during that period.

5. I use the term white nationalism here in order to indicate the continuity between English colonial and Afrikaner interests in dispossessing Africans of land, and in ensuring political and economic control over all black South Africans.

6. The apartheid state defined the Bantustans as the independent countries for separate ethnic "tribes." The reserves, constituting 13% of the land, would be modernized and become the Bantustans where the black majority, 79% of the total population, would become citizens.

7. Coloureds, who were 9 percent of the population, received 7 percent of the national income, while Asians, who constituted 3 percent, received 3 percent.

8. Infant mortality rate measures the number of children who die before their first birthday for every one thousand live births.

9. Leaders included Amina Cachalia, Lilian Ngoyi, Ray Simons, Helen Joseph, and Winnie Mandela.

10. The Gini coefficient is a measure of inequality. A Gini coefficient close to 0 indicates greater equality, while a coefficient closer to 1 reflects greater inequality. Trading Economics, n.d.

11. The term femocrats, first used by Australian feminists, refers to women who elect to be part of the state because they meet the state's gender quota but who may not support a feminist agenda, as well as feminists who seek to promote gender-sensitive policies within the administration.

12. Phumzile Hlambo Ngcuka is currently the head of UN Women.

13. These NGOs include the Network against Violence against Women and the Rape Crisis Centre, as well as the shelters for domestic violence survivors, such as St. Anne's Home and Saartjie Baartman Centre for women and children based in Cape Town; Masimanyane Women's Support Centre based in East London; and NISAA Institute for Women's Development and Tshwaranang Legal Advocacy Centre, both based in Guateng.

14. The national office responsible for gathering demographic data.

15. The South African law assumes that the accused is innocent unless proven guilty beyond all reasonable doubt. The onus rests upon the complainant and the state to prove irrefutable guilt. This is particularly difficult in rape trials when the complainant's testimony is the only evidence available (Smythe 2015).

16. Shukumisa means "to stir things up."

17. See also *Huffington Post* (Feb. 1, 2012).

ASIA

3

Pakistan's Women's Movement

Protests, Programming, and Revitalization

FARIDA SHAHEED

Introduction

In 2016, far more women and men than ever before are engaging with women's rights and gender equality in Pakistan. Yet the women's movement *qua* movement is less visible, in need of something that would coalesce disparate activities into a more easily recognizable identity that can rejuvenate ideas and ownership. Malaise about the state of women's movements is not confined to Pakistan.[1] Activists everywhere, it seems, confront a paradoxical reality: "Women's movements have arguably been leading the most successful social revolution the world has ever seen," but "gender inequality is still the most pervasive, systemic and universal form of discrimination on the planet" (AWID 2015). Feminists from both northern and southern hemispheres underscore the need to understand external factors as well as internal movement dynamics to explain (and overcome) the current "mobilizational lull" (Alvarez 1999).

Movements are never solely defined by the ideals, volition, actions, identities, and resources of their activists. They arise in and are inevitably shaped by the specific configurations of power they confront—in particular the character of the state—as well as by the international dynamics of politics and market forces, and contextual changes driven by other social movements and emerging trends. Responding and readjusting to changing circumstances, movements often assume different shapes at different moments.

The contemporary women's movement in Pakistan can be divided into three distinct phases of evolution. The first phase, in the 1980s, was defined by opposition to a military dictatorship bent upon rescinding women's rights. In a second phase in the 1990s, as democratizing processes within Pakistan and the trans-nationalization of women's movements coincided, activists readjusted strategies to set and negotiate the agenda with the state, using opportunities around several UN world conferences to leverage changes at home. Around 2000, the terrain for activism changed again, and activism moved beyond agenda setting to institutionalizing change. Despite significant legal and policy gains, the results for Pakistani women as a whole have been underwhelming, judging by Pakistan's ranking in the Global Gender Gap Index: second from last among 142 countries ranked in 2014 (World Economic Forum 2014). This brings us to today's "what next?" moment.

In this chapter I argue that the women's movement in Pakistan now needs a feminist transformation agenda providing unity of purpose that not only propels people into action but fires the imagination and association with a common projected vision. We have well-articulated feminist critiques of existing systems, structures, and norms—but no detailed blueprint for a feminist world. Also missing is an accepted roadmap for institutionalizing gender equality and reconfiguring state structures. How is change to be institutionalized? Activists must grapple with the difficulties of balancing the "political project of challenging inequality and promoting women's rights" with the "technical project of mainstreaming gender equality in policy, programmes and projects" (Mukhopadhyay 2005). They must calibrate the "work from the inside out" and "from the outside in" (Ewig and Ferree 2013).

To be effective, strategies must be anchored in a thorough understanding of women's different lived realities and of diverse local as well as transnational dynamics. The strength of the transnational women's movement(s) leading up to the Fourth World Conference on Women in Beijing lies precisely in bringing together analyses from disparate realities and struggles to inform a united front. Unfortunately, spaces for deliberating upon the broader issues confronting the movement have virtually disappeared in Pakistan.

Finally, the contemporary women's movement lacks an expressive dimension: a praxis that enables people to become part of the movement in their everyday lives through everyday actions, generating a collective identity beyond analytical discourses. Expressive dimensions are also a means of occupying the public sphere, an especially acute issue in Pakistan, as others, from the religious right to armed extremists, relentlessly deploy these expressive dimensions.

Today, the keys to overcoming the mobilizational lull and ensuring the movement's survival lie in two main arenas. The first is bridging the generational gap in activism, which necessitates connecting with and learning from younger women. The second key is creating discursive spaces to center a collective feminist identity, with all its overlays and underlays of tensions and debates.

The Movement Framework

Movements are galvanized by perceptions of no longer tolerable injustice, but not all actions combating injustice become movements. Protests can erupt without gaining sufficient traction to become a movement. Movements require continuity over time, and "an organized set of people vested in making a change in their position/condition..., building and pursuing a shared agenda for change... through collective action" (Batliwala 2014).

Movements may imply clarity in the proposed agenda and unity in actions taken to achieve those goals. In women's movements, however, agenda and actions have often emerged through lively debates and contestations over means, modalities, and even final objectives among activists. So the question is, to what extent do social actions or protests require a focused leadership, a clear-cut strategy for change, and organizational underpinnings to qualify as a movement? And how do we distinguish a women's movement from a feminist movement?

In Pakistan, people question whether the robust activism of women in the 1980s, acknowledged locally and internationally as a women's movement, qualifies as a movement given that it never became a mass movement and because activism remained so state-oriented. But movements can take many forms; they can be on the streets at one point and working within institutions at others. If the 1980s movement was unable to create a broad-based leadership at all levels of its constituency, it nonetheless had a unity of purpose and sufficient mass to effectuate change. Whether the movement was feminist is a separate question.

Contemporary usage has blurred terminology such that *feminist movement* is used interchangeably with *women's rights movement* or even *women's movement*. Meanings have shifted over time. The term *feminist* can refer to any and all actions ranging from improving "women's lives in some way" (Krook 2008) to a concept of pluralistic feminisms that, based on experiential differences, has led to distinctive "black" or "third world" feminisms (Phillips 2002).

The lack of definitional consensus suggests the need to clarify that *feminism* in this chapter is taken to mean "a discourse centrally concerned with gender inequality and women's empowerment" (Basu 2005b). For feminists, the essential problem is patriarchy as a system privileging males over females and disempowering women and girls, manifested in both state and social structures, and both within and beyond national boundaries. The aim, therefore, is to overturn patriarchy as a system in all its shapes and forms. For feminists, women's greater representation in decision-making forums, improved health, and better laws serve as stepping-stones to a restructuring of power relations, structures, and systems.

While the language of gender equality is relatively new, the powerful concepts of justice and injustice resonate deeply in most contexts. History is replete with examples of people's initiatives to combat various forms of injustice, including on the basis of gender. Many more people join social movements because of a perceived injustice than as a result of a theoretical understanding. Indeed, theoretical understanding often emerges and is honed in the process of action.

Distinguishing between a *feminist movement* and a *women's movement* is perhaps more useful. Many of those who catalyzed the Pakistan women's movement in the 1980s were feminists who valued the broader women's movement, including all those working to bring about more gender-equal rights and greater autonomy for women, whether or not they questioned the structures of state and society. This resembles Maxine Molyneux's differentiation of those concerned with women's strategic as well as practical interests versus those concerned only with the latter (Molyneux 1998b).

Making this distinction can be a challenge in Pakistan. Terminology for *women's movement* and even *women's rights movement* exists in local languages and is commonly used, but there is no equivalent for *feminism*. Thus even the language facilitates the suggestion—aggressively promoted by opponents of women's rights—that feminism is a North

American and European agenda. At worst, and often, Pakistan's feminists are condemned as agents of Western imperialist agendas. Consequently, even a significant number of women demanding greater rights
and opportunities for women feel discomfort with the feminist label.[2]
The deliberately promoted myth that women who struggle for women's
rights are Westernized and alien to their own societies must be robustly
contested; there is a rich legacy of women's assertions for rights as
women and for social justice across space and time, including in Muslim contexts (Shaheed and Shaheed 2005).

Regardless of terminology, to survive and thrive, the broader wom-
en's movement needs a feminist core that ensures a continuous analysis
of changing terrains for action, interrogates the basis for action, and
articulates a discourse that others can associate and identify with, or
contest. This resonates with Sonia Alvarez's important point that feminists not based in activist organizations:

> feel internally accountable to … [the] "women's movement" or
> "feminist movement" not as an aggregation of organizations nor an
> aggregation of individual members but a discourse…a set of chang-
> ing, contested aspirations and understandings that provide con-
> scious goals, cognitive backing, and emotional support for each
> individual's evolving feminist identity. (1999:27)

Ultimately, if the movement's "street theory and working ideals are
to remain responsive to what is going on in women's lives, it will always
involve internal combat" (Alvarez 1999:183). Indeed, a lively discursive
tension is what gives the movement its vitality, ensuring that it does not
become stultified.

The scholarly literature distinguishes between movements whose
principal agenda is redistribution, sometimes called instrumentalist
movements, and movements that seek recognition based on the formation or preservation of identity. Although specific movements may
place greater emphasis on one or the other aspect, most have dual faces
that "dialectically combine demands with an expressive dimension"
(Stammers 1991). For example, demands for quotas in jobs and in political processes are often made on the basis of creating, strengthening,
or redefining a collective identity (e.g. in movements demanding regional autonomy in Pakistan). The absence of proactive expressive dimensions within the Pakistan women's movement poses a challenge,

especially in view of the concentrated attention to this aspect in the movements of political Islamists. The Pakistan experience suggests that when movements arise in the context of defending rights and resisting change, their engagement with identity is likely to be one of defending expressive dimensions rather than seeking to institute new signifiers. This can be problematic. I am convinced that the women's movement needs to strategically develop the expressive dimensions of its activities to reshape the cultural contexts in which it operates, both by interjecting new elements and by appropriating and refashioning existing or older facets. An expressive dimension coupled with a dynamic theoretical base is needed to counter the incursions of the religious right. Quite separately, an expressive dimension is likely to help draw women into the movement at different levels, including women who may not wish to be part of the movement's institutional bases, but do identify with its aims.[3]

Historical junctures greatly influence which issues are addressed, how demands are articulated, the arenas for contestation and negotiation, who is considered an ally, and the nature of the relationships forged with other movements. To be sustained, movements must respond to external factors and circumstances that realign the terrain for activism. In Pakistan, this terrain has undergone several significant shifts since the start of the contemporary women's movement in 1981. While many of the issues taken up remained constant, the institutional base of the women's movement, arenas for contestation and negotiation, and modalities changed. External factors—threats as well as opportunities—combined with internal dynamics have led to the mobilizational lull in the movement today, including the absence of forums and attendant discursive tension needed for deepening analyses and sharpening strategies.

From State-focused Protests to Negotiations and Groundwork (1957–1988)

Within a decade of independence (1947), martial law derailed the political process that had been crucial for women's activism in the anticolonial period. Activists dispersed, and in the decade from 1957 to 1968 the struggle for women's rights ceased to be visible as a movement, although women able to access the corridors of power through informal social networks lobbied for women's rights. Gender inequality did not feature in the agenda of socialist groups active in the 1960s and 1970s despite the presence of some women; as in India, they never broached women's issues in these forums (Desai 1997). The rare feminist groups formed in this period were viewed by those in socialist groups as diverting focus and energy from the main class struggle.[4]

When women activists burst onto the scene in 1981, therefore, they came seemingly out of nowhere. The character of the state is always pivotal in defining the terrain for activism, but in the 1980s, combating state measures was urgent and paramount enough to virtually preclude a proactive agenda. The context of this first phase of the women's movement was a new military dictatorship under Zia-ul-Haq that, having "arrogated to itself the task of Islamizing the country's institutions in their entirety" (Khan 1985:127), sought to systematically rescind women's (and non-Muslims') rights. (For a detailed account see Mumtaz and Shaheed 1987.) The unprecedented convergence of the military and religion in state power brought an almost casual snuffing out of rights. The introduction of barbaric punishments and religiously wrapped rhetoric by the state and its allies stifled democratic voices and dissent. All felt the impact, but as the least powerful segments of society, women and minorities became special victims. The state systematically sought to push women back into the confines of the idiomatic "veil and the four walls" (the home), reverse their rights, and curtail their liberties— with devastating impact.

Focused on resisting immensely problematic legal and policy changes, women's activism largely ignored international arenas. During the Zia years (1977–1988), activists maintained personal connections with feminists and women's rights groups abroad, but felt unable to spare the time to engage more fully with transnational women's movements.

When women's rights activism started in Pakistan, allies were hard to find. Social movements were all in retreat. The labor movement had not recovered from the early and brutal suppression of workers' strikes. The elected prime minister Z. A. Bhutto had been deposed by Zia and hanged, and the protests (including dozens of self-immolations) to save Bhutto's life had subsided into despair. With all political parties and their activities banned, there was no parliament with which to engage. Nor was there an identifiable women's movement that could have provided an institutional base and networks.

The spark igniting women's activism in 1981 was the case of a couple who fell victim to the soon-to-be-infamous Hudood Ordinances promulgated by the military regime as part of its so-called Islamization. The provisions covered rape, abduction, and other sexual crimes, but also criminalized all forms of consensual sex outside marriage, leading to incredible injustices, as evidenced in this case (Mumtaz and Shaheed 1987; Jahangir and Jilani 1990). Fehmida, a college student, had eloped with the driver of her college bus. Trying to annul the marriage, Fehmida's parents registered a case of abduction without realizing that the Hudood Ordinances empowered the police to register a case of "illicit relations" when they found no evidence of abduction and insufficient documentary proof of marriage. A lower court handed out the maximum possible sentences: death by stoning for the already married Allah Bux, and a hundred lashes of the whip for Fehmida.[5]

A small feminist collective in Karachi, Shirkat Gah – Women's Resource Centre,[6] horrified at the notion that such barbaric acts had legal sanction, sounded the alarm after reading a little news item tucked inside the newspaper. Acutely conscious of the limited impact their ten-member volunteer collective was likely to have, they started mobilizing to rally opposition to prevent the sentences from being carried out.

Men's responses were either dismissive or defeatist.[7] In contrast, many women were outraged by this case, but also wanted to take action more widely to counter the threats posed by the regime's Islamization agenda. The increased harassment of women in public arenas and the questioning of women's status and role in workplaces and at home catalyzed responses, especially amongst women from the professional and upper-middle classes who, having gained the most since independence, also stood to lose the most. Women mobilized by Shirkat Gah went on to form the Khawateen-Mahaz-e-Amal, better known by its English name, Women's Action Forum (WAF).

Created to accommodate the widest possible array of women and women's groups, WAF became the vanguard of the women's movement. Launched in Karachi as a platform, a lobby-cum-pressure group, WAF brought together individual women and women's organizations across the political spectrum on a minimum agenda. To encourage wide participation, groups and individuals could join or dissociate from specific actions. WAF chapters were soon also established in Lahore and Islamabad. Working committees met weekly to manage affairs, and general membership meetings were held at least monthly.

WAF mobilized allies consisting of women's organizations across a remarkably wide spectrum. These included largely welfare-oriented groups such as the well-established All Pakistan Women's Association (APWA), professionally-oriented groups such as the Business and Professional Women's Association, and the socialist-oriented Democratic Women's Association that focused on demanding better life conditions for women of the oppressed classes. WAF also linked up with the Sindhiani Tehreek, a women's grassroots mass organization in Sindh province affiliated with the political sub-nationalist Sindhiani Movement. Hardly any of these organizations considered themselves part of a women's movement before their association with WAF, including those that, like APWA, had in the past demanded women's rights. The feminist underlay of the movement was provided by a handful of activists who were crucially involved in the daily organizing.

In this period, Pakistan's women's rights movement emerged as a defensive movement, resisting very real threats to existing rights. Activists had to contend with identity issues since the military regime and its politico-religious cabinet allies used a hegemonic "Islamization" discourse (Toor 1997) backed by brute military force. There were two interlocking sides of identity: the Islamizing discourse of new laws and directives and the state's remodeling of Pakistani womanhood.

Especially targeting the upper and middle classes, the regime systematically promoted a straitjacketed Pakistani womanhood, preferably invisible, silent, and self-sacrificing, and defined, among other things, by new dress codes. Notions of the good "Muslim" or "Islamic" woman were forwarded and frequently counter-posed to professional women who were projected as undermining Eastern values and family traditions. The state monopoly over broadcast media, backed by coercive directives, pushed these notions. During the previous era, Z. A. Bhutto had popularized unisex *awami* (people's) clothes, and some women had discarded the *dupatta* (lightweight headscarf) [8] altogether. In 1977, female TV announcers and program hosts were instructed to cover their heads with their *dupattas*; that directive was extended to female teachers in 1980. In March 1982, a new directive made the heavier chador obligatory for all female government employees, teachers, and students above class IX (grade 9). Underscoring the new look, women were regularly gifted with chadors at state functions. State-sponsored dress codes also pushed many rural women to abandon their traditional sarong-like clothes and gypsy skirts.

In parallel, in May 1982, the government launched a so-called anti-obscenity campaign aimed at removing women's images from public view. In 1988, cinemas were ordered to take down billboards with images of women. More comprehensively, a committee was established to ensure that TV programs, plays, and advertisements were not "un-Islamic." Thereafter, not only were women appearing on television obliged to cover their heads at all times—including actors supposedly asleep in bed—but TV dramas could no longer have scripts in which women "abandoned the family" by walking out of even abusive domestic situations (Mumtaz and Shaheed, 1987, chapter 6). The state did promote new dress codes for men, replacing western suits with a version of the local apparel, but labeled these as "national" rather than Eastern or Islamic (and never handed them out as presents).

The state discourse found resonance among conservatives and traditionalists who amplified the message. For the regime, these essentially cosmetic changes made far more convenient showcases of progress on its purported Islamization program than did instituting structural changes, although the major overhaul of the judicial system and revised educational content had major long-term impacts. Virtually every day brought new measures. This included proposing that women's political participation should be contingent on being over fifty years of age and having husbands' permission, and laws detrimental to women and non-Muslims in particular.

In the 1980s, the most vociferous opposition to Islamization came from women's groups (Toor 1997). While human rights and constitutional provisions were always a reference point, between 1981 and 1991 WAF selectively used an Islamic framework for countering measures proposed in the name of Islam. The three WAF chapters had differing approaches. Karachi's approach stood out in particular for its more distinct human rights framework, with frequent references to the United Nations Charter, and stressed Pakistan's obligations under it. It was not until its 1991 convention that WAF unequivocally declared it was secular and started promoting gender equality as an equal citizenship agenda.

The use of the Islamic framework was always hotly debated amongst WAF activists. Several considerations propelled its use. The human rights framework could not galvanize popular support against the regime's ordinances because for believers, the UN Charter would never trump an Islamic law. Furthermore, not engaging the powerful discourse on Islam would leave the field open for demagogues. Without an Islamic framework it would be difficult to mobilize sufficient numbers of women for whom Islam was a "lived reality" (Khan and Saigol

2004a:164-179). People, especially potential women activists, required reassurance that speaking out only against the proposals of a fallible regime did not mean speaking against their religion. And finally, laws and policies passed in the name of religion were nearly impossible to overturn.[9]

If "buying into the terms of the debate set by the Islamicists" affirmed the Islamicists' hegemony, it is also true that by linking up with other anti-martial law groups and those opposed to the imposition of supposedly religious laws, WAF successfully "built up an effective counter-hegemony" (Toor 1997:113, 121–122). How effective WAF's campaigns would have been had all its chapters adopted a secular approach is a moot point, but as Khan and Saigol say, it is likely that campaigns opposing legal propositions in the name of Islam "would not have been anywhere near as effective" (2004a).

Striving to counter the regime's proposals to reverse women's legal rights and reduce their presence in public arenas, the movement concentrated on the state apparatus, adopting actions characterized by intensive, high-profile, and attention-getting protest. In internal discussions, activists recognized that bringing about sustainable social change required reaching out and working with women at the grass roots.

Given the genesis of Pakistan's women's movement, violence was on its agenda from the start and remained a central concern both in terms of public campaigns and unpublicized actions helping survivors. From state violence—that is, corporal punishments, incarceration, and the torture of women political workers—activists quickly incorporated other facets of gender-based violence. The analysis was similar but the terminology was not. Within its first year, WAF organized two seminars on "crimes against women" in Karachi and Lahore. WAF newsletters used *crimes against women* in much the same way as *violence against women* or *gender-based violence* are currently used, encompassing systemic and structural violence in addition to interpersonal forms of violence. Seminars, pamphlets, public protests, press conferences, and press releases regularly highlighted *crimes against women*.

Although not known in Pakistan by this cumbersome term, the importance of *intersectionality* had already surfaced in practice (rather than from study of feminist theory or external links) in the 1980s. While the women's movement eventually embraced the causes of differently situated women, especially with respect to class and religion, learning about women's diversities and addressing them comprehensively was neither instant nor smooth, and entailed learning from past mistakes. The first lesson came about in 1984, when a woman trade union leader requested support from WAF activists in dealing with the harassment of female union members by the management of a pharmaceutical company. WAF supported the women in terms of the sexual harassment they were confronting (sexual harassment being an unambiguously gendered issue), but did not extend support when the union women were fired from their jobs (Mumtaz and Shaheed 1987).[10]

Obviously, much cried out to be done, but activists concluded that they had to concentrate on defensive measures while under the ceaseless barrage of proposals and promulgations of retrogressive laws and policies (WAF Convention Report 1982). Key organizers of WAF decided that although they wanted to engage in feminist politics, the need of the hour was a broad women's movement, bringing together all those who wanted to resist the rescinding of rights. The broader and more fluid women's movement thus would encompass institutions and individuals who took up women's rights issues without necessarily opposing patriarchy as a system. Indeed, few of the women associated with the movement of the 1980s would have identified as feminists. In the Pakistani context of this period it seems more appropriate therefore to speak of a women's movement with feminist underpinnings or, to use phraseology suggested by Amrita Basu (2005b), a women's movement with feminist demands.

There were limits to what the movement could take on. Activists opposed the anti-obscenity campaign, but not as a main campaign plank. Apart from one instance of spontaneously burning chadors during a demonstration in Lahore, there were no collective actions to oppose the new dress directives, only individual defiance.

In these early years of activism many women who did not join in actions nevertheless connected with the WAF discourse. In those days, WAF activists quite frequently met (mostly working) women in fairly remote small towns who, having read about WAF, would tell us, "We are with you." And the fact that the trade union leader approached WAF, as well as the trust of violence survivors and their supporters who sought WAF's help in individual cases, is clear evidence of a recognized women's movement in the 1980s, one not only able to address matters of the state, but able to effect change in personal lives.

How did feminist discourse reach people? In the 1980s, the most important vehicle was the news media, specifically newspapers. The unprecedented space accorded women in the print press stemmed from several factors. First, the continuous public protests by women, especially in Lahore, were unparalleled and coincided with the ban on political parties that left unused space in the media. Second, Karachi activists included a number of journalists who ensured coverage and mobilized support from sympathetic editors and other journalists. Third, several non-journalist activists started writing articles for the press.[11] Other modalities had far less reach. Lahore and Karachi WAF chapters brought out newsletters for a while but this was more an internal communication tool for the movement. Position papers and other documents prepared by activists circulated in select circles. Seminars and workshops would occasionally draw in new people, but the lack of regular study circles or opportunities to hold seminars and workshops in academic institutions was a hindrance to mobilizing new adherents and activists.[12]

Operating under the constraints of dictatorship, activists sought to leverage open space by widening the wedge separating "women's issues" from "politics" in the popular imagination. WAF deliberately called itself nonpolitical until 1991, when it amended this to "politically nonaligned." The non-political label had a dual purpose: to minimize hostile state reactions, and to allay concerns about political engagements among the wider WAF membership and potential women activists.

Maintaining a non-political stance presented challenges, however. Very few activists belonged to political parties but a significant number of those on the working committees had been associated with leftist movements and groups. They and other WAF activists regularly joined anti-martial law or prodemocracy demonstrations in their capacity as individual citizens and not as WAF. In practice, the distinction between activism within the women's movement and activism in the anti-martial law movement was lost; newspapers regularly reported the presence of WAF at such demonstrations and meetings. In retrospect, however, this engagement probably helped women's rights activists gain a measure of respect from and linkages with mainstream politicians that subsequently helped their lobbying after the restoration of democracy.

Formal engagements with political parties were limited. The movement did, however, reach out to all the political parties active in the 1980s Restoration of Democracy Movement, demanding that women's issues be addressed in manifestos. This was surprisingly successful and by the 1990s, most parties had done so, unexpectedly including the religious party Jamaat-i-Islami. Also unexpectedly, Zia doubled the number of seats reserved for women in the national assembly (from ten to twenty).

Joining others in demanding the restoration of democracy, WAF took up general human rights issues as well. Women's rights activists helped to develop Pakistan's human rights movement. The Human Rights Commission of Pakistan (HRCP), an independent civil society organization, is considered the leading voice on human rights today, but when the first meeting was called to launch the HRCP in 1986, women activists had already been waging their battle to defend women's rights for five years. Those activists were present in large numbers at the HRCP's inaugural meeting and were among its founding members.

The movement in the 1980s successfully put women on the national agenda of the state and diverse political actors including its opponents in politico-religious parties, such as the Jamaat-i-Islami. That women stayed on the agenda, however, has as much to do with the international and national developments and aid conditionalities in the 1990s as with the women's movement. The first opportunity for the women's movement to be proactive came after the providential demise of Zia in 1988 and the return of democracy.

Setting a Women's Agenda: Democratic Restoration and Transnational Engagement (1988–2000)

The restoration of democracy in 1988 heralded a new era for the women's movement. In the 1990s, the movement was reshaped by both internal and external factors. Internally, the ranks of WAF-associated activists thinned as the return of democracy dissipated the earlier sense of urgency to resist state moves. Externally, political parties and trade unions started operating again. Civilian courts fully resumed work, albeit saddled with new problematic laws and restructuring. This opened new avenues for engagement, but democracy was highly unstable. There were four elected and as many interim governments between 1988 and 1999, when the military resumed control. Finally, activists' explorations of how best to engage with a civilian government coincided with the 1990s UN summits. Two things happened simultaneously: first, unprecedented opportunities enabled Pakistani activists to meet other activists in transnational events; second, the preparations for the Beijing process provided mechanisms and opportunities for engaging the state as well as an anchor for formulating a national as well as global change agenda.

Transformations of Activism

The nature of activism changed, as the arena for activism shifted from street protests to the courts and other state institutions. Activists had to develop new skills and realign strategies in order to lobby effectively for better laws and policies. More nuanced, detailed responses were needed. Formulating counterproposals entailed analyzing ground realities as well as existing and proposed state measures, and learning from successful initiatives in other countries. Proposals were first discussed among women activists and with potential allies before being negotiated with decision makers.

The focus on legal reform continued on a range of matters, from the repeal of the Hudood Ordinances to criminalization of domestic violence. Seeking progressive legislation from a government bent on rescinding rights had seemed pointless, but influencing subsequent governments was still a slow process yielding uneven results. Broader issues were taken up and in 1990, WAF mobilized beyond women's groups to oppose the Shariat Bill that would have converted Pakistan into a Saudi Arabia-inspired civilian dictatorship (Shaheed and Hussain 2007). The resulting Joint Action Committee for People's Rights, a civil society coalition, provided an important platform for uniting the voices of activist groups with diverse institutional agendas.[13] Another high-profile success of WAF in this period was preventing the privatization of the First Women's Bank Limited that had been established in 1989 as an affirmative action by filing a writ petition in the Lahore High Court. (For details see Zia 1998.)

Greater attention was devoted to effectuating change in individual lives. Having learnt from the Zia era just how quickly rights can be overturned when so few women even knew about, much less enjoyed, their legal entitlements, activists initiated work not reliant on the state: setting up women's shelters, spreading legal awareness, providing legal aid, and building women's capacity to seek rights. Activists tried to widen the movement's base; women's organizations—a number of them formed by WAF activists—reached out more systematically to women outside the major urban centers.

Combating violence against women elicited the greatest response at the grass roots and was taken up by women's and other rights-oriented groups in smaller towns and more remote areas. Once the movement broke the silence around so-called honor crimes, groups in remote areas of Sindh and South Punjab took independent actions to document and report such crimes. New activists joined in major demonstrations and events, traveling for hours by bus to other cities. Often, grassroots activism was catalyzed by the work of urban-based women's groups that enhanced knowledge, skills, and linkages, and provided support networks.

Local activists took on a variety of issues from forced marriages to police failure to register rape cases, directly engaging with the state apparatus, frequently for the first time. They also innovated. After reading about "women's courts" in India in a women's newsletter, one women's organization established a Women's Panchayat (a dispute resolution forum), appropriating the term for the traditionally male-run institution, and started directly addressing issues of gender-based violence in their city. The preponderance and atrocity of violence highlighted by activists catalyzed support from people outside the women's movement, including serving and retired members of the judiciary and doctors. In 1994, for the first time, the government held a high-profile seminar on violence against women.

Movements are shaped in part by the preexisting networks of communication activists can mobilize and rely on (Freeman 1999). Women activists had largely mobilized through personal connections and networks, but activism enabled new connections. Enhanced interaction with other social movements and groups, especially those engaged in promoting labor and human rights, led to at least some women's issues being taken on board by those outside the movement, amplifying the voices for women's rights.

Thanks to the earlier involvement of women trade union leaders in the women's movement, this period saw the establishment of groups such as the Working Women's Organization and Women Workers Helpline. In parallel, labor-focused civil society organizations (CSOs) such as the Pakistan Institute of Labor Education and Research began to research women's working conditions and other issues in collaboration with feminist scholars, to include gender in training programs (mainly for male unionists), and to establish centers for women workers.

In contrast, WAF's earlier attempts to forge closer links with professional associations (for example, telephone operators and nurses) produced neither lasting ties nor new initiatives, only time-bound collaborations. In retrospect, these associations were perhaps too narrowly focused on the problems in their particular institutions and may not have seen themselves as part of the wider labor movement; they certainly never joined the women's movement.

In this second phase, while WAF continued to be the main vehicle for articulating a collective demand, the groundwork and organizing were increasingly carried out by specific women's groups, initially especially by WAF member organizations. Activists in women's groups or other institutions took the lead in specific areas, such as family law matters, domestic violence, and education. Work on women's political representation and the demand for an independent women's commission, for example, was led by Shirkat Gah, which had grown from a small volunteer collective to three offices with some 100 staff, and Aurat Publication and Information Services Foundation, another nationwide organization. Together they undertook research, formulated policy proposals, and organized forums bringing together political party representatives, bureaucrats, and civil society groups. The campaign was picked up and supported by numerous human rights-oriented civil society groups as well as other actors.

Women's organizations and individual activists increasingly functioned as gender experts in development forums, using their respective institutional bases to raise public concern around movement issues, in particular domestic violence. In 1990, Hina Jilani, an internationally renowned lawyer and human rights activist, established the first autonomous women's shelter. Later, galvanized and sensitized by activists to the issue of violence against women, others followed suit, including some former judges. Activists persuaded the federal government to adopt new guidelines drafted by them for government-run shelters for women in 1996, but the guidelines collected dust on bureaucrats' shelves, while the jail-like conditions of the government-run shelters persisted for another decade.

Across the three WAF chapters, the number of activists dropped; many who had put their lives on hold for almost a decade resumed interrupted careers. Activists' different political orientations, submerged under martial law, resurfaced and led to disagreements on strategies. In Islamabad, the country's capital, internal conflicts eventually made the WAF chapter dysfunctional. In Lahore, the capital of the country's largest province *and* considered the central arena for political contestations,

WAF had adopted the most radical actions, maintaining high street presence. Consequently the burnout there was more severe. WAF survived best in the mega-city of Karachi, the country's commercial and industrial hub, where regular WAF meetings and activities continued, although with fewer activists, and the chapter succeeded in mobilizing new and younger activists. Still, the crucial change in this period was that reduced attendance at meetings diminished the vibrancy of the discursive space within WAF.

Impact of the UN Conferences

These internal changes coincided with the game-changing UN conferences: the World Conference on Human Rights in 1993, the 1994 International Conference on Population and Development (ICPD), and the 1995 Fourth World Conference on Women (FWCW) held in Beijing. The processes around these conferences provided unprecedented spaces for thinking, sharing, and strategizing across various other identities (Bunch and Carrillo 2016; Olcott 2016). Only a handful of activists from Pakistan engaged in the 1993 human rights conference or the 1994 ICPD. The 1995 Beijing conference was qualitatively different. For the first time, an international event found deep resonance across a wide cross section of differently situated women. The palpable excitement of being part of the "women of the world" can be attributed in part to the hard work of activists in the 1980s and early 1990s, but it equally reflects the financial support made available by international funders both to the government for preparatory meetings and women's groups for holding country-wide discussions and participating in the UN process.

However, WAF was rarely the primary participant in these events, and with time its role as the collective voice of the movement was diminished. Although then, as today, some participants introduced themselves as WAF in development-focused gatherings, activists attended related forums abroad and at home in their non-WAF institutional capacity. Several factors explain this: WAF is not a registered entity; internal decision rules made it a herculean task to get approval to speak on behalf of WAF; and WAF as a matter of principle has never accepted institutional funding for any of its activities, including for attending events (see section on NGO-ization below).

The most remarkable aspect of this period is the commonality of analysis and sense of solidarity that transcended highly differentiated realities and struggles across the world, overcoming sometimes serious disagreements. Equally remarkable is that activists in Pakistan connected so easily with this international women's movement, even though very few of them participated in such events before 1993.

Few issues better illustrate the consensus emerging from different quarters than that of violence against women. In Pakistan, activists only started using the term *violence against women* in the early 1990s, replacing the earlier phrase *crimes against women*, indicating the greater engagement of local activists with the international arena and the adoption of language made popular not just by feminists but by the United Nations. This second phase saw understanding coalesce across countries in a new language of shared analyses.

Working with differently situated women brought to light how untenable it was for the women's movement to demand rights for women exclusively in terms of the narrow yardstick of whether discrimination was based on "sex alone," ignoring the differences in women's lived realities. (*Sex alone* is the term qualifying the constitutional prohibition of gender discrimination, now judged inadequate by women's rights and general human rights activists.) It took years for the issues arising from power differentials of intersectionality to be fully comprehended and, indeed, the issue demands constant (re)interrogation and review.

A new modality emerged in this phase, starting with the first-ever collaboration with the government. The government's own lack of expertise on women's issues propelled it to recruit and engage with activists and women's organizations as "experts" to facilitate the Beijing process and follow-up. This enabled activists wearing their "expert" hats to greatly influence the National Plan of Action for Women (NPA), the domestic policy for implementing the Beijing Platform for Action. UN processes provided the impetus, but collaborations only happened because the key woman responsible for the process in the incumbent government was sympathetic and had the ear of Pakistan's prime minister, Benazir Bhutto. She also accepted the women activists' condition: that their participation was contingent on the government's making no changes in the final text of NPA. The resulting document incorporated the language of activists and virtually all the measures they formulated.

Prepared in 1996, the NPA was not launched until 1998, since Benazir Bhutto's government was dismissed the night the draft plan was completed. The new government dragged its feet. The NPA was considered to be a significant step in institutionalizing the agenda of the women's movement and encouraged collaboration on the 2002 National Policy for Women's Development and Empowerment. Activists then used that policy and the NPA as accountability and negotiation tools in dealing with government.

In tandem, the movement pushed for greater representation of women in legislatures during this second phase. The impetus was the lapse of the constitutional provision for women's reserved seats in provincial and national assemblies, following the post-Zia 1988 general elections. Without this affirmative action, the number of women in the national parliament dropped from the (then) historic high of twenty-four in the 1988 assembly to only two in the following assembly.

Reserving a certain number of seats (quota) for women in legislatures predates independence, so it has never been a particularly controversial subject. In a first-past-the-post system for general seats, voting for reserved seats is not by franchise but by an electoral college comprised of directly elected representatives. Arguing that this made women representatives accountable to their largely male colleagues, rather than to women constituents, activists advocated for modalities that would directly link women with territorial constituencies. They finally succeeded in getting a 33 percent quota for directly elected women introduced in the new local government system in 2000.[14] In 2002, reserved seats for women were revived in the assemblies and, as demanded by activists, introduced in the Senate, the upper house of the bicameral parliament.[15] Modalities remained unchanged, however, and other proposals that would oblige all parties to field women candidates, have women in their executive bodies, or penalize parties without sufficient women members were ignored, despite their inclusion in the NPA.

The revival of democracy in 1988 and then 2002 has seen the number of women in the political process steadily increase. In this second phase, activists established effective linkages with both women and men representatives. A handful of activists have entered mainstream politics, facilitating a fruitful alliance.

Institutional efforts, on the other hand, had uneven and unstable results. The Women's Division, which had been established in 1979 as a special federal unit under the federal cabinet to look after women's affairs[16], was upgraded to a full ministry in 1989 under Benazir Bhutto. Nawaz Sharif however then merged it with several other portfolios, such as Social Welfare. Provincial Women Development Departments, essential for policy implementation, were established soon after the Beijing conference, in response to demands by women activists in 1996. Unfortunately neither ministry nor departments ever received the financial or human resources necessary for effectiveness. The demand for a permanent watchdog body brought the establishment in 2000 of the National Commission on the Status of Women, which has proven to be an effective ally for the movement, not least because the last two chairpersons have been movement activists.

More problematically, this period saw the UN-derived term *nongovernmental organization* or NGO gain currency, with implications discussed below.

Concretizing or Losing the Political Agenda? NGO-ization, Representation, and Generational Change (2000–2016)

The new millennium has been a period of contrasts and contradictions. The end of 1999 saw the return of military rule, but this time under an "enlightened moderation" banner. The first elections in 2002 under General Musharraf saw religious political parties gain ground and, thanks to new criteria determining who could stand, form an elected government in one province for the very first time (North West Frontier Province, now renamed Khyber-Pakhtunkhwa).[17] The rise of the Pakistani Taliban, who installed a reign of terror in several northern areas, brought unprecedented violence, including the targeted killing of women and men human rights defenders. The combined impact has been a growing religiosity in everyday discourse and a silencing of secular voices.

Ironically, significant progress has been made in terms of legal and policy reforms. The far greater number of women legislators (close to 20 percent in the national assembly since 2002) has had its own impact. Women have proposed more bills than their far more numerous male colleagues, and have taken up issues of domestic violence and child marriages, for example, with support from activists and women's organizations. Although the "illicit relations" sections of the infamous Hudood Ordinances were not repealed, the law was amended radically enough to render those provisions toothless. Two provinces (Sindh and Balochistan) have passed Domestic Violence Acts.[18] Sindh also revised the minimum age for marriage of girls to eighteen, at par with boys. A National Commission on the Status of Women was established as a statutory body in July 2000, followed by two provincial commissions in Khyber-Pakhtunkhwa and Punjab. The Sindh commission has been approved but is not yet operational.

These contradictions would shape the third phase of the women's movement, which started to emerge around 2000, following the five-year review of progress on the Beijing Platform and the launch of the UN's Millennium Development Goals (MDGs). Agenda setting gave way to efforts aimed at the realization of the agenda, partly facilitated by governments serving out their five-year terms.

As elsewhere, and in conjunction with a general growth in the non-profit sector, numerous women's groups emerged in Pakistan. But, as the agenda implementation splintered into specialized areas, it started to lose its mooring from an overall feminist analysis. Simultaneously, the UN's need to distinguish governmental from non-governmental voices meant that human rights and development groups were all labeled NGOs, denoting funded activities, and they were expected to follow the agendas of their funders.[19] Worries surfaced that NGOs were undermining the movement. In parallel, these years saw the relocation of discussions around women's rights issues (recast as "gender") into spaces neither controlled by activists nor autonomous.

This shift was particularly significant in Pakistan, where forums for rigorously reviewing and debating the changing character, gaps, and needs of women's activism are rare. In retrospect, the very lively and often heated debates integral to the activism of the first 1980s phase were crucial even if carried out on the run, between urgent campaigns, protests, and picket lines. Until 2000, meetings around the UN summits did provide spaces for discourse and analysis, especially as most movement activists entered such national spaces on consciously and carefully negotiated terms. Later, free thinking and academic endeavors continued to be undermined by the growing influence of the religious right in academic institutions. Academic institutions rarely provide the freedom necessary for inquiry and interrogation of accepted knowledge and truths. Today, academic research and writing, activism, and development work seem to move in parallel streams with little bridging.

NGO-ization and Its Effects

The MDGs marked a critical change of perspective in the international community. Activists viewed them as a setback, given their more technocratic approach that lacked the political analysis evident in the Beijing Platform. While funding continued and drove the creation of more NGOs, funding priorities shifted. In the years before and following Beijing, women's organizations could mobilize financial support for programs they themselves framed. Around 2000, donors started tying funds to a *projectization* of their own agendas, using a bidding process and boxing ideas into SMART outputs (specific, measurable, achievable, relevant, and time-bound). Government attitudes also shifted. The agenda defined by women activists seemed to be slipping away. Pakistan is not unique in this respect; other chapters in this volume point to similar dynamics in other settings. The consequence has been a narrowed scope for independent agendas, autonomous actions, and innovation.

In the meantime, efforts refocused from policy statements defining the agenda to concrete measures for its realization and institutionalization. Confronted with the challenge of how to inject feminist ideals into resistant bureaucratic reality, interventions became more complex. With respect to domestic violence, for example, the guidelines for government-run shelters drafted by activists in the 1990s had never been implemented. It took more than ten years of effort to prepare new research-based guidelines that maintained a rights perspective but were acceptable to bureaucrats, and to persuade the Punjab provincial government to officially adopt these. The Sindh province followed suit a few years later.

Efforts for effective implementation meant more than changing bureaucrats' perspective; they expanded to encompass assessing the operational constraints confronting staff, translating the English-language guidelines into the vernacular, persuading the head of the lead department to officially ask all other departments to extend the cooperation outlined in the policy, writing a manual of operations to help shelters' staff, and preparing training modules and running orientation sessions for staff, local government officials, and local activists. This went far beyond the press releases and broad policy demands of the second phase.[20]

As activists immersed themselves in more technical and specialized work, the wider movement became less visible. Work fragmented into specialized silos, such as sexual and reproductive health and rights, violence against women, economic rights, and political participation. Institutionalizing changes does demand specialization, but when activities become disconnected from an overall feminist analysis, this creates tunnel vision. In Pakistan as elsewhere, activities shifted away from "the political project of challenging inequality and promoting women's rights" toward a "technical project of mainstreaming gender equality in policy, programs and projects" (Mukhopadhyay 2005:1).

Political instability exacerbated the challenges of working with government. Regardless of whether the issue related to health, education, or law, start-and-stop processes and interminable delays devoured time and resources, depleting energies for other action. The year 2010 brought a new challenge. The 18th Amendment to the Constitution dissolved the federal ministry for women and devolved the women's affairs portfolio to the provincial governments, thus obliging activists to undertake five separate campaigns on any issue instead of a single national one.

In Pakistan today, almost all civil society organizations say they either work for women or have a "gender" perspective. Few however have either a feminist or movement perspective, and many can be criticized for being donor-driven and losing sight of downward accountability. Concerns about NGO-ization surfaced in Pakistan several years after others warned that NGO-ization could "reduce feminist NGOs' cultural-political interventions in the public debate...to largely technical ones" and channelize energies toward the state, privilege the well-educated, and further marginalize grassroots women (Alvarez 1999:183). A separate important issue, raised also in the context of the Arab Middle East by Islah Jad, is that NGO-ization disconnects decision making from the ability to mobilize people (Jad 2004).

Yet the criticism of NGO-ization in Pakistan, including from among feminist activists, is based on impressions rather than research, and fails to differentiate among organizations with dissimilar politics, institutional cultures, and practices. Criticisms seem particularly unfair when we consider feminist organizations. Although numerically insignificant, feminist organizations have been a vital part of the women's rights movement from the start, and most have been institutional members of WAF. Such blanket criticism of organizations feeds into the anti-NGO discourse propagated by elements opposed to all human rights.

Bangladeshi scholars note a parallel situation. Differentiating between feminist organizations and others, they conclude that while NGO-ization may have "diluted feminist political messages, it has increased outreach and helped to transmit feminist messages into other spheres" (Nazneen and Sultan 2012). In both Bangladesh and Pakistan, feminist groups that started as voluntary collectives in the 1970s and

1980s went through soul-searching before they accepted donor funding, and took steps to maintain organizational autonomy and aims.

New funding opportunities have enabled women's rights organizations to expand their scope of work beyond state-focused oppositional and advocacy work, to reach women beyond large cities and to establish programs supporting women. Their initiatives have strengthened links with community-based civil society groups and self-help organizations, spreading a feminist perspective. Catalyzing new groups, they have produced ripple effects to amplify voices for gender-equality state accountability.

Yet there has been a shift in funders' perspective, from supporting women's self-determined initiatives to reinforcing predetermined technical projects. Not only has funding for women's rights work declined relative to other human rights activities (Clark et al. 2006), but several major international funders have adopted a new business model deploying "technical management firms" to manage large grants. Driven by profit motives, these firms represent a new form of entrepreneurship around gender (and other issues), usually disconnected from the women's movement or any human rights goals. Moreover, large funds for women and gender equality do not necessarily benefit women's rights organizations.[21] Another unfortunate outcome of new funder policies is a credit-claiming competition among recipient organizations, which publicize only their own work so as to provide "supporting evidence" to funders—to the detriment of public-interest coalitions, lobbies, and movements. This fragments the collective identity of social movements.

Resources are, of course, crucial for the survival of all movements. Scanty resources shrink the activist base, excluding or marginalizing those unable to afford the costs of travel or the lost income that time devoted to activism implies. WAF deliberately kept its membership fee nominal to avoid such exclusion, but since it never became a mass organization, the funds generated were negligible. The primary source of funds for WAF has always been voluntary personal contributions, although it has occasionally mobilized support in kind, or as advertisements from sympathetic commercial establishments. Women's organizations have supported WAF activities, but the rule is that such support cannot be from a "donor project" or reported as such. No movement can survive and remain autonomous without mobilizing resources that have no strings attached. But to survive and flourish it is even more important that movements galvanize mass commitment to a cause and expand the number of activists, especially among younger people.

The Generation Gap: Age, Location, and Modalities

The women's movement cannot survive unless it overcomes the generation gap. The underlying reasons for the gap need more study; here, I only flag some key issues of age, location, and modalities shaping today's version of this primordial question.

A comparison with Bangladesh helps illuminate those issues. Young Bangladeshis describe a "feminist impasse" (Siddiqui 2011). There, studies find that younger women have a "more professionalized, meaning development-projectised" and "monetized" approach and are focused on development rather than the movement building orientation of older feminists. This is a paradoxical outcome of successful activism in the 1970s and 1980s to incorporate gender into academic programs and development organizations' training programs (Nazneen and Sultan 2012).

In Pakistan, too, younger women do appear to be more oriented to making money, but this has not been linked with gender studies. Instead, several younger women have explained that their great focus on money results from learning from older activists about the vital importance of economic independence for women and of not devaluing women's work.

The second factor identified by scholars in Bangladesh is the failure of more established women's or feminist organizations to provide sufficient space to younger women (Siddiqui 2011). This issue—identified decades ago—is of immediate relevance to Pakistan. Younger women do join and work in women's organizations, but they rarely join WAF, which has functioned for so long as the movement's principal institutional base. When new issues arise, it is still preponderantly the older generation "aunty brigades" in Pakistan who respond with public demonstrations. Why do younger people participate less in such oppositional politics?

Over the years, several efforts have been made to address and overcome the gap in Pakistan. One focused attempt to mobilize younger women took place in 2001, when the politico-religious parties formed a government in Khyber Pakhtunkhwa province.[22] Older activists, fearing backsliding toward the bad old Zia years, hoped to mobilize younger women to resist. Interactions over the course of several meetings revealed a real difference in perspective, with younger women questioning the need for a women's rights movement separate from a human rights movement. This response, however, only represents the views of the essentially urban, middle-class younger women at these meetings.

Outside urban centers, positive developments in 2015 signaled an important opportunity for revitalizing the movement. In rural settings and some poorer urban localities, women, especially younger women, participating in a feminist leadership program, started to knit together across locations and issues in a more grassroots movement for women's rights. The program built the capacity of more than three thousand women (and several hundred male supporters) through mentoring and more formal sessions aimed at introducing feminist ideas and movement building. One of the most striking outcomes emerged from a "branding" of local women's activism. Many women have adopted a purple chador with a logo of their (as yet unregistered) groups: Khwendo Tolana (Sisters' Group) in the Khyber Pakhtunkhwa province and New Dawn (in local dialects) in the other three provinces. Donning their chadors for all manner of activism, women have taken to calling themselves the Purple Women. This new collective identity provides a sense of strength and power. For example, women relate that when they previously visited police stations in their usual apparel, no one paid them attention. Today, when ten women enter in purple chadors, the police take notice. The Purple Women elicit similar reactions from families they visit in their communities to stop domestic violence or early-age/forced marriages.

The Purple Women have established scores of self-run and self-financed "sub-offices" to expand the number of activists and outreach. In practice, "sub-offices" are rarely more than the purple chador hung in a corner of a home, but the term coined by the women themselves links them with a wider movement. This new collective identity is a source of strength that underscores the vital role that expressive dimensions of activism can play.[23]

Another very recent positive development is that in large cities such as Lahore and Karachi, younger women have started feminist study circles in colleges and universities and initiated loose groups they call Feminist Collectives. Some have opened new spaces for discussion and interaction outside the NGO world, spaces like The Last

Word bookshop in Lahore, and the Dhabi Girls' feminist tea stalls they hope to develop into a teashop (café) in Karachi. The modalities used by urban-based feminists (and youth in general) to air their views, analyses, and self-expressions differ significantly from the forms of activism adopted by the older generation, which are derived from an understanding of the classic politics of street protests and negotiation with the state.

Younger feminists are trying out new ways to occupy and influence the public sphere. Some have experimented with readings in public spaces; others cycle collectively as a way of occupying public spaces. Social media networks, for example, form a crucial public sphere, dominated by younger voices. Younger feminists specifically raise the issue of widening the modes of activism, and engaging culturally.

To accommodate younger feminists necessitates a revitalization of the space for debate and dissent within the movement. Older activists have worked together for so long that they rarely now engage in the heated debates and disagreements that characterized decision-making in the earlier phases. Some older activists also resist change and novel ideas; the absence of older activists in Hyderabad may be one reason that the new WAF chapter there, run by younger women, has become the most active.

The most positive development has been the WAF national convention held in March 2016 after a hiatus of almost 10 years. The event was momentous and may signal a possible renewal. Bringing together newer and older activists from six cities across Pakistan with diverse socio-cultural and class backgrounds in intense two-day discussions, the convention has revitalized the sense of a movement. This was preceded by setting up a WAF Open Forum on WhatsApp that included many women not formally associated with WAF. The virtual forum has enabled women to connect and share separate activities and concerns under a common platform across the country. Following the convention, interactions between older and younger feminists have intensified and new younger members have become more active. The challenge is to tap into this energy, to ensure that the discussions and activism transcend cyberspace, and to meld the fresh thinking of youth with the grounded experience of older activists, while bearing in mind issues of intersectionality. Younger and older feminists need to come together and learn from each other to craft new modes of feminist activism.

Conclusion

Historical specificity influences which issues a movement addresses, the demands it articulates, and the arenas it utilizes for contestation and negotiation; it also affects who is considered to be an ally and the choice and nature of the relationships forged—or not—with other movements. The contemporary women's movement in Pakistan emerging in 1981 has gone through three distinct phases. The first intense efforts sought to prevent the state's erosion of rights in the name of Islam, placed women permanently on the national agenda, blocked some proposals, and had others revised. Starting in 1988, a second phase concentrated on proactively setting a gender-equality agenda in conjunction with transnational women's movements. The third phase, in the new millennium, focused on having the agenda implemented but led to more technical interventions.

In terms of the framework for action, the movement initially combined a human rights framework with the selective use of religious argumentation. After the Zia regime, WAF, still the singular voice of the movement, declared it was secular and started promoting gender equality as an equal citizenship agenda. Over the years, the movement has become more instrumental, ignoring the expressive dimensions. Despite numerous achievements, it has not been able to stem the progressive appropriation of public spaces and discourses by the religious right, most obviously through imposing various forms of dress code and the veil. Nor has it adequately taken up the personal dimensions of the feminist struggle (Khan and Saigol 2004a). This has led to the dissipation of a sense of identity of the movement *qua* movement.

A critical issue for identity aspects of movements is subjectivity, meaning how people think of themselves *vis-à-vis* others and their contexts. The general deficit of *citizen subjectivity* in Pakistan is acute among women, raising the question of how much resonance the human rights discourse can have. Located squarely within the parameters of nation-states, the human rights framework presumes that the state as the principal guarantor of rights has, or can be persuaded to have, the best interests of all its citizens at heart. The fallacy of this assumption is patently obvious in Pakistan's history. In confronting an authoritarian state, such as Pakistan under Zia, activists confronted a dilemma: while they rejected the military regime, they remained dependent on those in state power to reconsider or amend the measures being proposed.

Feminists in Pakistan as elsewhere have critiqued the nation-state
as inadequate for gender equality, (Hussain, Mumtaz and Saigol 1997)
yet activism has adopted the nation-state framework of rights. The human rights approach for achieving state-guaranteed rights also propels
energies and resources to "upward rather than downward linkages"
(Basu 2005b). This can easily take activism away from changing ground
realities through direct actions. Equally, although this is now starting to
change, the human rights framework prioritizes the rights of individual
citizens, with a tendency to overlook unequal power and attendant
structures that need to be fundamentally altered.

I do not mean to suggest that the human rights discourse or framework should be discarded. The human rights framework does provide
an important counterpoint, however inadequate, to the use of culture
and religion to justify the structures of patriarchy. Nevertheless, just as
rights activists need to spell out their political economy more con-
cretely, they must also seek to ground themselves in and reshape a dynamic indigenous culture. That this may be difficult and involve
conflicting views does not make it any less important.

Antonio Gramsci's argument about class struggle is relevant here:
the class (or alliance of classes) that emerges in dominant or "hegemonic" positions "will always attempt to secure a hegemonic position
by weaving its own cultural outlook deep into the social fabric" (cited in
Toor 1997:111). This is true with respect to gendered relations of power
that are reproduced in all aspects of social interaction and are justified
by and internalized as the given culture. Ultimately, rights can be enjoyed only if and when they have become an integral part of people's
culture, however this is defined.

The religious right's new forms of outward appearances and social
behavior must be seen for what they are: symbols of particular movements; of new subjectivities as an international "modern" Muslim identity (Maqsood 2015). This is not about preserving tradition. (The new
fashionable versions of the veil today are not derived from any traditional South Asian dress.) Expressive dimensions make use of and find
resonance with what people consider to be their own culture. The feminist movement, too, must consciously develop signifiers to mark the
collective identity of the gender-equality agenda, enabling people to express their identification with the women's movement in everyday acts.

In the first phase of the women's movement in Pakistan, activists
defied the ban on all political activities by holding protests and demon-

strations, but also deployed cultural interventions: using humor, songs, and poetry to project their views; in *jalsas* (somewhere between a large gathering and a festival); or in audio-cassettes of well-known artists performing movement-related songs. This type of cultural action almost disappeared in the latter two phases.

I believe the salience of the culturally expressive dimensions of movements for women's activism is grossly neglected. The interweaving of culture, economics, and the political domain deserves far greater attention from both academics and activists. In Pakistan, where the religious right has been successfully reshaping the public domains and discourse to its agenda, the need for the women's movement and more generally for human rights groups to develop a more conscious cultural presence seems urgent. It is especially vital to counteract the rewriting of history and culture by those who seek to build political constituencies through a self-serving political use of religious identity. The human rights framework needs to be complemented by a more effective use of the creative arts and cultural spaces that can resonate with people's everyday lives.

Today, the movement in Pakistan stands at a crossroads, and needs to revitalize its political agenda. This requires several changes, starting with the expansion of the movement's human base, not just in the number of activists, but also in terms of physical locations, class, age, and other differences that could infuse the movement with new thinking. Concomitantly, the movement must occupy a variety of public spaces more systematically, by further engaging with mainstream political processes and with other social movements, and must develop new modalities for occupying this space.

Effecting and institutionalizing gender equality necessitates engagement with the state, other political actors, and social movements, alongside direct actions seeking to change societal practices and norms. The challenge lies in ensuring that the political agenda, rather than the happenstance of openings and opportunities, drives technical projects of institutionalization and determines the balance between strategies to effect change from the outside in and inside out.

A clearly spelled-out feminist vision of the future would facilitate staying on course and avoid sliding into cooptation in place of negotiated collaboration. That requires at least some independent forums to ensure that discourse and debate can function as "social movement webs—the capillary connections among feminists and their sympathizers" (Alvarez 1998a), in a wide array of fields and locations.

Staying true to the compass of a feminist vision demands that the women's movement have a constantly evolving feminist ideology at its core. Only then would focused work in specialized areas remain connected to a political agenda, constantly weaving together the various strands of activism and critically interrogating ongoing work. In the last few years the movement in Pakistan has seemed to be missing such an anchor. Academic institutions do not fulfill this function. In the past, WAF provided such a core, as well as a base that was financially and politically independent. The 2016 convention gives hope that it can resume this role, provided it absorbs new blood and new thinking.

Movement building requires far greater engagement than simply acknowledging differences and endorsing each other's positions. To widen the movement, women's rights activists must embrace the concerns of differently situated women as integral components of the women's agenda. Contentious and vexatious though they may be, linkages with other social movements are critical for women's movements, for they facilitate and deepen a consciousness among activists about the complex interconnections of people's lives. Maintaining an independent agenda is crucial, but older activists must open themselves to the ideas, initiatives, and critiques of differently situated and younger women, and consider the new modes of activism they have adopted.

Today many more women call themselves feminists in Pakistan than in the 1980s, but most are urban, educated women who understand English. Still, with some younger women in remote towns and rural areas starting to use *feminism* in English, an older movement stalwart is advocating the adoption of the term *feminist* in Urdu "just as we use the English terms for television, community and other things."[24] The amazing energies and connections generated by the WAF national convention in 2016 need to be harnessed for a new phase of activism.

Notes

1. This was evident in the Roundtable on Building Feminist Leadership, organized by the *Women's Empowerment and Leadership Development for Democratisation* project (2012-2015; Kandy, Sri Lanka 2014) that brought together women across generations from nine countries of Asia, Africa, the Middle East, and North America.

2. Negative stereotyping is neither new nor unique to Pakistan, South Asia, or Third World countries (see, for example, Freeman 1999). Today this may be somewhat less of an issue in the West, but calling oneself a feminist tends to assume more overtly political dimensions in contexts such as South Asia (Forbes 2003).

3. This was pointed out by Indian feminist Pramada Menon at the 2014 Roundtable on Building Feminist Leadership. Supra note 1.

4. Personal communication by Aban Marker, founding member of Shirkat Gah – Women's Resource Centre, which was if not the first feminist women's organization in Pakistan, then certainly one of the very first. It was formed in 1975 as a non-hierarchical women's collective by young professional women aiming to raise consciousness and integrate women's rights and development, and functioned on a voluntary basis until well into the 1980s.

5. The case was later overturned. The maximum punishments have never been implemented in Pakistan.

6. See Supra note 4.

7. These were the responses we all seemed to have received when we approached men with the idea that we had to do something to prevent this sentence from being executed.

8. *Dupattas* are lightweight scarves traditionally worn with the *shalwar kameez* (tunic and baggy trousers), but in urban settings not necessarily worn covering the head. The chador is usually larger, of a heavier material, and worn in addition to the *dupatta*.

9. It would take 27 years for the Hudood Ordinances to be amended.

10. Similar discussions were held on whether WAF should support women political activists confronting state repression.

11. Whereas the press was a staunch ally in the early days and brought several violence cases to the notice of activists, with time and the return of democratic processes, the novelty of women's issues and activism wore off and attitudes became jaded.

12. Under General Zia's dictatorship, many progressive academics (the majority in some departments and institutions) left or were thrown out of their universities. Many relocated to the news media or civil society groups.

13. While sharing a common goal and human rights perspective, member organizations have their own specific focus on, for example, minorities, women, or labor, or an area of work, such as education or legal assistance. Some engage in development-oriented work and service delivery, while others, such as theater groups, concentrate on raising awareness.

14. Unfortunately, after the first round of elections inducted close to 40,000 women into the political process, the reduction of overall seats meant women councilors no longer constituted a critical mass, reducing effectiveness.

15. Out of a total of 342 seats in the national assembly, 60 seats were reserved for women and 10 for minorities. These seats were to be allocated on the basis of proportional representation to parties garnering at least 5 percent of the total general seats. In the provincial assemblies, out of the full 371-seat Punjab Assembly, 66 were reserved for women and 8 for minorities; in the 168-seat Sindh Assembly, 29 were for women and 9 for minorities; in the 124-seat North West Frontier Province Assembly, 22 were for women and 3 for minorities; and in the 65-seat Balochistan Assembly, 11 were for women and 3 for minorities.

16. Ironically the Division was a recommendation of the first Committee on Women's Rights commissioned by Zulfikar Ali Bhutto in 1976, but came into being after Zia-ul-Haq's 1977 coup.

17. A bachelors' degree was mandatory for standing for elections, but equivalencies were biased. "Graduates" of religious institutions (madrassahs) were given equivalency, whereas some chartered accountants were denied the same.

18. The Protection of Women Against Violence Act passed by the Punjab Assembly in March 2016 is highly problematic, as it does not criminalize acts of violence and only provides civil remedies.

19. Pakistan human rights activists struggled to resist this label. Eventually the term "civil society organizations" was accepted, but by that time NGO had become a widely used term, including in Urdu.

20. These activities were carried out by Shirkat Gah between 2007 and 2008, incorporating and complementing work done by others, such as Medecins Du Monde.

21. In Pakistan the UK-supported AAWAZ program is headed by a man and a five-member partnership of organizations, only one of which is a women's organization. Similarly the decision of the Dutch government in December 2015 to award grants under its new FLOW2 program to five international groups, only one of which is a women's group, was heavily criticized.

22. Led by the Jamaat-i-Islami, the Mutahida Majlis e Amal, consisting of six religious political parties, for the first time assumed control of a province through an electoral process.

23. The idea for the purple chadors was that of Humaira Shaikh, program director of Peace and Pluralism at Shirkat Gah. The impact of the chadors under the WELDD project (supra note 1) has been documented in a 2015 evaluation report. Starting in 2012, the project designed and ran five feminist leadership capacity-building modules, and followed up with mentoring, exchange programs, and large conventions. Women have established self-run and self-financed Purple Women sub-offices. The interventions included efforts to enhance the capacity of men from the same communities to function as supporters of women leaders.

24. This was the November 2015 closing meeting of WELDD (supra note 1); the activist was Tahira Abdullah.

4

The Indian Women's Movement Today

The Challenges of Addressing Gender-based Violence

POULOMI PAL

Introduction

December 16, 2012, was a watershed moment for the women's movement in India. A young para-medical student, Jyoti Pandey, on her way home from a movie theater with a male friend, was gang raped by six men in a moving private bus in New Delhi. The rapists beat up her companion and used a metal rod to brutally rape her, injuring her so severely that her intestines spilled out. They subsequently threw the two victims out of the bus and onto a highway. Several hours later, the police took them to a government hospital, where Pandey's friend recovered but she did not.[1] Jyoti Pandey died thirteen days later of sepsis and organ failure in a private hospital in Singapore, where the Indian government had flown her.

This government intervention was unusual: though 93 women are raped every day in India (Philip 2014), the government was forced to take action in this particular case because of unprecedented mass protests all over the country. Delhi, especially, saw public demonstrations by thousands of people from all walks of life, including many college students, which brought much of the city to a standstill. The December 16 protests, as they came to be known, were the biggest demonstrations against sexual violence to have taken place in India in recent times. Feminist activists and NGOs played an important role in these protests, demanding proper investigation, effective prosecution, and changing rape laws within the larger criminal justice system in India.

I open with this incident to call attention to how and why the horrific nature of sexual violence has been at the forefront of feminist concerns. As I describe further below, feminists' understanding of how the problem of sexual violence should be addressed differed from that of many of the other protesters who poured out onto the streets and sought immediate, punitive redress. This gang rape raised one of the central questions that this chapter explores, concerning the interaction between the women's movement and the state about sexual violence. As I will show, feminists played a major role in getting the government to establish the Justice Verma Committee to address gender-based violence. However, the law that the government eventually adopted ignored many of the progressive recommendations of both the committee and of feminists.

The women's movement from its outset has been deeply involved with challenging unjust laws and demanding new ones. Given the intrinsic relationship of the women's movement with legal jurisprudence, feminists have played an important role in the creation of landmark cases. Yet the legislation the state has adopted does not signify an unambiguous victory for feminists. The state has ignored some feminist demands while only partially conceding to others. It has failed to implement many laws it has passed. Often, the infrastructure and budgetary allocations are not in place for effective implementation of legislation. Moreover, we should not regard either the state or the women's movement as monolithic entities. During certain periods of time, under certain regimes, feminists have played an active role in government bodies, whereas at other times, including the contemporary period, they have had a more conflictual relationship with the state.

What does it mean to work with the state while maintaining a critical stance toward it? Who sets the agenda for the women's movement and where are the voices of marginalized women (Dalit [Scheduled Caste], *Adivasi* [Tribal], Muslim, disabled, and sexual minorities, for example)? How critical and self-reflective is the movement? What are some of the challenges it has faced and new ways of organizing it has attempted? These are some of the concerns this chapter will explore.[2] The first section will discuss the characteristics and development of the women's movement, up to the contemporary period. The next section will determine what role non-governmental organizations (NGOs) play in the women's movement. The following section will focus on some government initiatives on the issue of sexual violence and feminist responses to them. Finally, the chapter will chart the existing challenges for the women's movement and ways of addressing them looking ahead.

The Women's Movement in India

The women's movement in India today includes autonomous women's groups, NGOs, feminist women's studies centers, research institutions working on gender, feminist academics and publishers, and women's wings of left political parties. Various groups that are not part of the women's movement popularize its ideals and support its campaigns. For example, people's movements, trade unionists, and feminist artists (theater activists, feminist filmmakers) have added to the perspectives and texture of the women's movement in contemporary times.

This movement emerged through its association with other important movements in India. The nationalist movement, which eventually led to independence from British colonial rule in 1947, provided the first opportunity for women's mobilization. Whatever the blind spots of nationalist politics—and there were many, including a lack of attention to sexual violence—it encouraged women's activism and laid the foundations for women's professional and political advancement.

What is termed the Indian women's movement comprised a number of rural and urban movements that fostered women's activism and protested sexual inequality. In the 1970s this included such diverse groups and organizations as the *Shramik Sangathana* movement in Dhulia district, Maharashtra, a movement of landless tribal laborers against exploitation by Hindu landowners; the land rights movement in Bodh Gaya; the Self-Employed Women's Association (SEWA) in Gujarat, which organized women who work in the informal sector to protest low wages, poor working conditions, and lack of access to credit; and what became known as the *Chipko* movement in northern India, which opposed deforestation and the displacement of subsistence farming by commercial agriculture. The activities and demands of all of these movements were consistent with the most stringent definitions of feminism: in all of these cases large numbers of women played leadership roles and fought against sexual exploitation.

The late 1970s witnessed the emergence of autonomous women's groups, which deliberately sought to maintain a distance from political parties. These were groups that were comprised primarily of women and sought to challenge patriarchy and gender inequality. However, while these groups retained their autonomy from parties and stayed out of the electoral domain—aside from the collaboration of some groups with the communist parties—they worked closely with the courts and the bureaucracy. Correspondingly, the most important gains women achieved were in the courts and bureaucracy, not in the electoral arena. The government appointed women to some key posts and created bodies to investigate women's conditions and make recommendations. The National Commission of Women (NCW) was the most significant among them.

Working through these state institutions entailed some important costs. Struggles that got lodged in the courts often remained there for a long time, legal battles diverted women's attention from grassroots struggles, and the focus on rights was associated with narrow constructions of women's interests and identities. Nonetheless, these battles provided women with arenas within the state in which they could seek redress, while placing pressure on the courts and segments of the bureaucracy to address the conditions of marginal groups.

Over the years the women's movement has addressed a broad set of issues, which include rights to health, education, environmental preservation, livelihood, sexuality, reproductive health, work[3], property, maintenance, inheritance, and custody. The women's movement has also challenged the state's neoliberal policies, which have been associated with the growing feminization of poverty, and development projects that have resulted in massive displacement. In addressing the question of contraception and abortion, the women's movement has sought to pressure the state to ban the use of the drug Depo-Provera, because of its potentially negative health consequences, and of amniocentesis for the purposes of sex-selective abortions. It has been active in addressing the issue of the declining ratio of females to males, which results from son preference. Since the 1990s, the women's movement has also worked with women's wings of left political parties, demanding a 33 percent quota of women in parliament, among other demands (Menon 1999). The women's movement has engaged in struggles against right-wing and anti-religious fundamentalist forces and grappled with how to carve out a distinctive position that calls for reform within Personal Laws or the creation of a code which is gender just .

The women's movement has increasingly grappled with the complexity of intersectional gender and sexual identities. Many early feminists were from privileged backgrounds (based on class, religion, and sexuality). The same was true of their caste backgrounds. Upper-caste women were over-represented in the leadership of the movement. Over time Dalit, poor, and minority women have become increasingly politically active and have often fought gender inequality. Renu Addlakha from the Centre for Women's Development Studies (CWDS) notes that only feminists with disabilities brought out issues of disabilities within the discourse of the women's movement (CWDS 2013) The question of sexuality became increasingly important to the movement as a result of the growth of gay and lesbian activism and sex workers' collectives. The politics of trans identity (especially trans men) and its inclusion within the women's movement is something the movement is grappling with. At the same time, the women's movement should be credited with providing a space for debate and dialogue, which distinguishes it from other social movements.

The nature and texture of the women's movement today differs from the movement in the 1970s and 1980s. On the one hand, there are few autonomous (non-funded, non-party-affiliated) groups and networks, and on the other there are increasing numbers of feminist NGOs, which are part of the women's movement. Many of these NGOs receive external funding and work closely with the state machinery. This has led to the institutionalization of feminism. Many feminists are working closely with the government and NGOs, leading scholars to ask whether donor-driven agendas or co-option by the state has diluted earlier and more radical struggles. The movement has been criticized as having been "NGO-ized" since the 1990s.

The Role of NGOs

The role of NGOs in the women's movement is controversial. Some observers believe NGOs should be excluded from the women's movement. They fear that NGOs have dissipated the energies of feminist activism through their bureaucratized structures and their service orientation. They also worry that NGOs are overly dependent on foreign funding and thus are donor driven. I share some of these reservations and concerns, but argue that a more nuanced evaluation is necessary.

As I show below, some NGOs are working closely with the state machinery and thus may at times lose their critical edge. However, I do not believe that this is inevitable. Moreover, NGOs face twin challenges: avoiding dependence on and co-optation by both the state and by international donors. Within the current political climate, in which the state has become more hostile toward NGOs and less sympathetic to feminist demands, women's groups face an especially important dilemma.

I suggest that some—but not all—NGOs form part of the women's movement. Two important criteria are useful in determining which NGOs should be considered a part of the women's movement: whether the NGOs are committed to feminist goals and methods of organizing, and the extent to which they maintain autonomy from both international donors and the state, so that they are in a position to critique these entities if they feel that their core principles are being compromised.

Women's rights NGOs in India work on various aspects of gender-based violence: intervening to prevent violence (as crisis centers); changing patriarchal mindsets; creating safe spaces (public and private); addressing specific issues (domestic violence, sexual violence, sexual harassment at work, child sexual abuse, and violence based on caste, class, religion, disability, sexual preference, and religion); promoting rights (legal rights, health rights, sexual rights, right to decent work and livelihood); running campaigns (against dowry [bride price during marriage], *sati* [widow immolation], and rape; against the Uniform Civil Code; for a 33% quota for women in parliament; against the commodification of women); and addressing gender-based violence in conflict situations, communal (sectarian) violence, and natural disasters. Some NGOs work on specific issues and others work on interrelated overlapping issues.

Many NGOs engage in service delivery and work alongside the state to implement government schemes and policies. For instance, many NGOs are registered as service providers under the Protection of Women from Domestic Violence Act (PWDVA). Representatives of women's rights NGOs are often part of expert committees set up by government ministries to formulate amendments to legislation, draft protocols and guidelines, and engage in other policy interventions. Apart from working in collaboration with the state, many women's rights NGOs engage in generating empirical evidence, participating in fact-finding missions, raising awareness, training, capacity building, monitoring, evaluation, and policy change.

Funding for NGOs mostly comes from international donors, state agencies, and private trusts. Donor agencies such as the Ford Foundation, the International Development Research Centre (IDRC), and UN Women have funded many women's rights NGOs. The Ford Foundation transitioned from funding family planning and population control in the 1950s and 1960s, to nutrition and maternal and child health, to supporting coercive policies of population control by the state in the 1970s and 1980s, with a shift in the following decade to funding NGOs that mostly worked on sexuality. Starting in the 1990s, international donors began providing more funding for sexual rights, particularly for the treatment and prevention of HIV/AIDS. This led to an increased focus on other forms of sexual rights within the broad rubric of health and human rights, including reproductive rights, sex workers' rights, and domestic violence against women. IDRC has funded several projects on gender justice and state impunity in South Asia, as well as groups working on policy protocols for sexual and domestic violence.

A major challenge for the women's movement has been the growth of the Hindu nationalist political party, the Bharatiya Janata Party (BJP), which occupied national office from 1999 to 2004 and returned to power in 2014. The BJP government, representing the national government and in some states, has curtailed the activities of NGOs and some of the government programs that advanced women's interests. The BJP government has often blatantly supported communal violence, crushed citizens' democratic rights, and restricted the space for dissent.[4] Since attaining power in 2014, the BJP government has denied some NGOs authorization to work in India, and restricted foreign funding to NGOs (targeting funders such as the Ford Foundation) through the Foreign Contribution Regulation Act (FCRA). It has targeted organizations like Lawyers Collective, Amnesty International, Sabrang Trust, and Greenpeace. The BJP government has restructured government bodies such as the Planning Commission (now *Niiti Aayog*) and the National Mission for Empowerment of Women (NMEW), drastically scaling down their operations. The government made NMEW withdraw from projects that NGOs had already undertaken and withheld extensions for projects. The NMEW was started in 2010 by the United Progressive Alliance (UPA) government to work on gender convergence across ministries as a part of the Ministry of Women and Child Development. In recent times, women's rights NGOs have not articulated criticism of groups working in collaboration with the

BJP government. The one exception was after the BJP state government supported the Gujarat pogrom in 2002, when many women's rights organizations criticized SEWA for not taking a stand against the government, perhaps because it was receiving government funding. Many feminists argued at that point that one should look at the ends (outcomes in terms of work) and not the means (where the funding came from). Given the political climate of India today, it is important to reexamine the compromises women's groups make when they work with the state.

Some of the work funded by IDRC (Majlis Legal Centre)[5], UN Women (Special Cells, Lawyers Collective Women's Rights Initiative), the Ford Foundation, and Novib Tata Social Welfare Trust (Centre for Enquiry into Health and Allied Themes [CEHAT]) has been especially important to the women's movement's attempts to address sexual violence and to institutionalize their initiatives. Below, I selectively examine initiatives to monitor and evaluate state machinery from a feminist standpoint to effectively implement legislation (Lawyers Collective Women's Rights Initiative and Majlis Legal Centre); change perspectives of police (Special Cells); and work closely with medical institutions (CEHAT) and with legal cases and courts (Majlis Legal Centre). In the larger framework of work around sexual violence, it is important to understand the roles played by the police, courts, and medical establishments in the grassroots implementation of legislation. I discuss these feminist NGOs' interventions around sexual violence (including domestic violence) while working in collaboration with the state machinery.

Lawyers Collective Women's Rights Initiative, from 2008 to 2012, in collaboration with the government, published the "Staying Alive" monitoring and evaluation reports on the implementation of the PWDVA to map the gaps in the implementation of this legislation.[6] In 2012, the Majlis Legal Centre entered a Memorandum of Association with the Commissionerate of the Department of Women and Child Development, Pune, to monitor and evaluate the PWDVA in Maharashtra-*Mohim*. As a part of this initiative, Majlis Legal Centre organizes trainings and monitors the work of stakeholders (the judiciary, police, medical services, shelter homes, legal aid, NGOs, and civil society) under the act.

Although not an NGO, the Special Cells initiative was established in 1984 as a collaborative effort between Tata Institute of Social Sciences (TISS) and the Bombay Police. This initiative placed a social worker in police stations to help survivors of violence, for effective coordination with women's groups for short-term crisis intervention as well as long-term development.[7] The initial Memorandum of Association in 2001, which allowed Special Cells to be functional in the state, was signed between UNIFEM (now UN Women), TISS, and the Government of Maharashtra (Department of Home and Department of Women and Child Development). It was later, in 2005, that the Department of Women and Child Development instituted funds for the Special Cells. Currently there are 144 Special Cells sanctioned for Maharashtra, and many more states have established them.[8] TISS mostly provided technical support, including coordination, training, monitoring, and framing implementation guidelines.

In 2001, CEHAT started a crisis center (*Dilaasa*) for women facing domestic violence, in association with Municipal Corporation of Greater Mumbai. The center provides feminist counseling, emergency shelter, and legal counseling for victims or survivors of violence.[9] In 2006, the hospitals took responsibility for running *Dilaasa*, with support from CEHAT. The *Dilaasa* model has since been established in two more hospitals in Bombay and various other states.[10] CEHAT has also drafted guidelines and protocols for medico-legal care for survivors or victims of sexual assault for the Ministry of Health and Family Welfare, Government of India, and the World Health Organization (WHO).[11]

Majlis Legal Centre for victims of sexual assault and child sexual abuse, in association with the Department of Women and Child Development, started *Rahat*, which ensures socio-legal support for victims and survivors. Its services include legal assistance during investigation and trial; developing protocols and guidelines, generating awareness, and documenting best practices for the state; and helping the survivor access hospitals, trauma centers, counseling facilities, shelters, education, and other assistance. Majlis Legal Centre has devised a convergence model that includes engagement with all the stakeholders over the years.

These NGO initiatives have been important to the women's movement in India, but working closely with the state machinery creates many challenges—including co-optation. The state machinery is highly bureaucratic and patriarchal, and it often takes years for feminist women's rights NGOs to initiate substantive changes. The case of Majlis Legal Centre illustrates these challenges.

On March 25th, 2016, one of the founding members of Majlis—filmmaker, curator, and cultural activist Madhushree Dutta—wrote an open letter of resignation. The note was titled, "Why I Am Not Celebrating 25 Years of Majlis." Among other things, the letter claimed that Majlis had been co-opted by the state and other funding organizations, and had violated its founding feminist principles. Dutta described the Majlis Legal Centre as having become alienated from the larger women's movement, and argued that it prioritized legal work over the cultural critique of patriarchy. Some of her concerns are germane to the issue of NGOs working with the state machinery:

> My organization Majlis has even acquired the distinction of opposing all other women's organizations in the court in favor of the state....The state is happy because we are not only bringing legitimacy to their lip service but also doing the field work for them. The funding agencies are happy as only through State networks can we manufacture magic numbers of 'beneficiaries' and proudly fill up the column on deliverable and outreaches....The progressive lawyers, legal activists, and women's organizations from the city [are alienated] to such an extent that Majlis is now popularly considered as a counsel of the state. (Scroll 2016)

In response to this letter, many feminists called for more dialogue within the women's movement to discuss these issues. The Forum Against Oppression of Women (FAOW) Bombay called for NGOs to be more accountable to marginalized communities and to the broader women's movement in keeping with feminist principles of decentralized decision-making practices.

Another contentious issue is to what extent working with the state necessitates representing the state in the court of law. In July 2014, Majlis defended the Department of Women and Child Development in Maharashtra against a petition by various women's rights groups opposing a government-issued circular which declared that counseling or mediation between the parties in domestic violence cases could only be conducted by stakeholders at the order of a magistrate. In another instance, CEHAT and Lawyers Collective filed an Intervention Petition opposing the gender insensitive protocols developed by Government of Maharashtra, whereas Majlis supported them. This, according to CEHAT, caused a rift between tertiary and primary health care providers.

FAOW aptly critiqued Majlis as having wholly sacrificed its autonomy to the state in the following statement: "...This is not about working with the State any more it is working as the State and against the very same feminist comrades and organizations that we all claim to have a legacy from."[12]

Although one should not discount Majlis's contributions over the last three decades, it is time for some women's rights groups to be more self-critical of their work and reevaluate their stance in relation to the state.[13] However, this does not suggest that feminist organizations like Majlis have stopped critiquing the state in other instances: this will be discussed in relation to the feminist critique of One Stop Centres in the next section.

Sexual Violence

The issue that the women's movement in India has addressed most consistently is violence against women. This violence has assumed many forms, including but not limited to child marriage, child sexual abuse, trafficking, dowry, sati, custodial rape, rape, sexual assault, sexual harassment at work, domestic violence, honor killings, witch hunting, acid attacks, female feticide, female infanticide, communal violence, and police violence.

The greatest challenge the women's movement faces in addressing sexual violence is deeply entrenched misogynistic attitudes in Indian society. These attitudes are pervasive in media reports; comments by politicians, lawyers, and judges; and the verdicts of the *khap panchayats* (unelected village elders in northern states of India, especially in western Uttar Pradesh and Haryana). A few examples are illustrative. In 2016, unmarried women and girls below age eighteen in Gujarat were banned from using cell phones. In a case on domestic violence in Bangalore, a High Court judge, Justice Bhaktavatsala, justified domestic violence as long as the husband is "taking care" of the wife. *Khap panchayats* are known to impose social boycotts, fines, and order honor killings. In August 2015, a *khap panchayat* in Meerut ordered gang rape as punishment for two Dalit sisters because their brother had eloped with a girl from the upper-caste Jat community. A Bihar minister blamed rape on people who eat non-vegetarian food. In 2014, Mulayam Singh Yadav, chief of the ruling Samajwadi Party in Uttar Pradesh, justified rape by saying: "Boys will be boys....They commit mistakes....Will they be hanged for rape?" (Firstpost 2015).

The growth of Hindu nationalist BJP and affiliate organizations, particularly the Vishwa Hindu Parishad (VHP) and Rashtriya Swayam Sewak Sangh (RSS), has resulted in increasing misogyny. These organizations have engaged in moral policing, upheld patriarchal notions of women's sexuality and social position, and threatened minority groups. In 2013, the news website Cobra Post revealed how BJP state government resources in Gujarat were used to stalk a young woman from Bangalore who was under constant surveillance by the police on the orders of Amit Shah, the Minister of State, Home, at the time. The surveillance involved the Crime Investigation Department (CID) crime branch anti-terrorist squad: a clear case of the misuse of power with no legal basis (Khetan and Chowdhury 2013).

Sexual violence is also a manifestation of state militarization and caste-based oppression. The 2006 Khairlanji massacre and the 2014 Badaun case saw brutal caste-based gang rapes of Dalit women, and women were paraded naked and hanged (The Hindu 2010; BBC News 2015). Soni Sori, a teacher from Dhantewada, Chhattisgarh, was arrested in 2011 on charges of being a Maoist. She was raped and tortured in police custody; stones were found in her vagina. The Assam Rifles sexually assaulted and murdered Thangjam Manorama in Manipur in 2004; this incident illustrates the atrocities that are committed by the police and army under the Armed Forces Special Powers Act (AFSPA). In Kunan Poshpora, Shopian, Gujarat, and Muzaffarnagar, mass rapes were used as a tool of communal violence at different points in time. These incidents have constantly reminded feminists of the need to struggle against state-led violence.

The women's movement has been responsible for putting pressure on the government to enact laws with respect to gender inequality and sexual violence. Landmark cases concerning rape, custodial rape, and sexual assault that led to substantive changes in the law have histories of feminist struggle behind them.

In 1972, Mathura, a minor tribal girl, was gang raped by policemen while she was in custody in Maharashtra. The Supreme Court reversed the High Court's conviction of the policemen in 1978 on grounds that Mathura was "habitual to sex," did not "raise an alarm for help," and that there were no "injuries on her body or signs of struggle" (Murthy 2013). Four feminist law professors[14] wrote an open letter to the Chief Justice of India in protest, in which they distinguished between "submission and consent" and called for not questioning the past sexual history of the rape victim and shifting the burden of proof to the accused. In 1978, Rameeza Bee, a Muslim woman, was gang raped by four policemen. Although the policemen were found guilty by the enquiry commission, the Supreme Court transferred the matter to a District Judge who acquitted the accused. Decades of struggle from the women's movement against cases like these finally led to the Criminal Law Amendment Act of 1983, which shifted the burden of proof to the accused in custodial rape cases. A minimum punishment of ten years imprisonment was instituted in cases of custodial rape, gang rape, and rape of pregnant women and girls under twelve years, and of seven years in all other cases (Agnes 1992).

Due to persistent struggles from the women's movement, the Criminal Amendment Act of 1983 included Section 498A to address domestic violence, the Dowry Prohibition Act was amended, and the Immoral Traffic in Women and Girls Act was replaced by the Immoral Traffic (Prevention) Act in 1988. Other legislation such as the Indecent Representation of Women Act of 1986 and the Schedule Caste and Schedule Tribe Prevention of Atrocities Act of 1989 were also instituted. The women's movement raised the issue of Muslim women's right to maintenance in the Shah Bano case, which eventually was reflected in the enactment of the Muslim Women (Protection of Rights on Divorce) Act of 1986. Many feminists have critiqued some provisions of this act, however, and have also questioned the process of introduction of this law as the Congress government's attempt to appease a group of Muslims, given the backdrop of the Babri *Masjid* agitations[15].

The women's movement has also played an important role in instituting laws against sexual harassment in the workplace. In 1992, Bhanwari Devi, who worked as a *saathin* ("friend," or volunteer social worker in this context) as part of the Women's Development Project in Rajasthan against child marriages, was gang raped by five upper-caste men. In 1995 all the men were acquitted. Women's groups were outraged and to this day no justice has been done. However, in 1997, the court came out with the Vishakha Guidelines on sexual harassment in the workplace. It took a more than decade-long struggle for the women's movement to get the Sexual Harassment at Workplace (Prevention, Prohibition and Redressal) Act of 2013 passed. The new act had many loopholes, however; the most glaring one was the clause on false and malicious complaints, with a provision of punishment for the complainant.

For the first time, under the NCW in 1992, women's groups were part of a subcommittee to formulate a bill on sexual assault, which expanded the definition of penetrative sexual assault to include a category of "aggravated sexual assault," and highlighted the continuum of sexual violence. These groups demanded the repeal of Section 377 (which criminalizes "unnatural offenses against the order of nature," targeting mostly same-sex consensual relationships and also consensual sexual acts like oral and anal sex) and the inclusion of marital rape within the purview of rape. They recommended excluding the conduct and character of women as evidence that could be raised in court, as well as shifting the burden of proof onto the accused. The most contentious recommendation was a gender-neutral clause for both the victim and the accused. Many LGBT (Lesbian, Gay, Bisexual, Transgender) groups disagreed with the gender-neutral clause for the perpetrator because they contested the notion that women could perpetrate sexual violence. This was followed by the recommendations of the Law Commission's 172nd Report in 2000, which included most recommendations discussed above and added a new section on sexual harassment at work. However, this report did not include marital rape within the purview of rape.

Due to suggestions and recommendations from women's groups, the Law Commission Report in 2000 suggested sensitivity during the medical examination of the rape victim, especially during evidence-gathering with child sexual abuse victims. It also proposed greater punishment (with discretionary powers for judges during sentencing) for rape committed by people in a fiduciary relationship with the victim: public servants, relatives, people in positions of trust and authority, or the management and staff of hospitals (Law Commission of India 2000). Following this, women's groups made recommendations to include sexual violence as part of the All India Democratic Women's Association (AIDWA) Bill on sexual assault in 2002. This bill made provisions for child sexual assault, included marital rape within the purview of rape, defined sexual assault as a gender-specific crime, and repealed Section 377 . However, especially in a context where same-sex consensual relationships were not recognized by law, there wasn't any consensus within women's groups on their stance on same-sex sexual assault.

Finally, due to agitation from the women's movement, in 2002, the government enacted an amendment to the Criminal Law stating that victims of rape could no longer be questioned about "past sexual conduct" and "immoral character." Later, the Criminal Amendment Bill of 2010 and the Criminal Law (amendment) Bill of 2012 were placed before parliament. The 2012 bill introduced acid attacks and prescribed punishment for the failure of public servants to perform their duties. The Protection of Children from Sexual Assault Act also came into effect in 2012; this incorporated many of the demands from women's and child rights groups. Feminist groups were still debating the provision of gender neutrality for laws on sexual assault and rape, and asking for the inclusion of gradations of sexual assault to include stripping/public parading, and reducing the age of consent to 16 years from 18 years (Bali 2012).

This history of demands from women's groups and the interaction of the women's movement with the state is important context for the events surrounding the brutal gang rape of December 2012 discussed in the introduction to this chapter. The protests against the gang rape made the government more receptive than it previously had been to feminist demands. Feminists were critical of the media for its coverage of the Jyoti Pandey gang rape and made a distinction between feminist and non-feminist demands. They rejected widespread public demands that rapists be subject to the death penalty and chemical castration. They condemned Sushma Swaraj—then a BJP member of the opposition—who referred to the victim (still alive at that point) as "Zinda Laash" (living corpse), as a justification for giving the death penalty to the rapists. Along with this call for a punitive response to rape was the tendency to idolize Jyoti Pandey, thereby denying the everyday nature of violence against women in India. Since legal statutes in India do not allow public disclosure of a rape victim's identity, the media and the masses framed Jyoti Pandey's identity as an upper-caste Hindu. She was given appellations like "nirbhaya" (fearless), "damini" (lightning), "jagruti" (awareness), and "amanat" (treasure), all of which feminists critiqued.

From a feminist standpoint, rape is a violation of bodily integrity and a lack of consent, rather than a violation of patriarchal ideas of shame and honor (Bekhauf Azadi Campaign 2013). In the realm of sexual violence, feminists agreed that marital rape should be criminalized; that men should be recognized as perpetrators in sexual assault laws but the victims' and survivors' identities should be gender-neutral; that sexual assaults on Dalit and Tribal women should be recognized as aggravated sexual assaults; that Section 377 should be repealed; that the

AFSPA in Kashmir and the Northeast should be amended; that the
death penalty for those convicted of rape should be abolished; and that
the definition of rape should be expanded beyond penile-vaginal penetration and should include rape by objects other than a penis. Lastly,
they agreed that the age of consent should be shifted to 16 years from
18 years, as the present law criminalizes consensual relationships of
persons between the ages of 16 and 18. Women's groups and feminists
have pushed these concerns with the government for the last two decades. Amongst other issues, there have been debates on the contentious issue of same-sex sexual assault within the women's movement,
especially with LGBT groups.

In December 2012, the government formed the three-member Justice Verma Committee to formulate recommendations for the rape
laws and the criminal justice system. Many demands from the women's
movement were reflected in their report. Women against State Repression and Sexual Assault's submission to the Justice Verma Committee
stated:

> We believe that sexual crimes form a continuum, and that the graded
> nature of sexual assault should be recognized, based on concepts of
> harm, injury, humiliation and degradation by using the well estab-
> lished categories of sexual assault and sexual offences. (WSS 2013)

The Verma Committee's report focused on laws related to rape, sexual harassment, trafficking, child sexual abuse, police, medical examination of victims, and electoral and educational reforms. Reflecting
the demands from the women's movement, the Justice Verma Committee retained the term "rape," expanding the definition beyond penile-vaginal penetration to include penetration by any other object into
the vagina, anus, urethra, or mouth. It recommended criminalizing
marital rape, and retained the gender-neutrality clause for victims and
survivors, as demanded by women's groups and LGBT groups. It widened the legal definition of sexual violence to include intent to disrobe
a woman, acid attacks to disfigure, stalking, and voyeurism as forms of
assault. It recommended the age of consent be 16 years of age, and
banned the two-finger test.[16] It also introduced "breach of command
responsibilities," whereby senior public servants were to be held responsible for acts of mass sexual violence—for example, in the event of
communal violence (Justice Verma Committee Report 2013).

JVC did NOT work

However, feminists were critical of two features of the report. First, it left out their recommendation that Section 377 be repealed. Second, it also criminalized sex work by redefining and expanding the definition of trafficking. This was critiqued by many sex workers' rights organizations.

Soon the government instituted the Criminal Law (Amendment) Ordinance, which followed the enactment of the Criminal Law (Amendment) Act of 2013. This act introduced a new Section 375 to the Indian Penal Code, which expanded the definition of rape and sexual violence to include disrobing, voyeurism, stalking, and acid attacks. However it ignored many demands of the women's movement and recommendations by the Verma Committee. It introduced the death penalty, though in the "rarest of rare" cases, in which a victim dies or is left in a permanent vegetative state. The act did not include marital rape in the definition of rape, did not recognize sexual violence against Dalit and tribal women as aggravated assault, and the age of consent remained 18 years. Rape laws ignored feminists' demands that victims/survivors of sexual assault should be considered gender neutral. Rape was still seen as "outraging the modesty of women," thus reiterating the patriarchal stereotype of rape within a discourse of shame and honor. Finally, the act did not amend the AFSPA, making it difficult to prosecute armed forces personnel accused of sexual assault and rape.

In the aftermath of the December 2012 rape, the government immediately instituted six fast-track courts in Delhi to address rape and sexual assault, and established the Nirbhaya Fund, which kept aside 1000 crores (Approximately $185.19 million USD) in each financial year (starting in 2013-14) to provide services for survivors of gender-based violence. The government also introduced amendments to the Juvenile Justice Act. Based on the recommendations of the Usha Mehra Committee report,[17] the government also started "Nirbhaya Centres" or "One Stop Centres (OSCs)" to provide services to survivors of gender-based violence. Feminist activists were highly critical of such makeshift institutional initiatives. They argued that instead of critically addressing the loopholes in existing institutional bodies, the government created new ones without incorporating the inputs offered to the Ministry of Women and Child Development, which was drafting the policy for these centers.

The centrally sponsored OSCs were designed to provide referrals with regard to medical assistance, police assistance, pyscho-social counseling, legal aid, shelter, and video conferencing for women facing violence.[18] Integrated with helplines, the pilots of twenty such centers were planned, either to be housed within a government hospital or to be constructed within two kilometers of the hospital premises. The guideline for the policy and the policy document itself had elaborate descriptions of structure and levels of governance, including management committees, approval boards, reporting formats, and construction specifications, but did not elaborate on the basis of hiring staff or protocols for counseling. All the staff engaged in the OSCs were entirely voluntary; and the central government would disburse the money to state governments, which had discretion to determine how to "outsource" the services (MoWCD 2015). The policy undermined the role of the Ministry of Women and Child Development by highlighting the roles and responsibilities of other partner Ministries without any framework of accountability.

While it might seem that the state responded promptly and effectively to this incident of sexual assault, in fact its response was highly contentious. This is because in the actual policy document, the Ministry dropped the word "crisis" and hence undermined the recommendation from the XII Plan Working Group on Women's Agency and Empowerment.[19] The formulation of names for these centers (from "Nirbhaya Centers" to "One Stop Crisis Centre" to "One Stop Service Centre" to "Rape Crisis Centre" to "One Stop Centers") was also reflective of the government's stance on addressing sexual violence.[20] As part of the policy, the Ministry sent a model based on the National Building Construction Corporations (NBCC) design for construction of such centers, with elaborate description of floors and rooms. However, there was no allocation of funds for building ramps for any disabled women who would need to access such centers.

The government proposed a very small window for a consultative process and did not include a single substantive suggestion from women's groups. The petition from women's groups asked for consultations before the plan was finalized. Although the budget was adequate to initiate such centers in each district of every state, the OSCs were only piloted in twenty districts. The policy, according to feminists, underscored the replicability of crisis centers already in place in hospitals in Maharashtra (*Dilaasa*) and police stations in several states (Special Cells). They were highly critical that the government recommended including religious leaders as part of "community involvement."

The Lawyers Collective Women's Rights Initiative recommended the integration of existing institutions and functionaries to address all forms of violence. It pointed out that the OSCs were not equipped to conduct forensic tests for medico-legal cases of sexual assault. Coordination between the hospital and police station and the OSC was missing from the plan, an important flaw. The group recommended that a dedicated person in police stations, courts, and hospitals conduct this coordination; that doctors, lawyers, and police should also do an update of each case history to represent a full picture; and that a team of legal aid panel lawyers be made available on call to assist the public prosecutor, particularly to support the woman survivor through court proceedings. The group was highly critical of the appointment of retired police officers to facilitate the filing of the First Information Report (FIR). The ministry later removed "retired" from the plan.

Majlis pointed out that the government has not designated Protection Officers (POs) to work independently on domestic violence cases as specified by the PWDVA; instead, POs on the ground are often given additional responsibilities. Majlis also pointed out that the convergence model that would involve POs, shelter homes, hospitals, legal aid, and the court has not been achieved. Given that the plan does not address violence against girls below the age of 18, Majlis criticized the disregard for cases of child sexual abuse and the plan's inability to contextualize the Protection of Children from Sexual Offences Act and its child-friendly provisions. Most importantly, Majlis highlighted the duplication of institutions and flagged the victim/survivor's urgent need to access these services directly from the police station and hospitals instead of visiting such centers.

As part of setting up the OSCs, the guidelines and protocols for medico-legal care for survivors/victims of sexual violence, which had been developed by the Ministry of Health and Family Welfare and WHO in association with CEHAT and other experts, were attached in the initial drafts of the plan along with guidelines for feminist counseling. These were later removed. This points out how often existing models and protocols developed through consultative processes by one wing of the government (Ministry of Health and Family Welfare) are not incorporated by another (Ministry of Women and Child Development).

The government initiative, while well intentioned, was ultimately shortsighted and not cognizant of women's needs. It ignored many feminist demands. The state's policies often reflect selective and makeshift attitudes rather than addressing demands the women's movement has generated over decades to either transform the criminal justice system or institute effective gender-just plans to address gender-based violence.

Challenges Before the Women's Movement

The gang rape of Jyoti Pandey raised questions about which groups of women have been recognized as victims and agents in India. Clearly all women are subjected to gender-based violence, regardless of their class, caste, religion, region, sexual orientation, age, or gender. However, all women are not equally subject to violence. Women who live in the Northeast, Chhattisgarh and Kashmir, or are poor, Dalit, Muslim, lesbian, or disabled have faced more extreme and persistent violence than middle-class Hindu women in India's metropolises. Over the years these marginalized women have become increasingly politically active, articulating their particular positionalities within the women's movement. Interestingly, many of these groups do not believe that the autonomous feminist movement adequately addresses their interests and demands.

Another important challenge that feminists face is how to use the law to advance their claims without becoming overly reliant on the law. Clearly, feminists have achieved many victories through the courts. However, the striking down of Section 377 by the Delhi High Court and the reversal of this by the Indian Supreme Court in 2013 raised issues and concerns regarding the rights of LGBT communities in India. Although the order striking down Section 377 was a big victory for LGBT groups as well as the women's movement, the reversal of the order (which led to the criminalization of same-sex relationships, among other things) has led gay and lesbian activists within the women's movement to reevaluate their strategy for addressing this issue.

The courts have addressed the rights of transgender communities, but their decisions do not reflect activists' demands. In April 2014, the Supreme Court ruled that transgender persons should be given third gender status. This was a landmark judgment on a Public Interest Litigation filed by the National Legal Services Authority (NALSA). The ruling differentiated between gender identity and sexual orientation, based on the principle of "person autonomy" and "self determination." The *Hijras* (eunuchs) and "gender identity in opposite sex based on self identification" came under its purview. Under this new judgement, these groups were treated as "Other Backward Classes," and so became eligible for affirmative action in education and employment (Feminist India 2014). Based on this judgment, the Ministry of Social Justice started drafting the Rights of Transgender Persons Bill in 2015.

However, several trans men wrote an open letter to the Ministry, which questioned this bill. They felt that the bill specifically addressed Hijra communities, without adequately addressing the concerns of male-to-female and female-to-male transgender individuals. The activists also expressed discomfort at being labeled "Persons Assigned Gender Female at Birth" (PAGFB) in meetings and reports (LABIA 2013).

There are many challenges in implementing progressive legislation. With regard to disabled women, the government has included the aggravated nature of violence against disabled women[21] in the Criminal Law (Amendment) Act of 2013. However, given the lived realities of disabled women, and the insensitivity and discrimination they face from hospital authorities, police, and the courts, it would be a big challenge to implement the provision effectively. Women's groups working on disability rights have negotiated these rights with the state machinery by referring to "state obligations" under the United Nations Convention on the Rights of Persons with Disabilities (UNCRPD), which has been ratified and signed by the Indian government.

Another challenge is to recognize the intersectional nature of gender identities against international and domestic pressures. A case in point concerns bar dancers. The Indian government claimed that dance bars were fronts for trafficking and forced prostitution, especially of minor girls. In 2003 the Bombay High Court banned bar dancing, which left around 70,000 dancers unemployed. Some feminists argue that one reason the government banned bar dancers was because it conceded to pressures by the US State Department, which instructed governments to put policies in place to combat trafficking, or face certain adverse consequences. However, other feminists point out that the ban was based on issues of morality, caste and class hierarchy. In 2013, the Supreme Court overturned the judgment, but the women bar dancers were not compensated.

Studies conducted before and after the ban on dancing at bars showed that the women from dancing communities had no skills or sources of income other than dancing. According to the FAOW survey, 62 percent of the bar dancers interviewed were from migrant and nomadic groups (traditional entertainer communities), Dalit, or lower caste (SNDT and FAOW 2005 & 2006). The framing of the caste question in the Bombay Bar Dancers case created distance between feminists working on caste issues and others who looked at the issue as one of livelihood and the right to work. The issue created a rift between Dalit women, who saw bar dancing as a form of caste oppression, and many feminists who defended women's rights to earn a livelihood. Many of the bar dancers were Dalit women and the arguments of many feminists in the women's movement did not articulate the linkages between caste oppression, patriarchy, and the right to work. The women's movement has continually grappled with the question of caste. As Sandhya Gokhale points out:

> The silence on caste in women's movements is also linked to the caste/class composition of the leadership. Dalit women have also been silenced by the patriarchy of their own organizations. It was in the Calicut Conference in the 1990s that caste questions were raised for first time. Muslim women's issues had been raised around personal law reform by 1985 and the Shahbano case, but not on caste. Queer politics entered with the case of the two Dalit policewomen in MP who got married in 1987. But it did not occur to anyone at the time that they were Dalit – it was their lesbian identity that took centre-stage. (WSS 2015)

Working alongside the state machinery is a challenge for the contemporary women's movement. The NCW, the Ministry of Women and Child Development, and the NMEW have mandates to uphold women's rights and gender justice, but their understanding of gender inequality and gender violence is more limited than that of feminists. "Women's empowerment" defined within these institutional spaces often reiterates gender stereotypes in terms of gender roles and the gendered division of labor. This is in contrast to the feminist articulation of gender justice, which encompasses redefining and questioning such stereotypes. The government has delayed passing reforms and different government bodies often work at cross-purposes. Feminists also critique these bodies for being overly bureaucratized and institutionalized. An even bigger challenge emerges when the state is an accomplice to sexual violence.

The women's movement is at an important juncture with respect to its membership. Since December 2012, there have been many youth-led protests that share feminist concerns about women's mobility, choice, autonomy, and consent, but do not ground their analyses in a systematic understanding of class, patriarchy, and intersectionality. The Pink *Chaddi* campaign and Pub *Bharo* campaigns were started in response to attacks by a fundamentalist right-wing group against women in a pub in Mangalore. Although Hindi words such as "chaddi" (underwear) were used to give the campaign a mass appeal, the campaigns themselves were urban and elite in nature. The "Kiss of Love" protests in Kerala and different parts of India against moral policing by right-wing fundamentalist forces were also youth-led. Delhi saw flash mobs and "slut walks" organized by young women addressing gender-based violence. Many feminists were critical of some of these initiatives as being urban and middle class. Yet at the same time, there seems to be a clear need to have a second tier of leadership within the women's movement. While the older feminists have made invaluable contributions, it is important to allow a younger generation of feminists to grow and flourish.

At the same time, there have been some exciting attempts to link the activities of women across this generational divide. The "feministsindia" online portal started in 2009: this internet group moderated by Ramlath Kavil keeps readers abreast of news, judgments, open statements, and information on feminist campaigns and concerns. This is an intergenerational space for virtual debates and knowledge sharing, reflecting many different feminist perspectives. The online portal of Feminist Law Archive started by the NGO Partners for Law in Development charts out debates and has archived many landmark cases related to legal jurisprudence in the realm of gender-based violence. Zubaan, a feminist publishing house, started the "Poster Women" project, which is an online portal. As a part of women's history archives and memories, it is a remarkable documentation of the lives, struggles, and politics of the feminists in the women's movement.

In addition to these urban online initiatives , one noteworthy mention is Khabar Lehriya (News Waves), a local-language newspaper brought out by a collective of forty women journalists across six hundred rural villages in two states of India (Uttar Pradesh and Bihar). Part of a Delhi-based women's rights NGO, Nirantar, the Khabar Lehriya newspaper is run exclusively by rural women, from conceptualizing to publishing and distribution. Its growing popularity is evident from the fact that it started in one language (Bundeli) and now publishes in four more local languages.

The women's movement in India has been a space of ideas, debate, dissent, action, and growth of various feminist worldviews. Feminist organizing has been ongoing in different parts of India, often in local languages, making linkages with local, state, and global struggles. The relationship with the state machinery has been challenging, but at the same time has offered a learning opportunity for feminists within the movement. Institutionalization of feminist interventions by the state is both a strength and a weakness: autonomy and space for dissent must be preserved, especially when collaborating with a right-wing state machinery. In the case of sexual violence, feminist legal jurisprudence has played an important role. As of now legislation on violence against women has been targeted to end "a particular kind of violence" and does not create an environment of anti-discrimination based on caste, class, gender, sexuality, disability, and religion. There is need for broad-based anti-discrimination legislation in place of laws that address only one part of broader, intersecting identities (Rashida Manjoo 2014).

The women's movement in India has come a long way from articulating the concept of violence against women to that of gender-based violence, violence perpetrated by patriarchy not only toward cisgender women but also toward LGBTQ and gender-nonconforming people. There has been a concerted effort to question heteronormative relationships and to evolve some critique of marriage as an institution. The movement has a long way to go in grappling with issues of non-monogamy and the conceptualization of the non-heterosexual family within the legal framework and outside of it. The legacy of the women's movement's struggle for gender justice and the politics of "personal is political" will always guide feminist activism in India.

Notes

1. Many feminists later critiqued the role of the police and the cause of this delay, as the police spent a lot of time determining issues of jurisdiction and which police station should be registering the case.

2. Gender critique of political economy, especially after the neoliberal policies of the state in 1991, is beyond the limited scope of this chapter.

3. Specifically: questions around women workers in the unorganized sector, on minimum wages, on equal remuneration, on maternity benefits, and on women as sex workers and domestic workers.

4. The BJP government banned the possession and consumption of beef in Maharashtra in a bid to protect the cow, which is considered holy. This led to the lynching of a man by an entire village in Dadri, Uttar Pradesh in 2015, on the assumption that the family was consuming and storing beef. More recently, the BJP has been implementing

its right-wing agenda in major Indian universities, such as the Jawaharlal Nehru University, the Film and Television Institute of India, The University of Hyderabad, and the Indian Institutes of Technology. There has been a concerted drive by the government to restrict the space for dissent, while supporting unethical caste-ist policies in universities. The BJP has been directly implicated in major incidents of communal violence and mass rapes in the country: in the Babri Masjid Demolition of 1992, the Gujarat riots in 2002, and the Muzaffarnagar riots in 2013. Given the state of affairs in India today, the Communal Violence Bill (pending in parliament) and the recommendations of the Sachar Committee Report 2006 might be difficult to enact and implement with BJP in power.

5. Majlis includes Majlis Legal Centre and Majlis Cultural Centre. The discussion here mostly addresses Majlis Legal Centre.

6. Lawyers Collective Women's Rights Initiative, established in 1981, has played an important role within the women's movement by engaging in legal aid, litigation, research, documentation, and human rights advocacy. It is one of the organizations that drafted the PWDVA and led the national campaign for the enactment of the law.

7. Services offered are: negotiating with police, providing shelter, working with men, giving access to economic assets, counseling, and offering legal aid.

8. The state governments of Rajasthan in 2011, Haryana in 2008, Delhi in 2010, and Gujarat in 2013 have already institutionalized these. Special Cells have been working in various states: Madhya Pradesh since 2010, Odisha since 2011, and Andhra Pradesh since 2011.

9. The hospitals were to provide governance space, staff (a full-time social worker, a part-time doctor, and a part-time clinical psychologist), 24-hour shelter, and medical and referral support; CEHAT would train staff, provide technical assistance in setting up the crisis center, and secure funds.

10. Replication of the *Dilaasa* model has been initiated at a medical college hospital in Indore, a civil hospital in Shillong, and primary health care sites in Bangalore. Also under the NUHM (National Urban Health Mission) scheme, the *Dilaasa* center is being replicated in nine municipal peripheral hospitals in Bombay.

11. CEHAT's work has highlighted the role of medical professionals in evidence collection, questioning unscientific practices justified by forensic science textbooks, and gender bias and attitudes entrenched in the police, health, and judicial systems. Their work has added enormously to our understanding of gender-based violence from a health perspective.

12. Response of FAOW to Madhushree Dutta's Open Letter, email to the Feminist India list serve, April 4, 2016.

13. Majlis is known for its litigation and campaigns (against the Uniform Civil Code, to reform the Personal Laws, against child sexual abuse, for compensation for rape/acid attack victims, in defense of bar dancers, for matrimonial property and rights) and its work on sexual violence and domestic violence.

14. Upendra Baxi, Lotika Sarkar, Vasudha Dhagamwar, and Raghunath Kelkar.

15. On December 6, 1992, the Babri Mosque was demolished by Hindu right-wing forces claiming that the mosque was built on the land where Lord Rama (a Hindu god) was born. The aftermath of this saw massive Hindu-Muslim riots in many parts of north India.

16. The end of the two-finger test, which is used to determine if a survivor of sexual assault is "habituated to sexual intercourse" and therefore whether their claim of rape

is true, had been one of the major demands of the women's movement, since the test can further traumatize a survivor.

17. The Ministry of Home Affairs had appointed a Commission of Enquiry, the Usha Mehra Commission, after the Delhi gang rape of December 2012, under the Commission of Enquiry Act of 1952.

18. The staff of the OSC would be the center administrator, case worker, police facilitation officer, paralegal personnel/lawyer, paramedical personnel, counselor, IT staff, multipurpose helper, and security guard/night guard. Day-to-day functioning of the OSC would be entrusted to a designated Implemented Agency. The District Programme Officer/Protection Officer appointed under PWDVA would be entrusted with the day-to-day coordination of the OSC.

19. The recommendation was to set up One Stop Crisis Centres on a pilot basis for providing shelter, police desk, legal, medical, and counseling services to victims of violence under one roof, integrated with a 24-hour helpline. Historically in many countries, crisis intervention centers address the need for women facing violence to get immediate services in one place rather than going to the police station and hospitals when the assault takes place. In India, since the OSCs were referral centers, the idea of crisis intervention was taken away from their conceptualization.

20. The government's stance on removing "crisis" or "rape" from the names of these centers points to the fact that firstly the government did not understand the immediacy of services for rape victims; and secondly to the stigma attached to rape in India—women would not be encouraged to access these centers if they were called Rape Crisis Centres.

21. As reflected in Section 376 of IPC (Indian Penal Code) of the Criminal Law (Amendment) Act 2013.

5

Feminist Struggles in a Changing China

WANG Zheng

Introduction

Embedded in political, social, economic, and cultural transformations, gender has been a highly salient site of contention since the Chinese elite started to search for a modern China in the late nineteenth century. Having risen to become the world's second largest economy in the twenty-first century, China nonetheless witnesses growing conservative social and political forces that have importunately attempted to reinstall and consolidate gender and class hierarchies in the context of global capitalism. This chapter examines roughly three cohorts of Chinese feminists as a way to illustrate shifting settings and constant contentions over gender equality: state feminists of the socialist period, post-socialist NGO feminists around the Fourth World Conference on Women (FWCW), and young feminist activists ascending onto the public stage in recent years. Each cohort has adopted distinct strategies for their diverse agendas, conditioned by their particular historical contexts and social and political parameters.

But continuities remain. While the first generation of socialist period feminists has long left the historical stage, some of its legacies have persisted, especially in terms of its institution-building in the form of an official mass organization—the All-China Women's Federation. The relationship between feminism and the state remains central to feminist struggles in China even when state socialism has long evolved into state capitalism, and a rapid privatization of the economy has produced 250 million citizens who do not work in the state sector (Xing 2015). And just as Chinese feminism's inception was inseparable from a global context a century ago, today it is as deeply embedded in processes of globalization as ever. Contemporary China is in a time of "compressed temporalities," in the sense that various contentious discourses over the past century have neither reached closure nor faded out, but rather have often been reenacted and remobilized simultaneously against a drastically changed historical setting. This chapter traces both continuities and changes in Chinese feminist struggles while critically examining constraints and possibilities for further development.

A Brief Overview of Chinese Feminism in the Early Twentieth Century

Feminism was one of the many ideologies that educated Chinese have embraced in their pursuit of modernity and rejection of an ancient dynastic system underpinned by a hierarchical sex-gender system that held chastity as the supreme value of women in the interest of patrilineal kinship. Just as the imagination of a modern China has never been singular, feminism has also been understood in diverse ways that, nevertheless, express a shared concern with gendered social arrangements. At the turn of the twentieth century, anarchist, socialist, liberal, evolutionary, eugenic, and nationalist positions shaped various feminist articulations. In their proposals for changing gender hierarchy, rooted in ancient Chinese philosophy and gender norms based on Confucian ideals of gender differentiation and segregation, feminists expressed different imaginings of a better future: a more humane society that centered on social justice and equality, a modern society that allowed individuals to break away from the constraints of Confucian social norms embedded in kinship relations as well as the control of an imperial polity, and a stronger nation that turned China from being the prey of imperialist powers into a sovereign state. Regardless of their diverse political positions, reformers, revolutionaries, professionals, and educated women and men from elite social backgrounds who embraced various versions of feminism agreed on the necessity of changing gender practices in transforming their ancient civilization, which had fallen into deep crisis in a time of imperialist and colonialist expansion. The confluence of diverse and often contradictory ideas and practices rapidly made a neologism a key phrase in twentieth-century China: "equality between men and women" (*nannü pingdeng*, a Chinese rendition of the English phrase "sexual equality" that had been circulating globally since the late nineteenth century). Signifying a conscious rejection of the foundation of Confucian social order prescribing differentiation between men and women, "equality between men and women" became a badge of modernity that social groups and political parties adopted to assert a progressive identity.

After the collapse of the Qing dynasty in 1911, educated women from elite families who had joined the revolution against the Qing government launched a women's suffrage movement to demand equal political rights in the new Republic polity. Suppressed by a dictatorial president in 1913, the suffragists turned to women's education and careers to lay a social foundation for women's political rights. Radical male intellectuals launched a New Culture movement in 1915 to challenge the dominant Confucianism, which provided renewed critical feminist thrust. Gender hierarchy, gender differentiation, gender segregation, sexual double standards that demanded chastity of women while legitimizing polygamy, and cultural practices ritualized in the service of maintaining a deeply entrenched hierarchical society that was fundamentally based on the dominance of men over women, were highlighted as quintessential symbols of the backwardness of Confucian culture, defined as "feudalist." "Feminism" was enthusiastically embraced as a powerful weapon to combat the "feudalism" that had dominated China for millennia.

The small circle of cultural radicals, which included the future founders of the Chinese Communist Party (CCP), rapidly expanded its social and intellectual influence after May 4th, 1919, when college and secondary school students spearheaded a nationwide patriotic movement. Incensed by the treaty signed by world powers at the Versailles Conference, which transferred all of Germany's rights in Shandong Province to Japan after World War I, the May Fourth Movement, with its vehemently anti-imperialist female and male students as major constituents, became a powerful vehicle that carried the New Culture's advocacy of anti-feudalism, including the promotion of feminism, into mainstream urban society. Equal educational and employment opportunities for women, and their freedom to socialize with men, ending centuries of gender segregation, were seen as the foundation for women's liberation. Pursuing equality in all spheres of life and achieving an independent personhood became the hallmarks of the May Fourth women's feminist subjectivities. Many May Fourth feminists—by definition educated women and men—later played important roles in China's political, social, and cultural transformations (Wang 1999). From two cohorts, older New Culturalists and younger student participants in the May Fourth Movement, emerged a small group of men and women, disillusioned with the Western liberal but imperialist powers, who in 1921 formed the CCP—modeled after the Communist Party of the Soviet Union—and openly endorsed "equality between men and women" in its platform (Gilmartin 1995).

Even though many high-profile May Fourth feminists joined the CCP, the term "feminism" began to lose favor within the party when CCP feminists came into contact with Western socialists and communists and adopted their view that "feminism" was "bourgeois"—a discursive practice that had originated out of the rivalries between radical suffragists and socialist women in the early twentieth century (Boxer 2007). Nonetheless, CCP feminists kept alive the May Fourth feminist agendas of women's liberation, simply replacing the discredited Chinese translation of "feminism" *nüquan* with "women's rights" *funü quanli* and maintaining the pressure on the party to promote those rights. They mobilized women for the revolution with yet another new term: "women-work" (Davin 1976).

Managed by a Women Department or a Women-Work Committee in various periods, women-work was a major platform for CCP feminists engaged in pursuing gendered social justice and equality, especially for lower-class women, as well as an important branch of the CCP specialized in mobilizing women's participation in the Communist Revolution. In urban areas, the underground CCP feminists targeted women factory workers as the major constituents of women-work; in the CCP military bases in rural areas, peasant women were the target for feminist organization and mobilization. Running literacy classes and raising both class and gender consciousness were part of the women-work among factory workers; addressing abuse of women in patriarchal families, opposing arranged marriage, and promoting freedom to divorce were issues adopted by CCP feminists in rural base areas, though the latter item was dropped after the CCP moved to the northern base areas in late 1930s. The CCP could not afford to antagonize male peasants, who were their major recruitment targets in a time of war. So the focus of women-work shifted to enhancing women's economic status in rural families by encouraging them to participate in gainful, productive work.

The inner logic of the two-pronged agenda of women-work was that in order for the CCP to succeed in attracting women to the Communist Revolution, which promised women's thorough emancipation down the road, the party had to address women's particular and immediate needs and interests. In practice, the two dimensions of women-work presented an inherent source of tension that required tremendous wisdom for the CCP feminists to juggle skillfully, as male leaders at all levels tended to treat institutionalized women-work as an auxiliary instrument to fulfill various tasks of the party. After all, the wars against Japanese invaders and the Nationalist Party provided them with an excuse not to prioritize women's gender-specific interests, but instead to demand women's contribution to the Revolution.

Socialist State Feminist Transformative Practices

China in 1949 was an agrarian society with about 90 percent of its total population of 540 million residing in rural areas, 90 percent of women illiterate (*Zhongguo renquan nianjian* 2007:580), and an economy devastated by decades of war. Economic recovery with women's participation and increasing women's literacy were high on the CCP's agenda for a socialist modernity. The victory of the CCP in 1949 enabled feminists in the party to wield socialist state power to materialize their feminist dreams. Only 530,000 of the CCP's 1949 membership of 4.49 million were women, but many of these CCP women rose to official positions in administrations ranging from the central government to urban street offices and rural townships, depending on their party seniority and level of education. Although we do not claim that each CCP woman was a conscious feminist, the numbers and power of Chinese socialist state feminists in the early People's Republic of China were arguably unprecedented in feminist histories of the world. This was a consequence of a feminist-informed Communist Revolution in the world's most populous nation that attracted female constituents with equality between men and women as an integral goal of the revolution. Upon the founding of the PRC, many CCP feminists in their official capacities vigorously initiated and promoted transformative programs to cash the party's promissory note of women's thorough liberation in a socialist country. This belies the general assumption in much of the scholarship in English that these women were passive followers of a male-dominated party.

The first National Women's Congress, organized by senior CCP feminists Deng Yingchao and Cai Chang in March 1949,[1] resolved to set up a national women's organization, All-China Democratic Women's Federation (ACDWF was changed to All-China Women's Federation in 1957, hence ACWF), an umbrella organization that horizontally united all pro-CCP women's organizations, and an official institution that vertically reached down to the rural villages and urban neighborhoods nationwide. This vast organizational reach enabled socialist state feminists to effectively carry out many transformative actions nationwide. The very first law adopted by the socialist state, the 1950 Marriage Law, drafted by a feminist committee led by Deng Yingchao, was a centerpiece in the socialist feminist mission of transforming Chinese "feudalist" culture. The law enforced dismantling of traditional marriage practices such as arranged marriage and underage marriage, and granted women freedom to divorce and to remarry, establishing new gender norms of equality between men and women with state power. Women's literacy, equal employment and equal pay, political participation, reproductive health, and new public facilities to reduce working women's burden of childcare and housework were also areas of remarkable feminist achievement in the early PRC. Their efforts to involve and engage rural and urban lower-class women, particularly in all the transformative programs aiming to eliminate class and gender hierarchies, expanded urban elite-based concepts and practices of "women's rights" from the first half of the twentieth century. That said, the socialist state paradoxically widened the gap between the rural and urban by setting up a two-tier household registration system that offered urban residents more privileges and material goods in order to speed up industrialization.

Socialist feminists' comprehensive vision of Chinese women's liberation crucially hinged on transformation of subjectivities. Senior feminists were acutely aware that without undoing the patriarchal culture that saturated the psyche of the people and the CCP members, efforts to achieve women's equality in all spheres of life would encounter severe obstacles and resistance. Cultural production was thus also an important realm in socialist feminist transformation, a heritage from the May Fourth New Culture Movement when progressive intellectuals (a cohort that included many men) produced a massive amount of literature and drama to condemn a "feudalist" patriarchal tradition embodied in Confucianism. The Chinese term "feudalism" in socialist film (a state-owned industry led by female and male feminist leaders), novels, and operas decidedly represented the "Other" of socialist new China. It actually became a gender-inflected key word encompassing everything we today call sexism, masculinism, patriarchy, male chauvinism, and/or misogyny. Even illiterate women in rural areas could deploy the term effortlessly to accuse men of chauvinism (Hinton 1984). "Equality between men and women" and "women's liberation," popularized via state-owned media, especially the ACWF's magazine *Women of China* and socialist films accessible even to rural communities, became household slogans intimately connecting gender equality with the authority of the new socialist state. A socialist feminist gender discourse rapidly rose to the mainstream discourse in the early PRC.

Chinese socialist state feminists in the early PRC were an integral part of the international women's movement of the socialist camp that was represented by the Women's International Democratic Federation (WIDF). On December 10, 1949, only two months after the founding of the PRC, the All-Asian Women's Congress, attended by 197 representatives from 23 countries, was organized by the ACDWF in its new role as a member of the WIDF (Haan 2010). Hosting an international conference on women when only about 10 socialist countries had established diplomatic relationships with the PRC indicated the CCP leadership's full support for this initiative, as well as the state feminists' high capacity for global networking. The event certainly expressed state feminists' conscious efforts to merge the women's movement in the PRC with socialist women's movements globally. With the Chair of the ACDWF, Cai Chang, serving as the Deputy Chair of the WIDF, Chinese socialist state feminists also played a leading role in the international women's movement until the 1960s, when the CCP split with the Communist Party of the Soviet Union.

The CCP feminists' firm identification with the party both empowered and constrained them because of the contradictory political environment. Ideologically, the party's platform endorsed a feminist pursuit of "equality between men and women" that was written into the Constitution of the People's Republic of China. Institutionally, however, male Communists assumed leading administrative positions. Many male officials did not eschew male chauvinism during the Communist Revolution even though they vowed to strive for an egalitarian society.

Women of China in the early 1950s exposed many sexist behaviors of male officials, including blocking women from entering gainful employment (Wang 2016:Chapter 3). Feminists in the Women's Federation system found their proposals for women's benefits often pushed aside by male officials. Even the institutionalization of a women's mass organization did not resolve the problem of gender hierarchy in the party. The ACWF[2], after all, was organized as a party-led mass organization that was responsible for advocacy rather than as an executive branch of the government, although everyone in the WF system was also on the government payroll.

As each level of the Women's Federation subordinates to the party committee of the same administrative level, WF women officials often encountered party officials who showed little interest in equality between men and women or women-work. Party Chairman Mao Zedong was apparently well aware of this situation. On November 12, 1952, in a meeting the ACWF leaders had requested, he instructed them on dealing with different levels of party committees with these colorful words: *yi song* (first, submit proposals to the party committee); *er cui* (second, push the party committee to respond); *san maniang* (if the first two methods did not work, third, just curse and swear) (Luo and Duan 2000: 126).[3] Apparently, though never an intentional policy, neglecting women's interests was a common practice within the party that continued into the socialist period; and significantly, the chairman's support stopped at the level of advice without offering any structural rearrangement of power relations. Actually, quite a few WF officials who followed Mao's advice were labeled as "rightists" for their candid criticism of their party leaders in the Anti-Rightist Campaign in 1957. The subordination of the gender-based mass organization to the male-dominated party led to subsequent institutional marginalization of WF in the state structure of the PRC, which in turn conditioned the routine experiences of feminists in the CCP that women-work was of lesser value, except for those moments when some item on the party's central agenda required that women be mobilized.

Historically, some CCP male leaders used the label of "narrow bourgeois feminism" as a political stick to beat down those outspoken feminists who insisted on the priority of women's interests or raised a critical voice against male chauvinism in the CCP. In this historical context, state feminists in the WF system routinely operated in a *politics of concealment* in their endeavors to promote feminist agendas. Since singularly and openly raising a demand on behalf of women would have a slim chance of eliciting the support of male authorities, WF officials learned to insert feminist items into the party's agenda in order to gain legitimacy and resources for actions with a clear gender dimension. One example was when the Shanghai Women's Federation organized a large-scale women's rally against American imperialism in 1951 at the request of the municipal party committee. Utilizing the support from the municipal and district governments on this legitimate party "central task," WF officials swiftly expanded the WF's institutional development in Shanghai neighborhoods by setting up grassroots women's organizations (Wang 2016:Chapter 1). Articulating their strong support of the party's central tasks, state feminists often embedded a "hidden transcript" that intended to advance women's diverse interests. In other words, camouflaging a feminist agenda with dominant party language was a major principle in the politics of concealment. The concealing and self-effacing maneuver appealed to the authority of the party and glossed over their own struggles behind the scenes.

Receding into the shadows, socialist state feminists were unknown to either the public in China or scholars outside China. Women's dramatic advancements in education, employment, and political participation in the socialist period were noticed by many observers outside China, but without any knowledge of state feminists' endeavors these observers generally attributed all the accomplishments to a patriarchal party-state that supposedly showed sporadic benevolence to women. A dominant conceptualization of a monolithic socialist state in the field of China studies has disabled scholarly imaginations of possible feminist visions and contentions inside the socialist state.

Socialist state feminists' efforts to eliminate both gender and class hierarchies and transform a patriarchal culture were halted in 1964, when a Maoist class struggle against revisionism and capitalism rapidly ascended to become a dominant agenda of the CCP. The ACWF stopped functioning in the heat of the Cultural Revolution, when all government branches were paralyzed. While the effects of state feminists' social and cultural transformations in the first fifteen years of the PRC persisted, and institutional mechanisms they developed for gender equality in education and employment continued, their feminist agenda of further transforming gender relations was suppressed by a Maoist class struggle beginning in 1964. While working-class young women had more opportunities to be promoted to leadership positions

in the Cultural Revolution because of Mao's wife Jiang Qing's prominent position in the power center, a New Culture agenda highlighting
anti-patriarchy in cultural production was condemned by Jiang Qing
and other radicals as an expression of revisionism. Suppressing a conscious agenda of feminist cultural transformation by state feminists in
and outside the ACWF, Maoist radicals did serious harm to the feminist revolutionary cause. When the ACWF revived its function in 1978,
the political landscape had already changed so drastically that the sur-
viving first cohort of state feminists found their previous accomplishments for gender equality under severe attack.

A major erasure of socialist state feminists arose in the production
of historical knowledge of socialism since the late 1970s, when the CCP
began to depart from the socialist course after Mao's death in 1976. In
Chinese intellectuals' concerted critique of the CCP's crimes under
Mao Zedong's dictatorship, descriptions of the socialist period were
mainly limited to condemnations of its ills, and Mao became synony-
mous with socialism. The antisocialist discourse was both grossly reduc-
tive and openly masculinist. In post-socialist intellectuals' efforts to
dismantle both the CCP's authoritarian rule and socialist egalitarian
values and practices, socialist state feminist gender ideology and practices that promoted equality between men and women were characterized as the Maoist state's imposition of gender sameness, a crime of the
CCP that distorted women's natural femininity and masculinized them.

In an article published in the prestigious Chinese academic journal
Sociological Studies, Zheng Yefu argued that contemporary China was
falling far behind developed countries in terms of the level of a knowledge economy, as well as the levels of social and material wealth. At the
same time, he pointed out Chinese women's liberation surpassed all
countries in the world in terms of women's equal employment and
equal pay. Deploring what he viewed as a cause-and-effect situation,
Zheng offered a critique that condensed key elements in the backlash
against socialist women's liberation:

> The immediate consequence of a government enforced women's
> liberation "outpacing" socio-economic development is dysfunc-
> tional family relations . . . We have failed to explore a new gender
> division of labor in family life **because, through supporting the
> weak and suppressing the strong, a strong administrative
> power has interfered and destroyed the normal division of**

labor between the strong and the weak in family. It has even made the weak mistakenly think they are not weak, and made the strong lose confidence in themselves. **Ultimately, it has deprived Chinese society of "real men." . . . A women's liberation promoted by politics has also made China lose its women.** (Zheng Yefu 1994:110; bold in the original)

Restoring gender differentiation was promoted by the urban elite's conflicting proposals: embracing a Western capitalist modernity symbolized by sexualized and commodified women in advertisements, or reviving a Confucian tradition by retrieving so-called "Oriental female traditional virtues," which women could express by being self-sacrificing, virtuous mothers and good wives. Rearranging gender practices by promoting a discourse of femininity has become a prominent theme in elite proposals to undo socialist modernity since the early 1980s. The preferred Chinese rendition of "feminism" as *nüxing zhuyi* (feminine-ism) since the early 1990s partly reflects the hegemonic power of this discourse of femininity.

The CCP's turn to privatization and marketization was accompanied by a dismantling of socialist institutional mechanisms that safeguarded gender and class equalities for those working in the public sector, such as equal education, equal employment, equal pay, and state-funded health care and childcare; the state's departure from a socialist egalitarian distribution system was also crucially legitimized by propagating a neo-liberalist ideology that harped on social Darwinism, a discursive maneuver that many male intellectuals eagerly adopted. The slogan "Getting rich is glorious" was promoted by the party's media, and the poor were blamed for being incapable. The much-abused concept of a Maoist "class" became a convenient excuse for the CCP to abandon class as an analytical category in its embrace of global capitalism.

The profound social, economic, and ideological ruptures that were concealed by one major continuity—that is, the continuous authoritarian political system that sustained the CCP's rule—coincided with the retirement of the first generation of state feminists. Having barely returned to their posts after the ACWF's ten-year hiatus during the Cultural Revolution, the top feminist leaders used the limited time before their retirement to promote compilations of source materials and histories of the Chinese women's movement in diverse locations nationwide, manifesting their will to pass down the heritage of a socialist feminist history. They also started to organize national conferences on research on women, in an attempt to address the myriad problems women confronted in the era of marketization by insisting on a "Marxist theory of women's liberation." This theory's fundamental thesis is that women's liberation is based on their participation in social production. Propagating this Marxist theory of women's liberation was the WF feminists' important discursive struggle to resist tremendous masculinist pressures in and outside the government to push women back to the kitchen as a solution to the increasing unemployment in marketization. These initiatives recruited and relied on scholars who were showing interest in women's issues, and quickly stimulated a high tide of research on women nationwide beginning in the early 1980s. Discrimination in women's employment and education in a market economy and protection of women's legal rights in marriage and at work were among the hot topics for scholars who aimed to affect public policies with their research. In this period, Chinese scholars heavily relied on the WF's funding and organizational network as well as institutional legitimacy to get involved in research on women; however, feminist scholars from the West tend to ignore the crucial role state feminists played in this research boom, instead focusing on leading women scholars' activities in their effort to identify an "autonomous" feminist movement *vis-à-vis* the supposedly party-controlled women's movement. Literary scholar Li Xiaojiang has been credited as a pioneer of research on women in the 1980s, while much of the work state feminists in the ACWF have done since the late 1970s to initiate and support research on women has gone unnoticed.

In their old age and declining health, many members of the first generation of state feminists vigorously engaged in writing and publishing memoirs and autobiographies. These moves expressed their conscious resistance to the discursive erasure of Chinese socialist feminist struggles. However, when the CCP led by Deng Xiaoping had already made decisive moves to merge with global capitalism, which was characterized in the media as a new vision of Chinese modernity, socialist state feminists' claims of their accomplishments in socialist revolution could have little purchase, sounding outdated. Few cared about what these feminists remembered of a time that was condemned as a dark age dominated by Mao's dictatorship in the rising hegemonic discourse of anti-socialism. Thus, this cohort of socialist state feminists as well as their endeavors failed to enter the constructed public memory, or historical knowledge, of a socialist past in the age of capitalist globalization.

The Fourth World Conference on Women and Feminist NGOs

The state accelerated privatization and marketization in the 1980s while opening China to transnational corporations. Urban women workers bore the brunt of this "economic reform," as they became the first to be fired and last to be hired. The labor laws of the socialist period still existed, which required enterprises to pay for reproductive costs including paid maternity leave and daycare. Seeking to maximize profits in a changed economic system, even state-owned sectors began to lay off women disproportionately as well as close down publicly funded daycares and canteens in the name of "optimizing" management and improving "efficiency." The one-child policy initiated in 1979 placed rural women in a deep predicament, as the simultaneous de-collectivization in rural areas installed a household responsibility system, which increased patrilineal peasant families' demands for male labor and male heirs. Female infanticide and forced abortion increased rapidly, resulting in a seriously skewed sex ratio at birth: 117.8 boys born for every 100 girls in 2011.

In the context of a severe backlash against socialist women's liberation in male-dominated public discourse and the state's dismantling of socialist egalitarian institutional mechanisms in a state-controlled market economy, the beneficiaries of socialist gender equality policies rose to form a significant feminist force. A cohort of urban, educated women who were positioned in academic institutions in the 1980s began to participate in research on women in collaboration with the same cohort in the Women's Federations in large cities with the intention to influence public policies. When the Chinese government decided to host the Fourth World Conference on Women (FWCW) in the aftermath of the state suppression of the 1989 Tiananmen Square demonstrations, this cohort of feminists swiftly seized the opportunity to push the political boundaries that curtailed spontaneously organized activities after 1989. Many of these women founded feminist NGOs with resources from international donors as well as legitimacy granted by the NGO Forum that was held in tandem with the FWCW and attended by about forty thousand feminists from all over the world. The ACWF's presence in NGO activities preparing for the FWCW was challenged by global feminist communities due to its ambiguous status as a mass organization on the government's payroll, subordinate to the CCP. A new term, "GONGO"—government organized non-governmental organization— legitimized its participation in the NGO Forum, an ironic moment that made NGO a desirable status even in the eyes of a worried Chinese government. In any case, the monopoly of the ACWF in leading a Chinese women's liberation movement was deconstructed by the rise of feminist NGOs, though the two kinds of organizations worked more in collaboration than in competition in the decade following the FWCW. Two articles published in 2010 presented detailed examinations of the rise of Chinese feminist NGOs in the context of China's hosting of the FWCW (Zhang and Hsiung 2010; Wang and Zhang 2010). This section will highlight a few key features in this cohort of feminist activism from the hindsight of a changed political milieu in 2015.

First, the introduction of a key feminist concept, gender, proved to be enabling and empowering. Gender as a feminist concept was introduced to China by Chinese feminists in diaspora in the process of preparing the FWCW to critically engage with both post-socialist discourse of femininity naturalizing gender hierarchy and a limited Marxist theory of women's liberation unable to explain gendered power relations in all modes of productivity. For this cohort of feminists, who were deeply shaped by the socialist gender discourse of "equality between men and women," feminist gender theory provided a powerful critical lens through which to see weaknesses in a state-endorsed and instrumental gender discourse. Li Huiying, a leading feminist scholar/activist of the Central Party School, articulated the significance of feminist gender theory for her in these words:

> I think it was a very sad situation in women's pursuit of rights since China's liberation, because women's pursuit of rights has been turned into a means to the end. But now in the concept of gender, the highlighted "rights" is about human autonomy and agency. People should know what rights they have and then should struggle for those rights (UM Global Feminisms Project: Interview of Li 2004).[4]

The attraction of "gender," rendered in Chinese as *shehui xingbie* (social sex), in Li's emphasis, lies in an empowering notion that women should and can control their own destiny without subjecting themselves to the demands of a patriarchal state. The concept of "rights" here is deployed to demand citizens' rights against an authoritarian state. For this cohort of urban-educated women, "liberation" had been defined for them by the socialist state. In the 1990s, gender theory that emphasized women's agency and explicated gendered power relations and structures illuminated the limitations and constraints of that liberation. It brought about a sort of consciousness-raising for these urban feminists who began to see the potential of exercising citizen's rights to demand gender equality beyond statist definitions. The expression of citizen's agency, which had been amply demonstrated since the 1980s and brutally suppressed in 1989, now found a vehicle in a timely and legitimate notion of NGOs backed by the FWCW.

Second, the decade after the FWCW witnessed Chinese feminists' innovations in widely circulating the Platform for Action, the Beijing Declaration, and the Convention on the Elimination of All Forms of Discrimination against Women (which the Chinese government signed in 1980) to hold the government accountable, and translating global feminist concepts to local practices. They initiated programs to address a wide range of issues, such as domestic violence, gender and development, feminist curricular transformation in higher education, legal aid for women, rural women's political participation, sex-ratio imbalances, vocational training for rural women and unemployed urban women, and cultural productions that challenged sexist sexual norms, such as staging a Chinese version of *The Vagina Monologues*. Among all kinds of feminist activities, a creative form of gender training was widely adopted. Utilizing the UN agenda of mainstreaming gender as the basis for legitimate feminist actions, Chinese feminists promoted gender training as an important mechanism of social and cultural transformation. Various feminist NGOs conducted gender-training workshops as an integral part of their feminist projects, on themes such as anti-domestic violence, gender and development, and women's psychological counseling hotlines, to enhance all the participants' gender sensitivity. The workshops were also offered to various levels of government officials whose responsibilities related to women's interests. In the context of a rising neo-liberalist discourse in China since the 1980s, and when the state had collaborated with the intellectual elite to make a Marxist concept of class a taboo subject in the process of China's turning into a global sweatshop, promulgating the concept of gender equality as a mandate from the UN was also a feminist strategy to uphold social justice as a legitimate goal to pursue, and to hold the state accountable for its verbal commitment to equality between men and women.

The third feature most saliently demonstrates the specificity of Chinese feminism: the collaborative relationship between the Women's Federations at different levels and feminist NGOs in diverse locations. Instead of drawing a distinct divide between the two kinds of organizations, feminists from both WF and NGOs often participated in the same projects initiated by NGOs. And in some cases, feminists in the WF even organized NGOs when they felt constrained and limited by the official women's organization (UM Global Feminisms Project: Interviews of Wang 2003 and Gao 2005). Feminist NGO organizers and feminists in the WF were mostly in the same cohort, shaped by the same socialist ideology and practices of women's liberation. Moreover, feminists who organized NGOs in most cases were respectable academics in universities and academies of social sciences, all run by the government. The two groups thus were not only from the same cohort but also the same urban elite class who enjoyed social prestige and resources due to their positions in the state system. Fundamentally, the collaborative relationship was conditioned on the ACWF's switch from their target constituency, women of lower classes—the masses—in the socialist period to an orientation toward urban professionals in the context of class-realignment and social reconfiguration mandated by the state as it merged with global capitalism. Urban professionals' expertise was eagerly sought after in the rising discourse of a scientific modernity in post-socialist China. NGO feminists' scholarly titles allowed them to present themselves as experts to state officials, including the WF system. NGO feminist organizers who were consciously maintaining an independent position in terms of initiating and managing feminist projects nevertheless needed the vast institutional reach of the Women's Federations at six administrative levels as well as the official status WF offered to effectively promote feminist issues and influence policy making.

The unique collaboration allowed effective feminist intervention in state processes, or to use a less sensitive term, "implementation of gender mainstreaming," in the context of increasing state monitoring of NGO activism. Many issues identified and advocated by feminist NGOs have been incorporated by different levels and regions of the government, and have even entered legislation. Chinese feminists had no leverage to stem the state's merge with global capitalism, which has resulted in officials' massive profiteering from their power to dispose public assets and regulate the labor of the lower classes, and thus has increased gender gaps as well as class polarization. However, feminists have forged ahead with diverse programs ranging from legislating domestic violence and promoting rural women's participation in village management, to transformation of patrilocal marriage systems and land distribution policies to raise rural women's status in villages and change patriarchal cultural norms of son preference. The ACWF also promoted the Reproductive Security Fund at the municipal government level to mitigate the severe impacts on urban women workers of eliminating socialist benefits for women's reproductive work that had previously been guaranteed by state-owned enterprises. The momentous success of this collaboration between feminists in and outside the official system is China's first anti-domestic violence law, passed on December 27, 2015, after two decades of persistent feminist struggles following the FWCW.

Feminist actions and accomplishments have been quite impressive, but they were mostly known only within Chinese feminist circles. The goal of affecting policy-making and intervening in government agenda-setting in the context of the Chinese political system requires the strategy that socialist state feminists had long adopted: maneuvers behind the scenes, utilizing personal networks and institutional resources. Friends, colleagues, relatives, and classmates positioned in powerful posts can all be accessed for a particular project in a society whose operation heavily relies on the lubricant of personal ties. This cohort of feminist leaders of either NGOs or WFs, in this sense, also has acted as lobbyists who absolutely have no intention to publicize their crucial maneuvers. Keeping a low profile is in the best interest of the cause they fight for.

The legitimate concern about the effectiveness of their operations via the state power, however, could also become a source of self-censorship. This cohort's conscious subversive feminist actions have made them very sensitive to the political parameters set by the state, which paradoxically place them under the influence of a state constantly monitoring NGOs. The state's punishment of the very few feminists who dared to openly raise a dissenting voice and work on taboo issues forcefully demarcated a forbidden zone: issues related to so-called "national security," such as labor organizing, ethnic conflicts, and violation of citizens' rights in any form by any government branch. One prominent case is that of feminist literary scholar Ai Xiaoming of Zhongshan University,

who bravely made documentary films recording struggles of village
women and men against corrupt officials, rural victims of HIV-contami-
nated blood in the so-called "plasma economy" promoted by provincial
governments, the injustice of a court ruling in a date rape case, and so
on (UM Global Feminisms Project: Interveiw of Ai 2005).[5] Her actions,
which crossed the line of an exclusive focus on less risky "women's issues," resulted in the discipline of the state in the form of her forced
early retirement and non-renewal of her passport. The personal price is
high if one dares to defy the authoritarian state, which has been increasingly corrupt and coercive in the two decades following the FWCW.

The political context, thus, has served as a critical factor in feminists' choices of what actions to take and what strategies to adopt, and
limits what may be accomplished. The constraints of the context also
largely explain this cohort's preoccupation with the feminist concept of
gender. Legitimized by the UN mandate, gender has been carved out
as a relatively safe zone for feminists to pursue social justice and equality without an open challenge against multiple systems of oppression in
the process of a repressive state capitalism. "Gender mainstreaming" is
a circumscribed feminist agenda in comparison to the vision of this cohort's revolutionary foremothers, who pursued women's thorough liberation via political, economic, cultural, and social structural changes. It
nevertheless has quietly created new areas of feminist intervention that
their foremothers did not envision or where they were unable to intervene. Last but not least, this cohort's tremendous efforts in gender
training, especially their efforts to develop women's and gender studies
curricula in higher education and to promote feminist knowledge production, have inserted a critical feminist discourse in contemporary
China's media and knowledge production, otherwise dominated by blatant sexism and neo-liberalism. Such discursive endeavors have paved
the way for the rise of a younger generation of daring feminists who
reject the ambiguous term *nüxingzhuyi* (feminine-ism) and openly embrace *nüquanzhuyi* (women's right/power-ism), a Chinese rendition of
feminism shunned by the mainstream society for its emphasis on wom-
en's demand of both rights and power.

New Style of Feminist Actions of Young Feminists

In the second decade following the FWCW, the dynamics in the field
of Chinese feminist struggles changed again due to drastic shifts in

China's social and economic transformations as well as its political environment. The feminist pioneers who formed NGOs with the opportunity of the FWCW inspired other groups to follow suit in establishing issue-oriented NGOs nationwide. The rapid growth of various NGOs with massive financial support from diverse international donors alarmed the CCP, which was insecure about its rule and was confronting increasing class and ethnic conflicts domestically and the impact of "color revolution" globally. A decade after the NGO Forums hosted in China, the CCP started to tighten up its monitoring and regulation of Chinese NGOs and to restrict their international funding sources as well as to subvert and co-opt Chinese NGOs.

At the same time, a younger generation of feminists emerged on the stage of social activism, disregarding the tightening political control. Many of the students of the first cohort of feminist NGO leaders, now situated in various urban professions including universities, the media, and WF, carry on feminist struggles in new forms and styles. This cohort of feminists in their late thirties to early forties is joined by an even younger group of feminists who are recent college graduates in their twenties. One commonality across the age groups is that they have grown up in post-socialist China, when socialist institutional mechanisms such as equal employment and equal pay guaranteed along with a position in public enterprises had been largely dismantled in the process of privatization and marketization. In tandem with institutional changes, the socialist gender discourse of equality between men and women by the 1990s was already overshadowed by a discourse of gender differentiation that celebrated a "natural femininity" attained by "modern" consumption of feminine products and by resuming the traditional role of a virtuous mother and good wife, and a hegemonic masculinity embodied in the "successful" men who possess power, wealth, and women. The strong attraction of these young, educated women to feminism is not accidental in a particularly limiting and blatantly sexist political culture.

A demographic factor in combination with China's drastic economic development has prepared the rise of these young feminists. The one-child policy since 1979 has resulted in an unprecedented number of single daughters (the lucky ones who were not aborted) who enjoyed all the resources their families from both parents' sides could afford for their education and personal development. The coming of age of these "little princesses" coincided with China's huge expansion of college education, which tapped the educational market based on an expanding middle class. The college enrollment in China jumped from 2.28 million in 1978 to 29.07 million in 2008 (*Xin Zhongguo liushinian jiaoyu chengjiu zhan* 2009). As a result, the number of female college students rapidly rose from about 37 percent before 1999 to 51.03 percent in 2012, and female Master's degree holders also rose to 51.46 percent in 2012 (Zhang and Cai 2012). This college sex ratio, which indicates an opposite trend to the skewed sex ratio in the population, demonstrates female students' superb academic performance, since each applicant has to pass national college entrance examinations to be accepted by various universities according to their test scores. The gender of applicants whose test scores rank among the top regardless of disciplines and locations has also shown a continuous change, with the male top testers declining from 66.2 percent in 1999 to 39.7 percent in 2008 (Zhang and Cai 2012). The consistent high performance of female students has led to an outcry in male-dominated media about *yingsheng yangshuai*—a so-called gender imbalance with a flourishing female (*ying*) and declining male (*yang*). Many universities have adopted discriminatory admission policies that set a higher score for female students to be considered, on the grounds that many enterprises would like to accept more male graduates than female graduates. Indeed, blatant gender discrimination in employment has been a well-known reality since the economic reform, and even many government branches have jumped on the bandwagon of posting only male wanted job advertisements.

A large cohort of well-educated young women from diverse social and economic backgrounds with high aspirations for themselves as well as high expectations from their families, contradictorily, has encountered excessive gender discrimination and pervasive masculinist sexual norms that openly treat women as sex objects and secondary citizens. Inspired by feminism, young women nevertheless have few social resources to make their voices heard, let alone to participate in the policy-making process as the feminists of older cohorts have been able to. As a feminist organizer of this young cohort commented on the feminist strategy of the second cohort working quietly with/in the official system to generate policy changes, "Their experience is very difficult to replicate. At the time of the FWCW they usually already had some managerial positions in the official system, and they had a circle of friends who were in the decision-making or advisory positions. These factors have served as the lubricant between their NGO programs and the government" (Li 2015). It is a sober assessment of the relative deprivation of young urban educated women's social, economic, and political power versus that of the cohort growing up in the socialist period.

Where to find new resources for feminist activism? What forms of actions are viable for the young feminists who have hardly any ties with those who have power in the official system? It turns out that social and economic marginality does not necessarily disempower the young educated urban feminists who have been brought up in the age of cyberspace and of new conceptual frameworks circulating globally. The young feminists have quickly identified a powerful medium for feminist engagement: the Internet. And because they are not embedded in the official system and have no circumventing considerations associated with those who have some social status, they are far less restricted in conceptualizing the possibilities of their actions. As a result, we have witnessed many innovative actions initiated by young feminists who have nothing to lose.

Most prominent among those who engage in online feminist organizing are Feminist Voice in Beijing and New Media Women's Network in Guangzhou. Feminist Voice is an offshoot of Women's Media Monitor Network, a feminist NGO in Beijing founded in 1999. Led by a committed feminist, Lü Ping, who quit her job in the ACWF's newspaper to become a freelance writer to enact her vision of autonomous feminism, Feminist Voice has formed a loosely connected feminist network via its website and its electronic journal circulated via email. In particular, it has attracted young feminists who have neither prestigious social status nor available social resources, but who nevertheless possess abundant imagination and creativity. A loose coalition of young feminists all over the country named Young Feminist Activism (YFA), working closely with Feminist Voice, operates vigorously via website, email, *weibo*, and WeChat, with provocative topics and self-initiated actions. Because their intention is to call public attention to violations of women's rights in all aspects of Chinese society as a way to engender feminist social and cultural transformation, they deliberately create shocking images in public spaces and then take photos of their actions to circulate online. Their strategy drastically departs from the older cohort of feminist NGO leaders, who are good at maneuvering behind the scenes and inconspicuously running gender training workshops indoors. Visuality becomes a crucial method for these younger feminists to enable visibility of many unseen and untold violations of women's rights.

YFA members have staged many public performance actions that have successfully attracted public attention. They occupy men's rooms in public to demand change in the design of public bathrooms with gender equity; they shave their heads to protest gender discrimination in college admission; they protest sexual harassment on the subway with signs saying "I can be slutty, yet you can't harass me"; they adorn themselves in "blood"-stained white wedding gowns in public to protest domestic violence and post topless photos online collectively to inscribe anti-domestic violence slogans on their bodies; they launched a feminist cross-country walk to circulate feminist messages; and they engage in many more such innovative actions. As the Introduction to the YFA photo exhibition in New York City in the fall of 2015 states, "These young people are full of inspiration, talent and bravery at the intersectional space of art, body politics and social movement. Feminism has no doubt become the fountain of their wisdom" (YFA Photo Exhibition 2015. [6]

The YFA's most influential performance action took place on March 7, 2015, with the "assistance" of the police who detained five young activists preparing to post anti-sexual harassment stickers on public transportation as part of their activities to commemorate International Women's Day. The detention of the Chinese Feminist Five at the moment when global feminists launched Beijing + 20 to evaluate feminist progress since 1995 led to a global mobilization. Feminists in many countries staged protests and over 2 million people from all over the world signed the online petitions demanding their release. Chinese feminist activism entered the global spotlight.

Domestically, the detention of the Feminist Five epitomizes the tightening political control of social movements by the state, but nevertheless has galvanized more feminist awareness and support among the young generation. After the release of the Feminist Five, not only have they resumed feminist activities while still on probation, many more young women have joined online discussions of feminist issues to promulgate and expand a feminist discourse via the Internet. The term *nüquan zhuyi* (women's right/power-ism), unambiguously embraced by this cohort of feminists, is gaining increasing purchase among the young generation.

The New Media Women's Network in Guangzhou was initiated and led by journalist Li Sipan, and sustained by a core group of young faculty members in universities in Guangzhou, many of whom had been active participants in feminist programs organized by Prof. Ai Xiaoming before her forced retirement. The location of Guangzhou is congenial to social activism, as it is adjacent to Hong Kong. Ideas and resources for civil society have long flowed from Hong Kong to Guangzhou via various channels. The New Media Women's Network has creatively launched colorful public activities such as public lectures and art exhibitions as well as online feminist activism. One of the most prominent cases initiated by this group is the anti-sexual harassment campaign in higher education in China. The group succeeded in collecting about 260 signatures from Chinese professors and scholars transnationally on two petitions: one to the Ministry of Education demanding the implementation of anti-sexual harassment mechanisms in Chinese universities, and one to the president of Xiamen University demanding due punishment of a professor's systematic sexual harassment of his female graduate students. All the transnational mobilization was accomplished via email and WeChat, with the active participation of the YFA as well as older feminists situated in academic institutions. The widely circulated petitions resulted in the temporary removal of the male professor from his teaching post at Xiamen University (a mild punishment unsatisfactory to feminists and his victimized students), and the Ministry of Education's regulation to forbid sexual harassment at universities (at the moment remaining on paper without enforcement mechanisms).

A recent successful action by the New Media Women's Network was the massive online discussion on the meaning of International Women's Day, launched by Li Sipan as a blog post a few days before International Women's Day in 2016. By March 8, it had received 101 million visits: hundreds and thousands of young people joined a public discussion on how to continue a feminist heritage, join global feminist struggles, and resist capitalist consumerist co-optation of a feminist event as a way to commemorate International Women's Day. Feminism, *nüquanzhuyi*, has never received such massive public attention in China. The Feminist Five and many more YFAs also actively participated in the celebration and debates online and even re-circulated the anti-sexual harassment stickers which had been evidence of their "crimes" a year before. This huge success of cyber action demonstrates the existence of a rapidly expanding social force that is eager to be informed of feminist heritages as well as to get involved in feminist actions.

As the Guangdong area has been a center of manufacture for global markets, concentrating tens of millions of migrant workers, feminists in Guangzhou have developed contacts with women workers' organizations in recent years, turning increasing attention to the intersection of class and gender. The efforts of young, urban, educated feminists to seek coalition with a more marginalized social group, with full knowledge of the politically sensitive nature of their action, indicate their conscious challenge of political boundaries with an expanding feminist vision. In their online communications, these college-educated young feminists, fluent in English, frequently demonstrate their familiarity with current transnational feminist issues as well as feminist critiques of capitalist globalization. The critical concept of class has been consciously deployed by this cohort in their articles circulated via WeChat, analyzing migrant women workers' marginality and their predicament, conditioned by both gender and class power relations in today's China. It was also featured prominently in the online discussion on International Women's Day.

Finally, the most prominent feature distinguishing this young cohort from the previous two cohorts of Chinese feminists examined in this piece is their open defiance of heterosexual normativity. Unlike older feminists, who generally avoid open discussion of sexuality, the young cohort displays their diverse sexuality with ease and analyzes the oppressive nature of compulsory heterosexuality with depth. Some young feminists are also active members of gay and lesbian organizations. The determined break from the grip of dominant heterosexual normativity is often inseparable from the empowerment of these courageous young women and men's exposure to feminism, and embracing a feminist activist identity seems logical to many of them. They are not afraid of being singled out as a minority, sexually or politically, in a largely conformist society. Any individual challenge against homophobia or discrimination based on sexuality receives strong support from this young cohort of feminists.

Feminist Voice and the New Media Women's Network are physically located in two different regions far away from each other. However, both are national or even transnational in the sense that their overlapping members are scattered all over the world (some Chinese students studying abroad are active members), unrestricted by geographic location, as both groups operate mostly via cyberspace. YFA as well as some of the older cohort of feminists can be found in actions initiated by either organization. The confluence of these young feminist's innovative and spontaneous efforts on diverse fronts has formed a viable and dynamic feminist movement in the face of a tightening state control of social movements in China.

Conclusion

In 2013 at a meeting with the ACWF leading body, President Xi Jinping instructed: "Special attention should be paid to women's unique role in propagating Chinese family virtues and setting up a good family tradition. This relates to harmony in the family and in society and to the healthy development of children. Women should consciously shoulder the responsibilities of taking care of the old and young, as well as educating children. . . ." (Xi 2013). Emphasizing traditional familial roles for women articulates both a masculinist imperative to restore China's pre-socialist gender order and an increasing social crisis since the state has shed its responsibilities for the care of children, the old, and the sick. The privatization of reproductive labor and the recent population policy that switches from one child to two children added new fuel to the fundamentalist neo-Confucian agitation for reviving patriarchal order, making gender contentions ever more ferocious.

Chinese feminist activists are confronting grave challenges, as the male-dominated authoritarian state is turning openly conservative in its gender policy and further tightening its political control. How to deal with the state power with dwindling numbers of feminist agitators inside the official system (the first cohort has passed away, and the second cohort is mostly retired)? And as the state expands its restrictions on international donors' support of the Chinese NGOs, how are the resource-poor young feminists going to obtain necessary material support to continue their activism? Most seriously, the Chinese authority has also accelerated its control of cyberspace. State censorship is a daily experience for Chinese netizens, when the cyber police constantly delete texts circulating online or via WeChat, or shut down websites. The very space and means of young feminist activism is under the direct surveillance of the police.

Paradoxically, Xi Jinping gave a speech at the Global Women's Summit jointly hosted by the UN and the Chinese government in

September 2015, reiterating the Chinese state's commitment to gender equality. Certainly a stunt by state feminists operating behind the scenes to make the event possible, the verbal commitment by the top authority maintains the discourse of gender equality as an official one, providing legitimacy for feminist activism in China. In this sense, the politics of concealment of the first cohort of socialist state feminists has continuously been visible in the maneuvers of the second cohort, though the anti-feudalism of the first cohort has been replaced by gender-mainstreaming as a legitimate feminist agenda with the backing of the UN. Such an official feminist agenda can certainly provide some space for the third cohort to maneuver as well. However, the goal of the young feminists is beyond the boundaries of officially legitimate zones. Rather, young feminists have functioned as a conscious monitoring group constantly holding the state accountable to its verbal commitment to gender equality by initiating feminist projects beyond the scope of state feminists. This function of exerting public pressure from outside the official system is extremely important in a context where the ACWF has long lost its first cohort of revolutionary feminist leaders; the second cohort of feminist officials fostered in the socialist period with a commitment to women's liberation is mostly retired; and the organization has become part of the state bureaucracy with officials who have less commitment to gender equality than interest in career advancement. While conscious feminists still operate in the official system here and there, institutional constraints often seriously limit their capacity for feminist initiatives. With neither state power nor ties to those with official power, the young cohort of feminists nonetheless is producing a loud feminist critical voice in China's extremely contentious discursive arenas. We have confidence that the savvy young feminists who have reached a critical mass will be able to forge ahead with even more innovations and creativity to boldly and cautiously navigate the rough seas of feminist political, social, and cultural interventions, in between the gaps and fissures of multiple conflicting discourses and power structures.

Notes

1. Cai Chang joined the CCP in 1923 and Deng Yingchao joined the CCP in 1925. Their party seniority allowed them to enjoy tremendous respect, especially since they did not pursue high political position with their party seniority. Cai married Li Fuchun in 1923, who became Vice Premier of the PRC, and Deng married Zhou Enlai in 1925,

who became the Premier of the PRC. The informal power Cai and Deng enjoyed in the party was beyond the reach of their successors in the ACWF.

2. The acronym ACWF has two meanings: one, the national women's organization that has six administrative levels paralleling the state administrative structure; two, the national headquarters of the mass organization based in Beijing. In the following, ACWF is used strictly to refer to the national headquarters while WF means the whole system of the national women's organization.

3. Mao's original phrase *san maniang* was changed by women officials into *san piping* (third, criticize) in their public talks, perhaps because of the apparent gender offensiveness of the original and class connotation. Cursing and swearing in profane language were some times adopted by lower class women as a powerful weapon in their resistance, but were forbidden for women of "respectable" families.

4. University of Michigan's Global Feminisms Project can be accessed at http://umich.edu/~glblfem/ch/china.html. The quotation is from the interview of Li Huiying. *Gender and Public Policy* (2002), edited by Li, was the first publication on public policy in China adopting gender as an analytical framework.

5. Of a range of documentaries made by Ai Xiaoming, *Taishi Village, Stories of the Plain*, and *The Heavenly Garden* boldly exposed violation of citizens' rights by corrupted officials in different locations and at various levels.

6. The photo exhibition *Above Ground: Forty Moments of Transformation: a photography exhibition of young feminist activism in China*, was organized by YFA in New York City, in September 2015 to parallel the UN Global Summit on Women.

EUROPE AND THE UNITED STATES

6

Varieties of European
Women's Movements

SILKE ROTH

Introduction and Overview

European women's and feminist movements reflect European (and world) history, along with cultural and political differences.[1] The mobilization of women and feminists in Europe has been shaped by various revolutions, colonialism and post-colonial relations, fascism, two World Wars, the Cold War, and varieties of capitalism as well as varieties of secularism. It has been influenced by the strength of labor movements and the Catholic Church as well as by transnational political opportunity structures[2], in particular the European Union.[3] As of 2016, twenty-eight countries belonged to the European Union (EU). This transnational opportunity structure has been an important resource for the promotion of gender equality in member states and candidate countries since 1957.[4] Each enlargement of the EU—Western in the 1970s, Southern in the 1980s, Northern in the 1990s, and most recently Eastern in the 2000s—has shaped women's movements and feminist mobilization in candidate and member countries.

While there are some commonalities, there are also persistent distinctions between European women's movements. European countries are characterized by a variety of welfare and gender regimes (Walby 2004) that result in different relationships between feminist movements and the state. Furthermore, countries joined the European Union at various times and EU membership had distinct consequences depending on the state of gender equality and gender policies prior to joining the EU. There are also significant diversities within regions, for example, with respect to variations in an authoritarian past, welfare regimes, and the role of the Catholic Church.

In this short chapter, I discuss the diversity of European women's and feminist movements and how they have been shaped by historical, political, and cultural forces. It needs to be kept in mind that the EU is not identical with Europe. For example, Switzerland and Norway do not belong to the EU, and Turkey is a candidate for membership; while at the time of writing, the UK is preparing to leave the EU. The chapter is structured as follows: First, I will present national and regional differences in women's movements. Then I will survey transnational opportunity structures and (virtual) networks. This is followed by a brief discussion of minority women and their organizations. Finally, I will turn to "market feminism" (Kantola and Squires 2012) and women's responses to austerity measures. I argue that contemporary European women's movements can only be understood in the context of European history and the variety of gender and welfare regimes.

Varieties of European Women's Movements

The diversity of European women's movements[5] can only be understood from a historical and comparative perspective. The development of European women's movements has been shaped by the political developments of the past two hundred years or so, beginning with demands for women's right to vote at the time of the French Revolution, when women were excluded from *"liberté, egalité, fraternité"* (freedom, equality, brotherhood) (Sanborn and Timm 2016). There are some common characteristics of the emergence of European women's movements. At the end of the nineteenth century, bourgeois, socialist, and cultural women's movements, often referred to as *first wave feminism*, emerged throughout Europe. While bourgeois women's movements were primarily concerned with women's access to higher education and the right to vote, socialist women's movements were keen to improve the situation of working class women and their families. Cultural women's movements were concerned with "separate spheres" and the re-evaluation of women's values. In the first half of the twentieth century, women won the right to vote and access to education and employment in many countries (Paxton et al.

2006). World War II opened up employment opportunities for women when men joined the armed forces. In the 1970s, women's liberation movements emerged in many European countries: this is usually referred to as *second wave feminism*, followed by a *third wave* in the 1990s and a *fourth wave* at the beginning of the millennium.[6] In this section, I will introduce and compare the women's movements in different European regions and highlight the diversity of European women's movements.

Western European Women's Movements

Germany provides a good starting point to assess "varieties of feminism" (Ferree 2012) and provides us with a useful backdrop to compare and contrast the trajectories of women's movements in different parts of Europe, since German history combines experiences under fascism, during the Cold War, and within the European Union. German women's movements emerged in the 19th century when different branches—socialist, cultural, and bourgeois—represented women's interests, including the right to enter the public sphere (Ferree 2012). The different streams of the women's movement represented working class and middle class women and engaged in conflicts and coalitions around political rights for women, workers' rights, access to education, and family planning. German women's movements took different sides during the Weimar Republic and Third Reich. Pacifist women who participated in the Women's International League for Peace and Freedom (WILPF) sought to prevent the First and Second World Wars (Rupp 1994). Jewish, socialist, and communist women faced prosecution and death, while some bourgeois women's organizations aligned themselves with the Fascist regime.

After World War II, different types of women's organizations emerged in West and East Germany. Some belonged to the socialist party in East Germany, or to political parties and trade unions in West Germany. In the context of the student movement of the 1960s and 1970s in West Germany, an autonomous women's movement emerged which strongly distanced itself from male-dominated structures, including leftist parties. Body politics, violence against women, and reproductive rights played a central role in the second wave of the women's movement. The West German autonomous women's movement distanced itself from women who participated in mixed-sex—and male-dominated—structures who sought to put women's issues on the agendas of trade unions, political parties, and other institutions. With the formation of the Green Party, which included women who had been active in the West German autonomous women's movement, a dialogue between outsider and insider activists became institutionalized (Ferree 2012).

Throughout the 1980s, state feminism—the establishment of women's equality officers and ministries charged with women's affairs—was established at the level of the *Länder* (or states) of the Federal Republic as well as in national government. After unification, such equality officers were also established in the *Neue Bundesländer*— the new states—in the former GDR. At the same time, the NGO-ization of the women's movement was observed in East Germany and other Eastern European countries (Lang 1997). The critical assessment of NGO feminism reveals a complex relationship between NGOs and the state—dependent on state funding, NGOs may co-opt feminist expertise and take on state responsibilities (Guenther 2010). In the late 1990s and 2000s, the women's movement in Germany was characterized by involvement in transnational activism (Ferree 2012), which I will discuss further below.

Like the German women's movements, the women's movements in the United Kingdom first formed in the 19th century when groups such as the Fawcett Society were founded and suffragettes fought for the right to vote. After women gained equal political rights in 1928, a decline of the women's movement could be observed. The "new feminism" of the 1930s focused on health and welfare programs (Pugh 2000). By the 1970s, radical and socialist feminism came to play an important role in the United Kingdom. Whereas the 1970s and 1980s saw prominent examples of feminist protest, in the 1980s feminism started to engage with the state and the number of women in parliaments increased. The Equal Opportunities Commission was established in 1975 to oversee the Sex Discrimination Act, which has been supported by all political parties (Lovenduski 1995). The increasing involvement of women in traditional political institutions and legislation supporting gender equality, such as the Equal Pay Act (1970) and Sex Discrimination Act (1975), resulted in changing feminist repertoires of contention and a women's movement in abeyance (Baggueley 2002) in the 1990s. However, equality legislation did not mean the end of outsider activism. A prominent protest event bridging feminism, anarchism, socialism, pacifism, and queer feminist politics was the Greenham Common Women's Peace Camp (1981–2000) in Berkshire, established to prevent the deployment of cruise missiles (Roseneil 2000). Women participating in this protest came from all parts of the UK and from different social and political backgrounds and age groups.

Women's engagement in a wide variety of governmental and non-governmental organizations is well documented in the UK (Newman 2012), and the country is characterized by a well-established universe of women's organizations (Lovenduski 1995, Knappe and Lang 2014), including black feminist and ethnic minority organizations (Roy 1995; Mirza 1997; Patel 1997).[7] Moreover, although usually associated with the 1970s, at the beginning of the millennium radical feminism focusing on patriarchy and male violence and arguing in favor of women-only spaces has resurfaced, bringing together older and younger generations (Mackay 2015). In the early 21st century, the women's movement in the UK was characterized by a resurgence of offline and online protest and activism (Dean and Aune 2015; Evans 2015). Furthermore, due to frustration about the lack of inclusion of women and women's issues in politics, the Women's Equality Party was founded in 2015, within a year 45,000 members joined and the party participated in the London mayoral elections in 2016 (Evans and Kenny 2016). In 2015, women represented 25 percent of the House of Commons in the UK and 29 percent in the House of Lords (Women in Parliaments 2016) and women's issues had entered institutional politics. After the referendum to leave the European Union in June 2016 and David Cameron's subsequent resignation, Theresa May became prime minister of the conservative government.

In France, women participated in the French Revolution, and in 1791, Olympe de Gouges published the "Declaration of the Rights of Women." However, despite their contributions to overthrowing the *ancien régime*, women were excluded from political rights and the increasingly important public sphere (Timm and Sanborn 2016). During the revolutionary Paris Commune in 1871, women briefly gained political rights, but lost them when the uprising was repressed. French women gained the right to vote only in 1944 after the liberation from German occupation, and thus much later than in other European and non-European countries. When the EEC formed in 1957, however, France was the only country among the founding members that guaranteed equal pay for equal work, a legacy of women's employment during World War II.

The French women's liberation movement of the 1970s was highly diverse and could be roughly divided into two branches: the *materialists* influenced by leftist traditions, in particular Marxism, who concentrated on the gendered division of labor and considered women a class; and the *differentialists*. The latter, also known as French Feminists (Irigaray, Cixous, Kristeva), were influenced by psychoanalytic theory, in particular Derrida and Lacan, and challenged both phallocratic thinking and the feminism of the materialists by emphasizing "the feminine" and "fundamental differences between the sexes." Both of these currents had in common a focus solely on gender, thus ignoring class, sexuality, and other aspects of the heterogeneity of women's identities and interests (Lépinard 2007). While some of the materialist feminists were involved in leftist organizations, including trade unions and leftist parties, radical fringes of the women's liberation movement distanced themselves from traditional political institutions. Men were involved in feminist activism in a number of ways—in mixed-sex groups, as coalition partners, or in men's groups—either as part of their political or personal identities (De Wolf 2015).

In the early 1990s, influenced by international developments including European soft laws[8], French feminists started to discuss increasing women's political participation (Lépinard 2007:387), which resulted in the campaign for parity (1992–2000). In 2000, France introduced a law requiring political parties to have equal numbers of male and female candidates or face penalties (Jenson and Valiente 2003; Lépinard 2007). While this campaign resulted in significant changes in women's political participation and the feminist movement, the diversity of women's experiences and interests has not been addressed, as was the case during the women's liberation movement of the 1970s, thus continuing the marginalization of minority women.

In contrast to other Western European women's movements, the Irish women's movement was shaped to a far greater extent by the strong influence of the Catholic Church on Irish society and politics. Reproductive rights and women's participation in employment and politics were much more restricted in Ireland than in other Western European societies. In the late 1960s, the Irish women's liberation movement emerged, including liberal reformist as well as socialist groups (Mahon 1996). In 1970, the Commission on the Status of Women (CSW; later renamed National Women's Council of Ireland) was formed to coordinate Irish women's organizations and monitor recommendations of the European Commission (Cullen 2008).

Transnational opportunity structures, such as the European Union which Ireland joined in 1973 and the United National International Women's Year in 1975 played a significant role in the Irish women's movement. In 1990, Mary Robinson, a feminist activist, became the first female president of Ireland. At the same time the Irish women's movement became more professionalized and the National Women's Council of Ireland (NWCI) participated in state policy setting (Cullen 2008). Diversity—referring to single parents, disabled women, indigenous ethnic minority or Traveller women, minority ethnic women, asylum seekers, and refugees—has been one of the key goals of the NWCI since the late 1990s (Cullen 2008:90).

Thus while Germany, the United Kingdom, France, and Ireland certainly share some similarities, including EU membership, they also represent four quite different Western European women's movements. In each of these countries, the women's liberation movement included a range of different organizations, including liberal reformist, socialist, radical, and autonomous groups. National gender equality legislation was introduced somewhat earlier in the UK than in Germany, France, and Ireland. France is the only one of the four countries that legally requires quotas for women's political representation, and France's insistence on equal pay legislation in all founding EU member states laid the groundwork for future EU gender equality legislation.

Mediterranean Women's Movements

Women's movements in Southern European countries such as Spain, Portugal, Italy, and Greece have been shaped by three factors: agricultural economies, authoritarian regimes, and the strong influence of the Catholic and Orthodox Churches. These factors hampered democracy and progressive movements in general and women's equality movements in particular. The end of fascism in Spain with the death of Franco in 1975, the Carnation Revolution in Portugal in 1974, and the end of the military junta in Greece in 1975 returned these countries to democracy. This section will focus Spain and Italy to illustrate broader points about the region's movements. Fascism ended earlier in Italy, when the Allies invaded and ousted Mussolini; the Fascist Party was banned in 1943. These changes provided new opportunities for progressive movements, which could build on the foundations laid by socialist and other dissident movements that had been active under authoritarian rule. Italy was one of the founding members of the European Union, but Greece, Portugal, and Spain joined the EU later, after their return to democracy in the 1980s: similarly to Ireland, they strongly benefited from this development.

In Spain, the organization Women's Catholic Action was formed in 1919 to spread Catholicism as a response to industrialization and modernization (Valiente 2015). Primarily involved in religious and charitable activities, the organization supported Franco during the Civil War (1936–1939). In 1960, the Catholic Seminar for the Sociological Study of Women (SESM) was created. These Catholic women's organizations were a site of feminist protest within the Catholic Church during a period when women's equality and status were undermined by the authoritarian Franco regime. Overall, the Catholic Church supported Franco until his death, though a part of the Church did provide shelter to dissident movements (Valiente 2015).

In addition to the Catholic women's organizations, during the Franco era women were organized in homemaker and neighborhood associations permitted by the regime, and—to a much smaller extent— in the left-wing opposition to the undemocratic regime of the late 1960s and early 1970s (Valiente 2015). Feminist groups that emerged in the left-wing opposition were fighting against the dictatorship as well as for women's rights. These groups were related to various leftist groups, parties, and trade unions. Their close relationship with these leftist groups meant that the majority of the women's movement did not develop autonomously. Furthermore, due to differences between the women's groups after the end of the Franco regime no unifying umbrella group formed (Valiente 2003).

In the 1970s and 1980s, due to the regionalization of Spanish politics and Spain's recent EU membership, the movement reoriented itself to the regional and European levels (Valiente 2003). The European Union provided the women's movement in Spain with important resources that allowed Spain to transform from a backward country with respect to gender equality to "the vanguard in European gender equality policies" (Valiente 2008) after the government led by the Spanish Socialist Workers' Party adopted the Act on Gender Violence (2004) and the Gender Equality Act (2007). The latter required firm-level equality plans in companies with over 250 workers, a 40 percent quota for women on all electoral lists, and a longer parental leave for fathers (Valiente 2008:103).

Like Greece, Spain, and Portugal, Italy experienced a period of fascism and authoritarianism; however, this period ended earlier in Italy than in the other three countries due to the defeat of Mussolini in 1943. As in the other Mediterranean countries, as well as Ireland and Poland, women's movements in Italy have also been characterized by opposition to the Catholic Church and affinities to the old and new left. Like other European women's movements, the Italian women's movement of the 1970s was diverse and included an emphasis on equality and difference, and a focus on "cultural transformation rather than institutional reform" (Della Porta 2003:52). Consciousness-raising engaged in alternative politics and addressed reproduction, sexuality, and personal relations. In contrast to the French women's liberation movement, concern with difference was not restricted to male-female differences, but included differences among women (Della Porta 2003). As in France and Spain, women were involved in leftist groups such as parties and trade unions. These organizations simultaneously supported women's equality (to some extent), and also marginalized women—a fact that was criticized by feminists. Based on a study of the women's movement in Florence, Della Porta notes a wide variety of women's organizations in Italy, many of them involved in cultural activities, which are characterized by a "high degree of pragmatism" (2003:55). Over time, these groups increasingly professionalized and formalized and shifted their activities from protest to service provision for associates or clients. In the 1990s, two agencies responsible for fostering gender equality at various government levels were created: the Equal Status and Equal Opportunities Commission and the Equal Status Committee for the Implementation of Equal Treatment and Equal Opportunities for Men and Women (Della Porta 2003:62). At the same time, there was increasing interest in women's inclusion in political institutions, and the Italian women's groups belonging to the European Women's Lobby campaigned for parity in women's political participation (Della Porta 2003:53).

In addition to the strong influence of the Catholic Church and the conflict between leftist and authoritarian political movements, what characterizes Mediterranean countries is that for long periods in the nineteenth and twentieth centuries, they tended to be senders rather than recipients of migrants.[9]

Scandinavian Women's Movements

Whereas EU accession strengthened women's rights and provided opportunities for women's movements in Western and Southern European countries, women in Scandinavian countries were concerned that joining the EU might jeopardize what they had already achieved. With respect to gender equality legislation, the Nordic countries were ahead of the European Union and its member states. While Norwegian women successfully lobbied to prevent accession to the EU, the accession of Sweden and Finland strengthened EU gender equality legislation with the adoption of "gender mainstreaming"[10] in the Maastricht Treaty (1993) and the Treaty of Amsterdam (1995).

The Nordic countries are characterized by social-democratic welfare states which place a high emphasis on equality, including gender equality. This has had a significant impact on the strategies of women's movements. Whereas French, West German, and British autonomous and radical women's movements distanced themselves from the patriarchal state, in Scandinavian countries, women were integrated early on in political institutions, which impeded the development of autonomous movements that address gender inequality (Borchorst 2000).

In Sweden, for example, women represented 44 percent of Members of Parliament (Lower House) in 2015 (Women in Parliaments 2016). The strong representation of women in the public sphere in Sweden ensures that women's interests are articulated in political parties, parliament, and government agencies, and that gender inequalities are articulated in gender-neutral frames—as workers' rights, parents' rights, or citizens' rights (Hobson 2003). At the same time, gender differences are obscured through this emphasis on universalism, solidarity, and equality, which makes it difficult to articulate gender interests and makes gender-specific measures suspect (Elman 1995). Moreover, gender segregation in the labor market persists and mitigation of sexual harassment and violence against women is missing. Furthermore, the official discourse on gender equality makes it difficult to address issues of gendered power relations (Sandberg and Rönnblom 2013). Sweden thus presents a paradox, combining a strong presence of women in the public sphere—the labor market and politics—with a weak autonomous women's movement and less attention to gender-based violence. Elman (2003) describes how the Swedish state in fact marginalized the shelter movement, pursuing its own anti-violence initiatives. However, a discursive shift in the 1990s that moved the Swedish gender politics from equal opportunities to acknowledging gender relations as structural relations of power issues involved framing issues of abortion and prostitution as women's bodily rights (Freidenvall 2015). Moreover, in 2006 the Feminist Initiative, a women's party, was founded in Sweden. It considers itself a social movement and has participated in several Swedish and European elections (2006, 2010, 2014). In 2014, the Feminist initiative won a seat in the European parliament and the Swedish Prime minister "declared the new Swedish government feminist" (Thorin 2015:1).

In Norway, a campaign of the National Council of Women run in 1967 was highly successful in bringing about a higher representation of women in politics. In the 1970s, the socialist and liberal political parties as well as the Norwegian government adopted quotas for women's participation. In the early 1970s, a women's campaign mobilized against membership in the European Union due to the fact that at that time, women's organizations had not yet achieved consultative status and gender equality policies in the EU were still limited (Predelli et al. 2012). Also in the 1970s, Norwegian women successfully mobilized for abortion on demand, which was achieved in 1978, and gender equality legislation was adopted, including the far-reaching Equal Status Act of 1978, which covered not only working conditions, but also the private sphere. The Gender Equality Act of 1981 required a minimum representation of 40 percent of each gender on councils and committees. However, since the 1990s, Norwegian state feminism was transformed and women's movements organizations lost some influence and access to government and public financial support (Predelli et. al. 2012). In the following years, a resurgence of feminist and women's rights activism could be observed in Norway, including the forming of a 'Norwegian Women's Lobby', an umbrella organization of women's organizations (Halsaa 2016).

Thus, the Nordic model of gender equality goes beyond state feminism and includes feminist mobilization from below. Since the 1980s, three *Nordiskt Forums* were organized – 1988 in Oslo, 1994 in Åbo and 2014 in Malmö. All three events obtained public financial support, however, while the first forum in Oslo was initiated by the Nordic Council of Minister's Gender Equality Committee, the Forum in Malmo was a grassroots endeavor and the included the organizing of an alternative Feminist festival (Stoltz and Halsaa 2016).

Central and Eastern European Women's Movements

Women's organizations existed before, during, and after socialism. Poland, Hungary, the Czech Republic, Slovakia, Slovenia, and other CEE
countries had been independent states, including some democracies,
before they became satellites of the Soviet Union after 1945. In several
of these countries, bourgeois and other women's movements had existed as early as the 19th century and the interwar period (1918–1939).

Women's equality was an important aspect of socialism, and communist states believed they had solved the women question. This was
achieved through the inclusion of women in the public sphere, resulting in high employment rates and a high proportion of women among
party members. Furthermore, socialist states provided support for reproductive labor, including public childcare from the earliest years and
access to abortion in most countries (except Romania). Compared to
Western capitalist societies, women's full-time employment was much
higher in these socialist states. However, the high level of inclusion of
women in the public sphere did not result in an equal share of men
doing housework. And even though women entered male-dominated
sectors of the labor market at a higher rate than in Western states, job
segregation still existed and the familiar patterns of gendered organizations—providing men with better access to resources, prestige, and decision-making power—existed under socialism. An exception among
socialist women's organizations, the Committee of the Bulgarian Wom-
en's Movement (CBWM) criticized government policies and acknowledged that socialism had "not yet solved all of women's problems"
(Ghodsee 2012:53).

The end of the Cold War led to exchanges between East and West,
including disappointment and conflict as well as transnational cooperation (Roth 2007). The end of socialism meant high unemployment for
men and women and the dismantling of existing welfare provisions. Initially, women were presented as the "losers" in the transition, and some
suggested that it was more difficult for women to find re-employment
than men. However, the employment and unemployment rates of men
and women varied by country and job sector. For example, in Bulgaria
women dominated in the post-socialist tourism industry (Ghodsee
2005), while men were adversely affected by the declining mining industry (Ghodsee 2010). Furthermore, the involvement of Western
scholars, donors, and activists in the emerging women's movements in
Central and Eastern Europe was criticized for promoting Western

feminism, which did not address the situation and needs of the countries in transition (Kapusta-Pofahl 2002; Ghodsee 2004). The relationship of Central and Eastern European women to feminism is complex—the term "feminism" has been rejected both as a rejection of socialism as well as of Western feminism; at the same time, women in post-socialist societies do mobilize for equal rights and against gender discrimination, as I will discuss below, using the cases of Poland and the Czech Republic as examples.

The origins of the Polish women's movement go back to the 19th century, when the first women's congresses were held and women were involved in the struggle for independence (Fuszara 2005). The Polish Society for Equal Rights for Women was established in 1907, and in 1918 women gained the same political rights as men. In the period between the First and Second World Wars, over 80 different women's organizations were established. The transition to socialism after the end of World War II brought an end to independent civil society organizations. Grassroots women's organizations were replaced by the Women's League, which was created in 1945 to "promote women's professional work, to organize assistance in everyday life, and educational activities" (Fuszara 2005:1063). The first women's grassroots organizations emerged in socialist Poland in the context of democratization processes and the founding of Solidarity in 1980 (Fuszara 2005:1064).

Like other post-socialist societies, Poland after 1989 was characterized by retraditionalization, and given the central role of the Catholic Church, attacks on abortion rights. Even though some observers declared an absence of feminism or a women's movement in Poland (Tatur 1992; Graff 2003), in fact a wide variety of women's organizations emerged after 1990 (Fuszara 2005), including informal anarchist as well as Catholic women's organizations. Some of these organizations cooperated with the government, in particular with the Office of the Government Plenipotentiary for Equal Status of Women and Men.[11] A number of women's networks, including the KARAT Coalition (discussed below) and the Network of East West Women–Polska (NEWW Polska), were formed. Women's organizations working to achieve equality between men and women did not cooperate with the conservative and pro-family Catholic women's organizations.

The proliferation of Polish women's organizations coincided with Poland's application to join the European Union and the preparations that followed. Like any other candidate country, Poland—which experienced multiple changes in government, including right-wing governments—had to bring its legislation in line with EU standards, providing opportunities to those mobilizing for women's equality (Regulska and Grabowska 2008). Furthermore, the enlargement process enabled and required Polish women's organizations to engage in networking across European borders, with the financial support of the EU and EU member states (Roth 2007; Regulska and Grabowska 2008). Women's NGOs played an important role as mediators between the EU and the Polish government (Regulska and Grabowska 2008:150). Another strategy to promote women's rights in Poland was engagement in strategic litigation. Fuchs (2013) discusses this with respect to reproductive rights and employment rights, and argues that it not only influenced law and legal practices, but had an impact on public opinion by shaping the legal consciousness of the population.

Czech women were involved in the nationalist and socialist movements of the 19th century and gained the same political rights as men in 1918. In fact, the president of the First Republic, Tomas Garrigue Masaryk, was a feminist and supported women's rights from the 1880s until his death in 1937 (Ferber and Raabe 2003:411). The lack of civil and political rights under National Socialism (1938–1945) and communism (1948–1989) resulted in solidarity among men and women, and the Catholic Church played a smaller role than in Poland (ibid). In 1948, the Communist Czechoslovak Women's Union (CSWU) was established, replacing existing feminist organizations (Hašková 2005). While women were involved in the underground civic sphere that emerged in the late 1960s and 1970s, they did not form women's groups (Hašková 2005). After 1989, a wide range of small, informal women's groups addressing a variety of private, professional, and political issues emerged in urban centers, relying on voluntary engagement and small grants from Western donors (Kapusta-Pofahl et al. 2005). Hašková reports that by the early 1990s, 70 such groups already existed, which addressed

> the situation of women in the labour market and the public sphere, violence against women and trafficking in women, reproductive health and social services in child care, minority women's issues (e.g. Roma women and lesbian women), environmental and eco-feminist issues, and issues of increasing gender sensitivity, awareness and education among the public. (2005:1083)

EU accession negotiations had a "profound impact" on women's civic groups in the Czech Republic (Hašková 2005:1087). In the context of EU accession, the conditions for funding of all programs changed, including for programs related to women's movements, resulting in competition for larger funds that were fewer in number and more constrained. The consequences of project-oriented funds[12] were increasing formalization, professionalization, and reform orientation (Kapusta-Pofahl et al. 2005). EU directives strengthened women's ability to lobby in favor of gender equality legislation and government support, and resulted in the adoption of the EU equality *acquis*[13] into Czech legislation and the establishment of equality bodies at the government level (Hašková and Křižková 2008). EU membership resulted in access to funding through the European Structural Fund (ESF) and an expansion of Czech women's NGOs, a "golden era" that was followed by a period of retrenchment and precariousness (Lorenz-Meyer 2013:413). However, not all activism was project-based, reform-oriented, or state-centered. In 2000, anarcho-feminist groups emerged in preparation for the celebration of International Women's Day 2001, and the Global Women's Strike was critical both of gender relations in the anarchist movement as well as of institutional feminism (Kapusta-Pofahl et al. 2005:45f). Lorenz-Meyer (2013) distinguishes different phases of post-socialist women's organizing which are to some extent shaped by funding opportunities, but also by localized encounters and the biographical availability of activists.

The countries of Central and Eastern Europe vary with respect to feminist mobilization—stronger in Poland, weaker in Hungary. EU accession benefited women's organizations in Central and Eastern Europe, as it forced candidate countries to adopt equal opportunity policies through top-down reforms. With respect to Hungary, Kakucs and Petö speak of "gender equality policies for women without feminist participation" (2008:179). However, although the EU demanded the adoption of gender equality legislation, it has had no impact on its implementation.

European Women's Movements Outside the European Union

Of course, Europe is not identical with the European Union. But, the EU has an impact even on countries that do not yet belong to it; this applies particularly to candidate countries. Turkey is one such candidate country, with a long-standing relationship with the EU dating to the Ankara Treaty of 1983. Turkey officially applied to become an EU member in 1987 and in 1999, the EU officially recognized Turkey as a candidate (Marshall 2008). As in the countries discussed above, Turkey has to bring its legislation in line with EU requirements. In 2002, when the Central and Eastern European countries discussed above were accepted into the EU, Turkey's progress with respect to human and minority rights was considered insufficient. In 2005, Turkey entered into accession negotiations with the European Commission, which required the implementation of EU directives, including the gender equality directive. This means that, like other countries joining the EU, Turkey had to change civil and legal codes to improve women's status and gender equality. These requirements strengthened the position of feminist groups mobilizing against violence against women (including rape, honor killings, and sexual assault) and promoting women's political participation. The Turkish women's movement mobilized at the grassroots level and feminists participated in the EU parliament, the European Women's Lobby, as well as in UN meetings, combining local and transnational activism (Marshall 2013).

In contrast to Turkey, Switzerland has never sought membership in the European Union. Furthermore, Switzerland is unusual among Western democracies, as women were only given the vote in 1971. In the late 1960s, radical feminist groups emerged in Switzerland that criticized patriarchal structures in the private and public spheres and argued that the vote alone was not enough to transform Swiss society (Burgnard 2011). In addition to the cases of Turkey and Switzerland, women's organizations in the former Yugoslavia should be mentioned; these formed in response to the ethnic conflicts and violence against women in the 1990s (Cockburn 2013).

Thus, just as the women's movements in the EU member states differ widely, so do women's movements in European countries that do not belong to the EU. Those which are candidate countries, like Turkey, need to bring their legislation in line with EU law as a precondition to join. Just as in other countries discussed above, this can strengthen women's movements, as I address in the next section.

The EU as Transnational Opportunity Structure

The EU is acknowledged as a supranational institution influencing gender equality policy in its member states—as well as in candidate countries—even against their preferences (Ellina 2003). The initial gender equality legislation of the EEC was an unintended side effect, restricted to questions of equal pay. It was introduced at France's demand, as France was the only country with an equal pay provision and it feared that the rule was potentially a barrier to fair and equal competition. Article 119 of the Treaty of Rome (1957), guaranteeing equal pay for equal work, could be used as a basis for national equal pay campaigns and provided a starting point for further gender equality legislation. The EU therefore provided an opportunity structure for women's movements, as it was often more open to feminist demands than national governments. In addition, due to the northern enlargement of the EU in 1995, the proportion of women in the European parliament increased. As noted above, the new member states Finland and Sweden had a strong existing commitment to equal opportunities for women and considerable experience in mainstreaming gender in their national policies. In fact, Euro-skeptic Swedish women feared that joining the EU would have a negative impact on gender equality in their country, and therefore successfully sought to "export" Swedish gender equality policies. Their access to the EU as well as the UN conferences played a crucial role in strengthening the EU's position on women's equality (Ellina 2003). The impact of EU policy on the member states varied, depending on the gender equality policies already in existence. As noted above, EU membership contributed to strengthening gender equality policy in Spain and Ireland as well as in the former socialist countries.

Over time, EU policies on women's rights became broader, eventually addressing the reconciliation of employment with family life and, more recently, gender mainstreaming (Ellina 2003). In the 1970s and 1980s, a number of directives addressing tax and social security measures, child care facilities, education, training opportunities, and affirmative action programs on behalf of women were adopted (Morgan 2008; Wahl 2008; Zippel 2008). However, it was up to the member states to implement these directives and allocate funds promoting gender equality. The impact of EU policies varies not only between member states, but also in different policy areas. While there are binding legal directives for employment regulation, this is not the case for other key areas of gender equality, including sexual preference, abortion, and violence against women (Walby 2004).

Due to this variation, it is therefore not surprising that the assessment of the EU's importance for gender equality policies in the member states also differs. Some see it as extensive, others as limited (Walby 2004). Furthermore, the EU approach to gender equality represents a hybrid model encompassing principles of liberalism and social democracy as well as innovative ideas of global women's movements (Ferree 2012). It encompasses opportunities as well as threats to feminist achievements: for example, an emphasis on gender equality might jeopardize programs targeted at women and girls only, or a focus on diversity might take away attention from gender issues. In the 1980s and 1990s, when European women's groups were dissatisfied with respect to achieving equal rights at the national level, they became more and more involved in international women's networks. In addition to the European Union the UN conferences contributed to the emergence and consolidation of an international network (Keck and Sikkink 1998). The next section introduces transnational mobilization across Europe.

European Women's Networks

Women's activism and international networks like the European Women's Lobby played a central role in the expansive development of EU gender equality legislation and the introduction of gender mainstreaming (Cichowski 2002). Such networks provide opportunities for information dissemination, the coordination of lobbying and protest events, and mutual support (Roth 2007; Roth 2008; Agustin and Roth 2011; Agustin 2013; Lang 2013). The end of socialism and EU accession changed the agenda and composition of women's networks in Europe. I will briefly describe a range of networks representing different constituencies and issues. Some of these organizations still existed at the time of writing, while others were no longer active.

Women in Development Europe (WIDE), was established in 1985 after the Third UN Women's Conference in Nairobi in order to create a European network focusing on women and development. It engaged in information exchange, solidarity work, lobbying for the integration of women's concerns in development policies, and monitoring global macroeconomic and trade institutions. EU enlargement led to WIDE's involvement in Central and Eastern Europe (Harcourt 2011). In 2016, WIDE and the European Women's Lobby were organizing a two-day international conference to analyze global issues in Europe (WIDE 2016).

The *European Women's Lobby (EWL)* was the largest alliance of women's non-governmental organizations in Europe. According to Lang, "No other European transnational women's network comes close to having EWL's institutional influence, transnational membership base, or yearly funding from the European Union" (2013:171). It was founded and established its secretariat in Brussels in 1990 (Helferrich and Kolb 2001; Lang 2013). The EWL received long-term core support from the EU Commission, which is relatively safe from budgetary challenges (Cullen 2005:75). However, in the context of the 2008 economic crisis and the associated austerity measures, the EWL experienced a contraction, as gender equality was seen as "too costly" (Cullen 2015). The activities of the EWL included lobbying, policy and advocacy work, projects, and information-related activities. When the 1997 Amsterdam Treaty broadened "equal opportunities" beyond gender, and when in 1998 and 1999 policy proposals to extend anti-discrimination were discussed in the Platform of European Social NGOs, the EWL was concerned that the greater emphasis on race, disability, and religion might come at the expense of gender (Cullen 2005; Bygnes 2012). Since the late 1990s, the EWL has increasingly emphasized the diversity of women and addressed racism, thus challenging a separation of racial discrimination from gender discrimination (Agustin 2013:71f). In 2016, the EWL addressed a range of issues including violence against women, women's economic independence, immigration, integration and asylum, international action and young women in Europe.

The *Network of East-West Women (NEWW)* was founded in 1991 in Dubrovnik by activists and researchers interested in the situation of women in Central and Eastern Europe and the Newly Independent States (NIS). NEWW members came from over 30 countries: predominantly from CEE and NIS countries but also from the US, Spain, and Germany. NEWW was funded by Western foundations and monitored the effects of the transition to capitalism on women in the former socialist countries, focusing on their economic situation and involvement in decision-making processes as well as human rights issues (e.g. violence against women, trafficking, and reproductive rights). In June 2016, the organization held two celebratory birthday parties in order to discuss the future of feminisms, these and other activities are documented on the website and the Facebook page of the organization.

The *Women Against Violence Europe (WAVE)* network was founded in the context of the World Conference on Women in Beijing in 1995, with the objective of combating violence against women and children as well as promoting women's and children's human rights (Montoya 2013). The network received funding through the EC DAPHNE program in 1997, which enabled the setup of a coordinating office and the development of WAVE's organizational structure. The organizations belonging to the network ran women's shelters, counseling centers, and help lines, as well as prevention and training programs. In 2016, WAVE published the findings of a survey of service provision for women survivors of violence which documents limited availability of women's helplines, shelters and centers. In the same year, the organization was preparing its 18th conference (WAVE 2016).

The organization *Young Women from Minorities (WFM)* emerged in the context of a youth campaign (*All Different—All Equal*) that was launched by the Council of Europe (CoE) in 1995. This network included individuals and organizations and received financial support from the CoE. The main objectives of WFM were information provision, training, and projects relating to social integration: overcoming discrimination and exclusion with the aim of improving the participation of young minority women, as well as promoting projects initiated by young minority women. In 2016, the website of WFM was no longer working and the entry in the Yearbook of International Organizations was last updated in 2003.

In 1997, *KARAT Coalition* was formally established by representatives of ten CEE countries in Warsaw in order to develop its own agenda without influence from the West (Roth 2007; Lang 2013). KARAT was supported by American donors and later started to cooperate with WIDE. The coalition initially concentrated on monitoring the implementation by Central Eastern European/Commonwealth of Independent States (CEE/CIS) governments of their international commitments, especially those made at the Beijing Conference. In 2002, KARAT also began lobbying at the EU level, but rather than joining the EWL, KARAT decided to develop its own agenda and collaborate with the lobby. The focus of the newly formed coalition was on gender economic and social justice, labor market issues, and the impact of the EU enlargement process on the CEE/CIS region as a whole. After the Eastern EU enlargement, KARAT Coalition included members in EU countries as well as in CEE countries that did not belong to the EU. In 2016, KARAT reported about the monitoring of the implementation of the CEDAW convention in Poland, in the previous year, the organization completed a project focusing on girls in non-traditional occupations (KARAT 2016).

The *Black European Women's Council (BEWC)* was formed in the context of the European Year of Equal Opportunities for All (2007). It was officially launched during the European Year of Intercultural Dialogue (2008). The BEWC used EU institutional contacts extensively during the first years of its existence. It focused heavily on strategic lobbying and networking *vis-à-vis* the EU institutions. The network addressed diverse needs and interests, reflecting the heterogeneity of the African diaspora. Objectives of BEWC included female empowerment, challenges faced by black youth (with the objective of eliminating racism in the educational system), mental health issues of black women and children faced with racism, barriers in relation to the recruitment of black personnel, and the political participation of women of the African diaspora (Agustin and Roth 2011; Ellerbe-Dueck 2011a). At the time of completing this book chapter, BEWC was preparing to celebrate its 10th anniversary in December 2016.

These organizations ranged from large umbrella organizations like the EWL to smaller networks including individuals as members, like WFM. They differed in their main objectives, size, and sources of funding. The EWL was the largest of these networks, had the broadest range of objectives, and was most secure in terms of funding. However, BEWC, the youngest and smallest of these organizations, also intended to pursue a broad range of areas, in particular giving women of the African diaspora a voice and a safe space. This organization was least secure in terms of funding compared to the others. Each organization had a different approach to political intersectionality (Agustin and Roth 2011). Furthermore, while these networks had different foci and constituencies, they informed each other about their work and collaborated on conferences, campaigns, and publications, in some cases quite closely.

Women's movements and women's networks have not only been transformed by political and historical events, but also by technological change. The impact that information and communication technologies (ICTs) have had on social movements in general and women's mobilization in particular cannot be overestimated. These technologies have given rise to new forms of online activism—which often coexist with offline activism—and have also provided an infrastructure for women's networks. ICTs thus provide new "interactive communication repertoires" (Knappe and Lang 2014). However, women's organizations varied in the extent to which they made use of web-based communication. Based on a comparison between German and UK women's networks, Knappe and Lang found that UK NGOs were more likely to engage in interactive communication, whereas German organizations use the web more for one-way information (2014:367). These communication preferences seem to be reflected in different network patterns. Whereas the German advocacy network was "highly centralised and institutionalised," the UK network was "more densely connected" (ibid.:366). In addition to these country-specific differences, the networks themselves employed different strategies, as discussed above. Moving from the national to the transnational level, the European Women's Lobby was primarily linked to other networks in Europe rather than to non-European networks, in particular networks in the global South. This can be explained with the mission—and funding—of the European Union, but it indicates that its transnationalism was intra-regional rather than global (Pudrovska and Ferree 2004:134).

Diversity and Political Intersectionality

In the previous sections, I have only minimally referred to diversity and political intersectionality. European countries—whether they belong to the European Union or not—differ widely with respect to the situation of ethnic minorities and migrants as well as sexual minorities. Some countries—like France, the United Kingdom, and Belgium—are former colonial powers that experienced migration from their former colonies after independence. Other countries—for example West Germany and Austria—invited "guest workers" during times of economic growth in the 1950s and 1960s rather than encouraging women's full-time employment. In contrast, Sweden supported full-time employment and avoided migration as a means to address labor shortages. European countries also differ widely with respect to citizenship rights and citizenship models. Sauer (2009) distinguishes the civic-assimilationist model, the ethno-cultural model, and the multi-cultural model. The civic-assimilationist and multi-cultural models provide relatively easy access to citizenship (*ius soli*), while the ethno-cultural model is based on descent (*ius sanguinis*) and makes it more difficult to obtain citizenship.

With respect to head-scarf regimes, for example, not only citizenship regimes and integration policies matter, but also church-state relations, the recognition of religious communities, traditions of gender policies, institutions of antidiscrimination, and the role of women's movements and Muslim women (Sauer 2009:81). Sauer (2009) provides a comparison of women's movements and the voice of Muslim women in Germany, the Netherlands, and Austria. She found that in Germany and the Netherlands, the women's movement was divided concerning a ban on the head scarf, but that overall the support for the head scarf was weak and Muslim women's voices were marginalized. In contrast, in Austria Muslims were involved in public debates on religious issues and the Austrian women's movement did not take a stand on the head scarf. Laic countries such as France and Turkey, which insist on the separation of church and state, prohibited wearing a head scarf in the public sector (e.g. in schools, universities, or public sector employment). The case of head-scarf regimes indicates that with respect to minority women, a range of dimensions need to be analytically distinguished: citizenship status and nationality, ethnicity and "race" as well as religion, resulting in a diversity of interests and experiences.

Organizations of migrant and minoritized women emerged in the late 1970s in many European countries and took on a marginal place in women's and feminist movements (kennedy-macfoy 2012). This marginality was due to a reluctance to adopt the label "feminist" as well as experiences of racism within feminist contexts. However, majority and minority women's organizations experienced both competition for funding and solidarity across difference. Based on her study of minority women's organizations in Belgium, Norway, and the UK, kennedy-mcfoy (2012) concludes that overall, minority women felt ignored and excluded from mainstream feminist movements. They therefore formed their own organizations. Based on an analysis of 224 migrant women's organizations in Germany, Lenz and Schwenken (2002) found that the majority of women participating in these organizations came from different countries of origin, rather than organizing along national and ethnic belongings. Furthermore, the organizations tended to combine self-help, counseling, and capacity-building with political activism. The groups mobilized successfully for the independent legal status of foreign spouses and addressed trafficking in women, racism, and xenophobia. Migrant women's groups experienced racism in as well as support from the majority women's movement. The mobilization of ethnic minority and racialized women in Europe includes local, national, and transnational organizations that provide safe spaces (Ellerbe-Dueck 2011b).

European countries also vary with respect to intimate citizenship, which is concerned "with the processes, practices and discourses that regulate and shape the exercise of agency in intimate life: both the laws and policies, and the social relations between individuals and groups within civil society" (Roseneil et al. 2012:42). Similar to the variations of women's movements described earlier in the chapter, lesbian and gay movements emerged at different points in time in European countries and faced different political opportunity structures (Ayoub 2016). By the early 1950s, homosexuality had been decriminalized in the Nordic countries, Belgium, the Netherlands, Luxembourg, Italy, and Greece, whereas this took place later in the UK (1967), East and West Germany (1968 and 1969), Spain (1979), and Ireland (1993). The legal situation shaped organizational development, as gays and lesbians could organize openly in countries that accepted homosexuality. This resulted in moderate organizations in these countries, while in countries that repressed homosexuality, more radical organizations and subcultures emerged (Kollman and Waites 2009). Roseneil et al. (2012) provide a comparison of Norway, the UK, Portugal, and Bulgaria. In the UK and Norway, campaigning began in the 1950s and became more radical in the 1970s. Whereas the movement found political support in Norway, the opposite was the case under the conservative Thatcher government in the UK. Mobilization for gay and lesbian rights emerged later in Portugal and Bulgaria; activists in the latter benefited from the EU accession process (Roseneil et al. 2012:47). Lesbian women participated both in LGBT and women's movements, felt marginalized in both, and formed their own organizations. For example, in the UK, a group called Lesbian Avengers split from the radical activist organization Outrage!, which had formed in 1990 in the context of AIDS activism (Waites 2009). A study of transnational LGBTQ activism in Poland found that feminists were core actors in protest events like equality marches (Binnie and Klesse 2012). Polish activists successfully established coalitions that not only included feminists, gays, and lesbians, but also a broad spectrum of leftist groups.

Political intersectionality requires coalition-building across diversity, privilege, and disadvantage. This might be easier said than done, as a comparison of anti-racist and gender equality activists in Europe indicates (Nielsen 2013). Although the gender equality organizations referred to intersectionality in their publications, interviews with anti-racist activists pointed to "more inclusive understandings of diversity and less willingness to hierarchy specific equality concerns as compared with the gender equality activists" (Nielsen 2013:291).

Feminist Transformations and Responses to Austerity

Over the past fifty years, European women's movements have achieved an increased presence of women in the public sphere, new policies addressing intimate citizenship, and a growing awareness of an effort to engage in political intersectionality. The success story of feminist movements is intertwined with the neoliberal turn of the 1980s, and the affinity between (liberal) feminism and neoliberalism has been noted (Fraser 2009). In a tricky way, the demands of women's movements for self-determination, self-reliance, individual liberty, and autonomy are compatible with the logic of globalized markets. What does that mean? Neoliberalism involves the transfer of tasks that were previously covered by the state to the private sector or civil society, as well as an emphasis on personal responsibility and efficiency. This meets with feminist demands for self-determination and opens up possibilities for women's NGOs and gender consultants. Kantola and Squires (2012) characterize these changes as a shift from state feminism to market feminism. While it is welcome that the expertise and services of feminists are compensated adequately, the reliance on project and performance-bound funding includes the risk of co-optation and de-politicization. However, the consequences of professionalization processes need to be carefully assessed. Overall, paid positions in NGOs and social movement organizations tend to be precarious and short-term; thus, a lot of the work that is done by NGO staff is actually low or un-paid. In addition, radical critique and pragmatic action change frequently in the political biographies of feminist activists (Newman 2012). Thus, rather than considering state funding and offering diversity training to companies, these relationships and activities should be understood as a "march through the institutions" and unobtrusive mobilization (Katzenstein 1990). However, this requires ongoing critical reflection from activists engaging with institutions in order to prevent the selling out or watering down of feminist principles.

The financial crisis of 2008 had a significant impact on women and women's movements in Europe. Initially labelled the "he-cession," as the male-dominated private sector was hit first, the impact of public sector cuts on women losing jobs, services, and benefits was soon evident (Prügl 2012; Pearson and Elson 2015). However, despite welfare retrenchment a variety of welfare regimes (Ferragina and Seeleib-Kaiser 2011), and thus variations in gender regimes and familialism (Leitner 2003; Javornik 2014), exist. Public sector cuts, which particularly affect women and women's organizations, were more extreme in liberal welfare regimes such as the UK and Ireland, as well as in Southern European welfare states, than in the social democratic Nordic welfare states and some continental countries. In many countries, anti-austerity measures resulted in feminist and anti-austerity mobilization. For example in the UK, between 2010 and 2012, the coalition Women Against the Cuts, including Southall Black Sisters, Million Women Rise, Fawcett Society, London Feminist Network, and Women Against Fundamentalists, joined protest events such as the TUC March for an Alternative (Saunders et al. 2015). Women's organizations like the Fawcett Society (founded in 1866) have monitored and responded to austerity in Britain with campaigns such as Cutting Women Out, while the Women's Budget Group regularly published critical analysis of the UK budgets and their consequences for women (Women's Budget Group 2015). Budget cuts have significantly affected the funding for organizations addressing violence and domestic abuse and threaten coalition building across difference (Bassel and Emejulu 2014). However, as both Occupy and the Gezi uprisings in Istanbul show, anti-austerity protests constitute broad coalitions across gender, class, ethnicity, and sexuality (Potuoglu-Cook 2015). This shows that the relationship between feminism and neoliberalism is complicated and contradictory. The feminist ethos of autonomy, agency, and self-determination aligns well with the neoliberal emphasis on entrepreneurialism. However, this is only one side of feminist demands, which also include an emphasis on care and redistribution and a keen awareness that women are particularly affected by public sector cuts.

Conclusion

Writing about women's movements in Europe inevitably requires a comparative perspective to identify the degrees and patterns of institutionalization (Mazur et al. 2015). Rather than juxtaposing Western and Eastern European women's movements, it makes sense to assess similarities and differences between women's movements that are strongly influenced by the Catholic Church (for example Ireland, Poland, and Spain) and to compare women's movements with an authoritarian past (for example Germany, Hungary, and Greece). Women's movements in Europe vary with respect to their relationship to the state and their forms of mobilization. Moreover, state restructuring—including downloading to the regional level as well as uploading to the European Union—has shaped women's movements (Banaszak et al. 2003). As I have shown in this chapter, they are also shaped by the cultural and political legacies of fascism, socialism, and the Cold War, as well as by different welfare and gender regimes. Furthermore, joining the European Union at different points in time has had different consequences for women's movements in the member states. Thus, while there is an ongoing interaction among European women's movements, that does not necessarily mean convergence. European women's movements have experienced state feminism and professionalization processes at different points in time and to varying degrees. They are characterized by diversity within and across countries, combining insider and outsider activism.

Notes

1. Europe is the second largest continent (the westernmost part of Eurasia), comprising about 50 sovereign states (some with limited recognition) as well as a few dependencies, in which over 200 different languages are spoken.

2. Transnational opportunity structures include state and non-state actors as well as international institutions which enable and constrain international activism (see Tarrow 2006).

3. Of course, the European Union is not the only important transnational political opportunity structure: the United Nations has a pivotal role.

4. In 1957, Belgium, the Federal Republic of Germany, France, Italy, Luxembourg, and the Netherlands formed the European Economic Community (EEC), later renamed the European Union (EU). For the sake of simplicity, I will refer to the European Union throughout this chapter rather than to the EEC. In 1973 Denmark, Ireland, and the United Kingdom joined the EU (then called the EEC); in 1981 Greece followed; in 1986 Portugal and Spain became members; in 1995 Austria, Finland, and Sweden joined the EU; in 2004 Cyprus, the Czech Republic, Estonia, Hungary, Latvia, Lithuania, Malta, Poland, Slovakia, and Slovenia became part of the EU; in 2007 Bulgaria and Romania followed; and most recently, Croatia joined in 2013. In 2016, a referendum in the United Kingdom resulted in a majority for leaving and negotiating a new relationship with the European Union.

5. If not otherwise noted, when I refer to women's movements in this article, I have feminist movements in mind. Following Martin (1990) I understand movements or movement organizations as feminist if they are concerned with gender equality. This does not mean that they would necessarily adopt the label "feminist." They might reject it for strategic reasons, because they feel that they might alienate supporters. Furthermore, understanding women's movements as feminist movements—or movements for gender equality—allows for inclusion of men as supporters of these movements.

6. However, as I will show later in this chapter, the character of European women's movements has been shaped by changing political opportunity structures and alliances, which makes the use of the wave metaphor questionable (Dean and Aune 2015) and highlights that it is in fact exclusionary (Evans and Chamberlain 2015).

7. The relationship between majority and minority women and their organizations will be discussed in a later section of this chapter.

8. Soft law does not have legally binding force and is traditionally associated with international law, for example, resolutions and declarations of the UN General Assembly.

9. This has changed in the early 21st century, as more and more refugees have made the dangerous journey across the Mediterranean Sea to reach Southern Europe. Furthermore, Spain and other Southern European countries have become destinations for retirees from higher income countries, for example the United Kingdom.

10. Gender mainstreaming was first discussed at the UN Women's Conference in Nairobi (1985) and entered EU policy making in 1991 in the Third Action Programme on Equal Opportunities.

11. In the context of EU accession, the agency was initially formed as Plenipotentiary for Family and Women's Affairs. After the election of a right-wing government in 1997, it was renamed Plenipotentiary for Family Affairs (Regulska and Grabowska 2008:142f). From 2001 until 2006 it existed as Plenipotentiary for Equal Status of Women and Men. In 2006, the Department for Women, Family and Counteracting Discrimination within the Ministry of Labor and Social Policy took on gender equality policy (EIGE 2016).

12. Project funding is allocated for specific projects, and cannot be spent on other goals, in contrast to funding that can be freely allocated by organizations receiving it.

13. The acquis communautaire—shortened acquis—refers to EU law and legislation. Countries which want to join the EU have to bring their national legislation in line with the acquis.

7

Russian Women's Activism

*Grassroots Persistence in the
Face of Challenges*

LISA MCINTOSH SUNDSTROM

Introduction

Women's activism in Russia has undergone dramatic transformation since the collapse of the Soviet regime in 1991. Formally organized women's groups grew exponentially after the early 1990s, and women activists became savvy managers, fund-raisers, and organizers. Many established strong ties with global feminist networks to strengthen their effectiveness. But enormous weaknesses remain, to the point that it is difficult to truly say there is a significant "women's movement," whether feminist or not, in the country. Overall, women's post-Communist activism on the issue of gender-based violence has been rewarded with a number of mobilizational victories (albeit limited and unstable), while activism on women's economic inequality and political representation has been more muted and produced less tangible improvement.

Self-identifying feminists are few in Russia, and they struggle to persuade public officials and citizens at large to consider their ideas seriously. Feminists have had only minor and sporadic influence on Russian society, and most Russians have a decidedly negative orientation toward the term *feminism*, although their actual beliefs about gender equality vary greatly. While a dramatic growth in women's organizing occurred in the 1990s immediately after the collapse of the Soviet regime, for most of that time there was little collective sense of purpose among organizations. After the early 2000s, the visibility of these organizations and their ability to work for change contracted substantially.

Much of this decline occurred due to reduced foreign-donor funding for civil society organizations, as well as mounting government restrictions on civil society organizing more generally, which seriously depleted the resources of formal women's organizations and endangered their ability to continue working. As of 2010, a new wave of informal and avowedly feminist groups began to organize, without any donor funding, and often through social media platforms. While this activism was small in scale and has since subsided, the women involved displayed a sense of shared collective aims and a willingness to protest publicly. In this sense, perhaps a seed has been sown to allow for a re-emergence of feminist activism from hibernation once the political environment allows.

Some Historical Context: Gender Politics in the Soviet Period

Russia's twentieth-century history would seem at first glance to be conducive to strong feminist activism and gender equality in society. Soviet women were extremely well educated relative to Soviet men, and women's presence in higher education increased steadily throughout the Soviet period. By 1985, 58 percent of Soviet higher education students were women (Ratliff 1995:20), although this varied strongly by "nationality" (ethnic background), with Central Asian nationalities having the lowest proportions of female students and Russian nationalities the highest (Lapidus 1978:153). High female labor-force participation developed relatively early compared to most other countries; by the 1970s, over 87 percent of Soviet working-age women were either working outside the home or studying full-time.

Russian women gained the right to vote just before the Bolshevik Revolution that founded the Communist regime, under the Provisional Government that existed between the February and October 1917 revolutions. Those rights were enshrined later in the 1918 Soviet Constitution. The early Soviet government instituted (though did not always implement) various labor and welfare rights that women still struggle for in many countries: for example, equal pay for equal work, rights to maternity leave with full pay for eight weeks before and after birth, and

equal entitlement to employment-related
(Buckley 1989:34–35). The state lifted divorce
riage as a decision of mutual consent between
abortion (ibid.:35–37).

Bolshevik feminists at the time of the revolution
reorganization of family structures to emancipate wo.
pression of bourgeois marriage. Aleksandra Kollontai
mand, for example, argued that family as a social institut.   ved
women (ibid.:44). Kollontai argued that "the individual i ...sehold is
dying" and that under socialism, brigades of domestic workers (both
men and women) would do society's housework (ibid.:45). Lenin, following Engels, was sympathetic to these ideas, but viewed gender inequality as a problem that would disappear naturally once Communism
established itself, since he believed that women's inequality was fundamentally rooted in economic inequality and bourgeois capitalism
(Zetkin 1934).

During the Soviet period, the party's ideology both reified and tried
to break existing gender stereotypes. Beginning in the 1920s the regime's commitment to gender equality weakened in the face of insufficient resources to truly collectivize domestic tasks and a great deal of
hostility among both men and women toward these goals (Buckley
1989:chap. 1; Lapidus 1978:chap. 2; Aivazova 1998). Ultimately, the
Soviet state warped the ideas of the Bolshevik feminists in ways that
ended up increasing the burdens of Soviet women, requiring that they
fulfill traditional domestic roles while participating full-time in public
life (Waters and Posadskaya 1995; Temkina and Rotkirkh 2002:9). Because the development of communal services to reduce women's domestic labor time lagged behind the pace at which women were
entering the paid employment sector, Soviet women endured the
"double burden" of domestic and paid labor. It is estimated that nearly
75 percent of all domestic tasks fell exclusively to women in Soviet
households in the 1970s (including far more time-consuming ones
than women in the industrialized West endured, due to the lack of la-
bor-saving household devices and shortages of consumer goods, which
led to long hours searching and lining up for basic necessities), in addition to full-time work outside the home (Lapidus 1978:272). More
recent studies indicate little change in this pattern of housework responsibilities (Vannoy et al. 1999; Ashwin 2006), despite increased
standards of living.

the state closed the issue of gender equality when Stalin shut
the Women's Department (*Zhenotdel*) that Armand and Kollontai
had founded, declaring the "woman question" officially "solved" (Buckley 1989:108). Thereafter, the only women's organizations the government permitted were the official Soviet Women's Committee (SWC) and the vast official network of small women's councils (*zhensovety*) in cities, towns, and workplaces across Russia. The government originally created the SWC in 1941 as a mechanism for mobilizing women in the war effort. In the 1980s, Gorbachev put the SWC in charge of leading the network of women's councils, creating a single hierarchical network supposedly representing women's interests. Yet the network's primary mission was not to act as an advocacy organization to communicate women's demands or lobby for their interests at the national level. Rather, it was to transmit government and Communist Party messages to women to encourage them to fulfill regime goals in their daily lives (Buckley 1989). In other words, to use Molyneux's taxonomy, the network was an example of "directed mobilizations" rather than "autonomous mobilization" (Molyneux 2005:216). The SWC had a secondary mission: to promote a rosy image of Soviet women's status to the outside world. As Zoya Khotkina (1999) has stated, the SWC "had, like Janus, two faces: one for Soviet women and another for Western women." The legacy of Communist rhetoric as well as policy efforts to promote women's equality in some areas while undermining it in others has left women equal in law but not in practice. Once marketization penetrated and a laissez-faire model of the state became popular among political and economic elites, gendered labor segregation increased, and women's representation in politics declined. Yet the myth that the Soviet regime had already made women equal to men persisted. That myth, coupled with a sense that Soviet equality had ruined women's femininity, and with the renewed popularity of the Russian Orthodox Church, has led to an open resurgence of some traditional gender ideals of women as nurturing mothers, keepers of the hearth, and sex goddesses, and of men as strong providers (Sperling 2015:223; Jurna 1995:477). Moreover, this history has made it difficult for post-Soviet Russian feminists to mobilize successfully by framing political claims as demands for gender equality. Yet the situation is complicated and in flux: as I discuss below, these reactions *against* Soviet gender ideals are matched by enduring *positive* orientations toward women's labor-force participation, which themselves stem from Soviet labor patterns.

The Beginnings of Independent Women's Activism

In the 1970s and 1980s, when autonomous, non-state organizing remained illegal prior to the collapse of the Soviet Union, there were
some small groups of underground feminists working in Russia, including publishers of the *samizdat* (self-published) journals *Women and
Russia* and *Maria*. The Soviet government punished these activists severely, exiling some and sentencing others to hard-labor camps for advocating "bourgeois feminism" (Waters 1993; Dyukova 1998). In the
late perestroika period, when citizens were permitted to independently
associate with one another more openly, many women's organizations
were established informally, but they were not yet allowed to register
formally as legal organizations.

A crucial organizational moment for these nascent groups came
when several of them arranged two forums for independent women's
organizations, called the First and Second Independent Women's Forums. The first took place in March 1991 and the second in late 1992,
both in the small city of Dubna, outside Moscow. The forums proved
crucial for the early mobilization and networking of the post-Soviet
women's movement. Forum participants created a loose network of
women's organizations, scholars, and activists called the Independent
Women's Forum (IWF) (V. Sperling 1999:20). The IWF never really
mobilized formally except when some of its members later created an
organization called the Information Center of the Independent Wom-
en's Forum. Three other women's networks formed around that same
time, with somewhat overlapping memberships across the multiple
networks. The Women's League emerged out of a conference in Moscow in 1992 called "Women and the Market Economy." While independent of the state, the Women's League was more moderate in
outlook than the IWF (ibid.:21). Another network, the Union of Russian Women (URW), emerged in 1991 as a renamed version of the no
longer state-sponsored SWC. The URW also took a number of other
fairly mainstream women's organizations under its umbrella. The final
network was the US-NIS Consortium, later renamed the Russian Consortium of Women's Nongovernmental Organizations. The Consortium
was cofounded by Russian and US women activists in 1994 and brought
together an "uneasy coalition" of members from the IWF and the
Women's League (ibid.). Eventually, the Consortium outlived the IWF
and the Women's League, remaining one of the most prominent

women's networks in Russia during the 1990s, while the other two became relatively dormant.

As Russia transitioned from Soviet rule to multiparty democracy in the early 1990s, some women in the prodemocracy movement were fairly sympathetic to feminist ideas but did not identify openly with feminism or women's rights. Examples include Galina Starovoitova (a politician murdered in 1998 in a targeted assassination), Irina Khakamada (who rose to the senior leadership of one of the more liberal democratic parties, the Union of Right Forces), and, at more grassroots levels, many of the women involved in human rights organizations. But some feminists were actively involved, such as Olga Lipovskaya, a feminist poet widely recognized as a leader in the development of the Russian women's movement. Lipovskaya edited the samizdat journal *Zhenskoe chtenie* (Women's Reading) in the Soviet period and was active in the St. Petersburg division of the Democratic Union in the late Soviet and early post-Soviet period. She became head of the St. Petersburg Center for Gender Issues when it was founded in 1992.

However, Russian feminists or women's groups actively participated in the democracy movement significantly less than in, for example, Latin America (Jaquette and Wolchik 1998:250; E. Friedman 1998; Franceschet 2003; Waylen 1994:347). In many other countries' prodemocracy movements, male activists' failure to include women's issues in the democracy agenda spurred the growth of a separate feminist movement (Waylen 1994:342–343; E. Friedman 1998:107–109). Women in many Eastern European countries experienced more of this galvanization through exclusion from elite democratic politics than did Russian women. In Poland, for example, this dynamic, as well as threats to women's access to legal abortions, led over time to the emergence of feminist public protests and a sizeable women's movement. While some Russian prodemocracy activists who were already feminists experienced similar frustration (Waters and Posadskaya 1995:364), such feelings of alienation did not promote the development of a significant autonomous feminist movement.

The Shape of Post-Soviet Women's Activism

What exactly is a women's movement? Maxine Molyneux refers to the term as implying "a social or political phenomenon of some significance, that significance being given both by its numerical strength but also by its capacity to effect change in some way or another whether this is expressed in legal, cultural, social, or political terms" (Molyneux 2005:68–69). Other social movement scholars, such as Mario Diani (2000:162), focus on the importance of "a shared collective identity" in defining a social movement. I would take from Molyneux the importance of a critical mass of women and their capacity to effect change in some way, and from Diani at least the sense among women that they are in fact part of a shared movement, even if their views and agendas are diverse.

In Russia, the only indication of "a social or political phenomenon" and "shared collective identity" among women's organizations is the interaction of informal networks in a sustained, albeit infrequent, manner. Self-identification as a member of a general women's movement is rare. In my interviews with Russian women activists over the years, those who used the term *movement* tended to employ it in reference to issue-specific mobilization (such as the movement against violence against women) or in reference to formal networks of women's organizations. For example, leaders in the large network of women's councils under the umbrella of the URW sometimes referred to their network as "our women's movement." Women in the political party Women of Russia also frequently referred to their network of local branches as a "movement," but in legal terms, their political party was a "political movement," so they probably used the term in its legal sense.

While some non-Russian scholars have deemed the configuration of women's activism to constitute a "women's movement," (Waters 1993; V. Sperling 1999; Henderson 1998), some Russian feminists have actively rejected the idea that a "women's movement" exists in Russia (Marianna Muravyeva in Sopronenko 2008). There is considerable justification for this assessment. The scale of women's activism in Russia, especially the small subset based on feminist ideas, is relatively small and lacks the kinds of sustained, mobilized networks of contention that exist in social movements.

Historically, most women activists in Russia have declined to call themselves feminists. For instance, in a directory of women's organizations produced in 1998, only 3 percent of surveyed organizations across Russia and the other countries of the former Soviet Union listed themselves as engaging in feminism (Abubikirova et al. 1998:15). There is no more recent survey, but as we will see below, in recent years there has been a brief surge in self-consciously feminist mobilization by Russian women—particularly young women who are new to activism generally and feminism in particular.

Women's organizations and networks among them newly flourished in the late Soviet and early transition period. The first real spike in creation of women's organizations began in 1990 when the state permitted independent organization. The peak in organizing came in 1994 (ibid.), encouraged by funding from foreign-aid agencies and private foundations for the development of civil society and gender equality in Russia. However, particularly since 2001, foreign donors' resources have shifted elsewhere, leaving Russian civil society groups, women's organizations included, with a huge vacuum in funding for their initiatives.

Overall, women's activism in Russia in the 1990s and early 2000s adopted a fairly moderate, even conciliatory outlook in terms of both feminist philosophical approaches and stances toward cooperation and dialogue with the Russian state (e.g., asserting that women have a special relationship to the environment or peace) (V. Sperling 1999:63). Radical feminism, in the sense of a feminist approach disavowing dialogue with a fundamentally patriarchal state, or consciously rejecting partnership with men, appeared only recently in the women's movement. Women activists in the post-Communist period through the early 2000s were generally willing to work with the state when it expressed interest in dialogue, but most shied away from attempting to influence state policies. Those who made the attempt rarely succeeded. The lack of interest in lobbying can largely be attributed to the widespread ineffectiveness of much of the post-Communist Russian state in the 1990s. But it also reflected an accurate perception that much political influence derives from male insider patron-client networks rather than open, transparent communication channels. Organizations providing services for women that could be conceived as welfare, such as shelters for women victims of violence, have joined forces with state agencies. Often those women's groups have found themselves wrestling with the more conservative orientation of state actors towards gender roles and family structures. We will see those dynamics play out in the section on violence against women.

In the past several years, the nature of activism has undergone remarkable changes, due in part to the possibilities afforded by new social media technologies. More explicitly and more radical feminist organizing has increased, particularly among young women. Around 2010, newer, unabashedly feminist groups began to organize in Russia in unprecedented ways. With no foreign funding (unlike their prede-cessors), several informal groups of women began to organize around their feminist views and observations, and in some cases even staged frequent public demonstrations to protest government policies or par-ticular events (Sperling 2015:245–251). Aside from their participation in anti-Putin opposition protests in 2011 and 2012, they organized small demonstrations on policies or events of particular concern to feminists, such as a draft law in 2011 that proposed significant restric-tions on access to abortion, which had been widely available in the So-viet Union (Sperling 2015:255–256; *Moscow Times* 2011). The feminist pro-choice demonstrations were emblematic of this period's mode of organizing: organizers largely recruited attendees through social net-working sites, such as the "Feministki" group on LiveJournal and the "For Free Motherhood" website (Za svobodnoe materinstvo n.d.). While many of these groups were dormant or dissolved by 2015, their emergence with an explicitly feminist and publicly active face con-trasted with the more intellectual focus of previous feminist leaders, suggesting a milestone in the evolution of feminist consciousness among Russian women.

No doubt, some of this new wave of underground mobilization has been inspired by the courageous public actions of the punk perfor-mance group Pussy Riot—especially by their uninvited February 2012 "punk prayer" performance in Moscow's Cathedral of Christ the Savior, which was highly critical of President Putin. There is considerable de-bate within Russia's feminist community about the extent to which Pussy Riot's work is truly feminist in nature, due to the images of vio-lence and domination often portrayed in their lyrics and performance art. But as Valerie Sperling points out, Pussy Riot "could fairly be char-acterized as the only group of self-proclaimed Russian feminists who generated widespread media attention" (Sperling 2015:224). And Pussy Riot members call themselves feminists and have been depicted as such in international media. In some sense, therefore, they have opened a way for women with feminist leanings to see a feminist iden-tity as a possibility.

Another group called Femen, founded in Ukraine but also active in Russia in recent years, specializes in public acts of protest using gen-der-stereotypical techniques that combine political dissent with some feminist ideas. Members of the group, typically young, tall, slim, and blonde, appear topless in public to protest on a range of issues, some clearly feminist (for example, protesting sex tourism in Ukraine) and others more generically political (criticizing the Putin government) (Zychowicz 2011). As with Pussy Riot, some feminist activists in Russia dispute the feminist label for Femen's actions since they "reinforced the notion that women's bodies were the main thing that women were capable of offering in the political marketplace" (Sperling 2015:241; Hrycak 2011:3). Femen's emphasis on stereotypical feminine beauty to express their demands, rather than employing feminist critique to challenge gendered ideals about women's appearance, can be linked to a widespread post-Soviet phenomenon of enthusiasm for feminine cosmetics and fashionable clothing as a reaction to previous Soviet-era shortages of such products (Jurna 1995:481; Drakulic 1993:21-30; Sperling 1999:68).

In the case of Pussy Riot, Russian citizens were not terribly sympathetic after their arrest for the cathedral performance (Adomanis 2015). A Levada Center poll in July 2012 showed that only 5 percent of respondents thought they deserved no punishment for their "punk prayer" act, while the vast majority felt they should be punished with anything ranging from a large fine, to mandatory labor, to imprisonment from a few months to more than two years ("Rossiane O Dele Pussy Riot [Russians on the Pussy Riot Case]" 2012). This widespread disapproval of Pussy Riot's protest actions is indicative of most Russian citizens' negative views of not only radical feminism but all forms of radical political dissidence.

LGBT Activism

Lesbian organizing historically has been only a tiny part of women's movement mobilization in Russia. Lesbian activism has been slow to develop in Russia, partially due to the fact that Soviet law and propaganda ignored the existence of lesbianism, and therefore lesbian experience remained largely absent from any public discussion until the perestroika period (Temkina and Rotkirkh 2002:11). Unlike male homosexuality, lesbianism was not prohibited by law, but during most of the Soviet period lesbian women were punished with forcible psychiatric treatment (Gessen 1994:17). A few lesbian and gay organizations, such as *Gei Laboratoriia* (Gay Laboratory), existed despite extreme KGB repression in the 1980s. The situation changed at the turn of the decade, when the Moscow Association of Sexual Minorities was founded with Libertarian Party leader Evgeniia Debrianskaia as its head, and, in Laurie Essig's words, "queer activism in Russia found its voice" (Essig 1999:58). In the early 1990s other organizations, such as the Moscow Association of MOLLI (Moscow Organization of Lesbian Literature and Art) and the umbrella association *Treugol'nik* (Triangle) were formed, but were soon riddled with internal battles and fell apart (Essig 1999:62–66).

In the ensuing years, LGBT social and cultural spaces began to flourish in major cities (Stella 2014). However, mobilization for civic and political rights did not immediately follow. Even within this muted context, lesbian voices have certainly been less audible than male ones. "If shouts of queer subjectivity have barely been heard above that din that is post-Soviet Russia," writes Essig, "then queer women's voices have never been louder than a whisper" (Essig 1999:92-93).

Although legal by the 1990s and early 2000s, organizing publicly based on homosexual identity still requires extreme courage in Russia, as homophobic attitudes are deep and widespread (Essig 1999; Sperling 2015:chap. 5). This has led to an LGBT movement in which the majority of organizations focus on advocating for "tolerance" of LGBT people, rather than making more radical claims for equal legal rights (Kondakov 2013). Yet a major political backlash has followed even the growing social visibility of LGBT identities (Stella 2014:40). This backlash began with local anti-homosexual policies, signaling that the state would tolerate rampant and even violent homophobic behavior. The City of Moscow banned gay rights parades in 2011, and a number of regions banned "gay propaganda" in 2011 and 2012. In 2013 the State Duma, the more powerful lower house in the national legislature, brought this trend to a peak by passing a national law against "gay propaganda." This law bans the spreading of "propaganda of non-traditional sexual relations" among minors, and outlaws distribution of material on gay rights (Elder 2013).

Still, activism by LGBT groups has become more visible in recent years, both prior to—and counter-intuitively, after—passage of the propaganda law. Some alliances have also formed between feminist and lesbian initiatives. Sperling notes that the feminist activists she interviewed in 2012 all protested jointly with LGBT groups at various times, and that, in contrast to most civil society groups involved in opposition politics in Russia, feminist groups actively rejected homophobic views (Sperling 2015:204). Most civil society organizations, including many human rights groups, have remained silent on the topic of LGBT rights. Encouragingly, however, some mainstream Russian and international human rights organizations have recently taken up the cause of LGBT groups' rights to free expression as well as pursuing cases of homophobic hate crimes (Sundstrom and Sperling 2014:15-16). This is a surprising development; Russian human rights organizations have *not* generally had friendly or collaborative relationships with women's organizations (Sundstrom 2006).

We turn now to some specific areas in which women, whether avowed feminists or not, have mobilized to improve the status of Russian women. Three particular areas of concern are violence against women, women's economic inequality, and women's political representation. Mobilization on these issues has brought varying degrees of success, whether in attracting supporters or in winning actual improvements in women's equality.

Violence Against Women

During the Soviet period, domestic violence was not a frame of reference for state understandings of crime, nor for academic research, never mind in public discourse. Official policy dismissed the idea that widespread patterns of violence against individuals could exist in Soviet society (Zabelina 2002:6). The Soviet state concealed crime statistics, including on domestic violence (Stickley, Timofeeva, and Spären 2008:483). Crimes occurring within families were not addressed by the Soviet state until the perestroika era, and no analysis tried to quantify family violence until the early 1980s (Gondolf and Shestakov 1997:65).

Statistics regarding the frequency of intimate partner violence are still unclear. While rape is categorized as a specific crime under Russian law, domestic violence is not. We do know that in 2013, Russian courts issued 4,720 convictions for the crimes of rape and sexual assault under Articles 131 and 132 of the Criminal Code (Supreme Court of the Russian Federation 2014). According to the director of the Sisters' (Syostri) Rape Crisis Center in Moscow, and in keeping with rape reporting patterns in other countries, there is significant underreporting of rape to the police; only 10–12 percent of the rape victims who turn to Syostri choose to bring their cases to the attention of law enforcement (Mokhova 2014).

rape → domestic violence

A few small-scale surveys give a sense of the scale of domestic violence, although numbers may be inaccurate. One survey of one thousand women in Moscow in the 1990s showed a quarter of respondents having experienced physical abuse in their relationships; another survey of 3,900 women in the smaller regional cities of Novgorod, Perm, and Berezniki in 2000 found that 15 percent of women suffered from intimate partner violence (Stickley, Timofeeva, and Spären 2008:484). That violence is often lethal. The Ministry of Internal Affairs in 2008 estimated that 65 percent of all Russian homicides are related to domestic violence (Gentleman 2015). One frequently cited figure that has circulated since the mid-1990s and that was reported by officials in the Russian Ministry of Internal Affairs in 2008 is that approximately fourteen thousand women perish in Russia each year as a result of domestic violence (ANNA, 2010, 6, ft. 7). However, this figure is certainly inflated. In 2009, only 15,954 homicides *in total* occurred in Russia. By a process of extrapolation, given statistics on the percentage of women homicide victims in Russia, and typical worldwide estimates of female homicide victims who are killed by their partners, one can arrive at a likely figure closer to approximately 1,500 women per year killed in Russia by their partners—about one-tenth of the usual figure claimed (Sundstrom and Sperling 2014:6). Yet even this number is high relative to many Western countries: one cross-national study in the 1990s indicated that Russian women may be two and a half times more likely to be killed by their partners than American women (Gondolf and Shestakov 1997:70).

The deck is stacked against victims. They must contend with a widespread belief among law enforcement officials and the general public that victims are responsible for provoking the violence against them (Johnson 2009:28; Sinelnikov 1998; Attwood 1997:99; Human Rights Watch 1997). Police and state prosecutors are often unwilling to take on cases of violence against women because their performance incentives are primarily based on their "clearance rate" (the percentage of investigations that successfully proceed to the next stage) and speed of clearing prosecutions. This motivates them to prefer simple cases that arise from police-initiated investigations rather than from citizen complaints (Paneyakh 2013:126), and they never wish to see a case ending in acquittal or with a victim retracting an accusation (McCarthy 2015:113-119). The incentives work against accepting cases in which women file complaints about assaults by strangers or about violence without witnesses in complex long-term relationships.

Yet as a small movement against gender-based violence did begin to grow in Russia, the problem began to emerge from the shadows of discussion, and public awareness rose. Transnational links were crucial for the developing antiviolence movement, particularly in the early years, when the first crisis centers were set up. In the early 1990s several American feminists were involved in the founding of Syostri (Sisters), while a Swedish crisis center and the US-based Family Violence Prevention Fund mentored Marina Pisklakova-Parker, the founder of ANNA (the acronym for the "No to Violence" Association) (Chernenkaia 1999; Potapova 1999). Almost a decade later, other Western feminists, including a lawyer working at the American Bar Association's Central and East European Legal Initiative, continued to provide advice to antiviolence activists. Many of the slogans and methods used by women's crisis center NGOs are adopted from Western feminist crisis centers (Sundstrom 2006).

The first crisis centers in Russia were founded in Moscow and St. Petersburg between 1993 and 1995. The first three centers were ANNA and Syostri in Moscow (the former focusing mostly on domestic violence and the latter on sexual assault), and the St. Petersburg Crisis Center, which began unofficially in 1991 and was formally registered in 1994 (Johnson 2009:49). All three primarily offered a telephone hotline and in-person counseling and, usually with financial support from Western donors, began to spread this model across Russia. Most of the resulting crisis centers provided telephone hotlines for victims of sexual and domestic violence as the mainstay of their activity. Many also offered face-to-face counseling sessions. This particular model of crisis counseling was inexpensive and therefore well suited to the meager resources of 1990s Russia, compared to the investment required to open overnight shelters for women trying to escape violence (ibid.:52).

A national organization linking crisis centers for women, called the Russian Association of Crisis Centers for Women (RACCW), was formed in the 1990s, launched through a project funded by the US Agency for International Development and implemented by IREX (the International Research and Exchanges Board, a US-based nongovernmental organization).[1] The RACCW was officially registered in 1999 and by 2002 had formed a network of forty organizations in cities across the country (Johnson 2009:55). According to the RACCW, in the year 2001 more than 65,000 women turned to their member centers for help in instances of domestic violence and sexual violence (Zabelina

2002:8). The total number of crisis centers operating across Russia in 2004 was estimated at approximately two hundred (Johnson 2009:43). This is an astounding accomplishment over a period of barely more than a decade of activism on the issue of violence against women.

Many of these organizations are also active in public education campaigns and political advocacy work, seeking to influence the practices and views of social workers, doctors, police, lawyers, and judges who deal with victims of violence. They battle stereotypes, often with posters that mimic the startling images and slogans of anti-domestic violence organizations in the United States. Since very few lawyers are knowledgeable about how to approach domestic violence cases, ANNA has recently launched a program to train lawyers from all over the Russian-speaking former USSR to prosecute such cases (Pisklakova-Parker 2014).

A few of the key organizations, such as ANNA and Syostri, have become involved in public policy lobbying, contributing their expertise for the drafting of legislation. In the early 2000s, some activists participated in a working group within the State Duma Legislation Committee to draft legislation to prevent trafficking of women (Schatral 2007:50). They had lobbied repeatedly since 1995 to have several bills on domestic violence introduced in the State Duma, and provided input on the draft legislation to the legislative working group (Gondolf and Shestakov 1997:66). None of those earlier bills passed into law. Curiously, as the government overall has become more authoritarian in nature during President Putin's era, domestic violence legislation desired by activists has come closer to fruition. In 2011, a more promising process began, when a working group began a new attempt to draft a viable law on domestic violence. By 2014, a draft law had been written, largely by two lawyers collaborating with ANNA, and had received extensive commentary from Russian judicial and law enforcement agencies, as well as high-level support within the Russian government (Pisklakova-Parker 2014). Eventually, on July 3, 2016, President Putin signed a version of the draft legislation into law as part of a package of amendments to Russia's overall Criminal Code (Government of the Russian Federation 2016). The most important improvement for women included in these amendments was the inclusion of domestic violence (or "battery of close relatives") into the list of crimes that public prosecutors and investigators must pursue once they are reported—a change from the previous situation in which Russian law required a victim to build a case herself, through private prosecution procedures (Davtian 2016).

The movement combating violence against women has scored some important successes in changing the attitudes of law enforcement officials, judges, medical professionals, and other government officials and professionals who interact with victims of violence. A major indication of the movement's persuasiveness has been the increasing involvement of regional and municipal governments in either founding their own crisis centers or materially supporting or even absorbing formerly nongovernmental crisis centers. This development carries both advantages and drawbacks. One positive element is that state funding is usually more reliable than short-term funding from Western donors. And only state crisis centers have sufficient reliable resources to maintain overnight shelters where victims of domestic violence can safely stay while rebuilding their lives. But state funding too is subject to the whims of individual local politicians and bureaucrats. And state crisis centers typically have a much more family-centered, less feminist outlook on the problem of violence (Jäppinen 2008; Johnson 2009:57). A small pilot survey of Russian crisis centers for women found that only a minority of centers considered feminism important to their work, but NGO-based crisis centers were far more likely than state-run crisis centers to embrace feminism. A few NGO-based centers even considered themselves "feminist organizations" (Johnson 2008:10). Thus, operation as a state institution in Russia does seem to deradicalize crisis centers and limit their effect on gendered power relations in society.

Despite the mobilizational victories of the movement, in the past decade, as foreign donors have shifted resources to other causes and other regions of the world, many of the NGO-based crisis centers in Russia have faced their own crisis of resources. Reports cited by Johnson found only nineteen nongovernmental women's crisis centers remaining by 2007, while 40 percent of crisis centers could not afford to pay any staff and an additional 50 percent could not pay a decent living wage and therefore experienced high turnover of qualified staff (Johnson 2009:67).

This funding crisis hit RACCW hard. After criticism of its organizational structure from USAID, it lost that funding stream. By 2008, with no substantial funding, the association had lost its office space and no longer had any grants from donors to support building a crisis center network and conducting training for crisis center professionals. Eventually, the association dissolved and was replaced by a more modest "network" of crisis centers that included state-funded shelters for victims of violence as well as nongovernmental actors (Pisklakova-Parker 2014). ANNA now coordinates the Russian members (they report over one hundred organizations associated) of a broader pan-European network called Women Against Violence Europe (WAVE), who now focus on sharing knowledge and strategies among professionals working with victims of violence. ANNA itself has survived, with funders including UN Women, the Council of Europe, the EU Delegation in Russia, and Women Against Violence Europe.

As a result of the departure of previous Western donors, Syostri found itself on the verge of financial collapse in December 2014, owing back payments for rent and utilities (Kolotilov 2015). Eventually help came from the liberal Yabloko political party, which sponsored an online petition for help. The petition was signed by an impressive 45,000 supporters in two months; eventually a Russian charitable foundation called "Nuzhna Pomoshch" (Help Needed) that collects online donations contacted Syostri and placed the center's donation request on its site. This rescued the center for the time being, but they remain financially insecure (Kolotilov 2015).

Crisis centers have continued to struggle with contradictions between the restrictions on gender-based approaches to violence that state affiliation often imposes, and the perpetual instability of funding that reliance on foreign donors entails. However, with the development of a network that includes Russian state and non-state organizations as well as international connections, there is hope that feminist perspectives on violence can take hold in Russian society and that this change in social norms will help to foster a more stable resource base.

Women's Economic Inequality

Women's economic inequality in Russia occurs in multiple arenas: hiring discrimination, occupational segregation, and a significant gender wage gap. All have their roots in entrenched societal views about distinct "men's jobs" and "women's jobs." As in the post-Communist world more generally, economic inequalities between the sexes have increased with the expansion of the market economy (Johnson and Robinson 2007:6). According to Marina Baskakova, while Russian women's wages in the 1980s and early 1990s were 60 to 70 percent of men's (largely due to occupational segregation), by 1999 they were only 56 percent of men's (Baskakova 2000:63). A detailed analysis of national employment survey data for 2003 showed that, after all reasonable explanations for salary differences between men and women (such as skills differences and sectoral employment variations) had been accounted for, approximately 15 to 18 percent of men's wage advantage over women remained unexplained, and therefore could be attributed to gender-based discrimination alone (Oshchepkov, A. Iu. 2006).

There is widespread and open sex discrimination in hiring. Elena Gerasimova found in research conducted in 2009 that 27 percent of job ads specify the sex of desired applicants (and often the desired age limit as well) (Gerasimova 2010:15). According to reports by Russian women on social media sites as late as 2015 (zzzzuka 2015), this practice is still widespread, despite amendments to the Russian federal Law on Employment of Russian Federation Citizens (Article 25(b)) in 2013 that specifically prohibit such discriminatory language in employment postings (Rossiiskaia gazeta 2013). On job applications and in interviews women are frequently asked whether they have children, and what age the children are; men are not (Gerasimova 2010:15). Women with young children or who are planning to have children in the future encounter significant problems finding a job. It is practically impossible for a pregnant woman to get hired into a new job, although it is illegal to refuse to hire a woman for that reason (Gerasimova 2010).

Despite widespread gender stereotypes, Russian women do have one advantage in the labor market: Russian society generally views women's labor participation as a desirable and normal phenomenon, thanks to the Soviet-era practices encouraging women's full-time work outside the home. However, norms undermining women's role in the paid labor force began to emerge during the 1990s economic reforms. Public opinion surveys also show that many Russians accept such ideas. For example, the massive World Values Survey found in 2011 that 28.3 percent of Russian respondents agreed that: "When jobs are scarce, men should have more right to a job than women." In contrast, only 2.0 percent of Swedish respondents, 5.7 percent of US respondents, and 12.0 percent of Spanish respondents agreed (World Values Survey 2011). Russian views on this question are similar to those of many Eastern Europeans citizens: in Poland and Ukraine, agreement with the statement was also in the high-20 percent range.

Russian women know that they face discrimination in competition with men on the labor market, but mobilization on the issue has been slow in coming. Women's organizations at first lobbied at very formal levels for changes in legislation concerning employment equality. Lobbying has produced some legislative victories affecting women's economic status. The Consortium of Women's Nongovernmental Organizations claimed that Russian pension legislation was amended as a direct result of its lobbying efforts. The amendment allowed women's years of maternity leave to be included in their accumulation of employment years contributing to their state pension levels (Ershova 1998). The Consortium also argued that it was influential in amending two clauses of the draft Russian Labor Code. One clause concerned women's labor in heavy or dangerous forms of work (women's organizations argued for specifying a narrow list of jobs rather than generally banning women from dangerous labor). The other concerned employment protection for pregnant women and mothers with children under one and a half years of age (Sundstrom 2006:87; Levina 2001). Indeed, these amendments survived an extremely contentious and drawn-out debate period of nearly two years over the content of the new Russian Labor Code. Vigorous battles between Russian trade unions and employer groups resulted in modification of many aspects of the code, which was finally adopted only in December 2001 (Levina 2001).

More recently, attention has turned to addressing individual women employees' grievances and consciousness-raising campaigns about the injustice of employment discrimination. The organizations "Egida" in St. Petersburg and the Center for Social Labor Rights in Moscow (Tsentr Sotsial'no-Trudovykh Prav) have begun to litigate in domestic and international courts as well as to lobby government officials to prevent and obtain remedy for cases of labor discrimination (St. Petersburg Egida n.d.; Tsentr sotsial'no-trudovykh prav n.d.). In an encouraging move towards more grassroots mobilization, during the financial crisis of 2008–2010, these groups also helped to support a movement of mothers protesting employers' failure to pay out government-provided parental leave benefits to employees on leave (Center for Social and Labor Rights et al. 2013:19). Eventually, at the end of 2012, their joint advocacy efforts resulted in an amendment to federal law on benefits payments, to allow employees to obtain their parental benefits directly from the state Social Insurance Fund, and later this provision was extended to employees in the event of an employer's "disappearance" or lack of funds (Center for Social and Labor Rights et al. 2013:8-9; Tsentr sotsial'no-trudovykh prav 2011)._

This more activist and public orientation is an encouraging development, as through the 1990s and early 2000s, feminist activism had generally been confined to seminars with politicians and bureaucrats or to writing "gender expertise" reports on the implications of government legislation and welfare policies (Sundstrom 2006:88; 2005:436–437). It is possible that the shift toward activism built from widespread protests against wage and benefit losses by many social groups, which began in the mid-2000s and deepened in the wake of the 2008 global financial crisis that hit the Russian economy extremely hard (see Evans 2012:236-238).

Women's Political Representation

Women in post-Communist Russia have generally lost representation in political institutions compared to the Soviet period, when quotas for women existed at various legislative levels. In the Soviet system, generally one-third of the USSR Supreme Soviet and Congress of People's Deputy seats were reserved for women. Once quotas were removed when multiparty democratic elections were introduced, women's parliamentary representation fell to single-digit lows in several countries in the region—Russia included—with Ukraine having the lowest women's representation at 3 percent in 1990 (Kostadinova 2007:425). This pattern, shared across the post-Communist states of Eastern Europe and the former Soviet Union, underscores the well-known impact of gender quotas on improving levels of women's descriptive representation in legislative assemblies (Kostadinova 2007:425).

Even in the Soviet era, however, the more powerful the party or state institution, the less present were women. In the Central Committee of the Communist Party, fewer than 5 percent of deputies were women (V. Sperling 1999:116), while only a handful of women were ever appointed to the Politburo, the most powerful decision-making body of the Communist Party of the Soviet Union (Noonan and Nechemias 2001:184). The low level of female representation at the executive level continues today. At the time of writing, there have only been three female regional governors in post-Soviet Russia: Natalia Komarova in the small ethnic republic of Khanty-Mansiisk, Marina Kovtun of Murmansk oblast, and Valentina Matvienko, governor of St. Petersburg (Mikhaleva 2010:63).

Matvienko has since moved on to holding the chair of Russia's (fairly weak) upper house of Parliament, the Federation Council. As of 2013, there is a female head of the Russian Central Bank, Elvira Nabiullina, a former minister of economic development; this is an impressive development as Ms. Nabiullina was the first woman ever to head a Group of Eight country's central bank (and the only one until Janet Yellen became head of the United States Federal Reserve) (Kiryukhina 2013; Tsang 2013). Only three of thirty-one federal cabinet members at the time of writing are female: the ministers of health and education and the deputy prime minister for social affairs, two traditionally female cabinet portfolios in Russia and in many other countries due to their "caring" responsibilities often associated with women. The number of women in the cabinet has rarely risen higher than that in post-Soviet Russia.

An early high point of women's parliamentary representation in the post-Communist period was in the 1993 elections to the lower house of the national parliament, the State Duma. Three major women's organizations (the Union of Russian Women, the Association of Russian Businesswomen, and the Union of Women of the Naval Fleet) collaborated in 1993 to form a women's party called Women of Russia (WOR). The leaders of the organization were Alevtina Fedulova of the Union of Russian Women and Ekaterina Lakhova, adviser to the Russian president on family, mothers, and children. While the party advocated many social policies that would benefit women and children, promoted efforts to combat severe human rights violations against women such as the sex trade and sexual harassment, and campaigned for women's and children's rights, its candidates' relationship with feminism was an uneasy one, as they often advocated policies that reinforced women's traditional roles as mothers and caregivers (Nechemias 2000:211–212).

In their inaugural electoral participation during the Russian Duma elections of 1993, WOR attained a surprising high-water mark of 8 percent of the popular vote, resulting in twenty-three seats in the Duma, which at that time had a mixed electoral system with half of the seats elected by proportional representation (PR) and half by plurality in single-member districts. Then, in the parliamentary elections only two years later, WOR fell just short of the 5 percent vote threshold necessary to win PR seats in the Duma (Schevchenko 2002:1201). In the years that followed, the WOR leaders Fedulova and Lakhova parted ways, and Lakhova joined the Otechestvo party, which eventually merged into the pro-Kremlin United Russia party. In 1999, WOR attained barely over 2 percent of the national vote, and faded into obscurity, failing to mount campaigns in any subsequent elections.

The overall number of women in the Duma paralleled the trend in votes for WOR while it was a political force. Most other political parties include very small minorities of women among their candidates and have tended to place women near the bottom of party lists ranking candidates for PR seats, as there are no laws mandating gender quotas on the lists, and no parties have adopted such policies on their own. For example, in the 2003 elections, Ekaterina Lakhova, who had by that point migrated to the dominant United Russia Party, was the top-ranked woman on the party's candidate list—at position number 20 (Arkhiv politicheskoi reklamy n.d.). Lakhova retained her seat due to United Russia's strong share of votes (38 percent) and has since been appointed a senator in Russia's unelected upper legislative chamber, the Council of the Federation. But in general, women have tended to lose out when votes translate into seats.

Women won only sixty seats (13 percent) in the Duma in 1993, and their numbers declined steadily over subsequent elections until, surprisingly, in the December 2007 elections, a record sixty-four women (14 percent) were elected. In the 2011 election, the number fell to sixty-one (Inter-Parliamentary Union 2015). This remains a poor result for elected female representatives by world standards: Russia falls in one-hundredth place among 190 countries monitored by the Inter-Parliamentary Union (Inter-Parliamentary Union 2015; Kiryukhina 2013). Even the modest improvement in 2007 seems to have resulted from a combination of temporary electoral system reforms that were reversed for the 2016 election: a shift to purely proportional representation from party lists, eliminating the 50 percent of seats that were previously single mandate; and a 2007 amendment to increase the minimum-vote threshold for parties to win Duma seats from 5 percent to 7 percent. With regard to the first change, as generally observed in electoral systems worldwide, more women tend to be elected under proportional representation systems than first-past-the-post systems (Kostadinova 2007:416). With regard to the second change, as President Putin had intended, raising the vote threshold for parties to obtain seats reduced the number of parties elected to the Duma (only four parties succeeded in 2011), and thus each of the parties crossing the threshold was able to elect candidates farther down its list. Hence, even though they still placed lower on the party lists, more women were elected. This is a surprising side effect of the increased minimum-vote threshold, which is otherwise seen as harming democratic representation in Russian politics.

The proportion of women candidates is still dishearteningly low. In 1993 only 7 percent of Duma party-list candidates were female, while by 2007 the proportion had increased to 17 percent (Aivazova 2000; Russia Profile n.d.; "Predvybornye spiski partii" n.d.). By the 2011 Duma elections it was difficult to locate information on the total percentage of female candidates on all party lists, but a calculation from the list of candidates for United Russia—by far the dominant party, with 53 percent of the Duma seats—revealed that the percentage of female candidates remained roughly the same at 18 percent (Central Electoral Commission of the Russian Federation 2011).

Some women's organizations with a keen interest in formal politics have allied with political parties during election campaigns, but this has been rare. As Suvi Salmenniemi (2003) has remarked, "Elections do not seem to attract much attention in the Russian women's movement." While WOR held Duma seats, women's NGOs had fairly friendly and mutually responsive relationships with WOR Duma deputies, and women activists obtained greater access to Duma committee discussions and drafts of legislation. Yet the alliance was never formal. Feminist women's NGOs did not actively campaign for WOR, most likely because many feminist activists viewed WOR as too much a part of the political establishment and not sufficiently feminist in orientation (V. Sperling 1999:127–128). Women's NGOs have advocated for minimum quotas for women's representation in the Duma, or for female candidates in political parties, but their efforts have not borne success. There have been several attempts to lobby for seat quotas over the years, including Ekaterina Lakhova's sponsorship of a proposal for a 30 percent women's quota, for inclusion within the draft law that created the 2005 electoral system. The Duma rejected the quota proposal, after a debate accompanied by some politicians' statements discounting women as serious political figures (Abdullaev 2005). During the 2000, 2004, and 2008 presidential election campaigns, the Russian Consortium of Women's Nongovernmental Organizations repeatedly appealed to presidential candidates to endorse a proposal to ban any party with more than 70% of a single gender of candidates in its ranks from participating in elections. Most candidates responded negatively, a few lukewarmly or vaguely positively, but none provided a firm commitment to work towards such a legal change if elected (Aivazova 2008:72-81).

Of course, it must be noted that since 2007, with only Kremlin-loyal parties in the State Duma[2] and with higher barriers to mobilization by opposition parties, it is unclear whether participation in formal national politics is worthwhile for women who wish to challenge existing laws or the ever more socially conservative agenda of the Putin government.

Transnational Linkages of Russian Women Activists

Connections with transnational actors have been extremely important for Russia's self-proclaimed feminist activists. They have developed links with global feminist networks for the purposes of solidarity, support, and strategic development. The influence of those ties is palpable. In the area of violence against women, for example, many of the terms used in Russia have been translated directly into Russian from English (for example, "violence against women," "domestic violence," "violence in the family") (Johnson 2007:44). The term "gender" itself is transliterated letter for letter from English into Russian, with a hard "g" sound. But probably the most influential transnational connection that Russian women activists have established is with Western funding organizations. These linkages have been sources of strength in some respects and of weakness in others.

Activists' linkages with Western donor organizations as explored in the discussion of violence against women reveal some general patterns in transnational funding for Russian women's activism. Funding from Western (especially American) donors in the mid to late 1990s was crucial to the crisis center movement and the progress that activists were able to make in combating violence against women. However, these relationships with Western donors have also been undependable and have sometimes diverted women's organizations from their core missions. Donors provided substantial support in the mid to late 1990s for women's activism against violence, and in particular for fighting domestic violence. But by the early 2000s, their enthusiasm (at least among the largest American donors) had begun to shift towards initiatives to combat trafficking of women. This led some crisis centers to reorient part of their programmatic focus into antitrafficking, not because of genuine interest in the issue, but rather in order to sustain themselves financially.

Transnational linkages—through both funding and networking— have also been widely criticized for their tendency to strengthen the elitist nature of the Russian feminist movement. Leaders of women's

NGOs who speak English fluently have been particularly privileged in their relationships with Western donors and the global feminist movement (Sundstrom 2003:150; Richter 2002:37). Indeed, an unpublished article by Natalia Abubikirova and Marina Regentova in the 1990s argues that the English language is used as a "means of power and control" and "a convertible currency" in the Russian women's movement (Richter 2002:37). This privileging of English-language abilities has helped to create new hierarchies and reinforce some already existing in Russian society. Highly educated members of the intelligentsia (who are more likely to take a feminist stance toward issues affecting women) are more likely to speak English than women with less education and income, while women in major cities are also more likely to possess a good command of English than women in rural areas. More recently, and building on those initial hierarchies, those who have been trained in the West or already worked with Western organizations have a considerable advantage over those without such privileged backgrounds.

It is difficult to gauge the impact that Western funding has had on the degree of radicalism in women's groups' agendas. Certainly, Western funding accelerated the professionalization and formalization of women's organizations' activities—a process that is widely noted in the literature as typical of social movement organizations over time. There is significant debate in feminist literature concerning how positive or negative this kind of institutionalization is—positive in the sense that the longest-lasting organizations and movements tend to be highly institutionalized, but negative in that they tend to lose a degree of radicalism in their demands and are forced to create hierarchical decision-making structures (Ferree and Yancey 1995:474). Some Russian feminist activists have lamented that Western donors have forced them to formalize their organizations and create strict hierarchies in their governance procedures in order to be eligible for grant funding. This erodes feminist models of decision making, which aim for egalitarianism and consensus building (Ferree and Yancey 1995:474). One could argue that *perhaps* the Russian women's movement would have been more vocal or radical in its public claims in the absence of Western funding; the more radical stance of young feminists in subsequent years, without the intervention of such funding, further points to this possibility. Yet in my interview research on women's organizations across seven Russian cities in the late 1990s, I found that the few organizations that had engaged in demonstrations were nearly all funded by

Western donors (and most were women's crisis center activists) (Sundstrom 2001:188–193). Western funding may well have allowed these organizations to feel sufficient financial autonomy from the Russian state to protest in public. In short, in the Russian case, with a still weak culture of charitable giving outside the state, groups are likely to be caught in a choice between the Scylla of Western donors and the Charybdis of state funding if they are to receive any funding at all. Both of those options tend to discourage radical viewpoints or tactics. It is only the loosely organized, purely voluntary feminist initiatives that vocally promoted radical social change to achieve feminist goals.

Foreign funding of Russian women's NGOs institutionalized recipient organizations in some ways, but only temporarily. The NGOs secured initial funding through which they could begin to function on a full-time, professional basis, and by which they could begin to construct networks with other women's organizations. Yet in other ways foreign funding has profoundly harmed institutionalization. It has deterred NGOs from locating other domestic mechanisms for resource mobilization (such as domestic philanthropists, individual volunteers, or donations), so that when foreign donors began to withdraw support for feminist organizations in Russia, the organizations found themselves at a loss to locate other resource bases. Now, with Russian legislation hindering Western donors' ability to operate in the country, as well as the "foreign agents" law in force since 2012, funding from outside the country is exceedingly difficult to secure (International Center for Not-for-Profit Law 2015; RFE/RL 2015). The foreign agents law requires any NGOs that engage in (vaguely defined and broadly interpreted) political activities and receive funding from foreign organizations to declare themselves publicly in all their materials to be "foreign agents," or face fines and eventual dissolution (Russia Beyond the Headlines n.d.).

Conclusion

Women's organizing in Russia—particularly feminist women's organizing—faces serious obstacles for the foreseeable future. While some obstacles are specific to women's organizations, such as societal hostility to feminist ideals, many are equally troublesome for other social movements in Russian civil society today. Regardless of the kind of movement, independent activists in Russia face serious resource-mobilization challenges, including having to choose between a meager and unreliable existence as an NGO with ever more constrained foreign funding, or a more stable existence as a state-supported organization dependent on government approval. Increasingly draconian laws limiting NGOs' criticism of the government, and regular legal crackdowns on those that are critical, are forcing activists to minimize their public visibility and thus to become less active.

The trajectory of the women's crisis center movement illustrates many aspects of the challenges facing Russian women's mobilization in general. An initial blossoming of organizations in the 1990s, many supported by Western donors, ended when foreign donors moved programs elsewhere in the world or to different issues in Russian society. What seemed at one point to be a growing women's movement has stalled in recent years, leading many feminists to look for sustainable careers outside the activist realm. In a country where individual charitable donations are extremely rare and political participation by citizens is extraordinarily low—never mind the general hostility to feminism— in the medium-term the prospects for the growth of a mass-supported women's movement are exceedingly slim.

Yet some activists continue heroically in their missions and do manage to attain small victories through sheer persistence. Gender studies programs, which did not exist until the 1990s, are now flourishing in many universities around Russia, inspiring a new generation of feminists. And in recent years, small bands of young feminists have shown admirable courage in their willingness to protest sexism and discrimination publicly. Perhaps this is where hope lies: in the gradual emergence of activists and the changing of societal norms on an incremental basis.

Notes

1. The association is now officially called the "Let's End Violence" Association of Crisis Centers for Assistance to Women Victims of Violence (Assotsiatsiia krizisnykh tsentrov pomoshchi zhenshchinam, perezhivshim nasilie "ostanovim nasilie").

2. The parties with seats in both the 2011 and 2016 Dumas are United Russia (Putin's party), the Communist Party, A Just Russia, and the Liberal Democratic Party of Russia. They are all nearly entirely loyal to the Putin government's policies.

Women's and Feminist Movements in the United States

The Contradictory Effects of Class-based Success

BENITA ROTH

Introduction: US Feminisms of the Past Fifty Years

Women's and feminist movements in the United States present a set of puzzles. Why does a country that gives so much room to women's and feminist organizing in the civil society sector do so poorly when it comes to international markers of women's successful integration into the public sphere? Why have reproductive rights been under attack since the day they were "won" through the Supreme Court's *Roe v. Wade* decision in 1973? Why are paid family leave and other care-oriented policies—which could make easier the lives of working women all along the class spectrum—so glaringly absent on the national level? Why do wage gaps and promotion gaps still plague those working women? Why have institutional responses to rape, child sexual assault, and domestic violence seemingly stalled?

In the following essay, I first consider several of the ways in which US feminist efforts, which held so much promise in the last half of the twentieth century, and which did accomplish so much to change women's lives, have seemingly stalled. I will begin with several areas where the stall in progress is quite evident. I next turn to the contemporary scene, where feminist ideas seem to be at once "everywhere and nowhere" (Reger 2012) in US political culture. I then consider how US "second wave" feminist organizing was split into different organizationally distinct movements, and how liberal feminism, with its class-based feminist "associationalism" (Katzenstein 2003) became ascendant, leaving behind the issues of women on the lower rungs of the economic ladder.[1] I then argue that feminist organizing had important spillover effects (Meyer and Whittier 1994), sparking other social movements, especially but not limited to the movement for LGBT (lesbian, gay, bisexual, and transgender) rights. US feminist organizations today are best characterized by a commitment to intersectionality (Crenshaw 1995) and coalitional work. I show an example of how intersectional feminist ideas have been incorporated into the DNA of recent social movements like Black Lives Matter. Before turning to my conclusion, I consider how US feminist organizations have turned some attention to transnational feminist issues, despite a seeming lack of interest on the part of the American public about the transnational. I conclude that US feminisms' ability to transcend the stall in feminist policy progress will depend on the continuing but intensified commitment to a broadly based intersectional politics, especially one that tackles economic burdens still faced by American women.

Gains and Stalls in US Feminist Organizing

The second wave of US feminist protest—the upsurge in organizing during the 1960s and 1970s—generated both institutionalized feminism and grassroots feminist responses to local and national problems. Thousands of feminist groups and institutions across the country still act as the "tangible evidence of the movement in many feminists' lives and in the social and political life of the nation" (Ferree and Martin 1995:4). The National Organization for Women (NOW), the largest of the umbrella feminist organizations that came out of the second wave 1960s, today claims half a million contributing members and 500 chapters and campus affiliates ("FAQs | National Organization For Women" 2016). But even as former First Lady, Senator, and Secretary of State Hillary Clinton vies for the presidency, the US has yet to reach the global goal of having women make up 30 percent of its national legislature (Sengupta 2015). The US Senate still has not ratified the UN

Convention on the Elimination of All Forms of Discrimination against Women (CEDAW), thirty-five years after President Carter signed this international women's bill of rights ("UNTC" 2016).

As for reproductive rights, although the fundamental right to abortion in the first trimester of pregnancy established by *Roe v. Wade* has been preserved to date, in practice, safe and legal abortion has become more and more difficult to obtain. Some 89 percent of US counties have no abortion clinic—which limits the availability of abortion for almost 40 percent of women living in the US ("United States" 2016). Since 1977, when the so-called Hyde Amendment forbade the use of federal funding for abortions save in cases of rape or risk of death—a law upheld by the Supreme Court a few years later in *Harris v. McRae*—poor women in the US have had few options when it came to obtaining a low-cost, safe abortion (Davis 2008). The restrictions on the poor's access to abortion have emboldened state legislatures to pass law after law interfering with a woman's right to choose: imposing waiting periods, legislating intrusive intra-vaginal ultrasounds, and forcing young women to obtain parental consent. In late 2015, Planned Parenthood became a whipping post for right-wing Republican lawmakers, although to date the organization has withstood Republican-led efforts to defund it.[2] Even the passage in 2010 of the Affordable Care Act health insurance reform—"Obamacare"—has been attacked by foes of abortion and even contraception, who have argued on religious grounds against coverage of these crucial parts of women's health care. The highly worrisome 2014 Supreme Court decision in *Burwell vs. Hobby Lobby* established the right of employers to interfere in the reproductive decisions of employees on the basis of religious liberty. This decision, even though it is, as of now, limited to family-owned corporations, clearly discriminates against women and conflicts with women's civil rights (Liptak 2014).

If we look at the US in terms of its care policies—policies that would allow working women (and men) the time to raise children, care for elders, take time out for sick family members and for themselves if necessary—it is clear that despite some progress, the US falls far short of international standards. It has the dubious distinction of being one of the very few countries in the world lacking some form of a national paid family leave law. The Family and Medical Leave Act (FMLA), passed in 1993, gives a limited number of American workers the right to *unpaid* family leave of up to three months. One of the first studies of the

FMLA (Gerstel and McGonagle 2006) showed that the law was unequal in its effects. In order even to use the FMLA for leave, one had
to be able to afford up to three months without income. To be eligible,
workers had to have worked full time for at least twelve months at a
company of at least fifty employees, meaning that part-time or seasonal
workers or those employed in smaller businesses could not benefit;
these workers comprise up to 40% of the workforce. Even the FMLA's
gender neutrality resulted in inequality, with men much more likely to
take leave to care for themselves than other family members. As for a
national child care policy, the last time nationally subsidized child care
had a reasonable chance of passing was in the 1970s, when a bill with
bipartisan support was vetoed by then-President Nixon (Morgan 2001).

Estimates vary as to how much American women who work full
time make compared with their male counterparts, but a gender wage
gap remains; a recent White House report (April 2015) estimated the
median wage gap for women working full time as 78 cents on the dollar
compared to the median man's wages (White House 2015). The gap is
due primarily to gender segregation in the work force and women's primary responsibilities for raising children (England 2005). Recent ex-
hortations like that by the highly successful COO of Facebook, Sheryl
Sandberg, for women to "lean in" at work in order to cut the gender
promotions gap received an outsized amount of attention in the media
(Sandberg 2013). Sandberg's "lean in" call is itself a reflection of the
"glass ceiling," the barrier that working women face at the higher levels
of the class ladder (Ragins, Townsend, and Mattis 2006). Media discussion of the challenges faced by women at the top of the class ladder has
bracketed their experiences from those on the lower rungs, even when
privileged women have tried to show more awareness of the structural
barriers that less privileged women face. Anne-Marie Slaughter, for example, formerly a high-level State Department political appointee,
wrote about having to give up career dreams in order to be more present for her children (Slaughter 2015), but the kind of common-sense
policy recommendations she and others have proposed for paid leave,
sick leave, paid vacation time, subsidized child care, and the like are
seen as political non-starters. The recent critiques of business's un-
friendliness toward the actual work of making families echo concerns
long voiced by feminists about the "stalled revolution" of the feminist
second wave.[3] But these critiques seldom acknowledge how distant a
dream work/home balance is for American women employed in

low-wage service and retail industry jobs, where they often cannot expect even a regular schedule from an employer.

Lastly, efforts to eradicate violence against women have also seemingly stalled. Second-wave feminist activists were the ones who put the problem of violence against women onto the political agenda, resulting in both a grassroots shelter and hotline movement and some success at the federal level. For example, Title IX, a comprehensive federal law barring discrimination on the basis of sex in education, passed in 1972, and has been used to mandate efforts by colleges and universities to battle and investigate sexual assaults on college campuses. But surveys since the turn of the century indicate that one quarter of young college women will experience some kind of sexual assault during their college years (Perez-Pena 2005). The Violence Against Women Act passed in 1994, providing funding for prevention of rape and battering, funds for victim services and the collection of evidence, a federal criminal law against battering, and mandates that states enforce orders of protection ("History Of VAWA | Legal Momentum" 2016). VAWA has been continuously renewed despite recent attempts to stop renewals by conservative politicians. According to a 2010 census done by the National Network to End Domestic Violence, there were close to 2,000 programs aimed at victims and survivors of domestic violence, serving over 70,000 people on any given day (National Network to End Domestic Violence 2010). About half of those victims were in shelters or other forms of transitional housing. Over 80 percent of the programs who responded to the survey reported increased demand for their services, while 77 percent reported a decline in available resources.

Government monies came at a price, as the federal government and state agencies used VAWA money to further their ends as much as or more than feminist ones. As Nancy Whittier has argued in her work on the anti-child sex abuse movement, the state's "selection processes" (2011:11) reacted to feminist demands in a way that

> proceeded to incorporate child sexual abuse into the expansion and retrenchment of the prison system, proposing and implementing ever harsher laws requiring sex offenders to register with police, requiring community notification about local sex offenders, and permitting indefinite detention for offenders judged to be incurable sexual predators. (2011:9)

Similar selection processes have absorbed anti-violence against women efforts into the federal and state agencies, and struggling grass-roots groups trade autonomy and "activities that might alter social relations more fundamentally" for access to state resources (Matthews 1995:304). The trade-offs have all but drained the feminist content out of many efforts to combat violence against women. Conversations about the root causes of such violence have changed little since 1975.

The Origins of the "Everywhere and Nowhere" Character of Contemporary US Feminism

How should we think about the puzzles presented by the constant everyday contradictions of the political landscape that feminists and women's movement activists face in the United States? Media attacks and political backlash have contributed to an atmosphere where feminism is often pronounced "dead," despite the presence of feminist organizations, women's caucuses in mainstream civil and political organizations, and grassroots feminist groups. The enduring presence of women's and gender studies programs and departments in American colleges and universities—some 650 to 900 depending on the source—is never part of the calculations that go into these pronouncements of the death of feminism, nor do the proclaimers factor in the longevity of national women's political organizations like NOW (Reynolds, Shangle, and Venkataraman 2007).[4] For proponents of the "feminism is dead" camp, the very visibility of women in the public sphere is evidence that there is no longer a need for feminist praxis.

Clearly, feminist activists and scholars don't accept the feminism-is-dead argument, but they do point to a US political landscape where, in the words of sociologist Jo Reger, feminism is at once "everywhere and nowhere." Reger sees feminism everywhere because, as she explains, "as social movements continue over long periods of time, their ideas and goals are pervasive, becoming part of everyday cultural beliefs and norms" (2012:5). Feminist success in the US has contributed to the sense that feminism in the US has become "like fluoride, it is simply in the water" (Baumgardner and Richards, cited in Reger, page 5). But fluoride is undetectable as well—and thus as the social movement of feminism becomes pervasive, it also disappears. Such an assertion of feminism's "nowhereness" is similar to arguments two decades earlier about the second wave's influence, such as Judith Stacey's (1996) argument that Americans lived in a "post-feminist" era. According to Stacey, elements of a feminist political and cultural agenda had been depoliticized and incorporated into the lives of Americans both female and male, but without instilling in them a feminist consciousness. As such, feminist movements themselves seem to disappear.

Given this landscape of everywhere and nowhere feminisms, we should ask what we might be expecting from feminists going forward. Is it even necessary that those seeking to better the situation of women in the US organize as feminists? As Maxine Molyneux (1998), among others, has noted, women were quite active in modern progressive movements for social change before and alongside organized feminism. In previous work, I have argued that feminist organizing is only one form of women's public political action and social movement participation, and that "[t]he emergence of a feminist social movement is infrequent, analogous in its rarity as a response to gender oppression to that of revolutionary movements as working-class responses to class domination" (Roth 2004:14). In the next sections, where I trace the origins, the problems, and the promise of second wave US feminism, the reader should keep in mind that organizing as feminists is always one choice among many for women, and that claiming a feminist label is contingent on women's opportunities and relationships in and with other social movements.[5]

The History of Second-Wave Feminist Organizing in the US

In the latter half of the twentieth century, US feminists organized around collective identities constructed in dialogue with other political currents. Feminist organizing in the 1960s and 1970s was facilitated from above by liberal elites (Banaszak 2010; Hartmann 1999). At the same time, "parent" movements on the left created opportunities for feminists emerging from different communities to self-organize, and it made sense that varieties of feminist organizing emerged. (Blackwell 2011; Cobble 2005; Harris 2011; B. Roth 2004; S. Roth 2003; Springer 2005). Thus, because feminists had "shared political investments with men" (Rupp and Taylor 1999:364), second wave US feminism is best characterized as being composed of femin*isms* with different emphases and sometimes very different agendas.

Two general sets of agreements about the differences among feminisms have emerged from scholars' work, primarily revolving around the activism of white middle-class women. The first agreement identifies the origins of feminisms in specific social bases that gave rise to feminist organizing. Scholars posited two distinct social bases from which feminist organizing emerged: one social base of older women attracted to feminist politics in a bureaucratic mode, who formed hierarchical organizations like NOW, and another younger branch attracted to more collectivist forms of organization (Buechler 1990; Carden 1974; Freeman 1973, 1975; Hole and Levine 1971; Ferree and Hess 1985, 1994). The second agreement describes ideological divisions. Ideologically, the older, bureaucratic strand advocated liberal feminist politics, which stressed equality of opportunity for women and their full inclusion into the public sphere. The younger branch gave rise to two ideological strands: radical feminist politics that explored women's oppression at the hands of longstanding patriarchal practice, and socialist feminism, which married a critique of patriarchy with a critique of capitalism.

The "two social bases, three ideological tendencies" view of the landscape of American feminism had won general acceptance by the end of the 1970s, but more recent work has critiqued the scheme as overly simple. The tripartite ideological division of liberal, radical, and socialist feminism fits poorly when describing the politics of racial/ethnic feminists, whose claims often combined elements of all three tendencies, and whose politics are better captured by the concept of *intersectionality*. Intersectional ideologies of change look at intersecting oppressions in the lives of marginalized social actors and seek to account "for multiple grounds of identity when considering how the social world is constructed" (Crenshaw 1995:358). Furthermore, studies of feminist women working in the state and mainstream institutions have demonstrated that these women can hold relatively radical views and push from within for radical feminist political goals (Banaszak 2010; Katzenstein 1998). Scholars like Myra Marx Ferree (2012:4) have argued that feminist radicalism itself has to be seen in relation to the structures of power that produce it: "that which is radical stands at the margins, conflicts with institutionalized patterns of power, and in the long or short term undermines the pattern itself."

However poorly the tripartite ideological division may describe American feminisms, one thing is clear: liberal feminist goals have come to define feminist goals in the public sphere. In the US context of a neo-liberal, minimal welfare state, the Anglo-American variant of "equality" feminism is the one most easily digested. The state, elite institutions, and mainstream political media have selected liberal feminism as legitimate feminism, and this has led to a class-based depiction of feminism that relies on the fiction that feminists share a single ideology.

Class-based Associational Feminist Efforts

Between the dominance of liberal political discourse in the US, the selection processes by state and other institutions toward an assimilative feminist politics, and the staying power of a liberal feminist umbrella organization like NOW, it isn't surprising that liberal feminism has come to be conflated in the public sphere with feminism itself. This much seems over-determined. But it is important to understand the kinds of practices that enabled the success of middle-class feminists—and the unavailability of such practices to working-class and poor women.

Mary Katzenstein (2003:212) has argued that liberal feminists organized through a politics of "associationalism"; that is, they created "support networks, data and information gathering clearinghouses, networking agencies," and the like in a variety of institutions. Note that this definition of associational politics differs from Maxine Molyneux's (1998:7) use of associationalism, as Molyneux uses the word to mean feminist efforts to literally associate with non-feminist groups. Molyneux's use of the term associationalism resembles what movement scholars in the US tend to see as "coalition formation." Katzenstein's definition instead refers to feminist organizing that takes place within non-feminist institutional sites like various levels of the government or mainstream organizations, and does not presuppose the existence of independent feminist organizations, let alone their active alliances with institutions. She argued that middle-class women in the US made claims upon institutions and the state at a time when the US state was becoming more and more neoliberal. The rights and liberation movements of the 1960s were able to counter some of the US's deep-seated "bifurcation" (Katzenstein 2003:204) of racial/ethnic and gendered citizenship. The 1960s "rights revolution" was a real one, exemplified by the passage of the 1963 Equal Pay Act and the 1964 Civil Rights Act, and by the executive orders issued in 1965 and 1968 tasking national government agencies with assuring equality in wages, hiring, and promotion. But the effects of the new policies were mostly felt by middle-class women, and only privileged women were able to hold on to these enlarged rights and entitlements as they self-organized within institutions. While low-income women benefited from changes to the Fair Labor Standards Act, such as amendments that extended coverage to agricultural workers in 1966 and domestic workers in 1974, other social rights important to the poor, like welfare, were not established.

Middle-class feminists in institutions were able to "make their power felt through workplace and institution-based associational politics" (Katzenstein 2003:205). But associational politics did not work for poor women as the state retreated from its responsibilities for social welfare in the 1980s and 1990s. And social movement gains by poor women of color, like those in the National Welfare Rights Organization, were rolled back during the 1980s, as the neo-liberal state offloaded its responsibilities for care of the poor (ibid 208). The aforementioned Hyde Amendment curtailed meaningful reproductive rights for poor women by barring the use of federal funds for abortions. Public housing authorities privatized. As a result, Katzenstein argues, middle-class associationalist feminism made lives better for many women, but was limited in its reach:

> The 1960s restoration of social citizenship for women of economic means was not undone. The right to equal pay, to merit-based employment and promotion, to reproductive choice, to credit and to insurance (free of provisions that discriminate based on sex) are all still fundamentally in place assuming the "means" are there to make women competitive applicants and economically viable clients.... For poor women, the story is very different. (ibid.:209)

Poor women were ill-served by associational politics because the key institutions they interacted with were state-based, and provided no easy access to the inside unless one had a middle-class education. Their lesser place in the social order was further cemented by so-called welfare reform, the Personal Responsibility and Work Reconciliation Act of 1996, which was enacted under a Democratic president, Bill Clinton (Hays 2003; Reese 2005, 2011). The reform eradicated a number of federally run programs in favor of giving block grants to states, tellingly changing the very name of such programs from Aid to Families with Dependent Children to Temporary Assistance to Needy Families programs. Welfare rolls were cut even as poverty levels remained constant. Twenty years later, the National Women's Law Center's analysis of 2013 US Census data shows 18 percent of American women living in poverty—about one in five—with much higher rates in communities of color; nearly 40 percent of women-headed families were living at poverty levels ("No Improvement In Women's Poverty Rate; One In Seven Women Lives In Poverty, Says NWLC - NWLC" 2014). The 1996 act included funds for states to run so-called "healthy marriage" initiatives to encourage poor women to marry or stay married as a means of keeping them off welfare (Heath 2012; Johnson 2014; Silva 2015). Countering the secular nature of the US state but in line with the religious character of much of right-wing politics, some of the funds earmarked for healthy marriage initiatives were made available to faith-based groups who counseled couples to maintain traditional gender roles in marriages. Scholars who have critically studied the effects of these programs have argued that they have had next to no effect; meanwhile, younger cohorts of lower-middle-class and working-class women are delaying marriage or not bothering with it at all, and marriage looks increasingly like a rite practiced by the well-off (Heath 2012; Johnson 2014; Silva 2015).

Katzenstein's analysis of the class-based associationalism of US feminist efforts helps explain how feminism seems to be "everywhere" in the US, as she shows how liberal feminism has entered the mainstream of US political culture, thereby legitimating a culture-wide discourse of equal rights for women. At the same time, she notes that a feminist politics based only on the "equal opportunity doctrine...subverted the links between activists of different class backgrounds that might under some conditions be forged" (2003:215). After facing an intense anti-feminist backlash from the ascendant Republican Party in the 1980s, and as a result of critiques by racial/ethnic feminists unhappy with liberal feminism's exclusive focus on gender, many US-based feminists turned toward coalitions with others seeking more intersectional battles for social justice. As Ferree (2012:229) has put it, "[t]he energy of American feminism has spread into related movements, including the effort to reinvigorate the union movement, the antipoverty struggle in the cities, the battle for lesbian and gay rights, and the resistance to anti-immigrant and anti-Black mobilizations." I next turn to social justice efforts that have been closely allied with feminisms through "spillover" effects and coalitional efforts, and I consider how feminist DNA has been incorporated into related struggles for social justice. Following that, I look at efforts to transnationalize US feminist organizing before concluding that it will take broad-based, intersectionally based and globally aware efforts by feminists to further progress for women and restart the US's stalled feminist revolution.

Feminist Movement Spillover and Coalitional Efforts

Social movement spillover occurs when "[t]he ideas, tactics, style, participants, and organizations of one movement . . . spill over its boundaries to affect other social movements" (Meyer and Whittier 1994:227). Feminist efforts have spilled over into other successful movements since the beginning of the twenty-first century, with the most prominent successes coming in the marriage equality movement that has resulted in the legalization of same-sex marriage throughout the United States. Liberal feminism's ascendance in the American political sphere, with its emphasis on equal rights and equal protection under the law, made political space for the more assimilationist goals of the lesbian, gay, bisexual, and transgender (LGBT) movement.[6] The successful movement for marriage equality coexisted alongside another assimilationist movement for LGBT equality, which focused on the right of LGBT people to serve openly in the nation's armed services. In 2011, President Obama lifted the infamous Clinton-era "don't ask, don't tell" policy, and established the right of LGBT soldiers to serve openly in the US's volunteer-only armed forces. That right has helped normalize the idea of LGBT people as equal citizens (Shane III 2015).[7]

As for the marriage equality movement, the stunning fall, state by state, of laws that restricted marriage to heterosexual couples culminated with the US Supreme Court's decision, *Obergefell et al. vs. Hodges,* striking down remaining barriers to same-sex marriage. Social movement scholars find in this instance a fertile case study of how grassroots and national organizations can coordinate to expand rights in a federal system (Bernstein and Taylor 2013). Groups like the Human Rights Campaign, a nationwide LGBT organization, featured marriage equality as a prominent part of their umbrella platform; local efforts like MassEquality in Massachusetts (Kosbie 2013) organized complex coalitions of LGBT actors, civil rights organizations, feminist groups, and unaffiliated progressives in order to sway the minds of legislators, judges, and the public.

Dissenting voices in the LGBT community have questioned the wisdom of the fight for marriage equality and the way that battle reflected the priorities of white middle-class members of the LGBT community. LGBT people of color have questioned the relevance of the marriage battle for the making of their "invisible families" (Hunter 2013; Moore 2011; Stein 2013). Moreover, *Obergefell et al. vs. Hodges* did not overturn state laws that ban adoption by same-sex couples, nor did it establish nationwide statutes to protect LGBT people from discrimination in housing or work. There is evidence that Americans, while willing to grant formal rights to same-sex couples, are still uncomfortable with giving "informal privileges" of inclusion to LGBT couples and families (Long, Loehr, and Miller 2014). Still, for the two million same-sex couples to date who have taken advantage of the new definition of marriage and tied the knot, the guarantee of new rights has had real effects in legitimizing their "alternative" relationships and families; at the same time, legitimating same-sex marriages expands US states' power to determine what a "normal" family looks like.

Beyond the spillover effects of feminism for the LGBT rights movement, US feminist energies have been incorporated into a variety of coalitions with progressive causes, leading once more to both the everywhereness and nowhereness of feminism, insofar as feminist labels as such may not be used (Cobble, Gordon, and Henry 2015; Ferree 2012; Staggenborg and Taylor 2005). Feminists' coalitions with others in progressive causes manifest themselves in two ways: through the expanded list of concerns among mainstream feminist organizations, and through the feminist DNA in progressive organizations organized around other, extra-feminist social aims. Examples of both tendencies are easy to find.

Mainstream feminist groups like NOW and the Feminist Majority tackle a variety of issues in a broad manner. For example, NOW's economic justice platform "advocates for a wide range of economic justice issues affecting women, from the glass ceiling to the sticky floor of poverty. These include welfare reform, livable wages, job discrimination, pay equity, housing, social security and pension reform" ("Economic Justice | National Organization for Women" 2016). Although mainstream feminists have been criticized for narrowly focusing on abortion to the exclusion of other kinds of reproductive rights issues that affect poor women and women of color, NOW's platform regarding reproductive rights includes a call for comprehensive healthcare for all women (ibid.). Similarly, the Feminist Majority positions itself as opposing any type of discrimination—"on the basis of sex, race, sexual orientation, socio-economic status, religion, ethnicity, age, marital status, nation of origin, size or disability"—and in favor of promoting equality for women and men. The organization further explicitly "supports workers' collective bargaining, pay equity, and end of sweatshops," and encourages the membership to work towards preserving the environment ("About" 2012). Taken together, these two feminist organizations demonstrate that even mainstream feminism has come to promote a broad political agenda on all women's behalf.

For some groups on the left the goal of eradicating gender inequality can seem to be part of a laundry list of targeted oppressions, leading to a kind of surface intersectional activism, but other groups have incorporated intersectional feminism into their DNA. One example of such a group is Black Lives Matter (BLM), which was founded in 2013 by Patrisse Cullors, Opal Tometi, and Alicia Garza as a means of fighting the continuing violence perpetrated by law enforcement against ordinary Black women and men.[8] The three founders of BLM had been and continue to be involved in other social justice groups. Cullors works for the Ella Baker Center for Human Rights in Oakland, California, a predominantly Black community; Tometi, the daughter of Nigerian immigrants, works at the Black Alliance for Just Immigration; and Garza is the special projects director of the National Domestic Workers Alliance.

The Twitter hashtag "#BlackLivesMatter" took social media by storm. Garza describes BLM's "herstory" as having been formed by Black queer women, whose existence was subject to erasure. In rejecting, for example, the "#alllivesmatter" trope that emerged in reaction to BLM, Garza and her cofounders insist on the specificities of the Black experience in the US as an underpinning for progressive social change (Garza 2014). Garza characterizes what she sees as the mission of BLM:

> Black Lives Matter is a unique contribution that goes beyond extra-judicial killings of Black people by police and vigilantes. It goes beyond the narrow nationalism that can be prevalent within some Black communities, which merely call on Black people to love Black, live Black and buy Black, keeping straight cis Black men in the front of the movement while our sisters, queer and trans and disabled folk take up roles in the background or not at all. Black

Lives Matter affirms the lives of Black queer and trans folks, disabled folks, Black-undocumented folks, folks with records, women and all Black lives along the gender spectrum. It centers those that have been marginalized within Black liberation movements. It is a tactic to (re)build the Black liberation movement.

BLM's simultaneous insistence on inclusivity in forming a community for liberation while specifically naming what Black people in America have faced, has garnered a great deal of attention from social and other media, and the group has endured a host of criticism for going against standard American discourses of democratic access through political pluralism by maintaining a focus on Black lives as such. BLM *was* sought out by candidates for the US presidency for endorsements; they announced that they would endorse no one (Lewis 2015). The group has begun to get support from more mainstream feminists; the New York Women's Foundation awarded Garza, Tometi, and Cullors its "Walking Stick Award" for political trailblazers, an award previously given as well to Hillary Clinton ("NYWF'S 2015 Celebrating Women Breakfast Event Recap" 2015). Even *Cosmopolitan*, a women's magazine better known for its tips on sex than politics, interviewed Garza, Tometi, and Cullors recently for a short but remarkably direct piece where the three women conveyed their intersectional perspective on racial/ethnic, gender, and economic justice (Ohikuare 2015).

To discuss BLM as an example of the fruit of coalitional feminist politics is not to argue that they are "really" or "essentially" feminist, instead of what they say they are. Rather, BLM offers a salient example of how intersectionality, a political concept rooted in the feminist activism of women of color, has become more common, if not yet ubiquitous, in American political discourse. Intersectionality as social analysis lends itself to a politics of coalition formation. The idea of intersectional oppressions has become very much part of US feminisms, and those same feminisms have helped shape the identity of other groups.

Transnationalizing US Feminisms

It is difficult to explain why most feminist groups in the US have not prioritized making international or transnational linkages; US feminist neglect of the transnational may be linked to class-based associationalism, but also seems to have a racialized component, as some racial/ethnic feminists in the 1960s and 1970s claimed membership in transnational diasporic communities, and asserted allegiances with national liberation struggles by calling their groups by names like the Third World Women's Alliance and Las Hijas de Cuauhtémoc (Anderson-Bricker 1999; Blackwell 2011; Roth 2004; Springer 2005). In general, though, it seems likely that the US's position as the last remaining super-power—that is, its geopolitical hegemony—has led to neglect of the transnational. As Ferree (2012:220) noted, "most US feminists have little awareness of UN mandates"; arguably, this lack of a transnational perspective on US feminists' part contributes to the narrowness of their political discourse. Arguably as well, the inability of US feminist organizations to gain media attention for transnational efforts leads to an impoverished discussion of policy options for the betterment of women's lives.

There have been exceptions to such US feminist isolationism. One important leader was and is lesbian feminist pioneer Charlotte Bunch, who was active in the Washington, D.C. area, and helped found the journals *Women's Liberation* and *Quest: A Feminist Quarterly*. Bunch went on to found the Center for Women's Global Leadership at Rutgers University, which is both an academic research center and an NGO with consultative status with the UN.[9] Bunch and the Center were part of the global movement to have women's rights recognized as human rights. Beginning by attending the first UN World Conference on Women in Mexico City in 1975 as an "anti-imperialist feminist," Bunch went on to attend and organize around all the subsequent UN conferences on women, despite what she describes as "backlash and anti-feminist forces [who] have gained ground in a number of countries and often at the UN as well" (Bunch 2012:220). Bunch, like many other transnational activists, also thinks that US reactions to the 9/11 attacks have hampered activist ties beyond borders, but she nonetheless maintains hope given the kinds of connections that feminists have made and continue to make.

Mainstream feminist organizations as well have included global feminist organizing as part of their umbrella agendas. An example of coalitional and transnational efforts to place the country's gender politics in a global context can be seen in the NOW Foundation's help in researching and writing the 2006 *Report on Women's Human Rights in the United States under the International Covenant on Civil and*

Political Rights (ICCPR) otherwise known as the US "Gender Shadow Report" (Erickson 2006). The report itself was then endorsed by the National Council of Women's Organizations, an alliance of two hundred member organizations representing ten million individuals. The shadow report strongly criticized the lack of formal constitutional guarantees for gender equality, the failure of the US to ratify CEDAW, the elimination of federal initiatives designed to research and remedy job and wage discrimination against women, the over-incarceration of non-violent offenders, the treatment of immigrant women and asylum seekers, the federal government push toward abstinence-based sex education, and the effective denial of abortion rights to poor women, among other items. However the shadow report received little to no coverage in the US press.

The NOW Foundation's global actions aim chiefly at giving American women a voice at the UN. Other US feminist organizations seek more direct encounters with women on the ground, including the Global Fund for Women, founded in 1987 in Palo Alto, California, by Anne Firth Murray, Frances Kissling, Laura Lederer, and Nita Barrow ("Mission and History" 2016). As its name implies, the Global Fund gives money directly to what it considers to be "grass-roots women-led movements." As a public foundation, the Global Fund began modestly, but has grown to the point where it now gives out over $100 million a year. The fund merged with the International Museum of Women in 2014; the Museum was originally based in San Francisco and now features online exhibits about women's issues worldwide. In 1992, Jessica Neuwirth, formerly of Amnesty International, helped found Equality Now, a feminist organization which "advocates for the human rights of women and girls around the world" ("Our Work | Equality Now" 2016). Equality Now has offices in New York, Nairobi, and London, with "presences" in Amman and Washington, D.C. The specific issues it tackles include legal discrimination, violence against women, female genital cutting, and trafficking. The organization says that it does not take "direct funding from any government." Gloria Steinem sits on its board of directors. Neuwirth and Steinem are also involved in another, newer organization, Donor Direct Action ("About - Donor Direct Action" 2016). Donor Direct Action is actually directed by Jessica Neuwirth, with the guidance of a Steering Committee co-convened by Steinem and other well-known feminists. The organization operates as a donor and clearinghouse for projects on such issues as female genital mutilation, trafficking, violence against women, women in armed conflicts, and women's rights and the law.

It is fair to say that there is more awareness of global women's issues among US feminists than there was in the 1960s and 1970s, but as feminist organizations have formed everywhere in the American political landscape, only a small subset of feminists have been consistently involved in transnational organizing. Connections have been and are being made between individual feminists involved in UN and other kinds of networks, but unsurprisingly, given the stalled feminist revolution in the US, feminist organizing that centers on transnationality has not been a real priority for most.

Conclusion: Partial Transformations and Ongoing Conversations

I have argued in this chapter that feminists in the US face the reality of a stalled revolution. Their sisters in many other countries have made stronger headway in obtaining the kinds of policies that make the lives of working women easier (although those policies have not always come as a direct result of feminist organizing). Violence against women is still a major concern. Women's representation in electoral politics, although better than it once was, has reached a seeming plateau. Economic gains *vis-à-vis* men have been tenuous, gaps remain, and all American workers face a labor market with less secure and less remunerative employment. Reproductive rights are under constant and unrelenting attack. Transnational efforts directed toward feminists in other countries are real but limited. And yet grassroots feminist efforts continue to flourish, and some degree of feminist political discourse around equal rights and equal opportunity has gained wide acceptance. Liberal feminism, with its traditional emphasis on allowing women access to participation in the nation's institutions as they are, stands legitimated throughout most of the body politic.

Liberal feminism must be challenged in order to jumpstart feminist politics out of the stall it is in, and make future gains for women. There have been and still are intersectionally based challenges to liberal feminist hegemony. Women's and gender studies programs in the academy continue to take an intersectional approach to the study of women as socially situated members of communities—some privileged, some not—in a way that makes clear to many students that gender oppression is linked to other kinds of oppressions and that addressing gender oppression in isolation is a political non-starter. The spillover of feminist efforts into the LGBT movement is a bright spot despite the selection processes that rewarded assimilationist goals of participation in the social institutions of the military and marriage. Arguably, winning same-sex marriage rights, and continuing to struggle for the formation of nontraditional families headed by LGBT parents, will enable feminists to broaden their base. Transgender issues, the long-neglected "T" in the acronym, are currently part of popular culture and political debate (Ball 2015).[10]

What kind of organizing can intersectionality as feminist politics lead to? I would argue that an intersectional perspective toward the situated reality of gender oppression can incorporate positions that umbrella agenda groups like NOW and Feminist Majority take; intersectionality is already typical of the politics of many grass-roots feminist efforts. An intersectional feminist approach requires that we think of US feminist politics as a coalitional collection of diverse voices, where the "strategic interests," to use Molyneux's term, will only be created by having difficult discussions among coalitional partners (Ferree 2012:225). There is reason for hope. Beyond the successes of the LGBT movement, some slow progress is being made on the question of family leave, with several states using funding for disability insurance for workers to cover pregnant women for short periods of time (Milkman and Appelbaum 2013). Although minimal, this kind of government involvement, with its potential to affect a broad swath of workers, is preferable to the kind of top-down, company-bestowed benefits that some workers at the top of the class ladder can take. Another bright spot linked to feminists' coalitional efforts is the growing acceptance of the idea of a living wage for workers in low-wage service and retail work. Despite intense opposition and predictions of job loss, a number of municipalities and states are committed to raising low-wage workers' hourly pay to $15 an hour, or twice the current federal minimum, and women have been very visible from the start in the leadership of these struggles (Abramsky 2014).

Feminists have transformed the political and social landscape in the US. To argue otherwise is both inaccurate and strategically useless; the defeatism of such statements plays directly into the hands of those who would declare feminism irrelevant. But it is also clear that the feminist transformation of the real lives of American women has been incomplete, and that it was destined to be so, in the absence of a thoroughly intersectional vision of social change. The intersectional visionaries exist everywhere on the ground. They help move feminist politics, in the words of bell hooks (1984), "from the margin to the center" of American life.

Notes

1. The "wave" metaphor has been criticized by authors who see evidence of a more continuous American feminist movement (see Cobble, Gordon, and Henry 2015) and those who argue that the waves are defined by rises and falls in white middle class women's organizing (Springer 2002). While I am sympathetic to both critiques, I use the wave metaphor to signal the upsurge in US public political discussion of women's issues in the 1960s and 1970s.

2. The fact that such funding comes chiefly in the form of Medicaid reimbursements for contraceptive and other health care that Planned Parenthood provides to poor women has not generally been recognized; see Teresa Tritch, "What Defunding Planned Parenthood Would Really Mean," October 7, 2015, *The New York Times,*

3. Arlie Hochschild (with Anne Machung) wrote about the "stalled" feminist revolution in her classic 1989 book *The Second Shift: Working Families and the Revolution at Home,* and again in 2001, with *The Time Bind: When Work Becomes Home and Home Becomes Work.* Hochschild's work, as well as that of other scholars who address the missing home/work balance in the U S, always come back to the deficit of care policies for American workers as a cause: see Williams (2010); Heymann (2006) has argued that global neo-liberal policies which pull all adults into the labor force have made such care policies necessary for families in all countries, given that they can no longer rely on unpaid female caretakers at home to raise children.

4. *Ms.* Magazine estimated that there were about 900 women's studies departments and programs in the US in 2009 ("Ms. Magazine Online | Winter 2009". 2016. *Msmagazine.Com.*); The National Women's Studies Association's 2007 "National Census of Women's Studies Programs" gave a smaller estimate of 650 (Reynolds, Michael, Shobha Shangle, and Lekha Venkataraman. 2007. *A National Census of Women's and Gender Studies Programs In U.S. Institutions Of Higher Education.* University of Chicago).

5. The idea of feminism as a political choice is part of the "collective identity" approach to defining feminism (Rupp and Taylor 1999), which acknowledges that feminist collective identities exist in relation to other social movement organizations and communities. The collective identity approach dovetails with other visions of defining women's interests—and feminist women's interests—as constructed in particular historical/cultural moments (Molyneux 1998).

6. Steven Seidman (2005) distinguishes between "assimilationist" and "liberationist" goals in LGBT organizing.

7. The wars of opportunity fought by the US in the early twenty-first century have led to expanded discussion of women's role in the armed forces. The so-called "combat exclusion" has been almost completely lifted, opening up more career pathways for women in the armed forces. That these efforts take place at the same time as the military wrestles with the endemic presence of sexual assault within its ranks shows the limits of formal incorporation of outsiders into the unreconstructed realms of male-dominated institutions. New York Senator Kirsten Gillibrand has repeatedly

sponsored bills in Congress designed to address the sexual assault epidemic in the armed services by removing prosecution of such cases from the military chain of command. The bills, despite widespread support, have so far failed to reach the threshold needed for passage in the Senate; Shane III, Leo. 2015. "Military Sexual Assault Reform Plan Fails Again." *Military Times*.

8. The group's website is http://www.blacklivesmatter.com; it also has a Facebook page (https://www.facebook.com/BlackLivesMatter/?fref=ts) with over 200,000 "likes."

9. See https://www.facebook.com/pages/Charlotte-Bunch/103132416394050?fref =ts and https://www.facebook.com/pages/Center-for-Womens-Global-Leadership /138646046157269?fref=ts .

10. As I write, the rights of transgender people to use the locker rooms and the bathrooms of the gender they identify as has become a political football. Opponents of transgender rights raise the specter of "real" men in "real" women's bathrooms as a fear-mongering tactic to defeat local rights ordinances. At the same time, some municipalities are requiring that single stall bathrooms in public spaces be designed and designated as gender neutral. See Ball, Aimee Lee. 2015. "In All-Gender Restrooms, The Signs Reflect The Times". *New York Times*.

LATIN AMERICA

9

Seeking Rights from
the Left

Gender and Sexuality in Latin America

ELISABETH JAY FRIEDMAN

Introduction

As it has many times before, the Latin American region seems to be undergoing a swing of the political pendulum. After more than a decade in which the majority of Latin Americans lived under left or center-left governments, right-wing parties have begun a new ascendancy. Following twelve years out of power, the opposition won the presidency in Argentina; after fifteen years with little institutional impact they gained the congressional majority in Venezuela. In Bolivia, Evo Morales lost a referendum that would have allowed him to run for a fourth term. A free-market comedian took the presidency in Guatemala; at the time of this writing, the Brazilian right is avidly seeking to impeach Workers' Party president Dilma Rousseff. Across the region, the so-called "Pink Tide" is ebbing.

As the Pink Tide recedes, the time is ripe for an evaluation of the Left in power across a range of issues. Given the shared commitments of governments and progressive movements to issues of social justice, it might seem logical to expect state cooperation with feminist, women's, and LGBT[1] movements and support for their political, economic, and social demands. Historically, however, the political Left has an uneven record in this regard. How have contemporary left governments compared?

The answer, based on a comparative study of Argentina, Chile, Bolivia, and Venezuela, is one that echoes the historical record. These governments improved the well-being of many women by promoting social welfare. But beyond that bedrock achievement, support for women's access to the state (including decision-making positions), issues of bodily autonomy (including reproductive rights), and identity recognition (including the recognition of same-sex unions and gender identity) was less consistent. Even the most left-wing presidents seemed unwilling to frontally challenge gender and sexual hierarchies, in part because the Catholic Church and many evangelical denominations defend—and depend on—these constructs.

In Venezuela and Bolivia powerful leaders paid at least lip service to women's demands as they mobilized them on behalf of distinct, yet related, transformative political projects, but they offered women and LGBT people inconsistent opportunities to advance their rights. In the more stable political systems of Chile and Argentina, female heads of state presented quite different opportunities for feminist action even as they backed some forms of identity recognition.

In all cases, feminists and women from other social movements championed women's human rights in the face of political repression, economic austerity, and everyday violence. But their periodic collaboration has alternated with disagreement and distance over priorities, strategies, and allies. This chapter focuses on women's activism and its outcome with respect to women's rights and gender equality within the larger political context of the region. It also takes into account parallel organizing among lesbian, gay, bisexual, and transgender (LGBT) people, given their common challenge to the conservative Catholic inheritance of patriarchy and heteronormativity by championing bodily integrity and autonomy.[2]

To trace the connections between past and present, this chapter begins with a definition of the terms *feminism* and *women's movements* in the Latin American context. It then moves to a historical overview of the relations among feminist, women's, and LGBT movements, focusing on external influences including regime change, left parties and movements, religious authorities, and transnational organizing opportunities. The section traces such activism through the 1990s. The second half of the chapter offers a four-case study com-

parison of more recent developments under left-leaning governments, ranging from feminist state-society relations to sexual rights.

Gender and Sexuality-based Movements in
Latin America: Negotiating Boundaries

In this region, movements of women have assumed three forms: feminist movements, women's movements, and movements in which women
play significant roles. The first seek to end women's subordination, or
the existence of hierarchies based on gendered relations of power, by
challenging the traditional roles of women and men; following an early
scholarly characterization, in Latin America these movements have
been called movements for women's "strategic gender interests" (Molyneux 1985). The second focus on a range of issues, including basic material survival, defense of human rights, and even conservative demands
such as the continuance of an authoritarian regime. Movements composed of and led by poor and working-class women who do not explicitly
challenge gender roles, but often organize in order to be able to fulfill
those roles, have been called movements for "practical gender interests"
(ibid.). The third are movements in which women are primary actors
but include men and are often led by them, such as those demanding
respect for indigenous and Afro-Latin peoples.

These movements have not developed independently of one another, and the considerable cross-fertilization of activists, issues, and
ideas has meant that it is difficult, if not counterproductive, for both
analysts and activists to try to make bright-line distinctions. Unlike in
the United States and Western Europe, for example, in Latin America
the "Second Wave" middle-class feminists of the 1970s emerged from
leftist movements. Thus they understood both class and gender oppression as fundamentally structuring society, and initially prioritized poor
and working-class women's issues (Sternbach et al. 1992:402). Moreover, observers note the extent to which all women's movements, regardless of their explicit goals, always implicitly challenge traditional
gender roles: they are vehicles for women to actively engage with the
male-dominated world of public affairs. Moreover, nearly half a century
of coalitional feminist work has resulted in many indigenous, environmental, antipoverty, anti-imperial, and peace movements accepting
women's participation and equality as central to their goals. Indeed,

different movements of women have sought areas of confluence on which to work together, whether on gender-specific issues such as violence against women, or more general challenges, such as the detrimental impact of neoliberal and/or extractivist[3] economic development on their families, communities, and geographies.

Nevertheless, periodic attempts to draw boundaries around feminism have taken place in the region. From the emergence of "First Wave" feminism at the end of the nineteenth century, feminists have debated the relevance of theories and approaches, issues and allies. As women's movements sought to engage the places and spaces of Second Wave feminism in the 1970s, veteran activists grew frustrated by the impact of new participants who often brought new issues to the table at national and regional feminist meetings. Analysts have called these moments "crises of expansion and inclusion," and their resolution has been far from easy (S. Alvarez et al. 2003:541). At one regional meeting, when more experienced feminists insisted on a narrower and deeper focus on what they considered to be core feminist issues, including power struggles within autonomous organizations, they were met by more recent activists' sarcastic rejection of a feminist yardstick (*feministómetro*). Veterans' proposal to hold separate meetings for experienced and inexperienced feminists in the future was met by hundreds of women, from backgrounds including grassroots urban movements and union organizing, chanting "We are all feminists!" (*"Todos somos feministas!"*) (Sternbach et al. 1992:421). An outcome of these controversies has been the differentiation of a range of feminist positions, such as autonomous feminist, lesbian feminist, and "popular" feminist, a term originally used in the Chilean context by those focused on the needs of working-class women (Schild 1998:108).

From opposite ends of the political spectrum, some female advocates for women have rejected the label *feminist* as associated with middle-class women whose primary intent is to critique men. They picked up on the term *gender*, which diffused from academic into policy circles in the 1990s. Although many feminists found that state actors' adoption of *gender*, *gender theory*, and *gender perspective* co-opted the original intent of gender analysis, which was not only to identify gender inequality but also to seek to change it, other advocates embraced the new terminology. In an ironic move, gender theory "was defended both by working-class women who thought that the feminists were not sufficiently concerned about ending class inequality and by right-wing women who thought that the feminists were too concerned about ending class inequality" (Kampwirth and Gonzalez 2001:16). In a more recent backlash prompted by right-wing Christian activists, often nurtured by international links to partners in the United States, the term *gender ideology* has been used to critique feminist activism and policy recommendations as inherently threatening to Latin American culture and values.

Latin American feminism is multifaceted. Understanding its richness means foregrounding women's agency on the issues that women identify as central for survival. Privileging safe abortion over prenatal care or equal pay over microcredit, or excluding issues of race or ethnicity from a liberal or even radical interpretation of feminism, risks neglecting the situated meaning of women's interests in societies crosscut by multiple sources of oppression.

Women's Organizing in Historical Context

In the late nineteenth and early twentieth centuries, First Wave feminists in Latin America sought social reform under the banner of women's "different mission" from men, similar to the Catholic precept of gender "complementarity." Believing that women's proper focus was on issues of home and children, many early activists did not prioritize their own rights (Miller 1991). However, others realized that without the vote, their efforts would be stymied. Leaders such as Bertha Lutz, founder of the Brazilian Federation for Feminine Progress, sought transnational alliances, collaborating with the International Women's Suffrage Alliance in advancing Brazilian women's suffrage in the 1920s (Hahner 1990:138–161).

Avid feminist participation in left parties did not always result in support for suffrage. Male leaders assumed that the enfranchisement of women would give the Catholic Church increased political influence, considering women's perceived attachment to the institution. Suffrage was championed by parties that supported the Church's role in society, which were pleased with such potential results, and by communist and socialist parties that did not often hold power. Following World War II, however, left-leaning nationalist and populist parties mobilized women. They decreed female enfranchisement and incorporated women through women's branches or affiliated parties such as the Peronist Women's Party (Miller 1991:chap. 5). Though women gained political access, they were seen as the "housekeepers" of the public sphere, responsible for the daily life of the party organization rather than the promotion of their own interests (E. Friedman 2000:38–39).

The Second Wave feminists of the 1970s also had mixed experiences with the Left. Although they often cut their political teeth on the revolutionary Left or left-leaning parties, they became frustrated with the subordination of gender-based to class-related goals in both theory and practice: women found themselves, and their issues, neglected by male leadership (Luciak 2001). While some chose to create feminist organizations, others opted to engage in "double militancy," fighting from within their movements and parties to put gender on the agenda. This division between feminists (*feministas*) and party cadre (*militantes*) led to intense debates over whether the former were enjoying the latest imperial bourgeois import from the United States or Europe or the latter sacrificing their feminist ideals to mobilize masses for the socialist patriarchy. Despite their differences, both sides agreed that their natural constituency was the poor and working-class, and often indigenous or Afro-descendant, women who made up the majority of female Latin Americans. But because *militantes* often sought to recruit activists from women's movements to serve only party interests and *feministas* insisted that gender oppression was as important as class oppression, both found it difficult to create lasting multiclass alliances. Mobilized by the economic decline and political repression that characterized the region from the late 1960s through the 1980s, women's movements grew in strength and numbers, informed by—but always in uneasy tension with—the feminist ideals and organizing principles of largely middle- and upper-class white and *mestiza*[4] women.

The rise of military or military-backed governments intent on protecting their national security (and, eventually, free markets) against what they perceived as a communist threat led to a wave of repression across the region. In forerunner Venezuela, the 1950s dictatorship of General Marcos Pérez Jiménez drove political parties underground and their leadership into exile as his National Security force imprisoned hundreds in a concentration camp and terrorized through torture and assassination. In Argentina, the military council overseeing what would become known as the "Dirty War" (1976–1983) attacked all manner of progressive social and political organizations, with an estimated toll of 60,000 murdered and many more suffering torture and imprisonment. In Chile, the dictatorship of Augusto Pinochet (1973–1989) resulted in at least 3,000 deaths, tens of thousands imprisoned, and many more who fled into exile. In Bolivia, the military in power between the mid-60s and early 1980s sought to smash union and peasant organizing, often relying on paramilitary death squads.

In reaction to this long wave of repression, women mobilized through several arenas. Some organized on behalf of authoritarian governments, in agreement with a conservative ideology that claimed the traditional family was the cornerstone to restoring order to society, polity, and economy (Power 2001). Against authoritarianism, the now-famous "mothers' movements," which sought information about their missing children and partners, often formed the backbone of a growing opposition movement (Jaquette 1991; S. Alvarez 1990:chap. 3). In Chile, Brazil, and elsewhere, poor and working-class women organized for family survival, creating communal soup kitchens. Chilean women transformed a traditional craft into a tool for protesting human rights violations with their "arpillera" tapestries portraying the impact of repression on their families and communities. Sent around the world, these scraps of fabric and thread raised awareness of life under the dictatorship. Often such efforts took place under the protection of the Catholic Church, particularly where repression of left parties and unions was the most draconian. The Church was an inconsistent ally for women: while it protected grassroots organizations, and recognized the difficulties poor women faced in supporting their families and communities, it held the line against women's bodily autonomy. Where parties organized clandestinely, such as in Venezuela, women proved to be ideal underground cadres, as their gender made them less suspect in the eyes of the authorities (E. Friedman 2000:chap. 3). Finally, feminists, often inspired by ideas acquired during exile in Western Europe, made connections between authoritarianism in the polity and the family, fighting for "democracy in the country and the home" (Baldez 2002:161).

The growth of opposition movements provided an opportunity for women to form cross-class and nonpartisan coalitions to demand an end to authoritarianism. Women's gender solidarity, based on their common identification as "political outsiders," often allowed them to unite where men were unable to cooperate. For example, in Chile, the mass organizations Women for Life (1983) and Coalition of Women for Democracy (1988) brought women together across class and party lines to unify the opposition against Pinochet, and then to make gender-based demands on the new democracy (ibid.:chaps. 7–8; S. Alvarez 1990:chap. 5; E. Friedman 2000:117–121). Although this coalition building did not survive the transition to democracy intact, it fostered relationships and shared understandings, particularly the saliency of a human rights framework for women's struggles, that would continue to inform organizing.

In the Cuban and Nicaraguan revolutionary regimes, women played key roles in achieving state power. Mass women's organizations, the Cuban Women's Federation (FMC) and the Luisa Amanda Espinoza Association of Nicaraguan Women (AMNLAE), were created as the official channel for women's integration. While important gains—workplace-equality measures, antisexist education, day-care provision, and, in the case of Cuba, access to legal abortion—were made, women's rights were often subordinated to national needs. Both the FMC and the AMNLAE mobilized women on behalf of the revolutionary states, whether that meant taking on significant community work or postponing their demands in order to fight against the Contra War in Nicaragua (L. Smith and Padula 1996).

Early LGBT activists had similar experiences to feminists *vis-à-vis* the Left in the 1970s (Mongrovejo 2000; Babb 2003). Although they were stalwart members of left parties, these activists' sexuality was seen as a taboo subject, contrary to "revolutionary morality." This attitude was reflected in the homophobic policies and practices of the revolutionary regimes in Cuba and Nicaragua. Thus, some activists split off into separate gay liberation groups that included men and women.

For lesbians, the move from partisan to identity-based organizing was often unfulfilling. Although they participated in the formation of a political identity distinct from partisan ideology, they often found themselves and their issues sidelined or ignored by gay men. They thus turned to burgeoning feminist and women's movements, directing their energies to "larger" women's issues such as reproductive rights and ending violence against women. But here again they found themselves sidelined, if not silenced. Many feminists feared their movements would be "tainted" by association with lesbianism, given the widespread societal assumption that feminists were driven by hatred for men rather than for patriarchal structures of power, and refused to directly engage with issues of non-normative sexuality or family structure.

As a result of their double marginalization, some lesbians began organizing autonomously in the 1980s, often forming the most radical feminist groups, such as the Bolivian group "Women Creating." The

AIDS crisis led to rapprochement between mixed-gender groups and feminists. Although the disease tragically deprived movements of some of their most committed supporters, it created new sources of national and international financial and institutional support for LGBT groups, as well as opening up public dialogue on sexuality (Pecheny 2003). Following on these developments, coalitions between LGBT and feminist movements emerged around issues of bodily integrity and autonomy in the 1990s.

With the region-wide transitions to liberal democracy beginning in the 1980s, many feminists began to engage directly with the state. While it nurtured the feminist policy sector, democratization paradoxically debilitated movements by opening new avenues of action within the formal political arena. Some feminists continued in or rejoined party politics. In Brazil and Chile women demanded, and received, a full-fledged ministry of women's affairs. Opportunities for policy development and implementation also stimulated a process of professionalization of feminist movements, as many middle-class and elite women formed nongovernmental organizations (NGOs) to work on issues such as microcredit, domestic violence, and women's leadership (S. Alvarez et al. 2003:548). This dramatically changed the nature of feminist efforts, given that NGOs were subject to the demands of granting agencies, whether international foundations, organizations, or governmental ministries. Organizations often adapted their structure, projects, or even missions to coincide with the priorities of funders.

Moreover, engaging with the state provoked tensions with allies and the very women organized feminists sought to help. Feminists entered the state precisely as such states were beginning to shed their responsibilities for social welfare and economic growth under the dictates of neoliberal economic models. Those who remained outside the state criticized the resulting "gender technocracy" that supported the "global neoliberal patriarchy" by teaching poor and working-class women how to cope with neoliberal citizenship (Monasterios 2007:33–34; S. Alvarez et al. 2003:547; Schild 1998). The division between the self-proclaimed *autonomas*, who continued to work in movement arenas, including those of the political Left, and those they identified as *institucionalizadas*, who sought change through more formal institutions, marked another painful rending of feminist energies. The four case studies below help to shed light on the question of the extent to which "institutional" feminism helps to realize its goals or weaken its bases.

In addition to national politics, transnational networking remained critical to Latin American women. This networking, which included the circulation of ideas, strategies, resources, and people themselves, was facilitated by both formal state-oriented UN world conference processes and movement-based transnational meetings. The Latin American and Caribbean feminist *encuentros* (encounters) began in 1981. Intended to bring together movement activists from throughout the region, *encuentros* have taken place in Argentina, Brazil, Chile, Colombia, Costa Rica, the Dominican Republic, El Salvador, Mexico, and Peru. While changing in format and theme to reflect the interests and preoccupations of the national organizing committees, these multiday experiences provide a host of different ways for activists to interact, from encounter-type small group sessions to major presentations in large plenary meetings. Although they have provided spaces in which activists across the region can find community, the *encuentros* have also been a site for deep debate over feminist practices, ideals, and goals in the face of the economic, social, and political challenges of the region. Over time, they have become "key transnational arenas where Latin America–specific feminist identities and strategies have been constituted and contested" (S. Alvarez et al. 2003:539).

In the 1980s and 1990s, the *encuentros* inspired the creation of regional networks, including the 28 September Campaign for the Decriminalization of Abortion in Latin America and the Caribbean; the Network of Latin American and Caribbean Women's Health; the Network of Afrolatinamerican and Afrocaribbean Women; and the Latin American and Caribbean Feminist Network against Domestic and Sexual Violence. These networks coordinated their own face-to-face meetings as well as making use of new technologies to circulate information and strengthen regional campaigns.

These regional networks helped feminists prepare for a series of UN world conferences: on the environment (Rio de Janeiro, 1992), human rights (Vienna, 1993), population and development (Cairo, 1994), women's rights (Beijing, 1995), and habitat (Istanbul, 1996). Preparations for the conferences mobilized women's rights activists. The conferences themselves produced documents, such as the Vienna Declaration and Programme of Action and the Beijing Declaration and Platform for Action, that women used to legitimate demands at home. But it was not a one-way process: Latin Americans were at the forefront of the transnational movement that famously established that "women's rights are human rights" at the human rights meeting in Vienna. Their experiences fighting authoritarian rule had left them with a keen awareness, and a profound analysis, of the power of the human rights discourse to unite those seeking justice, equality, and inclusion. They shared these insights through international women's rights networks in preparation for the Vienna meeting, where they took on key roles organizing non-governmental participation and lobbying (E. Friedman 1995).

However, feminists became frustrated at the degree of backlash they experienced at the follow-up and other social conferences in the 2000s, as more conservative governments and NGOs, led by the Vatican, attempted to roll back gains. Moreover, many found that the conferences provided paltry results in comparison with the enormous effort invested in organizing around them, given the roadblock that global neoliberal economic policies threw in the way of improving most women's lives. Upon the initiation of the World Social Forum in Brazil in 2001, activists turned to this social movement–oriented "counter-hegemonic transnational space." Brazilian feminists became aware that gender analysis and issues were absent from the initial programming and quickly organized transnationally to convince the organizers to rectify this omission (César de Oliveira 2002). Since that time, Latin American feminists have sought to have an impact on the forum as a whole, continuing to debate whether carving out their own spaces or bringing feminist perspectives into other arenas is more effective (S. Alvarez, Faria, and Nobre 2004).

Transnational actions had a mixed outcome. Formal international opportunities helped Latin American feminists legitimate their demands at the national and local levels. In many countries these opportunities energized organizing and nurtured transnational connections, as Chapter 10 makes clear. But they exacerbated the divisions among feminist groups and between feminist groups and women's movements. International resources, often targeted at the most professionalized groups, and discourses, such as the importance of "mainstreaming a gender perspective," reinforced the split between those focused on policy making and those focused on movement building. Engaging with formal international processes drew resources and attention away from national contexts, sometimes "unsettling intra movement solidarities while accentuating class, racial-ethnic, and other inequalities among activists" (S. Alvarez et al. 2003:554).

Less-official forums such as the *encuentros*, oriented to the agendas of activists, strengthened solidaristic contacts, particularly through regional networks, and circulated new conceptualizations of issues. Despite their often-idyllic settings in places such as the Brazilian and Dominican coasts, they were not free from conflict over funding and inclusion. At times they magnified national controversies that might not have otherwise diffused as rapidly and destructively, such as when a group of Chilean feminists oriented the seventh *encuentro* around their bifurcation of the feminist world into autonomous and co-opted camps (S. Alvarez et al. 2003:554–557). However, deliberations made possible by this unique space continue to push the limits of what feminism is and who feminists are. Jumping to the thirteenth *encuentro* in Lima, Peru, in November 2014, organizers and attendees grappled with the intersections of gender and ethnic identity and oppression; transmasculine[5] participants questioned why participants must identify as women; and young women critiqued "adultcentrism" (E. Friedman 2015).

As important as transnational opportunities have been, national contexts of the 1990s remained key to the mediation of women's demands. Although feminists could now lobby democratic governments, they operated in a center-right context with inconsistent left support, and in many countries the Catholic Church had renewed legitimacy as a political actor following its staunch opposition to authoritarian rule. Moreover, growing evangelical denominations, whose promises of a better life after death and social support in this one appealed to many, often joined the Church in reinforcing traditional family structures and gendered expectations. However, key successes included the nearly region-wide adoption of statutory candidate gender quotas and legislation prohibiting domestic violence. Argentina and Costa Rica pulled ahead of other countries in female representation in their lower houses at almost 40 percent, although a regional advance was evident: in 2008 the percentage of women representatives in countries with quota provisions reached 20.5 percent, an increase of nearly 60 percent from a decade earlier (Llanos and Sample 2008; Inter-Parliamentary Union 2008b).

The negotiations for these laws and other proposals did not show a clear correspondence between feminist demands and left party support. Right-wing parties, influenced by religious forces, ensured that family values underpinned much of the antiviolence legislation, and some parties recognized that including women on party lists might benefit them at the polls (Macaulay 2006; Baldez 2004). Meanwhile, the Left refused to spend political capital supporting the feminist demand for reproductive rights, given the unpopularity of abortion in opinion polls across the region and active lobbying by the church. In 2006, in the most notable contradiction between left governance and reproductive rights, Nicaragua criminalized therapeutic abortion under the leadership of former revolutionary Daniel Ortega. Ortega's compromises with the Right and the Catholic Church, his political manipulation to defeat former allies, and the still-unresolved accusations by his stepdaughter of sexual slavery alienated feminists (Kampwirth 2008).

Left parties and revolutionary governments thus incorporated some feminist demands but subordinated women and their issues to "larger" goals—and for political expedience. The agenda for social change around gender and sexuality proceeded without consistent support from the Left.

The 21st Century Left on Gender and Sexuality: Making a Difference?

The historical context outlined above took place with the Left out of power—or fighting for the survival of a revolution. Although its dominance has recently been challenged, did the Left's entry into democratic governance made a difference? To answer this question, the remainder of the chapter provides a comparison of four countries: Argentina, Bolivia, Chile, and Venezuela. These countries offer a seemingly wide spectrum of political transformation. Chile is a representative democracy based on principles of political competition and separation of powers, underpinned by neoliberal economics. Argentina, while formally similar, has been characterized by executive dominance and the heavy influence of parties claiming the legacy of the charismatic historical figure of Juan Perón; its economic policy in the 2000s challenged market principles. Although Venezuela and Bolivia run elections, they have consolidated executive power and promote more direct participation through national popular movements, undergirded by even more state direction of economic development. Some analysts have offered normative distinctions among them, characterizing Chile as part of the "right Left," seeking to promote (neo)liberal democracy and equitable social policies, and condemning the others as a more radical "wrong Left," mired in an outdated, power-hungry, and free-spending populism (Castañeda 2006). But as the rest of this chapter will show, similarities across the "good-bad" divide, differences within each side, and each country's complex contextual realities with regards to gender and sexuality complicate such dichotomous assessments. Using gender and sexuality as lenses reveals a distinct reality of the Latin American Left.

To assess change within each country and across them, the rest of this chapter focuses on six areas pertaining to women's status and rights, as well as addressing LGBT rights. It first presents the record with respect to improvements in women's socioeconomic status. To demonstrate the impact of left governance on feminist state-society relations, the next section examines contemporary feminist and women's movements and their relationship with state feminism in the form of national women's machinery. The following section evaluates women's representation in national decision-making. The final three sections look at three key policy issues: violence against women, reproductive rights, and sexual and gender identity rights.

To briefly summarize the findings of this analysis: Venezuela's twenty-first century socialism has depended on the mobilization of women, but, as with its twentieth-century predecessors, predominantly to support the Chavista political project, named after former president Húgo Chávez, who was in power from 1998 until his death in 2013. Although they have made some important rhetorical gains, feminists have struggled to convince political decision-makers in the executive and legislative branches to implement gender-equitable policies. There are clear parallels in Bolivia: reflecting the impact of a women's coalition, the most recent constitution in Bolivia offers progressive language on gender-related rights, and there has been an astonishing leap in terms of women's national political representation; Bolivia currently has the second highest in the world at 53 percent. President Evo Morales has acknowledged the important political role of indigenous women, while reproductive rights and LGBT rights have been largely stymied. In Chile, two-term President Michelle Bachelet has sought to advance women's political, social, and economic rights despite stiff opposition on more controversial issues, and has signed civil unions into law. In Argentina, LGBT movements have been more successful in pressing for identity recognition than feminists have been in achieving long-sought decriminalization of abortion. President Cristina Fernández de Kirchner approved both same-sex marriage and gender identity recognition legislation. Despite robust legislative representation for women, she has been less open to including feminists in her administration or on her political agenda.

Women's Socioeconomic Status

These countries seemed to have made good on the leftist promise to ameliorate the material inequalities of their male and female citizens, albeit through a traditional understanding of their different social roles. In particular, all have addressed the welfare of poor women and their families. They even ensured it during and after the 2008 global recession, although the more recent moves toward austerity in the wake of the commodities crisis imperil these gains. In 2003, Chávez's administration introduced a parallel social service infrastructure at the national level called *misiones*. Focused on basic needs ranging from literacy to health care to housing, these programs incorporated large numbers of poor and working-class women as recipients, volunteers, and employees; since 2001 the national Women's Bank has offered microloans for poor entrepreneurs. In 2009, the Morales administration, under pressure from the indigenous women's movement, began a conditional cash transfer (CCT) program, Bono Juana Azurduy, through which women receive funds for participating in prenatal and postpartum programs, giving birth in a hospital, and attending child health education programs, as well as taking young children for regular checkups and vaccinations. Argentina implemented three waves of CCT programs under successive Kirchner administrations. While earlier ones were oriented more at ameliorating the lack of employment for both men and women, requiring a work component, later versions enforced traditional familial gender relations. Plan Familias focused on supporting poor mothers with regards to their children's welfare, an orientation continued with the next iteration of the CCT program (Tabbush 2010). Although Bachelet has not implemented national programs at the same scale, she has taken action on senior health care, education, and employment for the poorest sectors (Savelis 2007:73). The "Chile Grows With You" poverty reduction program included support for poor women across their adult lives: more than eight hundred new day-care centers for poor children opened during Bachelet's first administration, and minimum non-contributory pensions, expected to largely benefit poor women who have not worked consistently in the formal economy, were put into place (Thomas 2015).

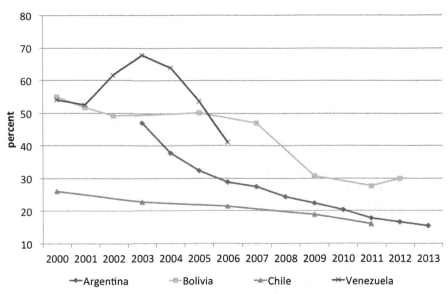

FIGURE 9.1 Proportion of female-headed households in poverty
Source: SEDLAC (CEDLAS and The World Bank).
Note: Poverty level defined as less than US$4.00 per day.

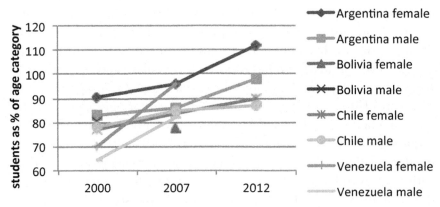

FIGURE 9.2 Combined gross enrollment ratio: Primary to tertiary
education
Source: Human Development Reports

As Figure 9.1 demonstrates, the focus on poor women's life conditions clearly paid off. There was a marked decrease in the percentage
of female-headed households living in poverty in these countries. While
it is hard to determine cause and effect, over the past decade these
kinds of programs seemed to be linked to other positive effects. As the

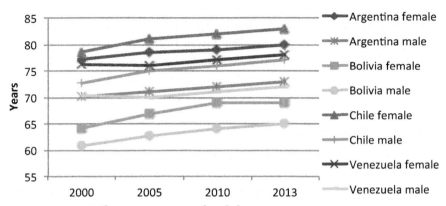

FIGURE 9.3 Life expectancy at birth by sex
Source: Human Development Reports

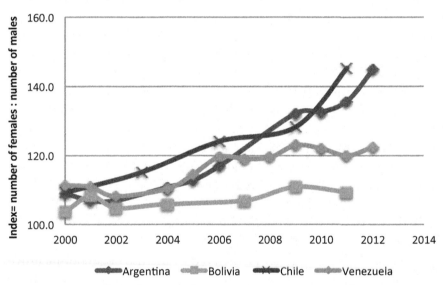

FIGURE 9.4 Index of women living in poverty compared to men
Source: CEPALSTAT

snapshots of figures 9.2 and 9.3 show, women had largely higher rates of educational enrollment and found improvement in life expectancy. This evidence suggests that left governments did make a difference in material elements of women's status. However, as Figure 9.4 shows, women made up a steadily growing number of the poor in these countries, with the exception of Bolivia; and they were two to four times as likely as men not to have their own income (Montaño Virreira 2015:34). Thus, although poor women were better off overall under these governments, they faced structural impediments to their taking advantage of employment opportunities. These indicators reveal a troubling gendered dimension of well-being that, if anything, worsened under the Left.

Feminist State-Society Relations

In moving from women's socioeconomic status to questions of whether feminist voices are heard by and can have an impact on state institutions, the picture of Left support blurs. Left governments often incorporate feminist activists and, in some cases, expand the abilities of their national women's machinery. But to what ends? Sometimes it has been to further national projects, rather than advance women's rights per se. This goal can exacerbate preexisting tensions between feminist and women's movements, as state actors seek to mobilize the latter. However, feminists within the state can make a difference on the direction of policy.

Although affected by the political polarization that characterized Chávez's rule, feminist activists in Venezuela advanced some issues from their "minimum agenda": the application of antiviolence statutes, the decriminalization of abortion, gender parity for electoral lists, prohibiting gender stereotyping in advertising, and achieving a minimum wage for homemakers. The incorporation of feminists from left parties into Chávez's government facilitated the institutionalization of agenda elements. For example, feminist intervention in the 1999 constitutional convention resulted in the prohibition of gender discrimination and the promotion of gender equality, illustrated by the use of gender-inclusive language throughout the constitution (for example, *cuidadanos y cuidadanas* [male and female citizens]). It also protects maternity, allows women to transfer their citizenship to foreign spouses, and recognizes housework as an economic activity. However, activists were not successful at getting the majority of women on board with the agenda (Espina 2000, 2007).

In contrast, the Chávez government made an effort to incorporate women into the "Bolivarian Revolution."[6] Although Chávez did not establish the highly institutionalized mass women's organizations that characterized the Cuban and Nicaraguan revolutions, his National Women's Institute (INAMUJER) attempted to bring together a "Bolivarian Women's Force" made up of members of the 22,000 *puntos de encuentro*, or "encounter points," which are small state-supported women's groups. These groups have been able to access microcredit and participate in health and women's rights campaigns, as well as national women's meetings (INAMUJER 2008). Even though men hold leadership roles in the social service *misiones* programs, women's participation in such opportunities has led to their empowerment (Fernandes 2007b).

In general, INAMUJER followed in the footsteps of other revolutionary women's organizations: its primary goal was to mobilize women for state ends. As a prominent example, the International Women's Day marches it sponsored focused on protesting the US invasion of Iraq, Colombia's violation of Ecuador's sovereignty, and Exxon's actions against the Venezuelan state oil company. These marches, attended by thousands of women, did not focus on their condition or rights. Recognizing the importance of women to the Bolivarian project, Chávez promoted INAMUJER to a full ministry, the Ministry of Woman's Popular Power and Gender Equality (MINMUJER), in 2009. Its intersectional focus sought women's integration across issues of race, ethnicity, and class into the Chavista project. But this integration focus often resulted in clientelistic relations between the poor women who depended on state resources and those who organized them through state-led organizations and programs (Elfenbein 2015).

In Bolivia, the movement sector was not able to overcome the preexisting polarization between feminists who worked with pre-Morales governments and those who rejected engagement with the state (Monasterios 2007). The latter, while small in terms of numbers, have been symbolically important both in Bolivia and in the region, seeking to support grassroots women while espousing radical, antipatriarchal politics. The anarcho-feminist group Mujeres Creando (Women Creating) in particular is famous for its direct action orientation, including graffiti, street theater, and protests. While one founding member became a consultant for the Morales government, others have insisted that he remains as patriarchal as previous male leaders and continue their work in public and community spaces.

As in Venezuela, some feminists used the opportunity of a constitutional convention to create and lobby for a common agenda. Over two years the Mujeres y Asamblea Constituyente (Women and Constituent Assembly) project, run by a group of feminist and development NGOs, organized more than 400 opportunities across the country for approximately 20,000 women to take part in formulating a consensus around their demands for the new constitution (Rousseau 2011:21). In a first for the country, if not the region, the NGOs who began the project succeeded in nurturing collaborations across ethnic and class lines by working with indigenous women's organizations (ibid.:25). The project's notable influence on the draft constitution is evident in many articles, some of which are discussed below.

Reflecting Chávez's efforts, Morales began direct dialogue with low-income indigenous women organized through neighborhood councils and the Bartolina Sisa National Federation of Peasant Women. That organization has grown tremendously under successive Morales administrations; it currently boasts over 100,000 members across the country (Villarroel 2011). However, indigenous men and women have participated in great numbers in opposition to the Morales' administration's extractivist economic orientation, which they believe is violating former commitments to environmental preservation and justice (Achtenberg 2013).

Morales has not used his women's machinery as a tool for mobilization; instead he chose to make the office less important. He threatened to get rid of the Vice Ministry of Women, under the Sustainable Development Ministry, as a "form of discrimination": since "women will be ministers," there would be no reason to have a special office for the sector. In sharp contrast, women within Morales's MAS party and the leader of the Bartolina Sisa Federation insisted they would fight to keep it, and even transform it into a full-fledged "Gender Ministry." Nevertheless, the office was downgraded to Vice Ministry of Gender, Generational, and Family Issues in the Justice Ministry (Bolpress 2006; NotiEMAIL 2006).

Under the four Concertación governments Chile has had since re-democratization, prominent feminists in this dominant political coalition have established close relationships with state actors or entered the state. As in Bolivia, radical autonomous feminists critiqued those who engaged with the state, seeing them as co-opted by a liberal, capitalist, patriarchal system. Moreover, as in Venezuela, there was a disconnect between those feminists professionally active in the state and nongovernmental organizations and those active in grassroots organizations of women (Ríos Tobar 2007).

Some of this disconnect, paradoxically, came through the relative success of Chile's national women's ministry. Compared to Venezuela and Bolivia, Chile's National Women's Service (SERNAM) is well established (begun during the Chilean transition to democracy) and has considerable political clout. Bachelet increased its budget by 13 percent in 2007, making it "one of the biggest, best-funded and highest-ranked national women's agencies in Latin America" (ibid.:28). Like the rest of the Chilean government, SERNAM has relied more on the technical expertise of professionals than on the incorporation of grassroots organizations, marginalizing nonelite actors (ibid.). However, Bachelet's appointment of a feminist to lead the ministry had an immediate impact, including increased attention to domestic violence. In her second term, the president further solidified support, giving SERNAM institutional stability as a ministry (Thomas 2015).

Turning to Argentina, the National Women's Council has suffered from politicization since its inception. Initially supported by feminist and women's movement activists who fought to both open and maintain the space at near-ministerial level (Guzmán 2001:21), the failure of presidents to support leadership committed to women's rights has resulted in tense or broken alliances with activists. The council lost both relevance and budget under President Kirchner (and her husband Nestor Kirchner, her immediate predecessor); its president was appointed for her partisan loyalties rather than links with feminism. As further evidence of the council's lack of feminist commitment, the subsecretary in charge of policy on violence against women publicly stated her opposition to abortion and lack of knowledge about pay inequity (Tabbush et al. 2016). Surprisingly, right-wing president Mauricio Macri has appointed a long-time feminist to head the council, but it remains an office inside the family section of the Ministry of Social Development.

This overview of feminist state-society relations under left governments reflects historical patterns but shows new trends as well. In line with his revolutionary predecessors, Chávez attempted to mobilize women within his "Bolivarian Revolution." His national women's machinery was crucial in this endeavor, prioritizing national goals over the fulfillment of women's rights. Morales also sought to incorporate grassroots women into his national project, but instead of relying on Bolivia's women's machinery, he diminished its role. Although his "mainstreaming" view ("women will be ministers") may garner political legitimacy in a society where ethnicity and class are more politically articulated than gender, the defense of women's machinery by his supporters showed its

continued relevance. In these "more left" cases, other political opportunities have been more fruitful for the articulation of feminist concerns. The constitutional reform processes overseen by Chávez and
Morales stimulated women's mobilization; in both countries they had
an impact on fundamental legal structures. In Argentina, the fate of the
women's machinery showed its vulnerability to executive manipulation
as well, although the Argentine system does not attempt to mobilize
women to the extent of the Venezuelan. In Chile, feminist alliances
with left parties have given them access to the state, and executives
have championed long-standing and high-profile women's machinery.
But the coexistence of state support for feminist issues and co-optation
of movement energies continues, given the governments' commitments
to technocracy and neoliberalism. Each country attests to the historical
dependence of state feminism on the political will of the executive, as
well as inequality of access between women with and without class and
race privilege.

Women's Representation in Decision-Making Positions

The percentage of women in national parliaments is often taken as a
proxy for gender equality—for example, as part of the United Nations
Development Program's "Gender Empowerment Measure." Certainly,
the number of women in decision-making positions indicates the extent
of gender equality in descriptive representation. However, descriptive
representation is not equivalent to substantive representation; female
leadership does not automatically translate into the promotion of a
feminist agenda. This is especially true when women's crosscutting
identities have saliency. For example, in Bolivia, "elite urban women
linked to the leadership of right-wing parties mainly benefited" from
gender candidate quotas under former president Sánchez de Lozada,
bringing their own political, class, and geographic perspectives to their
governance objectives (Monasterios 2007:34). They took advantage of
an opportunity for women to promote conservative policy, much like
their historical predecessors in the region. In addition, party systems
and structures have an impact on what women are able to accomplish
for women: strong parties in stable systems will be more able to exert
discipline over all their members, whereas weak parties and fragmented
systems will lead to more independence in their members' actions. Because these institutional outcomes can cut either way in terms of the

outcomes for gender-based interests, party platforms can have more impact on substantive representation than legislators' gender. Finally, if power is concentrated in the hands of executives, legislative representation may be less than salient in terms of real change.

With the difference between counting and consciousness in mind, this section examines the extent to which women participated in national representation and decision making in the governments of Chávez, Morales, Kirchner, and Bachelet. The following discussion is based on the percentage of women in the lower or single house of parliament, the global comparative measure of women's representation, during the past fifteen years. The section also examines policies to address the underrepresentation of women and women's cabinet positions. This survey reveals that left governments have been no guarantee for women's descriptive representation.

The Venezuelan "Bolivarian Revolution" did not result in high descriptive representation for women. After the constitutional reform of 2000 that consolidated power under President Hugo Chávez, women's representation jumped from 10 to 17 percent, an impressive increase. However, it hung there until its more recent decline to just over 14 percent after the opposition took control in late 2015.[7] Those results came despite the passage that year of a gender parity law that specifies that all electoral lists must present an equal number of male and female candidates in alternating positions, or, in cases where parity is not possible, that no less than 40 percent of either sex be represented. However, the law came into force after primaries had been held (PARLINE n.d.).

Quite a different picture emerges in Bolivia. When Morales was elected, the percentage of women in parliament declined slightly from 18.5 to 16.9, but, foreshadowing later developments, 74 percent, including the president of the assembly, were from his MAS party (Draper 2006). In addition, 86 of the 255 elected members of the 2007 Constituent Assembly were women, achieving a quota of one-third of the representatives. The Women and Constituent Assembly movement lobbied for this quota and its fulfillment, as well as encouraging turnout among women (Coordinadora de la Mujer et al. 2007). They also succeeded in having gender parity quotas written into the constitution. This has resulted in an astonishing upward trend in women's descriptive representation, which doubled between 2010 and 2015 to hit 53 percent. Bolivia currently ranks as the country with the second-highest percentage of women in its parliament (after Rwanda).

Bachelet has sought to improve the percentage of women in the Chilean lower house. It has risen slowly in the last three elections, from 10.8 percent to 15 percent. Recognizing her country's below-average status in regional terms, Bachelet introduced a bill in October 2007 to achieve equal political participation between men and women, specifying that party lists and party leadership positions can be no more than 70 percent of either gender. Parties opting to include more women than the minimum are eligible for extra state funds (Bunting 2007). Although she confronted a recalcitrant legislature during her first administration, under her second one, quota legislation to ensure that either gender makes up at most 60% of candidates has gone forward as part of a general electoral system reform. It has yet to be implemented in national elections.

Argentina, the regional leader with a legislated quota for female candidates of 30 percent going back to 1991, enshrined positive action in the highest law of the land by including a stipulation in the 1994 constitution that no future law can lower the quota. Although a female candidate had to bring a complaint of non-compliance all the way to the Inter-American Commission on Human Rights (IACHR), in 2001 that body brokered a so-called "friendly settlement" in which the Argentine executive agreed to issue a decree reinforcing quota legislation. Since that time, left-leaning governments have overseen quota fulfillment, with between 36 and 38 percent of the congress made up of female representatives.

Cabinet positions, appointed by executives and changed at their discretion (with congressional oversight), are a sensitive measure of the commitment of executives to gender equality in decision-making posts. The finding that left presidents are likely to appoint women to their cabinets is partially confirmed here (Escobar-Lemmon and Taylor-Robinson 2005; executive branch websites for each government). Bachelet famously implemented gender parity in her first appointments; in her second term, she dropped to 39 percent; Chávez had a 30 percent female cabinet, which his successor, Maduro, dropped to 22 percent; and Morales's cabinet is 28 percent female, including, at first, Justice Minister Casimira Rodríquez, a Quechua Indian and head of the union of domestic workers. Although she has since left the cabinet, her position continues to be held by a woman. Finally, Cristina Fernández de Kirchner's final cabinet was 24 percent female, divided between more and less traditional posts; her successor has only appointed three women (9.5 percent).

This section shows that more equitable distribution of decision-making positions has been the result of women's mobilization. In Argentina, female candidates insisted on the realization of quota legislation; in Bolivia, the key feminist demand was written into the constitution, with remarkable results. Cabinet making, controlled by the executive, provides a more sensitive measure of executive commitment to gender equality. Here Bachelet has made a significant effort; Maduro has not matched his predecessor's commitment, such as it was; Morales has yet to reach 30 percent female; and, while Kirchner was not concerned with parity, Macri is even less attentive to gender in his appointments. The gender of the executive does not seem to be relevant to descriptive representation at the cabinet level.

The 21st Century Left on Gender and Sexuality: Towards Rights and Protections

Violence Against Women

Moving from counting to consciousness, this section examines the first of three policy areas that, given the depth of their challenge to gender and sexual power relations, offer crucial evidence of the influence of advocates on left governments. New legislation against violence against women is reflective of feminist positions, although governments have been uneven in promoting it.

Bolivia's 1995 Law Against Domestic and Family Violence reflected the regional trend of protecting the family rather than addressing the gender-related nature of much violence in the home. Although a powerful regional-level statute, the Organization of American States' Inter-American Convention on the Prevention, Punishment, and Eradication of Violence Against Women, was developed and adopted in the early 1990s, across the region its feminist perspective, which insists that signatory states sanction violence against women whether committed by private or public actors, was (mis)translated at the national level (Friedman 2009). In reaction, feminist and women's movements pressured for change. In Bolivia, the Women and Constituent Assembly movement offered new language for the constitution that embodied a more feminist perspective on violence against women: "All people, women in particular, have the right to not suffer physical, sexual or psychological violence, as much in the family as in society." Moreover, the state is obliged to take the remedies necessary to "prevent, eliminate, and sanction gender violence" (Bolivian Constitution, Article 15, paragraphs 2–3). This constitutional precept was finally translated into a major reform of the legislation: in 2013, the comprehensive bill to guarantee women a life free from violence sanctioned both physical and psychological violence, as well as femicide (killing based on female gender), sexual violence, and spousal violence. However, implementation remains a stubborn problem: a lack of funding and training of public officials, crucially the police, has resulted in outcomes such as the conviction of only eight men in the reported 206 femicides that took place between 2013 and 2014 (Mullenax 2015).

A similar story has played out in Venezuela. Venezuelan women's organizations, outraged by the attorney general's 2003 decision to suspend restraining orders against batterers, successfully lobbied for the replacement of the Law on Violence Against Women and the Family with the 2006 Law on the Right of Women to a Life Free from Violence (Espina 2007:21). But the government delayed its implementation: the first antiviolence courts were slow to open their doors, and INAMUJER's promised nationwide provision of women's shelters was marred by delayed openings. By 2011, only three shelters existed in Venezuela (Elfenbein 2015).

Although organized pressure from civil society can have an impact on legislative change, a comparison of Chile and Argentina shows the importance that the national women's machinery can have in ensuring effectiveness on this issue by providing institutional support for feminist demands. Both countries adopted more family-oriented legislation in 1994, at the beginning of the regional wave of anti-violence statutes. And, under pressure by feminist advocates, both countries revised their initial legislation to more clearly reflect the need to challenge gender relations. In 1994, during the Christian Democrat–dominated era of the Concertación coalition, Chile adopted the law Establishing Standard Procedures and Penalties for Acts of Violence Within the Family. Advocates considered this legislation unsatisfactory, given the leeway that judges had over the fate of abusers and its lack of criminal sanction. Under Bachelet, the executive took the side of feminist legislators, backing a significant revision to the legislation that provided for criminal sanction; it also established family courts to deal with domestic conflicts and new shelters, walk-in assistance, and counseling centers for battered women (Estrada 2007; Haas 2007). Although Argentina's revised law widened the ambit of violence prevention beyond the family, eliminated reconciliation between spouses as a legal resolution, and offered victims guaranteed services, Chile's reform is superior. It is both more powerful, given its outright criminalization of domestic violence and state responsibilities for prevention, and better implemented, in terms of education, training, and victim services (Franceschet 2010: 2, 9). The role of SERNAM in this policy success is undeniable: its ability to develop and propose legislation, as well as its robust support from Bachelet, could not be more different from the weak institutional position and support from Argentine executives for the National Women's Council (ibid.:3). As a result, Chile is adding a reported 24 shelters to the existing 16 (Scruby 2014; Franceschet 2010:19). Although Chile is reported to have a "pandemic" of domestic violence, with the highest reported cases in the region (Scruby 2014), those statistics themselves may reflect the better infrastructure for monitoring this scourge. In Argentina, more than 1,800 women were victims of femicide between 2008 and 2014: or one woman killed every 36 hours. After two notorious murders of young women at the hands of their partners in early 2015, the obvious impunity for perpetrators of gender-based violence and the weak implementation of anti-violence legislation inspired a massive outcry across Argentina in the form of hundreds of thousands of protestors from all walks of life who took to the streets in June, mobilized by the slogan #NiUnaMenos (Not One Less) (Goñi 2015). Although it remains to be seen if demands to implement the law will be heeded by the government and judiciary, one important step has been the appointment of one of the protest organizers and a long-time anti-domestic violence advocate, Fabiana Túñez, as the head of the Argentine women's machinery.

On the issue of violence against women, legislative efforts have improved older statutes by incorporating feminist perspectives contained in a regional statute. But, with the exception of Chile, the state is far from taking the lead; implementation in every case depends on hard work from advocates.

Reproductive Rights

In the area of reproductive rights, especially the lightning-rod issue of abortion, left governments seem unable or unwilling to resist the strong opposition from the political Right and religious leaders. This is true in all four countries, despite a vocal regional reproductive-rights movement.

Although feminist and LGBT activists lobbied hard to use the 2007 constitutional convention in Venezuela to advance reproductive rights, women's ability to interrupt pregnancies in the first trimester was not included. Religious leaders joined with secular politicians in defeating this effort. Implementation of other reproductive rights has been more rhetoric than reality. For example, while the government has stipulated that the health care system must guarantee women and men's access to contraception, and claimed that it has done so, research indicates that only 30 percent of sexually active women have access to family planning. With only 10 percent of sexually active adolescents using contraception, Venezuela has the highest rate of teenage pregnancy in South America (Elfenbein 2015). Eighty out of every 1,000 girls between the ages of 15 and 19 gave birth in 2014 (worldbank.org).

In Bolivia some headway was made during the constitutional convention. The 2009 constitution states that: "men and women are guaranteed the exercise of their sexual and reproductive rights" (Article 66), and an attempt to protect life from the moment of conception was unsuccessful (Friedman-Rudovsky 2007). However, women were far from united in demanding reproductive autonomy, with indigenous women's movements as a whole opposed to abortion legalization. In a limited success in early 2014, feminist advocates convinced the Constitutional Court to remove the requirement that women seeking abortions in the legal cases of rape, incest, or extreme risk to health need court approval (although they must present a police report in the former two situations or doctor's diagnosis in the latter). Breaking with Morales, a female indigenous MAS representative brought the original case challenging the constitutionality of the restrictive abortion law (Achtenberg 2014).

In Chile, President Bachelet—who as health minister allowed the legalization of the so-called morning-after pill—decreed that all contraception, including this method, be provided free of charge in public clinics to all girls and women over the age of fourteen. This move was denounced by the Catholic Church and the Right. Right-wing politicians took the policy to the Constitutional Tribunal, claiming that the distribution order for the morning-after pill violated the constitution's protection of the right to life from the moment of conception. The tribunal ruled in their favor in April 2008, in a decision that cannot be appealed. Meanwhile, although Bachelet's party has stated its support for the decriminalization of therapeutic abortion, and Bachelet herself introduced a decriminalization measure in early 2015, the political opposition to this measure has meant a stalemate.

Despite an increasingly vocal and massive movement for abortion decriminalization—including 338 organizations across the country—advocates have encountered stiff resistance from decision-makers at the top of the Argentine hierarchy. Even though decades of activism have resulted in more than 60 legislators signing on to the most recent decriminalization bill, President Kirchner and her supporters prevented it from coming to the floor. In a new approach, feminist lawyers have begun to seek judicial support, and a 2012 Supreme Court decision came down in favor of allowing women to obtain abortions without a police report or court order if they have become pregnant after non-consensual sexual relations (Tabbush et al. 2016).

The impact of more than a decade of Vatican-inspired social mobilization against abortion and many forms of contraception is evident. Often trying to balance demands of political allies on a topic that has been characterized as a matter of moral absolutes, left executives seem either unable or unwilling to back a policy that deeply challenges gender roles—and religious belief (Htun 2003:chap. 6, 168). Activists have been more successful in persuading judiciaries to allow abortions in those limited exceptions to their prohibition.

Sexual and Gender Identity Rights

Although national legislation on sexual rights and gender identity remains uneven across these countries, there is no denying that, in contrast with reproductive rights, significant national efforts, and some successes, have gotten underway in this area. Like feminists, LGBT activists have made use of constitutional reform openings, and certain executives have responded positively to their demands for human rights.

In Venezuela's first constitutional reform in 1999, the Catholic Church blocked the addition of a clause stipulating nondiscrimination on the basis of sexual orientation. Eight years later, the clause was included in an unsuccessful attempt to further modify the constitution in 2007. However, between 2010 and 2012, the government took legislative and executive action promoting equality in banking, housing, policing, and employment regardless of sexual orientation. Moreover, since 2009, citizens have been able to change their name if it does not correspond with their gender identity (Elfenbein 2015). In Bolivia, the 2009 constitution promises a radical shift in antidiscrimination policy: Article 14 states, "The State prohibits and punishes all forms of discrimination based on sexual orientation [and] gender identity." This radical development places Bolivia in the vanguard of constitutional protection of gender identity. And in mid-2016, the Bolivian Congress made further progress with a law enabling people to change their gender on official documents. However, the constitution's definition of marriage as between a man and a woman reflects the continued power of the Catholic Church.

During the second Concertación government, in 1998, the Chilean parliament repealed the section of the penal code that criminalized same-sex relations between consenting adults. The reiterated backing of Bachelet and her Socialist Party during her first administration is now bearing fruit for civil unions: in April of 2015, she signed them into law. However, the Law to Establish Measures Against Discrimination remains frozen in the congress (Movimiento de Integración y Liberación Homosexual 2008). In terms of gender identity, the Civil Registry now allows for name and sex changes without undergoing sexual reassignment surgery, and the Labor Bureau will investigate claims against unjust firing on the basis of homophobia or transphobia.

As with quota legislation, Argentina has become both a regional and global leader on LGBT rights. A politically connected and savvy movement for same-sex marriage framed it as part of the human and equal rights trumpeted as central to Kirchnerist governance. They built civil society-based coalitions, but also venue-shopped across Argentina's federal system, seeking friendly municipalities and provinces and different levels of the judiciary. They also sought allies across the political spectrum in both the legislative and executive branches. In contrast with the weak support of national women's machinery for feminist demands, the movement found support from the governmental agency charged with promoting non-discrimination, the National Institute Against Discrimination, Xenophobia, and Racism. Drawing on the resources and rhetoric of their Spanish counterparts, whose own equal marriage reform passed in 2005, the movement was successful: Argentina became the tenth country to legalize same-sex marriage in 2010 (E. Friedman 2012). Immediately building on its success, the movement expanded its coalition and quickly and successfully advocated for the most progressive gender identity law anywhere in the world, which enables people to change their gender identity without recourse to medical or juridical approval, as well as obtain state assistance for sex-change medical intervention. Although the Catholic Church came out in strong opposition to the first development, President Kirchner ultimately supported it; and the second law saw no significant opponents (Tabbush et al. 2016).

Venezuelan and Bolivian constitutional reforms promised antidiscrimination clauses, although with one reform stymied and the other just passed, it is unclear what impact they will have. In Chile, Bachelet has taken steps to recognize sexual rights, even as legislative action has proved impossible. Argentina is at the forefront, a leader in international norms with respect to sexual rights and gender identity.

Conclusion: Seeking Rights from the Left— Advances and Challenges

The findings of this chapter reflect the historical record: having the Left in power makes a difference in some areas and not others. The Left has included grassroots women through attention to their "practical" interests and put more women into decision-making positions. But it has offered uneven support for policies challenging gender and sexual hierarchies.

In terms of gains, the attention paid to socioeconomic inequality, a hallmark of these governments, has had a positive effect on women and their families. "Participatory" democracies such as Venezuela and Bolivia, as they seek to include women in "twenty-first-century" socialist or indigenous nationalist projects, echo revolutionary experiences in Nicaragua and Cuba, and although not on the scale of their predecessors, they do rely on women's mobilization (Fernandes 2007a). They have also opened periodic opportunities for cross-class and cross-ethnic collaboration.

Meanwhile, the representative democracy of Chile has effectively wielded executive branch resources, such as its powerful women's machinery, to advance rights when legislative avenues are closed. Here state feminism has been more effective at promoting feminist goals, pointing to the importance of three elements: feminist leadership inside the state, good relations between state and civil society actors, and finding common ground to build upon. In Argentina, with its weaker machinery, such coincidences have been more effective for LGBT rights.

Left governments are less willing to undertake direct challenges to gender and sexual power relations in the face of religiously inspired opposition. The church-state politics of the twenty-first century do not follow predictable lines, as the actions of Daniel Ortega, and, periodically, Cristina Fernández de Kirchner indicate, and right-leaning politicians and civil society groups have been energized by their own transnational networks, whether Catholic or, increasingly, evangelical. Social benefits have been distributed to the poor in such a way to reinforce continued assumption of women as primarily homemakers. The implementation of antiviolence statutes, with all they imply for disrupting familial hierarchies, is weak. The decriminalization (let alone legalization) of abortion faces implacable opposition and little executive support. Where executive support exists for sexual rights, legislatures are often slow to move.

But the alliances that feminist, female, and LGBT activists have struck up over the past decades, as well as their transnational influences, continue to inform those seeking deeper transformation of left governance today. The human rights framework, which gained powerful meaning in the fight against authoritarianism, continues to provide a legitimating discourse and a basis for cooperation across movement arenas. LGBT activists' demands for nondiscrimination clauses in constitutions, or "the same rights with the same names" in their struggles for marriage equality, show their strategic use of the human rights framework (E. Friedman 2012). The transnational frame of women's rights as human rights was key to regionwide diffusion of antiviolence statutes (E. Friedman 2009). And even reproductive rights advocates have tried to use it, whether in the more neutral framing of reproductive rights as a "right to health," drawing directly from language formulated at the 1990s UN conferences, or the "right to abortion" demanded by some advocates. Cooperation among feminist, women's, and LGBT organizations is a vital resource for advancing unmet demands, and mobilization around the Venezuelan and Bolivian constitutional reforms and antiviolence legislation has demonstrated this potential.

But what of the challenges looming ahead, or already in full flower in countries where legislatures or executives are now in the hands of parties on the right? Because the Right in Latin America is generally closer to religious hierarchies in terms of both ideology and political alliances, feminists and LGBT activists can expect even stauncher resistance to their more transformative demands. With the end of the commodities boom that fueled left-leaning policy delivery, and the alignment between neoliberal economics and right-wing politics, poor women and men can expect less attention to pressing socioeconomic needs. If Argentina is any guide, a period of retrenchment is on the horizon. President Macri has done away with gender parity in his cabinet and through male appointees to the Supreme Court, and in his attempt to swing Argentina in the neoliberal direction has called for austerity measures challenging social welfare provisions, including a 50 percent reduction in the education budget, public employee layoffs, and a reduction in subsidies for basic utilities. Mothers and transgender people are losing healthcare access as community clinics are closed. As with other right-wing governments in the region, the Macri government and its allies in the provinces have begun to criminalize protest as a response to the rise in opposition mobilization (Friedman and Tabbush 2015; Kozameh 2016).

However, as one activist explained, "the social movement groups have learned a lot in the last fifteen years" (Kozameh 2016). After over a decade of negotiating with their states and each other, pressuring for more descriptive and substantive representation, organized women and LGBT people are in a very different place than they were with regard to the last wave of right-wing governments. And sometimes, a common challenge can bring allies closer together, or create fresh coalitions. No strangers to organizing under the most difficult of conditions, they are well positioned to carry their demands into an uncertain future.

Acknowledgements: This chapter draws from my article "Gender, Sexuality, and the Latin American Left: Testing the Transformation" (*Third World Quarterly* 30 [2]). I would like to thank Janet Chavez for her efforts obtaining the quantitative research, Amrita Basu and Kate Hartford for their helpful suggestions, and Kathryn Jay for her editing assistance.

Notes

1. Although this chapter uses the acronym LGBT, it varies across countries and specific movements, reflecting the dynamics and demographics of local activist communities.

2. One example of such a collective challenge is the campaign for an Interamerican Convention on Sexual Rights and Reproductive Rights, which can be found at http://www.convencion.org.uy/ (accessed August 24, 2016).

3. That is, dependent on the exploitation of natural resources for export.

4. This term refers to the mixed race ancestry of many Latin Americans, who descended from Spanish or Portuguese colonists, indigenous peoples, and African slaves. However, many across the region identify primarily as indigenous or Afro-Latin, while others claim exclusively European lineage. The racial and ethnic map of Latin America has a varied topography, with countries such as Bolivia being majority indigenous (though from different indigenous cultures) while others such as Venezuela having a more mestizo population. As the movement relations portrayed above attest, race and ethnic identity is deeply implicated in social hierarchies dominated by those with lighter skin.

5. Transmasculine describes transgender people assigned the female sex at birth who self-identify as masculine. They may or may not chose to take on traditional or stereotypical expressions of masculine gender.

6. Chávez has named his political project after Simón Bolívar (1783–1830), the "liberator of South America," in part because of Bolívar's (ultimately unsuccessful) plan to unite the Andean region following the defeat of the Spanish.

7. All the data on female representation are from Inter-Parliamentary Union (www .ipu.org).

10

State Feminism and Women's Movements in Brazil

Achievements, Shortcomings, and Challenges

CECILIA M. B. SARDENBERG AND ANA ALICE ALCANTARA COSTA

Inequalities = AMONG = women

Introduction

Over the past four decades, women in Brazil have engaged in several struggles in a context of deep social, cultural, economic, and political inequality. Not all women have benefited equally from the collective achievements. The combined effects of sexism, racism, lesbophobia, ageism, and other matrices of inequality and domination in Brazilian society have sustained inequalities among women, in spite of a narrowing of those between women and men. In pursuit of gender justice, women have also waged struggles for social and economic justice. The interweaving of these struggles has given rise to numerous different identity "feminisms" (Sardenberg and Costa 2014). As a result, feminisms in Brazil have expanded and diversified considerably, to the point that it is always best to refer to feminisms in Brazil in the plural. Indeed, within Latin America—and even beyond—Brazilian feminisms have been regarded as "perhaps the largest, most radical, most diverse, and most politically influential of Latin America's feminist movements" (Sternbach et al. 1992:414; see also Sardenberg 2015).

299

Contemporary feminist activism in Brazil emerged in a moment of political upheaval and played an important role in the process of redemocratization, stretching the very concept of democracy in the process (S. Alvarez 1990; Pitanguy 2002). Although self-proclaimed feminists represent a small segment of Brazilian women's movements (Soares et al. 1995; Costa 2005), their impact far exceeds their numbers. In late 2015, nearly thirty thousand black women from all over the country marched in Brasília, the capital, to demonstrate against racism and violence against women—under the coordination of black feminist organizations. Earlier that same year, the "March of Margaridas" brought more than fifty thousand rural women to Brasília—also with the help of feminist organizations. Feminist "SlutWalks" and Lesbian Walks, fighting against sexual violence and for lesbian rights, have been conducted all over the country. In just a few weeks toward the end of 2015, feminists repeatedly demonstrated in the streets of major cities, denouncing a setback in women's rights brought about by the very conservative National Congress, in a movement that has been termed by the media the "women's spring."[1] Close to three hundred thousand women were involved, directly or indirectly, in local and state conferences in preparation for the Fourth National Conference of Public Policies for Women called by the Federal Government and scheduled to take place in Brasília in March 2016.

Brazilian feminisms have made important contributions, not only to changing values regarding women's roles but also toward building a more gender-equitable society (Costa and Sardenberg 1994; Soares et al. 1995). Feminisms in Brazil have been instrumental in the passage of new legislation promoting gender equity and in the formulation of public policies for women, such as the Maria da Penha Law, a complex domestic violence package (Sardenberg 2011), and crafting new spaces in state machineries and apparatuses to implement and monitor them (Costa 2005; Sardenberg 2004). "Women's machineries" have expanded significantly, as seen in the growing numbers of councils and bureaus for women's rights at all governmental levels, and in the creation of state-sponsored networks and special courts to confront domestic violence against women. Brazil's *state feminism* has thus arisen through a gradual process of state institutionalization of the demands of feminist and women's movements.

"State feminism" was first used in relation to the activities of feminists in government (femocrats), but now refers also to the state's response to the demands of feminist and women's movements.

↳ *why did it have to be separate?*

Lovenduski defines state feminism as "the advocacy of women's movement demands inside the state" (2005:4); others see it as pertaining to all "activities of government structures that are formally charged with furthering women's status and rights" (Stetson and Mazur 1995:1–2). In general, the term also refers to state-sponsored women's and equality machineries, or Women's Policy Agencies (WPAs), which can be defined as the government structures in charge of materializing women's demands for gender justice.

This chapter provides a periodized overview of Brazilian feminist and women's movements since the 1970s, showing how dialogues with the state began and eventually led to the establishment of WPAs at different governmental levels (municipal, state, and federal), as well as in the different branches of government (executive, legislative, and judiciary), to deal with the demands of these movements.

In reflecting upon these achievements as well as the challenges facing feminisms in contemporary Brazil, however, it pays to consider one scholar's observation that the expansion of state feminism usually results from blockages to women's participation through more traditional processes (party politics, for instance). In such circumstances, one alternate strategy "is to enter and work directly through the state bureaucracy." Therefore, state feminism could be seen as "a post-liberal democratic solution and one possible institutional channel for giving voice to women." But state machineries alone cannot be expected to effect significant policy changes without feminist constituencies to support them, and state feminism tends to depoliticize women's movements, thus cutting short the very basis of its support (Razavi 2000:210).

This chapter argues that such demobilization is not a foregone conclusion. Although patriarchal culture in contemporary Brazil, as in the past, has continued to block women's participation in formal politics, a participatory form of state feminism is at work. Not only has it strengthened the demands of feminist and women's movements, but it also formulates its policies for women—at least at the federal level—in a more participatory fashion.

This *participatory state feminism* has emerged in Brazil both as a result of growing activism and articulation of feminist and women's groups, and as a response to the persistence of a patriarchal political system and political culture resistant to the empowerment of women. The situation presents a major paradox: on the one hand, we see the presence of a wide and well-articulated women's movement, and on the other, a notorious absence of women in decision-making positions (Costa 2008). Executive, legislative, and judicial branches have remained resistant to the inclusion of more women. One of the consequences of this state of affairs is that we still lack a "critical mass" of women to push for the implementation of new state institutions and policies, such as those designed to confront violence against women (Sardenberg 2007a). There is also little legislative or judicial support for greater advances concerning women's sexual and reproductive rights.

Participatory state feminism has been fostered by the rise to power of more progressive parties, such as the Workers' Party (Partido dos Trabalhadores, or PT), and their commitment to participatory forms of governance (Cornwall and Coelho 2006), such as councils, which operate with equal representation from government and civil society. This does not mean that participatory state feminism has erased the tensions between feminist and women's movements and the state, or that feminisms have not resisted state co-optation. Yet, despite women's poor representation in the upper echelons of all three branches of government, participatory state feminism has made it possible for feminists to take a greater part in the formulation and monitoring of public policies that build a more gender-equitable society.

Feminists' role has been especially evident in the creation of councils for women's rights, with the participation of civil society representatives, as well in the occasional conferences to propose public policies for women (2004, 2007, 2011, and 2016), promoted by President Luis Inácio (Lula) da Silva's administration and continued under President Dilma Roussef. Conferences such as these form a participatory governance structure parallel to the representative democratic system, and are a part of the democratization process in Brazil. At national, state, and local tiers of government, secretariats for sectors such as health, education, women, and the environment are invited to hold regular conferences with organized civil society to shape and monitor public policies. Like the councils, conferences have equal numbers of civil society and state participants, thus offering a significant opportunity for social movements to engage with the state (Sardenberg and Costa 2014).[2] For the 2016 Conference, civil society participation was raised to 60 percent, making room for a wider representation of the different segments that make up feminist and women's movements in Brazil at present.

But we also need major political reforms in order to expand women's presence in top positions. And we need to make sure those women have an eye to guaranteeing the exercise of women's reproductive rights and the implementation and application of domestic violence legislation, two of the major challenges we still face.

Meeting these challenges will inevitably entail some tensions, but tensions have been an integral part of the outstanding capacity of feminism in Brazil to diversify. Diversification refers to the joining of forces of women from different segments of the population—black women, Brazilian indigenous women, rural women, women from remaining runaway slave societies, gypsy women, working-class women—thus mirroring the diverse character of Brazilian society. But this pertains to more than the incorporation of different segments of women's movements into the ranks of feminism. Carving out new spaces of action, be they in the state apparatuses or in the nongovernmental organizations, universities, unions, and political parties that make up the institutions of civil society—and in local, national, or global arenas—is equally important (S. Alvarez 2000; Costa 2005). This process impels the *professionalization* of feminist activists (S. Alvarez 1998b) and the development of what we might characterize as new feminist careers, including academic ones. Professionalization, by means of special training for women and the emergence of nongovernmental feminist organizations, speaks to the need for more feminists trained to meet the challenges of incorporating a feminist gender perspective—that is, one geared to women's empowerment—within the state apparatus and in the different institutions of civil society. Both diversification and professionalization have been positive developments for feminisms in Brazil, in spite of the tensions that accompany them.

In the chapter that I wrote together with Ana Alice Costa for the 2010 edition of this collection, we highlighted both the major achievements and the shortcomings and challenges of feminist struggles in contemporary Brazil. Since then, much has changed, including the election in 2010 and re-election in 2014 of Dilma Rousseff, the first woman to hold the presidency of the Brazilian Republic. Nevertheless, she faces one of the most conservative Congresses in our history, with a large minority of religious fundamentalists who have pushed through legislation taking rights away from women and from lesbians, bisexuals, gays, and transgender people (LGBT). I will demonstrate that, despite these setbacks, state feminism *in its participatory form* continues to be an important instrument in the fight for gender equality in Brazil.

To better address the issues here raised, I begin with a periodization of feminist struggles in Brazil, tracing the emergence and consolidation of state feminism and the challenges it encountered. Next, I examine how state feminism in Brazil has furthered women's struggles: in combating their underrepresentation in formal politics, confronting violence against women, and advancing state support for the exercise of women's reproductive rights, focusing on the legalization of abortion.

As a feminist who has engaged in activism inside and outside academe, I have traced these different paths of feminist activism in Brazil and engaged in many of the struggles discussed in this chapter. My expectations and frustrations regarding feminisms and women's movements in Brazil will inevitably emerge in this analysis, revealing the complexity of the "engaged objectivity" (Santos, B 2007) of anyone who, like me, attempts both to engage in and to analyze transformative actions in society.

Feminist and Women's Movements in Brazil

While women have been active in many social movements, I regard as *women's movements* only those centered on gender-based interests, that is, as Maxine Molyneux suggests, "those arising from the social relations and positioning of the sexes and therefore pertained, but in specific ways, to both men and women" (1998a:231–232). Molyneux has further distinguished women's interests as "practical" or "strategic." Practical interests are "based on the satisfaction of needs arising from women's placement within the sexual division of labour." Strategic ones "involv[e] claims to transform social relations in order to enhance women's position and to secure a more lasting re-positioning of women within the gender order and within society at large" (ibid.:232). *Feminist movements* are here considered as those that are centered on women's strategic gender interests. But we must recognize that these interests are contextually defined: they will vary by time and place, and by the social location of the women involved.

Feminism may be understood as critical thinking as well as political action (Ávila 2007)—be it initiated by men or women—challenging the existing gender order and seeking to improve women's position in society. By this definition, feminism has a long history in Brazil (Sardenberg and Costa 1994; Soares et al. 1995). From the last quarter of the nineteenth century into the first three decades of the twentieth, the so-called First Wave (Chinchilla 1993) of feminists in Brazil defended women's educational rights and struggled in parliament for the extension of suffrage to women, which was granted in 1932. "Second Wave" feminisms emerged in the mid-1970s, bringing into the public arena women's demands for the criminalization of domestic violence, equal pay for equal work, and equity in decision-making spheres. That wave lasted close to fifty years in Brazil, although it incorporated new discourses, diverse strategies, and different forms of organization over the decades.

In discussing the unfolding of feminist campaigns in Brazil, Jacqueline Pitanguy distinguishes three major periods:

> The first, running from the mid-seventies to the mid-eighties, marks the appearance of feminism as a political actor and its struggle for legitimacy and visibility. The second period, which occurred in the eighties, is dominated by the inclusion of a feminist agenda in public policies and normative frames. The third, in the nineties, sees the internationalization of this agenda through transnational coalitions that will play a major role in the re-conceptualization of human rights language. (Pitanguy 2002:1–2)

We could add a fourth period, from 2000 on, characterized by the strengthening of state machineries for the promotion of gender equity and, thus, *participatory state feminism*. This came in response to demands made by women's movements, feminists in particular, aided by international agendas on human and women's rights. The expansion of "identity feminisms" (Costa 2005) as well as the widening of the spheres of feminist activism, particularly evident since the mid-1990s, also contributed to this process. However, the success of this activism has incited a backlash, particularly with the rise of religious fundamentalism in Brazil. Since 2010, there have been repeated attempts to rob us of our rights, leading feminist and women's movements back to street action. This new phase would represent a fifth period in the unfolding of feminist movements in Brazil.

The Dual Struggles of the 1970s

As in other countries of the so-called Southern Cone, contemporary feminisms emerged in Brazil in the context of democratic struggles and resistance against the military regime, which came into power with the coup of 1964. In this first period feminisms had a dual role, fighting for both the reestablishment of democracy and the inclusion of gender equality as a "central democratic theme," thus broadening the democratic agenda (Pitanguy 2002). This also involved the redefinition of the concept of politics in order to include the "personal," for the practices of everyday life should also be considered in the realm of the exercise of citizenship. This perspective was not easily accepted by progressive forces at that time (S. Alvarez 1990).

Feminists in Brazil participated in a much wider women's movement that included in its ranks groups with different interests and forms of organization. Following similar tendencies within Latin America at the time, the women's movement comprised three major "streams" or segments: human rights groups, popular women's movements, and feminist groups (Vargas 1992). In Brazil, however, human rights groups such as the Feminine Movement for Amnesty were never as strong as their counterparts in Argentina and Chile, nor did they take a major leadership role in the wider women's movement. They faded away after 1980, when amnesty was conceded to those in exile, in prison, or otherwise condemned for political reasons. In contrast, both popular women's movements and feminist groups became more visible and have remained much more active than their Brazilian human rights counterparts since the 1980s. During the 1970s, popular women's movements grew around the *clubes de mães* (mothers' clubs) organized by the more progressive sectors of the Catholic Church in the crowded poorer neighborhoods on the outskirts of the larger cities. These "clubs" grew in number and visibility as they came to lead the Movement Against the High Cost of Living, which gained nationwide attention.

Brazilian feminist movements in the 1980s were part of a wide and heterogeneous movement that integrated struggles against the oppression of women in society with the fight for redemocratization of the country. Some other social movements against the military dictatorship downplayed women's strategic interests (Lobo 1987). Nevertheless, feminist organizations strove to expand the discussion on gender inequality by bringing new issues into public debate: domestic violence, the discrimination against women in the labor force, and women's exclusion from decision-making arenas. Although feminists also raised issues such as sexuality, contraception, and abortion, they did so "gradually and awkwardly, since these issues were considered taboo by the

Catholic Church and rejected by democratic forces allied with the church against the military" (Pitanguy 2002:2).

In the 1980s women in neighborhood movements spearheaded a campaign for the creation of community day-care centers (see Sardenberg 2011). They gained support from feminists and formed partnerships and coalitions within the wider women's movements. Most feminist activists in this period were women from middle-class families and had had access to college education. But they had not lived lives of unmitigated privilege: many came from organizations of the "Revolutionary Left" that espoused a Marxist perspective. These feminists, along with other activists, suffered through the experiences of armed struggle, clandestine living, imprisonment, torture, and exile. The bitter irony was that they encountered authoritarianism and sexism not only from repressive state mechanisms but also from their left-wing comrades (Costa 2005). In spite of their critical stance toward these left-wing organizations, Brazilian feminists promoted a wider project of social reform that mobilized women from the popular sectors (Molyneux 2003;269).

The 1980s: Initiating Dialogues with the State

The 1980s ushered in the redemocratization process, in which social movements asserted new demands on the state. As political bodies formulated a new federal constitution with state and local ones to follow, feminist and women's movements enriched the redemocratization process by gathering support for popular amendments to be presented to the national and state congresses and to municipal councils. At the same time, participation in democratization efforts also strengthened women's movements, facilitating the opening of dialogues with the state. Two developments intensified this process: the granting of amnesty to political prisoners and those in exile, and the reform of political parties (Pinto 2003). The amnesty brought leftist activists back to Brazil; among them were many women who had participated in feminist groups in Europe and the United States. Their return strengthened feminisms in Brazil, particularly by creating more demands for the legalization of abortion and the criminalization of violence against women. At the same time, policies regarding the creation of new political parties, a change from the two-party system imposed under the dictatorship, opened the door to the creation of new progressive parties, and thereby created room for women's movements to negotiate alliances with parties that supported their demands.

Feminists also developed an agenda for the formulation of public policies for women (Pitanguy 2002). One of the major policies related to women's health: the 1983 launch of the Program of Integral Assistance to Women's Health (Programa de Assistência Integral à Saúde da Mulher, or PAISM) helped open an important and much-needed dialogue between officials in the Ministry of Health and feminist activists (Villela 2001).[3] As a result of campaign negotiations with opposition candidates in the state of São Paulo, "state-sponsored feminism" also first appeared, with the creation and expansion of state "machinery" to implement public policies for women. In 1983, for example, the Council for the Condition of Women was created, followed in 1985 by the implementation of the first major public policy related to combating violence against women, with the creation of Police Stations for Battered Women (Delegacias Especializadas de Atendimento à Mulher, or DEAMs). By 1992 there were 141 DEAMs across the country; two decades later, there were more than five hundred (Brasil- Secretaria de Políticas para Mulheres 2012). The creation of local and state councils for women's rights moved at a slower pace, but a crucial change came with the creation, in 1985, of the National Council for Women's Rights (Conselho Nacional dos Direitos da Mulher, or CNDM). The CNDM, a mixed council that included governmental and civil society participants, played a leading role in the campaign for the inclusion of women's rights in the new constitution, organizing, along with local women's forums, the gathering of signatures in support of popular amendments throughout the Brazilian states.

Before this period, government-appointed organizations had limited autonomy in making critical decisions. The new councils should have had room for independent decisions and greater efficacy in meeting women's interests; in response to feminist demands, feminist organizations appointed at least half of their members.[4] However, many of the councils were made up of party recruits, which eroded their autonomy (Pinto 2003:71). Some segments of the feminist movement therefore refused to participate in the councils because of their lack of autonomy. This became a controversial issue in the National Feminist Encounter held in 1986 in Belo Horizonte (Sardenberg and Costa 1994).

Indeed, participation in the new organizations and state support for the new policies would create dilemmas for feminists concerning the movement's relationship with the state. Because the state was no considered the "common enemy" (Costa 2005), feminists had to rec nize the capacity of the state to influence society as a whole, and no only through coercive means. It was important to look at the state as a potential ally in the transformation of the condition of women (Molyneux 2003:68). Feminists also began to understand the role of the state in guaranteeing the viability of social, economic, and political rights for the entire population and in amplifying citizenship rights (Costa 2005).

The emergence of state feminism led to the involvement of feminist and women's movements in the formulation of the 1988 constitution.[5] A direct-action campaign, led by the CNDM and supported by social mobilization and political pressure, convinced parliament to include the great majority of women's demands in the new constitution, among them, the principle of equal rights on the basis of sex.[6]

The Women's Caucus or *Bancada* in the National Congress also played a fundamental role in the defense of women's rights in the new constitution. The Bancada included twenty-six women elected for the 1986–1990 legislative mandate, representing several different political parties. Only one was a self-identified feminist. Nevertheless, the women in the Bancada assumed a suprapartisan identity, presenting thirty constitutional amendments to protect women's rights (Pinto 2003:74–75). They were backed by women's groups all over the country who, under the general coordination of the CNDM, collected signatures in support of these amendments.

Under Jacqueline Pitanguy's presidency of the CNDM, the council achieved widespread support throughout the country. As its power increased, it directly challenged institutional sexism and racism. Eventually, however, the Ministry of Justice moved to curtail the CNDM's autonomy and leadership role. A new Minister of Justice not only cut the council's annual budget but also restricted its autonomy. This precipitated the resignation of Pitanguy and all other members and staff of the CNDM. That act had the support of feminist and women's organizations throughout the country, but it took nearly a decade before a national council equally representative of Brazil's feminist and women's movements could be formed again (Sardenberg and Costa 1994). It made sense to step out, however, rather than remain as mere decorative objects!

The 1980s saw the emergence of new segments within the wider women's movements, many of them open to in-depth dialogues with

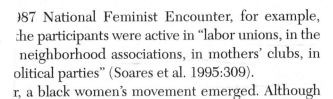

87 National Feminist Encounter, for example, the participants were active in "labor unions, in the neighborhood associations, in mothers' clubs, in olitical parties" (Soares et al. 1995:309).

r, a black women's movement emerged. Although been a part of the Second Wave of feminism in Brazil since its emergence in the mid-1970s, it was only during the 1987 meeting that they came together to mark a black women's movement within Brazilian feminisms. Since then, several national and regional encounters of black women have taken place, and a number of black feminist NGOs have been created in Brazil, leading to the formation of the Forum of Black Women's Organizations (Bairros 1995; Cardoso 2012; Ribeiro 1995).

The 1980s also saw the emergence of academic feminism. In national scientific and academic organizations and in universities throughout the country, research and study groups on women's and gender issues were formed (Costa and Sardenberg 1994), leading to calls for new professionals and thus the creation of new feminist careers. Academic feminism has been expanding ever since, with the proliferation of women's and gender studies groups, primarily in public universities throughout the country, and in numerous special events, publications, theses, and dissertations in this field of study (Sardenberg 2004).

The 1990s: Professionalization and Transnationalization of Feminisms

During the 1990s, the increase in the number of government agencies promoting women's public policy, such as DEAMs, spurred the growth of the demand for professionals specializing in gender and women's issues (Hautzinger 2007). Feminists began to assume the task of expert lobbying for policies for women, in many cases becoming planners and practitioners. This has engendered the emergence of feminist NGOs, many of them springing from the formalization of feminist women's groups (Thayer 2001). These NGOs have taken the lead in lobbying the state (S. Alvarez 1998b). They have engaged with other feminist NGOs on a global level, leading Brazilian feminisms into transnational feminist struggles.

In the early 1990s Brazilian women were active in a number of different organizations emerging from various segments of Brazilian society, giving rise to distinct "feminist identities" (Lebon 1997). Women of the working classes—also known as *classes populares*—were organized in neighborhood associations, in women's departments of factory workers' unions and national union coalitions, and in rural workers' organizations. These groups constitute different segments of the wider women's movement that began to self-identify with feminism, thus joining the ranks of what has since become identified as "popular feminism"; that is, a feminism that involves women from the working classes, as well as a nonwhite feminism. Black feminist associations continued to grow and amplify the feminist political agenda and the parameters of feminist struggles themselves, such that, in Brazil, in accordance with Sonia Alvarez's observations regarding Latin America as a whole, "the existence of various feminisms, with diverse points of view, major issues, means of organization and strategic feminist priorities were widely recognized in the 1990s" (1994:278).[7]

The growth of popular feminism, by diluting the ideological barriers and resistances to feminism, had a major impact on the wider women's movements. The diversity of feminisms in the Brazilian women's movement was already apparent in the preparations for the Fourth World Conference on Women, which convened in Beijing in September 1995. Women from the different segments actively participated in this process (Costa 2005). Indeed, the preparations for Beijing brought new energy into the Brazilian feminist movement. They stimulated the creation of local Women's Forums[8] in cities in which they did not previously exist or had been inactive. They sparked the formation of new coalitions and the establishment of new women and gender departments in unions and in other institutions of civil society. Pre-Beijing preparatory meetings were held in twenty-five of Brazil's twenty-seven states, involving more than eight hundred women's organizations. The Articulation of Brazilian Women (AMB) was formed in 1995 precisely to organize Brazilian women's participation for the Beijing conference.[9]

The AMB was able to achieve important advances. In spite of the lack of support from the CNDM, then languishing in the hands of conservative leadership, feminists were able to establish, for the first time in Brazilian history, a participatory dynamic for the drafting of the Brazilian government's official report to the Fourth Conference. The Ministry for External Relations (MRE), the agency responsible for that report, facilitated the participatory process by creating a special working group that included notable feminists, who organized and integrated dozens of activists by means of special seminars.[10] Many of the recommendations presented by activists in these seminars were included in the final report. This collaboration of feminist and women's groups guaranteed that the Brazilian government would present a representative report; it also ensured that government's approval of the Beijing Platform—the programmatic document adopted at the Beijing conference—in its entirety. More important, it ensured the federal government's greater acceptance of the demands raised by women's movements.

The experiences of Brazilian feminists in these regional meetings, as well as in the transnational spaces of the UN conferences, introduced new strategies and discourses in national activism (S. Alvarez 2000, 1998a; Pitanguy 2002). In particular, the affirmation of women's rights as human rights lent greater legitimacy to feminist struggles in Brazil, opening the way for the expansion and strengthening of state feminism throughout the next decade.

The 2000s: Strengthening State Feminism

The new millennium inaugurated transnational feminisms in the World Social Forum Conferences. The first three of these, held in 2001, 2002, and 2003, all took place in Porto Alegre, Brazil. Brazilian feminists were active not only in these transnational spaces on their home ground, but also in the WSF Conferences held elsewhere (such as in Mumbai), organizing panels, events, and public demonstrations, whether as part of their organizations and groups or as members of regional or global networks (Conway 2007; Vargas 2003).

Brazilian feminists' presence in these international and transnational spaces boosted their position locally and nationally to fight for public policy for women (S. Alvarez 2000). Margaret Keck and Kathryn Sikkink (1998) call this the "boomerang effect" of influence, the cycle of transnational coalitions pressuring more powerful states and international agencies so that they, in turn, attempt to "convince" a particular government to implement a policy change in the desired direction.

Indeed, the national and transnational articulation of feminists in the Beijing conference process eventually paid off with the creation of the position of the national secretariat of women's rights in 2002. One of the first tasks of the new organ was to draft Brazil's first report to the Convention for the Elimination of All Forms of Discrimination Against

Women (CEDAW), a report more than ten years overdue. The secretariat commissioned a number of feminist NGOs for the drafting.[11]

As a result of an initiative of the AMB, the feminist movement also mobilized in 2002 to draw up the Feminist Political Platform (Plataforma Política Feminista, or PPF), to be presented to all candidates in the 2002 presidential elections. The PPF represented an important shift in feminist discourse: instead of focusing strictly on women's issues, feminists voiced their positions on issues of general interest, formulating a proposition for the construction of a more equitable society on the basis of the principles of a nonracist, nonhomophobic, and anticapitalist feminism. The formulation of this platform involved participation in state conferences by women active in local women's forums throughout Brazil's major cities. The process culminated with a Brazilian women's conference held in Brasília, at which more than one thousand women represented various "feminist identities," and concluded with the presentation of the feminist platform to the candidates.[12]

The platform expressed the need to combat the inequalities among women in Brazil and the class hierarchy and inequalities that have characterized Brazilian society. It also defined a feminist stance against racism, lesbophobia, and homophobia (Sardenberg and Costa 2014). The PPF combined recognition of diversity among women and the emergence of new identity-based women's movements with the need for "equality, redistribution of wealth and for social justice" (CFEMEA 2002).

As a result of a proposition formulated by feminists involved in the Worker's Party (PT) presidential campaign, a process modeled after the PPF conference shaped a series of important national policy conferences. The conferences grew out of steps taken by the Lula government, which established 2004 as Women's Year by federal decree. As part of the year's events, the Special Secretariat for Women's Policies (Secretaria Especial de Políticas para Mulheres, or SPMulheres), a cabinet-level position created by the Lula government in 2003, organized the First National Conference on Policies for Women (I CNPM) in Brasília in July 2004. Nearly two thousand women delegates, elected by their peers in state conferences held all over the country, attended.[13] The stated purpose of this nationwide process was to establish a dialogue between civil society and government—from the municipal through the federal levels—for the formulation of the First National Plan of Public Policies for Women (I PNPM), toward the eradication of gender inequalities in Brazil (Sardenberg and Costa 2014).

A second conference, the II CNPM, met in Brasília in August 2007, and a third one, in August 2010. Each brought together more than two thousand delegates from all over the country to evaluate the National Plan of Public Policies for Women and suggest needed adjustments.[14] The documents resulting from these conferences have affirmed some important achievements, such as the launching of the Pact Against Violence and the passage of comprehensive legislation to combat domestic violence, known as the Maria da Penha Law (discussed below). Likewise, the demand for the legalization of abortion was also reaffirmed by a wide margin (Sardenberg 2007a).

The II and III CNPMs included the issue of "gender and power" and women's empowerment. Feminists were successful in securing inclusion of the principle that "to widen women's participation in power and decision-making spheres is to work for the consolidation and perfection of Brazilian democracy" (SPM 2008:118; our translation). This principle has fostered the creation of government machinery at the municipal and state levels to oversee the implementation of the policies in question, including the establishment of councils for the defense of women's rights, formed by representatives of civil society.

Since 2010: Expansion and Backlash?

According to Sonia Alvarez (2014), feminist discourse and practices in Brazil have expanded both vertically in a process termed "mainstreaming"—moving upward within the state apparatus—and horizontally in "sidestreaming"—overflowing into parallel sectors of civil society, with the resulting multiplication of feminist action fields. Indeed, in the past five years, state feminism in Brazil has continued to expand with the multiplication of women's rights councils and bureaus of public policies for women in different states and major cities, as well as in terms of machinery geared toward confronting domestic violence.[15] This expansion of state feminism responds, in turn, to the expansion and diversification of feminist and women's movements, which find expression in other social movements as well. Parallel developments have occurred in other social movements: the black movement, the landless people's movement, and the LGBT movements, among others, and also in formal institutions of civil society like political parties and labor organizations (Sardenberg and Costa 2014).

At the same time, new feminist struggles have gained the streets. Of special note is the "SlutWalk" movement, inspired by the protest march in Canada in 2011 against rape culture, which soon expanded into a transnational movement. In Brazil, this is mostly a young women's movement, with SlutWalks happening in all major cities throughout the country. Young women are also behind the numerous feminist protest marches that have taken over the country since October 2015, when the National Congress passed legislation that curtails access to "safety kits" to women victims of sexual violence. As noted earlier, this movement has brought thousands of women, young and old, to the streets—the Women's Spring—calling for the ouster of the President of the National Congress, Congressman Eduardo Cunha, an evangelical pastor.

Congressman Cunha, although accused of corruption, holds enough strings to pull Congress his way, particularly among the opposition and religious leaders. In a seeming backlash against feminist and LGBT movements, these conservatives have also voted against the inclusion of gender issues in national education programs. Such a move, along with budget cuts slicing into government programs, has brought to a halt important gender and sexuality sensitizing programs, such as those designed for teachers and other civil servants through federal universities.

Curtailment of government expenditures required by Congress has forced the shrinking of the state machinery, including the downgrading of SPMulheres from an autonomous ministry with cabinet status to one of the secretariats in the newly created Ministry for Women, Racial Equality and Human Rights. This has also meant cuts in personnel and funding, further restricting an already limited budget for programs geared toward promoting gender equality. Nonetheless, preparations for the National Conference on Public Policies for Women slated for May 2016 continued at full force, mobilizing women of the many different segments of feminist and women's movements all over the country.

Women's Underrepresentation in Power Structures[16]

Despite actively participating in the so-called informal political spheres, as a group, women in Brazil have not been able to break into the traditional political structures. During the recent 2014 elections, of the 513 seats available in Congress, only fifty-one were occupied by women, whereas in the federal Senate, of a total of eighty-one seats, women occupied only thirteen. In terms of the proportion of women in major legislative bodies, Brazil sits at the bottom of the list of the twenty countries that make up Latin America, above only Haiti.

This low rate of representation contrasts sharply with the strength, reach, and political influence of Brazil's feminist movement. Despite three decades of vibrant activism and evolving engagement with the state, increasing women's political participation has remained a seemingly insurmountable challenge. This remains a key paradox in Brazilian feminism: it has succeeded, through its political strength, in putting women's demands on the table, but it has failed to open formal political spaces to women themselves.

Two types of factors have contributed to the historical exclusion of women from these spaces: first, women's social trajectories, directed as they are to the domestic sphere; and, second, elements more directly related to the political system: political party structures, the electoral system, and a political culture traditionally based on patronage and patriarchal values (Araújo 2003). Despite women's participation in informal political arenas such as social movements, it was only in the 1980s that significant numbers of women became active in formal politics and institutions. The process of redemocratization also opened the way for the greater presence of women in those arenas. After 1986 this process slowed, emerging from a hiatus only with the 2002 elections, and then mainly within the more progressive-leftist parties. Nevertheless, the electoral system requires all candidates to have a party affiliation, and because feminists—wary of party control of social movements and wanting to claim autonomy—have tended to steer away from party involvement, success has been difficult for feminist candidates.

Feminists first organized to address women's political representation in 1995. Working closely with federal congresswomen and -men, they pushed for and won passage of the "Quotas Law," which stipulated that 20 percent of all candidates in proportional elections (town councilors and state and federal deputies) should be women. Although it was applied in the municipal elections of 1996, the new legislation fell short of reversing women's exclusion. In 1997 a second law was approved, raising the mandatory female-candidate percentage to 25 percent for the 1998 elections at all levels, and to 30 percent for subsequent elections. All parties should meet the quotas; however, the quotas have not translated well into practice. Since the law specifies no penalty for parties failing to meet the quota, many simply ignore it. In addition, the quota law provides no concrete support for female candidates, such as public campaign funds or free television and radio advertising. Finally, it neither establishes nor offers incentives for political parties to create mechanisms encouraging women's political development and education.

Increasing the proportion of women in public office in Brazil has remained an elusive goal. Aware of this fact, in June 2007 the revitalized CNDM and the Women's Caucus in the National Congress, with the support of the SPMulheres, organized a public demonstration with the theme "Not more or less: just equal," held in front of the National Congress. They aimed to call attention to the persistent exclusion of women from decision-making spheres, and by pressing for Congress to pay attention to gender issues in proceeding with political reform, particularly the introduction of more effective quota laws, demonstrated their commitment to political reform while demanding greater space for women in the parliament (SPM 2008:117). A few weeks later, in the midst of the heated discussions going on in Congress, our own research center, the Nucleus of Interdisciplinary Women's Studies (NEIM) of the Federal University of Bahia, together with two feminist NGOs and the Women's Caucus at the National Congress, held an international seminar in the Congress Hall, to provide examples of successful international experiences in affirmative action.[17] Participants included representatives from Argentina and Costa Rica, countries that hold the highest percentages of women in parliament in Latin America (30 and 40 percent, respectively), and from Rwanda, where women occupy 49 percent of seats in Congress. The presentations made it clear that, to be effective, quota systems need to include sanctions for parties that fail to comply. Unfortunately, this lesson has yet to be incorporated in Brazil.

Clara Araújo (see also Araújo 2003), also present at the seminar, keenly analyzed the Brazilian experience, identifying a number of weaknesses in the political system—in particular, practices that have consistently kept women (among others) outside the decision-making sphere. This analysis was confirmed by the reform process that ensued that very same week, when a new Political Reform Project was being formulated. Despite a unified set of proposals backed up by international experience and strong partnerships between the government and civil society, feminists and their allies in the Brazilian legislature were able to secure only a few measures aimed at ensuring gender parity in political representation. Very few of women's demands were incorporated into the Political Reform Project's official report, and still fewer made it onto the list of final reforms.

The Brazilian women's movement is accustomed to transforming experiences of struggle into opportunities for learning. It managed to guarantee that free television and radio advertising for political parties would address the political participation of women, and it succeeded in ensuring that 20 percent of public campaigning funds would be set aside for female candidates (less than the desired 30 percent, which would correspond to the current quota). Despite the overall defeat, women used the political reform process to organize, raise awareness, build new alliances, and strengthen existing collaborations with members of the executive branch and with female legislators in both houses of the National Congress.

But it is important to emphasize that not only in the legislative bodies but also in the executive and judicial branches, women's exclusion from the higher offices continues to be notorious. In fact, women's participation in top positions in the executive branch—despite showing an increase from 13 percent during President Cardoso's terms to 19 percent with President Lula and 30 percent with President Dilma Rousseff—still falls far behind that of men. Of course, women in positions of power do not necessarily represent women's interests. However, the success in passing legislation favoring women in the 1988 National Constitution suggests that a critical mass of women in positions of power can make a positive difference.

Criminalizing Domestic Violence Against Women: The Maria da Penha Law

One area in which this positive difference is badly needed is in the judiciary, particularly concerning the implementation of the Maria da Penha Law regarding the criminalization and prevention of domestic violence, sanctioned by President Lula in 2006. This legislation came after more than thirty years of feminist organizing and campaigning for the criminalization of violence against women. As we shall see below, despite progress, its implementation has encountered significant obstacles from judicial authorities.

This law increases the period of imprisonment for violent acts against women, and allows preventive arrests and other measures to protect women. The law was formulated on the basis of a legal document drafted by a consortium of feminist networks and organizations, passing through a long process of discussion and reformulation by a working group formed by representatives of several government ministries coordinated by the SPMulheres. It recognizes different forms of violence—physical, psychological, sexual, moral, and patrimonial—and stipulates not only punitive measures against aggressors, but also much needed protective and assistance measures to aid victims, as well as important preventive measures at large. It also mandates the creation of special courts in all twenty-six states and in the federal district (Brasília). It requires the combined actions, in each city, of the federal and state public safety agencies, public health agencies, referral centers, battered women's shelters, and labor agencies—among others—in addition to the courts. More importantly, it defines new roles and tasks for the Police Stations for Battered Women (DEAMs), nearly doubling the demands placed on them and increasing the need for well-trained staff (Bonetti and Pinheiro 2009).

The first step in implementation was creating more DEAMs, ideally staffed by policewomen. The first such station was created in São Paulo in 1985. Today, there are more than five hundred DEAMs across the country. Many states also created referral centers and shelters for battered women, as well as a network of services, including medical examiner's offices (responsible for examining women who suffer physical violence), hospitals, and so forth, to assist women victims of violence.

In 2006 a national hotline sponsored by the federal government, Ligue 180, opened to respond to the public on issues concerning violence against women. According to the SPMulheres, the number of calls rose steadily during its first years of operation. In the first six months of 2009 the calls increased by nearly one-third compared to the same period in 2008; from 2009 to 2010, the calls doubled. By June 2010, SPMulheres registered a six-month total of 343,063 calls. Among the calls received during that period, nearly one-fifth reported violent acts. However, a similar proportion called to register complaints about DEAMs and other public services that were supposed to tend to women in situations of violence (Brasil, Secretaria de Políticas para Mulheres 2010). In analyzing the 2014 data, SPMulheres found that just over half of the calls referred to physical violence, while nearly one-third reported psychological violence (Brasil, Secretaria de Políticas para Mulheres 2014).

Despite the clear advances in combating domestic violence, however, a number of problems have frustrated the implementation of the Maria da Penha Law. It is a federal law and thus of national scope, but it depends on state and municipal organs and agencies to be properly implemented. That situation has given rise to different local policies and practices that fall short of fulfilling the law's aims.

Nowhere is the problem more evident than in the courts. According to the Brazilian National Justice Council, of 75,829 court cases of violence against women initiated from July through November 2008, considerably less than 3 percent resulted in successful convictions of abusers. Legislation that criminalizes domestic violence has not been easily accepted. Several judges have claimed that the Maria da Penha Law is unconstitutional because it "discriminates" against men.

Aware of the various obstacles to implementing the Maria da Penha Law, the SPMulheres wrote and has been strengthening the National Pact for Combating Violence Against Women with the twenty-seven state governments, with the objective of consolidating the National Policy for Combating Violence Against Women. SPMulheres has also created a mechanism to monitor the implementation of the Maria da Penha Law throughout the twenty-seven states, by means of a consortium. That consortium, Observe (the Observatory for Monitoring the Implementation of the Maria da Penha Law), conducted research in state capitals, revealing in 2010, that in nearly four years since the passage of the new legislation, few strides had been made toward its implementation, with the greatest obstacles to be found in the creation of the needed courts (Gomes, Tavares and Sardenberg 2010). The study also revealed that feminist and women's movements have been active in pushing for the implementation of the law, as it is clear that it will not be enacted without pressure from interested groups—women from all walks of life.

SPMulheres has tried to coordinate the different services available to women in situations of violence by creating the "House of the Brazilian Woman" (Casa da Mulher Brasileira) in the major state capitals. These installations will offer all services in one location, from DEAMs to special courts. While these will facilitate access to justice for women living in these cities, they can only tend to a very small percentage of women victimized by gender-based violence.

Data regarding violent deaths involving women show that much remains to be done. According to the Institute of Applied Economics

Research, for instance, between 2002 and 2012, over fifty thousand women were victims of femicide in Brazil. An average of thirteen women are murdered in Brazil every day due to gender-based violence. Over those ten years, the murders increased by nearly one-fourth. Most of the women were killed by people very close to them. The "Violence Map 2015: Homicides of Women" showed that fully half of femicides in Brazil were committed by family members, and one-third by partners and ex-partners (Brasil, Secretaria de Políticas para Mulheres2015). While the number of white women dying in femicides declined by nearly 10 percent from 2003 to 2013, femicides of black women increased by half (Brasil, Secretaria de Políticas para Mulheres 2014). It is no wonder Brazilian women, especially black women, have marched in Brasília protesting against this situation.

In March 2015, President Dilma Rousseff promulgated a law known as the "Femicide Law," which amended the Brazilian Penal Code to redefine "femicide" as a type of qualified homicide, including it in the list of "hateful crimes"—that is, among those considered extremely grave and deserving more severe sentences, with no possibility of bail or of sentence reduction. Domestic violence against women is now classified as a "crime qualifier," carrying sentences up to two-and-a-half times longer than those for "simple" homicides.

This change spells an important advance in the fight against gender-based violence against women, made possible by the work of state feminism pressured by feminist and women's movements. Such pressure also brought a response from the Ministry of Education: the 2016 annual ENEM, the equivalent to the ACT exams, not only had a question citing Simone de Beauvoir, but also had as an essay theme "The Persistence of Violence Against Women in Society," requiring more than five million youngsters to reflect upon this serious national problem.

Despite progress, many gains are still under threat, as we will see below: both the gains for victims of sexual violence and those for the reproductive rights of all Brazilian women.

The Fight for Reproductive Rights: Legalization of Voluntary Abortions

Given their controversial character and strong opposition from religious groups, campaigns for women's reproductive rights are sustained mostly by self-declared feminist activists. Although this struggle in

Brazil spans the past thirty years, it has grown in prominence since 2003, with the coming to power of more progressive governments.

Abortion is a major public health issue in Brazil. Since the 1940s abortions in Brazil have been legal only when pregnancy occurs as a result of rape or when it endangers the life of the mother. In spite of its being prohibited in all other instances, however, it is believed that between seven hundred fifty thousand and one million clandestine abortions are performed in Brazil every year. Nearly two hundred fifty thousand women have to be admitted to public hospitals due to abortion-related complications; nearly 10 percent of them die, and close to 20 percent suffer severe damage to their reproductive organs (Sugimoto 2005; Martins and Mendonça 2005).

For the most part, these women are black and poor, since middle- and upper-class women are able to find safe abortion services in clandestine clinics. Studies in recent years have shown that abortion was more common among women with lower educational levels, and that the highest percentages were to be found in the Northeast Region, the poorest part of the country. The percentage of black women who had had abortions was double that of white women (Diniz and Medeiros 2012; Brazilian Institute of Geography and Statistics [IBGE] 2013).

Even in the cases permitted by law, it was only in the late 1980s, with the launching of the PAISM health program for women, that national and state health programs began to provide legal abortions in the state of São Paulo.

It was not until the 1990s that similar services emerged across the country, when a "change of mood" regarding abortion sparked public debate around the issue. This change began with the launch of the September 28 Campaign for the Decriminalization of Abortion in Latin America during the Fifth Latin American and Caribbean Feminist Meeting in 1990. That campaign garnered support from women in twenty-one countries and seven regional networks. A series of international conferences followed—Rio in 1992, the 1994 International Conference on Population and Development in Cairo, the Copenhagen Conference in that same year, and the 1995 International Conference in Beijing—that increasingly supported women's struggles for reproductive rights.

Since 1990, when the September 28 Campaign was first launched, it has gained supporters across the country. Indeed, the Feminist Network for Health, Reproductive Rights, and Sexual Rights, or simply the

Feminist Health Network in Brazil has been a major actor, leading the September 28 Campaign jointly with CLADEM, a Latin American network with similar goals. They have focused on three major paths of action: working with the Ministry of Health and local health officials and professionals to guarantee the availability of services for legal abortions; building and monitoring changes in public opinion in favor of legalizing abortion (included monitoring the media on the issue); and dealing with the law, particularly with the situation in the legislature (Villela 2001; Soares and Sardenberg 2008).

During the first decade of this century, the legalization campaign benefited from the rise to power of more progressive political parties, such as the PT, which brought Lula to the presidency for eight years beginning in 2003. During Lula's first term (2003–2006), the Minister of Health was especially supportive of the legalization of abortion, building a strong argument centering on public health (Sardenberg 2007a). SPMulheres also pressured the government from within to change the law. Nevertheless, growing opposition came from conservative religious groups, particularly elements of the Catholic Church that were strengthened by the visit of Pope Benedict XVI to Brazil in 2007 (Sardenberg 2007a).

Brazilian feminists have responded to religious opponents by avoiding a head-on collision, instead directing campaigns and other efforts toward creating the conditions for a more favorable public opinion. This is a strategic choice, as polls indicate fluctuations in Brazilian public opinion, with sometimes strongly conservative turns. In 1993, 54 percent of those polled defended the maintenance of abortion laws as they stood, while 23 percent supported full legalization; in 2007, a poll in *Folha de São Paulo* suggested that the percentage favoring legalization had fallen to 16 percent (ibid.). More recent polls have detected a change of mood. For instance, in 2010, IBOPE, under the coordination of the Brazilian branch of Catholics for the Right to Choose (CDD), conducted a survey on attitudes toward induced abortion. Of the approximately two thousand people interviewed nationwide for the survey, 70 percent agreed that a woman should be able to terminate a pregnancy when it posed health risks, or when the fetus had no chance of extra-uterine survival. Agreement was lower for pregnancy resulting from rape, with only 52 percent favoring a right to abortion. However, 96 percent believed that a woman should not be punished for having an abortion in this situation. A strong majority (61 percent) of those

interviewed believed women should be the ones to decide about inter-
rupting an unplanned pregnancy, while only 5 percent thought that
social institutions, such as the Church, the National Congress, the judiciary, or the president of the republic should have the right to decide
in such matters. Even among Catholics, the majority favored a woman's right to decide, thus standing against the teachings of the Church.

In any event, it is clear that the Catholic Church has emerged as a
major enemy of women's rights and women's lives. The Church has the
financial resources and the reach, through its parishes, to allow it to
wage a strong campaign, and it is not scrupulous about the means used.
One such campaign involved the distribution—with full support from
the local bishop—of plastic "aborted fetuses" to people who attended
Sunday mass in Rio de Janeiro's parishes in December 2010. The
Church has also been behind local legislation prohibiting the distribution of the morning-after pill through the public health system in cities
such as Recife in Pernambuco, and Jundiaí in São Paulo. Even though
such laws have been overturned as unconstitutional, they have an impact on public opinion. The Church has scored two major points: it was
instrumental in defeating a project formulated by the Tripartite Committee formed by SPMulheres in the Congressional Committee for Social Security and the Family, and it is backing the Parliamentary
Investigating Committee to investigate abortion practices in Brazil.

The 2010 presidential elections in Brazil brought an important novelty: of the three candidates, two were women, and the two won nearly
70 percent of the votes. Precisely because there were women candidates, legalization of abortion became a major issue, and candidates
had to take a public position on it. Although legalization of abortion has
been on feminist agendas for over three decades, it remains controversial in Brazilian society at large and thus is used by conservative parties
as a weapon against more progressive ones. The issue came up again in
the 2014 elections, for similar reasons, placing President Dilma Rousseff in a difficult position. Her program for her second term omitted
reproductive rights, affirming that decisions regarding this issue were a
prerogative of Congress.

The National Congress has been threatening regressions in reproductive rights. A congressional committee has approved the passage of
Law Project 5069, which forbids the provision of morning-after pills to
women victims of sexual violence and makes over-the-counter sales of
the pills illegal. The Law Project was proposed by Dep. Eduardo

Cunha, now president of the National Congress, and under investigation for a number of illicit acts and corruption. It is against this Law Project and for removing Cunha that women in Brazil have taken to the streets, leading the marches that have become known as Brazilian Women's Spring.

Despite the backlash in Congress against the gains obtained for women regarding reproductive rights, the campaign for the legalization of abortion in Brazil will continue. The state conferences for public policies for women have maintained safe and legal voluntary abortions as one of the major propositions to carry to the National Conference in March 2016. In late 2015, feminist organizations were already campaigning for its approval. As we move forward, the conservative forces in our society resisting women's reproductive rights will continue to push for patriarchal restrictions on our full autonomy. Combating these forces will constitute a major challenge to feminists in the years to come.

Conclusion

In a comparative study of state feminisms in Chile and Nigeria, Philomina Okeke-Ihejireka and Susan Franceschet (2002:440) observed that "incoming governments that replace authoritarian regimes" often attempt to gather support "by responding to the needs of marginalized groups, including women," independent of the patterns of women's mobilization. However, they point out that state feminism has not succeeded in furthering women's citizenship everywhere. They identify three factors that encourage more progressive state responses to women's demands: 1) the existence of a "coherent and unified women's movement" with the capacity to make political demands; 2) the presence of "patterns of gender relations" which can make way for women's access to political arena; and 3) the existence of local cultural notions that women can use to further their struggles (ibid.:441).

They observe that these factors combined to lead to the emergence of women's policy machinery in Chile that has yielded important achievements guaranteeing women's rights. They point out that in Latin America as a whole, feminist and women's movements made alliances with broad-based popular movements and human rights movements, organizing across class to fight the authoritarian regimes, and making good use of a conceptual link between authoritarianism and patriarchy in pushing for their demands. This has certainly been true of

Brazil, as Sonia Alvarez (1990) demonstrated; so, I hope, has this chapter. Feminists in Brazil joined forces with other social movements in fighting for redemocratization of the country, thus carving out a space to join with the opposition forces, gain access to political arenas, and lodge their demands. They could therefore initiate a dialogue with the state early in the process of redemocratization, resulting in the creation of women's machineries, such as the Police Stations for Battered Women, councils for the defense of women's rights, and the creation of PAISM, the special Health Program for Women through the Ministry of Health.

As S. Razavi (2000) notes, the establishment of state feminism by means of such machinery, or WPAs, flourishes in those circumstances in which patriarchal political culture blocks women's access to formal political positions for the formulation of policies. This is the case in Brazil. To this day, despite having a woman president, women's presence in electoral posts, particularly legislative ones, remains very low. WPAs, therefore, have expanded and multiplied all over the country, under the pressure of very influential feminist and women's movements.

Unlike other countries, however, state feminism in Brazil has become more participatory, particularly with the coming to power in 2003 of a more progressive party, which fosters parallel participatory policy formulation. Periodic conferences with the participation of civil society delegates have been the hallmark of that participation in Brazil. In the next National Conference of Public Policies for Women, in fact, the percentage of these delegates will rise to 60 percent, and government delegates will be reduced to 40 percent. State agencies have expended much effort and financial support for the creation of councils for women's rights in all Brazilian states and major cities, with the goal of coordinating and monitoring the implementation of public policies for women. This seems to be a consolidated policy area, which, as Maria Bustelo (2014) has affirmed with respect to Spain, also "has enough elements to survive and to keep on developing," even in the face of economic downturn and conservative reversals.

State feminism in Brazil is not imposed from the top. It is a response to pressures from the feminist and wider women's movements. Furthermore, it has become *more* participatory within the past decade, as more participatory mechanisms like councils and conferences, from the local to the national levels, have played an important part in the formulation and monitoring of public policies for women. Finally, the new decision-making positions in the state machineries that are being created, particularly at the federal level, are being occupied by feminists; they are the ones pushing forth, advancing the National Plan of Public Policies for Women. Of course, as a result of party pressure, there are spaces in these machineries occupied by women who are not in the movement. In the absence of pressures from the movement, these state machineries become mere bureaucratic bodies; they do not achieve the same gains as those in the hands of feminists.

Indeed, the success of the present Special Secretariat for Women's Policies lies in its recognition of the importance of the feminist movement for the public policies that will make a difference in women's lives. Thus far, participatory state feminism has brought new energy to feminisms in Brazil, providing the means for more participatory channels for the formulation, implementation, and monitoring of public policies for women.

For feminism, it is not enough to have a state mechanism; it is necessary to have people committed to feminist causes advancing the issues at hand, as well as a more participatory form of governance. Thus, feminist organizations and women's forums monitor the actions of those in power and give or withhold their support. If feminisms in Brazil are to continue expanding into the state apparatus, rather than allowing the state to control the movement, building feminist constituencies will continue to be a fundamental challenge for feminisms in the decades to come.

This is a revised version of the chapter originally published in the 2010 edition, which was written in partnership with Ana Alice Alcantara Costa. Ana Alice, my dear friend and colleague for over thirty years at NEIM—the Interdisciplinary Women's Studies Nucleus at the Federal University of Bahia, Brazil, passed away on December 26, 2014. Most of the ideas here contained express her thoughts regarding participatory state feminism in Brazil, but when "I" is used in this text it refers only to me, Cecilia.

Notes

1. Because Brazil is a southern hemisphere country, the seasons are reversed; spring is late in the calendar year.

2. In November 2015, I participated as delegate to the State Conference of Bahia, when close to 1,300 women, the majority self-declared feminists, gathered to elaborate on policy proposals and forge strategies to enlarge and strengthen women's presence in decision making positions in all of Brazil's three branches of formal power: executive, legislative, and judiciary.

3. Indeed, as a result of this "dialogue," abortion services in the cases prescribed by law began to be performed in public hospitals for the first time, the city of São Paulo being the first to provide these services (Pinto 2003). Since the 1980s feminists have worked closely with health secretariats and numerous integrating health councils throughout the country to promote campaigns on issues regarding women's reproductive health (Villela 2001).

4. The process differs by state, but, in general, feminist and women's organizations nominate women to the councils, half of the members being chosen from this pool of women and the other half appointed by different state bureaus and agencies. The governor or other authority in charge then formally approves the nominees.

5. During the military regime, a severe constitution, taking away all citizenship rights, was put into effect. With the process of redemocratization, a new constitution had to be elaborated.

6. In accordance with the procedures established by the National Congress, these demands had to be presented in the form of amendments, each being supported by at least thirty thousand signatures. Four such amendments were presented by feminist and women's groups, one of them containing a "package" of demands, approved in its entirety, including, among others, changes in the wording of the law to include women, issues regarding women's health, equality for partners in marriage, medical and psychological support to women victims of sexual violence, freedom in family planning, and women's rights to ownership of land. For a more detailed discussion of these demands and of women's participation in the writing of the new constitution, see Pinto 2003:72–79.

7. See Carneiro 1999; Ribeiro 1995.

8. The Fóruns de Mulheres (Women's Forums) are noninstitutionalized entities, constituted by feminist groups or organizations, women's groups in unions and other organizations, and independent feminists (*feministas autônomas*) operating in Brazil's major cities. They are responsible for organizing, articulating, and implementing campaigns, events, and other mobilizations of the feminist and women's movements throughout the country. The *fóruns* maintain thematic coordinations without a deliberating or representative power, except when such power is explicitly authorized by the participating women and organizations. At present these fóruns constitute the most organized manifestation of so-called autonomous or independent feminism in Brazil. Cecilia Sardenberg and Ana Alice Costa, authors of this paper, participated in the creation of the Women's Forum of Salvador, Bahia, and we have been active members for close to two decades.

9. Indeed, speaking of the impact of these conferences on women's movements in Brazil, Maria Aparecida "Shuma" Shumaher, one of the coordinators of the AMB, has observed, "This mobilization provoked and constituted [women's] Forums/Articulations in twenty-five Brazilian states, and the promotion of nearly 100 events (state meetings, seminars, research projects, etc.), involving more than 800 organizations. In the history of Brazilian women's movements, I do not know of any other international event that has counted on such an intense mobilization in the country. In some Brazilian counties, the Beijing event stimulated the creation of new spaces for debate. For the first time, women's movements elaborated twenty-two documents/diagnostics that showed the complex nature of inequality among women in the country, giving us the opportunity to evaluate the degree of organization of the movement in each one of these states, assess regional priorities, and propose the design of policies to be implemented" (Pinto 2003:114–115; our translation).

10. Ana Alice Alcantara Costa integrated this work group, being responsible for the coordination of the Conference on Gender and Power, held in Salvador, Bahia, organized by NEIM/UFBA. Cecilia Sardenberg participated in this conference as co-coordinator.

11. The report was created in 2002, during the presidency of Fernando Henrique Cardoso, but it was discussed by CEDAW only in the following year, with the presence of Minister Emilia Fernandes, nominated by the Lula government, who assumed the task of implementing the CEDAW committee recommendations.

12. Ana Alice Alcantara Costa participated in this conference as part of the delegation from Bahia.

13. Cecilia Sardenberg, the first author of this paper, participated in the I CNPM as a delegate from the state of Bahia and in the II CNPM as a delegate from the Ministry of Education, representing the Nucleus of Interdisciplinary Women's Studies of the Federal University of Bahia. Ana Alice Alcantara Costa participated in the II CNPM as group coordinator.

14. This time, a total of 2,559 were elected in the 600 municipal, regional, and state conferences that were part of this process, implying, once again, the direct or indirect involvement of more than 300,000 women across the country.

15. According to data gathered by the Secretariat of Public Policies for Women,, there has been a marked increase in the number of women's rights councils and organisms for public policies for women at the state and municipal level. Whereas in July 2007, there was a total of 155 such organisms, two years later, in July 2009, this number had jumped to 239. Nearly all of Brazil's 27 states now have state councils for women's rights, and there has been a sharp increase on municipal councils: from 163 in September 2007, to 345 in June 2009. http://www.observatoriodegenero.gov.br/eixo/politicas-publicas/conselhos-e-organismos

16. Portions of this section were published in Costa 2008.

17. This seminar was part of the Pathways of Women's Empowerment Research Program Consortium in which NEIM participates as a partner institution. See, for example, http://www.pathways ofempowerment.org. DFID, the Brazilian Congress, and the Pathways of Women's Empowerment RPC were the major funders of the event.

THE MIDDLE EAST

(11)

Feminist Movements in
the Maghreb

VALENTINE M. MOGHADAM

Introduction

Women's movements are varied in their composition, objectives, and activities, but *feminist* or *women's rights* mobilizations have more in common with each other, despite their different priorities across space and time. As scholarship and the historical record show, feminist movements respond to women's oppression or subordination or second-class citizenship, and aim for women's autonomy or legal equality or enhanced participation. In this connection, they engage with states, civil-society actors, and their fellow citizens, though not without tensions.

In the Middle East and North Africa (MENA), women's mobilizations historically revolved around support for nationalist movements or demands for women's education. Since the 1980s, their goals and activities have centered on reforms of patriarchal family laws, the criminalization of violence against women (including so-called honor crimes and sexual harassment), establishment of equal nationality rights (so that women married to foreign-born men may pass on their nationality to their children), and enhanced economic and political participation. Like feminist movements everywhere, their collective action repertoire includes research, lobbying, advocacy, and movement-building. Depending on the political context, feminist groups also may hold street demonstrations or join coalitions that organize such public rallies. All women's rights organizations know about the UN-sponsored global women's rights agenda, including such international agreements as the Convention on the Elimination of All Forms of Discrimination against Women (CEDAW), the Beijing Declaration and Platform for Action, and Security Council Resolution 1325 on women, peace, and security. Some are also aware of the International Labor Organization's conventions pertaining to working women's conditions and rights. Feminist groups draw on these international standards and norms, on aspects of their nations' history and culture(s), and—where relevant—on their countries' constitutional guarantees to make the case for women's equality, participation, and rights.

The Maghreb region of North Africa—Algeria, Morocco, and Tunisia—has seen audacious feminist mobilizations as well as some policy achievements and legal reforms. For example, following a dozen years of feminist research, lobbying, and advocacy, Morocco achieved a landmark family law reform in 2004. The countries form a geocultural subregion: they are contiguous in territory; share an experience of French colonialism; retain some francophone identity as well as French-influenced institutions such as the educational system, the judiciary, and trade unions; and are home to a well-known transnational feminist network, a collective of scholar-activists known as the Collectif 95 Maghreb-Egalité. They share a pattern of attention to labor and social rights as well as to the enhancement of women's civil and political rights. Maghrebian women are major contributors to and participants in civil society and democracy movements, seeing a democratic polity as both a desirable alternative to authoritarianism and a pathway to their own equality and rights. Until 2013, the only MENA countries with women political party leaders were in the Maghreb: Algeria's Louisa Hanoune and Tunisia's Maya Jribi led left-wing parties, while Algeria's Khalida Toumi-Messaoudi co-led the ruling party. In 2016, Algeria and Tunisia had the highest levels of elected female political representation in the MENA region, at 31 percent.

This chapter examines the history and evolution of feminist mobilizations in the Maghreb, first discussing the region as a whole, and then considering the differences across the three countries. Although non-feminist forms of activism among women—most notably among women associated with Islamist movements and parties—exist in the Maghreb, this chapter focuses on *feminist* activism, which aims for the achievement of women's full and equal citizenship through the reform of religiously based family laws (also known as personal status codes), programs to end violence against women, and the removal of reservations and qualifications to the ratification of CEDAW.[1] I show that despite the challenging environment within which Maghreb feminists have worked—characterized by economic difficulties, political Islam, conflicts and wars, and regime changes—they have managed to effect legal and policy changes and have helped to diffuse and legitimize the notion of women's rights to equality and dignity. The chapter draws on the relevant secondary sources, my observations during visits to the region since 1990 and especially during 2013-2015, and interviews I have conducted with activists and academics from Algeria, Morocco, and Tunisia.

The State, the World-System, and Women's Mobilizations

A body of scholarship in Middle East women's studies has identified *state feminism* (Hatem 1992, 1994; Joseph 2000) as a characteristic of the modernizing regimes in the region. That is, authoritarian modernizing regimes sought to involve women in state-building, development, and modernization projects, albeit within limits. Thus most countries saw increases in female literacy and educational attainment; women's employment as teachers, health workers, and civil servants; and the establishment of what the UN called the "national women's machinery," or state-led women's policy agencies tasked partly with adhering to UN mandates and partly with mobilizing a population of loyal female citizens. Egypt under Gamal Abdel Nasser (1956–1970) and Tunisia under Habib Bourguiba (1956–1987) were regarded as quintessential state-feminist regimes, but the two differed in that Muslim family law was retained in Egypt, with the result that women's participation and rights were more circumscribed there than in Tunisia. Tunisia's 1956 Personal Status Code (Code du Statut Personnel or CSP)—introduced by President Bourguiba, a French-educated lawyer, even before the promulgation of the country's first constitution—was at the time the most liberal in MENA and remains a document cherished by the country's feminist movement. One feminist scholar calls it "Bourguiba's gift to women and to the nation as a whole," because it banned polygamy and gave women the right to divorce. Bourguiba's notion of women's emancipation, however, was limited by the attitudes of his time. While encouraging women to enter the workforce, for example, he emphasized fields suitable for women's "natural dispositions" (Arfaoui 2015).

The postcolonial period of the 1950s and 1960s saw women involved almost exclusively in either official and state-run women's organizations or charitable associations. In the 1970s, activism expanded. Women with left-wing or liberal ideals formed study groups on women and development. Some were able to attend the UN's World Conference of the International Women's Year (first in the series of world conferences on women), which convened in Mexico City in 1975 and was followed the next year by the UN's Decade for Women. In 1976, Moroccan feminist sociologist Fatima Mernissi, who had studied in France and the United States, published *Beyond the Veil: Male-Female Dynamics in Modern Muslim Society*. The book influenced a generation of scholar-activists and set the stage for the fields of North African women's studies, Middle East women's studies, and the study of women and Islam. Mernissi's bold sociological analysis laid bare a key problem in women's status and gender relations in Muslim societies generally and in Morocco in particular: the application of sharia-based family law privileged men, subordinated women, and prevented companionate marriage.

In the 1980s, academics, artists, and journalists, many with left-wing or secular worldviews, mobilized to warn about the growing Islamist influence. Their concerns were crystallized in the 1987 edition of Mernissi's book, with a new introduction that examined Islamic fundamentalist movements, finding them the products of the contradictions of modernization, including changes in gender relations and women's roles. As she memorably noted in her preface: "If fundamentalists are calling for a return of the veil, it must be because women have been taking off the veil" (Mernissi 1987). In the latter part of the 1980s, Mernissi helped form a Maghreb-wide anti-fundamentalist network of scholars and activists, which produced seminars and a number of books on women and the law.[2]

The woman-owned publishing house Editions Le Fennec, based in Casablanca, Morocco, produced a series of analyses on women and the law in the three Maghreb countries. Founded by Leila Chaouni in 1987, Le Fennec published writing by and on women while also collaborating with male and female members of research groups and organizations linked to women's rights. Le Fennec's multidisciplinary and multilingual research on women in North Africa strengthened regional research networks of Moroccan, Tunisian, and Algerian activists, media professionals, and academics (Skalli 2006). It published novels, academic studies, and advocacy texts in both Arabic and French to cater to larger circles of writers and readers, and it encouraged men and women researchers and activists to work, write, and publish together.

In the early 1990s, during the run-up to the UN's Fourth World Conference on Women, feminists in Algeria, Morocco, and Tunisia created another network, this one called the Collectif 95 Maghreb-Egalité. With the support of European foundations, some UN agencies, and several international women's NGOs, the Collectif drew on the global women's rights agenda and the proliferation of women's rights groups across the region to advance the case for egalitarian family codes and full and equal citizenship for women. Members attended the Beijing Conference's forum for non-governmental organizations, where the Collectif distributed a pamphlet on the measures needed to reform family law toward women's equality and organized a number of panel discussions (author's personal observation).

Those who had coalesced around Mernissi's network and later the Collectif objected to the notion of men's guardianship over women, polygamy, and unequal family inheritance. An argument that developed in the new century was that such clauses were insulting to women's dignity and were at odds with the social reality, given that women were increasingly helping to support their families. This point was highlighted in the Collectif's advocacy book on family law, published in 2003 in both French and Arabic (Collectif 2003, 2005:66). The book's French title, *Dalil pour l'égalité dans la famille au Maghreb,* deployed the Arabic word *dalil* to suggest the kind of analysis underpinning the book: a careful reading or reinterpretation of Islamic texts, references to contemporary social conditions, and advocacy for women's equality and rights.

Composed of Algerian, Moroccan, and Tunisian women who were (and remain) active in national women's rights groups and professional associations, the Collectif continued to hold meetings in the three countries well into the new century, cooperating on seminars, books, and media activities, and advocating for repeal of discriminatory laws. In addition, the Collectif forged ties with other transnational feminist networks: first with Women Living Under Muslim Laws (WLUML), formed in 1984 in opposition to Islamic fundamentalism and discriminatory family laws; and later with the Women's Learning Partnership for Rights, Development, and Peace (WLP), established in 2000 with an international partnership of twenty women's organizations across Asia and Africa and a secretariat in Bethesda, Maryland. Two years after the Collectif produced its 2003 book on family law, the WLP issued an English-language version, *Guide to Equality in the Family in the Maghreb* (Collectif 2005). Members of the Collectif also took part in activities of the World March of Women (Marche Mondiale des Femmes), a transnational initiative of Québecoise feminists against poverty, patriarchy, and violence.

At the national level, the 1980s and 1990s saw the emergence of a number of women's rights associations in Algeria, Morocco, and Tunisia, formed largely by women from the left. Women were becoming prominent in the professions, making inroads into previously male-dominated associations of lawyers, journalists, judges, scientists, and human rights advocates. In Algeria in 1992, as the Islamist armed rebellion was getting underway, it was a woman judge who read the decree officially dissolving the Front Islamique du Salut (FIS). The trade unions had women's sections, staffed largely by teachers and health workers as well as working-class women members.

In all three countries, officials responded to feminist advocacy with speeches, new policy agencies, or legal reforms. Algerian women mobilized in the 1980s and 1990s to contest the 1984 family law and the emergence of political Islam, and in the new century launched a campaign for gender justice called 20 Years Is Enough (*20 ans Barakat*), spearheaded by groups such as SOS Women in Distress and the Center for Information and Documentation on the Rights of Children and Women (CIDDEF). Women in several fields—the academics Cherifa Bouatta and Doria Cherifati-Merabtine, the novelist and essayist Assia Djebar, and the filmmaker Horria Saihi—sought to uncover Algerian women's roles in the 1950s liberation movement and the building of the new state and society, and boldly criticized fundamentalist thinking and Islamist terrorism. Saihi's documentary, *The Algeria of Women (Algérie des Femmes)*, recounted the horrors of kidnapping, torture, and rape inflicted on women by violent Islamist extremists during the 1990s (Ryan 1998). In 2002 Algeria's women were rewarded with five cabinet positions;[3] in 2003, President Bouteflika referred to the problem of violence against women in his International Women's Day speech; and some amendments, albeit insufficient, were made to the family law in 2005 (Cheriet 2014; Moghadam 2013: chap. 8; Salhi 2010).

Morocco's Democratic Association of Moroccan Women (Association Démocratique des Femmes du Maroc, ADFM) and the Women's Action Union (Union d'Action Féminine, UAF) began to agitate for reform of the country's very patriarchal family law, the Mudawana.[4] In 1993, the UAF launched the One Million Signatures drive to change the law, and in alliance with a new progressive government in 1998 promoted the National Action Plan for Integrating Women in Development (Moghadam and Gheytanchi 2010). Morocco had a number of well-known women's rights advocates associated with the Collectif and family law reform—such as Latifa Jbabdi, Rabéa Naciri, and Amina Lemrini—and some associated with political parties, notably Aicha Belarbi and Nouzha Skalli.[5] In 2001, women politicians from the main political parties—Independence (Istiqlal), Socialist Union of Popular Forces (Union Socialiste des Forces Populaires), the Party of Progress and Socialism (Parti du Progrès et du Socialisme), and the Popular Movement (Mouvement Populaire), among others—established a network advocating for a women's quota system. The quota was adopted in 2002, when the Electoral Code introduced a "national list" with a minimum 10 percent female parliamentary quota, or thirty reserved seats (subsequently raised).[6] Women members of parliament subsequently played an important role in the adoption of key laws (Sater 2007); most were associated with or sympathetic to the women's rights organizations. A new cabinet formed in Morocco in October 2007 included seven women, the highest female representation in the cabinet since independence.

Tunisia's two main women's rights organizations, formed in 1989, were the Tunisian Association of Democratic Women (l'Association Tunisienne des Femmes Démocrates, ATFD, known in Tunisia as *les femmes démocrates*) and the Association of Tunisian Women for Research on Development (l'Association des Femmes Tunisiennes pour la Recherche sur le Développement, AFTURD), both of which engaged in research and advocacy. In 1993 the ATFD established the Maghreb's first listening and counseling hotline (*centre d'écoute*) for women victims of violence (Chékir and Arfaoui 2011; Tchaicha and Arfaoui 2011). Tunisia's state feminism provided for the government-funded Center for Research, Studies, Documentation, and Information on Women (Centre de Recherche, d'Etudes, de Documentation et d'Information sur la Femme, CREDIF), which produced numerous studies on problems of women's legal status and social positions. The ATFD became known for its independence and assertive stances. As Tunisians grew more dissatisfied with the authoritarian rule of the Ben Ali regime and the corruption of his extended family, the ATFD issued a statement in 2008 declaring: "Our work on behalf of women's empowerment is also aimed at political change and is part of the movement for democratization" (Khedija Arafoui, personal communication). As new communication technologies expanded, Tunisians took activism to cyberspace; these included young female bloggers like Lina Ben Mhenni, author of the blog "A Tunisian Girl," and Emna Ben Jemaa, who took part in the May 2010 anti-censorship protest (Khalil 2014:189).

On the eve of the Arab Spring in 2011, therefore, the Maghreb had experienced three decades of feminist organization and mobilization, exhibiting the acquisition of civic skills and significant contributions to civil society. The combination of women's cultural production, advocacy efforts, mobilizing structures, access to various media, use of new information and communication technologies, and engagement with various publics had generated "a gradual feminization of the public sphere" in North Africa (Moghadam and Sadiqi 2006). The political parties were still largely run by men and in an authoritarian setting were weak anyway, but women's presence in political society was growing.

Structural Opportunities, Strategies, and Constraints

At least three sets of factors converged to generate the flurry of feminist organizing in the 1990s. *First* were the changes in the characteristics of the female population, notably greater educational attainment, the rising age at first marriage, smaller family size, and women's presence in an array of professional fields and occupations. The wide gender gap in educational attainment that had prevailed in the immediate postcolonial period was rapidly narrowing and more young women were attending university. In turn, this increased the age at first marriage to around twenty-four; later marriage and access to contraception lowered the fertility rate from close to 5 in the 1970s to 3 in the 1990s (and 2.3 in Tunisia), giving educated women more time for professional and advocacy work.[7] Travel abroad, access to satellite TV, and knowledge of information technology facilitated women's international connections and began to foster civic and feminist activism. Participation in media and cultural production, including a feminist press, enhanced women's presence in the public sphere. Engagement in national debates and dialogues and collaborations with newly established human rights organizations were additional changes that led to new aspirations for a new generation of educated women.

As a participant in the world economy and world society, the Maghreb is vulnerable to the vagaries of global capitalism, but also open to global discourses. Thus a *second factor* was the diffusion of the global women's rights agenda, promoted by the United Nations and its specialized agencies from the mid-1970s onward. Maghreb women who attended the various UN conferences on women—such as the Third World Conference on Women in Nairobi in 1985, the 1994 International Conference on Population and Development in Cairo, and the Fourth World Conference on Women in Beijing in 1995—embraced CEDAW, the Nairobi Forward-looking Strategies, and the Beijing Platform for Action, and the promotion of these conventions became part of the Maghreb feminist collective action repertoire and framing strategy.

The *third factor* was the waning of the golden age of Third World development, as fundamentalist movements spread contemporaneously with the implementation of structural adjustment policies. Thus, when Maghreb states began privatizing previously state-owned enterprises and limiting public sector employment from the 1980s into the 1990s, unions protested on the streets, while burgeoning feminist groups wrote critiques in their domestic publications and in documents prepared for the Nairobi and Beijing conferences. The spread of Islamic fundamentalism (known as *intégrisme* in the Maghreb) and of Islamist politics alarmed many of the women's rights advocates and provided a strong incentive for women to organize and mobilize in new ways.

One of the strengths of women's rights movements in the Maghreb lies in their inclination toward broad social bases, collaborations, and coalitions, including action in concert with men, religious and secular women, young people, and more veteran activists. Although their critics have long faulted women's rights groups for supposed westernization, cultural alienation, atheism, and so on, the reality is that their mode has tended to be broadly inclusive, not exclusionary. Women's rights groups have worked with human rights organizations and trade unions to push for reform, raise public awareness, and build institutions. The various hotlines established by feminist groups arose from activists' attention to the concerns of working-class women, and other women who experienced violence or harassment at home, on the streets, or at workplaces. Maintaining the hotlines has required collaboration with other domestic actors as well as with international donors. Feminists have framed the issue in terms of the urgent need to combat all forms of violence against women, the rights and dignity of women, and the importance of healthy working environments conducive to women's participation and their contribution to development. Tunisia's ATFD, which established the region's first hotline in 1993, also conducted the advocacy that led to the passage in 2004 of the country's first law against sexual harassment. Algeria's first hotline was hosted by the country's main trade union. Subsequently, Moroccan feminist groups helped form a coalition with physicians' groups and human rights organizations, called the Springtime of Dignity, to urge the government to reform the penal code and criminalize all forms of violence against women in order to preserve "the dignity of women, their physical and psychological integrity, and their autonomy."[8] In November 2014, Tunisian activists took part in the international campaign 16 Days of Activism against gender violence and for human rights. At its conclusion, ATFD joined with another feminist group, Beity, and with the International Federation of Human Rights (FIDH), to hold a joint North Africa regional seminar on "Best practices for combating violence against women" in Tunis on December 9 and 10, 2014 (FIDH, ATFD, and Beity, 2014).

Indeed, transnational links to international human rights organizations or to transnational feminist networks are an important feature of Maghrebian feminist organizations. While Algerian feminists remained closest to counterparts in Muslim countries through Women Living Under Muslim Laws (WLUML), Morocco's ADFM became an active partner within the more broadly international Women's Learning Partnership (WLP), and engaged in peer-to-peer activities with Iranian, Mauritanian, Lebanese, Malaysian, and other network partners. As recounted by founder Mahnaz Afkhami, a WLP conference put Moroccan and Iranian feminists in contact with each other, leading to the adoption by the Iranian feminists of the one million signatures petition drive that the UAF had spearheaded over a decade earlier (personal communication, Jakarta, April 2010).

Attention to labor laws to address the needs of women in the workforce is another feature of these movements. In February 2004, a coalition to ensure the implementation of Morocco's new labor law was launched by the Center for Human Rights (le Centre des Droits des Gens), the Democratic League for Women's Rights (la Ligue Démocratique pour les Droits des Femmes), and the Moroccan Association for Women's Rights (l'Association Marocaine des Droits des Femmes), and in November of that year it was joined by the Moroccan Labor Union (l'Union Marocaine du Travail), the Democratic Confederation of Labor (la Confédération Démocratique du Travail), and the Moroccan Association for Human Rights (l'Association Marocaine des Droits Humains). The campaign issued a report entitled *Protection of Women's Rights* (*Protection des droits des femmes*), which, among other things, pointed out that Morocco had yet to sign and ratify ILO Convention 183 on maternity protection.[9] Ratification was finally achieved in 2011. More recently, Tunisian feminist trade unionists launched a campaign for ratification of the ILO convention.[10]

Constraints and weaknesses persist. Mobilizing across a country and across social classes was never a simple matter for activists in an authoritarian context. In this respect, feminist groups (as well as other civil society organizations and left-wing political parties) were at a disadvantage compared with the growing Islamist movements, which were able to utilize a preexisting and widespread religious frame, as well as mosques and various religious bodies, to advance their agenda. Women's rights groups also remained small, compared with the trade unions, which were able to acquire membership throughout the country because of industrialization and other forms of economic development. The leverage of the women's rights groups therefore remained limited. Nonetheless, their commitment to social change and especially to improvements in the legal status and social positions of women generated an array of actions, from research to street demonstrations, and brought policy achievements. (See Table 11.1.) In what follows, we spotlight some of the key feminist campaigns and strategies for each of the three Maghreb countries under consideration.

Algeria: The Long and Winding Road to Women's Equality

Although women played prominent roles in the national liberation movement of the late 1950s and early 1960s, the rise of a radical women's movement and of feminist organizations began only in the 1980s and 1990s. Whereas Algerian women were once intimately connected to the projects of national liberation and postcolonial state building through a version of Arab socialism, the new women's movement extricated itself from those projects to demand rights, equality, and security—and all in the language of secular feminism. Though they never separated themselves from the project of building a

TABLE 11.1 Women's Rights Organizations in the Maghreb: Issues and Results, 2003–2015

Organizations	Issues, Priorities, Campaigns	Results
Regional:		
Collectif 95 Maghreb-Egalité (formed 1993)	Awareness-raising on women's rights issues Adherence to UN's global women's rights agenda Full and equal citizenship for women	2003: Advocacy book, *Dalil pour l'égalité dans la famille au Maghreb* At national level: see below
Algeria:		
SOS Femmes en Détresse Centre d'Information et Documentation sur les Droits de l'Enfant et de la Femme (CIDDEF) (both formed between 1990 and 1992)	Repeal of the Family Law and its replacement by an egalitarian law; abolition of polygamy and unilateral male divorce; and equality in division of marital property Criminalization of all forms of violence against women Social and psychological support for victims of the 1990s violence; Coalition *20 ans Barakat*	2004: Amendment to Article 341 of penal code, making sexual harassment an offense 2005: Amendment to nationality code, to permit an Algerian woman married to a non-Algerian to confer citizenship on her children 2012: Parliamentary quota adopted; women candidates win 31 percent of parliamentary seats in National Assembly 2014: Seven women appointed to the cabinet, constituting 20% 2015: Stronger legislation adopted on domestic violence and sexual harassment
Morocco:		
L'Union d'Action Féminine (UAF) (formed 1987) Association Démocratique des Femmes du Maroc (ADFM) (formed 1985)	Reform of Moudawana and replacement with more egalitarian family law Lifting of reservations to CEDAW "Spring of Dignity" coalition of 30 associations for penal code reform (e.g., address marital rape; decriminalize abortion); consolidating democracy; empowering rural women	2007: The Claiming Equal Citizenship campaign achieves a success when Morocco changes its nationality code, allowing women who are married to foreign Muslim men to pass their nationality on to their children. 2008: King Mohammed VI pledges to bring the country's domestic laws into compliance with CEDAW. 2009: A three-year campaign overturns century-old laws

(continues)

TABLE 11.1 (*continued*)

Organizations	Issues, Priorities, Campaigns	Results
Morocco (continued):		denying equal land rights to Soulaliyates (rural, tribal) women to share, transfer, and benefit from 30 million acres of communally owned land. 2011–2013: The amended constitution stipulates that the state will work toward gender parity; Morocco lifts all reservations to CEDAW 2013: New law on gender parity: political parties should achieve at least 30% female representation
Tunisia: Association Tunisienne des Femmes Démocrates (ATFD) Association des Femmes Tunisiennes pour la Recherche sur le Développement (AFTURD) (both formed 1989)	Women's equality in all areas, including inheritance, democracy, and rights Full implementation of CEDAW, including equal inheritance rights; support for working women	2003: State women's agency creates sexual harassment and domestic violence hotline. 2004: Tunisia forms the first sexual harassment and domestic violence hotline. 2011: Transitional government declares gender parity in elections and lifts remaining reservations on CEDAW. 2012: Large protests by feminist groups and supporters defeat attempt by Ennahda-dominated Constituent Assembly to replace "equality" between women and men with "complementarity" in the new constitution. 2014: The new constitution codifies gender parity and bans violence against women. 2012–2014: ATFD and AFTURD extend networks to Sfax, Sousse, Bizerte, Kairouan; members join coalitions and political parties to prevent Ennahda victory in November 2014 parliamentary elections; women candidates win 31 percent of seats

modern and progressive Algerian polity, feminists have insisted that women's rights are necessary for the achievement of democracy and modernity.[11]

In the late 1980s, Algeria experienced profound economic and political crises that led to constitutional reforms and the emergence of an incipient civil society as well as many new political parties and the FIS (Entelis and Arone 1994; Layachi 1995). Twenty women's associations took part in the first national meeting that convened in late 1989, and in 1993 perhaps as many as twenty-four were present (Bouatta 1997). These included women's studies and research associations, social-professional associations (such as one that sought to promote and assist women in business), a number of service-delivery organizations (for legal aid, literacy, and reproductive health), and several notable feminist organizations.

Elsewhere, I have described three waves of feminist organizing and mobilization in Algeria from the 1980s through to the new century. The first wave was the struggle around the controversial 1984 Family Code (Moghadam 2013: chap. 8). Two prominent feminists and political figures who emerged during this period were Khalida Messaoudi and Louisa Hanoune, who helped found the Association for the Equality of Rights between Women and Men (Association pour l'Egalité des Droits entre les Femmes et les Hommes, known as Egalité) in May 1985. Cherifa Bouatta, a participant in the movement, succinctly summarizes the origins of Algerian feminism:

> Under the shadow of the one-party system, the political monolith [le pouvoir], some women attempted to create spaces of independent expression through cultural and trade union groups. Psychology students created a working group and a cine-club. In Oran, study and reflection workshops on Algerian women were organized in early 1980, with contributions from historians, economists, sociologists and psychiatrists. The proceedings of these workshops were published and the organizers created a women's journal, *Isis*. Other groups were then created, such as the *moudjahidates* collective and groups that studied and criticized official proposals for a new Family Code. This latter effort gave life to the women's movement, and is indeed regarded as the spark that led to the emergence, the objective and the strategies of Algeria's feminist movement. (Bouatta 1997: 4)

In the second wave of Algerian feminism, the period 1989-1994 was dominated by anti-Islamist activism, with the formation of such feminist organizations as the Independent Association for the Triumph of Women's Rights (l'Association Indépendante pour le Triomphe des Droits de la Femme, also known as Triomphe); the Association for Women's Emancipation (l'Association pour l'Émancipation des Femmes, or Emancipation); the Association for the Defense and Promotion of Women (l'Association pour le Défense et Promotion des Femmes, known as Défense et Promotion); the Algerian Gathering of Democratic Women (Rassemblement Algérien des Femmes Démocrates, RAFD); Women's Cry (Cri de Femmes); Women's Voice (Voix des Femmes); El Aurassia; and the aforementioned SOS Women in Distress. The organizations called for the abolition of the Family Code; full citizenship for women; enactment of civil laws guaranteeing equality between men and women in areas such as employment, marriage, and divorce; abolition of polygamy and unilateral male divorce; and equality in division of marital property. At the time, left-wing women dominated the Algerian women's movement, which may account for its audacity and organizational capability. When Egalité was formed in 1985, its officers and members were associated with the Socialist Organization of Workers (OST, which had Trotskyist tendencies). Members of Emancipation belonged to the Socialist Workers Party (PST), and those of Défense et Promotion belonged largely to the Parti de l'Avant-Garde Socialiste (PAGS, the former Communist Party), as Bouatta (1997:15) has explained.

The 1990s was a decade of Islamist terror and fierce military reprisals, but elections continued. In the 1997 municipal and parliamentary elections, eleven women were elected to the National Assembly, among them several well-known activists and feminists. With the end of the terrorism period, Algerian women were able to enjoy a number of advantages, such as cabinet positions and new legislation. The emergence of a feminist politics critical of both fundamentalism and the state shaped the composition and orientation of the newly elected women. Among them were Louisa Hanoune, leader of the Workers Party, Khalida Messaoudi, who joined the Rally for Culture and Democracy, and Dalia Taleb of the Socialist Forces Front.[12] All three women were known for their radicalism. Professionally, too, Algerian women were making gains. In 2006, women reportedly represented 50 percent of teachers, 53 percent of medical doctors, and 37 percent of magistrates, or prosecutors and judges (Marzouki 2010:6). At the turn of the new century, Algeria had the highest proportion of women judges not only in the Maghreb but in all of MENA (see Saad-Zoy 2010; Sonnefeld and Lindbekk, forthcoming).[13]

The network and campaign called 20 Years Is Enough (*20 ans Barakat*), part of the third wave for gender justice, was formed in 2003 to continue lobbying for family law reform and for prosecution of all perpetrators of violence against women during the decade of terror. In another display of activism for women across social classes, the Wassila network began in 2000 and consisted of women's NGOs and individual professionals, many of whom were psychologists addressing post-conflict traumas; one was Cherifa Bouatta, who founded the Society for Psychological Assistance, Research, and Training (Société pour l'Aide Psychologique, la Recherche et la Formation). The Center for Assistance of Women Victims of Sexual Harassment (Centre d'Écoute et d'Assistance aux Femmes Victimes d'Harcèlement Sexuel) was a hotline and counseling service hosted by the country's main trade union, the UGTA. By one account, after the center's opening, there were thousands of calls from women victims and supporters (Algeria Watch 2005). The work of the union, the women's commission, and the Algerian League of Human Rights resulted in the government's adoption of a new policy against sexual harassment. CIDDEF, a prominent organization mentioned earlier in this chapter, advocates for children's rights and welfare as well as women's equality, and its representatives were present at the World Social Forum in Tunis in March 2013 (personal observation).

In October 2004, Algeria's National Popular Assembly adopted an amendment to article 341 of the Algerian penal code. Sexual harassment was now an offense; it was defined as abusing the authority conferred by one's function or profession in order to give orders to, threaten, impose constraints on, or exercise pressure on another person for the purpose of obtaining sexual favors. A person convicted of this offense would be subject to imprisonment of two months to one year and a fine of fifty thousand to one hundred thousand dinars (Algeria Watch 2005). However, the amendment left unaddressed the legal loophole allowing a rapist to escape prosecution by marrying his victim, which was the subject of much discussion at feminist sessions at the 2013 World Social Forum (personal observation). A stronger law was passed by parliament in 2015 and came into effect in February 2016, specifying harsh penalties for perpetrators of domestic violence and sexual harassment (Al-Arabiyya 2015; CBS News 2016).

One effect of the Arab Spring was the adoption of a parliamentary quota for women, resulting in a 31.6 percent female share of seats won in the May 2012 elections, giving Algeria the distinction of being part of an elite group of thirty-five countries with female representation of 30 percent and above. Indeed, Algeria ranked twenty-sixth among the 142 countries listed.[14] In May 2014, Bouteflika's reelection to the presidency brought the appointment of seven women to the cabinet, with portfolios in education; land-use planning and environment; culture; family and women; tourism; handicrafts; and post, information technology, and communication. This 20 percent female share of cabinet seats is high not only by Arab but also by international standards. In June 2014, three women were promoted to the rank of general in the Algerian military, joining Fatima Arjoun, who had been made a general in the national army (Armée Nationale Populaire) in 2010. The four constitute the largest number of high-ranking women army commanders in the Arab world; a news report called the appointments "a sign of the liberalization of Algeria's closed military organization" (Al-Arabiyya 2012).

Dissident Algerians view these developments as window-dressing, or see the women in political leadership as regime women and the state (*le pouvoir*) as hopelessly cynical. For example, among the countries that held elections in 2011–2012, Algeria alone did not elect an Islamic government, although the Islamic Green Alliance had expected to win the elections and called the results fraudulent. Perhaps to counter negative perceptions from religious citizens, the regime has sought to show its own Islamic credentials by starting construction on what will be the largest mosque in the world, and by showing intolerance for religious diversity (Ghanem-Yazbek 2015). For example, in Algeria (as in many Muslim-majority countries), a woman is not permitted to be married to a non-Muslim unless he converts to Islam. Algeria's military expenditure since 2010 has consumed between 4 percent and 5.5 percent of GDP— and this in a country with very high youth unemployment. In addition, cracks in the feminist movement appeared in the context of post-conflict "normalization" during the presidency of Bouteflika. Louisa Hanoune's tendency to placate the Islamic opposition irked many Algerian feminists; so did Khalida Toumi-Messaoudi's ascent to the position first of advisor to the president and then of cabinet minister, which was seen as compromising her independence.[15] There seems to be some consensus that the Algerian women's rights movement is currently in abeyance (Boutheina Cheriet, personal communication, Washington DC, November 2014). Nonetheless, the presence of a critical mass of women in political leadership, the women military officers, the women lawyers and judges, and the large proportion of women teaching at the country's universities (38 percent in 2013) and at schools has the potential to change images of and cultural attitudes toward women in what remains a male-dominated society.

Morocco: Family Law and Constitutional Amendments

Toward the end of his life and long reign, King Hassan II, under pressure from Western allies, allowed elections that in 1998 brought to power a socialist party that supported the family law reform campaign. Although that party was defeated in the next parliamentary election, the new king, Mohamed VI, proved amenable to feminist demands for family law reform, while also accommodating civil society demands for acknowledgement and repudiation of the repressive "years of lead" under Hassan II. The Consultative Council of Human Rights and the Equity and Reconciliation Commission, institutions newly created in 2003, signaled both reconciliation and democratization. The new monarch also formed a Royal Commission to examine the family reform bill. Thanks to the twelve-year feminist campaign led by the UAF and the ADFM, Moroccan women, long subject to the highly patriarchal Mudawana family law, saw its replacement in 2004 with a more egalitarian set of laws and norms for marital life and family affairs. ADFM summarized some of those gains:

> The new law embodies the principle of shared family responsibilities between the spouses. It was the product of extensive public discussion of challenges women faced under the previous law, as well as analysis of the implications of human rights standards and religious texts. To help ensure effective implementation of the new rights that have been guaranteed, the legislative changes were accompanied by the creation of dedicated Family Courts, and the Ministry of Justice is enhancing the provision of support services and training for judges and court officials. (ADFM 2009)

The new family code formed part of a broad wave of important reforms in Morocco, including changes to the electoral code (in 2002), which introduced a "national list" that reserved thirty parliamentary seats for women; to the labor code (in 2004), which banned sexual harassment in the workplace; and to the nationality code (in 2007), which gave women and men equal rights to transmit nationality to their children as required by CEDAW's Article 9. Morocco also signed the ILO convention on maternity protection in 2011 (see table 11.1), although many would argue that the statutory fourteen weeks of paid maternity leave is inadequate.

Morocco's Arab Spring in 2011 took the form of peaceful street protests calling for better public services and expanded citizen rights. Calling itself the 20 February Movement (M20F), it had the backing of progressive political parties and—according to Fatima Sadiqi (2016)—at least half the protesters were women. Sadiqi highlights the role of a young blogger, Nidal Hamdache Salam, who had initiated a Facebook forum for discussion of social and political issues and helped mobilize the protests (see pp. 61-62). Others have drawn attention to the self-immolation of Fadwa Laroui, a young solo mother of two who had been denied social housing, as another trigger. These events galvanized the country's youth, intellectuals, and women.

In May 2011, the ADFM hosted a regional seminar in Rabat on Women and Democratic Transitions in the MENA region, which was attended by representatives from civil society, women's rights organizations, UN Women and other international organizations, and the diplomatic corps from Morocco, Tunisia, Egypt, Syria, and Lebanon. The Moroccan Minister of Women's Affairs at the time, Nouzha Skalli, announced that after years of tireless advocacy by women's rights organizations, the Moroccan government would officially ratify CEDAW's Optional Protocol, which permits the CEDAW Committee to receive and consider communications from non-state actors such as feminist groups. Minister Skalli, well known for her commitment to women's equality and to social rights, discussed the challenges and prospects for equality in the constitutional reform process in Morocco; she also noted that women made up five of the eighteen members of the Consultative Commission for the Constitutional Reform Coalition (WLP 2011).

The uprisings in Tunisia and Egypt from late 2010 to early 2011 created a political opportunity for the reform of the Moroccan constitution, with the possibility of institutionalizing the principle of gender equality in the reformed constitution (Darhour and Dahlerup 2013). Popular pressure, along with strategic decision making by the king, resulted in the constitutional amendments restricting the king's vast powers (to some extent) and institutionalizing the rights of women as well as the cultural and language rights of the Amazigh or Berber ethnic community. The new constitution, approved in a referendum in July 2011, reserved 15 percent of seats in the national parliament for women and 10 percent for youth.[16] In parliamentary elections that year, the Islamic Party of Justice and Development (Parti de la Justice et du Développement, PJD) won 26 percent of the seats, also winning the right to name a prime minister. Prime Minister Benkirane's first cabinet had just one female minister, Bassima Hakkaoui, who was considered very conservative; subsequently, he appointed a number of female deputy ministers, for higher education, foreign affairs, mines, and the environment.[17] Because of the new quota law, the female share of seats in parliament rose to 17 percent, up from 11 percent. Nabila Mounib became the first woman elected to lead a major Moroccan political party, the United Socialist Party (PSU). A critic of the Islamist agenda and of the power of the *makhzen* (royal palace), and an activist in M20F, she declared that the PSU "respects Moroccan women and places women's rights at the center of the democratic struggle," adding that "my election is a victory for all women struggling for equality and dignity" (Belamri 2012).

CEDAW reservations were removed as part of measures to harmonize domestic laws with each other and with the international women's rights agenda. But more remained to be done. Women's rights groups in the Springtime of Dignity Coalition continued their advocacy to lift the criminalization of abortion and remove the legal loophole allowing a rapist to escape punishment by marrying his victim. In June 2014 they held a press conference and rally to protest the prime minister's comments that "women's role" should be focused on the family (WLP 2014).

Morocco continues on the road to more openness. Some government-led projects may improve the quality of life for lower-income citizens and might generate jobs for the numerous young people who remain unemployed. Yet activists of the M20F continue to speak out, to join the frequent demonstrations of young people for jobs, to call for full implementation of Amazigh cultural rights, and to decry what they

deem to be excessive police presence at universities.[18] In the course of
a visit to Rabat in May 2014, I learned that many dissident Moroccans
regard the 2011 constitutional amendments as falling short of codify-
ing genuinely democratic and egalitarian principles; some look forward to what they call the "Spanish model" of a monarch who reigns
but does not rule, and a stronger parliamentary system. Morocco's feminist organizations remain active and prominent, working within civil
society and with progressive political parties to further women's rights
and well-being.

Tunisia: Feminism and Revolution

Over the decades, Tunisian feminists had the advantage of a modernizing regime that presented itself as a champion of women's rights, albeit
within an authoritarian context. Even under authoritarianism, feminists
built an institutional base that enabled them later to emerge as formidable political actors. With the launch of the Arab Spring in Tunisia and
the collapse of the Ben Ali government in January 2011, feminist groups
mobilized to ensure a democratic transition *with* women. Fearing that
the Jasmine or Dignity Revolution in which they had taken part would
come to favor Ennahda[19]—the Islamist party that had been banned
since the early 1990s—and recalling that party's regressive stance on
women's issues in the past, Tunisian feminists staged a protest on the
eve of Ennahda leader Ghannouchi's return from exile in January 2011.
They also encountered a new phenomenon made possible by the political opening: the public presence of bearded men and heavily veiled
women wearing the all-encompassing *niqab* who espoused an aggressively fundamentalist (*salafist*) worldview and opposed the country's
secular institutions. In the secular-religious divide that characterized
the country's politics for the next few years, Tunisian feminists sided
with the secular parties and politicians.

During the 2011 transitional period that prepared the way for elections and a National Constituent Assembly (NCA), four High Commissions were established to run the country, and women were present in
varying capacities in all four (Khalil 2014). The transitional government
declared a gender parity law, removed CEDAW reservations, and began to enact programs for rural and poor women. The elections for the
NCA brought about a 27 percent female share of deputies, or fifty-eight
women altogether. Forty were from Ennahda, but the others were very

assertive.[20] Because it held only a plurality, Ennahda formed a coalition government with two secular political parties, governing until the new constitution was adopted in January 2014. Throughout this period, Tunisian women were active participants in political and civil society. Of the 107 parties legalized in August 2011, three were led by women. The Modern Democratic Pole, a left-wing political coalition party that included El Massar and the party led by Maya Jribi, had featured a significant number of women at the head of their electoral lists in 2011. Indeed, El Massar had a policy of gender parity and sent outspoken left-wing women, such as Nadia Chaabane, to the NCA. Chaabane had links to the anti-globalization movement (known in French as *alter-mondialisation*), and she and other Tunisian feminists received considerable support from French, Québécoise, and other international women's rights groups. In part because of the prominence of Tunisian feminists within the local organizing committee, a focus on women's rights was a key feature of the World Social Forum in Tunis in March 2013 and again in March 2015.[21]

Tunisian women showed that they could mobilize very effectively against attempts by conservative forces to undo the gains of the past or to compromise women's rights through new constitutional language. Feminist groups held rallies, marches, and demonstrations in 2011 and 2012, where women of various ages held placards reading "Hands off my rights" (*Ne touche pas à mes acquis*, referring to the 1956 Personal Status Code and subsequent rights). AFTURD and ATFD organized marches in 2011 and 2012 for "liberty, dignity, equality." In 2013, when the Ennahda members of the NCA sought to replace the term "equality" with words like "complementarity" or "partnership" in the new constitution, women's rights activists and their male supporters in the secular and left-wing parties took to the streets and to the domestic and international media in protest. Ennahda was compelled to retreat. When a political crisis emerged following the assassinations of two left-wing political figures and protests ensued over those incidents and the country's socioeconomic problems, four civil society groups led by the large and powerful General Union of Tunisian Workers (Union Général des Travailleurs Tunisiens, UGTT) stepped in to mediate between Ennahda and its main secular opposition.[22] As a result, the government agreed in October 2013 to resign and make way for a caretaker government and new elections once the new constitution was finalized and adopted.

That occurred in January 2014, and the new constitution received much domestic and international acclaim. Article 46 of the new constitution confirms that women's rights will remain in place. Hafidha Chékir, a well-known scholar-activist and law professor who was part of the council of experts for the Constituent Assembly, said: "This has been a victory. It's not the constitution of the Islamists but of civil society." Still, she remained concerned about Article 7 (regarding the state's support for the family) and insisted that women's equality would come about only through the harmonization of domestic laws with CEDAW, notably on the issue of equality in inheritance. Samia Letaief, trade unionist and women's rights activist told me: "We are very happy with the equality article in the constitution. But ... [w]e still have lots to do, with laws and so forth, and anyway Ennahda is still here. So I can't celebrate yet." (Author interviews, Tunis, March 2014.)

Interviews with ATFD and AFTURD activists in March 2014 revealed that the open political environment and balance of political forces now enabled the women's organizations to establish sections outside Tunis, in Sfax, Sousse, Bizerte, and Kairouan, and—in coalition with the UGTT, the Human Rights League, and figures from the progressive political parties—to work toward the formation of an electoral bloc to prevent another Islamist victory in the next elections. In spring and summer 2014, a "political academy" organized by Women's Voice (Aswat Nissa), a new women's rights NGO, was preparing women to stand in the 2015 municipal elections. The new constitution's promised decentralization of power offered a chance for more women to enter politics, especially local politics. An activist in Women's Voice pointed to three main areas of women's training and capacity building: gender-sensitive budgeting; confidence building of women to engage with the public; and presenting women's issues to the political parties and convincing them to incorporate them in their electoral programs (Cordall 2015).

Emna Aoudi—feminist, syndicalist, and longtime activist of the left—insisted that constitutional guarantees needed to be elaborated in the form of new laws and policies to protect women's participation, rights, and working conditions, especially in the private sector. As she said:

We need work on the national budget and a development plan that includes measures for a more equitable distribution of national

wealth so that we do not find ourselves in the future in a position
whereby only rich people access political power and other decision-making positions. We have to combat women's poverty, marginalization, exclusion, and exploitation with a gender budget,
which will make it more possible for more women to access jobs.
(personal interview, Tunis, March 12, 2015)

The needs are stark. Despite decades of modernization and development, a recent ATFD study found that 40 percent of women in rural
areas are illiterate; 60 percent suffer from health problems, mostly
work-related; and just 10 percent have access to health care. Among
the needs, especially for rural women, are infrastructural projects such
as roads, more health-care facilities, and better schools. One attempt to
address these needs can be seen in the new Amal program, a three-year
series of activities rolled out in Tunisia (as well as in Morocco, Yemen,
and Palestine) by Oxfam and fifteen local organizations with funding
from the Swedish International Development Authority (Elrahi 2015).
A group associated with Amal presented at the World Social Forum
2015 to make the case for women's development priorities. Amal works
alongside the League of Tunisian Women Voters, ATFD, and AFTURD
to empower rural and marginalized women with the skills, tools, and
knowledge to challenge political systems in five of Tunisia's regions:
Kef, Kasserine, Sousse, Ben Arous, and Kelibia (Elrahi 2015).

When in March 2014 I visited the Tunis office of AFTURD, I was
struck by the many posters, flyers, and leaflets associated with numerous rallies, marches, and demonstrations. AFTURD also produces
books and pamphlets in Arabic and French (see also AFTURD n.d.).
The language of women's rights in the various AFTURD publications,
as well as those by AFTD, is assertive and uncompromising. Both feminist associations are committed to ensuring women's full citizenship,
which includes socioeconomic rights as well as civil and political rights
for women.

Tunisia remains a test case of the prospects for a women-friendly
democratic transition after the Arab Spring, and the evidence thus far
is promising. As noted, the principle of parity has been established in
Tunisia's political system, and in the fall 2014 elections, women participated in large numbers, though not necessarily at the head of party
lists. Sixty-seven women were elected: thirty-three from Nidaa Tounes,
twenty-seven from Ennahda, three from Popular Front, two from Free

Patriotic Union, and one each from Democratic Trend and The People Want ("Tunisie législatives" 2014). For the first time, there was a woman presidential candidate: Kalthoum Kennou, a well-known and highly regarded judge, former president of the Association of Tunisian Magistrates and an advocate of judicial independence, who opposes religious extremism (Ghribi 2014). Kennou was endorsed by AFTURD, but many ATFD women preferred to cast their votes for a candidate more likely to win: Beij Caid Essebsi, the veteran politician who became the country's first democratically elected president in November 2014. But at least the new president publicly acknowledged the importance of the women's votes.

Conclusions

The effects of socioeconomic development and the contradictions of globalization in the Maghreb have produced at least two generations of organizing women. Educated and employed women with smaller families and more time to devote to civic activities are a significant demographic group that has contributed in large measure to the growth of civil society and the onset of democratization in the region. The global women's rights agenda and the UN conferences of the 1990s created a favorable opportunity structure for the proliferation of feminist organizations and women-led NGOs in the Maghreb and for links with feminist groups elsewhere. In Algeria, increasing state conservatism and the rise of Islamism forced women's organizations and feminist leaders to assume an assertive stance on women's rights, one that was also more independent of the state and often critical of it. In Morocco and Tunisia, alliances with supportive government officials and civil society groups made legal reform and policy change possible. Although democratization and feminist activism are at different stages, feminists in all three countries have pursued institution building and reform of those legal codes and public policies that impede women's empowerment and equality.

Feminism has emerged in the Maghreb as an alternative to the master narrative frame of religio-nationalism, offering a different vocabulary, critique, and set of objectives. In the discourse of contemporary Maghreb feminism, the ideal society is one in which women participate fully in the development of their societies, have equal status with men in the family, and are able to function within civil society and the political process to expand civil, political, and social rights of citizenship to all.

The Islamist-feminist divide remains wide in the region. As the Moroccan scholar and women's rights advocate Fatima Sadiqi writes, the philosophical and ideological concepts from which secular feminists and Islamic women draw are inherently divergent (Sadiqi 2016). For many Islamists, women's rights begin and end with the right to wear the veil, including the *niqab*. Tunisian feminists complain of the "unprecedented violence and threats to gains and all forms of freedom," including alcohol, dancing, mixing of sexes, and so on (Arfaoui 2015). Security concerns loom large in the national discourses. Tunisia in particular has been rocked by Islamist terrorist attacks, a result partly of its more open atmosphere, and partly of its porous border with Libya, the neighbor that turned anarchic following its "liberation" by NATO in 2011.

In addition, socioeconomic difficulties—low growth, high youth unemployment, rising cost of living, and poor public services—spell a major challenge. In all three countries, women's unemployment rates are very high, and working mothers lack the necessary institutional supports that would enable them to enter and remain in the labor force. In the future, the feminist organizations in these countries will likely strengthen ties with the women's sections of the trade unions, along with the progressive political parties, to ensure that economic and social policies advance rather than undermine the participation and rights of working-class women. Advocacy for more generous support structures for women in the labor force, from longer paid maternity leaves to subsidized quality childcare centers, would be especially effective in achieving fuller economic citizenship for working-class women.[23] As Tunisian feminist Khedija Arfaoui has stated, democracy will be achieved when the political class includes the status of women in its vast program against poverty, against radical Islam, against unemployment, and against terror.

Notes

1. Family laws in Muslim-majority countries are based on sharia interpretations and may differ somewhat across countries with different Islamic jurisprudential traditions. In general, however, they place a female under the control of first her father and then her husband; this is the concept of male guardianship over women. Men may divorce far more easily than women; the father has automatic custody and guardianship over the child in any divorce; a man may marry up to four wives; and sons inherit twice as

much as their sisters. Such family laws also were the basis for the "reservations" that were placed on state ratification of CEDAW; that is, the state reserved the right to ignore a CEDAW article if it contravened the country's family law. Both the family laws and the CEDAW reservations have been contested by women's rights/feminist activists but largely defended by women associated with the Islamist parties.

2. Some of the network's activities and publications were co-financed by the United Nations University, and Mernissi held a large conference at the UNU's research institute in Helsinki, Finland, in 1989, shortly before I became coordinator of the Institute's research program on women and development (March 1990-December 1995).

3. For their names and tenure, see http://www.guide2womenleaders.com/Algeria.htm.

4. ADFM was formed in 1985 by women from the communist Party of Progress and Socialism (Parti du Progrès et du Socialisme) and UAF in 1987 by women from the Organization of Democratic and Popular Action (l'Organization de l'Action Démocratique et Populaire).

5. Aicha Belarbi was state secretary for foreign affairs in the Abdelrahman Yousefi government of 1998-2002 and later ambassador to the European Union; she is a founder of the Moroccan Organization of Human Rights. Nouzha Skalli of the Party of Progress and Socialism (PPS) was elected to parliament in 2002 and in 2007-11 was minister of Solidarity, Women, Family, and Social Development.

6. Between 2002 and 2007, the number of women representatives in the major political parties was no more than six women each, though given the total seats won by the parties, the Justice and Development Party (PJD) had the highest proportion, with a 14% female share. See Darhour and Dahlerup (2013).

7. For details see Moghadam 1993, Tables 4.3 and 4.4, pp. 122-123; Moghadam 2003, Table 4.1, p. 140; Karshenas, Moghadam, and Chamlou 2016.

8. WLP [Women's Learning Partnership for Rights, Development, and Peace], 2010. "Springtime of Dignity: Coalition for a Penal Code That Protects Women from Discrimination and Violence." http://www.learningpartnership.org/lib/morocco-spring time-dignity-coalition. The coalition also sought a lifting of the ban on abortion, which tends to harm poor, low-income, and working-class women far more than upper-class Moroccan women. Personal communication, Rabéa Naciri, Jakarta, 12 April 2010.

9. *Protection des Droits des Femmes: Agissons pour l'application effective de la législation du travail* was produced by the advocacy group Tanmia. I originally accessed the document in 2006, and although it no longer seems available online, the website does have commentary on more recent events. See http://www.tanmia.ma/fr/.

10. Interviews with two feminist trade unionists, members also of AFTURD, in Tunis in March 2014 and March 2015.

11. For details on Algeria's gender politics, see Lazreg 1994; Moghadam 2013, ch. 8; Salhi 2010; Khalil 2014, ch. 3.

12. The Workers Party is Trotskyist. The RCD's goals are "secularism, citizenship, a state based on rights, the repeal of the Family Code, recognition of Algeria's Berber dimension, social justice, educational reform, etc." (Messaoudi and Schemla 1995:94). Likewise, the Socialist Forces Front stands for democracy and Berber rights.

13. For figures on women judges, see Saad-Zoy (2010), specifically chapters by Boutheina Cheriet on Algeria, Fouzia Rhissassi and Khalid Berjaoui on Morocco, and Monia Ammar on Tunisia. See also Sonnenfeld and Lindbekk (forthcoming).

14. Turnout for the May 2012 parliamentary elections was small, but the FLN won 220 of 462 seats. Islamists came in third. Some 7,700 women ran, winning 145 seats. In

terms of the breakdown: 68 women were from the ruling FLN; 23 from the RCD; 15 from the Islamic Green Alliance; 7 from the FFS; 10 from the PT; the remaining 12 spread across five other parties. See http://themoornextdoor.files.wordpress.com /2012/05/screen-shot-2012-05-14-at-7-28-14-pm.png.

15. Personal communications from two Algerian women's rights activists at a regional women's rights conference held in Marrakesh, Morocco, July 2002.

16. Law No. 27-11 increased the national list reserved for women from the earlier 30 seats to 60 (out of a total of 395 seats, representing 15%). In addition, and in response to the pressure from the youth under the Arab Spring, 30 seats were to be reserved for young men under the age of 40 (Article 23). For details, see Darhour and Dahlerup (2013).

17. Morocco's environment minister, Hakima el-Haite, has been active in promoting solar energy for Morocco. See Neslen (2015).

18. See   http://www.al-monitor.com/pulse/security/2014/05/morocco-violence -universities-factions-political-integration.html. In Rabat on May 27, 2014, I witnessed a demonstration of unemployed young people in front of the Justice Ministry. On Amazigh dissatisfaction, see http://www.al-monitor.com/pulse/originals/2015/05/Morocco -language-Amazigh-constitution-education.html.

19. Here I use the Tunisian spelling, also transcribed as An-Nahda or Al-Nahda.

20. A note on the women members of the National Constituent Assembly: some writers have claimed that there were forty-eight female deputies; a deputy that I interviewed in 2013 told me there were sixty-three; an NDI report (2011) states the figure of fifty-eight female deputies.

21. Interviews with Nadia Chaabane, Tunis, March 2014 and via phone and email, April 2015. I first met Ms. Chaabane at the WSF in Tunis in March 2013.

22. The National Dialogue Quartet, as it came to be known, won the 2015 Nobel Peace Prize.

23. For an elaboration of such coalitions involving feminists and trade unionists, see contributions in Moghadam, Franzway, and Fonow (2011).

12

The Palestinian Women's Movement

ISLAH JAD

Introduction

Palestinian women's movements in the Palestinian Occupied Territories face two major tasks while pressing for women's rights: continuing
the national struggle and participating in state building. Palestinian
women's movements contend with both old agendas of mobilization
and liberation (from the Israeli Occupation) and new ones concerning
women's equality and empowerment (here, under the "rule" of the Palestinian Authority, or PA). Even under normal circumstances, strad-
dling these two agendas is difficult; the difficulty nears impossibility
when the very existence of the Palestinian "state" and society is threatened by the Israeli Occupation.

Since the conclusion of the Oslo Accords in 1993, changes in local
and national political and societal structures—particularly, the establishment of the Palestinian Authority in 1994 and of all the quasi "state"
apparatuses that followed—have had profound impacts on the Palestinian women's movements, both locally in Palestine and in the wider exile.
The importance of state-building dynamics cannot be underestimated.
In fact, the dual dynamics of state building and an accompanying phenomenon of "NGO-ization" have led to increasing fragmentation and
demobilization of all Palestinian social movements.

There are several reasons for this. First, both the nature and the
limited life cycle of projects funded by donors induce fragmentation.

361

Nongovernmental organizations (NGOs) typically aim to advocate for
or to educate a target audience, usually defined for and limited to the
period needed to implement a project. Here, the constituency is not a
natural social grouping but is artificially constructed. Equally important, the targeted group is typically a temporary passive recipient rather
than an ongoing active partner in the initiative. This relationship carries a cultural dimension, promoting values that favor dependency,
lack of self-reliance, and new modes of consumption.[1] NGO-ization
also introduces changes in the composition of much of the women's
movement, bringing to the fore a middle-class, professional women's
elite at the expense of rural and refugee women activists from grassroots organizations. Such a transformation (Goetz 1997) results in a
shift in power relations.

Each of the factors just mentioned contributes to a significant difference between NGOs and social movements—two phenomena that are
often conflated. According to Maxine Molyneux, the term *women's
movement* implies a social or political phenomenon of some significance,
due to both its numerical strength and its capacity to effect change,
whether in legal, cultural, social, or political terms. A women's movement does not have to have a single organizational expression and may
be characterized by diversity of interests, forms of expression, and spa-
tial location. It will comprise a substantial majority of women, although
it may not be exclusively made up of women (Molyneux 1998b:226). For
Sidney Tarrow, movements require "sustainable networking," whereby
ties are made, nurtured, and maintained; what specifically characterizes
social movements is that "at their base are the social networks and cultural symbols through which social relations are organized. The denser
the former and the more familiar the latter, the more likely movements
are to spread and be sustained" (1994:2). The same can be said of wom-
en's movements, as distinguished from "women in movement" (Rowbotham 1992, as cited in Jackson and Pearson 1998).

While many scholars view the proliferation of NGOs in the Middle
East as evidence of a vibrant civil society and as counterhegemonic to
Islamist discourse (Norton 1993, 1995; Ibrahim 1995; al-Sayyid 1993;
Moghadam 1997), little work has been done to evaluate the impact of
the proliferating NGOs on the empowerment of the different social
groups they claim to represent, much less on their capacity as viable
alternatives to Islamist groups. Nor are there attempts to verify whether
NGOs in fact succeed in mobilizing or organizing different groups in

pursuit of their rights. Indeed, few studies on the Middle East focus on how NGOs affect and interact with other forms of social organization—whether in the form of unions, political parties, or social movements involving students, women, or workers (Hanafi and Tabar 2002).

The transformation in the nature and role of Palestinian leadership in the PA era has left deep marks on the forms of women's activism. The creation of the PA, with its admittedly limited state-building mandate, pressured women's movements to shift their agenda from a combination of national struggle and women's emancipation to an agenda of targeting the state to promote women's rights. Many successful women's grassroots organizations were transformed into NGOs or came under the growing influence of NGO practices. A new Palestinian civil society emerged as a depoliticized arena that, while providing a forum to discuss democratization, human rights, and women's rights, effectively lost its previous capacity to organize and mobilize different groups, in particular women's groups aiming to combat the occupation.

In addition to the changes in the nature of NGOs and their efforts at state building, various traumatic developments have contributed in some measure to the evolution of the women's movement. These include the second uprising (*intifada*) in 2000, the separation of Gaza and the West Bank in 2003, the construction of hundreds of roadblocks throughout the territories, the election of Hamas in 2006, the complete closure of Gaza in 2007 (with 1.816 million people residing in Gaza and another 2 million in the West Bank), and the construction of the Separation Wall (begun in 2002 and still ongoing). The very real repression enacted daily by the occupying power has stifled any attempts to define or promote citizenship or to make progress of any kind in the West Bank or Gaza. Most Palestinian resources are hostage to Israeli control and punitive actions (Hilal and Khan 2004). The infrastructure and most development projects of the nascent PA have been subject to ongoing, systematic destruction. The Separation Wall has cut off Palestinians from their own land and water resources, as well as from one another. Complete lack of control over land, sea, and airspace; the inability of Palestinians to travel from town to town even in the "PA-controlled" areas; continual raids, invasions, targeted assassinations, and killings—these and countless other aspects of the Israeli Occupation all stymie attempts at development.

This chapter takes a broad look at Palestinian women's movements today to shed light on sweeping changes that have had impacts in several important areas: the legal contours of Palestinian citizenship and gender, the idealized images of women in official Palestinian and in Islamist discourse, forms of women's activism and participation in civil society, the waxing and waning of grassroots movements' ability to mobilize, and the balance between secular and Islamist forces.

I argue that the establishment of the Palestinian Authority has had a demobilizing effect on all social movements, including the women's movement, and that NGO-ization has further demobilized Palestinian civil society in a crucial phase of national struggle. I show how the weakening of the secular Palestinian national movement under Israeli Occupation, due in part to donor-funded attempts at promoting civil society, has provoked a progressive depoliticization of the women's movement. The vacuum created by this retreat, I suggest, has been increasingly filled by the militancy of the Palestinian Islamic Resistance Movement known as Hamas.

In what follows, I describe the paradoxical process of depoliticization and demobilization of the previously powerful and locally grounded women's grassroots committees after the initiative passed to the PA, which became the main political actor and job provider and defined the role for NGOs as complementary to the new "state." In order to examine whether this transition realized feminism and empowered women, I trace the trajectory of one of the "new" NGOs, as an illustrative example; describe the rise of "femocrats"; and contrast these developments with the gradual demobilization of an earlier grassroots women's organization. I also briefly trace the parallel process of the growing power of the Islamists, who are now taking up the lead in the national struggle.

One Century of Palestinian Women's Organization

Beginning early in the twentieth century, women in Palestine, as in neighboring countries in the rest of the Arab world, established their own charitable organizations in urban centers. The pioneering women in that domain were mainly Christians who had been empowered by missionary education. Muslim women too were encouraged to join the national struggle, establish their own organizations, and transcend religious boundaries. These women were urban, middle-class, and driven by the desire to "modernize" the "traditional" social order through the "uplifting" of rural women by means of education (Mogannam 1937; Fleischmann 2003).

Charitable work and urban elites dominated women's activism until the formation of the General Union of Palestinian Women (GUPW) in 1965 as one of the popular organs of the Palestinian Liberation Organization. At the peak of the "revolutionary" era, when the Palestine Liberation Organization (PLO) was settled in Lebanon after their expulsion from Jordan in 1972, activist women divided along factional lines controlled the GUPW. The GUPW played an important role in organizing and mobilizing Palestinian women in different localities throughout the diaspora. In the West Bank and Gaza, meanwhile, elite women conducting charitable activities continued to dominate the work and activism of the GUPW until women's grassroots organizations began forming in 1978.

Israel's conquest and occupation of the West Bank and Gaza in the war of June 1967 expanded Israeli rule to all of historic Palestine. This opened a new chapter in Palestinian resistance and ushered in new political, social, and economic realities that profoundly affected women and initially shaped the Palestinian women's movement. The women's movement contributed to both Palestinian national resistance and the creation of a new consciousness among Palestinian women. During this period the women's movement was linked inextricably to the nationalist movement and shared its fortunes, its burdens, and its vision of Palestinian independence. For both, the imperative to end the harsh rule of the Israeli military Occupation and attain national self-determination shaped the ideology.

Both the nationalist and the women's movements developed under a prolonged occupation and in the absence of a state. This absence, however deleterious to social and economic development, afforded space for mobilization and public activity that gave a special empowering character to Palestinian grassroots movements in the West Bank and Gaza, including the formation of the women's movement in the late 1970s. Embodied in the women's committees, the movement decisively widened the circle of activist women and played an important role in mobilizing women for the first *intifada*, the nationalist Palestinian uprising launched in December 1987.

During the Palestinian resistance, women formed organizations with the aim of enhancing women's participation in the battle for independence and defending the Palestinian people and cause, while simultaneously providing vital services for women in the realms of education, political participation, and cultural life. These women viewed realization of their social rights as a vital link toward the independence of Palestine. Their goals paralleled those of the nationalist movement, whose members also viewed these women as an integral component in the creation of the new nation-state.

Before the formation of the PA, Palestinian society was organized into political parties, grassroots mass organizations, and NGOs tied to political parties, all under the umbrella of the PLO, which nurtured and financially supported these parties and their satellite organizations. While Israel had banned the PLO and its affiliated political parties, their satellite organizations, primarily seen as service providers, were allowed some freedom to work in the Occupied Territories.

The Oslo Agreement (1993) ended the PLO's armed resistance and through negotiations allowed the organization to constitute itself as a quasi-state with the symbolic trappings of statehood—a flag, an anthem, an airport, and passports—but without sovereignty over its people, territory, or resources. The PA's failure to deliver national rights came as the Islamic Resistance Movement, or Hamas (launched in 1987), emerged to contest what it called the defeatist stand of the PLO. Hamas established itself as an Islamic national movement representing Palestinians' historical national right to self-determination and the right of refugees to return to their homeland. Hamas sought to mobilize and organize Palestinians in the West Bank and Gaza to resist the occupation, borrowing the old pre-PA ethos developed through the Palestinian national struggle led by the PLO: the core idioms of struggle, sacrifice, and suffering that constituted Palestinian national identity in the diaspora. As Islamist groups gained hegemony in civil society, other advocates lost out.

Women, Citizenship, and Gender in Official Palestinian Law and Discourse

Palestinian Authority Legislation Affecting Women's Interests

With the establishment of the PA, Palestinian citizenship became a dilemma. The Oslo Agreements granted the PA the right to issue only a Basic Law, not a constitution. In the March 2003 version of the Palestinian Basic Law, Article 12 specified the ways in which Palestinian nationality might be transmitted. Under pressure from the women's movement, the criterion for nationality was changed from blood ties through the father, used before 1984, to blood ties through either parent. For the first time in an Arab state, women were given the right to transmit citizenship to their children (Jad et al. 2003:9). In the last version of the Basic Law from 2003, however, the citizenship issue was removed altogether. Instead, Article 7 stated that "Citizenship will be regulated by Law," and the relevant law has not been promulgated to this day.

Earlier drafts of the Basic Law had already affirmed that Palestine respected and recognized a whole set of universal agreements and declarations, including the United Nations Convention for the Elimination of All Forms of Discrimination Against Women (CEDAW), which provide sources for legislation. In the first four drafts of the Basic Law, which were subject to popular discussion, sharia was not mentioned as a source of legislation, nor Islam as the state religion. Under pressure from Islamists, as will be described later in this chapter, both were later added by the Legislative Council, which consisted mostly of secular members at the time.

Despite the positive provisions, some revealing passages in the third version of the Basic Law dealing with work and motherhood suggest a less than full commitment to changing gender relations. Article 23, for example, declares that a "woman has the right to participate actively in social, political, cultural and economic life, and the Law will work to eliminate constraints that forbid women from fully participating in the construction of their families and society" (Jad et al. 2003:9). However, the major dilemma of women's unemployment was not clearly addressed in terms of job availability, employers' reluctance to hire women, the need for child care and a change in family protective mores, or guarantee of equal pay for equal work. Nor did the article define the constraints that the law would work to eliminate. The same article also stated that women's constitutional and sharia rights were protected, and that the law would stipulate punishment for any violations (ibid.). The proposed law's obscure language thus suits all ideological inclinations, whether secularist or religious, and leaves unclear which code, constitutional or sharia, would prevail if the two conflict. Motherhood, child care, and the family, all concepts central to Palestinian nationalism, were dealt with in most PA legal documents as the duty of society but without any official commitment on the part of the PA to help women carry out that duty (Jad, Johnson, and Giacaman 2000). Child care and maternity services, traditionally the task of women's organizations, did not receive enough support under the PA to keep them functioning. In many laws, such as the Civil Law and Civil Service Law, women were depicted as being dependent on men. More important, changes in the laws were not translated into policies, and the financial support required to develop policies and programs based on the new laws has not materialized to this day. Thus, the last version of the Basic Law, issued on March 18, 2003, has no mention of the articles dealing with women, and instead includes a provision common in Arab constitutions, stating in Article 9 that "Palestinians shall be equal before the law and the judiciary, without distinction based upon race, sex, color, religion, political views or disability" (al-Muqtafi 2016).

The PA also lacks a coherent set of policies to enforce the rule of law as an important guarantor of citizens' rights. The most visible policy is related to the security responsibilities assigned to the Authority by the Oslo Accords. The PA frequently uses detention without charge, torture, maltreatment, and harassment against the Islamic political opposition (Islamic Resistance Movement 1996). A higher security court was established by presidential decree as a parallel body to civil courts. Different security apparatuses created their own courts free of civil control (JMCC 2000a, 2000b, 2000c).

These repressive measures present women activists with a difficult dilemma. Various social organizations that demanded civil and social rights were already encountering antagonism from the PA; for women activists to criticize the PA's practices would invite similar repercussions. In order to strengthen their position, the women found it necessary to ally with other social organizations, such as Islamist groups, whose stances did not necessarily run parallel to their own. Failure to take a stand at all would have discredited the women activists, reducing their legitimacy in civil society.

In fact, certain grassroots women's organizations linked to Fateh, the ruling party, were discredited for precisely this reason. Most notable among these was the GUPW. When the PA was established, the leadership of the GUPW, an organization that Israel had previously banned in the Occupied Territories, returned from exile and set up an official organizational infrastructure to supersede the local unofficial committees that had constituted the women's movement when the entire West Bank and Gaza were solely under Israeli Occupation.

Conflict quickly arose between the returnee diasporic leadership and local leadership over a variety of issues. While the GUPW tried to present itself as a nongovernmental body, its actions and funding indicated otherwise. The organization was financially dependent on the PA, and the PA showered it with sometimes flagrant favoritism. The returnee leadership and its administrative staff, for example, received monthly salaries from the PA, and the PA also paid the rent for their luxurious offices, a fact that eventually led the local leadership to challenge the Union's claim that it was an independent NGO. [2] In the eyes of some, the GUPW had become a mere pawn for the PA. A woman from the local group put it this way in an interview:

> Every time we want to publish a leaflet or any political document, they [the GUPW returnee leaders] always insist that we have to add some glorifying sentences about the president; they ask us to display his photos. We are rebellious here; we are not used to that. Also, they objected to one of our leaders attending a conference in Amman because she was one of the signatories of a leaflet published by an opposition group criticizing the corruption in the PA. Of course we have to criticize the government. This is our right: we are not representing the government; we represent our people, our women. [3]

The GUPW returnees recognized the gender inequality being practiced by the national leadership; however, they chose not to protest it openly. As Agarwal put it, these women were compliant but not complicit with political hierarchy (1997:25).

Changes in law, then, reflected ambivalence on women's rights and equality, and even those laws that represented an improvement were not supported at the policy level, while the new situation placed women's organizations in a difficult position *vis-à-vis* the political hierarchy.

Ideology and the Ideal Woman in Palestinian Discourses

In addition to changes in legal status, changes in women's image and expected role also followed the establishment of the PA. In the historic discourse of the Palestinian national movement, women were typically portrayed either as militants or as self-sacrificing mothers (Peteet 1991; Jad 1990). In the face of death, dislocation, rejection, and annihilation, Palestinian poets glorified the woman who had a large number of children, especially male children. [4] The woman "freedom fighter" with a gun in her hand was an image glorified by different Palestinian factions, especially on the Left. However, the new situation required a different model for women.

In her study of Palestinian nationalism, Helena Schulz underlines the "ambiguity of Palestinian nationalism and national identity" (1999:156). In the new era of unachieved liberation the terms *belonging*, *loyalty*, and *commitment* have become the watchwords for the new regime around which the reconstruction of Palestinian nationalism is taking place. Belonging to Palestine is the main notion, without specifying which Palestine or whose Palestine. Belonging to Palestine is also extended to mean belonging to Fateh, still the main political party. This is manifested in the Fateh ideology whose core values include belief in the Palestinian cause, willingness to engage as a member of the Tanzim (i.e., Fateh) to carry out the responsibilities associated with the required commitment, and abiding by the stands, programs, and decisions adopted by the Tanzim with respect to political framework. This ideology extended to a broader national level and resulted in a proliferation of social organizations willing to follow the lead of the Palestinian Authority. The watchwords were still enforced among Fateh members after Hamas won the legislative election of January 2006.

As part of this process, media and propaganda signal the PA's "sovereignty" through two key symbols: the flag and the president.[5] Pictures of President Arafat in military uniform (replaced after the death of Arafat in 2004 with a portrait of Mahmoud Abbas in a Western suit and a tie) were hung in the streets, in stores, and in all PA offices. "Struggle" has been replaced with the "symbolic militarism"[6] reflected in many youth military marches and the use of military uniforms by young men and even children. This symbolic militaristic orientation is reinforced through the mushrooming of the PA's security apparatuses, each one in a different military uniform.

The new culture of symbolic militarism has come again to glorify the male fighter and to overshadow the image of the woman militant prominent during the PLO's years in Lebanon. In those days, the most respected women activists were those who got directly involved in the underground and militant activities of the political organization. Very few women were actually members of the Fateh political organization. In Fateh, "there was always a clear distinction between the military wing and other mass-based organizations, including women's organizations, and membership in the women's organization was insufficient for inclusion in the higher ranks of Fateh" (Rafidi 2001). In order to be a Fateh member, a woman had to prove herself as *"bint* Fateh" (a daughter of Fateh) (ibid.), constructed as masculine and tough, with short hair, simple trousers, a long shirt with long sleeves, and, as Islamism became popular, a head scarf. She had to be discreet, speak little, and remain steadfast under interrogation. The few but well-known women who headed militant cells were given male pseudonyms. As "Aisha," a former militant, remembers:

> I was known by the name of Abu Muhammad [Muhammad's father].[7] I talked, walked, and behaved exactly like men. If I showed my femininity, they [men] would take me as a weak, easy-to-crack person. I was tough, very tough. I had to show them that I was not less than they were, that I was a tough strong man. I only realized that I was a woman and that I should be proud of it after the establishment of the PA, when I joined a conference on what our gender agenda under the PA should be. (Maghassib 2001)

More recently, during the second *intifada* that began in September 2000, women again projected an image of themselves as militants and fighters when a number of women persuaded some militant groups to recruit them for military actions. Lately, Islamist women, like women in the PLO before them, have persuaded male leaders in the militant al-Qassam Brigades to recruit them (Palestine Media Centre 2005).

The PA, however, has attempted to replace the image of the woman militant with the image of the ideal woman as fertile, self-sacrificing, and steadfast. The fertile woman was deemed necessary because the outcome of the national struggle seemingly depended partly on the demographic balance between Jews and Arabs. An extension of the ideal of the self-sacrificing mother is the official glorification of mothers of martyrs.

Palestinian mothers, sisters, and daughters of martyrs receive contradictory messages from multiple discourses. While nationalist discourse glorifies women as mothers, uplifting their maternal suffering into national defiance and resistance, another feminist discourse urges women to be themselves, to express their true feelings and grief.[8] Feminist women's activism presents a new image for the woman as urban, professional, elegant, and claiming her individual rights from the PA, society, and family; it portrays the woman as a "taker." At the same time, Islamist groups depict the model woman today, as in the past, as modestly veiled, patient, a pious caretaker for her husband and children. She is, most important, the bearer of male children sacrificed in order to continue the resistance; to them, woman is the selfless "giver."[9] For its part, most Palestinian official discourse, prompted by the demands of foreign donors and UN agencies to "mainstream gender" and to take it into account in all projects, employs up-to-date, gender-friendly language. These myriad and contradictory discourses, each projecting its own image of the ideal Palestinian woman, all coexist in today's Palestine.

In sum, with the establishment of the Palestinian Authority, militarism has taken on an increasingly male complexion; women have had to retreat from this domain but have received confusing messages about their ideal role in society.

The Islamist Challenge

At this point, it is important to address the rise of what is sometimes called Muslim "religious fundamentalism." While there is a considerable volume of writing on contemporary Islamic movements (Hroub 1996, 2000; El-Hamad and Bargothi 1997; Abul-Omrein 2000), there has only been sketchy reference to their gender ideology, and very little attention has been paid to women activists themselves. Such an omission is surprising, particularly given the growing activism in Palestinian civil society of Islamist women, who are not considered by many feminists to be part of the women's movement.[10]

The increasing influence of Islamic movements in the Middle East is usually examined in the context of states' withdrawal from providing vital social and economic services to their citizens. This frame does not fit in the case of Palestine, where a sovereign nation-state has never existed. In both the West Bank and Gaza, the socioeconomic and political transformations produced by the Israeli Occupation were important in promoting the Palestinian Islamists directly or indirectly. The Israeli Occupation and the Jordanian regime colluded to boost the Palestinian Islamic Resistance Movement as a counterweight to the PLO, an offspring of the Muslim Brotherhood, in 1988, and it managed to build an impressive infrastructure of cultural, social, economic, and political institutions that proved crucial in sustaining the Islamic movement, mainly in Gaza. The PA's lack of delivery on national rights came as Hamas emerged to contest the hegemonic role of the PLO over the Palestinian communities. Hamas constituted itself as an Islamic national movement representing the historical Palestinian demand for self-determination and the return of Palestinian refugees to their homeland through the mobilization and organization of the Palestinians in the West Bank and Gaza to resist the Israeli Occupation.

The "new" Islamists differ from those active during the British Mandate or Jordanian rule. The older generation of Muslim Brothers came from the wealthier urban upper stratum; the new generation comes mainly from the peasant refugee population in the Gaza Strip. The older generation of founders were schoolteachers and minor members of the clergy. The second generation of leaders came from poor backgrounds in refugee camps, and were trained as doctors, engineers, headmasters, and university teachers at Arab universities (Abul-Omrein 2000:257; Al-Bargothi 2000:57–59). Their supporters consisted mainly of students, especially from poor and conservative families, as well as clergy and professionals (Al-Bargothi 2000; Abul-Omrein 2000). Emulating the secular and leftist political groups and in reaction to them, the Islamists adjusted their appeal to attract a wider constituency. As Islamist groups gained hegemony in civil society, other advocates lost out.

In December 1995 Hamas announced the establishment of the Islamic National Salvation Party (INSP). Its Women's Action Department is one of thirteen departments managing work ranging from public relations and cultural and political affairs to women's affairs. Unlike women's organizations in the secular national movement, the Women's Action Department of INSP has been able to integrate women not into a separate section (as in the case of secular national parties), but fully into its political appendages, whether in the leadership or in its popular base.

The party and its women's department opened its doors to the "new Islamic woman" who is highly educated, outspoken, modern, professional, and politically active. The "new Islamic dress" (long robe of plain color and a white or black head scarf) is seen as

> different from the *thub* (traditional peasant woman's dress) which is used by our mothers and grandmothers. [Islamic dress] is different in its meanings; it is a unifying symbol to our followers and members. If I see a woman wearing it, I will immediately realize that she

is *ukhot*[11] [a sister]. It indicates that we are educated and not like our mothers who are mostly illiterate. It gives us *heiba* [respect] as the dress of our *ulema* [religious clergy]. It is economic, simple, and modest." (Haroun and Salah 2000)

In this sense, women's new Islamic dress is regarded as a uniform of conviction, unlike the blind adherence to tradition that is presumed to explain clothing choices and other practices among the masses. Implicit in the Islamist veiling style is participation in a national social movement that lends the wearer a heightened sense of status, both moral (vis-à-vis secularists) and social (vis-à-vis women who cover instead of veiling). However, despite its political cachet, behind the social force of veiling, "one can discern the familiar principle of *himaya* (guidance and protection), by (and from) men" (White 2002:223).

Unlike in some other Islamic parties, in which Islamist women, once married, lose their "voice" when they retreat to the security and seclusion of the patriarchal family (White 2002), the INSP and its women's department made available an important venue for women who are highly educated (holding bachelor's and higher degrees) but have limited access to a restricted male-dominated labor market. In order to facilitate this integration process, the party and its satellite societies run a massive web of kindergartens with a minimal charge in which poorer women and wives of political prisoners are exempted from paying any fees. Running kindergartens was a common task formerly undertaken by nationalist and secularist women's organizations and later abandoned; the vacuum was filled not by the PA but by Islamist organizations. The Islamists thereby solved a major problem for working mothers and women's activists. However, it is significant that the two women who managed to make it to the top level of the party were both unmarried. The work in the politburo, according to Amira and Youssra, "is intense, diversified, needs lots of time and strong characters" (Haroun and Salah 2000). The times set for political meetings were identified by many feminists as a hindrance to women's participation in political parties, since these are usually set for the convenience of men rather than women (Waylen 1996). In this case, the veil facilitates mobility for politically committed women and gives them the required validation for transcending the social taboos that might ordinarily restrict unmarried women from mobility during late hours. Behavioral signals thus become important markers of the inapproachability and inviolability of Islamist women.

The Women's Action Department employs various strategies and methods for reaching and recruiting women. They work face-to-face, building cells in refugee camps as entry points. They give special attention in their activities to the large numbers of political prisoners and their families, who are now forgotten by almost all nationalist and secular women's organizations. The department organizes a yearly campaign for political prisoners, in the form of demonstrations against the Israelis and the PA—against the latter because of their "lack of democracy and to oppose the continuous harassments against the party offices and journal alongside the arrest of its leaders" (Haroun and Salah 2000).[12] In the yearly plan the activities directed toward women combine both a national and a gender-specific agenda. Cultural and educational activities are directed to women with higher education, while vocational education and material support target the poorer and less educated. The department organizes many workshops in political socialization, very similar to programs conventionally offered by secular leftist (Marxist) women's organizations. A program called "women's encounter," aimed at "linkage and mobilization," targets women lawyers, writers, journalists and media experts, doctors, and accountants. In addition, there is an annual course for women's cadre formation that borrowed its organizational form from Marxist groups and that sometimes lasts for a year.[13] These types of programs are innovative in comparison to those of the nationalist and secularist women's organizations, which fail to target this category of women in such a systematic and sustained manner.

As for specific women's issues, the Women's Action Department organizes a one-day women's conference annually, in which men and women participate by presenting papers on gender issues. The papers cover "hot topics" put on the agenda by secular nationalist women's groups or treat specific problems that women face in their respective fields of activity, such as work, political life, and culture. Some of the workshops are directed at the male members of the department and focus on topics such as socialization and involve thorough discussion of sharia family law.

The attitude of the party and of Palestinian Islamist women concerning sharia is "modified" and ever evolving. It both challenges the discourse of the feminist NGOs, which is based on a liberal, individualistic notion of rights, and ignores the plight Palestinians face under occupation, and the rather ambivalent Palestinian secularism that uses

Islam as a source of legitimacy. It is important to note that the motivations behind the call to reform sharia are in essence a move to change the internal power relations between males and females within the family structure. Some male members are receptive to change and support men and women participating jointly in the same activities, which enhances the image of the party and its women as "modern," while they continue to object to significantly deeper and less visible changes within the family. According to Amira, "Some topics elicit fierce resistance from men, as in the discussion of shari'a, while other topics like mixing (male and female) are contested and some male members are provoked by the separation between the sexes in our activities" (Haroun and Salah 2000). As one male member of the party put it, "As a party keen for the development of women, we should abolish segregation in the Party" (Zeyyad 2000).

Support for mixing, however, is not shared by all Islamists, many of whom encourage segregation among students in the university, a position that suggests that the veil is not enough to transcend sexual barriers. In the end, Hamas's gender ideology, while supporting the "new Islamic woman" and thus potentially contradicting the common perception of the Palestinian woman as a fertile womb, does, like the secular nationalist ideology, emphasize the more accepted role of women in reproducing the nation. By "Islamizing" Palestine and "nationalizing" Islam, the Islamists have proved successful in forging a brand of nationalism to which Islam is integral and that constitutes a mobilizing force for the masses.

As time goes on, the strict gender agenda and moral system inherited from the Muslim Brotherhood continue to evolve as Islamist women exert pressure on their leaders and empower themselves through their activism in the movement. The observation that "the text does not prohibit" was one that recurred throughout my interviews with women Islamists. What they meant was that religious texts are open-ended, making it possible for changing interpretations to forge a wider legitimate space for women in the public arena. Islamist women, even while disseminating the movement's gender ideology, are the first to push its boundaries and stretch their public presence. They have managed to build well-organized constituencies among highly educated and professional women, at times using more secular discourses based on sustainable development and women's rights, as well as new textual interpretations.

The Rise and Fall of Different Forms
of Women's Activism

As most doors closed on women's chances for militant action, especially in the West Bank, women's activism in Palestinian society has taken new forms. The changes in the NGO sector represent the most remarkable change of all affecting women's movements in Palestine; alongside these, the emergence of "femocrats" within the PA administration represents a major change in the role of older militant women leaders.

The NGO-ization of Women's Organizations

Before the formation of the PA, women activists belonged to what were known as "grassroots organizations," women's committees that were branches of political formations and sustained the first Palestinian *intifada*. The success of those women activists lay in organizing and mobilizing the masses, based on their skills in building relationships with people. It was important for a woman activist to be known and trusted by people in the community, to have easy access to them, to care about them, and to help them when needed. The task required daily tiring, time-consuming networking and organizing. These women activists knew their constituencies personally and depended on face-to-face human contact for communicating with them.

But even during the first *intifada* and following the signing of the Oslo Agreement in 1993, a significant change occurred. The NGO sector in the West Bank and Gaza began to be used as a channel for the foreign aid that enabled service delivery at the grassroots level in the form of clinics, schools, kindergartens, and income-generation projects. In 1991, when the Madrid Conference initiated the state-building process, women's movements were pressured to shift their agendas away from a program of combining the national struggle with women's emancipation, to instead looking to the "state" (which had none of the authority or powers of a true state) to fulfill women's rights. In the process, many previously successful women's grassroots organizations were transformed into advocacy NGOs or came under the growing influence of NGO practices. As a result, these NGOs became important actors, and acquired more power than their parent political parties.

The period from 1988 to 1994 witnessed a noticeable increase in feminist women's organizations in the form of NGOs. These new organizations included women's affairs centers in Nablus in 1988 and in Gaza in 1989. In Jerusalem, the Women's Study Center was founded in 1989, the Women's Center for Legal Aid and Counseling in 1991, and the Women's Affairs Technical Committee in 1991. The Women's Studies Program at Birzeit University was initiated in 1994 (Jad 2000:44). The growing number of institutions propagated a new discourse on women and women's status—paradoxically, in the context of a steady decline in women's mobilization. An unpublished study of five women's mass organizations found that membership declined by 37 percent after 1993 and that new enrollment in 1996 did not exceed 3 percent, with most of it occurring (probably due to patronage) in the Fateh women's organization (ibid.).

It is difficult to give an exact number of Palestinian NGOs. Sources vary in their estimates, from two thousand members in 1990 to one thousand in 2006. But undoubtedly, important changes in the landscape and composition of NGOs occurred after the signing of the Oslo Agreement in 1993 (Challand 2009:68). The Oslo years saw the establishment of many new NGOs: 37.6 percent of NGOs active in 2001 were created after the signing of the agreement. The funding received by this sector was huge, though impossible to state precisely. For instance, estimates for the year 1996 alone vary from $60 million to $240 million (ibid.).

The largest newcomer on the scene, the Palestinian Authority, embarked on gaining bureaucratic power and capturing funds from the NGOs. The PA co-opted some of the activists who had moved to the NGO sector and simultaneously separated them from their grassroots political base. Other activists formed autonomous advocacy NGOs, which viewed the PA as threatening their autonomy. Within the women's movement, power was granted by the PA to a new elite working within civil society in advocacy NGOs or within the PA apparatuses.

Along with the rise in the numbers of NGOs, a new category of women came into their own in the post-Oslo period with the formation of the PA. This is the category of women referred to as "femocrats" (i.e., women who work in the state bureaucracy).[14] Palestinian "femocrats" are not necessarily feminist, nor are they "employed within state bureaucratic positions to work on advancing the position of women in the wider society through the development of equal opportunity and anti-discrimination" (Yeatman 1990:65). Most Palestinian "femocrats," especially those in high-ranking positions, are nominated through patronage relations and not for their feminist credentials. However, patronage per se does not necessarily mean that the women are antifeminist or that they will not do their best to represent other women. Thus, while some use the gender agenda and their political access to promote their own interests, others work to develop a gender agenda despite the numerous constraints facing the PA and their position within it.

The locus of femocrats within the Palestinian quasi-state apparatus was the Inter-Ministerial Committee for the Advancement of Women's Status (IMCAW), until it was dissolved and replaced by the Ministry of Women's Affairs. IMCAW consisted of women in key positions in their respective ministries, mostly nominated by the president and assigned to mainstream gender issues (i.e., to integrate gender concerns in all policies, legislation, and programs) in their institutions. Success in fundraising and capacity building was seen as vital if women in IMCAW were to prove themselves as professionals. As the United Nations Development Fund for Women (UNIFEM) coordinator put it, "The members of IMCAW feel that they need lots of training on capacity building. They feel they lag behind the skills in the women's NGOs who all know how to fund-raise, how to formulate a strategy, how to manage and communicate, [while] they used to be mere freedom fighters. They did not need to fund-raise; they used to get funds through money collections and donations from the Arabs or the Palestinians in the diaspora" (al-Yassir 2001).

Thus, NGO-ization set the new model for the "old" militants and was their path to professionalization. Unfortunately, although the Palestinian Development Plan, 1996–1998 (Palestinian Ministry of Cooperation and International Relations 1996), assigned IMCAW the task of "developing" women and mainstreaming gender, it was not allotted resources. Lacking the financial means to develop and pursue an overall goal for development, IMCAW femocrats tended to focus instead on technicalities, such as how many workshops were needed to develop a mainstreaming plan. They fell into the trap Goetz (1997) describes: that of focusing on processes and means rather than ends, resulting in a preoccupation with the minutiae of procedures at all levels, rather than clarity about goals. The committee remained heavily dependent on donor aid, working as a GONGO (a governmental nongovernmental organization).

The new NGOs shifted from their roles as service providers to their communities and political facades for their parties to become advocates of democratization and citizens' rights. In their new role, they were portrayed and saw themselves as the voice of democratic, secular civil society, trying to define new boundaries between state and society. Whereas grassroots NGOs had worked to provide health, education, jobs, and child care for poorer communities, many of the newer NGOs turned to focus on donor-driven agendas such as good governance and violence against women, at the expense of national liberation and economic inequality. The so-called war on terror and the frenzied US effort to (purportedly) "democratize" the Middle East have intensified the tendency of many donors to concentrate on issues of government administration rather than economic or social needs. All of this has meant a power shift within what must now be categorized as the secular Palestinian women's movement, tilting it toward a more highly educated, middle-income and professional class at the expense of a female cadre with rural or refugee backgrounds.

The composition of today's NGOs contributes to this tendency. The typical NGO now consists of a board of seven to twenty members and a highly qualified professional and administrative staff, generally few in number, depending on the number and character of projects. The practical decision-making power frequently lies not in the hands of the board but with the director, who has to answer to the funders—who are themselves international NGOs or foreign government bodies. The power of the director stems from the ability to raise funds; to be convincing, presentable, and competent; and to deliver the well-written reports that the foreign donors require. Indeed, all administrative staff members are required to have highly professional skills. Sophisticated communication skills, including facility with English as the common language and use of modern technology, become vital, since donors promote the use of communications media, workshops, and conferences and of modern communication equipment including fax machines, computers, and mobile phones. This reliance on globalized, rather than local, tools automatically limits the pool of possible employees; and while it may not necessarily directly affect the relationship between an NGO and its local constituency, it often does.

In effect, since the typical structure of NGOs bars them from serving as mobilizing or organizing agents, however much they proliferate, they can neither sustain nor expand a constituency nor tackle issues related to social, political, or economic rights on a macro or national level.

Demobilization of a Grassroots Organization:
The Women's Committees for Social Work

Paralleling the rise of both the Islamist women's movement in Gaza and the new NGOs with their contingents of femocrats was the gradual *demobilization* of the grassroots organizations that had earlier played such a large role in both the nationalist movement and the building of consciousness around women's rights. The main grassroots women's organization was the Women's Committee for Social Work (WCSW), allied with Fateh. This was one of the women's committees which were connected to political parties and together had played an important role during the first *intifada*. The WCSW, however, had a wider outreach than the women's organizations in the leftist parties. Like the Islamists, the WCSW targeted villages and refugee camps and managed to organize young educated women. One activist explained the reason for WCSW's popularity among rural and refugee women:

> We use a simple language the people can understand; we give each one what he or she would like to hear. If they are religious, we use religious language; if they are leftist, we use leftist language. The most important thing was how to mobilize people to join the struggle, but for women, we paid special attention to providing services for them and their children. Women were lacking everything. In villages they have no services, no employment, and a striking level of poverty. (Azraq 2002)

For women from Fateh, the gender agenda was understood to equate to fulfilling women's basic needs: providing services, especially for poor women. Urban professional and academic women, for their part, were more inclined to join leftist organizations, seeing the WCSW as conservative and lacking a feminist vision.

With the establishment of the PA, many leaders of grassroots women's organizations faced a dilemma. If they joined the PA structure, they might lose the power base they had managed to build; if they didn't join the PA, they would leave the dividends of the process to the undeserving. It did not take long for almost all the women's leaders who supported the Oslo Accords to join the PA bureaucracy. Uncertain about the durability of the PA and its institutions, however, they did not want to risk leaving their base to other leaders. The lack of internal elections allowed them to keep both posts, although the pressure to prove themselves as professional femocrats meant they had little time for their grassroots organizations. Rabiha Deyyab, for example, then head of the WCSW, was put under tremendous pressure to choose between that post and her position as general director in the Ministry of Youth and Sports. She had to fight to preserve both, "as men do" (Deyyab 2001). Thus, the women who had previously built the grassroots organizations were co-opted, and their organizations were paralyzed by a lack of democracy.

When many women's leftist organizations and NGOs started making claims on the "state" for women's rights, the WCSW felt at a loss. The following excerpt reveals the dilemma felt by many women activists in Fateh:

> We in Fateh are not like women in the leftist organizations who raised the women's issues from the beginning of their work. We were more oriented to the national cause; we never dealt with or spoke about what should be the social status of women once we have a state; that was delayed until after liberation. When the PA was established we discovered our *matab* [impasse]. Now there is no national struggle; now it is a state-building era, and we have no vision about what we have to do.... We have great women militants who sacrificed a lot during the struggle, but they are not highly educated; they are not *motakhassissat* [professional]. We had very little money we needed to fund-raise for our organization. The PA did not help us financially, and we were obliged to register as an NGO to fund-raise for our own activities. We hoped that this might open new avenues and provide new contacts. (Azraq 2002)

As the WCSW oriented itself toward advocacy of women's rights, it became alienated from its previous vision and programs.

Meanwhile, events within Fateh were having a major effect on its women's organizations. Even before taking its place as the ruling party within the Palestinian Authority, Fateh had been subject to efforts by the Palestinian leadership to control it. Efforts ranged from nominating students linked to the internal security apparatus for positions on university campuses to sabotaging party elections. Without elections, Fateh began to experience internal decay. The attempts of different groups, including returnees and supporters of the Oslo process, to build new power bases within Fateh led to further fragmentation. The main division was between those who supported the Oslo Agreement and those who opposed it. Fateh's internal divisions were mirrored in the WCSW, which took a position critical of Oslo and was close to Marwan Barghouthi, a local leader who has been in prison since 2002, and who advocated "struggle" and "resistance" against Israeli oppression.[15]

The response of the PLO leadership was to dilute the old WCSW leadership by enlarging its membership. The addition of more women seemed on its face to increase representation of women in decision-making bodies, but in reality it was an attempt to control and weaken the grassroots organization. Original WCSW members criticized the newcomers: "The women they added have no political awareness and no organizational experience.... Many other members were more deserving to be in their place, but they were chosen to create patronage and not for any personal merit; they wanted to control Fateh locally by using women" (Azraq 2002.).

The newly enlarged WCSC "elected" a new leadership of thirteen members, which did not include Rabiha Deyyab, then head of WCSW. The PA president assigned the new incumbent the role of reorganizing women's participation in Fateh. This led to the creation of a new organizational body for women called the Women's Organization, which was strongly contested by women activists in the WCSW. They perceived the change as a replacement of militant activists, mainly from villages and refugee camps, by professional women who "never sacrificed their time and lives as we did." The activists also charged that "they wanted to put all women in a small hall to fight each other. The WCSW is the women's organization of Fateh, so why create another body and this time isolated from its base? They just wanted to marginalize us" (Azraq 2002.).[16]

The attempt to create a parallel women's organization ended as the second Palestinian *intifada* erupted in 2000, but by that time the largest Palestinian women's organization was already demoralized, divided, and losing its vision.

Palestinian Women in Politics: Fragmentation and Flawed Governance

The legislative elections of 2006 led to a sweeping victory for the Islamists of Hamas. The PA in the West Bank never agreed to cede power to the newcomers, and this led to the takeover of Gaza by Hamas, creating a political schism. The political schism divided the Palestinian political polity into West Bank and Gaza governments, and has altered the priorities of women in the West Bank and Gaza and impaired their capabilities for mutual accommodation. The fragmentation of the Palestinian national movement has resulted in two diametrically opposed approaches: one in the West Bank emphasizing state building, and one in the Gaza Strip continuing the national struggle by giving priority to the mobilization and empowerment of women in the resistance and defense of Palestinian rights and national existence.

The Ministry of Women's Affairs in the West Bank focuses on state building and institutionalizing equality within the Palestinian Authority (PA). It has followed the political line of the PA, and has been unable to take initiative either formally or informally to bridge the political gap between women in both governments. Connections between the West Bank ministry and the PA have helped the ministry in lobbying centers of power and the government to introduce some changes, such as introducing quotas for women in local and parliamentary elections, raising the marriage age for girls to eighteen, securing adoption of UN Resolution 1325 on protection of women in conflict situations, and partially amending the penal code. However, the PA remains shy of reforming the provisions of the personal status law for fear of a negative public reaction. The colonial context has rendered the PA ineffectual. Lacking control over resources or even its own fate, it has proven largely unable to satisfy women's demands for reform of the family law, gender equality, and full citizenship, and has at the same time weakened the political parties and social movements—including the civil society organizations—that were active within the Palestine Liberation Organization (PLO).

The ministry's counterpart in Gaza also relies on a network of relationships with and support from the Gaza government. Unlike the West Bank ministry, though, the Gaza ministry makes a great effort to mobilize women at the grassroots by emphasizing national struggle, pushing them to reach high echelons of power in both the executive and legislative branches. These branches, in turn, show a high propensity to respond positively to demands relating to the rights of widows and orphans and to the Islamic version of the Palestinian Women's Charter (a reference document for policymaking and legislation formulated and lobbied for by the national secular women's movement in 1997 and amended in 2008), partly because this discourse does not threaten the prevailing gender system, but rather tries to introduce improvements to it, targeting women and families of prisoners and those directly affected by occupation, and offering support and services to its mass base.

Clearly, there remains a need to consolidate and internalize the gains secured so far, both among women and in society at large. The mismatch between the visions of the two ministries exacerbates the current division between the West Bank and the Gaza Strip socially and intellectually. Each of the two ministries has a different referential framework and vision, as well as contrasting regional and international alliances. Lack of dialogue between the two ministries deepens this division further. Women in both governments bear part of the responsibility for bridging the gap. At the least, they should start a discussion on citizenship rights for women, as well as on priorities under the current situation, where the Israeli Occupation still dominates life in both the West Bank and the Gaza Strip.

Women in Ministries in the West Bank and Gaza

This part discusses the most important developments in and influences on the political life of women in the occupied Palestinian territory (the West Bank and Gaza Strip, including Jerusalem) in recent years, seen through the actions of the Ministry of Women's Affairs in the West Bank and Gaza. The impact of the ongoing instability on gender mainstreaming and the priorities of the Ministry of Women's Affairs can be analyzed as falling into three phases.

Phase I: The Formative Stage

The Ministry of Women's Affairs based its 2004 Plan on the 1997 National Strategy for the Advancement of Palestinian Women, which was based on international and regional conference documents, including the Convention on the Elimination of All Forms of Discrimination against Women (CEDAW 1979) and the resolutions of the Beijing Conference of 1995. However, the 1997 strategy reflected the approach and vision of feminist activists and the General Union of Palestinian Women at the time, and hence focused on national liberation, the role of women in opposing occupation, and the mobilization of international cooperation and solidarity to expose the crimes of occupation against women in particular and Palestinian people in general.

Nonetheless, a change in mission and vision regarding national liberation and gender mainstreaming led to a clear shift in emphasis toward "construction and development of the democratic Palestinian homeland, and consolidation of an effective civil society governed by national, cultural and humanitarian values"[17]. The three key objectives of the plan centered on a "social agenda" consisting of securing a government commitment to mainstreaming gender; supporting democracy and human rights issues in the policies, plans, and programs of the various ministries, as well as in legislation and regulations; linking lobbying activities to the development of policies and laws; and building a network of relationships with governmental and international women's organizations and human rights groups to exchange experiences in applying international conventions on women's and human rights, particularly CEDAW[18]. The plan also focused heavily on the institutionalization of the Ministry's work and on incorporating it within the body of government through an organizational structure, human resources, and a budget.

Phase II: Political Divide—2005-2007

The subsequent 2005–2007 plan focused on educational, vocational, and technical training of young women; support for women's access to decision-making positions; and poverty of young women, especially heads of households. These goals were based on the Beijing Platform for Action, as well as on consultation with governmental and other non-governmental institutions. Once again, this plan focused on development and capacity building, with an emphasis on women's access to decision-making positions. This was popular among women working in the various ministries, supporting them in their efforts to improve their job positions.

With the legislative elections in 2006, the Islamic movement, Hamas, came to power. The first Islamist Minister of Women's Affairs[19] set out to provide assurances. However, ambiguity or lack of clarity over the positions of Hamas *vis-à-vis* the demands of the feminist movement raised doubts in the minds of some feminist activists. For example, several meetings were held for women leaders, coordinated by The Palestinian Initiative for the Promotion of Global Dialogue and Democracy (MIFTAH), to understand the reasons behind the political "turning of the tables." The meetings called for a review of the work and discourse of women's organizations in order to extract lessons. The elitism of feminist work and its focus on educated groups of women in the central West Bank was criticized, emphasizing a need to change the means of communication with women in general. There was no acknowledgement, however, of the importance of opening dialogue with the official newcomer—the Islamist women of Hamas.[20]

The two Hamas ministers introduced amendments to the vision of the Ministry of Women's Affairs. Notwithstanding a continued prioritization of the fight against discrimination against women in the community and the need to support equality, anti-violence, and legal reform efforts (as indicated in the earlier strategic plans), a new element was added: support for certain groups of women, mainly young women and the wives and families of Palestinians who had been killed, detained, and imprisoned. This emphasized the national struggle agenda and its social ramifications for women and their families. This trend was to later become the main focus of the Ministry of Women's Affairs in Gaza after the split between Fatah and Hamas in June 2007. Islamist ministers' leadership of the Ministry of Women's Affairs in the West Bank led to paralysis resulting from internal conflicts that derived mainly from political rejection of the Islamist newcomers.

Phase III (Part One): The West Bank after 2007

After the political split, and in a newly charged political environment, a fresh strategy for the Ministry of Women's Affairs in the West Bank was developed for 2008–2010. The focus returned to the earlier priorities, with a new addition: combating violence, mainly domestic, against women, and building an appropriate related strategy for the period 2011–2015. The new strategy promoted government efforts to put into effect UN Security Council Resolution 1325—under which Palestinian women can file complaints concerning the violence of the Israeli occupation to international bodies, especially the International Criminal Court—and its clauses related to the participation of women in conflict resolution and peace-building. The recommendations did not address how this might be achieved, however.

The political division led the ministry in the West Bank to shift its focus away from the strategic needs of women (understood to be legal reform and an impact on policy-making) toward meeting the practical needs of women and implementing relief policies. This shift was reluctant since, according to the 2009 national report of the Ministry of Women's Affairs, such policies were considered to be "often in conflict with 'social justice'" and with the "state building" aspirations of "mainly secular [non-governmental organizations]"[21].

However, priorities soon changed again with the 2011–2013 strategy, which reverted to national issues, envisaging support for women in Jerusalem and women prisoners. The strategy included a number of sub-goals that were difficult to achieve within the specified period. Moreover, the priorities lacked consistency. Combating violence was understood to be directed at domestic violence, rather than violence perpetrated by the Israeli Occupation, whether in the West Bank or Gaza Strip, despite the bloody war waged on the Gaza Strip in 2008–2009. Furthermore, low budget allocations did not reflect a real commitment to national issues. Out of a total budget of NIS 43,813,240 or about $11 million, NIS 200,000 or 2.74 percent was allocated to family law and civil rights programming, while only NIS 128,400 (0.29 percent) was allocated to protecting the rights of women in Jerusalem and NIS 53,000 (0.12 percent) to supporting women prisoners.

Strategies of the Ministry of Women's Affairs in the West Bank were mainly based on the Declaration of Independence of 1988; Palestinian Basic Law; the Palestinian Women's Charter of 2008; international conventions, particularly CEDAW; and UN Security Council Resolution 1325 addressing women in times of war. The ministry made great efforts to raise awareness about these instruments, in particular Resolution 1325 and the Palestinian Women's Charter. It also succeeded in several other areas, the most important of which was the institutionalization of gender and women's issues in various ministries. The Council of Ministers decision (15/12/09 M.W/A.Q) of 2005 urged ministries, particularly larger ones, to establish units for women's affairs, where needed and possible. This decision was not mandatory, however, and was unclear. The ministry later worked to amend it and specify clearer tasks and an organizational structure. On July 28, 2008, it succeeded in gaining approval for a name change for these groupings, from "women's units" to "gender units," and is working on implementing this change.[22] Nonetheless, ministries are not required to establish such units.

There are currently 20 gender units in various ministries and official institutions. Their status varies from one ministry to another, depending on the capacity of staff, their positions, and their influence, in addition to the overall vision of the ministry and the political will of the minister. They need more time, effort, and capabilities to achieve their goals. Several continue to focus on women's access to decision-making positions, which translates to having more women in each ministry in senior or better positions. Some ministry units (such as in the Ministry of Labor and the Ministry of Local Government) have been active in forming coalitions with civil society activists in an effort to increase their influence, while some are still feeling their way.

The ministry also supported the establishment of women's communication centers in key provinces (Hebron, Nablus, Bethlehem, Jenin, and Ramallah) through partnerships with civil, government, local, regional, and international institutions designed to combat all forms of discrimination against women in all fields. According to documents issued by the ministry and the Palestinian Women's Charter, the aim is to empower women and enable them to participate in public life. Although undoubtedly this is an important step in mainstreaming women's issues in decentralized arenas, these centers suffer from a lack of essential human and financial resources.[23] In addition, women and children's departments were added on April 4, 2007, by presidential decree, to the structures of the various governorates, with the aim of supporting and developing the capabilities of women and children in all spheres: political, social, and economic. These units were not allocated budgets, however, that would enable them to implement the plans, programs, and activities assigned to them. This is a problem facing most of the structures that have been established to institutionalize gender.

Phase III (Part Two): Gaza after 2007

The two Hamas-affiliated ministers in the 2006-2007 government and in the 2007 government of national unity adopted the Palestinian Women's Charter with reservations.[24] However, once the governing regimes split after June 2007, the content of the document was changed by the Gaza Ministry of Women's Affairs. Significant changes made notwithstanding, it is to the credit of the Gaza Ministry that it has retained the document, which indicates that there is injustice and a need to develop an integrated rights and political framework, albeit in an Islamic context. Workshops were conducted to promote the contents of the sharply altered document. In a workshop held on June 5,

2009, the official in charge of policy and planning in the Gaza Ministry stated that the document serves as a legal base compatible with the special identity and culture of Palestinian society but that the original document promoted by the West Bank ministry is not based on Islamic law. He went on to say that "99% of the previous document promoted Western thought that is incompatible with Islam ... being grounded in leftist thought based on secularism. The current Ministry has modified it to bring it in line with Islamic law. Initial re-writing of the document will be accomplished through a series of workshops (26 workshops) to be held by experts to study and analyze various issues in the document."[25]

The main objection to the West Bank ministry's version of the document is "that it was based on the concept of gender, since it deals with individual rights of women, thereby promoting conflict between men and women." By advocating complete equality in all matters relating to gender, such as considering testimony of women in courts of law equal to that of men, that version of the document purportedly denies complementarity between men and women. [26] Nonetheless, as Al Sabti explains, the Gaza Ministry document advocates that Palestinian women have the right to vote and be nominated in general and local elections, the right to equal access to all public offices according to Islamic law[27], the right to form and join political parties, and the right to enjoy all educational, financial, health and social services granted to citizens by law. There is thus a contradiction between avowed rejection of the principle of full equality and these achievements that are based mostly on the principle of equality in civil rights and penal law. While foundational concepts in the original document, such as gender, are rejected, there is serious work underway, albeit indirect, aimed at encouraging women and engaging them in political, economic, social, and community roles that have been denied to them by society on the basis of their gender. However, the political split removed the possibility for a "dialogic engagement" between women on both sides. The West Bank Ministry fully abides by the international conventions on women's rights, and the Gaza Ministry was freed from pressure of national and secular activists to meet at a middle ground. Instead, the Ministry in Gaza is struggling to form its own vision on what women's rights should be from an Islamic perspective, relying on its wide networks through the Muslim Brothers movement and the support of Arab and Islamic countries.

Conclusion: What Hope in the Face of a Crippling Military Occupation?

The emergence of the PLO—a national secular leadership, especially after the Arab defeat of 1967—played an important role in consolidating Palestinian national identity based on core elements of struggle, return, and sacrifice. The new construction of Palestinian nationalism constituted women in contradictory images: on the one hand, the traditional, sacrificing mother whose main role was to reproduce her nation by providing male fighters, and, on the other, the revolutionary militant who should join the struggle hand in hand with her brothers to liberate the nation. This contradictory construction was contested by women activists, who started to challenge the prevailing gender order by pressuring their organizations for more equitable policies and legislation to redress this inequality. The unstable political situations in which the Palestinians and their leaderships have existed since 1947, however, have always worked against any serious push by women for social change. Nevertheless, the "revolutionary" era in the diaspora and the Occupied Territories was an important phase in the development of the Palestinian women's movement during which women's activism was successful in bridging the gap between urban elite women, rural women, and refugees. This linkage was an important shift to broader organization and mobilization for women at the grassroots level and the recruitment of new women activists who, for the first time, did not come from middle-class backgrounds.

The Oslo Agreement and the emergence of the PA triggered an ephemeral process in which civil society organizations shifted from sustaining their community to claiming citizens' rights. This shift brought the professional urban elites back to the fore at the expense of the rural and refugee leadership. The merger between the structures of the PLO with those of the newly created Palestinian Authority led to the marginalization and fragmentation of all grassroots organizations and their elites. A process of NGO-ization supported by foreign funding, mainly Western, added to the fragmentation and demobilization of all social movements in general and of the national secular women's movement in particular. The vacuum was immediately filled by new forms of activism, new forms of nationalism, and a new gender ideology developed by men and women in the Islamist movement (see, for example, Jad 2005).

The obstacles in the way of the development of an aware gender mainstreaming in Palestine are now so enormous that international blueprints for women and development may simply be incapable of overcoming them. The blueprints, brought by international aid agencies and international women's movements, assume a situation of political normality and stability, the existence of a state with functioning structures, and a stable and well-defined civil society. Clearly, none of these exist in Palestine. The Palestinian women's movement in its secular form forged important ties with international and transnational women's movements through attending conferences and global communication media. Through these linkages, women activists gained awareness about gender issues related to domestic violence and women's representation in public offices, and acquired important knowledge on universal conventions.

From the 1990s onward, however, the effects of NGO-ization started to appear in the formulation of the national agenda geared so far to resist the occupation. This position is credible since some of the main donors for Palestinian NGOs and activists in international women's movements insisted upon "correct political conditions" in an attempt to separate these organizations from politics.[28] Many women activists became involved in projects to bring both Israeli and Palestinian women to "reconciliatory conferences" to build "peace and reconciliation." Most of these activities ignored the painful reality of the occupation and its policies of land confiscation. These conferences may not have helped support the "peace process" but rather helped the intensification of the occupation policies by covering them up and directing international attention to the endless "peace process" that never leads to real peace. But, again, it would be an oversimplification to perceive NGOs as passive recipients and donors as simply following or executing their governments' policies. It was argued that local NGOs, as well as international actors, have a space to negotiate their mutual relationships. Cohen and Comaroff, for example, state that NGOs "do not respond to a need, but negotiate relationships by convincing the other parties of the meaning of organizations, events and processes. . . . They act as brokers of meanings" (1976:88, cited in Hilhorst 2003:191). I would argue that, besides their ability to convince international donors of the vitality of their work, "peace activists" are equally involved in this process, driven by their own interests. The involvement in "peace process" activities by many NGOs, aside from getting them funding, supports the NGOs' claim to acquire more power and legitimacy. "Peace process" activism might constitute a power base for the NGO elite to reach decision-making positions, whether in the PA or in the leadership of the Palestinian women's movements and other social movements.

The tendency of outside experts is to ignore the impact of structural and national instability and to pursue the implementation of externally designed projects for mainstreaming gender, despite the fact that the continuing military occupation and confiscation of land in the West Bank and Gaza render most development mechanisms useless. The freeze in the expansion of the GUPW, for instance, is related not only to the power struggle between returnees and locals but also to the facts on the ground created by Oslo. When Salwa Abu Khadra, head of the GUPW and the EC, was faced with persistent criticisms about the lack of new elections in the GUPW, she stated:

> What prevent elections from happening are very real and problematic issues such as the scope and location of the election. The members in the diaspora cannot all come unless the Israelis grant them permits, and the Israelis don't accept that because of the shaky political situation. We cannot organize in the diaspora as an issue of principle; the Occupied Territories are now the center of the headquarters of the leadership. Also it will be very costly to bring big numbers of women representatives from the diaspora, and the Union coffers are empty. And even if they restrict the election to members living in the homeland in Gaza and the West Bank, the members in Gaza cannot join because of the siege. (Abu Khadra 2001)

Thus, on top of the absence of gender-related policies on the part of the PA, and the conflict and confusion within the PA and within the women's organizations, there is no denying that the Israeli military Occupation has been and remains a primary factor in the shaping and in the eventual demise of the Palestinian women's movements in the West Bank and Gaza.

In the end, while providing a forum in which to discuss democratization, human rights, and women's rights, the relatively new forms of Palestinian civil society have effectively weakened the capacity that Palestinian society previously possessed to organize and mobilize different groups, in particular women's groups aiming to combat the occupation (Jad 2004). Ultimately, the transformation of Palestinian women's organizations from grassroots organizations capable of mass mobilization into NGOs was disempowering in that it weakened the mobilizing potential of secular feminist women's organizations and depoliticized their activism, leaving the Islamist women's movement as the main force contesting the previous hegemony of the secular women's movement. Reality contradicts the prevailing perception of women's secular feminist NGOs as modern and democratic "agents of civil society," whether in Palestine in particular or in the Middle East in general (Moghadam 1997:25; Kandil 1995). It problematizes the unqualified and interchangeable use of the terms *NGO* and *social movement* in the Palestinian case or in the greater Middle East (Bishara 1996; Beydoun 2002; Bargouthi 1994; Chatty and Rabo 1997; Shalabi 2001). Meanwhile, the growing power of the Islamists has considerably complicated the possibility of forming a unifying agenda for combating the occupation or achieving women's rights (Jad 2005). Despite the fact that they are seen by many of the secularists as undemocratic, "fundamentalist," and not part of a "true" civil society, the Islamists are now essentially carrying the cause of national struggle and national service, thereby further complicating the possibility of forming a unifying agenda for combating the occupation or achieving women's rights.

Notes

1. In advertisements in Palestinian newspapers, it is common to read about collective community actions organized by youth groups, such as cleaning the streets, planting trees, painting walls, and so forth, followed by a little icon indicating the name of the donors who funded these projects. It is also noticeable that many of the NGO activities are held in fancy hotels, serving fancy food, distributing glossy material, and hiring "presentable" youth to help organize the event. All this has led to the gradual disappearance of the traditional image of the casual activist with the peasant accent and look.

2. Interview with the author in Ramallah, April 9, 2001; the interviewee asked to remain anonymous.

3. Interview with the author in Ramallah, April 9, 2001; the interviewee asked to remain anonymous.

4. One such example is the poem "Ahmed al-Za'atar," by the famous poet Mahmud Darwish, which was written after the 1976 attacks by the Syrian army on the Palestinian refugee camp Tel al-Za'atar during the Lebanese civil war.

5. In a local television (Phalastine) interview on December 18, 1999, in the West Bank town of Jericho, after a physical assault in Jericho's prison on M.P. Abdel-Jawad Saleh (also former minister of agriculture), General Al-Tirawi, head of the Palestin-

ian Intelligence Service Office, declared, "We have two sacristans, the president and the flag."

6. I refer to it as "symbolic militarism" because when the Israeli troops invaded the PA area in April 2002, a national strategy for resistance, whether military or civil, was not on display. The political leadership denounced many local groups' or individuals' resistance actions as acts of "terror."

7. In Palestinian culture, it is common practice to give the name of the first male son to his parents. Thus, Abu Muhammad means the *father* of Muhammad. It is therefore an honorary nom du guerre. In 1997 Aisha was appointed to serve as the head of a local police station in Gaza but was later removed when a prisoner in her station escaped.

8. In the second intifada, many women's NGOs ran counseling programs for mothers and children so they could cope with the immense psychological stress of the Israeli violence.

9. Hamas issued many statements forbidding women from military activities since there are "enough men to continue the struggle." See Jad 2005.

10. I use the word *Islamists* to denote the supporters and militants of Islamic movements in Palestine. From the Islamists' point of view, there is hostility toward the use of the label "Islamic fundamentalism" as a foreign notion. I use *Islamic movement* to refer to a sociopolitical movement founded on an Islam defined as much in terms of political ideology as in terms of religion. This is the term that activists in the movement use to define themselves (Bassam Jarrar, one of the Islamist leaders in the West Bank, in Usher 1997:336). I reserve the term *Islamist women* for those who belong to the Islamist movement and are actively engaged in the public sphere in promoting what Keddie has called "an Islamic state that would enforce at least some Islamic laws and customs" (1988, in Karam 1998:16). Islamist women have only mobilized into a movement in Gaza, and there is little coordination between Islamist organizations in Gaza and the West Bank.

11. It is also worth noting that Fateh also used to call a woman member *ukhot* (sister), while in the leftist parties she is called *rafiqa* (comrade).

12. In 2001 the PA raided local party offices to confiscate all their equipment, documents, and computers and issued a rule to ban the party from all activities as well as to ban its journal, *al-Rissala*. According to Amira (Haroun and Salah 2000), the party functions at a very low level only from its headquarters in Gaza City. At this moment, even though the party managed to obtain a ruling on March 21, 2003, from the highest court canceling the PA ruling 113/2003 that allowed the PA to put its hand on the budgets of thirty-nine Islamic societies, the PA refuses to implement the ruling and renewed its own budget-taking powers with ruling 40/2004 (http://www.Palestine-info.net).

13. The course contains topics related to more "modern" and "scientific" issues such as self-assertiveness, self-building, effective communication, political awareness, socialization, program designing, and collective picnics.

14. In drawing on a similar situation in Africa, Amina Mama juxtaposes femocracy with feminism. In her view, feminism is defined as being the popular struggle of African women for their liberation from various forms of oppression, and "femocracy" is described as "an anti-democratic female power structure which claims to exist for the advancement of ordinary women, but is unable to do so because it is dominated by a small clique of women whose authority derives from their being married to powerful men, rather than from any actions or ideas of their own" (1995:41). She questions whether "femocracy" can result in improvement of the status of ordinary women or be

democratized, as well as whether state structures can act as vehicles for ordinary women's struggles or only serve the elite.

15. Women were close to Marwan Barghouti, a popular Fateh leader and PLC member who is currently serving several life sentences in an Israeli prison.

16. Khawla is an active member of Fateh and the WCSW from a refugee camp. Rabiha is from a poor village, as are most of women activists in the WCSW.

17. The Ministry of Women's Affairs, Strategic Vision and a Plan of Action, March 2004. Ramallah.

18. Ibid.

19. Mariam Saleh, the first minister of the Ministry of Women's Affairs in the tenth government (March 29, 2006 to February 15, 2007) spoke to leaders of women's organizations on November 5, 2006 (Al-Quds newspaper 2006). Amal Siam, her successor in the Government of National Unity (the eleventh government), which was formed on March 17, 2007 and ended with Hamas' takeover of the Gaza Strip on June 14, 2007, also called for a meeting with women's organizations and unions, but only a few responded (Al Hayat al Jadidah newspaper 2007).

20. Miftah, Women in Peace and Negotiation, Women Political Forum, third meeting minutes taken by the author on 26/2/2006, Miftah office. Ramallah.

21. Palestinian National Report Beijing + 15, ESCWA, Beirut (unpublished report)

22. Ibid.

23. Ibid.

24. Al Hayat al Jadidah Newspaper.

25. Haroun, Amira, The Palestinian Women's Bill of Rights, workshop, Gaza in 5/6/2009, http://www.mowa.gov.ps/news_details.php?id=10 , accessed on 12/8/2011.

26. Al Sabti, Randa The Most Important Pillars and Themes of Women's Bill of Rights, The Palestinian Women's Bill of Rights' workshop, Gaza in 5/6/2009, http://www.mowa.gov.ps/news_details.php?id=10 , accessed on 12/8/2011.

27. The position is actually ambiguous. There are those who reject the idea of women holding high state office or in the judiciary. However, views differ between the moderate current (Muslim Brotherhood) and some of the most stringent fundamentalist (Salafi) trends.

28. The head of USAID in Tel Aviv announced the intention to make further aid conditional on positive political developments. The formal statement made by the head of USAID, Larry Garber, announced that aid would stop if a declaration of independence were made by the Palestinian National Authority (Hanafi and Tabar 2002:35). In 2003 the same organization circulated a form on all Palestinian NGO recipients of its funds to "certify" that they don't support "terrorism" through their activities.

13

The Women's Movement and Feminism in Iran

Revisiting a "Glocal" Perspective

NAYEREH TOHIDI

Introduction

Women's status and rights in contemporary Iran and thereby the trajectory of Iranian women's activism and feminist movements seem paradoxical and complicated.[1] For instance, how could women under a conservative Islamist clerical state, which has pursued sex segregation and many extreme forms of legal and practical discrimination against women, show impressive educational attainment, even surpassing men in higher education? Why haven't women's remarkable educational achievements corresponded with their employment opportunities, economic and occupational mobility, or their representation in political decision-making? Why have Iranian women's labor force participation rates and share of representation in the Parliament remained among the lowest in the world, even in comparison to other Middle Eastern countries? Or how could Iran become exemplary in the world for its success in reducing fertility rates in a few decades by more than two-thirds, from 6.6 births per woman in the mid-1970s to about 2 births per woman in 2010 (Roudi 2009)?

Many factors have shaped women's contradictory status in present-day Iran, including the patriarchal and patrimonial patterns in Iranian history and culture, be it secular or religious (Islamic); the state policy and state ideology; and the influential ideological and intellectual trends such as nationalism, anti-imperialism, socialism, Islamism, and, more recently, liberalism and a human rights framework. External and international factors, especially Western imperial meddling have also influenced state policies and intellectual discourses pertaining to women's rights and gender issues. Another set of factors, of increased influence in recent years, involves increased processes of globalization and the international currency of the discourses of human/women's rights spreading through the United Nations, transnational feminist activism, and new communication technology such as satellite TV, the Internet, and social media. Increased globalization has intensified a "glocal" dialectic, meaning the interplay of local-national factors with global-international factors. The glocal and transnational dynamism in Iranian society have intensified in the past four decades due to the impact of millions of forced and voluntary exiles and emigrants, mostly settled in Western Europe and North America. This massive exodus of Iranians, mostly caused by politics, has become a drastic brain drain for the country. Yet, these many diasporic communities of Iranians include thousands of highly educated and accomplished professionals, many of them still devoted to the cause of human rights and democracy for Iran. This has offered Iran's civil rights and women's rights movements a well-connected new resource. Iranian diasporic feminist activism has made up a significant component of transnational connection, cross pollination, and the glocal process of socio-cultural change in Iran today (Tohidi 2005).

This chapter attempts to provide an overview of the current women's movement and feminism in Iran from a glocal perspective. Following a glance over the social and historical background of this movement, a brief discussion is offered on the methodological and theoretical issues encountered in researching the women's movement in Iran. Then the chapter traces the trajectory of women's activism after the 1979 Revolution and discusses the ironies and challenges of the emergence of a growing women's movement and feminist discourse under an Islamist state. Special attention is paid to transnational, diasporic, and international interplay with local-national factors such as state policies, oppressive laws, and patriarchal cultural traditions as well as socioeconomic and demographic changes.

Historical, Socioeconomic, and Political Contexts

The history of Iranian women's quest for equal rights and their collective actions for sociopolitical empowerment dates back to the formation of the modern social movements for constitutionalism and democratic nation-state building in the late nineteenth and early twentieth centuries. In Iran, as in other parts of the world, the women's movement and feminist discourse are byproducts of modernity and industrial capitalism. At the same time, the women's movement, especially feminism, has presented a challenge to and a critique of the androcentric and unjust aspects of modernity. Moreover, since modernity in Iran and in many other Middle Eastern countries has been associated with Western intrusion, colonialism, and imperialism, it has resulted in mixed feelings among many women and men: a fascination with progressive aspects of modernity and strong desire to become modern, yet at the same time a resentment of and resistance against Western domination.

Taking advantage of such anti-imperialistic resentments, the ruling patriarchal and despotic authorities in Iran have usually blamed Iranian feminists and characterized any quest for women's emancipation as an exogenous idea. This supposedly Western exported phenomenon is accused of promoting sexual license to penetrate the *dar ol-Islam* and the traditional family and thereby destroying the internal moral fabric of the entire society. Therefore, women activists aspiring for equal rights (who may or may not identify as feminist) have often found themselves in a defensive position. They have usually tried to assure their community of their moral virtue, loyalty, and patriotism. They have also tried to convince the ruling elites that not only do egalitarian and powerful female images have authentic and indigenous roots in Iranian pre-Islamic history, but also the quest for equal rights is not incompatible with progressive understandings of Islamic tradition (see, for example, Kar and Lahidji 1993; Tavassoli 2003; Milani 2011; and Vasmaghi 2014).

The women's movement in Iran, as in most other parts of the Middle East and North Africa (MENA), therefore, has been intertwined with nationalism and anti-colonial or anti-imperialistic sentiments. Although Iran was never colonized, the strong influence of the Russian and British Empires in Iran during the nineteenth and early twentieth centuries gave an anti-imperialistic orientation to many of the Iranian pro-modernity and pro-democracy groups. The constitutional movement (1905–1911) that sought to build a modern nation-state in Iran had to fight the despotism of the old monarchy and its imperial supporters at the same time. Anti-American sentiments were added to this after the CIA and British Intelligence Service supported the 1953 coup

against the secular and democratically elected Prime Minister Mohammad Mossadegh because of his agenda to nationalize the oil industry.

Within this context, women's rights advocates and feminists in Iran
(as in Egypt and many other MENA countries), have often felt compelled to show their distance from the imperialist "outsiders," prove
their loyalty and devotion to their nation, and then dare to fight the
patriarchal "insiders" and demand women's rights. They have been
carefully navigating between identity politics, a cultural pressure for
"authenticity," and the quest for national independence on the one
hand, and the aspiration for individual rights and universal values such
as equality, human rights, freedom of choice, and democracy, on the
other.

In their more than one-hundred-year history of collective activism,
Iranian women have made remarkable achievements in the realms of
education; scientific, literary, and artistic creativity; and to some extent
in economic productivity and sociopolitical participation. However,
they have not succeeded in gaining equal rights in many areas, particularly in the family (inheritance, marriage, divorce, and child custody).
During the process of rapid modernization under the Pahlavi dynasty
(from the 1930s through the 1970s), many institutions in Iran, including the public education and judiciary systems, were modernized and
went through secularization. But personal status and family law remained strictly on the basis of the old sharia (Islamic law).

In most Muslim-majority countries, except for Tunisia, Turkey, to
some extent Morocco, and the Muslim-majority republics in the Cau-
casus and Central Asia (such as Azerbaijan and Uzbekistan), egalitarian
reforms in family law, whether by revising and reinterpreting sharia or
by replacing it with secular law, have been painfully slow. This has been
due to several complex reasons; the most important is a patriarchal consensus (based on a tacit distribution of power) among the secular nationalist (usually military) elite and the religious Islamic elites, that is,
the clerics (*ulema*). Laws governing women's roles in the public domain
increasingly fall under the control of the secular modernizing state
elites, whereas laws governing women and children in the family (and
domestic gender relationships and personal status) remain under the
control of the clergy and religious authorities.

But with the rise of Islamism and after the establishment of the
theocratic state of the Islamic Republic in Iran since 1979, many of the
laws and policies in both the public and domestic domains have come

under the direct control of the clerics, who have furthered the extent of gender discrimination in favor of men. A few significant progressive reforms made in family law in the 1960s and '70s under the rubric of the Family Protection Law (FPL) (during the second Pahlavi) were repealed in the 1980s, and family law and the penal code regressed to the way they were in the 1930s and '40s (Kar 2008). Due to women's objections, however, and also because no replacement legislation was passed, in practice the FPL remained the guide for answering questions not explicitly addressed within sharia, which resulted in a later reversal of some of the initial regressions (see Mir-Hosseini 2002:167, 187).

In short, after the establishment of sharia-based rule in the Islamic Republic (IR) in Iran, women lost many rights in almost all spheres of life. According to the IR's laws of *Hudud* (punishments, such as stoning) and *Qisas* (retaliation, eye for an eye), which belong to pre-modern tribal societies, a woman is practically considered as subhuman. For instance, in case of murder, a woman's *Diyeh* (blood money or compensation rate) is worth half that of a man's. In cases of bodily harm, certain organs of a male person (for example, his testicles) are worth more than the whole body of a female person (Tohidi 1991:261-265; Ebadi 2000; and WLUML 2014). The women's movement in Iran, therefore, has remained predominantly rights oriented. Its main target is the legal system, which is full of discriminatory laws against members of any gender, ethnic, and religious groups other than the Shi'i male (Ahmadi Khorasani 2012). The demand for changes in the law and the role of lawyers in almost all women's organizations have become more prominent than ever.

Theoretical and Conceptual Considerations

I make a distinction between "women in movement" and "women's movement"(Rowbotham 1992). "Women in movement" refers to women's participation and active role in various social movements such as anticolonial nationalist movements and class-based labor movements. The "women's movement," however, pertains to social movements in which women are the leading and primary players and women's empowerment and gender equality in legal rights and sociocultural opportunities are the predominant goals. Women's movements usually have a feminist orientation, even though many of their actors may not identify themselves as feminist.

My empirical research and survey data among 57 leading Iranian women activists inside Iran show that many of them uphold an eclectic understanding of feminism, and many of their actions are organized around specific shared goals and intersectional concerns rather than any school of ideological inclinations.[2] These data also indicate that most leading activists are primarily middle class, urban, and highly educated and range in age from 22 to 67. Iranian women's activism, however, goes beyond such activists who are engaged in organized or semi-organized collective activities within feminist networks. It also includes women's day-to-day ordinary activities that either deliberately defy proscriptions of the ruling clerics or transgress the dictated norms of patriarchal culture. Although many of these defiant women may not describe themselves as feminist nor be directly connected to feminist networks, their resistance and contribution to a gradual change in Iran's cultural landscape can be seen as a component of a more extensive women's movement. As stated by activists such as Rezvan Moghadam, "Iranian women's movement is currently everywhere, in the public and private, even at the home of some ruling clerics whose wives or daughters are resisting male domination. They cannot kill this movement, not by resorting to Sharia, nor by the threat of jail and gun.")

Furthermore, the concerns and diverse voices of urban poor and working-class, rural, and ethnic minority women based in less developed provinces have occasionally been addressed through field reports published on various women's websites and in print publications (see for instance, Shojaee 2009 and Javaheri 2015). But the leading feminist groups have not yet succeeded in drawing a considerable number of rural or working-class women or women of ethnic or religious minorities into their semi-organized networks. This is mainly due to the more conservative and male-controlled milieu of those areas and the extra repression by the local authorities against any pro-democracy and feminist activities.[3] Issues concerning sexuality and sexual diversity (LGBT) are also rarely addressed by feminists inside Iran. On social media, among the diaspora feminists and cyber activists, however, many taboos have been broken and a few organized networks represent concerns and activism of Iranian sexual minorities (see, for instance, Raha Bahreini, et al. 2014 and Khadije Moghadam 2015).[4]

Several campaigns have been waged against discriminatory laws, policies, and violent or oppressive traditional customs that have reinforced violence, insecurity, and humiliation against women of all walks of life (Ebadi 1994, 2016; Kar 1999, 2001; Ahmadi Khorasani 2012; Rezvan Moghadam 2013; Masih Alinejad 2014[5] ; Jelveh Javaheri 2015; Asieh Amini 2016).

The very notion of a "women's movement" in Iran is still a contested subject. The ruling conservative Islamists deny the existence of such a movement. They portray women's activism for equal rights as a "harmful feminist deviation instigated under the Western influence,"[6] or as a disguise for the Zionist and American agenda toward "regime change" through a "velvet revolution." Thus, they react to it with smear campaigns, negative propaganda, arrest, and imprisonment (Tohidi 2008a). The most recent cases that drew international attention are those of Narges Mohamadi[7] and Homa Hoodfar. [8]

Many moderate Islamic reformers and secular progressive Muslim and non-Muslim intellectuals, however, express support for the demands of women and condemn the government's arrest and repression of women activists. Some people insist that there is no women's movement, citing the lack of organizational structure, etc. Others have begun writing about the movement with enthusiasm[9] characterizing it as an "inspiring model" for other civil society movements (see, for example, Alamdari 2008) or as a "definer of a true social movement" (see Keshavarz 2008 and Mashayekhi 2009).

Another approach, an interesting conceptual alternative to classical theorization of social movements, has been presented by sociologist Asef Bayat, who defines the current women's activism in Iran as "a women's non-movement." He argues that in an authoritarian and repressive context such as that of Iran, "collective activities of a large number of women organized under strong leadership, with effective networks of solidarity, procedures of membership, mechanisms of framing, and communication and publicity—the types of movements that are associated with images of marches, banners, organizations, lobbying, and the like," are not feasible. Instead, as Bayat cogently stresses, women's activism through their presence in the public domains and their daily resistance to the state's ideology of seclusion and policies of sex segregation and forced veiling remains significant. To be a woman activist in the Iran of today means to be able to defy, resist, negotiate, or even circumvent gender discrimination—not necessarily by resorting to extraordinary and overarching "movements" identified by deliberate collective protest and informed by mobilization theory and strategy, but by being involved in daily practices of life, by working, engaging in sports, jogging, riding bikes, singing, or running for public offices. This involves deploying *the power of presence*, the assertion of collective will in spite of all odds, by refusing to exit, circumventing the constraints, and discovering new spaces of freedom to make oneself heard, seen, and felt. The effective power of these practices lies precisely in their ordinariness (Bayat 1997:162).

Indeed, the *"power of presence"* and the *"ordinariness"* of women's resistance constitute important aspects of women's agency in Iran, probably more so than in democratic countries.[10] While I agree with Bayat's discerning analysis, I believe, as Bayat may also agree, Iranian women's activism in more recent years has actually evolved beyond "ordinariness." I would argue that some of the features of social movements mentioned by Bayat, also by those of the "new social movements," do exist in the recent trajectory of the collective women's activism in Iran, such as framing, networking, campaigning, generating discourse and symbols (hence collective identity), lobbying, mobilizing, and collective protests (though all on a small scale). New social movements that have emerged since the 1970s and 1980s in Europe, America, and other parts of the world around women's issues, feminism and sexuality, the environment, civil rights, and antiwar sentiment are categorically different from the movements in the past. Instead of formal organizational structure, new social movements, as the case of the Iranian women's movement represents, are "segmentary" (with several, sometimes competing, organizations and groupings), "polycentric" (with multiple and sometimes competing leaders), and "reticulate" (are linked to each other through loose networks) (see Gerlach 1999).

Stages of Feminist Formations and Women's Movements in Iran

The characteristics of feminist formation and the women's movement in modern Iran—their demands, strategies, tactics, effectiveness, and achievements—have varied in accordance with varying socioeconomic developments, state policies, political trends, and cultural contexts at national and international levels. This history can be roughly divided into eras similar to the ones presented by Parvin Paidar, 1995.

During the Constitutional Movement (1905–1925), the first generation of women activists emerged mostly through their involvement in anti-despotic, pro-constitutional and anti-imperialist activities through mostly semisecret associations. Their main demands included women's literacy; access to public education, hygiene, and vocational training; and abolition of women's seclusion, polygamy, and domestic violence.

The era of modern nation-state building (1920s–1940s) was associated with increasing literacy, women's entrance in universities, and gradual expansion in women's associations and women's press. However, the controversial state-dictated compulsory unveiling of women in 1935 under Reza Shah's rather progressive but dictatorial rule led to politicization of the veil. Although his son (Mohammad Reza Shah), stopped enforcing mandatory unveiling, that did not prevent the backlash of forced veiling under Khomeini and the Islamist state in 1979. Had Reza Shah respected women's freedom of choice and used his authority and the police to protect both unveiled and veiled women from harassment and attacks instead of ordering his police to take off women's head-covers by force, the issue of veil would have probably taken a different trajectory in Iran.

The era of nationalization of the oil industry (1940s–1950s) brought more women into the public and political activism within both nationalist and socialist ideological and organizational frameworks. Many reform projects and egalitarian ideas concerning women's roles and status were brought into the public discourse, yet neither the nationalist nor the socialist and Communist parties could succeed in bringing about legislative reforms concerning women's suffrage or changes in family law.

The era of modernization (1960s–1970s) saw growth in the number and social visibility of modern working and professional women in the rapid process of urbanization, and some positive and significant legal reforms concerning women's suffrage and family law. But increased centralization and dictatorship of the Shah led to erosion of women's autonomous associations, resulting in state control and a top-down process of autocratic modernization without democratization, thus creating a dual and polarized society.

The era of Islamist Revolution and Islamization (1979–1997) was associated with massive socio-political mobilization of men and women, but soon followed by many retrogressive and discriminatory laws and policies against women and religious and ethnic minorities, forced hijab, sex segregation, war and violence, political repression, massive emigration and exile of intellectuals and ordinary people, and overall socio-economic decline.

The post-Islamist era of reform and pragmatism under President Khatami (1997–2005) was associated with relative socio-political openness, civil society discourse, and neo-liberalism (which had actually begun under President Hashemi Rafsajani's "construction era," 1989–1997). But the growth of civil society organizations, the vibrant and relatively free press, including a feminist press, and relative economic improvement did not last long.

The Neo-conservative and populist backlash under President Ahmadinejad (2005–2013) was associated with a resurgence of Islamist fanatic groups, over-emphasis on nuclear ambition, belligerent and provocative foreign policy, and intensified hostility between the IRI, Israel, and the Western powers. This led to an increased danger of military attacks and war, increasing international sanctions and isolation of Iran, increased repression of the media and civil society organizations, including women's groups, introduction of anti-women bills, increased corruption, economic mismanagement, inflation, and rising unemployment.

Finally, the era of "moderation" under President Rouhani (2013 to present) has been associated with a remarkable attempt to shift foreign policy that led to success in resolving the nuclear crisis diplomatically and negotiation with the world powers. But so far attempts toward some openness and improvement in human rights and women's status have been practically blocked by the ruling hard-liners who still have the upper hand over the moderate president.

This chapter is limited to discussing some major turning points in women's status and feminist activities during the latter four eras only. For more elaboration on the earlier four eras, see Sanasarian 1982, Paidar 1995, Sedghi 2007, and Tohidi 2010a.

Islamist State and Rise of Feminist Responses (1980s–1990s)

The first sign of an emerging Iranian feminist opposition to the Islamist government that took power in 1979 appeared on the national and global scenes during the International Women's Day (IWD) on March 8, 1979. For the first time in many Iranian women's lives, women organized a number of independent mass demonstrations primarily for women's causes in line with the global feminist movement. Newly formed women's organizations such as the National Unity of Women (*Etehad Melli Zanan*), Association for Woman's Emancipation (*Anjoman*

Rahai Zan), and Society for Awakening of Woman (*Jamiát Bidari Zan*) (though many were still politically affiliated with male-dominated political organizations) joined their forces together in order not only to celebrate the IWD but also to protest retrogressive and sexist policies of the new regime such as compulsory veiling and other newly announced discriminatory measures (see Tabari and Yeganeh 1982: 203-230). Thousands of women took to the streets and shouted, "We did not make revolution to go backward!" and "Freedom is neither Western nor Eastern, it is universal!" (Shojaee 2009)[11]

Several spontaneous marches and sit-ins by women continued for the next week in front of the Ministry of Justice and the National Television Building to protest its refusal to broadcast the women's demonstrations; the University of Tehran; and the headquarters of two main secular leftist organizations (Fadaiyan Khalq and Mojahedin Khalq). A small group of veiled women waged a counterdemonstration demanding compulsory veiling for all women. Also, groups of zealot men armed with knives, clubs, and stones attacked women demonstrators and caused many injuries. While the revolutionary guards passively watched the assaults, some male supporters tried to protect the unveiled protesters. The vigor and extent of outrage expressed by women protesters and the leniency in the nature of the provisional government of Mehdi Bazargan (a rather liberal Muslim nationalist) led to a temporary retreat by the Islamists. But women's resistance soon lost momentum as the "hostage crisis" (1979–1981) and the start of the Iran-Iraq war (1980–1988) overshadowed all other matters.

During the war, as often happens in war, the general atmosphere turned into a repressive masculinist militarism from which only the Islamist and nationalist hard-liners could and did benefit. Soon gaining the upper hand in the state power organs, the Islamist hard-liners marginalized the Islamic moderates and repressed and banned all secular groups, including women's organizations. Critics were accused of being under the influence of either the West or the East, namely, the Soviet Union. Women's rights activists, ethnic and religious minorities, independent journalists, students, academics, newly formed labor councils, publishers, and progressive parties all became subjects of repression by the rapidly growing Islamist extremists who aimed to build a totalitarian system.

The emphasis on keeping women subordinated, especially the control over women's sexuality, has been central to the ideology, policy, and discourse of the ruling Islamists in Iran. During its formative years, the IR deliberately presented sex segregation and mandatory veiling as the hallmarks of its cultural and political identity. But women's lives and gender relations are not shaped by the law or state policies alone. The modern changes put in motion prior to the revolution, and the social dynamism of revolutionary and postrevolutionary Iran; the diversity and contradictions within Islamic thinkers, political groups, and even state policies; and the increasing influence of globalization would not allow the years of silence, conformity, and demoralization to last very long. Thanks to a widespread resistance from all sides, especially women, the project for a totalitarian theocracy, including the idea of creating a uniformed "Islamist womanhood," has not succeeded in Iran.

Divergence of Islamic Gender Politics

The extremist policies of the radical Islamists soon caused opposition in various degrees and forms from all sides. A growing split in the outlooks and policies of the hard-liners and moderates in the new ruling circles led to the resignation or marginalization of the latter. By the late 1980s and early 1990s, the following Islamic groups could be distinguished from each other, especially with regard to their gender ideology and attitudes toward democracy:

Traditionalist/conservative Islam is advocated mainly by traditionalist *ulema* and the traditional layers of popular classes, especially bazaar merchants. They insist on preservation of a patriarchal gender regime. They would like to confine women to the private domain and consider wifehood and motherhood to be the sole roles and obligations of women. Veiling is used as the main device for the maintenance of strict sex-based division of labor and segregated spaces. Traditionalists, however, are not necessarily political or interested in gaining state power.

Moderate/modern or reform Islam is advocated by new Islamic intellectuals (*naw-andishan dini*), some members of the ulema, and national-religious/Islamic (*Melli-Mazhabi*) groups that are usually members of the modern, educated, and urban middle class. Many of them believe that "true Islam" is defined by its egalitarian ethics and is essentially just and compatible with human and women's rights and democratic polity. They apply rationalist and "dynamic" (*pouya*) *ijtihad* (reasoning) and "dynamic" *fiqh* (jurisprudence) versus static or dog-

matic and "traditionalistic" (*sunnati*) jurisprudence. Thereby, they rein-
terpret Islamic texts (especially the Quran) in the context of the
twenty-first century's realities rather than those of fourteen hundred
years ago (Mir-Hosseini and Tapper, 2016). The advocates of reform or
modernist/liberal Islam have gradually entertained egalitarian gender
relations and feminist ideas. This is in part due to the influence of feminist critiques, growing women's movements, and modernist Muslim
thinkers' eagerness to distance themselves from the conservative traditionalists and fundamentalist Islamists. The more progressive among
them have embraced a growing number of Muslim feminist activists
such as Shirin Ebadi, Shahla Sherkat, Nargess Mohamadi, Sedighe Vas-
maqi, and reformist women deputies such as Fatemeh Haghighatjoo,
Elaheh Koolaee, Fatemeh Rakei, and Jamileh Kadivar who played active roles in legislative reforms in favor of women's rights during the
fifth (1996–2000) and sixth (2000–2004) Majlis (Parliaments).

Revolutionary Islamism, fundamentalist or radical Islam has posed
itself as a political alternative or solution for all of the social ills and
gender-related "moral decadence" experienced in both traditionalist
and modern systems. The Islamists' agenda with regard to gender issues is not always in line with the conservative traditionalists. In the
specific context of an Iran where Islamists have seized state power, they
have often pursued contradictory and instrumentalist gender policies.
In order to appeal to women as a constituency and counter the growing
feminist appeal, the Islamist state has not shunned women's education
and sociopolitical activism as long as those activities serve their state
power. At the same time, the ruling Islamists have tried to implement
sex segregation and reinforce sexual stereotypes in all spheres of life,
from school textbooks and the media to public buses and parks. By using the "Islamic *hijab*"[12] as an identity marker, Islamists try to keep
their women's identity and behaviors distinct from the gender regimes
and sexual mores promoted by secular modernists, liberals, socialists,
and feminists, all perceived by them as Westernized.

Convergence of Women's Responses

During the eight years of the Iran-Iraq war (1980–1988), socioeconomic hardship, repressive atmosphere, and intensive Islamization,
secular women activists mainly engaged in small group studies, reflecting on what went wrong and what could be done. They became

involved in feminist literary production, translation, research, and humanitarian work concerning those affected by the war. Many Islamist women, too, began questioning and criticizing the oppressive policies, the male-biased and "unjust" laws that seemed to contradict the state promise of an "Islamic just society." For example, they printed open letters to the religious leaders about hardworking divorced women, left with no support or alimony because their husbands wanted to marry younger women. Or they would complain against paternal in-laws that took children away from widows who had lost their husbands to the war, since children legally belong to paternal grandparents in the absence of fathers (Hoodfar 1999:32–34).

The increasing factional differences within the state came into the open by the late 1990s. Disillusionment with ideological dogmas and pragmatism became growing trends among both sides of the polity—Islamists and the secular Left—especially in light of the disintegration of the Soviet Union. This functioned as a sort of structural opportunity for many civil rights activists. Women grabbed any open space for exerting their agency; they tested the limits by utilizing any ambiguities or contradictions within legal, theological, or policy frameworks. For instance, many women in urban centers gradually turned the initial strict Islamic hijab and state-mandated dress code into more relaxed, colorful, and diverse forms of fashion. In short, specific shared concerns and available opportunities, rather than ideological agreements, have brought many women activists of diverse religious and secular backgrounds into a de facto collaboration.

Zanan magazine is an illustrative example of convergence among women activists of different ideological backgrounds. Right after the establishment of the Islamist regime, a young Islamist revolutionary, Shahla Sherkat, became editor of *Zan-e Ruz* (Woman of the Day), which used to be a state-controlled women's magazine under the Shah. Sherkat grew increasingly disillusioned with the growing discrimination within the dominant gender discourse and gender policies of the new Islamist regime. In 1992, she broke away from the state-controlled publishing house, Keyhan, which had not allowed her to take a critical and feminist direction. She then founded *Zanan* (Women) as a new independent feminist magazine. She identified herself as a Muslim feminist when the word *feminism* was still taboo. She invited secular feminists of liberal, nationalist, and socialist tendencies as well as Islamic writers to contribute to *Zanan* magazine, thereby helping to break down the old hostile divide between secular and religious thinkers (Najmabadi 1998). For example, Mehrangiz Kar and Shirin Ebadi, two prominent feminist lawyers, were among a growing number of secular feminists who used *Zanan* as a relatively open and diverse forum for dialogue on gender issues (Kar 2001).

Later, even Iranian feminists active in the diaspora began contributing to *Zanan*, which helped break not only the secular versus Islamic divide but also the "inside-Iran versus outside-Iran" divide. Such collaboration helped enhance the transnationalization of Iranian feminism (Tohidi 1995, 1996). Among other sections, in a series of interviews with prominent intellectuals and reformists, *Zanan* took male reformers to task for their negligence of gender issues and the significance of women's rights. *Zanan*, by far the most important and widely read feminist magazine in the Iranian history of the women's movement, was shut down in January 2008 under Ahmadinejad's presidency after publishing 140 issues and persevering through previous threats for sixteen years (Tohidi 2004a). Under Rouhani's presidency, Zanan was relaunched in June 2014 by its original founder Shahla Sherkat under the new name Zanan-e Emruz (Today's Women). After another period of shutdown due to the hardliners' pressure, Zanan Emruz resumed publication in October 2015, but more recently again (since August 2016) Zanan Emruz stopped publishing due to increasing pressure by the Islamic Revolutionary Guards Corps, an increasingly influential force that makes up the unelected military back of the ruling clerics and other hardliners.

Islamic and Secular Feminisms: Divergence and Convergence

To many observers of the women's movement in Iran, *Zanan* also represented "Islamic feminism," a feminist voice of Islamic reformation that has emerged in several Muslim-majority nations and among Muslim-minority or diaspora communities in the West. An illustrative example of this trend is "Sisters in Islam" in Malaysia, whose motto is "Justice, Democracy, and Equality" (Basarudin 2015).[13] "Islamic feminism" has been a subject of confusion, controversy, and debate, beginning with its very name and definition (Moghadam 2002). In the context of Iran, for example, two ideologically and politically opposite groups have expressed the strongest objection to this term and to any mixture of Islam and feminism, theoretically and practically. On the one hand are the right-wing conservative traditionalists and radical Islamists who adamantly oppose "Islamic feminism" because of their strong antifeminist views and feelings. On the other hand, are some secularist feminists (especially among the Iranian diaspora) who hold strong anti-Islamic views and feelings. Both camps essentialize and reify Islam and feminism and see the two as mutually exclusive, and hence the term *Islamic feminism* as an oxymoron.

Also, some scholars worry that this new categorization—coined mainly by secular Western-based feminist scholars—may entail more division and confusion (Abou-Bakr 2001:1-3). Theoretically or conceptually, a potential problem is a sort of orientalistic or essentialist Islamic determinism characterized by continually "foregrounding the Islamic spirit or influence as the regularly primary force in Middle Eastern societies, hence disregarding the complexities of social/political and economic transformations."[14] Elsewhere, I have suggested using the term Muslim feminist or Muslim feminism in reference to those Muslims who see their faith as compatible with feminism. The term Islamic feminism, however, can be used in reference to analytical categorization in the field of feminist theology or feminist exegesis within the Islamic tradition (Badran 2001; Tohidi 2003a).

In short, I see Muslim feminism or "Islamic feminism" as a multidimensional trend related to spirituality and faith, the search for gender justice, and identity politics in the post-colonial and global era. I use the term in reference to those Muslim women activists who challenge the orthodox Islamic teachings on differential rights and responsibilities, criticize the sexist policies of Islamic authorities, and "question Islamic epistemology as an expansion of their faith position and not rejection of it" (Cooke 2001). It may also reflect their insistence on, using Marnia Lazreg's phrase, a "decentering of feminism" from its supposedly Western central location. In the context of Iran, such Islamic feminists have been willing to collaborate with non-Islamic feminists around women's common demands within frameworks compatible with CEDAW. As a secular feminist, I see Muslim feminists (or Islamic feminists) not as a rival force, but as a welcome addition to the diverse spectrum of global feminisms, granted that they too would accept the diversity and plurality of feminist stands for equal rights. In the spirit of convergence, dialogue, and coalition building, I have suggested not only avoiding old and false binaries of East and West in this increasingly transnationalized and globalized era of deterritorialized identities, but also avoiding polarization or dichotomization of a "faith position" and a "secular position" with regard to commitment to women's rights. In practice and in many societies, feminists of all ideological and religious inclinations need to enter a common ground in their attempts to improve women's legal status and social positions. To set secular and Muslim (or Islamic) feminism in conflict can only benefit the reactionary patriarchal forces, be they of traditional or new Islamist patriarchy or secular modern male domination. Not all Muslims are against a secular state and equal rights for women, and not all secular states or secular people are pro-feminism or in favor of women's equal rights (see Tohidi 2003a; Badran 2009; Mir-Hosseini 2010).

Societal Changes and the Post-Islamist Reform Era (1990s–2005)

During the 1990s, due to a widespread disillusionment with Islamic revolution, Islamism, and any absolutist ideology, a reform and human/civil rights discourse began to take shape among many former Islamists and a few members of the clergy as well as secular leftist and liberal intellectuals. This ideological shift from Islamism to moderation and post-Islamism manifested itself most visibly by the surprise victory of a reformist cleric, Seyyed Mohammad Khatami, in the presidential elections of 1996. The active support lent by women and youth (half of them female) played the key role in this upset victory. Borrowed from Asef Bayat, the notion of "post-Islamism" is "defined both as a condition and a project characterized by the fusion of religiosity and rights, faith and freedom, Islam and liberty. Post-Islamism emphasizes rights rather than merely obligation, plurality instead of singular authoritative voice, historicity rather than fixed scriptures, and the future instead of the past." It represents "a critical break from and an alternative to Islamist politics." It "promises to make Islam compatible with democracy" (Bayat, 2013:xi).

This positive shift in political culture facilitated the growth of women's activism and the rising feminist movement in Iran. But such a shift could not have happened without a wide range of interconnected demographic and socioeconomic changes in recent decades, including rapid urbanization that intensified in the 1960s–1980s; a youth bulge (70 percent of the population being below age thirty); a rise in female literacy rates and educational attainment (as of 2005, more than 60 percent of university enrollment was female); a remarkable decrease in women's fertility rates; an overall improvement in women's health and life expectancy; increasing participation of women in economic activities, though mostly in the informal sector; changes in sexual attitudes and marriage patterns (particularly increasing delayed marriage) (Mahdavi 2008 and Afary 2009); increased access to the media, news, and information thanks to globalizing new communication technologies; and the ability to facilitate glocal interaction and growing awareness of alternatives to the state-propagated patriarchal Islamist discourse.[15]

Women's Rising Activism and Feminist Intervention

Cultural Production. Along with these changes in society at large, women's expanding roles in cultural and artistic production too have contributed to the rise of a new wave of feminist movement. Women writers and translators of both older and younger generations have written widely read works, including best-selling fiction and nonfiction (Milani 2011). Filmmakers such as Manijeh Hekmat, Rakhshan Bani-etemad, Tahmineh Milani, and Pouran Derakhshandeh have produced internationally acclaimed and award-wining films, many with feminist messages. The number of women publishers and journalists has also increased considerably. Women's press and periodicals such as *Zanan, Hoquq Zanan, Farzaneh, Zan, Jens Dovom*, and *Payam Hajar* have contributed to the richness and diversity of feminist discourse and many women journalists working within the conventional daily papers have raised gender issues from within the mainstream press. By the 2000s, many blogs, websites, and online journals (such as Feminist Bulletin, Feminist School, Meydan, Kanoon Zanan, and Bad Jens) replaced the banned print press of women. The intensified repression, censorship of literature and the media, and filtering of the internet under Ahmadinejad, especially during his second term of presidency, left a dampening impact on the press, cultural expression, and the artistic production of women and men.

Civil Society Building. In 1997 there were only 67 NGOs related to women's issues; in 2005 this number reached more than 480, a sevenfold growth thanks to the reform era. After the backlash under Ahmadinejad, however, the quantity and quality of the growing trend in civil and political activism faced remarkable decline, with a small recent rise again under President Rouhani. The number of women NGOs, for example, has risen much more slowly since 2005. Women are engaged in various civil society activities, including protection of the environment and promotion of sustainable development; establishment of local libraries, study groups, and cultural centers; awareness raising regarding AIDS and drug abuse; antiviolence training; protection of battered women; protection of children's rights, especially street children; improving living conditions of poor and working-class women through vocational training; and provision of legal advice to abused women. But because of the intense crackdown on student groups, journalists, and civil society organizations, along with crushing of the pro-democracy Green Movement (2009–2011), many of the leading activists (male and female) were imprisoned or felt compelled to leave Iran to avoid further persecution and imprisonment.

One very active new civil society organization of women created in the past two years is called "Women's Citizenship Center" (*Kanoon Shahrvandi Zanan*). It identifies itself as part of the women's movement, an NGO independent from any states and political parties (Iranian and non-Iranian) seeking to reform the discriminatory laws; raise awareness of and sensitivity toward gender issues and equal rights; and intervene in any social realms that can improve women's rights and opportunities by using civic and non-violent methods including campaigns, lobbying, and any other forms of civic protests.[16] One of the latest campaigns that WCC has helped wage is called "Campaign to Change the Masculinist Image of Majlis" in an attempt to improve women's representation in the parliamentary elections of 2016. More on this later.

Women's Political Participation

Iranian women play rather limited yet at times decisive roles in politics, both within and outside of state-approved boundaries at formal and informal levels. Due to the suppression of secular parties, each of the 240 registered political parties or organizations (eighteen of them being women's groups) in today's Iran has a religious orientation, or is at least willing to identify themselves religiously with an Islamic affix or suffix in their names, such as Hezb Mosharekat-e Islami (Islamic Participation Party). At the formal level, these registered political parties can be broadly divided along the "reformist," "conservative," and "hardliner" spectrum. Some women activists work mainly within these formal and state-recognized political entities, while many others reach out beyond these boundaries and interact with secular or Islamic women who side with oppositional politics. While most feminists have maintained their independence from the repressive state, they have not shunned collaboration and coalition building with women's groups who work within the reformist Islamic frameworks or lobby the state organs such as the Majlis (Parliament) for legislative changes.

Not only at the parliamentary level, but in rural as well as urban areas, women have been gradually but steadily participating in social spheres, including political and electoral competitions. For example, in the first municipal elections in 1999 (during the reform era), women made up 7.3 percent of candidates: 2,564 urban women and 4,688 rural women ran as candidates in the elections of city councils and village councils. Many of these women actually got elected: 1,120 women were elected in different cities, winning one-third of the seats in major cities. In all central cities of the provinces, except for Ilam, Sanandaj, and Yasuj, women were elected as the primary members of the city councils; that is, they won the highest number of votes. This unprecedented mobilization and electoral success of women, however, did not result in any tangible changes. Because of the structural obstacles in the political system, the hardliners were able to sabotage or prevent the elected reformists within city or village councils from any effective functions (Vasmaghi 2015).

Feminist Intervention in Presidential Elections

Elections in Iran are neither free nor fair. Candidates are screened and vetted by a conservative half-elected body called the Guardian Council.[17] Nevertheless, women's role in electoral politics—though mostly limited to voting rather than being elected—has proved significant. During the presidential elections of 1996, and to a lesser extent, of 2013, women's active support played a decisive role in the unexpected victory of Khatami, who ran under a reform platform (1997–2005) and Rouhani (2013–present), who ran under a moderation platform and promised to end Iran's international isolation caused by the nuclear crisis and intensified hostility under the Ahmadinejad and Bush administrations.

During the presidential elections since 2001, almost 5 percent of those registered to stand for elections have been women. But the

Guardian Council has not approved of their candidacies, though it has never openly admitted that disqualification of all women candidates has been due to their femaleness. This is related to a vague clause in the constitution that requires the head of the state to be a *rajol*, an Arabic word that can mean male or a politically experienced and knowledgeable person. Knowing this ambiguity and lack of consensus among the clerics about its meaning in this context, some reformist women activists, beginning with Azam Taleghani, a prominent Islamic reformer, have kept nominating themselves in various presidential elections. This political game with the conservatives is in line with taking advantage of any possible space for challenging the sexist law and raising women's presence and political profile.

During the ninth presidential election in 2005, the changing gender politics and the significance of women as a political constituency became more apparent in light of women's rights activism and factional politics in Iran. Unlike Khatami's campaign in 1997, which had mobilized massive, enthusiastic, and united participation of women and youth under a reform banner concerning political openness and human and civil rights, the ninth election (2005) suffered from disarray and low morale among the reform camp. Some prominent women activists such as Shirin Ebadi, angry with the undemocratic intervention of the Guardian Council in disqualifying many candidates, especially all women candidates, and disappointed with unfulfilled promises of Khatami due to structural barriers against his reforms, boycotted the ninth elections. Other activists called for a national referendum for the election of a new constitutional assembly and the establishment of a secular and egalitarian constitution compatible with the Universal Declaration of Human Rights. Many others, however, saw those relatively radical proposals as unfeasible and decided to support the reform candidate or relatively more moderate ones in order to prevent the victory of their hard-liner rival, Mahmoud Ahmadinejad.

Despite varying views and strategy *vis-à-vis* the election, all activists agreed to take advantage of the relative openness of the political atmosphere of the election period to bring women's demands into the public debates by taking each candidate to task. All the eight presidential candidates, conservatives as well as reformists, felt compelled to address women's issues in their platforms, on their Internet sites, and in their campaign speeches. They also formed special "Women's Committees" in their campaign headquarters. Mostafa Moìn, the main candidate from the reform camp went so far as to appoint a woman, Elaheh Koo-laee, as his spokesperson, and his wife accompanied him during some of his campaign trips. Hashemi Rafsanjani, too, appeared in some public scenes along with his wife, unprecedented for a high-ranking cleric.

As *Zanan* magazine indicated in a headline, a unique aspect of the ninth presidential election was the "Men's Race over Women's Votes."[18] Deliberate efforts to appease women and attract their votes extended to the instrumental use (by Hashemi and Qalibaf) of some young pretty women, girls, and boys in "un-Islamic" dress and appearance in order to appeal to the young and to women, the two groups that proved to be important constituencies during Khatami's victory.

Many activist groups chose to address more systemic problems, including discriminatory articles in the constitution (Shekarloo 2005). About 90 NGOs concentrating on women and gender issues, the environment, and education joined 350 prominent female writers, academics, lawyers, artists, activists, journalists, and 130 bloggers to call for a public protest against the breaches of women's rights in the Islamic Republic of Iran. The result was an unprecedented and unauthorized demonstration on June 12, 2005, just a couple weeks before the election. In spite of intimidation, about 3,000 women gathered at five in the afternoon in front of the main gate of the University of Tehran. The protesters were determined, well organized, and keen on making their voices heard, both inside and outside Iran. Their slogans and their ending statement stressed the necessity for changing the constitution and reforming the legal system. They identified the present laws, based on sharia, as the main obstacle to achieving equality and the empowerment of women. The security forces came in overwhelming numbers and tried to interfere, but the event was relatively peaceful, with no confirmed reports of arrest or serious injury. Due to certain glocal dynamics and the machinations of the electoral process, Mahmoud Ahmadinejad, a hard-liner backed by conservatives, won a surprise victory (Tohidi 2010). Nevertheless, the campaign process displayed a prominent and active gender dimension in Iran's political culture.

Feminist Intervention in Parliamentary Elections

Women also play a considerable role in parliamentary elections. During the sixth (1998) and seventh (2003) parliamentary elections of the reform era, 351 and 504 women, respectively, sat among the candidates (a considerable increase from 287 in the previous election) (see Bani-yaghoob 1384/2005). Nevertheless, the number of women deputies in the Majlis has remained very low (ranging from 9–14 women out of 290 total deputies, or 3 to 5 percent), far below the world average (22 percent) and even far below the regional average (Asia 19 percent, and Arab states 18 percent). However, the quality and composition of women deputies in the sixth Majlis of the reform era were encouraging. Due to their commitment to reform, women's rights, and outspokenness, some of them (Fatemeh Haghighatjou and Elaheh Koolaee, for example) were persecuted by hardliners in the judiciary power.

During the parliamentary election for the eighth Majlis in the winter of 2007, Islamist, conservative, and reformist women's groups formed separate coalitions among themselves. Despite their ideological and political differences, a common goal for all groups was to set a 30 percent quota on their respective parties' electoral lists.[19] But their attempts ended with failure, so much so that the number of women deputies in the eighth Majlis was even smaller than the previous ones (9, or 3 percent). In the seventh, eighth, and ninth Majlis, women deputies were overwhelmingly conservative and did little in support of women's rights.

During the latest parliamentary election for the tenth Majlis, held in February 2016, a campaign was waged (beginning on October 27, 2015) under the initiative of the NGO "Women's Citizenship Center" to "Change the Masculinist Image of the Majlis." They aimed to win 50 seats for egalitarian women, thus raising the share of women in parliament to at least six percent. Members of the campaign also formed three committees; "Red Cards for Anti-Women Candidates," "I Will Be a Candidate," and "50 Seats for Egalitarian Women" in order to both educate the public and also alert the incumbent and running candidates of negative implications of their stance against women (Mova-hed-Shariatpanahi 2016).

Despite the ruthless vetting of the Guardian Council that initially disqualified ninety percent of the reform-minded candidates, particularly women with known egalitarian backgrounds, eighteen were able to enter the tenth Majlis, increasing the representation of women legislators to 6 percent—twice as much as before. This was in part due to the more than threefold increase in the number of women candidates (over 1500), which made it more difficult for the hardliners to screen and disqualify all of them. Moreover, eight of the women elected this time were on a reformist-backed list of 30 candidates standing in the Tehran constituency known as "the list of hope."[20]

According to the campaign activists, despite all the barriers, there was some improvement in the composition, quality, and quantity of women deputies in the tenth Majlis, in part thanks to feminist intervention (Movahedi-Shariatpanahi 2016 and Family 2016). Moreover, for the first time in the history of the Islamic Republic, the number of elected women deputies in the Majlis is a bit more than the number of elected clerics (18 compared to 17). This is quite noteworthy for a male supremacist theocracy, especially when one considers the consistently declining number of clerics in the Majlis—from 164 in the first one in 1980 to 17 in 2016 (Ghazi 2016).

Feminist activists involved in the campaign expressed mixed feelings about the results of the elections. Nahid Tavassoli, for instance, stressed the importance of the process more so than the immediate results and the impact of such small yet positive changes in the long-run.[21] Many feminist activists in Iran have insisted on the power of the presence of women and feminist intervention, and that especially during election times some space for activism becomes inevitably available; "more ears and eyes are open to hear and see us," they say. In line with the characteristics of women's activism explained by Bayat and myself in previous pages, many activists tend to grab any possible opportunities, and are hardly willing to exit and withdraw to silent and passive position. But there are also those who say their efforts seem to go nowhere, thus may experience burnout and a sense of hopelessness or learned helplessness, resulting in passivity if not cynicism.

Already, we see how the bloody suppression of the Green Movement, triggered by the fraudulent elections in 2009, has made some feminist activists very pessimistic about any electoral participation. Some see the electoral process under the current regime as a "vicious cycle" that may not lead to any profound changes in a system in which unelected military and clerical organs such as the Islamic Revolutionary Guard Corps and the Guardian Council led by the supreme Leader (the "deep state") hold the upper hand. Some have argued that under the current repressive conditions, which have left feminists and democrats weak and in disarray, any participation in elections can only add to the regime's delusion of legitimacy and play into the hands of their sham "democracy game" (see, for instance, Mozaffari 2015). In response, those who believe in strategic engagement argue that, by staying away from the elections, we would leave the space completely to the anti-democracy and anti-women forces, enabling them to grab more power with no challenge. The Majles then would be monopolized by the totalitarian forces, leaving no progressive voices of dissent that can at least occasionally expose and oppose their dirty games. Furthermore, if the activism and electoral campaigns of the feminists had no positive impact on the political landscape, why then are such feminist interventions attacked with so much vigor by the hardliners' media outlets, and most of their meetings blocked by security forces?[22] Many women's groups have made de facto alliances with other civil rights groups, especially student movements, and some reformist parties. At the same time, they are mostly keen on retaining their autonomy and not pinning their hopes on national political groups and parties that may give attention to women and their issues only at election time or during political turmoil.

Many men and women in Iran are gradually getting ready to take women's rights seriously and accept women in leading political roles (Mortazi 2015). But it is mainly the ruling Islamist hardliners and their supportive traditionalist strata that keep trying to hold women back by forced sex segregation and by resisting any legal reforms. According to some Iranian feminist sociologists, several survey results indicate that patriarchal order within many families has been transforming toward a rather egalitarian and child-centered (rather than father-centered) orientation (Kian-Thiébaut 2008). Many contemporary Iranian men do not insist on holding control over the social appearance and activities of their wives or daughters. It is the state, however—specifically the ruling clerics and the supreme jurist (Leader) and its military arm, the Islamic Revolutionary Guard Corps—who see themselves as surrogate patriarchs who must monitor, control, and discipline the women of Iran in every private and public aspect of life (Ezazi 2015).

Women's Rights Campaigns

A backlash under Ahmadinejad took back some small achievements women and men had made under Khatami concerning personal, socio-economic, and political freedoms, but women's rights activists continued pushing for their goals through new forms and creative methods. Several rather organized and focused collective campaigns emerged that have constituted important components of the women's rights movement in contemporary Iran, including the One Million Signatures Campaign to change discriminatory laws, the Stop Stoning Forever Campaign, the Women for Equal Citizenship Campaign, Women's Access to Public Stadiums Campaign, National Women's Charter Campaign, and Mothers for Peace. Due to the limits of this chapter, I will discuss only two of these campaigns: the one with the sharpest focus, the Stop Stoning Forever Campaign, and one with a broader agenda and the largest and most influential grassroots supporters, the One Million Signatures Campaign. I will also present a brief review of the coalition against the patriarchal Family Protection Bill.

The Stop Stoning Forever Campaign

The target of this campaign was the practice of stoning adulterers, which is globally perceived as the most repugnant part of the penal code in Iran. Although it is practiced rarely and may directly affect only a few people, perhaps five to seven women and a few men per year, its practice and legality have important violent and patriarchal implications. For one, stoning is based on the assumption that women's sexuality and male-female sexual relationships are to be punitively controlled by religious authorities rather than the mutual consent of two adults. Moreover, the public ritual of torturous killing (usually women) by community members reinforces violence, cruelty, and misogyny at large. Therefore, the fight against stoning has broader significance that goes beyond protection of the human rights of a few adulterous people.

Although during the reform era the head of the judiciary had declared a moratorium on stoning, under the presidency of Ahmadinejad the practice resurfaced sporadically in different parts of Iran. In mid-2006 some young lawyers such as Shadi Sadr and Muhammad Mustafa`i, along with academics, activists, and journalists such as Mahboubeh Abbasgholizadeh and Asiyeh Amini, inside and outside Iran, came together to form a campaign to stop stoning forever.[23] The state authorities usually deny the enforcement of this law, while the practice goes on in some small towns. Since it has not been outlawed, some local judges (who are members of the clergy) see it as their own prerogative to issue stoning sentences against adulterers (usually women but occasionally men, too). The campaigners then saw it was necessary to first document the cases on the ground. In 2006 they succeeded in publicizing seven cases of imprisoned women and two men pending stoning (see Vahdati 2007 and Amini 2016).

This campaign brought to the surface the differences of opinion and interpretation among the *ulema* (Islamic scholars and clergy) with regard to the question of stoning. Many argue that there is no Quranic injunction about stoning. Some clerics have codified this outdated and inhumane punishment as part of the sharia in the IRI penal code only on the basis of some dubious instances in the *Hadith* (sayings attributed to the Prophet Mohammad).

Stoning recently resurfaced as a "community punishment ritual" in the Kurdish province of Iraq but not in the Iraqi penal code. Actually, Iran and the Sudan are the only Muslim-majority countries that have stoning in their criminal codes. Moderate jurists such as Ayatollah Yousef Sanei and Ayatollah Hussein Mousavi Tabrizi have called for the end of this practice for both theological and pragmatic modern-age considerations (see Alasti 2007).

By 2009, for strategic reasons, as announced by some of its leading activists, the Stop Stoning Forever Campaign continued its efforts on transnational levels in conjunction with the transnational network of Women Living Under Muslim Laws (WLUML). Following the widespread crackdown during the Green Movement, many of the leading members of this campaign joined many other activists seeking asylum in Europe or North America.

The One Million Signatures Campaign

One of the feminist campaigns in Iran that received the widest national and international attention and made the most effective use of glocal processes was the "One Million Signatures Campaign to Change Discriminatory Laws" (2006–2010). This campaign sought "Change for Equality" (*Taghyir Baray-e Barabary*) through the collection of one million signatures to be presented to the parliament demanding changes to the present discriminatory laws.[24] It evolved from two peaceful demonstrations demanding equal rights on June 12 in 2005 and in 2006. The police and plainclothes security forces violently attacked both demonstrations, especially the second. This led some activists to question the costs and effects of holding street demonstrations under Ahmadinejad's hard-liners' government. Following some internal debates and tension over various strategies (see such related discussions in Zanan magazine, issues 133–134, June–July 2006), the idea of the campaign was born and officially inaugurated during a seminar on August 27, 2006, in Tehran with the attendance of more than two hundred advocates of women's rights, including several prominent writers, lawyers (such as Simin Behbahani and Shirin Ebadi), journalists, and students (Ahmadi Khorasani 2007, 2009).[25]

Modeled after a similar campaign by Moroccan women that had begun in 1992 and produced progressive changes in family law in that country, fifty-four young and middle-aged women activists were the founding members of this campaign. Soon joined by hundreds of others, they pursued a face-to-face and door-to-door educational strategy for collecting signatures from women and men at places that women usually gather—parks, public buses, metro trains, shops, schools, offices, hair salons, or simply at their homes. During such contacts, they distributed an instructive pamphlet about the biases in the present laws and the way discriminatory laws reinforce violence and harm the well-being of women, men, and family life. Despite intimidation and arrests, this campaign grew into a network of thousands of activists with branches in 15 of the country's 31 provinces. It gained recognition and respect among various political and civil society organizations, intellectuals, journalists, and even some moderate clerics. Two special committees, Men for Equality (*Mardan baraye Barabari*) and Mothers of the Campaign (*Madaran-i Kampaign*), reflected the involvement of men, usually of the younger generation, and mothers, who were not otherwise activists as such (Tohidi 2006).[26] The campaign also mobilized support among Iranians abroad with branches in several other countries and gained increasing recognition and solidarity among transnational feminist networks and human rights organizations. The campaign and campaigners were recipients of several international awards and recognitions. Such prestigious international awards by nongovernmental entities have provided the women and civil rights activists in Iran with international recognition and moral support, also further strengthening transnational and global ties (not withstanding some unintended perils to be discussed later).

Thanks to the impact of this campaign and other pressures from different women's groups, there has been much more discussion among decision makers and even religious leaders about the need to reform laws on women (Tahmasebi 2008). Following the crackdown on the Green Movement, however, most of the better known and leading activists of The One Million Signatures Campaign felt compelled to leave Iran to escape further persecution. In retrospect, some have viewed this campaign as a desirable model for non-hierarchical, horizontal, leaderless networking for semi-organized activism. At the same time, some have attributed its shortcomings in achieving its stated goals in part to state repression and in part to its unrealistic and romanticized insistence on being "leaderless" and "structureless." Such structural problems, as some critics have argued, resulted in a lack of a clear and accountable division of labor and management responsibilities, which made the campaign susceptible to unaccountable and unelected leaders or the syndrome of "the tyranny of structurelessness," or "tyranny of powerlessness," similar to what many American feminist groups experienced during the early years of second wave feminism in the US (Freeman 1973; Molyneux 2002; Ahmadi-Khorasani 2007; and Tohidi 2010b).

Opposition to the "Family Protection Bill"

Instead of listening and yielding to the legitimate demands of the women's campaigns, the government of President Mahmoud Ahmadinejad proposed a bill named, in Orwellian fashion, the "Family Protection Bill." If passed it would have threatened the stability, equilibrium, and mental health of families by reinforcing and further facilitating polygamy, temporary marriage, and men's privileged position with regard to divorce (Tohidi 2008a). Shirin Ebadi, the Nobel Laureate for Peace, warned the authorities that she and her colleagues would stage a sit-in at the Majlis building should the bill be discussed on the Majlis floor. When it became clear that such a discussion was imminent, in an unprecedented action in the Islamic Republic of Iran, dozens of prominent women activists entered the Majlis building on August 31, 2008, met with members of parliament, and made compelling arguments against the bill, calling it the "Anti-Family Bill."

In addition to presenting a petition signed by more than three thousand activists and intellectuals, this diverse coalition of women's rights activists, which had gained the support of even some moderate clerics and politicians, persuaded a judicial commission to drop some of the most contested articles of the bill, and the parliament passed an amended version on September 9, 2008. This version maintains the present law that makes second marriage contingent upon the first wife's consent and does not attach any tax on the amount of dowry to be paid to the wife in case of divorce.

This small yet symbolically significant victory for women displayed the power in their unity around urgent issues and the effectiveness of building coalitions. It also brought Islamic and secular feminists together again around specific issues of common concern and demonstrated the effectiveness of combining different tactics that were used by various women's groups, including exerting pressure through media coverage, both printed and online; petitioning and signature collecting; lobbying; distribution of educational brochures; a letter writing drive; a phone call drive to the Majlis representatives; and finally direct public and physical presence in the organs of power, face-to-face communication, peaceful confrontation, and the threat of a sit-in (civil disobedience).

Feminist Aspects of the Pro-Democracy Green Movement

During the tenth presidential elections in June 2009, Iranian society faced a new upheaval. Conflicts within the ruling factions and between the people and the state came to the fore during and after the election, in which the incumbent president, Mahmoud Ahmadinejad, was declared the winner again. Iranian women figured prominently both in pre- and post-election political processes. They played an active and visible role in the large pre-election rallies and in the massive street protests that followed the vote, as opposition candidates and their supporters raised accusations of wholesale fraud in the official results and declared it an "electoral coup."

These protests faced a cruel and bloody crackdown that included almost 100 officially acknowledged deaths, thousands of arrests, hundreds of imprisonments entailing torture, rape, and some cases of murders of those in custody, and later the house arrest of the front runners Mir-Hussein Mousavi and his wife, Zahra Rahnavard, and Mehdi Karrubi, who had come to be seen as the symbolic leaders of the pro-democracy Green Movement. Despite severe repression, the Green Movement's open resistance continued for two years (2009–2011). The Green Movement "remains the most promising indigenous democracy movement in the history of Iran.... By asserting the republican principle of popular sovereignty, the Green Movement has posed a counter-claim of legitimacy against the Iranian theocracy" (Jahanbegloo

2011). Some scholars have argued that the revolts and uprisings of the Arab streets against corrupt dictatorships in Tunisia, Egypt, Libya, Algeria, and Bahrain (known as the "Arab Spring") that began in 2011 were in part inspired by and synchronized with the demands and rhythm of nonviolent demonstrations in Iranian cities during 2009–2011 (Hashemi and Postel 2011).

The international media, largely unaware of the brewing women's movement in Iran, was surprised to see women marching in the demonstrations in large numbers and braving the violent response by security forces, dramatically illustrating the clash between a changing society and an increasingly repressive government. Women's prominent and impressive role in that uprising for democracy, however, is a strong confirmation of the main precept of this chapter; that is, the women's rights movement has become a major agent of change, democratization, and modernity in present-day Iran. The emphasis on nonviolence, the prevalence of artistic images, songs, and poetry, especially the choice of the color green as the unifying symbol of the reform camp, gave a "feminine" ambiance to the electoral campaign that soon turned into a growing Green Movement for change in which the youth, especially young women, played a critical role.

The main characteristics of women's participation in the Green Movement indicated some continuity but also important changes from participation in the 1979 Revolution. This time, gender consciousness and demands for women's rights constituted an important component of the broader social movement for change. Though mostly young and urban middle class, women from all walks of life took part in both electoral campaigns and protests against the fraudulent results. Some, covered in traditional black chadors, seemed to be devotedly religious, while many others appeared in colorful scarves and secular and modern fashions. Unlike the government-orchestrated demonstrations of the past thirty- five years, the 2009–2011 demonstrations were not sex segregated. Women were marching not behind men but alongside men or even in the forefront.

The nightly cries of "Allah-o-Akbar" (God is great) and "Death to the Dictator" on the rooftops were similar to those during the 1978–1979 Revolution. However, unlike then, the Green Movement (GM) was non-Islamist, nonsectarian, nonideological, and nonviolent. Neither the revolutionary Islamism nor the revolutionary Marxist-Leninism of the guerrilla movements of 1970s Iran made up the predominant framework of the GM. While a populist, religious fundamentalist (Islamist), and anti-imperialist discourse led by Ayatollah Khomeini had become predominant in the Iran of late 1970s, during the GM a post-Islamist, rather democratic, and predominantly secular discourse based on human rights and civil rights made up the main framework.

It was only a few months before the elections that the overall mood shifted from political apathy and hopelessness to a sense of hope for change, and thus vast mobilization to participate in voting. This was mainly due to the progressive platforms for change presented by the two reformist front-runners, Mir-Hossein Mousavi and Mehdi Karrubi. What distinguished the reform candidates from the incumbent president, Ahmadinejad, was their promises to stop his onslaught on civil rights and to improve the rights of women and religious and ethnic minorities, to mend the mismanaged economy (marked by 25 percent inflation, rising unemployment, and soaring prices), and to change the hostile and confrontational foreign policy that had resulted in several UN resolutions against Iran, economic sanctions, increasing militarization, isolation, the threat of military attacks and war, and thus an overall sense of insecurity.

About three months before the elections, an increasing number of feminists and women's groups decided to take advantage of the relative openness of the political atmosphere again in order to render an active feminist intervention in the process. They formed a diverse coalition called the Convergence of Women (*Hamgarayi Zanan*) that represented forty-two women's groups and seven hundred individual activists that included many members of the One Million Signatures Campaign, the Stop Stoning Campaign, and others. As explained in its inaugural statement in the *Feminist School* (8 Ordibehesht 1388/2009), [27] this coalition aimed at pressing the presidential candidates on two specific sets of women's demands: ratification of CEDAW and revision of four specific articles (19, 20, 21, and 115) in the constitution that enshrine gender-based discrimination. This was a demand-centered (*motalebeh-mehvar*) coalition that did not endorse any particular candidate. Rather, it put each candidate on the spot to address women's issues and respond to the demands specified by the coalition.

Through their publications; appearances in the media, at street rallies, on the campaign trail, and in press conferences; interviews with the candidates; and networking and mobilization by an effective utilization of new communication technology (SMS and email via cell phone and the Internet), the coalition members were able to bring women's issues to the surface. Meanwhile, a film made by an internationally acclaimed Iranian feminist director, Rakhshan Banietemad, put all these efforts together in one documentary, including some revealing interviews with the presidential candidates along with their wives on women's issues, in which all but Ahmadinejad had agreed to participate. For more description on this wonderfully diverse and effective coalition, see reports on the online journal Feminist School (2009).

Change in the gender politics of the tenth presidential elections in 2009 was more visible than it had been during the ninth in 2005. For one, both front-running reform candidates promised to address women's demands raised by the coalition and also include woman ministers in their cabinets, should they get elected. The front-runner candidate, Mousavi, was usually accompanied by his wife, Zahra Rahnavard, holding her hand, a bold and unprecedented act in the Iranian sex-segregated political culture. Rahnavard is a prominent Muslim feminist; a highly accomplished academic, writer, and artist, and the first woman to become a university president in Iran. Her academic stature, strong personality, outspokenness about human and women's rights, colorful head scarf and a branch of flower in her hand were among the traits that added to the appeal of this couple as a promising choice for some positive changes.

The other reform candidate, Karrubi, also ran a more woman-friendly campaign than in his previous election campaign. Though he is a clergyman, his campaign team—composed of some respected reformers—included a prominent woman activist, Jamila Kadivar, as the spokesperson of his campaign headquarters. His wife, a strong professional woman, was also actively involved in his campaign management. The conservative candidate, Mohsen Rezai, too was seen accompanied by his wife at several campaign rallies. Even Ahmadinejad felt compelled to bring his wife along in public during one of his campaign occasions.

In short, both in symbolism and content, the tenth presidential elections signified considerable progress in gender politics. This was due to the years of feminist struggles, consciousness raising, cultural reconstruction, and equal rights campaigns (especially the One Million Signatures Campaign), and other feminist interventions that women's groups and coalitions had carried out slowly but consistently, especially in the past fifteen years.

In the vote's aftermath, millions of marchers flashed victory signs (instead of clenching fists) while carrying green-colored banners with a simple and modest yet profound slogan: "*Where is my vote?*" which signified a prevalent keenness on civil and political rights. The symbolism of the color green is not only rooted in the national Islamic as well as secular pre-Islamic mythology and poetry of Iran, but also in the global color of peace, nonviolence, and environmental protection. Even the first icon and martyr of the Green Movement was a woman: Neda Agha-Soltan, who was gunned down by the state-controlled militia while peacefully demonstrating. Her death was captured by a cell phone camera for all the world's eyes to see, inspiring more demonstrations and the outrage that followed (Tohidi 2009).

Despite increasing violent suppression, the GM remained less masculinist and less violent than the uprising in 1978–1979. A new women's group, the Mourning Mothers (Madaran-e Azadar), known also as the Mothers of Laleh Park, was initiated by mothers who lost their sons or daughters during the prodemocracy demonstrations.[28] In order to commemorate the martyrs and keep the spirit of resistance alive, and also demand government accountability for the deaths, arrests, and disappearances of their children, they kept meeting and rallying on Saturdays in Laleh Park in Tehran for almost three years.[29] Following a call by Shirin Ebadi on women around the world to hold similar rallies on a weekly basis in various parks as a show of transnational solidarity with the Mourning Mothers in Iran, several such groups took form and remained active.

What Next: The "Era of Moderation"?

During the second term of Ahmadinejad's increasingly unpopular government led by a military-clerical alliance, people experienced increasing violations of human rights, especially of women's rights; more restriction on the media and civil society organizations; the brutal crackdown on the pro-democracy Green Movement in 2009–2011; and new waves of exodus of activists from Iran and further brain drains. Moreover, the rising inflation (41 percent in 2012), budget deficit, unemployment, and overall economic hardship caused by the government's mismanagement and reckless spending on the one hand, and the expanding international sanctions, political isolation, and even a threat of military attack on the other, brought many in Iran to the verge of despair.

During this period, the main subjects of discussion among Iranian women activists inside and outside Iran included the need for a critical assessment of the role of the women's movement within the Green Movement; the need for an adjustment of tactics and framing of feminist activism under the rising repression, declining economic conditions, and increasing political crisis, militarization, and international tension; and the need to redefine and readjust the women's movement's transnational relationships, especially between the activists inside and the diaspora feminists outside Iran, as their composition had changed after the latest wave of exodus (Abbasgholizadeh 2010; Tohidi 2010b).

Another subject of discussion and debate among the feminist activists was related to the 2013 presidential elections. The unexpected first-round victory of a moderate conservative cleric, Hassan Rouhani, who ran against five ultra conservatives of mostly military background, was welcomed at home and internationally, as it was hoped to signal the beginning of the end of the era of erratic hardliners and extremism in Iran (Tohidi 2013). This was because Rouhani ran under a platform for change toward "moderation, hope, and prudence" while undercutting Ahmadinejad's domestic and foreign policies. As in most previous presidential elections, the primary drive behind many people's (including many women activists') reluctant participation in that election, after much initial hesitation, was the immediate goal of saving Iran from further troubles by preventing the electoral victory of another Ahmadinejad-type juggernaut, this time embodied in the most hardline candidate, Saeed Jalili. Many perceived Jalili to be the first choice of the establishment, namely the Leader and Islamic Revolutionary Guard Corps; this led to more support for Rouhani, who reminded people that "I am a scholar of law, not a colonel."

As feminist activists had during the past two decades, during the eleventh presidential elections in summer 2013, they again formed a coalition of diverse groups and individual women to do "Brain-Storming about Women's Demands."[30] This coalition represented three "forces for change" among women: certain members within the ruling factions connected to the state who advocated for women's rights; women activists within civil society who worked collectively within organized NGOs or semi-organized networks; and individual women who defied sexism and resisted in daily life in support of change for equality (Ahmadi Khorasani 2012). They tried to highlight commonalities among the concerns of these three forces and use the election as an opportunity to publicize and press for women's demands without endorsing any particular candidate (Mortazi 2013). Among the presidential candidates, the only one that had sent some representatives to sit in on the first seminar of this coalition and listen to their demands was Hassan Rouhani.

Their main demands included protection of women from state and domestic violence; respect for civil and human rights that can provide security for establishing women NGOs in order to do educational, cultural, and journalistic work toward promotion of egalitarian values; and elimination of discriminatory laws and policies—these were more modest than their demands in 2009. They also wanted the presidential candidates to promise appointment of qualified and egalitarian ministers, including women ministers, in their cabinet. The last meeting and statements issued by this coalition were about the "Required Criteria for the State Ministries" that was signed and supported by over 600 individuals.[31] This stress on setting clear criteria for appointment of ministers was in part a reaction to the tactical move Ahmadinejad had made in 2009 by unexpectedly appointing two women ministers to his cabinet in order to appease women, since women had made up his primary opponents during the Green Movement. Many activists however had dismissed his gesture as opportunistic, disingenuous, and at most too little too late.

Rouhani won the election with a small margin. During his campaign, albeit in some vague and general terms, Rouhani promised to "de-securitize" the general "atmosphere," and promote "justice" and "civil rights." He had also promised to respect and improve the status of ethnic and religious minorities and women (Tohidi 2013). Under President Rouhani, so far, there have been some moderately positive changes in the government's discourse and approach at the national and international levels. He has shown considerable success in his program's first priority, that is, improvement in foreign relations through negotiation and diplomatic resolution of the nuclear crisis. His second priority—economic improvement—is closely tied to Iran's foreign policy. It needs to be seen if the recent shift in economic policies can survive the sabotage of the corrupt mafia-style circles close to the hardliners. Unemployment rates have remained very high, especially among educated women.

So far, there has been very little success in improving the status of women, human rights, and the domestic political situation. While a number of political prisoners were released right after Rouhani's election, among them prominent women's rights defense lawyer, Nasrin Sotoudeh, many others (including journalists, lawyers, writers, and teachers) are still in jail. Narges Mohammadi, one of the leading and most courageous human/women's rights activists, has been imprisoned again, this time under Rouhani; Mohammadi's letters from prison have been a significant source of inspiration. Homa Hoodfar, an Iranian-Canadian feminist academic who has been highly respected for her ethnographic research on women across the Middle East, including Iran, as well on Muslims living in the West, was arrested by the Islamic Revolutionary Guard Corps on June 6, 2016. Despite her illness, she has been kept in solitary confinement for over 198 days so far because of "dabbling in feminism" and "propaganda against the state". [32]

Iran still continues to have one of the highest execution rates in the world.[33] President Rouhani's new Iranian "Citizen Rights Charter" met with mixed reviews and has yielded nothing real so far. We have seen reactivation of some NGOs and women's press, such as Zanan Emrooz, but they have remained under constant threat, both the print magazine Zanan Emrooz and online Feminist School have been forced to stop publication since summer 2016. Rouhani's appointment of four women in the cabinet as deputies or spokespeople, and of a few women mayors in underdeveloped provinces such as Baluchistan, has been welcomed by women activists. The most encouraging appointment has been that of Shahindokht Mowlaverdi as a woman vice president of "women and family affairs." Her background as an active member of women's rights coalitions at the civil society level, and her courageous resistance against attacks and harsh critiques by the hardliners have made her a rather popular ally of Iran's feminist groups. However, it remains to be seen how much Mowlaverdi can really achieve in the face of the relentless attacks on every progressive and egalitarian project she has tried to pursue so far. In one of her statements, she pointed to the reality that women's status cannot be changed simply by a woman minister who is being blocked from doing anything effective and is "being crucified" (Women Living Under Muslim Law, 2015).

Transnational and Diasporic Support

Many women activists in Iran are well aware of global feminism and transnational feminist networks. A turning point in gaining international recognition for the Iranian women's rights movement and expanding transnational activism was the awarding of the Nobel Peace Prize to a feminist lawyer, Shirin Ebadi, in 2003 because of her courageous advocacy for human rights, especially rights of children and women. The subsequent formation of the Nobel Women's Initiative for Equality and Peace with Justice, initiated by Ebadi and Jody Williams in 2006, has further facilitated such transnational connections.[34]

Thanks to new communication technology, an increasing number of computer-savvy, highly educated, multilingual women activists are effectively employing the Internet and transnational space in the service of women's movements. Dissident secular feminists, women of ethnic and religious minorities, and gender-egalitarian Islamic women reformers disillusioned with theocracy all actively seek these international connections. They have engaged in cross-cultural dialogues at the regional and international levels. Many have traveled abroad to take part in workshops and gender-training sessions sponsored by UN agencies or academic institutes, human rights organizations, or international donor agencies. The UN conventions such as the Convention on the Elimination of All Forms of Discrimination Against Women (CEDAW), and the UN-sponsored regional and international conferences and their outcomes, such as Nairobi's Forward Looking Strategies and the Beijing Platform for Action, have played a significantly positive role in gender sensitization, legitimization of the women's rights movement, and development of women's NGOs (for details, see Tohidi 2002a).

The UN Commission on the Status of Women, itself an outcome of global women's movements, has helped the engendering of state machinery in many countries, including Iran. As a UN member state, the IRI during the presidency of Hashemi Rafsanjani in the early 1990s created an Office of Women's Affairs to report to and advise the president on gender policies and plans. The new professional and highly educated Islamic women, well connected to state organs and the new bureaucracy, have benefited from this machinery. Their active presence at international conferences and work to establish international connections are supposed to be in the service of public relations and diplomatic strengthening of the Islamic state, especially in regard to its gender image. Yet due to their own experience with sexist barriers and their contacts and dialogue with the international community, especially secular women's organizations and feminist discourse, many of them have come to be less ideologically rigid, relatively more open-minded and pragmatic, and more conscious about women's rights.

The UN gender and development documents and criteria also provided independent women activists with a sort of blueprint and framework upon which they could argue for their issues and put pressure on state agencies to comply with the UN-demanded gender standards. Under Khatami's presidency, the functions of this office, now named the Office of Women's Participation, further expanded and emphasized women's participation in politics and civil society building. Building on his call for "dialogue among civilizations," women's NGOs, especially those connected to government resources, sought further international contacts at both intergovernmental and global civil society levels.

According to one research report encompassing thirty years after the 1979 Revolution, there have been ninety-seven Iranian women's groups outside Iran on four continents, in sixteen countries, and twenty-six cities (Navaeei 1999:18). This number has probably increased considerably after the latest exodus of activists from Iran in the aftermath of the bloody crackdown on the Green Movement. Although the addition of this new generation of exiles or refugees initially intensified activism in certain areas, their differences with previous communities of Iranian immigrants have at times furthered tension and division among the diaspora.

In general, diaspora women activists have been part and parcel of the Iranian women's movements while contributing to women's activism inside Iran at different levels (see for example, Nimeye Digar (1984-1999); Avaye Zan; Zannegaar; IranDokht; Iran Women Solidarity; Zanan TV; Justice for Iran; Iran Human Rights Documentation Center; International Campaign for Human RightsOne of the long-lasting and effective such forums has been the Iranian Women's Studies Foundation, holding annual conferences in Europe, Canada, and the United States for 25 years so far (Ghorashi 2007).

I should also point to a rich body of diasporic literature (novels, poetry, and biography) produced by Iranian women, many of them of feminist and transnational orientation. Biography writing by women is a new trend, and some are bold and revealing memoirs of political imprisonment or taboo-breaking private memoirs concerning sexuality, incest, and sexual abuse by family members during childhood (see for instance, Mahbaz 2008; Forouhar 2012; and Sanati 2014).

In more recent years, growing access to satellite TV, radio, Internet, social media, and cyber activism have intensified the impact of transnational feminism and facilitated dialogue and interaction between feminists inside and outside Iran. For instance, over a dozen websites have been created by diaspora women with a focus on gender and sexuality issues. A number of closed feminist dialogue groups are also active on Facebook and other social media (for example, "Feminist Dialogue," created by Nasrin Afzali in 2015). Some of the Iran-based feminist journals or websites, such as *Zanan Emrooz*; *Feminist School; Kanoon Zanan Irani; Bidar* Zani; and *Khoshounat Bas* are also utilizing social media, especially Facebook, to further readership and impact.[35] One of the most successful Facebook-based campaigns concerning women's rights, known as *"My Stealthy Freedom,"* was initiated in 2014 by a prominent Iranian journalist, Masih Alinejad, who had joined the new wave of exiles right after the suppression of the Green Movement. This ongoing campaign has gained wide online support (about one million followers) inside and outside Iran, and is focused on ending compulsory hijab and respecting freedom of choice. Although this campaign operates online only, the harsh reaction of hardliners inside Iran against Alinejad is an indication of its effectiveness (Carpenter 2014).

It is important to note that the glocal factor, foreign interventions, and international support (including of diaspora) at times have hurt rather than helped the women's rights movement in Iran. The Iranian diaspora is politically divided. The majority of it tend to be secular, nationalist, highly educated, resourceful, and overall progressive. A small but rich and vocal segment, mostly concentrated in Southern California, is composed of Jewish or Muslim Iranians who follow a pro-monarchy right-wing politics and were supportive of the neoconservative policies of the Bush administration. Their interventions in Iran's politics through a dozen satellite television channels based in Los Angeles have often been based on a nostalgic and nonrealistic past and vindictive agitation, instead of nourishing a democratic and egalitarian culture.

As pointed out at the beginning of this chapter, Iranian feminism has been intertwined with nationalism, and often women's rights have become stuck in the midst of political games and international rivalries.[36] Most arrested women activists have been charged with "endangering national security" or "contributing to the enemy's propaganda against the regime." Under such threats, most women's rights activists have been careful not to receive any donations or grants from international donors. This has deprived women's rights groups in Iran of international monetary resources available to women's groups in many countries. Even the international awards that have monetary values attached to them have occasionally become a source of tension and political divisions among the activists.[37] While some have developed an aversion to any financial help or even symbolic awards from Western agencies, many others see this as yielding to the hardliners' pressures and contrary to their practical needs and interests.

Feeling caught in a double bind, many Iranian feminists have resolved to oppose both internal and external masculinist hegemonic forces; they have no illusion about the Western promises of salvation through bombs and mortar shells as in the invasion of Iraq, nor do they side with the hegemonic ambitions of the Iranian regime and its militaristic and sectarian interventions in the region (Tohidi 2007b). Since the election of President Rouhani in Iran, who pursues a conciliatory and moderate approach toward foreign relations, and also the shift in the US from a militaristic neo-con approach under the Bush administration to dialogue and diplomacy under President Obama, Iranian people in general and human rights and women's rights activists in particular are expecting a considerable easing of tension locally and a gradual normalization of foreign relationships globally. A peaceful and mutually respectful international relations can also facilitate mutually beneficial transnational feminist connections for women activists, along with material and non-material support of civil society organizations and grant-offering foundations in the more resourceful and richer countries in the world.

Conclusion

Following a tumultuous trajectory, the women's movement in Iran is gradually growing into a seasoned and inspiring feminist model for those aspiring to equal rights and gender justice under repressive and authoritarian Islamist regimes. Iranian women's experiences; their resilience and courage; and their creative, flexible, and pragmatic strategies have significant practical and theoretical implications for local and global feminisms. For one, they have stayed away from both secularist infatuations with the "West"—so prevalent in Iran's polity of the previous eras—and romantic nativism. Despite the currently forced Islamism, many Iranian feminists are keen on rainbow colors of global feminisms that reflect a polycentric world rather than an Islamo-centric or Euro-centric world order.

Despite intense repression at the state and societal levels, personality friction, ideological divergence, and differences in strategy and tactics, Iranian gender activists have often converged in practice to collaborate over their common goals. While the patriarchal system has tried to keep Iran internationally insulated, women are becoming increasingly more informed of the current trends within global feminisms and more transnationally engaged, especially with regard to the mechanisms, tools, and machineries created through the UN gender projects and conventions such as CEDAW (Tohidi 2008b). Although due to the vetting power of the conservative Guardian Council, the attempts made by the reformist deputies in the sixth Majlis to ratify CEDAW did not succeed, most women activists, including some Islamic as well as secular ones, have been framing their demands within the CEDAW framework (Tohidi, 2003).

Nevertheless, due to increased repression and lack of access to the mainstream media in the country, the strong potential impact of the women's movement has not been actualized. Like most typical feminist women's movements, it is predominantly made up of the urban middle class in major cities. The movement has a long way to go to reach various classes and ethnic or religious minorities among the wider populace in small towns, provinces, and rural areas. Systemic political and structural barriers too have blocked the effectiveness of the otherwise hard and courageous struggles of women for equality and gender justice.

In today's increasingly globalized world system, feminists and women activists in many countries have been using at least three groups of strategies to empower women and bring about egalitarian changes: women's policy machinery within state institutions, building an issue advocacy network outside of formal institutions, and developing grassroots women's movement practices that are aimed at cultural production, consciousness raising, and knowledge creation (see Ferree 2006). The repressive, patriarchal, and authoritarian state in Iran has made it very difficult for Iranian feminists to utilize all these strategies effectively. Yet whenever such spaces become available due to changes and contradictions within the political system, women activists can and have utilized such small structural opportunities.

Islamism, as a totalitarian state ideology, has resulted in a prevalent aversion toward any ideological absolutism among intellectuals, feminists included. A pragmatic, social democratic or liberal democratic human rights framework has become the common denomination for collaboration and coalition building. Aside from some who still fight for an abstract utopian society based on certain ideologies, many tend to work for concrete changes toward improvement of the rights and living conditions of all citizens regardless of their gender, ethnicity, sexual orientation, and ideological stance.

Most women activists have adopted nonconfrontational, nonideological, nonsectarian, and reform-oriented strategies. Deploying the "power of presence," they have entered into a strategic engagement not only with the civil society at large, but also with some members of the ruling elite. They engage the political reformers inside and outside the government, the intelligentsia, the media, the law and lawmakers in the parliament, some members of the clerics, various social institutions, and ordinary people. This engagement takes various forms and tactics,:constructive criticisms within as well as outside of the framework of the existing laws and Islamic sharia toward revision, reinterpretation, and reform, as well as deconstruction and subversion. Their desire to stay away from both elitism and populism and also keep moving ahead pragmatically in the face of continuous repression by the ruling hard-liners has proved a most challenging task. Nevertheless, the Iranian women's rights movement has remained potentially vigorous and actually defiant. It has maintained its homegrown roots and independence both despite and because of all the national and international pulls and pushes (Ahmadi Khorasani 2012).

Many have hoped that with the latest successful nuclear deal between Iran and the "P-5 Plus 1" powers, Iran will enter into a new era of reconciliation with the West, end the cold war in US-Iran relations, and move toward a more rational and less repressive political system. But it is hard to keep hope alive, given the extremist trends evident in the current US presidential campaigns; the continuous power of hard-liners in Iran; the rising power of religious extremists such as ISIL in the MENA region; and the ongoing violent tragedy in Syria, which has grown into a locus of regional sectarian and hegemonic proxy wars, involving among others, Saudi Arabia, the most powerful bastion of patriarchy. But we can be sure of one thing: without vibrant civil society organizations, especially effective grassroots women's movements for equal rights and gender justice, Iran (or any other countries in the MENA, for that matter), cannot ever succeed in building a peaceful, secular, and democratic political regime: a regime that can be capable of pursuing sustainable human development inside the country locally, while also playing a constructive role outside the country globally toward resolving the current sectarian proxy wars in the region before they turn into another world war.

Notes

1. I am grateful to Amrita Basu, Katharine Moore, and Nikki Keddie for their very helpful comments on an earlier draft of this chapter. Part of this work was supported by the Keddie-Balzan Fellowship at UCLA awarded to me during 2005–2006.

2. Some of the information here is drawn from the findings of an open-ended long questionnaire carried out among fifty-seven leading activists inside Iran during 2006–2007. This survey aimed to document a sociological portrayal of the primary actors in the current women's movement in Iran.

3. See, for instance, the report on the arrest of 25 women activists in a training workshop of the Campaign in Khorram-Abaad, in Lorestan Province, September 14, 2007: http://www.dw.com/fa-ir

4. See also the Iranian Queer Organization (IRQO): http://www.irqo.org/english/ (In Persian)

5. On Masih Alinejad, see for instance: https://www.washingtonpost.com/blogs/she-the-people/wp/2014/06/07/iranian-journalist-faces-threats-false-report-of-rape-after-viral-facebook-success/

6. Even the supreme leader, Ayatollah Khamenei, has on a few occasions warned "Muslim sisters" against the danger of feminism. See Tohidi 2002a.

7. See: http://www.theguardian.com/global-development/2016/may/24/narges-mohammadi-iranian-activist-un-condemns-10-year-jail-sentence

8. See: https://www.washingtonpost.com/news/worldviews/wp/2016/06/09/iran-has-detained-an-iranian-canadian-professor-and-her-family-doesnt-know-why/

9. A series of interviews with some prominent male and female scholars about the question of whether there is a women's movement in Iran appeared in several issues of the magazine Zanan.

10. Such "dailyness" or "ordinariness" of women's activism is not unique to Iran. A prominent American feminist has discussed the significance of the dailyness of women's activism and feminist practice in the American context. See Aptheker 1989.

11. Actually, the commemoration of the IWD has gained a symbolic significance for the women's movement in Iran, both signifying an international solidarity with global feminisms and establishing a day of their own within a secular and non-state framework. See Shojaee 2009.

12. Some Islamists in Iran, unlike traditionalists, have come to accept a new "Islamic hijab" in place of the all-encompassing black chador. This new Islamic hijab constitutes a dark color (gray, black, brown, or dark-blue) long overcoat, pants, and large scarf that would cover the hair completely. This dress code is more mobile and practical than the chador, which keeps a woman's hands busy holding it tight.

13. See also http://www.sistersinislam.org.my/ ("Section 66A Has No Effect on SIS Judicial Review." Sisters in Islam (SIS). Accessed March 23, 2016. http://www.sistersin islam.org.my

14. Quoted from Hoda El-Sadda by Abou-Bakr in her article in the Middle East Women's Studies Review (Winter–Spring 2001).

15. "According to official statistics, the number of Internet users increased from 250 in 1994 to 4 million in 2006 and the number of blogs from just 1 in 2001 to more than 65,000 in 2009" (Kian-Thiébaut 2009:55).

16. See https://www.facebook.com/women.citizenship.center/info/?tab=page_info

17. Guardian Council is composed of 12 members, half of which must be Islamic clerics to be selected by the unelected Supreme Leader (himself a cleric); the other half must be jurists elected by the Majlis.

18. See Zanan 14, no. 121 (Khordad 1384/June 2005): cover page, 2.

19. The question of a parliamentary quota for women (introduced by a few reformist women) has not generated a successful public debate. Some research conducted by my colleagues (Homa Hoodfar and Shadi Sadr in Iran) indicate that women see the reform of family law to be more significant than having quotas for women in the parliament or having a woman president. Among the political parties, the Islamic Participation Party, which is the largest party among the modernist reformers, has established a 30 percent quota. This has been due to activities of women reformers within this party.

20. But one of the elected women from the reform list in the city of Esfahan, Minoo Khaleghi, was later blocked by the Guardian Council from entering the Majlis under the excuse that she has appeared in some pictures online without Islamic hijab. Ms. Khaleghi's case became a point of contention between the Interior Ministry (part of the elected moderate government) and the unelected hardliners backed by the Guardian Council, who eventually won the fight. Without this loss, the number of elected women deputies was actually nineteen.

21. Cited by Ghazi, Freshteh, Jan. 17, 2016: http://persian.euronews.com/2016/01/17/iran-equal-rights-for-women-in-elections/. See also Alipour, Zahra, Jan. 18, 2016: http://www.al-monitor.com/pulse/originals/2016/01/iran-parliamentary-elections-womens-campaign-more-seats.html#

22. Ghazi, Fereshteh. Dec. 23, 2016: See http://www.radiozamaneh.com/253066

23. See reports about this campaign at: http://www.meydaan.com/english/aboutcamp.aspx?cid=46

24. Most of this campaign's websites have been banned or retired. Visit the following available ones at: http://femschool.info/english/spip.php?rubrique3; http://archive.is/tgtEM

25. For a detailed description and analysis on the birth of the campaign and the related issues and concerns, see the book by one of its leading founders, Noushin Ahmadi Khorasani (1386/2007 and its English translation in 2009).

26. Visit the website of Men for Equality, http://forequality.wordpress.com/. On feminist men, see, for instance, "Babak Ahmadi der mosahebeh ba weblog Mardan Baraye Barabary: Der kooshesh baraye azadi digary ast ke azadi man tahaqoq miyabad" (Babak Ahmadi in an interview with the blog of Men for Equality: "It is in the quest for others' freedom that my freedom can actualize," October 14, 2008, http://forequality.wordpress.com/2008/10/14/babakahmadi/). (In Persian)

27. See http://www.feministschool.com/spip.php?article2461

28. For instance, Parvin Fahimi, mother of the second popular icon of this movement, Sohrab Erabi, a nineteen-year-old student who was killed while in the security

forces' custody, has been among the leading figures of this new group. Visit their Web site at http://www.mournfulmothers.blogfa.com/.

29. See, for instance, "Iran: 30 Members of Mourning Mothers Detained in Tehran". Payvand Iran News. 2010: http://www.payvand.com/news/10/jan/1089.html

30. See a report, video, and pictures of the participants at: http://www.feminist school.com/spip.php?article7316

31. See: http://feministschool.com/spip.php?article7343

32. See the international petition signed by over 5500 academics demanding immediate release of Homa Hoodfar: https://docs.google.com/forms/d/1z6ll5q8InnCcqp _9JDeYBodVMqMDaRV7vDYQqa8cyaM/viewform#responses

33. See: "UN Rapporteurs Urge Iran to Stop Executions." 2014. International Campaign for Human Rights in Iran. https://www.iranhumanrights.org/2014/01/un-executions/

34. See: https://www.youtube.com/user/nobelwomen#p/u/32/dM0TaJZfO2Q

35. See for instance: https://www.facebook.com/zananemrooz/; http://www.feminist school.com/; http://ir-women.com/;http://bidarzani.com/; http://basast.org/; http://www .iranzanan.com/iranzanan_network/cat-119/004394.php

36. Quoted from an activist Facebook page in 2011.

37. The case in point was the monetary value attached to the Simon de Beauvoir prize (30 thousand Euros) awarded to this Campaign in 2009, which caused heated debates among the campaigners, who finally decided to not accept the money but only the prize for its symbolic value.

Appendix

Country and Region Information

Algeria

Human Development Index ranking: .736
Gender Inequality Index: .413
Gender-Related Development Index value: .837

General

Type of government: Presidential Republic
Major ethnic groups: Arab-Berber 99%, European less than 1%
Language: Arabic (official), French (lingua franca), Berber or Tamazight (official); dialects include Kabyle Berber (Taqbaylit), Shawiya Berber (Tacawit), Mzab Berber, Tuareg Berber (Tamahaq)
Religions: Muslim (official; predominantly Sunni) 99%, other (includes Christian and Jewish) <1%
Date of independence: 1962
Former colonial power: France

Demographics

Population, total (millions): 39.9
Annual growth rate (%): 1.84
Total fertility (average number of births per woman): 2.78
Contraceptive prevalence (% of married women aged 15–49): 61.4
Maternal mortality ratio, adjusted (per 100,000 live births): 140

Women's Status

Date of women's suffrage: 1962
Life expectancy: M 75.29; F 77.96
Gross primary enrollment ratio, 2008: 95
Gross secondary enrollment ratio, 2008: 49
Gross tertiary enrollment ratio, 2009: 38
Literacy (% age 15 and older): M 81; F 64

Political Representation of Women

Seats in parliament (% held by women): 32
Legislators, senior officials, and managers (% female): 5
Professional and technical workers (% female): 35
Women in government at ministerial level (% total): 12

Economics

Estimated earned income (PPP US$): M 22,127; F 3,669
Ratio of estimated female to male earned income: .17
Economic activity rate (% female): 43.9
Women in adult labor force (% total): 15.2

Argentina

Human Development Index ranking: .836
Gender Inequality Index: .376
Gender-Related Development Index value: .982

General

Type of government: Presidential Republic
Major ethnic groups: white (mostly Spanish and Italian), mestizo (mixed white and Amerindian ancestry), Amerindian, or other non-white groups
Language: Spanish (official), Italian, English, German, French, indigenous (Mapudungun, Quechua)
Religions: Roman Catholic 92% (less than 20% practicing), Protestant 2%, Jewish 2%, other 4%
Date of independence: 1816
Former colonial power: Spain

Demographics

Population, total (millions): 41.8
Annual growth rate (%): .93
Total fertility (average number of births per woman): 2.23
Contraceptive prevalence (% of married women aged 15–49): 78.9
Maternal mortality ratio, adjusted (per 100,000 live births): 52

Women's Status

Date of women's suffrage: 1947
Life expectancy: M 74.46; F 81.09
Gross primary enrollment ratio, 2008: 123.7
Gross secondary enrollment ratio, 2008: 107.3
Gross tertiary enrollment ratio, 2009: 80.3
Literacy (% age 15 and older): M 98; F 98.1

Political Representation of Women

Seats in parliament (% held by women): 36.8
Legislators, senior officials, and managers (% female): 31
Professional and technical workers (% female): 53
Women in government at ministerial level (% total): 18

Economics

Ratio of estimated female to male earned income: .53
Economic activity rate (% female): 47.5
Women in adult labor force (% total): 55

Bolivia

Human Development Index ranking: .662
Gender Inequality Index: .444
Gender-Related Development Index value: .931

General

Type of government: Presidential Republic
Major ethnic groups: mestizo (mixed white and Amerindian ancestry) 68%, indigenous
    20%, white 5%, cholo/chola 2%, black 1%, other 1%, unspecified 3%; 44% of re-
    spondents indicated feeling part of some indigenous group, predominantly Quechua
    or Aymara
Language: Spanish (official) 60.7%, Quechua (official) 21.2%, Aymara (official) 14.6%,
    foreign languages 2.4%, Guarani (official) 0.6%, other native languages 0.4%, none
    0.1%
Religions: Roman Catholic 76.8%, Evangelical and Pentecostal 8.1%, Protestant 7.9%,
    other 1.7%, none 5.5%
Date of independence: 1825
Former colonial power: Spain

Demographics

Population, total (millions): 10.8
Annual growth rate (%): 1.56
Total fertility (average number of births per woman): 2.73
Contraceptive prevalence (% of married women aged 15–49): 60.5
Maternal mortality ratio, adjusted (per 100,000 live births): 206

Women's Status

Date of women's suffrage: 1938 (literate women/certain incomes) and 1952 (universal)
Life expectancy: M 65.9; F 70.9
Gross primary enrollment ratio, 2008: 90.9
Gross secondary enrollment ratio, 2008: 80
Gross tertiary enrollment ratio, 2009: 37.7
Literacy (% age 15 and older): M 97; F 92

Political Representation of Women

Seats in parliament (% held by women): 51.8
Legislators, senior officials, and managers (% female): 33
Professional and technical workers (% female): 45
Women in government at ministerial level (% total): 33

Economics

Estimated earned income (PPP US$): M 7,130; F 4,372
Ratio of estimated female to male earned income: .61

Economic activity rate (% female): 64.2
Women in adult labor force (% total): 66

Brazil

Human Development Index ranking: .744
Gender Inequality Index: .542
Gender-Related Development Index value: not available

General

Type of government: Federal Republic
Major ethnic groups: Portugese, Italian, German, Spanish, Japanese, Arab, African,
    indigenous people
Language: Portuguese
Religions: Roman Catholic (64.6%)
Date of independence: 1822
Former colonial power: Portugal

Demographics

Population, total (millions): 200.36
Annual growth rate (%): 0.8
Total fertility (average number of births per woman): 1.79
Contraceptive prevalence (% of married women aged 15–49) 2007–2012: 81
Maternal mortality ratio, adjusted (per 100,000 live births): 56

Women's Status

Date of women's suffrage: 1932
Life expectancy: M 70.4; F 77.6
Gross primary enrollment ratio, 2008: 95
Gross secondary enrollment ratio, 2008: 81
Gross tertiary enrollment ratio, 2009: 36.07
Literacy (% age 15 and older): M 92.2; F 92.9

Political Representation of Women

Seats in parliament (% held by women): 9.596
Legislators, senior officials, and managers (% female): 37
Professional and technical workers (% female): 55
Women in government at ministerial level (% total): 26

Economics

Estimated earned income (PPP US$): M 17,813; F 10,851
Ratio of estimated female to male earned income: .61
Economic activity rate (% female): 59.5
Women in adult labor force (% total): 43.7

Chile

Human Development Index ranking: .832
Gender Inequality Index: .338

Gender-Related Development Index value: .967

General

Type of government: Presidential Republic

Major ethnic groups: white and non-indigenous 88.9%, Mapuche 9.1%, Aymara 0.7%, other indigenous groups 1% (includes Rapa Nui, Likan Antai, Quechua, Colla, Diaguita, Kawesqar, Yagan or Yamana), unspecified 0.3%

Language: Spanish 99.5% (official), English 10.2%, indigenous 1% (includes Mapudungun, Aymara, Quechua, Rapa Nui), other 2.3%, unspecified 0.2%

Religions: Roman Catholic 66.7%, Evangelical or Protestant 16.4%, Jehovah's Witnesses 1%, other 3.4%, none 11.5%, unspecified 1.1%

Date of independence: 1810

Former colonial power: Spain

Demographics

Population, total (millions): 17.8

Annual growth rate (%): .82

Total fertility (average number of births per woman): 1.82

Contraceptive prevalence (% of married women aged 15–49): 64.2

Maternal mortality ratio, adjusted (per 100,000 live births): 22

Women's Status

Date of women's suffrage: 1931 (municipal) and 1949 (legislative/provincial)

Life expectancy: M 75.58; F 81.76

Gross primary enrollment ratio, 2008: 101.2

Gross secondary enrollment ratio, 2008: 89

Gross tertiary enrollment ratio, 2009: 74.4

Literacy (% age 15 and older): M 97.6; F 97.4

Political Representation of Women

Seats in parliament (% held by women): 15.8

Legislators, senior officials, and managers (% female): 24

Professional and technical workers (% female): 46

Women in government at ministerial level (% total): 39

Economics

Estimated earned income (PPP US$): M 28,849; F 14,245

Ratio of estimated female to male earned income: .49

Economic activity rate (% female): 49.2

Women in adult labor force (% total): 55

China

Human Development Index ranking: .719

Gender Inequality Index: .202

Gender-Related Development Index value: .939

General

Type of government: Communist Party–led state

Major ethnic groups: Han Chinese (91.6%); Zhuang, Uyghur, Hui, Yi, Tibetan, Miao, Manchu, Mongol, Buyi, Korean, and other nationalities (8.4%)
Languages: Mandarin; Cantonese; local dialects
Religions: Officially atheist; Buddhist; Daoist; Christians (5.1%); Muslims (1.8%)

Demographics

Population, total (millions): 1,355.6
Annual growth rate (%): .5
Total fertility (average number of births per woman): 1.55
Contraceptive prevalence (% of married women aged 15–49) 2007–2012: 85%
Maternal mortality ratio, adjusted (per 100,000 live births): 37

Women's Status

Date of women's suffrage: 1949
Life expectancy: M 73.09; F 77.43
Gross primary enrollment ratio: 128
Gross secondary enrollment ratio: 87
Gross tertiary enrollment ratio: 24
Literacy (% age 15 and older): M 98.2; F 94.5

Political Representation of Women

Seats in parliament (% held by women): 23.4
Legislators, senior officials, and managers (% female): 17
Professional and technical workers (% female): 52
Women in government at ministerial level (% total): 8

Economics

Estimated earned income (PPP US$): M 13,512; F 9,288
Ratio of estimated female to male earned income: .69
Economic activity rate (% female): 63.8
Women in adult labor force (% total): 43.6

Europe

Human Development Index Ranking: .738
Gender Inequality Index: .317
Gender-Related Development Index value: .938

Demographics

Population, total (millions): not available
Annual growth rate (%): not available
Total fertility (average number of births per woman): not available
Contraceptive prevalence (% of married women aged 15–49) 2009: 72.6
Maternal mortality ratio, adjusted (per 100,000 live births): 31

Women's Status

Life Expectancy: M 67.3; F 75.4
Gross primary enrollment ratio: 101

Gross secondary enrollment ratio: 95
Gross tertiary enrollment ratio: 50
Literacy (% age 15 and older): not available

Political Representation of Women

Seats in parliament (% held by women): 18.2
Legislators, senior officials, and managers (% female): not available
Professional and technical workers (% female): not available
Women in government at ministerial level (% total): not available

Economics

Estimated Earned Income (PPP US$): M 17,867; F 7.287
Ratio of estimated female to male earned income: .41
Economic activity rate (% female): 45.5
Women in adult labor force (% total): not available

India

Human Development Index ranking: .586
Gender Inequality Index: .563
Gender-Related Development Index value: .828

General

Type of government: Federal Republic
Major ethnic groups: Indo Aryan (72%); Dravidian (25%); other (3%)
Languages: Hindi, English; 16 other official languages and more than 1,000 others
Religions: Hindu (81.4%); Muslim (12.4%); Christian (2.3%); Sikh (1.9%); others (1%)
Date of independence: 1947; republic declared, 1950
Former colonial power: Britain

Demographics

Population, total (millions): 1,236.3
Annual growth rate (%): 1.2
Total fertility (average number of births per woman): 2.51
Contraceptive prevalence (% of married women aged 15–49) 2007–2012: 55
Maternal mortality ratio, adjusted (per 100,000 live births): 190

Women's Status

Date of women's suffrage: 1950
Life expectancy: M 66.68; F 69.06
Gross primary enrollment ratio: 113
Gross secondary enrollment ratio: 69
Gross tertiary enrollment ratio: 23
Literacy (% age 15 and older): M 81.3; F 60.6

Political Representation of Women

Seats in parliament (% held by women): 10.9
Women in government at ministerial level (% total): 9
Seats in lower house or single house (% held by women): 12

Seats in upper house or senate (% held by women); 12.8

Economics

Estimated earned income (PPP US$): M 7,833; F 2,277
Ratio of estimated female to male earned income: .28
Economic activity rate (% female): 28.8
Women in adult labor force (% total): 24.2

Iran

Human Development Index ranking: .749
Gender Inequality Index: .498
Gender-Related Development Index value: .847

General

Type of government: Islamic Republic
Major ethnic groups: Persian (61%); Azeri (16%); Kurd (10%); Arab (2%); other (11%)
Languages: Persian and Persian dialects (53%); Turkic and Turkic dialects (18%); Kurdish (10%); Arabic (2%); other (17%)
Religions: Muslim (99.4%; Shi'a 90-95%, Sunni 5-10%); Zoroastrian, Jewish, Christian, Baha'i (0.6%)

Demographics

Population, total (millions): 80.8
Annual growth rate (%): 1.3
Total fertility (average number of births per woman): 1.85
Contraceptive prevalence (% of married women aged 15–49) 2007–2012: 79
Maternal mortality ratio, adjusted (per 100,000 live births): 23

Women's Status

Date of women's suffrage: 1963
Life expectancy: M 69.32; F 72.53
Gross primary enrollment ratio: 106
Gross secondary enrollment ratio: 85
Gross tertiary enrollment ratio: 55
Literacy (% age 15 and older): M 91.2; F 82.5

Political Representation of Women

Seats in parliament (% held by women): 3.1
Legislators, senior officials, and managers (% female): 15
Professional and technical workers (% female): 35
Women in government at ministerial level (% total): 10

Economics

Estimated earned income (PPP US$): M 22,631; F 4,159
Ratio of estimated female to male earned income: .18
Economic activity rate (% female): 16.4
Women in adult labor force (% total): 18.4

Morocco

Human Development Index ranking: .628
Gender Inequality Index: .525
Gender-Related Development Index value: .828

General

Type of government: Parliamentary Constitutional Monarchy
Major ethnic groups: Arab-Berber 99%, other 1%
Language: Arabic (official), Berber languages (Tamazight (official), Tachelhit, Tarifit), French (often the language of business, government, and diplomacy)
Religions: Muslim 99% (official; virtually all Sunni, <0.1% Shia), other 1% (includes Christian, Jewish, and Baha'i); note: Jewish about 6,000 (2010 est.)
Date of independence: 1956
Former colonial power: France

Demographics

Population, total (millions): 33.5
Annual growth rate (%): 1
Total fertility (average number of births per woman): 2.13
Contraceptive prevalence (% of married women aged 15–49): 67.4
Maternal mortality ratio, adjusted (per 100,000 live births): 121

Women's Status

Date of women's suffrage: 1963
Life expectancy: M 73.64; F 79.94
Gross primary enrollment ratio, 2008: 97
Gross secondary enrollment ratio, 2008: Not reported
Gross tertiary enrollment ratio, 2009: 13
Literacy (% age 15 and older): M 76; F 58

Political Representation of Women

Seats in parliament (% held by women): 17
Legislators, senior officials, and managers (% female): 13
Professional and technical workers (% female): 36
Women in government at ministerial level (% total): 16

Economics

Estimated earned income (PPP US$): M 10,988; F 3,123
Ratio of estimated female to male earned income: .28
Economic activity rate (% female): 26.5
Women in adult labor force (% total): 50.5

Pakistan

Human Development Index ranking: .537
Gender Inequality Index: .375
Gender-Related Development Index value: .563

General

Type of government: Parliamentary Democracy
Major ethnic groups: Punjabi; Sindhi; Pashtun; Baloch; Muhajir; Saraiki; Hazara
Languages: Urdu (national and official); Sindhi; Siraiki; Pashtu; English and others
Religions: Muslim (96.4%) (Sunni 85-90%, Shi'a 10-15%); small minorities of Christian, Hindu, and others

Demographics

Population, total (millions): 196.2
Annual growth rate (%): 1.7
Total fertility (average number of births per woman): 2.86
Contraceptive prevalence (% of married women aged 15–49) 2007–2012: 27
Maternal mortality ratio, adjusted (per 100,000 live births): 170

Women's Status

Date of women's suffrage: 1947
Life expectancy: M 65.16; F 69.03
Gross primary enrollment ratio: 93
Gross secondary enrollment ratio: 37
Gross tertiary enrollment ratio: 10
Literacy (% age 15 and older): M 69.5; F 45.8

Political Representation of Women

Seats in parliament (% held by women): 19.7
Legislators, senior officials, and managers (% female): 3
Professional and technical workers (% female): 22
Women in government at ministerial level (% total): 5.6

Economics

Estimated earned income (PPP US$): M 7,439; F 1,707
Ratio of estimated female to male earned income: .22
Economic activity rate (% female): 24.4
Women in adult labor force (% total): 22.1

Palestine

Human Development Index ranking: .686
Gender Inequality Index: not available
Gender-Related Development Index value: .974

General

Type of government: Transition; limited self-rule
Major ethnic groups: Palestinian Arab; Jewish
Languages: Arabic; Hebrew
Religions: Muslim; Jewish

Demographics

Population, total (millions): 4.295
Annual growth rate (%): not available

Total fertility (average number of births per woman): 4.65
Contraceptive prevalence (% of married women aged 15–49) 2007–2012: 52.5
Maternal mortality ratio, adjusted (per 100,000 live births), 2010: 64

Women's Status

Date of women's suffrage: not applicable
Life expectancy: M 71.5; F 75
Gross primary enrollment ratio: 94
Gross secondary enrollment ratio: 83
Gross tertiary enrollment ratio: 49
Literacy (% age 15 and older): M 98.4; F 94.5

Political Representation of Women

Legislators, senior officials, and managers (% female): not available
Professional and technical workers (% female): not available
Women in government at ministerial level (% total): not available

Economics

Estimated earned income (PPP US$): M 8,580; F 1,651
Ratio of estimated female to male earned income: .19
Economic activity rate (% female): 15.2
Women in adult labor force (% total): not available

Russia

Human Development Index Ranking: .778
Gender Inequality Index: .685
Gender-Related Development Index value: 1.038

General

Type of Government: Federation
Major Ethnic Groups: Russian (77.7%); Tatar (3.7%); Ukrainian (1.4%); other (17.2%)
Languages: Russian (official); more than 140 other languages and dialects
Religions: Russian Orthodox; Muslim; Jewish; Roman Catholic; Protestant; Buddhist; other

Demographics

Population, total (millions): 142.83
Annual growth rate (%): .2
Total fertility (average number of births per woman): 1.61
Contraceptive prevalence (% of married women aged 15–49) 2007–2012: 80
Maternal mortality ratio, adjusted (per 100,000 live births): 34

Women's Status

Date of women's suffrage: 1918
Life Expectancy: M 61.8; F 74.4
Gross primary enrollment ratio: 99
Gross secondary enrollment ratio: 85
Gross tertiary enrollment ratio: 75

Literacy (% age 15 and older): M 99.7; F 99.6

Political Representation of Women

Seats in parliament (% held by women): 12.072
Legislators, senior officials, and managers (% female): 39
Professional and technical workers (% female): 64
Women in government at ministerial level (% total): 7

Economics

Estimated Earned Income (PPP US$): M 27,741; F 18,228
Ratio of estimated female to male earned income: .66
Economic activity rate (% female): 57
Women in adult labor force (% total): 49.1

South Africa

Human Development Index ranking: .658
Gender Inequality Index: .461
Gender-Related Development Index value: not available

General

Type of government: Democratic Republic
Major ethnic groups: Black (80.2%); White (8.4%); Colored (8.8%); Indian/Asian (2.5%)
Languages: eleven official languages, including Afrikaans, English, isiNdebele, Sepedi or Northern Sotho, Sesotho, Seswati, Setswana, Tshivenda, isiXhosa, Xitsonga, and isiZulu
Religions: Predominantly Christian; traditional African; Hindu; Muslim; Jewish
Date of independence: 1961; majority government, 1994
Former colonial power: Holland, England

Demographics

Population, total (millions): 53.2
Annual growth rate (%): 1.5
Total fertility (average number of births per woman): 2.23
Contraceptive prevalence (% of married women aged 15–49) 2007–2012: 60
Maternal mortality ratio, adjusted (per 100,000 live births): 140

Women's Status

Date of women's suffrage: 1994
Life expectancy: M 50.52; F 48.58
Gross primary enrollment ratio: 102
Gross secondary enrollment ratio: 102
Gross tertiary enrollment ratio: not available
Literacy (% age 15 and older): M 84.9; F 80.9

Political Representation of Women

Seats in parliament (% held by women): 41.1
Women in government at ministerial level (% total): 41.4

Economics

Estimated earned income (PPP US$): M 15,233; F 8,539
Ratio of estimated female to male earned income: .56
Economic activity rate (% female): 44.2
Women in adult labor force (% total): 44.6

Tunisia

Human Development Index ranking: .721
Gender Inequality Index: .24
Gender-Related Development Index value: .894

General

Type of government: Parliamentary Republic
Major ethnic groups: Arab 98%, European 1%, Jewish and other 1%
Language: Arabic (official, one of the languages of commerce), French (commerce),
   Berber (Tamazight)
Religions: Muslim (official; Sunni) 99.1%, other (includes Christian, Jewish, Shia Muslim, and Baha'i) 1%
Date of independence: 1956
Former colonial power: France

Demographics

Population, total (millions): 11.1
Annual growth rate (%): .89
Total fertility (average number of births per woman): 1.99
Contraceptive prevalence (% of married women aged 15–49): 62.5
Maternal mortality ratio, adjusted (per 100,000 live births): 62

Women's Status

Date of women's suffrage: 1957 (municipal) and 1959
Life expectancy: M 73.79; F 78.14
Gross primary enrollment ratio, 2008: 98
Gross secondary enrollment ratio, 2008: Not reported
Gross tertiary enrollment ratio, 2009: 43
Literacy (% age 15 and older): M 88; F 72

Political Representation of Women

Seats in parliament (% held by women): 31.3
Legislators, senior officials, and managers (% female): 15
Professional and technical workers (% female): 41
Women in government at ministerial level (% total): 4

Economics

Estimated earned income (PPP US$): M 17,003; F 4,690
Ratio of estimated female to male earned income: .28
Economic activity rate (% female): 25.1
Women in adult labor force (% total): 27

Venezuela

Human Development Index ranking: .762
Gender Inequality Index: .476
Gender-Related Development Index value: 1.03

General

Type of government: Federal Presidential Republic
Major ethnic groups: Spanish, Italian, Portuguese, Arab, German, African, indigenous
    people
Language: Spanish (official), numerous indigenous dialects
Religions: Roman Catholic 96%, Protestant 2%, other 2%
Date of independence: 1811
Former colonial power: Spain

Demographics

Population, total (millions): 30.9
Annual growth rate (%): 1.39
Total fertility (average number of births per woman): 2.32
Contraceptive prevalence (% of married women aged 15–49): 60.5
Maternal mortality ratio, adjusted (per 100,000 live births): 95

Women's Status

Date of women's suffrage: 1946
Life expectancy: M 70.2; F 78.5
Gross primary enrollment ratio, 2008: 91
Gross secondary enrollment ratio, 2008: 78
Gross tertiary enrollment ratio, 2009: 99
Literacy (% age 15 and older): M 97.8; F 93.6

Political Representation of Women

Seats in parliament (% held by women): 17
Legislators, senior officials, and managers (% female): 33
Professional and technical workers (% female): 66
Women in government at ministerial level (% total): 16

Economics

Estimated earned income (PPP US$): M 22,040; F 13,836
Ratio of estimated female to male earned income: .63
Economic activity rate (% female): 65.1
Women in adult labor force (% total): 55

Uganda

Human Development Index Ranking: .483
Gender Inequality Index: .538
Gender-Related Development Index value: .886

General

Type of government: Presidential Republic

Major ethnic groups: Baganda 16.9%, Banyankole 9.5%, Basoga 8.4%, Bakiga 6.9%, Iteso 6.4%, Langi 6.1%, Acholi 4.7%, Bagisu 4.6%, Lugbara 4.2%, Bunyoro 2.7%, other 29.6%

Language: English (official national language, taught in grade schools, used in courts of law and by most newspapers and some radio broadcasts), Ganda or Luganda (most widely used of the Niger-Congo languages, preferred for native language publications in the capital and may be taught in school), other Niger-Congo languages, Nilo-Saharan languages, Swahili, Arabic

Religions: Roman Catholic 41.9%, Protestant 42% (Anglican 35.9%, Pentecostal 4.6%, Seventh-Day Adventist 1.5%), Muslim 12.1%, other 3.1%, none 0.9%

Date of independence: 1962

Former colonial power: United Kingdom

Demographics

Population, total (millions): 38.8
Annual growth rate (%): 3.24
Total fertility (average number of births per woman): 5.89
Contraceptive prevalence (% of married women aged 15–49) 2009: 30
Maternal mortality ratio, adjusted (per 100,000 live births): 343

Women's Status

Date of women's suffrage: 1962
Life Expectancy: M 53.54; F 56.36
Gross primary enrollment ratio: 92
Gross secondary enrollment ratio: 15
Gross tertiary enrollment ratio: 4
Literacy (% age 15 and older): 73.2

Political Representation of Women

Seats in parliament (% held by women): 35
Legislators, senior officials, and managers (% female): 20
Professional and technical workers (% female): 42
Women in government at ministerial level (% total): 32

Economics

Estimated Earned Income (PPP US$): M 1,932; F 780
Ratio of estimated female to male earned income: .40
Economic activity rate (% female): 75.8
Women in adult labor force (% total): 77

United States

Human Development Index ranking: .914
Gender Inequality Index: .755
Gender-Related Development Index value: .995

General

Type of government: Federal Republic

Major ethnic groups: White (77.7%); Black (13.2%); Asian (5.3%); American and Alaskan Native (1.2%)

Languages: English; Spanish

Religions: Protestant (51.3%); Roman Catholic (23.9%); Mormon (1.7%); Jewish (1.7%); other or none (21.4%)

Date of independence: 1776

Former colonial power: Britain

Demographics

Population, total (millions): 318.8

Annual growth rate (%): .7

Total fertility (average number of births per woman): 2.01

Contraceptive prevalence (% of married women aged 15–49) 2007–2012: 79

Maternal mortality ratio, adjusted (per 100,000 live births): 28

Women's Status

Date of women's suffrage: 1920

Life expectancy: M 77.11; F 81.94

Gross primary enrollment ratio: 99

Gross secondary enrollment ratio: 94

Gross tertiary enrollment ratio: 95

Literacy (% age 15 and older): M 99; F 99

Political Representation of Women

Seats in parliament (% held by women): 18.2

Legislators, senior officials, and managers (% female): 43

Professional and technical workers (% female): 55

Women in government at ministerial level (% total): 32

Economics

Estimated earned income (PPP US$): M 63,163; F 41,792

Ratio of estimated female to male earned income: .66

Economic activity rate (% female): 56.6

Women in adult labor force (% total): 46.2

Indices

Human Development Index: This index measures factors relating to life expectancy, educational opportunities and achievement, and income. This index, which ranks each country between 0 and 1, is meant to serve as a frame of reference for both social and economic development.

Gender Inequality Index: This index measures gender inequalities in three aspects of human development—reproductive health measured by maternal mortality ratio and adolescent birth rates; empowerment, measured by proportion of parliamentary seats occupied by females and proportion of adult females and males aged 25 years and older with at least some secondary education; and economic status expressed as labor market participation and measured by labor force participation rate of female and male populations aged 15 years and older. The higher the GII value the more disparities between females and males.

Gender-Related Development Index Value: This index measures the same factors as the Human Development Index but takes into account the inequalities that exist between men and women in a given country. Measures of inequality include (but are not limited to) access to education and income disparity. A country's Gender-Related Development Index value is usually lower than its HDI value.

Key Terms

Condom use at last high risk sex: The percentage of men and women who have had sex with a nonmarital, noncohabiting partner in the last twelve months and who say they used a condom the last time they did so.

Contraceptive prevalence rate: The percentage of married women of reproductive age (15–49) who are using, or whose partners are using, any form of contraception, whether modern or traditional.

Enrollment ratio, gross: Total number of pupils or students enrolled in a given level of education, regardless of age, expressed as a percentage of the population in the theoretical age group for the same level of education. Gross enrollment ratios in excess of 100% indicate that there are pupils or students outside the theoretical age groups who are enrolled in that level of education.

Estimated earned income: Derived on the basis of the ratio of the female nonagricultural wage to the male nonagricultural wage, the female and male shares of the economically active population, total female and male population, and GDP per capita; given in purchasing power parity terms in U.S. dollars.

Fertility rate, total: The number of children that would be born to each woman if she were to live to the end of her child-bearing years and bear children at each age in accordance with prevailing age-specific fertility rates in a given year/period, for a given country, territory, or geographical area.

Labor force participation rate, female: The number of women in the labor force expressed as a percentage of the female working-age population.

Mortality ratio, maternal, adjusted: Maternal mortality ratio adjusted to account for well-documented problems of underreporting and misclassification of maternal deaths, as well as estimates for countries with no data.

Professional and technical workers, female: Women's share of positions defined according to the International Standard Classification of Occupations to include physical, mathematical, and engineering science professionals; life science and health professionals; teaching professionals; and other professionals and associate professionals.

Women in government at ministerial level: Includes deputy prime ministers and ministers. Prime ministers were included when they held ministerial portfolios. Vice presidents and heads of ministerial-level departments or agencies were also included when exercising a ministerial function in the government structure.

Sources

2014 Human Development Report: http://hdr.undp.org/en/data
CIA The World Factbook: https://www.cia.gov/library/publications/the-world-factbook/
World Bank World Development Indicators: http://data.worldbank.org/indicator
UNdata Contraceptive Prevalence Rate: https://data.un.org/Data.aspx?d=SOWC&f=inID%3A34

World Economic Forum The Global Gender Gap Index 2014: http://reports.weforum.org/global-gender-gap-report-2014/rankings/

"Women in National Parliaments" compiled by the Inter-Parliamentary Union: http://www.ipu.org/wmn-e/classif.htm

UNESCO "Adult and Youth Literacy: Statistics and Trends, 2985-2015": http://www.uis.unesco.org/Education/Documents/literacy-statistics-trends-1985-2015.pdf

Note:

Gross enrollment ratios in excess of 100% indicate that there are pupils or students outside the theoretical age groups who are enrolled in that level of education.

Bibliography

Abbasgholizadeh, Mahboubeh. 2010. "The Crisis of Agency in the Iranian Women's Movement: A critique from inside," Article presented at the 21st Annual Conference of the Iranian Women's Studies Foundation, Paris, July: http://shabakeh.de/opinion/347/.

Abdullaev, Nabi. 2005. "Duma Gives Its Vote to Big Parties," *Moscow Times* (18 April): https://themoscowtimes.com/sitemap/free/2005/4/article/duma-gives-its-vote-to-big-parties/223828.html.

Abou-Bakr, Omaima. 2001 "Islamic Feminism; what is in the name?" *Middle East Women's Studies Review* (Winter–Spring): 1–3.

"About." 2012. *Feminist Majority*. http://feministmajority.org/about/.

"About - Donor Direct Action." 2016. Donor Direct Action.

Abrahams, N., R. Jewkes, M. Hoffman, R. Loubsher. 2004. "Sexual Violence Against Intimate Partners in Cape Town: Prevalence and Risk Factors Reported by Men," in *Bulletin of the World Health Organization* 82 (5) 2004.

Abramsky, Sasha. 2014. "What if the Minimum Wage were $15 an Hour?" *The Nation.*

Abu Khadra, Salwa [head of the General Union of Palestinian Women, General Command]. 2001. Interview with Islah Jad, Ramallah, July 11.

Abubikirova, N. I., T. A. Klimenkova, E. V. Kotchkina, M. A. Regentova, and T. G. Troinova. 1998. *Spravochnik: Zhenskie nepravitel'stvennye organizatsii rossii i SNG* [Directory: Women's NGOs in Russia and the CIS]. Moscow: Women's Information Network.

Abul-Omrein, Khaled. 2000. *Hamas: Harakat al-moqawameh al-islameyya fi falastine* [Hamas: The Islamic resistance movement in Palestine]. Cairo: Marqaz al-Hadara al-'Arabeyya (the Arab Civilisation Center).

Achtenberg, Emily. 2013. "Contested Development: The Geopolitics of Bolivia's TIPNIS Conflict." *NACLA Report on the Americas.* https://nacla.org/article/contested-development-geopolitics-bolivia%E2%80%99s-tipnis-conflict (Accessed April 2, 2016).

———. 2014. "For Abortion Rights in Bolivia, A Modest Gain." *NACLA Rebel Currents Blog.*

ADFM 2009. "Report on the Application of CEDAW in the Arab World." http://cedaw.files.wordpress.com/2009/07/adfm-report-on-the-application-of-cedaw-in-the-arab-world.pdf.

Adomanis, Mark. 2015. "What Do Russians Think About 'Pussy Riot?' The Answer Might Surprise You." *Forbes.* http://archive.fo/nlKM9.

Afary, Janet. 2009. *Sexual Politics in Modern Iran.* Cambridge: Cambridge University Press.

Afkhami, Mahnaz, and Erika Friedl, eds. 1994. *Eye of the Storm: Women in Post-Revolutionary Iran.* London: I. B. Tauris.

After the Ban, Women working in dance bars, a study conducted by Research Center for Women's Studies, SNDT Women's University, and Forum against Oppression of Women, Mumbai (FAOW), December 2006

AFTURD. n.d. "Produits et publications." http://www.afturd-tunisie.org/14-2/.

Agarwal, Bina. 1997. "Bargaining and Gender Relations: Within and Beyond the Household." *Feminist Economics* 2, no. 1: 1–50.

Agnes. Flavia. 1992. "Protecting women against violence? Review of a decade of legislation, 1980-89", *Economic and Political Weekly*, 27: WS19–WS33.

———. 1994. "Women's Movement in a Secular Framework: Redefining the Agendas." *Economic and Political Weekly*, May 7, 1123–1128. Reprinted in *Women's Studies: A reader*, edited by Mary E. John, 501–508. New Delhi: Penguin Books India, 2008.

Agustin, Lisa Rolundsen (2013) *The Politics of Intersectionality. Gender Equality, Intersectionality, and Diversity in Europe*. New York, Palgrave Macmillan.

Agustin, Lisa Rolundsen and Silke Roth. 2011. "Minority Inclusion, Self-Representation and Coalition-Building: The Participation of Minority Women in European Women's Networks," in *Transforming Gendered Well-Being in Europe. The Impact of Social Movements*. Ed. A. E. Woodward, J.-M. Bonvin, and M. Renom, pp. 231–247. Farnham: Ashgate.

Ahmadi Khorasani, Noushin. 2007. "Jonbesh yek million emza: Ravayati az daroun" [The One Million Signatures movement: A narrative from inside]. http://www.femschool .info/campaign/spip.php?article86.

———. 2009. *Iranian Women's One Million Signatures Campaign for Equality: An Inside Story* (English translation by Women's Learning Partnership, Washington DC, 2009): http://www.learningpartnership.org/iran-oms-inside-story.

———. 2012. *Bahar-e Jonbesh-e Zanan* [The Spring of Iranian Women's Movement]: www.noushinahmadi.wordpress.com.

Aivazova, Svetlana. 1998. *Russkie zhenshchiny v labarinte ravnopraviia* [Russian women in the labyrinth of equal rights]. Moscow: RIK Rusanova.

———. 2000. "Zhenshchina i vlast': Liubov' bez vzaimnosti" [Women and political power: Unrequited love]. *Zhenshchina Plius* 1.

———. 2008. *Russian Elections: Gender Profile*. Moscow: Consortium of Women's Non-Governmental Associations.

Alamdari, Kazem. 2008. "Jonbesh yek-million emza, ulgouyi bara-ye jamèh madani dar Iran." 10 Farvardin/March. http://www.femschool.info/campaign/spip.php?article 210.

Al-Arabiyya. 2012. "Algeria appoints four female army generals," July 9, 2012. http:// english.alarabiya.net/en/News/2014/07/09/Algeria-appoints-four-female-army -generals-.html.

———. 2015. "Algeria passes law banning violence against women." http://english .alarabiya.net/en/News/africa/2015/03/06/Algeria-passes-law-banning-violence -against-women.html.

Alasti, Sanaz. 2007. "Comparative study of stoning punishments in the religions of Islam and Judaism." *Justice Policy Journal* 4, no. 1 (Spring).

Al-Bargothi, Eyyad. 2000. Al-islam al-seyassi fi falastine: ma wara al-seyassa (Political Islam in Palestine: Beyond Politics). Jerusalem: Jerusalem Media and Communication Center (JMCC).

Algeria Watch. 2005. "Harcèlement sexuel dans le milieu de travail" [Sexual harassment at work]. http://www.algeria-watch.org/fr/article/femmes/harcelement_sexuel.htm.

AL-HUDA Association. 1998. Al-mara' al-falestenyya wa mo'amrat al-'al-a'maneyyat [Palestinian woman and the plot of secular women], al Bireh: al-huda association. [In Arabic.]

Alliance for Rural Democracy. 2002. "Traditional Courts Bill: Zuma's doublespeak—the President concedes Bill is flawed but attacks those opposed to it." Press release. http://www.wlce.co.za/index.php/2013-04-30-11-57-18/press-releases/165-traditional -courts-bill-zumas-doublespeak-the-president-concedes-bill-is-flawed-but-attacks -those-opposed-to-it

———. 2014. "Statements by the Alliance for Rural Democracy on the Traditional Courts Bill—Gender Justice." Press release. https://za.boell.org/2014/02/03/statements -alliance-rural-democracy-traditional-courts-bill-gender-justice

Al-Muqtafi. 2016. "Public Rights and Freedom: Article 9." http://muqtafi.birzeit.edu /mainleg/14138.htm.

Al-Quds Newspaper. 2006. Nov. 5, No. 13192: 1, Jerusalem.

Al Sabti, Randa. 2009. "The Most Important Pillars and Themes of Women's Bill of Rights," The Palestinian Women's Bill of Rights' workshop, Gaza, May 6, 2009, http://www.mowa.gov.ps/news_details.php?id=10.

al-Sayyid, Mustapha K. 1993. "A 'civil society' in Egypt?" *Middle East Journal* 47, no. 2 (Spring): 228–242.

al-Yassir, 'Alya [UNIFEM]. 2001. Interview with Islah Jad, Ramallah, June 25.

Alvarez, Carmen. 2000. "Cosmovisión maya y feminismos: ¿Caminos que se unen?" In *La encrucijada de las identidades, mujeres feminismos y mayanismos en diálogo*, edited by Aura Estela Cumes and Ana Silvia Monzón, 19–31. Guatemala City: Serviprensa.

Alvarez, Sonia E. 1990. *Engendering Democracy in Brazil: Women's Movements in Transition Politics*. Princeton: Princeton University Press.

———. 1994. "La (trans)formación del (los) feminism(s) y la política de gênero em la democratización del Brasil." In *Mujeres y participación política*, edited by Magdalena Leon. Avances y desafios em América Latina. Bogotá: Tercer Mundo.

———. 1998a. "Latin American Feminisms 'Go Global': Trends of the 1990s and Challenges for the New Millennium." In *Cultures of Politics/Politics of Cultures: Revisioning Latin American Social Movements*, edited by Sonia E. Alvarez, Evelina Dagnino, and Arturo Escobar. Boulder: Westview Press.

———. 1998b. "Advocating Feminism: The Latin American Feminist NGO Boom." Conference made at the Latin American Studies Program, Mount Holyoke College, on May 2, 1998. http:// www.mtholyoke.edu/acad/latam/schomburgmoreno/alvarez.html.

———. 1999. "Advocating Feminism: The Latin American feminist NGO 'boom'", *International Feminist Journal of Politics* 1(2): 181–209.

———. 2000. "Translating the Global: Effects of Transnational Organizing on Local Feminist Discourses and Practices in Latin America." *Meridians: Feminism, Race, Transnationalism* 1, no. 1 (Autumn): 30–31.

———. 2014. "Para Além da Sociedade Civil: Reflexões sobre o Campo Feministas." *Cadernos PAGU*, (43):13-56.

Alvarez, Sonia E., Nalu Faria, and Miriam Nobre. 2004. "Another (Also Feminist) World is Possible: Constructing Transnational Spaces and Global Alternatives from the Movements." In *The World Social Forum: Challenging Empires*, edited by Jai Sen, Anita Anand, Arturo Escobar, and P. Waterman, 199–206. New Delhi: Viveka.

Alvarez, Sonia E., Elisabeth J. Friedman, Ericka Beckman, Maylei Blackwell, Norma Chinchilla, Nathalie Lebon, Marissa Navarro, and Marcela Ríos Tobar. 2003.

"Encountering Latin American and Caribbean Feminisms." *Signs: Journal of Women in Culture and Society* 28, no. 2: 537–579.

AMB—ARTICULAÇÃO de mulheres brasileiras. 2004. *Articulando a luta feminista nas políticas públicas.* Recife: [s.n.]. (Texto para discussão.)

American Anthropological Association. 1947. "Statement on human rights." *American Anthropologist* 49: 539–543.

Amini, Asiyeh. 2016. "War of Words: A woman's battle to end stoning and juvenile execution in Iran." In *New Yorker*, by Lara Secor, January 4: http://www.newyorker.com/magazine/2016/01/04/war-of-words-annals-of-activism-laura-secor.

Anderson-Bricker, Kristin. 1999. "Triple Jeopardy: Black Women and the Growth of Feminist Consciousness in SNCC, 1964–1975." In *Still Lifting, Still Climbing: Contemporary African American Women's Activism*, edited by Kimberly Springer. New York: New York University Press.

Aptheker, Bettina. 1989. *Tapestries of Life: Women's Work, Women's Consciousness, and the Meaning of Daily Life.* Amherst: University of Massachusetts Press.

Araújo, Clara. 2003. "Quotas for Women in the Brazilian Legislative System." Paper presented at the International IDEA Workshop, "The Implementation of Quotas: Latin American Experiences," Lima, Peru, February 23–24.

Arfaoui, Khedifa. 2015. "Women and Leadership in the Post-Arab Spring: The Case of Tunisia." Unpublished paper provided to the author.

Arkhiv politicheskoi reklamy. n.d. *Results of Elections to the State Duma of the Russian Federation (Itogi vyborov v Gosudarstvennuiu Dumu RF).* Retrieved from http://www.33333.ru/elections.php.

"Article 7—Public and Political Life." 2006. Chap. 5 of *Second and Third Alternative Report on CEDAW*. Delhi: NAWO.

Ashwin, Sarah. 2006. "The post-Soviet gender order: Imperatives and implications." In *Adapting to Russia's New Labor Market Gender and Employment Strategy*, edited by Sarah Ashwin, 32–56. London: RoutledgeCurzon.

Attwood, Lynne. 1997. "'She was asking for it': Rape and domestic violence against women." In *Post-Soviet women: From the Baltic to Central Asia*, edited by Mary Buckley, 99–118. Cambridge: Cambridge University Press.

Ávila, Maria Bethania, 2007. "Radicalização do Feminismo, Radicalização da Democracia," Cadernos de Crítica Feminista, Número 0, Ano I, Recife: SOS CORPO.

AWID. "The State of Women's Organizations: Fund Her Fact Sheet 1."

———. 2011. "Global Survey: Where is the Money for Women's Rights? Assessing Resources and the Role of Donors in the Promotion of Women's Rights and the Support of Women's Organizations."

———. 2015. "Feminist Donor List: Who Can Fund My Women's Rights Organizing?" August 12, 2015. http://www.awid.org/resources/feminist-donor-list-who-can-fund-my-womens-rights-organizing.

Ayoub, Phillip M. 2016. *When States Come Out: Europe's Sexual Minorities and the Politics of Visibility.* Cambridge, Cambridge University Press.

Azraq, Khawla [Fateh activist]. 2002. Interview with Islah Jad, Beirut, December 22.

Babb, Florence E. 2003. "Out in Nicaragua: Local and transnational desires after the revolution." *Cultural Anthropology* 18, no. 3: 304–328.

Badran, Margot. 2001. "Understanding Islam, Islamism, and Islamic feminism." *Journal of Women's History* 13, no. 1 (Spring): 47–52.

———. 2009. *Feminism in Islam: Secular and Religious Convergences.* Oxford: Oneworld Publications.

Baggueley, Paul. 2002. "Contemporary British Feminism: a social movement in abeyance." *Social Movement Studies: Journal of Social, Cultural and Political Protest* 1, no. 2: 169–185.

Bahreini, Raha. 2014. "Pathologizing Identities, Paralyzing Bodies." Amin, Shadi; Sadr, Shadi; McDermott, Nicola, eds. *Justice for Iran and Iranian Lesbian and Transgender Network* (6Rang).

Bainomugisha, A. "The Empowerment of Women." *Uganda's Age of Reforms: A Critical Overview.* Ed. Mugaju, Justus. Kampala: Fountain Publishers, 1999.

Bairros, Luiza, 1995. "Nossos Feminismos Revisitados." *Revista Estudos Feministas*, Vol. 3, No. 2, pp. 458–463.

Baldez, Lisa. 2002. *Why Women Protest: Women's Movements in Chile.* Cambridge: Cambridge University Press.

———. 2004. "Elected bodies: Gender quotas for female legislative candidates in Mexico." *Legislative Studies Quarterly* 29, no. 2: 231–258.

Bali, Kamayani. 2012. "Immediate Release—Petition for a comprehensive response to sexual violence submitted to Sonia Gandhi," *Kracktivist: Bridge the Gap, Bring the Change,* July 24. https://kractivist.wordpress.com/2012/07/24/immediate-realease-petition-sonia-gandhi/.

Banaszak, Lee Ann. 2010. *The Women's Movement Inside and Outside the State.* New York: Cambridge University Press.

Banaszak, Lee Ann, Karen Beckwith, and Dieter Rucht. 2003. *Women's Movements Facing the Reconfigured State.* Cambridge: Cambridge University Press.

Baniyaghoob, Zhila. 1384/2005. "Zanan der dowran-e riyasat jomhouri-ye Mohammad Khatami" [Women during the presidency of Mohammad Khatami]. *Gooya News,* 3 Shahrivar.

al-Bargothi, Eyyad. 2000. *Al-islam al-seyassi fi falastine: Ma wara al-seyassa* [Political Islam in Palestine: Beyond politics]. Jerusalem: Jerusalem Media and Communication Center.

Bargouthi, Mustafa. 1994. "Monazamat al-mojtama' al-madani wa dawreha fil-marhala al-moqbela" [Civil society organizations and their role in the coming era]. Paper presented at the conference "The Future of the Palestinian Civil Society," Birzeit University, May 13–15.

Baskakova, Marina. 2000. "Gender aspects of pension reform in Russia." In *Making The Transition Work for Women in Europe and Central Asia,* edited by Marina Lazreg. World Bank Discussion Paper no. 411. Washington, DC: World Bank.

Basarudin, Azza. 2015. *Humanizing the Sacred: Sisters in Islam and the Struggle for Gender Justice in Malaysia.* Seattle: University of Washington Press.

Bassel, Leah and Akwugo Emejulu. 2014. "Solidarity under Austerity: Intersectionality in France and the United Kingdom." *Politics & Gender* 10, no. 01: 130–136.

Basu, Amrita, ed. 1992. *Two Faces of Protest: Contrasting Modes of Women's Activism in India.* New Delhi: Oxford University Press.

———. 1995. *The Challenge of Local Feminisms: Women's Movements in Global Perspective.* Boulder: Westview Press, 1995.

———. 2000. "Globalization of the Local/Localization of the Global: Mapping Transnational Women's Movements," *Meridians: feminism, race, transnationalism.* (Vol. 1, No. 1, Autumn 2000)

———. 2005a. "Transnational Feminism Revisited." *Feminist Africa,* no. 5: 90–95.

———. 2005b. "Women, Political Parties, and Social Movements in South Asia." Occasional Paper 5. Geneva: UNRISD: 68–84.

————. 2010. "Introduction" in Amrita Basu (ed.) *Women's Movements in the Global Era: The Power of Local Feminisms.* Boulder: Westview Press.

Batliwala, Srilatha. 2014. "Linking leadership capacity building with movement building – some inputs for the WELDD Roundtable, 22 May 2014", Power Point presentation at the May 2014 WELDD Roundtable on Feminist Leadership, Kandy, Sri Lanka.

Baumgardner, Jennifer, and Amy Richards. 2000. *Manifesta: Young Women, Feminism, and the Future.* New York: Farrar, Straus, and Giroux.

Baxi, Upendra. 2005. "The Gujarat catastrophe: Notes on reading politics as democidal rape culture." In *The Violence of Normal Times: Essays on Women's Lived Realities*, edited by Kalpana Kannabiran. New Delhi: Women Unlimited in association with Kali for Women.

Bayat, Asef. 1997. February. *Street Politics: Poor People's Movements in Iran.* New York: Columbia University Press.

————. 2007. "A women's non-movement: What it means to be a woman activist in an Islamic state." *Comparative Studies of South Asia, Africa, and the Middle East* 27, no. 1.

————, Ed. 2013. *Post-Islamism: The Changing Faces of Political Islam.* Oxford University Press.

Beckwith, Karen. 2003. "The gendering ways of states: Women's representation and state reconfiguration in France, Great Britain, and the United States." In *Women's Movements Facing the Reconfigured State,* edited by Lee Ann Banaszak, Karen Beckwith, and Dieter Rucht. Cambridge and New York: Cambridge University Press.

Beale, J. 1990. "Picking Up the Gauntlet. Women Discuss the ANC Statement" in *Agenda 8 1990.*

Bekhauf Azadi Campaign. 2013. "Why the Government's Ordinance is Fraud and Mockery of the Justice Verma Committee Recommendations: Bekhauf Azaadi Campaign," *Kafila*, February 3. http://kafila.org/2013/02/03/why-the-govts-ordnance-is-fraud-mockery-of-the-justice-verma-committe-recommendations-bekhauf-azaadi-campaign/.

Belamri, Ramdane. 2012. "Moroccan Socialist Leader Blasts Islamists." http://www.al-monitor.com/pulse/tr/contents/articles/politics/2012/05/secretary-general-of-the-morocca.html#.

Bergman, Solveig 2002. *The Politics of Feminism.* Abo, Abo Akademi University Press.

Bernstein, Hilda. 1975. "Inside Apartheid's Gulad Archipelago," *Los Angeles Times*, 29 Janaury 1978.

Bernstein, Mary and Verta Taylor. 2013. *The Marrying Kind? Debating Same-Sex Marriage within the Lesbian and Gay Movement.* Minneapolis: University of Minnesota Press.

Berrío Palomo, Lina Rosa. 2008. "Sembrando sueños, creando utopías: Liderazgos femeninos indígenas en Colombia y México." In *Etnografías e historias de resistencia: Mujeres indígenas, procesos organizativos y nuevas identidades políticas,* edited by Rosalva Aída Hernández, 181–217. Mexico City: Publicaciones de la Casa Chata CIESAS/PUEG-UNAM.

Beuno-Hansen, Pascha. 2015. *Feminist and Human Rights Struggles in Peru: Decolonizing Transitional Justice.* Champaign: University of Illinois Press.

Beydoun, Aza S. 2002. *Nissa wa jam'eyyat: Libnaneyat bayna insaf el-that wa khedmat al-ghayr* [Women and societies: Lebanese women between self-assertion and caring for the others]. Beirut: Dar el-Nahar.

Binnie, Jon and Christian Klesse. 2012. "Solidarities and tensions: Feminism and transnational LGBTQ politics in Poland." *European Journal of Women's Studies* 19, no. (4): 444.

Bishara, Azmi. 1996. *Mossahama fi nakd al mujtam'a al madani* [A contribution to the critique of civil society]. Ramallah: Muwatin (the Palestinian Institute for the Study of Democracy).

Bissonnette, Nathalie. 2013. "Senegal, Governance Gets a Make Over." Uniterra. Ottawa, Canada: World University Service of Canada (WUSC) and Centre for International Studies and Cooperation (CECI).

Blackwell, Maylei. 2011. *¡Chicana Power!: Contested Histories of Feminism in the Chicano Movement.* Austin: University of Texas Press.

Bobo, K. A., J. Kendall, and S. Max. 2001. *Organizing for Social Change: A Manual for Activists.* 3rd ed. Cabin John, MD: Seven Locks Press.

Bolpress. 2006. "Evo dijo que la instancia sería borrada de la estructura del Ejecutivo." January 20. http://www.bolpress.com/.

Bond-Stewart, K. 1987. *Independence Is Not Only for One Sex.* Harare: Zimbabwe Publishing House.

Bonetti, Alinne and Pinheiro, Luana. 2009. "De Inovadora À Diabólica—Primeiros Resultados Da Lei Maria Da Penha." *Revista Pós Ciências Sociais.* v. 1 n. 11 São Luis/MA, published online.

Borchorst, Annette. 2000. "Feminist Thinking about the Welfare State." In *Revisioning Gender,* edited by Myra Marx Ferree, Judith Lorber and Beth B. Hess, 99–127. Walnut Creek: Rpwman & Littlefield.

Bouatta, Cherifa. 1997. "Evolution of the Women's Movement in Contemporary Algeria: Organization, Objectives, and Prospects." Helsinki: UNU/WIDER Working Paper No. 124 (February).

Boxer, Marilyn J. 2007. "Rethinking the Socialist Construction and International Career of the Concept 'Bourgeois Feminism,'" in *The American Historical Review,* Vol. 112, No. 1, pp. 131–158.

BRASIL. 2013. Instituto Brasileiro de Geografia e Estatística. IBGE.

BRASIL, Secretaria de Políticas para Mulheres—SPM. 2004. Conferência Nacional de Políticas Para As Mulheres, 1, 2004, Brasília. *Anais...* Brasília: SPM, 2004. http://www.presidencia.gov.br/estrutura_presidencia/sepm/.arquivos/integra_anais.

BRASIL, Secretaria de Políticas para Mulheres—SPM, 2012. "Em 2011, a Central de Atendimento à Mulher—Ligue 180—registrou 734.416 atendimentos." http://www.spm.gov.br/area-imprensa/ultimas_noticias/2011/02/em-2010-a-central-de-atendimento-a-mulher-2013-ligue-180-2013-registrou-734-416-atendimentos.

BRASIL, Secretaria de Políticas para Mulheres—SPM. 2014. "Balanço Ligue 180—2014." http://www.spm.gov.br/central-de-conteudos/publicacoes/publicacoes/2015/balanco180_2014-versaoweb.pdf.

BRASIL, Secretaria de Políticas para Mulheres—SPM. 2015. "Mapa da Violência apresenta aumento de homicídios de mulheres." http://www.spm.gov.br/noticias/mapa-da-violencia-apresenta-aumento-de-homicidios-de-mulheres.

Breaking the Binary. 2013. "Understanding concerns and realities of queer persons assigned gender female at birth across a spectrum of lived gender identities," *A study conducted by LABIA–A Queer Feminist LBT Collective,* April. https://sites.google.com/site/labiacollective/.

Breines, Winifred. 2006. *The Trouble Between Us: An Uneasy History of White and Black Women in the Feminist Movement.* Oxford and New York: Oxford University Press.

Buckley, Mary. 1989. *Women and Ideology in the Soviet Union*. Toronto: Harvester Wheatsheaf.

Buechler, Steven M. 1990. *Women's Movements in the United States: Woman Suffrage, Equal Rights and Beyond*. New Brunswick and London: Rutgers University Press.

Bunch, Charlotte. 2012. "Opening Doors for Feminism: UN World Conferences on Women." *The Journal of Women's History*, 24, no.2 (Winter): 213–221.

Bunch, Charlotte and Roxanna Carrillo. 2016. "Women's Rights Are Human Rights: A Concept in the Making" in *Women and Girls Rising: Progress and Resistance around the World*, eds. Ellen Chesler and Terry McGovern, 51–68. Routledge: New York.

Bunting, Helen. 2007. "Chile's Bachelet signs bill to promote women's participation in politics." *Santiago Times,* October 30. http://www.santiagotimes.cl/santiagotimes/.

Burgnard, S. 2011. "Second Wave Feminism and the Capability Approach: The Swiss Case." In *Tranforming Gendered Well-Being in Europe. The Impact of Social Movements.* Ed. A. Woodward, J.-M. Bonvin and M. Renom, pp. 67–81. Farnham: Ashgate.

Burk, Martha. 2008. "Why Hillary Is the Right Choice for Women." *Huffington Post,* February 3. http://www.huffingtonpost.com/martha-burk/why-hillary-is-the-right-_b_84718.html.

Bustelo, Maria. 2014. "Three Decades of State Feminism and Gender Equality Policies in Multi-governed Spain." *Sex Roles*. http://eprints.sim.ucm.es/29738/1/Bustelo%20three%20decades%20os%20state%20Sex%20Roles.pdf.

Butler, Judith. 2001. *El género en disputa: El feminismo y la subversión de la identidad.* Mexico City: Paidós/PUEG-UNAM.

Butler, J. R. Rotberg and J. Adams. 1978. *The Black Homelands of South Africa: The Political and Economic Development of Bophutatswana and KwaZulu*. Natal Berkley: University of California Press.

Bygnes, Susanne 2012. "'We Are in Complete Agreement': The Diversity Issue, Disagreement and Change in the European Women's Lobby." *Social Movement Studies*: 1–15.

Cai, Yiping, Wang Zheng, and Du Fangqi, eds. 1999. *Engendering the Study of History* Tiangin: Internal Publication (in Chinese).

Carden, Maren Lockwood. 1974. *The New Feminist Movement*. New York: Russell Sage Foundation.

Cardoso, Cláudia Pons. 2012. *Outras Falas: Perspectivas de mulheres negras brasileiras sobre os feminismos.* PhD dissertation presented to the Programa em Estudos Interdisciplinares Sobre Mulheres, Gênero e Feminismo—PPGNEIM—Universidade Federal da Bahia.

Carneiro, Sueli. 1999. "Black Women's Identity in Brazil." In *Race in Contemporary Brazil: From Indifference to Inequality,* edited by Rebecca Reichmann. University Park: Pennsylvania State University Press.

Carpenter, Julia. 2014. "Iranian journalist faces threats, false report of rape after viral Facebook success." *The Washington Post,* June 7: https://www.washingtonpost.com/blogs/she-the-people/wp/2014/06/07/iranian-journalist-faces-threats-false-report-of-rape-after-viral-facebook-success/

Castañeda, Jorge G. 2006. "Latin America's left turn." *Foreign Affairs* 85, no. 3: 28–43.

Causes of Farmer Suicides in Maharashtra: An Enquiry; Final Report Submitted to the Mumbai High Court, March 15, 2005. 2005. Tuljapur, India: Tata Institute of Social Sciences, Rural Campus.

CBS News. 2015. "New Law in Algeria Punished Violence Against Women." http://www.cbsnews.com/news/new-law-in-algeria-punishes-violence-against-women/

CEDAW. 2007. *Concluding Comments of the Committee on the Elimination of Discrimination Against Women: India*. 37th sess., January 15–February 2. http://www .un.org/womenwatch/daw/cedaw/cedaw37/concludingcommentsAU/India_Advance %20unedited.pdf.

Celis, Karen, Sarah Childs, Johanna Kantola, and Mona Lena Krook. "Constituting Women's Interests through Representative Claims." *Politics & Gender* 10, no. 02 (2014): 149–74.

Center for Social and Labor Rights, Heinrich Boll Stiftung, and Zhenskii Most: Women's Bridge. 2013. "The Solutions Are in Our Hands: Successful Women's Initiatives and Campaigns." Moscow.

Central Electoral Commission of the Russian Federation. *Federal'nyi spisok kandidatov v deputaty Gosudarstvennoi Dumy Federal'nogo Sobraniia Rossiiskoi Federatsii shestogo sozyva, vydvinytyi politicheskoi partiei "Vserossiiskaia politicheskaia partiia 'Edinaia Rossiia'"* [Federal list of candidates for deputies of the sixth session of the Federal State Duma of the Russian Federation forwarded by the political party "All-Russian political party 'United Russia'"].

César de Oliveira, Glaucira [political liaison and directorate member, CFEMEA]. 2002. Interview with Elisabeth Jay Friedman, Brasilia, Brazil, August 1.

CFEMEA. 2002. "Plataforma Política Feminista é aprovada em Brasília." *Jornal Fêmea* Número 113, June. http://www.cfemea.org.br/index.php?option=com_content& view=article&id=687:plataforma-politica-feminista-e-aprovada-em-brasilia&- catid=97:numero-113-junho-de-2002&Itemid=129.

Challand, Benoit. 2009. *Palestinian Civil Society: Foreign Donors and the Power to Promote and Exclude*. London and New York: Routledge.

Chatty, Dawn, and Annika Rabo. 1997. *Organizing Women: Formal and Informal Women's Groups in the Middle East*. Oxford: Berg.

Chékir, Hafidha and Khedija Arfaoui. 2011. "Tunisia: Women's Economic Citizenship and Trade Union Participation." In *Making Globalization Work for Women*, eds., Valentine M. Moghadam, Suzanne Franzway, and Mary Margaret Fonow, 71–92. Albany: State University of New York Press.

Cheriet, Boutheina. 2014. "The Arab Spring exception: Algeria's political ambiguities and citizenship rights." *Journal of North African Studies*, vol. 19, no. 2 (March): 143-156.

Chérif Chamari, Alya. 1992. *La Femme et la Loi en Tunisie*. Rabat: Le Fennec.

Cherifati-Merabtine, Doria. 1994. "Algeria at a Crossroads: National Liberation, Islamization, and Women." In *Gender and National Identity: Women and Politics in Muslim Societies*, edited by V. M. Moghadam, 40–62. London: Zed Books.

Chhachhi, Amrita and Sunila Abeysekera. 2015. "Forging a New Political Imaginary: Transnational Southasian Feminsisms." In *The Oxford Handbook of Transnational Feminist Movements*, edited by Rawdwida Bakshi and Wendy Harcourt. New York: Oxford University Press.

Cherkassov, Gleb. 2000. "Partii-autsaidergy" [Outsider parties]. In *Rossiia v izbiratel'nom tsikle 1999–2000 godov* [Russia in the electoral cycle of 1999–2000], edited by Michael McFaul, Nikolai Petrov, and A. Ryabov. Moscow: Moscow Carnegie Center.

Chernenkaia, Irina [former executive director of the Syostri Center for Victims of Sexual Assault]. 1999. Interview with Lisa McIntosh Sundstrom, Moscow, April 5.

China Project Group. 2004. "Enhance gender mainstreaming capacity and improve gender equality in employment policies" [Tigao shehui xingbei zhuliuhu nengli zhidao shouce]. Beijing: China Society Press.

Chinchilla, Norma S. 1993. "Women's movements in the Americas: Feminism's Second Wave." *NACLA Report on the Americas* 27, no. 1: 17–23.

Chow, Esther Ngan-ling, Naihua Zhang, and Jinling Wang. 2004. "Promising and contested fields: Women's studies and sociology of women/gender in contemporary China." *Gender and Society* 18, no. 2: 161–188.

Christensen, Hilda Romer, Beatrice Halsaa, and Aino Saarinen, eds. 2004. *Crossing borders: Remapping women's movements at the turn of the 21st century.* Odense: University Press of Southern Denmark.

Cichowksi, Rachel A. 2002. " 'No Discrimination Whatsoever'. *Women's Transnational Activism and the Evolution of EU Sex Equality Policy."* Pp. 220 – 238 in Women's Activism and Globalisation. Linking Local Struggles and Transnational Politics, edited by by Nancy A. Naples and Manisha Desai. London: Routledge.

"Clinton supporters turn to McCain." 2008. NPR, June 10. http://www.npr.org/templates /story/story.php?storyId=91356785.

Cobble, Dorothy Sue. 2005. *The Other Women's Movement: Workplace Justice and Social Rights in Modern America.* Princeton, NJ: Princeton University Press.

Cobble, Dorothy Sue, Linda Gordon, and Astrid Henry. 2015. *Feminism Unfinished: A Short Surprising History of American Women's Movements.* New York: Liveright Publishing Corporation.

Cockburn, Cynthia. 2013. "Against the odds: Sustaining feminist momentum in postwar Bosnia-Herzegovina." Women's Studies International Forum 37: 26–35.

CodePink. n.d. Mission statement. http://www.codepink4peace.org/article.php?list= type&type=3.

Cole, J. 1987. *Crossroads.* Johannesburg: Ravan Press.

Collectif 95 Maghreb-Egalité. 2003. *Dalil pour l'égalité dans la famille au Maghreb.* Rabat: Association Démocratique des Femmes du Maroc. Rabat: Collectif.

———. 2005. *Guide to Equality in the Family in the Maghreb.* Bethesda, MD: Women's Learning Partnership's Translation Series.

Combahee River Collective. 1986. *The Combahee River Collective statement: Black feminist organizing in the 1970s and 1980s.* Lanham, MD, and New York: Kitchen Table, Women of Color Press.

Conway, D. 2012. *Masculinities, Militarization and the End Conscription Campaign: War, Resistance in Apartheid South Africa.* Manchester: Manchester University Press.

Conway, Janet. 2007. "Transnational feminisms and the World Social Forum: Encounters and transformations in anti-globalization spaces." *Journal of International Women's Studies* 8, no. 3: 49–70.

Cooke, Miriam. 2001. *Women Claim Islam: Creating Islamic Feminism through Literature.* New York: Routledge.

Cooper, Barbara. 1995. "The Politics of Difference and Women's Associations in Niger: Of 'Prostitutes,' the Public and Politics." *Signs* 20, no. 4: 851–82.

Coordinadora de la Mujer, Católicas por el Derecho a Decidir, Oficina Jurídica de la Mujer, and CLADEM Bolivia. 2007. *Aportes y complementaciones al cuestionario presentado por el gobierno boliviano ante el Comité de la CEDAW.* http://www .iwraw-ap.org/resources/pdf/40_ shadow_reports/Bolivia_SR.pdf.

Cordall, Simon Speakman. 2015. "Tunisia's female politicians prepare to seize their chance in local polls." *The Guardian* (May 19). http://www.theguardian.com/global -development/2015/may/19/tunisia-female-politicians-woman-local-polls.

Cornwall, Andrea, and Vera Schatten Coelho, eds. 2006. *Spaces for Change? The Politics of Citizen Participation in New Democratic Arenas.* London: Zed Books.

COSEF. *Combats pour la parité. La Campagne "Avec la Parité, consolidons la démocratie."* Dakar: COSEF, 2011.

Costa, Ana Alice Alcantara. 2005. "O movimento feminista no Brasil: Dinâmicas de uma intervenção política." *Gênero* 5, no. 2: 9–36.

———. 2008. "Women and politics: The Brazil paradox." Open Democracy, November 3, 2008. http://www.opendemocracy.net/article/5050/political_representation_brazil.

Costa, Ana Alice Alcantara, and Cecilia M. B. Sardenberg. 1994. "Teoria e praxis feministas nas ciências e na academia: Os núcleos da mulher nas universidades Brasileiras." In "Anais do Simpósio Internacional, 'Formação, Pesquisa e Edição Feministas nas Universidades.'" Special issue, *Revista Estudos Feministas* (Rio de Janeiro, CIEC/ECO/UFRJ): 387–400.

———, eds. 2002. *Feminismo, ciência e tecnologia*. Salvador, Bahia: REDOR, NEIM.

Crenshaw, Kimberlé. 1989. "Demarginalizing the intersection of race and sex." *University of Chicago Legal Forum* 139.

———. 1995. "Mapping the Margins: Intersectionality, Identity Politics and Violence Against Women." In *Critical Race Theory: The Key Writings that Formed the Movement*, edited by Kimberlé Crenshaw, Neil Gotanda, Gary Peller, and Kendall Thomas. New York: The New Press (357–383).

———. 2008. "Should Clinton or Obama be first?" NPR radio transcript, March 11. http://www.npr.org/templates/transcript/transcript.php?storyId=88099579.

Crisis in Zimbabwe Coalition. 2003. December. Statement on the Occasion of the Commonwealth Heads of Government. Harare: Crisis in Zimbabwe Coalition. http://www.kubatana .net/docs/hr/crisis_orgviol_mar_030328.pdf.

Cullen, Pauline P. 2005. "Conflict and Cooperation within the Platform of European Social NGOs." In: *Coalitions across Borders. Transnational Protest and the Neoliberal Order*. Ed. by Jackie Smith and Joe Bandy. Lanham, Rowman & Littlefield: 71–94.

Cullen, Pauline P. 2008. "Irish Women's Organizations in an Enlarged Europe." In: *Gender Politics in the Expanding European Union. Mobilization, Inclusion, Exclusion*. Ed. by Silke Roth. Oxford/New York, Berghahn Books: 83–100.

Cullen, Pauline P. 2015. "Feminist NGOs and the European Union: Contracting Opportunities and Strategic Response." *Social Movement Studies* 14(4):410–426.

Cumbre de Mujeres Indígenas de las Américas. 2003. *Memoria de la primera cumbre de mujeres indígenas de América*. Mexico City: Fundación Rigoberta Menchú Tum.

"Curtain Falls on World Conference on UN Year of Women." 1975. *People's Daily*, July 4, 6.

Dahlerup, Drupe. 2006. "Increasing Women's Political Representation: New Trends in Gender Quotas." In Ballington and Karam, eds. *International IDEA. 2005: Women in Parliament. Beyond Numbers* (revised edition) and Drude Dahlerup, ed., *Women, Quotas and Politics*. Routledge.

Darhour, Hanane and Drude Dahlerup. 2013. "Sustainable Representation of Women Through Gender Quotas: A Decade's Experience in Morocco," *Women's Studies International Forum*, 41, Part 2: 132–142.

Darwish, Mahmoud. 2002. "A State of Siege." http://www.arabworldbooks.com/Literature /poetry4.html.

Das, Rahul. 2003. "Women *sarpanches* asserting their authority." *Chandigarh Tribune*, November 28.

Davin, Delia. 1976. *Woman-work: Women and the Party in Revolutionary China*. Oxford: Clarendon Press.

Davis, Angela. 2008. "Racism, Birth Control, and Reproductive Rights." pp. 86–93 in Nancy Ehrenreich, editor, *The Reproductive Rights Reader: Law, Medicine and the Construction of Motherhood*. New York: New York University Press.

Davtian, Mari. 2016. Facebook post on Russia's new domestic violence law. July 3. https://www.facebook.com/mari.davtyan.54/posts/641167662715572.

Dean, Jonathan and Kristin Aune. 2015. "Feminism Resurgent? Mapping Contemporary Feminist Activisms in Europe." *Social Movement Studies* 14, no. 4: 375–395.

Dei, George J. Sefa. 1994. "The Women of a Ghanaian Village: A Study of Social Change." *African Studies Review* 37, no. 2: 121–45.

Del Campo, Esther. 2005. "Women and politics in Latin America: Perspectives and limits of the institutional aspects of women's political representation." *Social Forces* 83, no. 4: 1697–1726.

Della Porta, Donatella 2003. "The Women's Movement, the Left and the State: Continuities and Changes in the Italian Case." In *Women's Movements Facing the Reconfigured State*. Edited by Lee Ann Banaszak, Karen Beckwith and Dieter Rucht, 46–68.Cambridge: Cambridge University Press.

Democracy Now. 2008. "Race and gender in presidential politics: A debate between Gloria Steinem and Melissa Harris-Lacewell." January 14. http://www.democracy now.org/2008/ 1/14/race_and_gender_in_presidential_politics.

Desai, Manisha. 1997. "Constructing/Deconstructing 'Women': Reflections from the Contemporary Women's Movement in India." In *Feminism and the New Democracies Resisting the Political*, edited by Jodi Dean, 110–123. New Delhi: Sage.

———. 2005. "Transnationalism: The Face of Feminist Politics Post-Beijing." *International Social Science Journal* (October).

Devi, Dr. Rama, cf. P. Sainath. 2004. "How the better half dies." *India Together*, August.

De Wolf, Philippe 2015. "Male feminism: men's participation in women's emancipation movements and debates. Case studies from Belgium and France (1967–1984)." *European Review of History: Revue européenne d'histoire* 22, no. 1: 77–100.

Deyyab, Rabiha [head of the union of Palestinian Woman for Social Work and general director in the Ministry of Youth and Sports]. 2001. Interview with Islah Jad, Ramallah, July 11.

Dhagamwar, Vasudha. 2005. "'The shoe fitted me and I wore it . . .': Women and traditional justice systems." In *The Violence of Normal Times: Essays on Women's Lived Realities*, edited by Kalpana Kannabiran, 46–66. New Delhi: Women Unlimited.

Diani, Mario. 2000. "The concept of social movement." In *Readings in Contemporary Sociology*, edited by Kate Nash, 155–176. Malden, MA: Blackwell.

Dicker, Rory. 2008. *A History of U.S. Feminisms*. Berkeley: Seal Press.

Diduk, Susan. 1989. "Women's Agricultural Production and Political Action in the Cameroon Grassfields." *Africa* 59, no. 3: 338–55.

Diniz, Debora and Medeiros, Marcelo. 2012. "Itinerários e métodos do aborto ilegal em cinco capitais brasileiras." *Ciência e saúde coletiva* [online]. Vol. 17, no. 7, pp.1671–1681.

Domestic Violence Counts 2010: A 24-Hour Census of Domestic Violence Shelters and Services, National Network to End Domestic Violence,. 2010. *Domestic Violence Counts 2010: A 24-Hour Census of Domestic Violence Shelters and Services*. Washington, DC.

Drakulic, Slavenka. 1993. *How We Survived Communism and Even Laughed*. New York: Harper Perennial.

Draper, Melissa. 2006. "Women and the mud ceiling." Democracy Center blog, October 3. http://www.democracyctr.org/blog/2006/10/bolivian-women-and-mud-ceiling.html.

Dyukova, Natalia. 1998. "Istoriia sozdaniia feministskogo dvizheniia v nachale 80-kh godov" [History of formation of the feminist movement in the early 1980s]. Paper presented at the conference "Society and Totalitarianism: First Half of the 1980s," St. Petersburg.

Ebadi, Shirin. 1994. *The Rights of the Child: A Study on Legal Aspects of Children's Rights in Iran* (Translated into English by M. Zaimaran). Tehran: UNICEF.

———. 2016. *Until We Are Free: My Fight for Human Rights in Iran*. New York: Random House.

"Economic Justice | National Organization for Women." 2016. *Now.Org.*

EIGE (2016) European Institute for Gender Equality. "Gender Mainstreaming. Poland/Structures." http://eige.europa.eu/gender-mainstreaming/structures/poland /office-government-plenipotentiary-equal-treatment.

Elder, Miriam. 2013. "Russia Passes Law Banning Gay 'Propaganda.'" *The Guardian*, June 11.

———. 2000. *History and Documentation of Human Rights in Iran*. Trans. Nazila Fathi. New York: Bibliotheca Persica Press.

Elfenbein, Rachel. 2015. "Towards Feminist Socialism? Gender, Sexuality, Popular Power, and the State in Venezuela's Bolivarian Revolution." Paper Prepared for the 2015 Latin American Studies Association Meeting, San Juan, Puerto Rico.

El-Hamad, Jawad, and Eyyad al-Bargothi. 1997. *Derassa fi fikr harakat al-moqawamah al-islameyya hamas* (A Study in the Political Ideology of the Islamic Resistance Movement, Hamas 1987–1996). Amman: Middle East Study Centre.

Ellerbe-Dueck, Cassandra. 2011a. "The Black European Women's Council: 'thinking oneself into the New Europe.'" *African and Black Diaspora: An International Journal* 4, no.2: 145–160.

———. 2011b. "Networks and 'Safe Spaces' of Black European Women in Germany and Austria." In *Negotiating Multicultural Europe: Borders, Networks, Neighbourhoods*. Ed. H. Armbruster and U. Meinhof, 159–184. Basingstoke:Palgrave Macmillan.

Ellina, Cassandra. 2003. *Promoting Women's Rights. The Politics of Gender in the European Union*. New York, Routledge.

Elliott, Carolyn. ed. 2008. *Global Empowerment of Women: Responses to Globalization and Politicized Religions*. New York: Routledge.

Elman, Amy R. 1995. "The State's Equality for Women: Sweden's Equality Ombudsman." In *Comparative State Feminism*. Ed. D. McBride Stetson and A. Mazur, 237–253. Thousand Oaks/London/New Dehli: Sage.

———. 2003. "Refuge in Reconfigured States: Shelter Movements in the United States, Britain and Sweden." In *Women's Movements Facing the Reconfigured State*. Ed. L. A. Banaszak, K. Beckwith and D. Rucht, 94–113. Cambridge and New York: Cambridge University Press.

Elrahi, Nay. 2015. "Rural women in Tunisia: We have been silent for too long." *The Guardian*, March 30. http://www.theguardian.com/global-development/2015/mar /30/rural-women-rights-tunisia-world-social-forum#img-1

"Em 2007, governo pagou 67, 32% do Orçamento Mulher." 2008. *Jornal Fêmea* 155. http://www.cfemea.org.br/jornalfemea/pesquisa.asp.

England, Paula. 2005. "Gender and Inequality in Labor Markets: The Role of Motherhood and Segregation." *Social Politics* 12, no. 2 (264–288).

Entelis, John, and Lisa Arone. 1994. "Government and Politics." In *Algeria: A Country Study*, edited by Helen Chapin Metz, 173–233.Washington D.C.: Federal Research Division, Area Handbook Series, Library of Congress.

Erickson, Jan. 2006. Testimony on Behalf of the U.S. Gender Working Group. Report on Women's Human Rights in the United States under the International Covenant on Civil and Political Rights. http://now.org/wp-content/uploads/2014/02/Testimony -on-Behalf-of-the-U.S.-Gender-Working-Group-2006.pdf.

Ershova, Elena [coordinator of the Consortium of Women's Nongovernmental Organizations]. 1998. Interview with Lisa McIntosh Sundstrom, Moscow, July 21.

Escobar-Lemmon, Maria, and Michelle Taylor-Robinson. 2005. "Women ministers in Latin American government: When, where, and why?" *American Journal of Political Science* 49, no. 4: 829–844.

Espina, Gioconda. 2000. "Sudden awakening in Venezuela: Venezuelan women active in placing controversial issues in parliament." *LOLApress* 13: 62. http://giocondaespina.com.ve/ GIOCONDA/mvenezolanas.php?itemmmvv=33.

———. 2007. "Beyond polarization: Organized Venezuelan women promote their 'minimum agenda.'" *NACLA Report on the Americas* 40, no. 2: 20–24.

Essig, Laurie. 1999. *Queer in Russia: A story of sex, self, and the other*. Durham: Duke University Press.

Estrada, Daniela. 2007. "Chile: High-profile trial opens dialogue on domestic violence." Global Information Network, May 9. http://www.globalinfo.org/.

Evans, Alfred B. 2012. "Protests and Civil Society in Russia: The Struggle for the Khimki Forest." *Communist and Post-Communist Studies* 45 (3-4), 233-242.

Evans, Elizabeth. 2015. *The Politics of Third Wave Feminisms. Neoliberalism, Intersectionality and the State in Britain and the US*. Basingstoke: Palgrave Macmillan.

Evans, Elizabeth and Prue Chamberlain. 2015. "Critical Waves: Exploring Feminist Identity, Discourse and Praxis in Western Feminism." *Social Movement Studies* Vol. 14, Issue 44: 396–409.

Evans, Elizabeth and Meryl Kenny. 2016. "Working for Women? The Emergence and Impact of the Women's Equality Party" Paper presented at the American Political Science Association's Annual Meeting, Philadelphia, PA 1-4 September.

Ewig, Christina and Myra Marx Ferree. 2013. "Feminist Organizing: What's Old, What's New? History, Trends, and Issues." In *The Oxford Handbook of Gender and Politics*, eds. Georgina Waylen, Karen Celis, Johanna Kantola, and S. Laurel Weldon.

Ezazi, Shahla. 2013. "Tajavoz-e jensi va baz-tolid-e hoviyyat-e mardanegi" ["Rape and the re-construction of masculine identity"] in Feminist School, Aban 27 1394: http://www.feministschool.com/spip.php?article7827

Family, Shirin. 2015. "Campaign taghyir chehre mardaneh Majles, gami boland baraye mosharekat-e siyasi zanan" ["The Campaign to change the male image of Majlis is a long step toward women's political participation]. 18 Bahman, 1394: http://www.feministschool.com/spip.php?article7884

Feminist School 2009. "What do the covergers of Iran's women's movement say?" 23 Tir, 1388: http://www.feministschool.com/spip.php?article2599

Ferber, Marianne and Phyllis Hutton. Raabe. 2003. "Women in the Czech Republic: Feminism, Czech Style." *International Journal of Politics, Culture and Society* 16, no. 3: 407–430.

Fernandes, Leela, Ed. 2014. *Routledge Handbook of Gender in South Asia*. New York: Routledge.

Fernandes, Sujatha. 2007a. "Barrio women and popular politics in Chávez's Venezuela." *Latin American Politics and Society* 49, no. 3: 97–127.

———. 2007b. "The gender agenda of the pink tide in Latin America." Zmag.org, October 7. http://www.zmag.org/content/showarticle.cfm?ItemID=13958.

Fernandez, Bina, and N. B. Gomathy. 2005. "Voicing the invisible: Violence faced by lesbian women in India." In *The violence of normal times: Essays on women's lived realities*, edited by Kalpana Kannabiran, 224–265. New Delhi: Women Unlimited.

Ferragina, Emanuele and Martin Seeleib-Kaiser. 2011. "Thematic Review: Welfare regime debate: past, present, futures?" *Policy & Politics* 39, no. 4: 583–611.

Ferree, Myra Max. 1994. *Controversy & Coalition: The New Feminist Movement Across Three Decades of Change.* 2nd ed. Twayne Publishers: New York.

———. 2000. *Controversy and Coalition: The New Feminist Movement Across Four Decades of Change.* 3rd ed. New York and London: Routledge.

———. 2006. "Globalization and Feminism: Opportunities and Obstacles for Activism in the Global Arena." In *Global Feminism*, edited by Myra Max Ferree and Aili Mari Tripp. New York: New York University Press.

———. 2012. *Varieties of Feminism: German Gender Politics in Global Perspective.* Palo Alto, CA: Stanford University Press.

Ferree, Myra Marx and Beth B. Hess. 1985. *Controversy & Coalition: The New Feminist Movement.* Twayne Publishers: New York.

Ferree, Myra Max, and Aili Marie Tripp, eds. 2006. *Global Feminism: Transnational Women's Activism, Organizing, and Human Rights.* New York: New York University Press.

Ferree, Myra Max, and Patricia Yancey, eds. 1995. *Feminist Organizations: Harvest of the New Women's Movement; Women in the Political Economy.* Philadelphia: Temple University Press.

FIDH, ATFD, et Beity. 2014. Seminaire regional sur les bonnes pratiques de lutte contre les violences faites aux femmes et aux filles, 9 & 10 décembre 2014, à Tunis.

"Finding women's security in the 21st century: A gendered perspective." 2002. Panel presentation and discussion organized by the National Council for Research on Women, New York, February 21.

Fleischmann, Ellen. 2003. *The Nation and Its "New" Women: The Palestinian Women's Movement, 1920–1948.* Berkeley and Los Angeles: University of California Press.

Forbes, Geraldine. 2003. "Reflections on South Asian Women's/Gender History: Past and Future." *Journal of Colonialism and Colonial History* 4, no. 1.

"Foreign funding of NGOs: Donors: Keep Out." 2014. *The Economist*, September 13.

Forouhar, Parastou. 2012. *In the Name of Iran: Darush and Parvaneh Forouhar* (Bekhan be nam-e Iran). Germany: Parastou Forouhar.

Franceschet, Susan. 2003. "'State feminism' and women's movements: The impact of Chile's *servicio nacional de la mujer* on women's activism." *Latin American Research Review* 38, no. 1: 9–40.

Franceschet, Susan. 2010. "Explaining Domestic Violence Policy Outcomes in Chile and Argentina." *Latin American Politics and Society* 52, no. 3: 1–29.

Frankovic, Kathy. 2008. "Age gap may start younger than thought." CBS News, April 25. http://www.cbsnews.com/stories/2008/04/25/opinion/pollpositions/main4045033.shtml?source=search_story.

Fraser, Nancy. 2003. "Rethinking Recognition: Overcoming Displacement and Reification Politics." In *Recognition Struggles and Social Movements: Contested Identities, Agency, and Power*, edited by Barbara Hobson. Cambridge: Cambridge University Press.

———. 2009. "Feminism, Capitalism and the Cunning of History." *New Left Review* 56(March-April): 97–117.

Freeman, Jo. 1973a. "The Origins of the Women's Liberation Movement." *American Journal of Sociology* 78:792–811.

———. 1973b. "The Tyranny of Structurelessness," *Ms. Magazine*, July, pp. 76–78, 86–89.

———. 1975. *The Politics of Women's Liberation.* New York and London: Longman.

————. 1999. "On the Origins of Social Movements." In *Waves of Protest: Social Movements Since the Sixties*, edited by Jo Freeman and Victoria Johnson, 7–24. Lanham, MD: Rowman and Littlefield.

Freidenvall, Lenita. (2015) "In Pursuit of Bodily Integrity in Sweden." In: *European Women's Movements and Body Politics. The Struggle for Autonomy*, edited by by Outshoorn, J., R. Dudova, A. Prata and L. Freidenvall. Basingstoke: Palgrave, 118-152.

Friedman, Elisabeth J. 1995. "Women's Human Rights: The Emergence of a Movement." In *Women's Rights, Human Rights: International Feminist Perspectives*, edited by Julie Peters and Andrea Wolper, 18–35. New York: Routledge.

————. 1998. "Paradoxes of Gendered Political Opportunity in the Venezuelan Transition to Democracy." *Latin American Research Review* 33, no. 3: 87–135.

————. 2000. *Unfinished Transitions: Women and the Gendered Development of Democracy in Venezuela, 1936–1996*. University Park: Pennsylvania State University Press.

Friedman, Elisabeth Jay. 2003. "Gendering the Agenda: The Impact of the Transnational Women's Rights Movement at the UN Conferences of the 1990s." *Women's Studies International Forum* 26, no. 4: 313–31.

————. 2009. "Re(gion)alizing Women's Human Rights in Latin America." *Politics & Gender* 5: 349-375.

————. 2012. "Constructing "The Same Rights with the Same Names": The Impact of Spanish Norm Diffusion on Marriage Equality in Argentina." *Latin American Politics and Society*, 54:4: 29-59

————. 2014. "Feminism Under Construction." *NACLA Report on the Americas* 47, no. 4: 20–25.

Friedman, Elisabeth Jay and Constanza Tabbush. 2015. "Contesting the Transformation." Paper in author's possession.

Friedman, Gil. 1999. *The Palestinian Draft Basic Law: Prospects and potentials*. Jerusalem: Palestinian Independent Commission for Citizen's Rights.

Friedman-Rudovsky, Jean. 2007. "Abortion Under Siege in Latin America." *Time*, August 9. http://www.time.com/time/world/article/0,8599,1651307,00.html.

Fuchs, Gesine. 2013. "Using strategic litigation for women's rights: Political restrictions in Poland and achievements of the women's movement." *European Journal of Women's Studies* 20, no. 1: 21–43.

Fuszara, Malgorzata. 2000. *The New Gender Contract in Poland*. SOCO/IWM Working Papers. Vienna: SOCO/IWM.

————. 2005. "Between Feminism and the Catholic Church: The Women's Movement in Poland." *Czech Sociological Review* 41, no. 6: 1057–1075.

————. 2006. "Udzial Kobiet we wladzy." Warsaw: Kobiety w polityce. http://www.cpk.org.pl/ images/artykuly/attach_82.pdf.

Gabriel Xiquín, Calixta. 2004. "Liderazgo de las Mujeres Mayas en las Leyendas y Mitologías según su Cosmovisión." Manuscript, Guatemala City.

Gaidzanwa, R. 1992. *The Ideology of Domesticity and the Struggles of Women Workers: The Case of Zimbabwe*. Zimbabwe: Institute of Social Studies.

Gaitskell, D. 1988. "Race, gender and imperialism. A century of black girls' education in South Africa." Unpublished seminar paper presented at African Studies, University of Witwatersrand.

Gallup Polling. 2008. March 26. http://www.gallup.com/poll/105691/McCain-vs-Obama -28-Clinton -Backers-McCain.aspx.

Gao, Xiaoxian. 2000. "Minjian funu zuzhi de minzhuhua jianshe" [Democratic construction of women's popular organizations]. *China Women's News*. http://www.westwomen.org/jigou/ 2007/1024/article_57.html.

———. 2001a. "Strategies and space: A case study of the Shaanxi Association for Women and Family." In *Chinese women organizing cadres, feminists, Muslims, queers*, edited by Ping-Chun Hsiung, Maria Jaschok, and Cecilia Milwertz, 193–208. Oxford: Berg.

———. 2001b. "Zhongguo minjian funu zuzhi de kongjian he celue" [Space and strategies for Chinese popular women's organizations]. In *Shen lin "qi" jing* [In "wonder" land], edited by Li Xiaojiang et al., 215–236. Nanjing: Jiangsu People's Press.

———. 2009a. "Cong heyang moushi dao shaanxi moushi: Tuidong nongcun funu canxuan canzheng de shijian yu sikao: Jianlun dangdai zhongfuo funu yundong de celue yu tedian" [From Heyang Model to Shaanxi Model: Practices and reflection on advancing rural women's participation in election and governance]. Paper presented at the First International Conference on Gender Studies in China, Shanghai, June 26–29.

———. 2009b. *Shiwu nian, women zou dao le nali.* [Where are we after 15 years].

Gao Xiaoxian, Jiang Po, and Wang Guohong. 2002. "Tudong Shehui Xingbei yu fazhan bentuhua de nuli" [Efforts in promoting indigenization of gender and development in China]. In *Shehui Xingbei yu fazhan zai zhongguo: Huigu yu zhanwang* [Gender and development in China: Looking back and forward], 1–20. Xian: Shaanxi People's Publishing House.

Garza, Alicia. 2014. "A Herstory Of The #Blacklivesmatter Movement By Alicia Garza—The Feminist Wire." *The Feminist Wire*.

Garza, Ana María, and Sonia Toledo. 2004. "Mujeres, agrarismo y militancia: Chiapas en la década de los ochenta." In *Tejiendo historias: Tierra, género y poder en Chiapas*, edited by Maya Lorena Pérez Ruíz. Mexico City: CONACULTA-INAH.

Garza Caligaris, Anna María. 2002. *Género, interlegalidad y conflicto en San Pedro Chenalhó.* Mexico City: PROIMMSE, UNAM / IEI, UNACH.

Geiger, Susan. 1997. *TANU Women: Gender and Culture in the Making of Tanganyikan Nationalism, 1955–1965.* Portsmouth NH: Heinemann.

Geisler, Gisela. 1995. "Troubled Sisterhood: Women and Politics in Southern Africa." *African Affairs* 94: 545–78.

Gentleman, Amelia. 2015. "Breaking the Taboo: The Moscow Women Taking a Stand against Domestic Violence." *The Guardian*, June 10.

Gerasimova, Elena. 2010. "Zhenshchiny v Trudovykh Otnosheniiakh v Rossii." In *Zhenskoe Dvizhenie v Rossii: Vchera, Segodnia, Zavtra: Materialy Konferentsii*, edited by Galina Mikhaleva, 15–18. Moscow, Russia: RODP "Yabloko" and KMK Publishers.

Gerlach, Luther. 1999. "The structure of social movements: Environmental activism and its opponents." In *Waves of protest: Social movements since the sixties*, edited by Jo Freeman and Victoria Johnson. Lanham, MD: Rowman and Littlefield.

Gerstel, Naomi and Katherine McGonagle. 2006. "Job Leaves and the Limits of the Family and Medical Leave Act: The Effects of Gender, Race, and Family." In *Workplace/Women's Place: An Anthology*, edited by Paula J. Dubeck and Dana Dunn, 340–350. Los Angeles: Roxbury Press.

Gessen, Masha. 1994. *The Rights of Lesbians and Gay Men in the Russian Federation: An International Gay and Lesbian Human Rights Commission Report.* International Gay & Lesbian Human Rights Commission.

Ghanem-Yazbek, Dalia. 2015. "Algeria's Islamist Revival." Beirut: Carnegie Middle East Center. Available at http://carnegie-mec.org/2015/06/26/social-and-cultural-re-islamization-or-trivialization-of-islamism-is-clear/ib67.

Ghazi, Fereshteh. 2016. "Recordha-ye Tazeh Majles Iran: Kamtarin rowhani, bishtarin zan" [New Majlis records: the least clerics and the most women], BBC Persian, May 1: http://www.bbc.com/persian/iran/2016/05/160501_l10_fgh_majlis_clerics_women

Ghodsee, Kristen. 2004. "Feminism-by-Design: Emerging Capitalism, Cultural Feminism, and Women's Nongovernmental Organisations in Post-socialist Eastern Europe." *Signs: Journal of Women in Culture and Society* 29, no. 3: 727–753.

———. 2005. *The Red Riviera. Gender, Tourism, and Postsocialism on the Black Sea.* Durham/London, Duke University Press.

———. 2010. *Muslim Lives in Eastern Europe. Gender, Ethnicity and the Transformation of Islam in Post-socialist Bulgaria.* Princeton/Oxford, Princeton University Press.

———. 2012. "Rethinking State Socialist Mass Women's Organizations: The Committee of the Bulgarian Women's Movement and the United Nations Decade for Women, 1975–1985." *Journal of Women's History* 24, no. 4: 49–73.

Ghorashi, Haleh. 2007. "Iranian women's voices across borders." In *Women, feminism, and fundamentalism,* edited by Ireen Dubel and Karen Vintges, 82–95. Amsterdam: Humanistics University Press.

Ghribi, Asma. 2014. "Tunisian presidential candidate Kennou takes on the patriarchy." http://transitions/foreignpolicy.com/posts/2014/10/10/.

Gilmartin, Christina K. 1995. *Engendering the Chinese Revolution: Radical Women, Communist Politics, and Mass Movements in the 1920s.* Berkeley: University of California Press.

Ginwala, F. 1990. "Women and the African National Congress 1912–1943." In *Agenda* 6 (8).

Global Network of Women Peacebuilders. 2012. *Women Count: Security Council Resolution 1325: Civil Society Monitoring Report 2012.*

Goetz, Anne Marie, ed. 1997. *Getting Institutions Right for Women in Development.* London: Zed Books.

———. 2003. "Women's political effectiveness: A conceptual framework." In *No Shortcuts to Power: African Women in Politics and Policy Making,* edited by Anne Marie Goetz and Shireen Haseem. London: Zed Books.

Gokhale, Sandhya. 2015. "FAOW Mumbai." In *Seminar Report, Resisting Caste and Patriarchy: Building Alliances,* organized by Women Against Sexual Violence and State Repression (WSS), December 10–11, New Delhi. https://wssnet.files.word press.com/2016/04/wss-seminar-resisting-caste-and-patriarchy-10-11th-dec-2015 -final-report.pdf.

Golley, Nawar Al-Hassan, and Pernille Arenfelt, eds. 2011. *Mapping Arab Women's Movements: A Century of Transformations from Within.* American University in Cairo Press.

Gomes, Márcia, Tavares, Márcia and Sardenberg, Cecilia, 2010. *A Aplicação da Lei Maria da Penha em Foco.* Salvador, Bahia : NEIM/UFBA, v.01.

Gondolf, Edward W. and Dmitri Shestakov. 1997. "Spousal homicide in Russia versus the United States: Preliminary findings and implications." *Journal of Family Violence,* 12(1), 63-74.

Goñi, Uki. 2015. "Argentine Women Call Out Machismo," *New York Times,* June 15.

Gouws, A. 2014. "Recognition and Redistribution: State of the South African Women's Movement 20 Years After Democratic Transition." *Agenda* 100 (28).

Govender, Pregs. 2007. *Love and Courage: A Story of Insubordination.* Johannesburg: Jacana.

Government of India. 1974. *Towards equality*. New Delhi: Government of India.

Government of the Russian Federation. 2016. "Federal Law from 03.07.2016 No. 323-F3 'On the introduction of amendments to the Criminal Code of the Russian Federation and Criminal Procedural Code of the Russian Federation on questions of improving the grounds and order of exemption from criminal responsibility'" ['O vnesenii izmenenii v Ugolovnyi kodeks Rossiiskoi Federatsii i Ugolovno-protsessual'nyi kodeks Rossiiskoi Federatsii po voprosam soverwhenstvovaniia osnovanii i poriadka osvobozhdeniia ot ugolovnoi otvetstvennosti']. http://publication.pravo.gov.ru/Document/View/0001201607040116?index=3&rangeSize=1.

Gqola, P. 2015. *Rape: A South African Nightmare*. Johannesburg: Jacana

Graff, Agnieszka. 1999. "Patriarchat po seksmisji." *Gazeta Wyborcza*, June 19–20.

———. 2003. "Lost between the Waves? The Paradoxes of Feminist Chronology and Activism in Contemporary Poland." *Journal of International Women's Studies* 4, no. 2: 100–116.

Grupo de Mujeres Mayas Kaqla. 2000. *Algunos colores del arco iris: Realidad de las mujeres Mayas*. Discussion paper. Guatemala City: La Palabra y el Sentir de las Mujeres Mayas de Kaqla.

Guenther, Katja. M. 2010. *Making Their Place: Feminism after Socialism in East Germany*. Stanford: Stanford University Press.

Guha, Ranajit. 1983. *Elementary Aspects of Peasant Insurgency In Colonial India*. Delhi: Oxford University Press.

Guzmán, Virginia. 2001. *La institucionalidad de género en el estado: Nuevas perspectivas de análisis*. Santiago de Chile: CEPAL, Unidad Mujer y Desarrollo. http://repositorio.cepal.org/bitstream/handle/11362/5878/S01030269_es.pdf?sequence=1 (accessed November 12, 2015).

de Haan, Francisca. 2010. "Continuing Cold War Paradigms in Western Historiography of Transnational Women's Organisations: The Case of the Women's International Democratic Federation (WIDF)," *Women's History Review* Vol. 19, No. 4, September, pp. 547–573.

Haas, Leisl. 2007. "The rules of the game: Feminist policymaking in Chile." *Política* 46: 199–225.

Hahner, June Edith. 1990. *Emancipating the Female Sex: The Struggle for Women's Rights in Brazil, 1850–1940*. Durham: Duke University Press.

Halsaa, Beatrice. 2016. "Changes and challenges: Norwegian feminisms." Labrys, etudes feminists, janvier/juillet 2016 http://www.labrys.net.br/labrys29/sumarios/mundo.htm

Hanafi, Sari, and Linda Tabar. 2002. "NGOs, elite formation, and the second intifada." *Between the Lines* (Jerusalem) 2, no. 18 (October): 31–37. http://www.between-lines.org.

Harcourt, Wendy. 2011. "Care Economies, Collective Well-Being in Contemporary European Feminist Organizing." In *Transforming Gendered Well-Being in Europe: The Impact of Social Movements*. Edited by Alison E. Woodward, Jean-Michel Bonvin and Merce Renom, 249–264. Farnham: Ashgate.

Haroun, Amira. 2009. "The Palestinian Women's Bill of Rights," workshop, Gaza on May 6. http://www.mowa.gov.ps/news_details.php?id=10.

Haroun, Amira, and Youssra Salah [Women's Action Department, Islamic Khalas Party]. 2000. Interview with Islah Jad, Gaza, October 1–2.

Harris, Duchess. 2011. *Black Feminist Politics from Kennedy to Obama*. New York: Palgrave MacMillan.

Harriss-White, Barbara. 1999. "Gender cleansing: The paradox of development and deteriorating female life chances in Tamil Nadu." In *Signposts: Gender Issues in Post-Independence India*, edited by Rajeswari Sunder Rajan, 124–153. New Delhi: Kali for Women.

Hartmann, Susan M. 1999. *The Other Feminists: Activists in the Liberal Establishment.* New Haven and London: Yale University Press.

Hashemi, Nader and Danny Postel (eds.). 2011. *People Reloaded: The Green Movement and the Struggle for Iran's Future.* New York: Melville House.

Hašková, Hana. 2005. "Czech Women's Organising under the State Socialist Regime, Socio-Economic Transformation and the EU Accession Period." *Czech Sociological Review* 41, no. (6): 1077–1110.

Hašková, Hana. and Alena Križková. 2008. "The impact of EU Accession on the Promotion of Women and Gender Equality in the Czech Republic." In *Gender Politics in the Expanding European Union. Mobilization, Inclusion , Exclusion.* Edited by Silke Roth, 155–173. Oxford/New York: Berghahn Books.

Hassim, Shireen. 2003. "The Gender Pact and Democratic Consolidation: Institutionalising Gender Equality in the South African State." *Feminist Studies* 29: 3.

———. 2005. "Terms of Engagement: South African Challenges." *Feminist Africa* 5.

———. 2006. *Women's Organizations and Democracy in South Africa: Contesting Authority.* Madison: Wisconsin University Press.

———. 2010. "Perverse consequences? The impact of quotas for women on democratization in Africa" in Shapiro, I., Stokes, S.C., Wood, E.J., and Kirshner, A.S. (eds.) *Political Representation*: Cambridge University Press.

———. 2014. *ANC Women's League: Sex, Politics, and Gender.* Johannesburg: Jacana Media.

Hatem, Mervat. 1992. "Economic and Political Liberation [sic; Liberalization] in Egypt and the Demise of State Feminism." *International Journal of Middle East Studies*, vol. 24, no. 2 (May): 231-51

———. 1994. "Privatization and the Demise of State Feminism in Egypt 1977-1990." In Pamela Sparr (ed.), *Mortgaging Women's Lives: Feminist Critiques of Structural Adjustment.* London: Zed Books.

Haussman, Melissa, and Birgit Sauer, eds. 2007. *Gendering the State in the Age of Globalization: Women's Movements and State Feminism in Postindustrial Democracies.* Lanham, MD: Rowman and Littlefield.

Hautzinger, Sarah J. 2007. *Violence in the City of Women: Police and Batterers in Bahia, Brazil.* Berkeley and Los Angeles: University of California Press.

Hawthorne, Susan, and Bronwyn Winter, eds. 2003. *September 11, 2001: Global feminist perspectives.* Vancouver: Raincoast Books.

Hays, Sharon. 2003. *Flat Broke with Children: Women in the Age of Welfare Reform.* New York: Oxford University Press.

Heath, Melanie. 2012. *One Marriage Under God: The Campaign to Promote Marriage in America.* New York: New York University Press.

Helferrich, Barbara and Felix Kolb. 2001. "Multilevel Action Coordination in European Contentious Politics: The Case of the European Women's Lobby." In *Contentious Europeans: Protest and Politics in an Emerging Policy,* edited by Doug Imig and Sidney Tarrow, 143–161. Lanham, MD: Rowman and Littlefield.

Henderson, Sarah. 1998. "Importing civil society: Western funding and the women's movement in Russia." Paper presented at the annual meeting of the American Political Science Association, Boston.

————. 2003. *Building Democracy in Contemporary Russia: Western Support for Grassroots Organizations*. Ithaca: Cornell University Press.

————. 2008. "Shaping civic advocacy: International and domestic policies towards Russia's NGO sector." Paper presented at the conference of the Canadian Political Science Association, Vancouver, BC.

Hernández, Daisy, and Bushra Rehman, eds. 2002. *Colonize This! Young Women of Color on Today's Feminism*. New York: Seal Press.

Hernández Castillo, Rosalva Aída. 1994. "Reinventing tradition: The women's law." *Akwe:Kon: A Journal of Indigenous Issues* 2, no. 2: 67–70.

————. 1996. "From the community to the women's state convention." In *The Explosion of Communities in Chiapas*, edited by June Nash, 20–52. Copenhagen: International Working Group for Indigenous Affairs (IWGIA).

————. 2002. "Indigenous law and identity politics in México: Indigenous men's and women's perspective for a multicultural nation." *Political and Legal Anthropology Review* 25, no. 1: 90–110.

————. 2006a. "Between feminist ethnocentricity and ethnic essentialism: The Zapatistas' demands and the national indigenous women's movement." In *Dissident Women: Gender and Cultural Politics in Chiapas*, edited by Shannon Speed, R. Aída Hernández Castillo, and Lynn Stephen, 57–75. Austin: University of Texas Press.

————. 2006b. "Fratricidal war or ethnocidal strategy? Women's experience with political violence in Chiapas." In *Engaged Observer: Anthropology, Advocacy, and Activism*, edited by Victoria Sanford and Asale Angel-Ajani, 149–170. New Brunswick: Rutgers University Press.

————. 2007. "State and gender violence: Backlashes on women's human rights in Mexico." Fray Bartolomé de las Casas Lecture, Latin American Studies Center, University of Oregon, April.

————. 2008. *Etnografías e historias de resistencia: Mujeres indígenas, procesos organizativos y nuevas identidades políticas*. Mexico City: Publicaciones de la Casa Chata CIESAS/PUEG-UNAM.

Heymann, Jody. 2006. *Forgotten Families*. New York: Oxford University Press.

Hilal, Jamil. 1999. *Al-mojtam' al-falastini wa iskaleyat al-dimocrateya* [Palestinian society and democracy problems]. Nablus: Center for Palestine Research and Studies.

Hilal, Jamil, and Mushtaq H. Khan. 2004. "State-society relationships, rent-seeking, and the nature of the PNA quasi-state." In *State Formation in Palestine*, edited by Mushtaq Khan, George Giacaman, and Inge Amundsen. London: Routledge.

Hilhorst, Dorothea. 2003. *The Real World of NGOs: Discourses, Diversity, and Development*. London: Zed Books.

Hirschkind, Charles, and Saba Mahmood. 2002. "Feminism, the Taliban, and politics of counter-insurgency." *Anthropological Quarterly* 75, no. 2 (Spring): 339–354.

"History of VAWA | Legal Momentum." 2016. *Legalmomentum.Org*.

Hobson, Barbara. 2003. "Recognition struggles in universalistic and gender distinctive frames: Sweden and Ireland." In *Recognition Struggles and Social Movements: Contested Identities, Agency and Power*. Ed. Barbara Hobson, 64–92. New York: Cambridge University Press.

Hochschild, Arlie with Anne Machung. 1989. *The Second Shift: Working Families and the Revolution at Home*. New York: Random House.

————. 2001. *The Time Bind: When Work Becomes Home and Home Becomes Work*. New York: Metropolitan Press.

Hofmeyr, I, S. Marks and S. Trapido. 1987. *The Politics of Race, Class and Nationalism in 20th Century South Africa*. London: Longman.

Hole, Judith, and Ellen Levine. 1971. *Rebirth of Feminism*. New York: Quadrangle Books.

hooks, bell. 1984. *Feminist Theory: From the Margins to the Center*. Boston: South End Press.

Holland, Dorothy, Gretchen Fox, and Vinci Daro. 2008. "Social movements and collective identity: A decentered, dialogic view." In "Meaning-making in social movements," special issue, *Anthropological Quarterly* 81, no. 1 (Winter): 95–126.

Holmgren, Beth. 1995. "Bug inspectors and beauty queens: The problems of translating feminism into Russian." In *Postcommunism and the Body Politic*, edited by Ellen E. Berry. New York: New York University Press.

Honderich, Ted. 1989. *Violence for Equality: Inquiries in Political Philosophy*. London and New York: Routledge.

Hoodfar, Homa. 1999. "The women's movement in Iran." *WLUML* (Winter).

Howell, Jude. 1997. "Post-Beijing reflections: Creating ripples but not waves in China." *Women Studies International Forum*, 20, no. 2: 235–252.

Hroub, Khalid. 2000. *Hamas Political Thought and Practices*. Beirut: Institute of Palestine Studies.

———. 1996. "Obstacles to Democratisation in the Middle East." *Contention* 14: 81–106.

Hrycak, Alexandra. 2011. "FEMEN-Ism: FEMEN and the Ukrainian Women's Movement." *Ukraine Analysis* 3, no. 4: 1–4.

Hsiung, Ping-chun, and Yuk-lin Renita Wong. 1998. "*Jie Gui*—connecting the tracks: Chinese women's activism surrounding the 1995 World Conference on Women in Beijing." *Gender and History* 10, no. 3: 470–497.

Htun, Mala. 2003. *Sex and the State: Abortion, Divorce, and the Family under Latin American Dictatorships and Democracies*. Cambridge: Cambridge University Press.

al-Huda Association. 1998. *Al-mara' al-falestenyya wa mo'amrat al-'al-a'maneyyat* [Palestinian woman and the plot of secular women]. al-Bireh: al-Huda Association.

Huffington Post. 2012. "South Africa Lesbian Zoliswa Nkonyana's Killers Sentenced." February 1. http://www.huffingtonpost.com/2012/02/01/south-africa-zoliswa-nkonyana-lesbian-killed-sentencing_n_1247320.html.

Hughes, Melanie M., Mona Lena Krook, and Pamela Paxton. 2015. "Transnational Women's Activism and the Global Diffusion of Gender Quotas." *Transnational Politics* Issue 2 Volume 59, May 27.

Hull, Gloria T., Patricia Bell Scott, and Barbara Smith, eds. 1982. *All The Women Are White, All the Blacks Are Men, But of us Are Brave: Black Women's Studies*. New York: Feminist Press.

Human Rights Watch. 1997. *Russia—too little, too late: State response to violence against women*. New York: Human Rights Watch.

Hunt, Nancy. 1989. "Placing African Women's History and Locating Gender," *Journal of Social History* 14, no. 3 (October).

Hunter, Marcus Anthony. 2013. "Race and the Same Sex Marriage Divide," *Contexts* (Summer) 12, no. 3 (74–76).

Hunter, Wendy, and Timothy Power. 2007. "Rewarding Lula: Executive power, social policy, and the Brazilian elections of 2006." *Latin American Politics and Society* 49, no. 1: 1–30.

Hussein, Khadija. 2010. "Rereading the Palestinian Women's Bill of Rights," Women's Affairs Committee: 17–18. Ramallah. Unpublished report.

IBGE. 2003. *Síntese de indicadores sociais.* Rio de Janeiro: IBGE (Instituto Brasileiro de Geografia e Estatística).

Ibrahim, Sa'd Eddin, ed. 1993. *Al-mujtama' al-madani wal tahawol al-dimoqrati fil watan al-'arabi* [Civil society and democratic transformation in the Arab world]. Annual report. Cairo: Markaz Ibn Khaldoun.

———. 1995. "Civil society and prospects of democratisation in the Arab world." In *Civil Society in the Middle East,* edited by Augustus R. Norton. Vol. 1. Leiden: E. J. Brill.

Ifeka-Moller, Caroline. 1973. "'Sitting on a Man: Colonialism and the Lost Political Institutions of Ibo Women': A Reply to Judith Van Allen." *Canadian Journal of African Studies* VII (1973): 317–18.

INAMUJER. 2008. "Puntos de Encuentro con INAMUJER." August 1. http://www .inamujer .gob.ve/index.php?option=com_content&task=view&id=21&Itemid=44.

Independent Task Force. 1999. *Strengthening Palestinian public institutions: Council on Foreign Relations.* Prepared by Yazid Sayiegh and Khalil Shaqaqi, June 28. http:// www.cfr.org.

"India's Badaun: Police investigate 'rape of two girls'." 2015. *BBC News,* April 2. http:// www.bbc.com/news/world-asia-india-32157223

Indian Feminism. 2016. "As Mumbai feminist group Majlis turns 25, co-founder resigns with a scathing open letter," *Scroll,* March 25. http://scroll.in/article/805688 /as-mumbai-feminist-group-majlis-turns-25-co-founder-resigns-with-a-scathing -open-letter.

International Campaign for Human Rights in Iran. 2015. "Narges Mohammadi Should Be Released Immediately and Given Medical Treatment": https://www.iranhuman rights.org/2015/10/narges-mohammadi-8/

International Center for Not-for-Profit Law. 2015. "Russia—NGO Law Monitor—Research Center."

International Initiative for Justice. 2003. *Threatened existence: A feminist analysis of the genocide in Gujarat.* Mumbai: International Initiative for Justice.

Inter-Parliamentary Union. 2008a. "Women in national parliaments." April 7. http:// www.ipu.org/wmn-e/classif-arc.htm.

———. 2008b. "Women in national parliaments, situation as of 25 January 1998." April 7. http://www.ipu.org/wmn-e/arc/world250198.htm.

———. 2015. "Women in Parliaments: World Classification." September 1. http:// www.ipu.org/wmn-e/classif.htm.

Islamic Resistance Movement. 1996. *The practices of the self-rule authority against the Palestinian civil society.* May 20. Document distributed by Hamas.

Jackson, Cecile, and Ruth Pearson, eds. 1998. *Feminist visions of development: Gender analysis and policy.* London: Routledge.

Jad, Islah. 1990. "From Salons to the Popular Committees: Palestinian Women, 1919– 1989." In *Intifada: Palestine at the Crossroads,* edited by Jamal R. Nassar and Roger Heacock. New York: Praeger.

———. 2000. *Palestinian Women: A Status Report—Women and Politics.* Palestine: Birzeit University, Women's Studies Institute.

———. 2004. "The 'NGOisation' of the Arab Women's Movement." In *Repositioning Feminisms in Development,* edited by Andrea Cornwall, Elizabeth Harrison, and Ann Whitehead. Sussex: Sussex University Press; *IDS Bulletin* 35, no. 4 (October).

———. 2005. "Islamist Women of Hamas: A New Women's Movement?" In *On Shifting Ground: Muslim Women in a Global Era,* edited by Fereshteh Nouraie-Simone. New York: Feminist Press.

Jad, Islah, et al. 2003. "Qiraah nassaweyya lemosswadat al dosstor al-falastini" [A feminist reading for the draft of the Palestinian Constitution]. *Review of Women's Studies* (Birzeit University) 1, no. 1: 8–12.

Jad, Islah, Penny Johnson, and Rita Giacaman. 2000. "Gender and Citizenship under the Palestinian Authority." In *Gender and Citizenship in the Middle East,* edited by Suad Joseph. Syracuse: Syracuse University Press.

Jahanbegloo, Ramin. 2011. Preface to *People Reloaded: The Green Movement and the Struggle for Iran's Future,* edited by Hashemi, Nader and Danny Postel. New York: Melville House.

Jahangir, Asma, and Hina Jilani. 1990. *A Divine Sanction? The Hudood Ordinance.* Lahore: Sang-e-Meel Publications.

James, Joy, and T. Denean Sharpley-Whiting, eds. 2000. *The Black Feminist Reader.* Malden, MA: Blackwell.

Jäppinen, Maija. 2008. "Tensions between familialism and feminism: A case study of a crisis centre for women in Udmurtia." Paper presented at the annual meeting of the American Association for the Advancement of Slavic Studies, Philadelphia, November.

Jaquette, Jane S., ed. 1991. *The Women's Movement in Latin America: Feminism and the Transition to Democracy.* Boulder: Westview Press.

Jaquette, Jane S., and Sharon L. Wolchik, eds. 1998. *Women and Democracy: Latin America and Central and Eastern Europe.* Baltimore: Johns Hopkins University Press.

Javaheri, Jelveh. 2015. "Ejazeh hamsar, rouy-e digar-e sekkeh esteqlal zanan" [Husband's Permission, the other side of the coin of women's independence], *Khoshounat Bas,* Azar 1394, Tehran, Iran: http://basast.org

Javornik, Jana. 2014. "Measuring state de-familialism: Contesting post-socialist exceptionalism." *Journal of European Social Policy* 24, no. 3: 240–257.

Jeffery, Patricia, and Amrita Basu, eds. 1998. *Appropriating Gender: Women's Activism and Politicized Religion in South Asia.* New York: Routledge; New Delhi: Kali for Women.

Jeffreys, Sheila. 2002. "Trafficking in women versus prostitution: A false distinction." Keynote address, Townsville International Women's Conference, James Cook University, Australia, July 3–7.

Jenson, Jane and Celia Valiente. 2003. "Comparing Two Movements for Gender Parity: France and Spain." In *Women's Movements Facing the Reconfigured State.* Ed. L. A. Banaszak, K. Beckwith and D. Rucht, 69–93. Cambridge: Cambridge University Press.

Jewkes, Rachel, et al. 2009. *Understanding Men's Health and Use of Violence: Interface of Rape and HIV in South Africa.* Medical Research Council Technical Report, Medical Research Council, Pretoria.

Jiang, Yongping. 2007. "Shehui xingbie yu gonggong zhengce yanjiu zongshu" [Overview on gender and public policy]. In *Zhongguo Funu Yanjiu Nianjian (2001–2005),* edited by Quanguo Fulian Funu Yanjiusuo, 59–68. Beijing: Shehui Kexue Wenxian Chubanshe.

Jiang, Yongping, and Tang Binyao. 2007. "Funu yu jingji yanjiu zongshu" [Overview on women and economic research]. In *Zhongguo Funu Yanjiu Nianjian (2001–2005),* edited by Quanguo Fulian Funu Yanjiusuo, 98–108. Beijing: Shehui Kexue Wenxian Chubanshe.

JMCC [Jerusalem Media and Communication Center, Palestine]. 2000a. *Palestine: Report* (February 23).

———. 2000b. *Report* (May 24).

———. 2000c. *Report* (June 14).

John, Mary E., ed. 2008. *Women's Studies: A Reader.* New Delhi: Penguin Books India.

Johnson, Janet Elise. 2007. "Contesting violence, contesting gender: Crisis centers encountering local government in Barnaul, Russia." In *Living Gender After Communism,* edited by Janet Elise Johnson and Jean C. Robinson, 40–59. Bloomington: Indiana University Press.

———. 2008. "The plight of women's crisis centers in Putin's Russia." Paper prepared at the annual meeting of the American Association for the Advancement of Slavic Studies, Philadelphia, November.

———. 2009. *Gender Violence in Russia: The Politics of Feminist Intervention.* Bloomington: Indiana University Press.

Johnson, Janet Elise, and Jean C. Robinson. 2007. "Living gender." In *Living Gender After Communism,* edited by Janet Elise Johnson and Jean C. Robinson, 1–21. Bloomington: Indiana University Press.

Johnson, Matthew D. 2014. "Government-Supported Healthy Marriage Initiatives Are Not Associated with Changes in Family Demographics: A Comment on Hawkins, Amato, and Kinghorn (2013)," in *Family Relations* 63, (April): 300–304.

Joseph, Suad (ed.). 2000. *Gender and Citizenship in the Middle East.* Syracuse, NY: Syracuse University Press.

Judge, M. 2012. "The Culture of the Chiefs Is a Setback for Gender and Sexual Rights." Unpublished paper.

Jurna, Irina. 1995. "Women in Russia: Building a movement." In *From Basic Needs To Basic Rights: Women's Claim To Human Rights,* edited by Margaret Schuler. Washington, DC: Women Law and Development International.

Justice Verma Committee Report. 2013. January. http://www.prsindia.org/parliament track/report-summaries/justice-verma-committee-report-summary-2628/.

Kabeer, Naila. 1998. *Realidades trastocadas: Las jerarquías de género en el pensamiento de desarrollo.* Mexico City: Ed. Paidos-PUEG-UNAM.

Kakucs, N. and A. Petö (2008) The Impact of EU Accession on Gender Equality in Hungary. In: *Gender Politics in the Expanding European Union. Mobilization, Inclusion, Exclusion.* Ed. by Silke Roth. Oxford/New York, Berghahn Books: 155-173.

Kampwirth, Karen. 2008. "Neither left nor right: Sandinismo in the anti-feminist era." *NACLA Report on the Americas* 41, no. 1: 30–43.

Kampwirth, Karen, and Victória Gonzalez. 2001. Introduction to *Radical Women in Latin America: Left and right,* edited by Karen Kampwirth and Victória Gonzalez, 1–28. University Park: Pennsylvania State University Press.

Kandil, Amani. 1995. *Civil Society in the Arab World.* Washington, DC: Civicus.

Kannabiran, Kalpana. 2005. Introduction to *The Violence of Normal Times: Essays on Women's Lived Realities,* edited by Kalpana Kannabiran. New Delhi: Women Unlimited.

———. 2006. "A cartography of resistance: The national federation of *dalit* women." In *The Situated Politics of Belonging,* edited by Nira Yuval Davis, Kalpana Kannabiran, and Ulrike Vieten. London: Sage.

———. 2008a. "Sexual assault and the law." In *Challenging the Rule(s) of Law: Colonialism, Criminology, and Human Rights in India,* edited by Kalpana Kannabiran and Ranbir Singh. New Delhi: Sage.

———. 2008b. "Violence and women's lifeworlds." *Journal of the National Human Rights Commission* (December 10).

Kannabiran, Kalpana, and Ekta. 2006. "Article 7: political and public life." In *Second and Third Alternative Report on CEDAW*, 53–60. Delhi: National Alliance of Women.

Kannabiran, Kalpana, and Vasanth Kannabiran. 1997. "Looking at ourselves: The women's movement in Hyderabad." In *Feminist Genealogies, Colonial Legacies, Democratic Futures*, edited by M. Jacqui Alexander and Chandra Talpade Mohanty. New York and London: Routledge.

Kannabiran, Kalpana, and Ritu Menon, eds. 2007. *From Mathura to Manorama: Resisting Violence Against Women in India*. New Delhi: Women Unlimited and International Centre for Ethnic Studies.

Kannabiran, Vasanth, Volga, and Kalpana Kannabiran. 2004. "Women's rights and Naxalite groups." *Economic and Political Weekly*, November 6, 4874–4877.

Kanogo, Tabitha. 1987. "Kikuyu Women and the Politics of Protest: Mau Mau." In *Images of Women in Peace and War: Cross-Cultural and Historical Perspectives*, edited by Sharon Macdonald, Pat Holdern and Shirley Ardener, 78–99. Madison: University of Wisconsin Press.

Kantola, J. and J. Squires. 2012. "From state feminism to market feminism?" *International Political Science Review* 33, no. 4: 382–400.

Kapusta-Pofahl, K. 2002. "'Who would create a Czech feminism?': challenging assumptions in the process of creating relevant feminisms in the Czech Republic." *Anthropology of East Europe Review* 20, no. 2: 61–68.

Kapusta-Pofahl, K., H. Hašková and M. Kolářová. 2005. "'Only a Dead Fish Flows with the Stream': NGO Formalization, Anarchofeminism, and the Power of Informal Associations." *Anthropology of East Europe Review* 23, no. 1: 38–52.

Kar, Mehrangiz. 2001. "Women's strategies in Iran from the 1979 revolution to 1999." In *Globalization, Religion, and Gender: The Politics of Women's Rights in Catholic and Muslim Contexts*, edited by Jane Bayes and Nayereh Tohidi, 177–202. New York: Palgrave.

———. 2008. "Discrimination against women under Iranian law." *Gozar* (Freedom House). December 8.

Kar, Mehrangiz, and Shahla Lahidji. 1372/1993. *Shenakht-e hovviyat-e zan-e irani dar gostareh-ye pish-tarikh va tarikh*. Tehran: Roshangaran.

———. 1999. *Mavane' Hoquqi Towse' siyasi dar Iran* [Legal Obstacles to Political Development in Iran]. Tehran: Qatreh Publications.

———. 1378/1999. *Sakhtar Hoquqi Nezam Khanevadeh dar Iran* [Legal Structure of Family System in Iran]. Tehran: Roshangaran Publications.

Karam, Azza M. 1998. *Women, Islamisms, and the State: Contemporary Feminisms in Egypt?* London: Macmillan.

KARAT (2016) Latest News. http://www.karat.org/.

Karshenas, Massoud, Valentine M. Moghadam and Nadereh Chamlou. 2016. "Women, Work and Welfare in the Middle East and North Africa: Introduction and Overview." In *Women, Work, and Welfare in the Middle East and North Africa*, eds., Nadereh Chamlou and Massoud Karshenas, 1–30. London: Imperial College Press.

Katzenstein, Mary Fainsod. 1990. "Feminism within American Institutions: Unobtrusive Mobilization in the 1980s." *Signs* 16, no. 1: 27–54.

———. 1998. *Faithful and Fearless: Moving Feminist Protest Inside the Church and the Military*. Princeton: Princeton University Press.

———. 2003. "Redividing citizens—Divided Feminisms: The Reconfigured U.S. State and Women's Citizenship." In *Women's Movements Facing the Reconfigured State*, edited by Lee Ann Banaszak, Karen Beckwith, and Dieter Rucht, 203–218. Cambridge and New York: Cambridge University Press.

Katzenstein, Mary Fainsod, and Carol McClurg Mueller. 1987. *The Women's Movements of The United States And Western Europe: Consciousness, Political Opportunity, and Public Policy*. Philadelphia: Temple University Press.

Kay, Rebecca. 2004. "Meeting the challenge together? Russian grassroots women's organizations and the shortcomings of Western aid." In *Post-Soviet Women Encountering Transition*, edited by Kathleen Kuehnast and Carol Nechemias, 241–261. Washington, DC: Woodrow Wilson Center Press.

Kayed, Aziz. 1999. *Takrir hawl tadakhol al-salaheyyat fi mo'assat al-solta al-wataneyya al-falastineyya* [A report on the overlapping of authority in the Palestinian National Authority]. Ramallah: Palestinian Independent Commission for Citizen's Rights.

Keck, Margaret E., and Kathryn Sikkink, eds. 1998. *Activists Beyond Borders: Advocacy Networks in International Politics*. Ithaca: Cornell University Press.

Keddie, Nikki. 2003. *Modern Iran: Roots and Results of Revolution*. New Haven: Yale University Press.

Kemp, A., et al. 1995. "The Dawning of a New Day: New South African Feminisms." In *The Challenge of Local Feminisms*, edited by Amrita Basu. Boulder: Westview Press.

Kennedy-Macfoy, M. 2012. "Remaking Citizenship from the Margins: Migrant and Minoritized Women's Organisatins in Europe." In *Remaking Citizenship in Multicultural Europe*. Ed. S. Roseneil, B. Halsaa and S. Suemer, 168–187. Basingstoke: Palgrave Macmillan.

Keshavarz, Nahid. 1387/2008. "Kampaign yek million emza be masabeh jonbesh-e ejtemayi." 15 Ordibehesht/April. http://femschool.info/spip.php?article550.

"Khairlanji: the crime and punishment." 2010. *The Hindu*, August 30. http://www.the hindu.com/opinion/Readers-Editor/khairlanji-the-crime-and-punishment/article 588045.ece.

Khalil, Andrea. 2014. "Tunisia's women: partners in revolution." In *Journal of North African Studies*, 19, no. 2 (March): 186–199.

———. 2014. *Crowds and Politics in North Africa: Tunisia, Algeria, and Libya*. Milton Park, UK: Routledge.

Khan, Nighat Saeed and Rubina Saigol. 2004a. "Women's Action Forum: Debates and Contradictions." In *Up Against the State*, edited by Nighat Saeed Khan, 146–191. ASR: Lahore.

———. 2004b. "Sindhiani Tehreek: Rural Women's Movement in Sindh." In *Up Against the State*, edited by Nighat Saeed Khan, 192–208. ASR: Lahore.

Khan, Omar Asghar. 1985. "Political and Economic Aspects of Islamisation." In *Islam, Politics, and the State: The Pakistan Experience*, edited by Asghar Khan, 127–163. London: Zed Books.

Khetan, Ashish and Raja Chowdhury. 2013. "The Stalkers: Amit Shah's Illegal Surveillance Exposed," *Cobrapost*, December 5. http://www.cobrapost.com/index.php /news-detail?nid=4054&cid=64.

Khotkina, Zoya [senior research affiliate and former codirector, Moscow Center for Gender Studies]. 1999. Interview with Lisa McIntosh Sundstrom, Moscow, March 27.

Khreishe, Amal [head of the Palestinian Working Woman's Society for Development]. 2002. Telephone interview with Islah Jad, March 29.

Kian-Thiébaut, Azadeh. 2009. "Social change, the women's rights movement, and the role of Islam." *Middle East Institute Viewpoints: The Iranian Revolution at 30* (January 29).

————. 2008. "From Motherhood to Equal Rights Advocates: The Weakening of Patriarchal Order," in Homa Katouzian and Hossein Shahidi, eds., *Iran in the 21st Century: Politics, Economics and Conflict* (London, UK: Routledge), pp. 86–106.

Kiryukhina, Yaroslava. 2013. "Will a Woman Reach the Top in Russian Politics?" *Russia Beyond the Headlines*, September 26.

Knappe, H. and S. Lang. 2014. "Between whisper and voice: Online women's movement outreach in the UK and Germany." *European Journal of Women's Studies* 21, no. 4: 361–381.

Kollman, K. and M. Waites. 2009. "The global politics of lesbian, gay, bisexual and transgender human rights: an introduction." *Contemporary Politics* 15, no. 1: 1–17.

Kolotilov, Vasily. 2015. "Russia's Sole Sexual Assault Center Struggles to Make Ends Meet." *The Moscow Times*. October 21.

Kondakov, Alexander. 2013. "Resisting the Silence: The Use of Tolerance and Equality Arguments by Gay and Lesbian Activist Groups in Russia." *Canadian Journal of Law and Society / Revue Canadienne Droit et Société* 28.3: 403–24.

Kondlo, Kwandiwe (editor). 2014. *Treading the Waters of History. Perspectives on the ANC*. Africa Institute of South Africa.

Kosbie, Jeffrey. 2013. "Beyond Queer vs. LGBT: Discursive Community and Marriage Mobilization in Massachusetts." Pp. 103-131 in *The Marrying Kind? Debating Same-Sex Marriage Within the Lesbian and Gay Movement*, edited by Mary Bernstein and Verta Taylor. Minneapolis: University of Minnesota Press.

Kostadinova, Tatiana. 2007. "Ethnic and Women's Representation under Mixed Election Systems." *Electoral Studies* 26, no. 2: 418–31.

Kozameh, Sara. 2016. "Argentina's Painful Return to Economic Orthodoxy." *NACLA Report on the Americas*. https://nacla.org/news/2016/02/08/argentina%E2%80%99s-painful-return-%E2%80%9Ceconomic-orthodoxy%E2%80%9D-0 (Accessed April 15, 2016).

Kozol, Wendy and Wendy Hesford. eds. 2005. *Just Advocacy?: Women's Human Rights, Transnational Feminisms, and the Politics of Representation*. Rutgers University Press.

Krook, Mona. 2008. "Quota Laws for Women in Politics: Implications for Feminist Practice." *Social Politics, 15* (3): 345–368.

Kuehnast, Kathleen, and Carol Nechemias. 2004. "Introduction: Women navigating change in post-Soviet currents." In *Post-Soviet Women Encountering Transition: Nation Building, Economic Survival, and Civic Activism,* edited by Kathleen Kuehnast and Carol Nechemias, 1–20. Washington, DC: Woodrow Wilson Center Press; Baltimore: Johns Hopkins University Press.

Kumar, Radha. 1993. *The History of Doing: An Illustrated Account of Movements for Women's Rights and Feminism in India, 1800–1990*, New Delhi: Kali for Women.

Kynsilehto, Anitta, ed. 2008. *Islamic Feminism: Current Perspectives*, Tampere Peace Research Institute Occasional Paper No. 96. Finland: University of Tampere.

Labidi, Lilia. 2007. "The Nature of Transnational Alliances in Women's Associations in the Maghreb: The Case of AFTURD and AFTD in Tunisia." *Journal of Middle East Women's Studies*, 3, no. 1 (Winter): 6–34.

Laclau, Ernesto, and Chantal Mouffe. 2014. *Hegemony and Socialist Strategy: Towards a Radical Democratic Politics*. New York: Verso Press.

Lala fanjiabao xiangmu [Anti-domestic Violence Project for Lesbians and Bisexual Women]. http://dv.tongyulala.org/.

Lang, S. 1997. "The NGOization of Feminism. Institutionalization and Institution Building within the German Women's Movement." In *Transitions, Environments, Translations: Feminisms in International Politics*. Ed. J. Scott, C. Kaplan and D. Keats, 101–120. New York: Routledge.

———. (2013). *NGOs, Civil Society and the Public Sphere*. Cambridge, Cambridge University Press.

Lapidus, Gail Warshofsky. 1978. *Women in Soviet society: Equality, Development, and Social Change*. Berkeley and Los Angeles: University of California Press.

Larana, Enrique, Hank Johnston, and Joseph Gusfield. 1994. *New Social Movements: From Ideology to Identity*. Philadelphia: Temple University Press.

Lau, Jaiven Ana. 2002. "El nuevo movimiento feminista Mexicano a fines del milenio." In *Feminismo en México: Ayer y hoy*, edited by Eli Bartra. Mexico City: Universidad Autónoma Metropolitana.

Lavinas, L. 1996. "As Mulheres No Universo Da Pobreza: O Caso Brasileiro." In *Estudos Feministas*, Vol. 4, No. 2, 464–479.

Layachi, Azzedine. 1995. "Algeria: Reinstating the State or Instating Civil Society?" In I. William Zartman, ed., *Collapsed States: The Disintegration and Restoration of Legitimate Authority*. Boulder, CO: Lynne Rienner Publishers.

Lazreg, Marnia. 1994. *The Eloquence of Silence: Algerian Women in Question*. London: Routledge.

Lebon, Nathalie. 1997. "Volunteer and professionalized activism in the São Paulo women's movement." Paper prepared for presentation at the 1997 meeting of the Latin American Studies Association, Guadalajara, Mexico, April 17–19.

Lee, Peggy. 2008. "Hate crimes against LGBTI in South Africa: Homophobic violence as patriarchal social control." Unpublished report prepared for the Triangle Project, July.

Legassick, Martin. 1974. "Legislation, Ideology and Economy in Post-1948 South Africa." In *Journal of Southern African Studies*, 50 1(1):5–35.

Leith-Ross, S. 1965. *African Women*. London: Routledge and Paul Kegan.

Leitner, S. 2003. "Varieties of familialism: The caring function of the family in comparative perspective." *European Societies* 5, no. 4: 353–375.

Lenz, I. and H. Schwenken. 2002. "Feminist and Migrant Networking in a Globalising World: Migration, Gender and Globalisation." In *Crossing Borders and Shifting Boundaries. Vol II: Gender, Identities and Networks*. Ed. I. Lenz, H. Lutz, M. Morokvasic-Mueller, C. Schoening-Kalender and H. Schwenken, 147–178. Opladen: Leske+Budrich.

Lépinard, E. 2007. "The Contentious Subject of Feminism: Defining Women in France from the Second Wave to Parity." *Signs* 32, no.(2): 375–403.

Levina, Yelizaveta. 2001. "Rewriting the labor code." *Russia Journal* 7 (November).

Lewis, D. 2007. "Feminism and the radical imagination." *Agenda* 72: 18–31.

Lewis, D. and Cheryl Hendricks. 1994. "Voices from the Margins." and the radical imagination." *Agenda* 20: 64.

Lewis, Taylor. 2015. "Black Lives Matter Activists Will Not Endorse A 2016 Presidential Candidate." *Essence.Com*.

Li, Hongtao. 2005. "Intervention and counseling strategies for men's domestic violence against women in Beijing." In *China History and Society: Women and Gender in Chinese Studies*, edited by Nicola Spakowski and Cecilia Milwertz, 64–73.

Li, Sipan. 2015. "Zhongguo ban nüquanzhuyi: qimeng dao zijue" [Chinese version of feminism: from enlightenment to consciousness], *Boke Tianxia* electronic journal, No. 4. http://www.duokan.com/shop/114/book/85058.

Li, Suwen. 1975. "Geguo funu yao zhengqu jiefang bixu jinxing fan di fan zhi fan ba douzheng" [To win liberation women of all countries must carry out the struggle against imperialism, colonialism, and hegaminism]. *People's Daily*, June 24, 5.

Li, Xiaoyun, and Wang Yihuan. 2007. "Nongcun funu yanjiu zongshu" [Overview of research on rural women]. In *Zhongguo funu yanjiu nianjian (2001–2005)*, edited by Quanguo Fulian Funu Yanjiusuo, Beijing: Shehui Kexue Wenxian Chubanshe.

Liang, Jun. 2001. "Cong xiaojia zouxiang dajia" [From small family to the large family]. In *Shen lin "qi" jing* [In "wonder" land], edited by Li Xiaojiang et al., 63–82. Nanjing: Jiangsu People's Press.

Liebling-Kalifani, Helen. 2004. "Ugandan Women's Experiences of Sexual Violence and Torture during Civil War Years in Luwero District: Implications for health policy, welfare and human rights." *Psychology of Women Section Review*, 6, 2, 29–37, autumn edition, British Psychological Society.

Likimani, Muthoni. 1985. *Passbook Number F 47927: Women and Mau Mau in Kenya*. London: Macmillan.

Lin, Zhibin. 2008. "Chinese women and poverty alleviation: Reflections and prospects for the future." *Chinese Sociology and Anthropology* 40, no. 4 (Summer): 27–37.

Liptak, Adam, "Justices Rule in Favor of Hobby Lobby," June 30, 2014, *The New York Times*.

Liu, Bohong. 2009a. "Jiang xingbei pingdeng leiru lifa guocheng" [Incorporating gender equality into the process of law making]. In *Xingbei pingdeng yu falu gaige* [Gender equality and law reform], edited by Huang Lei, 21–33. Beijing: China Social Sciences Press.

———. 2009b. "Lianheguo tuijin xingbei pingdeng de sange zhongyao wenshu he woguo zhixiang qingkuang" [Three important UN documents to promote gender equality and their implementation in our country]. In *Tamen yanzhong de xingbei wenti* [Gender issues in their eyes], edited by Tan Lin and Meng Xianfan, 179–194. Beijing: Social Sciences Documents Publishing House.

Liu, Wenming. 2007. "Funu yu zongjiao yanjiu zongshu" [Overview on women and religion]. In *Zhongguo Funu Yanjiu Nianjian (2001–2005)*, edited by Quanguo Fulian Funu Yanjiusuo, 171–179. Shehui Kexue Wenxian Chubanshe.

Llanos, Beatriz, and Kristen Sample. 2008. *30 Years of Democracy: Riding the Wave? Women's Political Participation in Latin America*. Peru: International Institute for Democracy and Electoral Assistance.

Lobo, Elizabete Souza. 1987. "Mulheres, feminismo e novas práticas sociais." *Revista de Ciências Sociais* (Porto Alegre) 1, no. 2.

Long Doan, Annalise Loehr, and Lisa R. Miller. 2014. "Formal Rights and Informal Privileges for Same-Sex Couples: Evidence from a National Survey Experiment." *American Sociological Review* 79, no.6: 1172–1195.

Lorenz-Meyer, D. 2013. "Timescapes of activism: Trajectories, encounters and timings of Czech women's NGOs." *European Journal of Women's Studies* 20, no. 4: 408–424.

Lovenduski, Joni. 1995. "An Emerging Advocate: The Equal Opportunities Commission in Great Britain." In *Comparative State Feminism*. Ed. D. McBride Stetson and A. Mazur, 237–253. Thousand Oaks/London/New Dehli:Sage.

———. 2005. 'Introduction'. In *State Feminism and Political Representation*, ed Joni Lovenduski. Cambridge Univ. Press.

Luciak, Ilja A. 2001. *After the Revolution: Gender and Democracy in El Salvador, Nicaragua, and Guatemala*. Baltimore: Johns Hopkins University Press.

Lughod, Lila Abu. 2013. *Do Muslim Women Need Saving?* Cambridge: Harvard University Press.

Lukose, Ritty, and Ania Loomba eds. 2012. *South Asian Feminisms*. Duke University Press.

Luo, Qiong and Duan Yongqiang. 2000. *Luo Qiong fangtan lu* [Interviews with Luo Qiong]. Beijing: Zhongguo funü chubanshe.

Macaulay, Fiona. 2006. "Judicialising and (de)criminalising domestic violence in Latin America." *Social Policy and Society* 5, no. 1: 103–114.

MacDonald, Laura. 2002. "Globalization and social movements." *International Feminist Journal of Politics* 4, no. 2 (August).

Mackay, F. (2015). "Political Not Generational: Getting Real About Contemporary UK Radical Feminism." *Social Movement Studies* 14, no.4: 427–442.

Mackie, Vera. 2001. "The language of globalization, transnationality, and feminism." *International Feminist Journal of Politics* 3, no. 2 (August).

Magallón, Carmen. 1988. "La participación de las mujeres en las organizaciones campesinas: Algunas limitaciones." In *Las mujeres en el campo,* edited by Josefina Aranda. Oaxaca: Instituto de Investigaciones Sociológicas.

Maghassib, Aisha Abu [Fateh member and ex-militant]. 2001. Interview with Islah Jad, Cairo, July 11.

Maharaj, Irma. 2008. Interview with Elaine Salo, Saartjie Baartman Centre, Cape Town, November 3.

Mahbaz, Effat. 2008. *Forget Me Not* [Faramoosham makon]. Sweden: Baran Publications.

Mahdavi, Pardis. 2008. *Passionate uprisings: Iran's Sexual Revolution.* Stanford: Stanford University Press.

Mahon, E. 1996. "Women's Rights and Catholicism in Ireland." In *Mapping the Women's Movement: Feminist Politics and Social Transformation in the North.* Ed. M. Threlfall, 184–215. London:Verso.

Maitrayee, Mukhopadhyay. 2007. "Gender Justice, Citizenship and Development: An Introduction." Pp 1-14 in *Gender Justice, Citizenship and Development* edited by M. Maitrayee and N. Singh. New Delhi: Zubaan and Ottawa: International Development Research Centre. Retrieved Dec.13, 2015. (http://www.idrc.ca/EN/Resources/Publications/openebooks/339-3/index.html).

Mama, Amina. 1995. "Feminism or Femocracy? State Feminism and Democratisation in Nigeria." *Africa Development/Afrique et Développement* 20: 37–58.

———. 1999. "Dissenting Daughters? Gender Politics and Civil society in a Militarized State." *CODESRIA Bulletin*, nos. 3–4.

———. 2001. "Challenging Subjects: Gender and Power in African Contexts." In *Sociological Review* 5 (2) 2001.

———. 2005. "The Ghanaian Women's Manifesto Movement," *Feminist Africa,* Issue 4.

Ma Qiusha. 2006. *Non-Governmental Organizations in Contemporary China: Paving the Way to Civil Society?* New York: Routledge.

Maqsood, Ammara. 2014. "'Buying Modern': Muslim Subjectivity, the West and Patterns of Islamic Consumption in Lahore, Pakistan," *Cultural Studies* 28, No. 1, 84–107.

Marcos, Sylvia. 1997. "Mujeres indígenas: Notas sobre un feminismo naciente." *Cuadernos Feministas* 1, no. 2.

———. 1999. "La *Otra* Mujer: Una propuesta de reflexión para el VIII Congreso Feminista Latinoamericano y del Caribe." *Cuadernos Feministas* 2, no. 9.

Marks, Shula and Stanley Trapido. 2014. *The Politics of Race, Class and Nationalism in Twentieth Century South Africa*. London: Routledge.

Marshall, G. A. (2008). "Preparing for EU membership: Gender policies in Turkey" in *Gender Politics in the Expanding European Union: Mobilization, Inclusion, Exclusion.* Ed. Silke Roth, 195–210. Oxford/New York: Berghahn Books: 195–210.

———. 2013. *Shaping Gender Policy in Turkey: Grassroots Women Activists, the European Union, and the Turkish State.* New York, SUNY Press.

Marsiaj, Juan P. 2006. "Expanding human rights: The Brazilian gay, lesbian, and travesti movement and the struggle against homophobic discrimination." Paper presented at the Twenty-sixth Latin American Studies Association Congress, San Juan, Puerto Rico.

Martin, Patricia Y.1990. "Rethinking Feminist Organizations." *Gender and Society* 4(2): 182-206.

Martins, Alaerte L., and Lígia C. Mendonça, eds. 2005. "Aborto: Mortes Previsíveis e Evitáveis; Dossiê Aborto Inseguro." http://www.redesaude.org.br/dossies/assets/docs/revista)05.pdf.

Marzouki, Nadia. 2010. "Algeria." In *Women's Rights in the Middle East and North Africa: Progress Amid Resistance,* eds. Sanja Kelly and Julia Breslin, 29–58. Lanham: Rowman & Littlefield; New York and Washington DC: Freedom House.

Mashinini, E. 1989. *Strikes Have Followed Me All My Life.* London: Women's Press.

Mashayekhi, Mehrdad. 1387/2009. "Iranian women placing the social movement in its proper place." 17 Esfand/February. http://www.femschool.infspip.php?article2235.

Matthews, Nancy. 1995. "Feminist Clashes with the State: Tactical Choices by State-Funded Rape Crisis Centers." In *Feminist Organizations: Harvest of the New Women's Movement,* edited by Myra Marx Ferree and Patricia Yancey Martin, 291–305. Philadelphia: Temple University Press.

Mazur, Amy, ed. 2001. *State Feminism, Women's Movements, and Job Training Policy in the Global Economy: Making Democracies Work.* New York: Routledge.

Mazur, A. G., D. E. McBride and S. Hoard. 2015. "Comparative strength of women's movements over time: conceptual, empirical, and theoretical innovations." *Politics, Groups, and Identities*: 1–25. http://www.tandfonline.com/doi/full/10.1080/21565550 3.2015.1102153

McCallum, Cecilia. 2007. "Women out of place? A micro-historical perspective on the black feminist movement in Salvador da Bahia, Brazil." *Journal of Latin American Studies* 39: 55–80.

McCarthy, Lauren A. 2015. *Trafficking Justice: How Russian Police Enforce New Laws, from Crime to Courtroom.* Ithaca, NY: Cornell University Press.

McClintock, A. 1995. *Imperial Leather: Race, Gender and Sexuality in the Colonial Conquest.* London: Routledge.

McFadden, P. 2002. "Becoming postcolonial: African women changing the meaning of citizenship." Paper presented at a conference at Queens University, Canada.

"MDC launch sets stage for bruising battle." 1999. *Financial Gazette,* September 16.

Medical Research Council. 2005. "Health systems trust health statistics." http://www.hst.org.za/healthstats/147/data.

Meena, Ruth, ed. 1992. *Gender in Southern Africa: Conceptual and Theoretical Issues.* Harare: SAPES Books.

Menon, Nivedita. 2012. *Seeing Like a Feminist.* Zubaan in Collaboration with Penguin Books.

———, ed. 1999. *Gender and politics in India.* Oxford India.

Menon, Ritu. 2007. "Alternative forms of protest." In *From Mathura to Manorama: Resisting violence against women in India,* edited by Kalpana Kannabiran and Ritu

Menon. New Delhi: Women Unlimited and International Centre for Ethnic Studies.

Mernissi, Fatima. 1987. *Behind the Veil: Male-Female Dynamics in Modern Muslim Society*. Bloomington: Indiana University Press, revised ed.

Messaoudi, Khalida and Elisabeth Schemla. 1995. *Unbowed: An Algerian Woman Confronts Islamic Fundamentalism*. Philadelphia: University of Pennsylvania Press.

Meyer, David S., and Debra C. Minkoff. 2004. "Conceptualizing political opportunity." *Social Forces* 82, no. 4 (June): 1457–1492.

Meyer, David S. and Nancy Whittier. 1994. "Social Movement Spillover." *Social Problems* 41:2 (May): 277-298.

Miftah, Women in Peace and Negotiation, Women Political Forum. 2006. Third meeting minutes taken by the author on February 26, Miftah office. Ramallah.

Miguel, Luis F. 2008. "Political representation and gender in Brazil: Quotas for women and their impact." *Bulletin of Latin American Research* 27, no. 2: 197–214.

Mikell, Gwendolyn. 1984. "Filiation, Economic Crisis and the Status of Women in Rural Ghana." *Canadian Journal of African Studies* 18, no. 1: 195–218.

Mikhaleva, Galina. 2010. "Est' Li Politicheskii Potentsial U Zhenskogo Dvizheniia v Rossii?" [Does the Russian Women's Movement Have Political Potential?]. In *Zhenskoe Dvizhenie v Rossii: Vchera, Segodnia, Zavtra: Materialy Konferentsii*, edited by Galina Mikhaleva, 62–73. Moscow: RODP "Yabloko" and KMK Publishers.

Milani, Farzaneh. 2011. *Words not Swords: Iranian Women and the Freedom of Movement*. New York: Syracuse University Press.

———. 1992. *Veils and words: The emerging voices of Iranian women writers*. Syracuse: Syracuse University Press.

Miller, Francesca. 1991. *Latin American women and the search for social justice*. Lebanon, NH: University Press of New England.

Milkman, Ruth and Eileen Appelbaum. 2013. *Unfinished Business: Paid Family Leave in California and the Future of U.S. Work-Family Policy*. Ithaca and London: ILR Press.

Milwertz, Cecilia. 2002. *Beijing women organizing for change: The formation of a social movement wave*. Copenhagen: NIAS Press.

———. 2003. "Activism against domestic violence in the People's Republic of China." *Violence Against Women* 9, no. 6 (June): 630–654.

"Minister Jaruga-Nowacka o Swoich Planach." 2002. *Gazeta Wyborcza*, January 24.

The Ministry of Women's Affairs. 2004. "Strategic Vision and a Plan of Action," March. Ramallah.

Ministry of Women and Child Development (MoWCD), Government of India, 2015, Proposal for One Stop Centre, accessed on May 1, 2016, Available at http://wcd.nic .in/sites/default/files/ProposalforOneStopCentre17.3.2015.pdf.

Minoo, Moallem. 2006. "Feminist scholarship and the internationalization of women's studies." *Feminist Studies* 32, no. 2 (Summer).

Minow, Martha. 1990. *Making All the Difference*. Ithaca: Cornell University Press.

Minutes of a one-day workshop organized by the Centre for Women's Development Studies and the Indian Council for Social Science Research on the issues before the women's movement on April 6th, 2013, accessed on May 1, 2016, Available at http:// www.cwds.ac.in/seminar.htm#Issues_before_the_Womens_Movement_at_Nehru _Memorial_Museum_and_Library,_New_Delhi,_April_6,_2013

Mir-Hosseini, Ziba. 2010. "Understanding Islamic Feminism." http://www.countercurrents .org/sikand070210.htm.

————. 2002. "Negotiating the politics of gender in Iran: An ethnography of a documentary." In *The New Iranian Cinema,* edited by Richard Tapper. London: I. B. Tauris.

Mirza, H. S., Ed. 1997. *Black British Feminism: A Reader.* London, Routledge.

Misra, Nirja, Shobhita Rajan, and Kavita Srivastava. 1993. "The gang rape of Bhanwri: Response of state, WDP, and women's groups." Paper presented at the Sixth National Conference on Women's Studies, Mysore.

"Mission and History." 2016. *Global Fund for Women.*

Mitchell, Timothy. 1991. "The limits of the state: Beyond statist approaches and their critics." *American Political Science Review* 85, no. 1: 77–94.

Mody, Perveez. 2008. *The Intimate State: Love Marriage and the Law in Delhi.* New Delhi: Routledge.

Mogannam, Matiel. 1937. *The Arab Woman.* London: Herbert Joseph.

Moghadam, Khadije. 2015. "I did not flee from my son's homosexuality, I faced it": https://www.tableaumag.com/2389

Moghadam, Rezvan. 2013. In an interview with Radio Zamaneh: http://www.radio zamaneh.com/189490 (In Persian)

Moghadam, Valentine M. 1993. *Modernizing Women: Gender and Social Change in the Middle East.* Boulder: Lynne Rienner.

————. 1997. *Women, Work, and Economic Reform in the Middle East and North Africa.* Boulder: Lynne Rienner.

————. 2000. "Transnational Feminist Networks: Collective Action in an Era of Globalization." *International Sociology* 15, no. 1 (March).

————. 2002. "Islamic Feminism and Its Discontents: Toward a Resolution of the Debate," in *Signs: Journal of Women in Culture and Society,* vol. 27, no. 4.

————. 2005. *Globalizing Women: Transnational Feminist Networks.* Baltimore: Johns Hopkins University Press.

Moghadam, Valentine M. and Suzanne Franzway, and Mary Margaret Fonow, eds. 2011. *Making Globalization Work for Women: The Role of Social Rights and Trade Union Leadership.* Albany, NY: SUNY Press.

Moghadam, Valentine M. and Elham Gheytanchi. 2010. "Political Opportunities and Strategic Choices: Comparing Feminist Campaigns in Morocco and Iran." *Mobilization: An International Quarterly of Social Movement Research* 15, no. 3 (September): 267–88.

Moghadam, Valentine M., and Fatima Sadiqi. 2006. "Introduction and Overview: Women and the Public Sphere in the Middle East and North Africa." *Journal of Middle East Women's Studies* 2, no. 2 (Spring): 1–7.

Moghissi, Haideh. 1996. *Populism and feminism in Iran: Women's struggle in a male-defined revolutionary movement.* New York: St. Martin's Press.

Mohanty, Chandra Talpade. 1991. "Under Western Eyes: Feminist Scholarship and Colonial Discourses." In *Third World Women and the Politics of Feminism,* edited by Chandra Mohanty, Ann Russo, and Lourdes Torres. Bloomington: Indiana University Press.

————. 2010. *Feminism Without Borders: Decolonizing Theory Practicing Solidarity.* New Delhi: Zubaan Books.

Mokhova, Maria. 2014. Interviewed by author and Valerie Sperling, "Sisters" Center, Moscow, June 16.

Molyneux, Maxine. 1986. "Mobilization without Emancipation." In *Transition and Development: Problems of Third World Socialism,* edited by R. Fagen et al. New York: Monthly Review Press.

———. 1998b. "Analyzing Women's Movements." In *Feminist Visions of Development: Gender Analysis and Policy,* edited by Cecile Jackson and Ruth Pearson. London: Routledge.

———. 2001. *Women's Movements in International Perspective: Latin America and Beyond.* London: Palgrave.

———. 2003. *Movimientos de mujeres en América Latina: Estudio teórico comparado.* Madrid: Colección Feminismos Ediciones Cátedra.

Molyneux, Maxine, and Shahra Razavi, eds. 2002. *Gender Justice, Development, and ights.* Oxford: Oxford University Press.

Montaño Virreira, Sonia. 2015. *Regional Review and Appraisal of Implementation of the Beijing Declaration and Platform for Action and the Outcome of the Twenty-Third Special Session of the General Assembly (2000) in Latin American and Caribbean Countries.* Santiago de Chile: UN/Economic Commission for Latin America and the Caribbean.

Monasterios, Karin. 2007. "Bolivian women's organizations in the MAS era." *NACLA Report on the Americas* 40, no. 2: 33–37.

Mongrovejo, Norma. 2000. *Un amor que se atrevio a decir su nombre: La lucha de las lesbianas y su relacion con los movimientos homosexual y feminista en America Latina.* Mexico: Plaza y Valdes Editores/CDHAL.

Montecinos, Verónica. 2001. "Feminists and technocrats in the democratization of Latin America: A prolegomenon." *International Journal of Politics, Culture, and Society* 15, no. 1 (September): 175–199. http://www.kluweronline.com/issn/0891-4486.

Montoya, C. 2013. *From Global to Grassroots: The European Union, Transnational Advocacy, and Combating Violence against Women.* Oxford, Oxford University Press.

Moore, Mignon. 2011. *Invisible Families: Gay Identities, Relationships, and Motherhood among Black Women.* Berkeley: University of California Press.

Moraga, Cherríe L., and Gloria E. Anzaldúa, eds. 2002. *This Bridge Called My Back: Writings By Radical Women Of Color.* Berkeley: Third Woman Press.

Morgan, Kimberly J. 2001. "A Child of the Sixties: The Great Society, the New Right, and the Politics of Federal Child Care." *Journal of Policy History* 13, no. 2: 215–250.

———. (2008). "Toward the Europeanization of Work-Family Policies? The Impact of the EU on Policies for Working Parents." *Gender Politics in the Expanding European Union. Mobilization, Inclusion , Exclusion.* Ed. Silke Roth, 37–59. Oxford/New York: Berghahn Books.

Mortazi-Langaroudi, Minoo. 2013, cited in a report by *Feminist School,* 22 Khordad 1392: http://www.feministschool.com/spip.php?article7316

———. 2015. "Mafrouzhayi dar bareh kandidahaye zan namayandegi Majles"[Some assumptions on woman candidates for Majles] in *Kanoon-e Zanan,* 24 Day, 1394: http://ir-women.com/spip.php?article11291

Moscow Times. 2011. "Church, Lawmakers Target Abortion," May 31.

Moser, Annalise. 2004. "Happy heterogeneity? Feminism, development, and the grassroots women's movement in Peru." *Feminist Studies* 30, no. 1: 211–239.

Moser, Robert G. 2001. "The effects of electoral systems on women's representation in post-communist states." *Electoral Studies* 20, no. 3: 353–369.

Movahed-Shariatpanahi, Jila. 2016. "Shoray-e negahban be grayeshhay-e zan-setizaneh bi etena ast" [The Gurdian Council does not care about the mysoginist tendencies]: http://entekhabkhabar.ir

Movimiento de Integración y Liberación Homosexual. 2008. *VI informe anual: Dere-chos humanos minorías sexuales Chilenas (Hechos 2007)*. Santiago, Chile: Movilh.

Mozaffari, Kaveh. 2015. "Aya faza-ye entekhabat mitavanad forsati baraye etelaf-e madani bashad?" [Can the election space be a good opportunity for a civil coalition?] in *Bidar-Zani*, 24 Azar/December 18, 1394: http://bidarzani.com/24532

"M.P. government declares Section 144 in Khargone to prevent public hearing by NCW: Women of 4 Narmada dams hold public hearing sans NCW chairwoman." 2004. NBA press release, December 6.

Mujeres y Asamblea Constituyente. 2007. "Quienes Somos." November 27. http://www.mujeres constituyentes.org/quienes_somos.php.

Mukhopadhyay, Maitrayee and Singh, Navsharan. 2007. "Gender Justice, Citizenship and Development: An Introduction," in eds. Zubaan, An Imprint of Kali for Women, ed. Zubaan, 1–14. New Delhi and International Development Research Centre: Ottawa.

"Mulayam's rape comment isn't a first: 5 quotes that prove Yadavs are the poster boys of misogyny." 2015. *Firstpost India*, August 20. http://www.firstpost.com/politics /mulayams-rape-comment-isnt-a-fir.

Mullenax, Shawnna. 2015. "De jure transformation, de facto stagnation: The status of women's and LGBT rights in Bolivia." Paper Prepared for the 2015 Latin American Studies Association Meeting, San Juan, Puerto Rico.

Mulligan, Diane, and Jude Howell, eds. 2005. *Gender and Civil Society: Transcending Boundaries*. London: Routledge.

Mumtaz, Khawar. 1998. "Political participation: Women in national legislatures in Paki-stan." In *Shaping Women's Lives: Laws, Practices, and Strategies in Pakistan*, edited by Farida Shaheed, Sohail Akbar Warraich, Cassandra Balchin, and Aisha Gazdar, 319–369. Lahore: Shirkat Gah.

Mumtaz, Khawar, and Samiya K. Mumtaz. Forthcoming. *Women's Participation in the Punjab Peasant Movement: From Community Rights to Women's Rights?*

Mumtaz, Khawar, and Farida Shaheed. 1987. *Two Steps Forward, One Step Back? Women of Pakistan*. London: Zed Books; Lahore: Vanguard.

Munusamy, R. 2016. "State Capture: Going Gets Tough for Zuma and the Guptas," in *Daily Maverick*, March 23.

Murray, C. 1981. *Families Divided: The Impact of Migrant Labor in Lesotho*. Cam-bridge: Cambridge University Press.

Murthy, Lakshmi. 2013. "From Mathura to Bhanwari." *Economic and Political Weekly*, 16–18.

Naihua, Zhang, with Wu Xu. 1995. "Discovering the positive within the negative: The women's movement in a changing China." In *The Challenge of Local Feminisms: Women's Movements in Global Perspective*, edited by Amrita Basu, 25–57. Boulder: Westview Press.

Najmabadi, Afsaneh. 1998. "Feminism in an Islamic Republic: 'Years of Hardship, Years of Growth.'" In Yvonne Y. Haddad and John Esposito, eds., *Women, Gender, and Social Change in the Muslim World*, pp. 59–84. New York: Oxford University Press.

Naples, Nancy A., and Manisha Desai, eds. 2002. *Women's Activism and Globalization: Linking Local Struggles And Transnational Politics.* New York: Routledge.

Narayan, Uma, and Sandra Harding, eds. 2000. *Decentering the center: Philosophy for a Multicultural, Postcolonial, and Feminist World.* Bloomington: Indiana University Press.

Nash, June. 1993. "Mayan household production in the modern world." In *The Impact of Global Exchange on Middle American Artisans,* edited by June Nash. Albany: State University of New York Press.

National Commission on the Observance of International Women's Year. 1978. *The Spirit of Houston: The First National Women's Conference.* Washington, DC: U.S. Government Printing Office.

National Democratic Institute. 2011. "Final Report on the Tunisian National Constituent Assembly Elections," October 11. https://www.ndi.org/files/tunisia-final-election-report-021712_v2.pdf.

National Organization for Women. 2008. "National Organization for Women PAC endorses Obama-Biden." September 16. http://www.now.org/press/09-08/09-16.html.

National Organization for Women. 2016. See FAQs. *Now.Org.*

The National Women's Law Center, 2014. "No Improvement in Women's Poverty Rate; One in Seven Women Lives in Poverty, Says NWLC."

Navaeei, Shahin. 1999. *Avaye Zan,* nos. 38–39 (Winter).

Nazneen, Sohela and Maheen Sultan. 2015. "Taking the Bull By the Horns: Contemporary Feminist Politics in Bangladesh" in *New South Asian Feminisms Paradoxes and Possibilities,* edited by Srila Roy.

Nechemias, Carol. 2000. "Politics in Post-Soviet Russia: Where Are the Women?" *Demokratizatsiya* 8, no. 2: 199–218.

Nemenyi, Maria. 2001. "The social construction of women's roles in Hungary." *Replika* 1.

Neslen, Arthur. 2015. "Morocco aims to be solar superpower." *The Guardian Weekly,* October 30.

Newman, J. 2012. *Working the Spaces of Power: Activism, Neoliberalism and Gendered Labour.* London: Bloomsbury Academic.

Newell, Andrew, and Barry Reilly. 1996. "The gender wage gap in Russia: Some empirical evidence." *Labour Economics* 3, no. 10: 337–356.

NGO Coordinating Committee for Beijing +5. 2000. *Pakistan NGO review: Beijing +5.* Lahore: Shirkat Gah.

Ngugi, Mumbi. c. 2001. "The Women's Rights Movement and Democratization in Kenya." Unpublished paper.

Nielsen, H. P. 2013. "Joint purpose? Intersectionality in the hands of anti-racist and gender equality activists in Europe." *Ethnicities* 13, no. 3: 276–294.

Nkomo, Boshadi. 2000. "New customary marriages act sees women as equal partner." http:// www.afro.com.

Nogueira, Rogério. 2005. *O Preceito de Diversidade e a Composição da Força de Trabalho no Setor Público.* Brasília: Universidade de Brasília, OPAS.

Noonan, Norma Corigliano, and Carol Nechemias, eds. 2001. *Encyclopedia of Russian women's movements.* Westport, CT: Greenwood Press.

Norton, Augustus Richard. 1993. "The future of civil society in the Middle East." *Middle East Journal* 47, no. 2 (Spring): 205–216.

———, edited by 1995. *Civil society in the Middle East.* Vols. 1–2. Leiden: E. J. Brill.

NotiEMAIL. 2006. "Diputada cree viceministerio Género es 'retroceso' para mujeres." October 2. http://bolivia.notiemail.com/.

Nussbaum, Martha C. 2004. "Sex equality, liberty, and privacy: A comparative approach to the feminist critique." In *India's Living Constitution: Ideas, Practices, Controversies*, edited by Zoya Hasan, E. Sridharan, and R. Sudarshan. Delhi: Permanent Black.

"NYWF'S 2015 Celebrating Women Breakfast Event Recap". 2015. *New York Women's Foundation*.

O'Barr, Jean. 1976. "Pare Women: A Case of Political Involvement." *Rural Africana* 29, 121–34.

Office on the Status of Women. n.d. "South Africa's national policy framework for women's empowerment and gender equality." http://www.womensnet.org.za/free-tags /office-status-women.

Ohikuare, Judith. 2015. "Meet The Women Who Created #Blacklivesmatter." *Cosmopolitan*.

Okeke-Ihejireka, Philomina and Susan Franceschet, 2002. "Democratization and State Feminism: Gender Politics in Africa and Latin America." *Development & Change*, 33 (3), 439–466.

Okin, Susan Moller. 1999. *Is Multiculturalism Bad for Women?* Princeton: Princeton University Press.

Olcott, Jocelyn. 2016. "From the Time of Creation: Legacies and Unfinished Business from the First International Women's Year Conference," in *Women and Girls Rising: Progress and Resistance around the World*, eds. Ellen Chesler and Terry Mc-Govern, 21–31. Routledge: New York and Oxon.

172nd report of the Law Commission of India on Reform of Rape Laws. 2000. Delhi: Law Commission of India.

"Orissa: Probing starvation deaths." 2002. *Economic and Political Weekly*, August 24, 3477.

Osava, Mario. 2007. "Brazil: Turning women's rights into reality." *Inter-Press Service*, August 16.

Oshchepkov, A. Iu. 2006. "Gendernye Razlichiia v Oplate Truda v Rossii." *Ekonomicheskii Zhurnal VShE*, no. 4: 590–619.

Othman, Zeyad. 1998. "Al-barlaman al-sowary, al-marah wal tashri' bayna al-tajdeed wal qawlaba" [The model parliament: Women and legislation between renewal and preservation]. *Al-seyassa al-falastineyya* [Palestinian Politics] 19.

"Our Work | Equality Now." 2016. *Equalitynow.Org.*

Outsjhoorn, Joyce, and Johanna Kantola, eds. 2007. *Changing State Feminism*. New York: Palgrave Macmillan.

Paidar, Parvin. 1995. *Women and the Political Process in Twentieth-Century Iran*. Cambridge: Cambridge University Press.

Palestine Media Centre. 2005. "Al-markaz al-falastini lil i'lam, qassamyyon wa qassameyyat" [Male and female *qassamis*]. August 18. http://www.palestineinfo.com /arabic/palestoday/reports/ report2005/qassameyoon.htm.

Palestinian Ministry of Cooperation and International Relations. 1996. *Palestinian Development Plan (PDP), 1996–1998*. Ramallah: Palestinian Ministry of Cooperation and International Relations.

Palestinian National Report Beijing + 15, ESCWA, Beirut. Unpublished report.

Paneyakh, Ella. 2013. "Faking Performance Together: Systems of Performance Evaluation in Russian Enforcement Agencies and Production of Bias and Privilege." *Post-Soviet Affairs* 30, no. 2-3: 115–36.

Park, Haeyoun and Iaryna Mykhyalyshyn. 2016. "L.G.B.T. People Are More Likely to Be Targets of Hate Crimes Than Any Other Minority Group," *New York Times*, June 16.

PARLINE n.d. "Venezuela National Asssembly." http://www.ipu.org/parline-e/reports /2347_e.htm (Accessed August 24, 2016).

Parpart, Jane. 1988. "Women and the State in Africa." In *The Precarious Balance: State and Society in Africa*, edited by Donald Rothchild and Naomi Chazan. Boulder: Westview Press.

Pascale Dufour, Dominique Masson, Dominique Caouette. 2010. *Solidarities Beyond Borders: Transnationalizing Women's Movements*. University of British Columbia Press.

Patel, L. 2008. "Getting it Right and Wrong: An Overview of a Decade of Postapartheid Welfare," in *Pratice Social Work in Action*, 20 (2).

Patel, P. 1997. "Third wave feminism and black women's activism," in *Black British Feminism*. Ed. A Reader. H. S. Mirza, 255–268. London: Taylor & Francis.

Paxton, P., M. M. Hughes and J. L. Green. 2006. "The International Women's Movement and Women's Political Representation, 1893–2003." *American Sociological Review* 71, no. 6: 898–920.

Paxton, Pamela, Melanie M. Hughes, and Mona Lena Krook. 2015. "Transnational Women's Activism and the Global Diffusion of Gender Quotas." *International Studies Quarterly* 59, no. 2 (June): 357–372.

"PDP Palestinian Development Plan 1996–1998." 1996. Ministry of Cooperation and International Relations. Palestine.

Pearson, R. and D. Elson. 2015. "Transcending the impact of the financial crisis in the United Kindom: towards plan F—a feminist economic strategy." *Feminist Review* 109: 8–30.

Pecheny, Mario. 2003. "Sexual orientation, AIDS, and human rights in Argentina: The paradox of social advance amid health crisis." In *Struggles for social rights in Latin America*, edited by Susan E. Eckstein and Timothy P. Wickham-Crowley, 253–270. New York: Routledge.

Penn, Shana. 2001. "The great debate: When feminism hit the headlines, Poland hit the roof." *Ms.*, January.

———. 2005. *Solidarity's Secret: The Women Who Defeated Communism in Poland*. Ann Arbor: University of Michigan Press.

Perez-Pena, "1 in 4 Women Experience Sex Assault on Campus," *New York Times*, September 21, 2005.

Peteet, Julie. 1991. *Gender in crisis: Women and the Palestinian resistance movement*. New York: Columbia University Press.

Petersburg Egida. 2013. "Uroki Zhenskogo Liderstva" [Lessons of Women's Leadership]. Report. St. Petersburg: Petersburg Egida.

Philip, Christin Mathew. 2014. "93 women are being raped in India every day, NCRB data show," *Times of India (TOI)*, July1. http://timesofindia.indiatimes.com/india/93-women-are-being-raped-in-India-every-day-NCRB-data-show/articleshow/37566815.cms.

Phillips, Anne. 1991. *Engendering Democracy*. Philadelphia: University of Pennsylvania Press.

———. 2002. "Does Feminism Need a Conception of Civil Society?" In *Alternative Conceptions of Civil Society*, edited by Simone Chambers and Will Kymlicka, 71–89. Ethikon Series in Comparative Ethics. Princeton: Princeton University Press.

Phiri, Brighton. 2006. "Ministry of Women's Affairs Was Created for a Party Cadre—Sikazwe." *The Post*, April 2.

Picheta, Sophie. 2008. "Brazilian president calls homophobia a 'perverse disease.'" Pink News, June 11. http://www.pinknews.co.uk/.

Pinto, Célia Regina Jardim. 2003. *Uma história do feminismo no Brasil*. São Paulo: Editora Fundação Perseu Abramo.

Pisklakova-Parker, Marina [Director, ANNA Center, Moscow]. 2014. Interview with Lisa McIntosh Sundstrom and Valerie Sperling, Moscow, June 19.

Pitanguy, Jacqueline. 2002. "Bridging the local and the global: Feminism in Brazil and the international human rights agenda." *Social Research* (Fall). http://findarticles .com/p/articles/ mi_m2267/is_3_69/ai_94227142.

Platzsky, L, and C. Walker. 1985. *The Surplus People: Forced Removals in South Africa*. Johannesburg: Ravan Press.

Potapova, Anna [executive director, ANNA]. 1999. Interview with Lisa McIntosh Sundstrom, Moscow, May 12.

Potuoglu-Cook, O. 2015. "Hope with qualms: a feminist analysis of the 2013 Gezi protests." *Feminist Review* 109: 96–123.

Power, Margaret. 2001. "Defending dictatorship: Conservative women in Pinochet's Chile and the 1988 plebiscite." In *Radical Women in Latin America: Left and Right*, edited by Karen Kampwirth and Victória Gonzalez, 299–324. University Park: Pennsylvania State University Press.

Predelli, Nyhagen and Halsaa, Beatrice. 2012. *Majority-Minority Relations in Contemporary Women's Movements: Strategic Sisterhood*. UK: Palgrave Macmillan.

Predelli, L., B. Halsaa, A. Sandu, C. Thun and L. Nyhagen. 2012. *Majority-Minority Relations in Contemporary Women's Movements*. Basingstoke, Palgrave Macmillan.

"Predvybornye spiski partii" [Preelection party lists]. n.d. http://www.kreml.org/topics /160523714.

Presley, Cora Ann. 1991. *Kikuyu Women, The "Mau Mau" Rebellion and Social Change in Kenya*. Boulder: Westview Press.

Prügl, E. 2012. "'If Lehman Brothers Had Been Lehman Sisters...': Gender and Myth in the Aftermath of the Financial Crisis." *International Political Sociology* 6, no. 1: 21–35.

Pudrovska, T. and M. M. Ferree. 2004. "Global Activism in 'Virtual Space': The European Women's Lobby in the Network of Transnational Women's NGOs on the Web." *Social Politics: International Studies in Gender, State & Society* 11, no. 1: 117–143.

Pugh, M. 2000. *Women and the Women's Movement in Britain*. New York: St. Martin's Press.

Purvis, June, Haan Francisca de Haan, Krassimira Daskalova, Margaret Allen. eds. 2012. *Women's Activism: Global Perspectives from the 1890s to the Present*. Routledge.

Qadeer, Imrana. 1998. "Reproductive health: A public health perspective." *Economic and Political Weekly*, October 10, 2675–2684. Reprinted in *Women's studies: A reader*, edited by Mary E. John, 381–387. New Delhi: Penguin Books India, 2008.

Quataert, Jean H. and Roth, Benita. 2012. "Guest Editorial Note: Human Rights, Global Conferences, and the Making of Postwar Transnational Feminisms," *Journal of Women's History* 24, no. 4 (Winter): 11.

Qunta, Christine. 1987. *Women in southern Africa*. Johannesburg: Skotaville Publishers.

Rafidi, Tami [Fateh activist]. 2001. Interview with Islah Jad, Ramallah, July 3.

Ragins, Belle Rose, Bickley Townsend, and Mary Mattis. 2006. "Gender Gap in the Executive Suite," in *Workplace/Women's Place*, edited by Paula J. Dubeck and Dana Dunn, 95–109. New York: Oxford University Press.

Rashida Manjoo, Report of the Special Rapporteur on violence against women, its causes and consequences, Addendum, Mission to India, April 1, 2014.

Ratliff, Patricia M. 1995. "Women's Education in the USSR: 1950–1985." In *Women's Higher Education in Comparative Perspective*, edited by G. P. Kelly and S. Slaughter. Springer Netherlands, 17–30.

————. 2008. "Women and forced migration." Trans. Kalpana Kannabiran from Telugu audio recording. Lecture delivered at the Workshop on Forced Migration organized jointly by the Asmita Resource Centre for Women and the Calcutta Research Group, Hyderabad, February 22–24.

Ray, Raka. 1999. *Fields of Protest: Women's Movements in India.* Minneapolis: University of Minnesota Press.

Razavi, Shahra. 2000. *Women in Contemporary Democratization.* Occasional Paper no. 4. Geneva: UNRISD.

Reddock, R. 1985. "Women and Slavery in the Caribbean: A Feminist Perspective," in *Latin American Perspectives* 12 (1). http://www.cfemea.org.br/temasedados/imprimir _detalhes.asp? IDTemasDados=151.

Reese, Ellen. 2005. *Backlash against Welfare Mothers: Past and Present.* Berkeley: University of California Press.

————. 2011. *They Say Cut Back, We Say Fight Back! Welfare Activism in an Era of Retrenchment.* New York: Russell Sage Foundation.

Reger, Jo. 2012. *Everywhere and Nowhere: Contemporary Feminism in the United States.* New York: Oxford University Press.

Regulska, J. and M. Grabowska. 2008. "Will It Make a Difference? EU Enlargement and Women's Public Discourse in Poland," in *Gender Politics in the Expanding European Union. Mobilization, Inclusion , Exclusion.* Ed. Silke Roth, 137–154. Oxford/ New York:Berghahn Books.

"Report on lesbian meeting: National Conference on Women's Movements in India, Tirupati, 1994." 2007. In *Sexualities,* edited by Nivedita Menon. New Delhi: Women Unlimited in association with Kali for Women.

"Report on Review of Rape Laws (172nd)." 2000. *Law Commission of India,* March 25. http://www.lawcommissionofindia.nic.in/rapelaws.htm, 2000.

"Representation by 'Women against Sexual Violence and State Repression' to the Justice Verma Commission." 2013. *FeministIndia: Sharing is Living,* January. http:// feministsindia.com/women-and-law/justice-verma-submissions/wss/.

Reynolds, Michael, Shobha Shangle, and Lekha Venkataraman. 2007. *A National Census of Women's And Gender Studies Programs In U.S. Institutions Of Higher Education.* University of Chicago.

RFE/RL. 2015. "The Crackdown on NGOs in Russia."

Ribeiro, Matilde. 1995. "Mulheres Negras Brasileiras: de Bertioga à Beijing." *Revista Estudos Feministas,* Vol. 3, No. 2, pp. 446–457.

Richter, James. 2002. "Promoting civil society? Democracy assistance and Russian women's organizations." *Problems of Post-Communism* 48, no. 1: 30–41.

Ríos Tobar, M. 2007. "Chilean feminism and social democracy from the democratic transition to Bachelet." *NACLA Report on the Americas* 40, no. 2: 25–29.

Robins, S. 2004. "'Long Live Zacky Long Live': AIDS Activism, Science and Citizenship After Apartheid," in *Journal of Southern African Studies* 30 (3) 2004.

Rompiendo el Silencio. 2008. "Partido Socialista apoyaría Ley de Unión Civil." March 16. http://www.rompiendoelsilencio.cl/.

Roseneil, S. 2000. *Common Women, Uncommon Practices: The Queer Feminisms of Greenham.* London/New York: Cassell.

Roseneil, S., I. Crowhurst, T. Hellesund, A. C. Santos and M. Stoilova. 2012. "Remaking Intimate Citizenship in Multicultural Europe," in *Remaking Citizenship in Multicultural Europe.* Ed. B. Halsaa, S. Roseneil and S. Suemer. Basingstoke, Palgrave Macmillan: 41–69.

"Rossiane O Dele Pussy Riot (Russians on the Pussy Riot Case)." 2012. *Levada Center*. July 31.

Rossiiskaia gazeta. 2013. "Izmeneniia v Zakon Rossiiskoi Federatsii 'O Zaniatosti Naseleniia v Rossiiskoi Federatsii' I Otdel'nie Zakonodatel'nye Akty Rossiiskoi Federatsii [Changes to the Russian Federation Law 'On Employment of the Russian Federation Population' and Separate Legislative Acts of the Russian Federation]." May 7.

Roth, Benita. 2004. *Separate Roads to Feminism: Black, Chicana, and white feminist movements in America's Second Wave.* Cambridge: Cambridge University Press.

Roth, Silke. 2003. *Building Movement Bridges: The Coalition of Labor Union Women.* New York: Praeger.

———. (2007). "Sisterhood and Solidarity? Women's Organizations in the Expanded European Union." *Social Politics* 14, no. 4: 460–487.

Roth, Silke, ed. 2008. *Gender Politics in the Expanding European Union: Mobilization, Inclusion, Exclusion*. Oxford, New York: Berghahn Books.

Roudi, Farzaneh 2009. "Youth, Women's Rights and Political Change in Iran,": *Population Reference Bureau (PRB)*. http://www.prb.org/Publications/Articles/2009/iran youth.aspx

Rousseau, Stéfanie. 2011. "Indigenous and Feminist Movements at the Constituent Assembly in Bolivia: Locating the Representation of Indigenous Women." *Latin American Research Review* 46:2: 5-28.

Rowbotham, Sheila. 1992. *Women in Movement: Feminism and Social Action.* London: Routledge.

Roy, A. 1995. "Asian Women's Activism in Northamptonshire," in *Feminist Activism in the 1990s*. Ed. G. Griffin. London, Taylor & Francis: 101–109.

Rupp, Leila J. 1994. "Constructing Internationalism: The Case of Transnational Women's Organizations, 1888–1945." *The American Historical Review* 99, no. (5): 1571–1600.

Rupp, Leila J. and Verta Taylor. 1999. "Forging Feminist Identity in an International Movement: A Collective Identity Approach to Twentieth-Century Feminism." *Signs: Journal of Women in Culture and Society* 24, no.2 (Winter): 363–386.

Russia Beyond the Headlines. 2015. "NGO Law." Russia Profile. Political parties and movements. *RussiaProfile.Org*.

Russia Profile. n.d. Political parties and movements. http://www.russiaprofile.org/resources /political.

Ryan, Nick. 1998. "Truth Under Siege." *Mother Jones* (August 11). http://www.mother jones.com/politics/1998/08/truth-under-siege.

Saad-Zoy, Souria (ed.). 2010. *Femmes, Droits de la Famille, et Système Judiciare en Algérie, au Maroc, et en Tunisie.* Rabat : UNESCO.

Saartjie Baartman Centre. 2007. *Annual report.* Manenberg, South Africa: Saartjie Baartman Centre.

Sadiqi, Fatima. 2016. "An Assessment of Today's Moroccan Feminist Movements (1946–2014)" in *Moroccan Feminisms: New Perspectives*, eds. Moha Ennaji, Fatima Sadiqi and Karen Vintges, 51–76. Trenton, NJ: Africa World Press.

Salhi, Zahia Smail. 2010. "Gender and Violence in Algeria: Women's Resistance against the Islamist Femicide," in *Gender and Diversity in the Middle East and North Africa*, edited by Zahia Smail Salhi. Milton Park, UK: Routledge.

Salmenniemi, Suvi. 2003. "Democracy without women? The Russian parliamentary elections and gender equality." http://www.balticdata.info/russia/elections/russia _elections_suvi.htm.

Salo, Elaine. 2004. *Respectable Mothers, Tough Men and Good Daughters: Producing Persons in Manenberg Township, South Africa.* Unpublished Ph.d dissertation, Emory University.

———. 2010. "South African Feminisms: A Coming of Age?" In A. Basu (ed.) *Women's Movements in the Global Era.* Boulder: Westview Press.

Sanasarian, Eliz. 1982. *The women's rights movement in Iran: Mutiny, appeasement, and repression from 1900 to Khomeini.* New York: Praeger.

Sanati, Mahdokht. 2014. *Women of Shadow* (Zanan-e Sayeh-Rowshan). Berlin: Gardoun Publications.

Sandberg, L. and M. Rönnblom. 2013. "Afraid and restricted vs bold and equal: Women's fear of violence and gender equality discourses in Sweden." *European Journal of Women's Studies* 20, no. 2: 189–203.

Sandberg, Sheryl. 2013. *Lean In: Women, Work, and the Will to Lead.* New York: Knopf.

Sandler, Joanne and Anne Marie Goetz. 2015. "Debating A 5th World Conference on Women: Defiance or Defeatism?" (https://www.opendemocracy.net/5050/anne-marie-goetz-joanne-sandler/debating-5th-world-conference-on-women-defiance-or-defeatism)

Sane, Idrissa. 2010. "Adoption de la loi sur la parité: Les actes-clé au cours de cette décennie," in *Le Soleil.* Dakar, Senegal.

Santilli, Kathy. 1977. "Kikuyu Women in the Mau Mau Revolt: A Closer Look." *Ufahamu* VIII, no. 1: 143–59.

Santos, Boaventura de Sousa. 2007. *Renovar a teoria crítica e reinventar a emancipação social.* São Paulo: Boitempo.

Sardenberg, Cecilia M. B. 2004. "With a little help from our friends: 'Global' incentives and 'local' challenges to feminist politics in Brazil." *IDS Bulletin* 35, no. 4 (October): 125–129.

———. 2011. "What Makes Domestic Violence Legislation More Effective?" Pathways Policy Brief. http://www.ids.ac.uk/publication/what-makes-domestic-violence-legislation-more-effective.

———. 2015. "Brazilian Feminisms in Global Spaces: Beijing and Beijing+20." IDS Bulletin , v.46, p.115–122.

Sardenberg, Cecilia M. B., and Ana Alice Alcantara Costa. 1994. "Feminismos, feministas e movimentos sociais." In *Mulher e Relações de Gênero*, edited by M. Brandão and M. Clara Binghemer, 81–114. São Paulo: Ed. Loyola.

———. 2014. "Feminisms in Brazil: Voicing and Channeling Women's Diverse Demands". In: S. NAZNEEN e M. SULTAN (orgs.), *Voicing Demands: Feminist Activism in Transitional Contexts.* 1 ed., London and New York : Zed Books Ltd., p. 56-81.

Sassen, Saskia. 2002. "Finding women's security in the 21st century: A gendered perspective." Panel presentation and discussion organized by the National Council for Research on Women, New York, February 21.

Sater, James M. 2007. "Changing Politics from Below? Women Parliamentarians in Morocco," *Democratization*, 14, no. 4 (August): 723–742.

Sauer, B. 2009. "Headscarf regimes in Europe: diversity policies at the intersection of gender, culture and religion." *Comparative European Politics* 7, no 1: 75–94.

Saunders, C., Silke Roth and C. Olcese. 2015. "Anti-Cuts Protests in the UK: Are We Really All in This Together?" in *Austerity and Protest: Citizens' Reactions to the Economic Crisis and Policy.* Ed. M. Giugni and M. Grasso, 171–190. Ashgate: Routledge.

Savelis, Peter M. 2007. "How new is Bachelet's Chile?" *Current History* 106.

Schatral, Susanne. 2007. "Stop violence: Framing strategies of Russian women's NGOs." In *Movements, migrants, marginalisation: Challenges of societal and political participation in Eastern Europe and the enlarged EU,* edited by Sabine Fischer, Heiko Pleines, and Hans-Henning Schroder, 43–56. Stuttgart: Ibidem-Verlag.

Schevchenko, Iulia. 2002. "Who cares about women's problems? Female legislators in the 1995 and 1999 Russian state Dumas." *Europe-Asia Studies* 54, no. 8: 1201–1222.

Schild, Verónica. 1998. "New subjects of rights? Women's movements and the construction of citizenship in the 'new democracies.'" In *Cultures of Politics/Politics of Cultures: Revisioning Latin American Social Movements,* edited by Sonia E. Alvarez, Evelina Dagnino, and Arturo Escobar, 93–117. Boulder: Westview Press.

Schulz, Helena Lindholm. 1999. *The Reconstruction of Palestinian Nationalism: Between Revolution And Statehood.* Manchester: Manchester University Press.

Scruby, Celia. 2014. "14 new shelters to aid vicitms of Chile's domestic abuse pandemic." *Santiago Times.*

Second and Third Alternative Report on CEDAW. 2006. Delhi: National Alliance of Women.

Sedghi, Hamideh. 2007. *Women and Politics in Iran: Veiling, Unveiling, and Reveiling.* New York: Cambridge University Press.

Seidman, Steven. 2005. "From Outsider to Citizen." In *Regulating Sex: The Politics of Intimacy and Identity,* edited by Elizabeth Bernstein and Laurie Schaffner, 225–243. New York and London: Routledge.

Sengupta, Somini. 2015. "U.N. Meeting on Women's Rights Brings More Discord for U.S. and China." *New York Times,* September 27, 2015, p. A8.

Shaheed, Farida, and Neelum Hussain. 2007. *Interrogating the Norms: Women Challenging Violence in an Adversarial State.* Colombo: ICES.

Shaheed, Farida, and Aisha L. F. Shaheed. 2005. *Great Ancestors—Women Asserting Rights in Muslim Contexts: A Book of Narratives.* Lahore: Shirkat Gah.

Shahla Zia. 1998. "Some Experiences of the Women's Movement: Strategies for Success," in Farida Shaheed *et al, Shaping Women's Lives.* Shirkat Gah. Lahore. 1998. pp. 371-414.

Shalabi, Yasser. 2001. "Al-ta'thirat al-dawleya 'ala tahdid ro'aa al-monathmat ghayr al-hokomeyya al-felastineyya wa-adwareha" [International and local impacts on the visions and roles of Palestinian NGOs]. Master's thesis, Birzeit University.

Shane III, Leo. 2015. "Military Sexual Assault Reform Plan Fails Again." *Military Times.*

Shekarloo, Mahsa. 2005. "Iranian women take on the constitution." Middle East Report Online, July 21. http://middleeastdesk.org/article.php?id=208.

Shojaee, Mansoureh. 2009. "The history of International Women's Day in Iran." March. http:// www.feministschool.com/english/spip.php?article253.

Siddiqui, S. 2011. "Sultana's Nightmare," *Forum: The Daily Star Monthly Magazine,* March 8, page 3.

Silva, Jennifer M. 2015. *Coming Up Short: Working-Class Adulthood in an Age of Uncertainty.* New York: Oxford University Press.

Sinelnikov, Andrei. 1998. "Russia: Inside the broken cell." Family Violence Prevention Fund. http://www.fvpf.org/global/gf_russia.html.

Skalli, Loubna. 2006. "Communicating Gender in the Public Sphere: Women and Information Technologies in the MENA Region." *Journal of Middle East Women's Studies* 2, no. 2 (Spring): 35–59.

Slaughter, Anne-Marie. 2015. *Unfinished Business: Women Men Work Family.* New York: Random House.

Smith, Lois M., and Alfred Padula. 1996. *Sex and revolution: Women in socialist Cuba.* Oxford: Oxford University Press.

Smythe D. 2015. *Rape Unresolved: Policing Sexual Offenses in South Africa.* Cape Town: UCT Press.

Soares, Gilberta, and Cecilia Sardenberg. 2008. "Campaigning for the right to legal and safe abortions in Brazil." *IDS Bulletin* 39, no. 3 (July): 55–61.

Soares, Vera, Ana Alice Costa, Cristina Buarque, Denise Dora, and Wania Sant'Anna. 1995. "Brazilian feminisms and women's movements: A two-way street." In *The Challenge of Local Feminisms: Women's Movements in Global Perspective*, edited by Amrita Basu. Boulder: Westview Press.

Sonnefeld, Nadia and Monica Lindbekk (eds.). Forthcoming. *Women Judges in the Muslim World: A Comparative Study of Discourse and Practice.*

Sopronenko, Igor. 2008. *Twenty Years Forward? The Contents and Discontents of Modern Russian Feminism.* Film produced by Beth Holmgren. Signature Media Productions LLC.

Sperling, Valerie. 1999. *Organizing Women in Contemporary Russia: Engendering transition.* Cambridge: Cambridge University Press.

———. 2015. *Sex, Politics, and Putin: Political Legitimacy in Russia.* New York: Oxford University Press.

Spink, K. 1991. *Black Sash: Beginning of a Bridge in South Africa.* London: Macmillan.

SPM. 2008. *II Plano Nacional de Políticas para as Mulheres.* Brasilia: Governo do Brasil, Secretaria Especial de Políticas para mulheres.

Springer, Kimberly. 2002. "Third Wave Black Feminism?" *Signs* 27, no. 4. University of Chicago Press: 1059–82.

———. 2005. *Living for the revolution: Black feminist organizations, 1968–1980.* Durham: Duke University Press.

Sriskandarajah, Dhananjayan. 2015. "Five Reasons Donors Give For Not Funding Local NGOs Directly," *The Guardian*, November 9. http://www.theguardian.com /global-development-professionals-network/2015/nov/09/five-reasons-donors-give -for-not-funding-local-ngos-directly.

St. Petersburg Egida. 2015. "O Nas [About Us]." Petersburg Egida. Retrieved from http://spb-egida.ru/pages/about.

Staggenborg, Suzanne and Verta Taylor, 2005. "Whatever Happened to The Women's Movement?" *Mobilization: An International Quarterly* 10, no. 1 (February): 37–52.

Stacey, Judith. 1990. *Sexism by a Subtler Name? Postindustrial Conditions and Post-feminist Consciousness in Silicon Valley.* In *Women, Class, and the Feminist Imagination: A Socialist-feminist Reader*, edited by Karen V. Hansen and Ilene J. Philipson. Philadelphia: Temple University Press.

Stammers, Neil. 1991. "Social Movements and the Social Construction of Human Rights." *Human Rights Quarterly* 21, no. 4.

Stein, Arlene. 2013. "What's the Matter with Newark? Race, Class, Marriage Politics, and the Limits of Queer Liberalism," in *The Marrying Kind? Debating Same-Sex Marriage within the Lesbian and Gay Movement*, edited by Mary Bernstein and Verta Taylor, 39–66. Minneapolis: University of Minnesota Press.

Stella, Francesca. *Lesbian Lives in Soviet and Post-Soviet Russia: Post/socialism and gendered sexualities.* Palgrave Macmillan, 2014.

Sternbach, Nancy S., Marysa Navarro-Aranguren, Patricia Chuchryk, and Sonia E. Alvarez. 1992. "Feminisms in Latin America: From Bogota to San Bernardo." *Signs* 17, no. 2: 393–434.

Stetson, Dorothy McBride, and Amy Mazur, eds. 1995. *Comparative state feminism.* Thousand Oaks, CA: Sage.

Stickley, Andrew, Irina Timofeeva, and Par Spären. 2008. "Risk factors for intimate partner violence against women in St. Petersburg, Russia." *Violence Against Women* 14, no. 4.

Sugimoto, L. 2005. "Uma Mulher Morre a Cada Três Minutos." *Jornal da Unicamp* (Salda de Imprensa) 305 (October 10–17). http://www.unicamp.br/unicamp/unicamp _hoje/ju/outubro2005/ ju305pag04html.

Sundstrom, Lisa McIntosh. 2001. "Strength from without? Transnational actors and NGO development in Russia." Ph.D. diss., Stanford University.

———. 2003. "Limits to global civil society: Gaps between Western donors and Russian NGOs." In *Global Civil Society and Its Limits,* edited by Gordon Laxer and Sandra Halperin, 146–165. London: Palgrave.

———. 2006. *Funding Civil Society: Foreign assistance and NGO development in Russia.* Stanford: Stanford University Press.

Sundstrom, Lisa McIntosh and Valerie Sperling. 2014. "Are Women's Rights Human Rights? Gender Discrimination Cases and the European Court of Human Rights in Russia." Paper presented at the Association for Slavic, East European, and Eurasian Studies (ASEEES) Convention, San Antonio, TX, November 21.

Supreme Court of the Russian Federation. 2014. "Osnovnye Statisticheskie Pokazateli Deiatel'nosti Sudov Obshchei Iurisdiktsii Za 2014 G." [Basic Statistics on the Activities of Courts of General Jurisdiction for 2014]. Judicial Department.

Tabari, Azar, and Nahid Yeganeh, eds. 1982. *In the Shadow of Islam: The Women's Movement in Iran.* London: Zed Books.

Tabbush, Constanza. 2010. "Latin American Women's Protection after Adjustment: A Feminist Critique of Conditional Cash Transfers in Chile and Argentina." *Oxford Development Studies* 38, no. 4: 437–459.

Tabbush, Constanza, Ma. Constanza Díaz, Catalina Trebisacce and Victoria Keller. 2016. "Trayectorias discontinues: Incidenia de los movimientos feministas y LGBTTI en las reformas legislativas argentinas." Paper prepared for the 2016 Latin American Studies Association Meeting, New York, NY.

TAC. 2007a. *Annual report, 2006/2007.* Cape Town: TAC.

———. 2007b. "Poor PMCT program: ALP letter on behalf of TAC to minister of health." October 1. http://www.tac.org.za/xommunity/node/2136.

———. n.d. "About TAC." http://www.tac.org.za.

Tahmasebi, Sussan. 2008. "Answers to your most frequently asked questions about the campaign." February 24. http://www.changeforequality.info/english/spip.php?article226.

Tarrow, Sidney. 2006. *The New Transnational Activism.* Cambridge, Cambridge University Press.

Tatur, M. 1992. "Why is there no women's movement in Eastern Europe?" in *Democracy and Civil Society in Eastern Europe.* Ed. P. G. Lewis. Basingstoke: Palgrave.

Tavassoli, Nahid. 1382/2003. "Nov-garayi dini va zan" [Modernist religiosity and woman]. In *Chera khawb-e zan chap ast?,* Nahid Tavassoli. Tehran: Nashr Qatreh.

Tchaicha, Jane D. and Khedija Arfaoui. 2011. "Tunisian Women in the Twenty-first Century: Past Achievements and Present Uncertainties in the Wake of the Jasmine Revolution." *The Journal of North African Studies.*

Temkina, Anna A., and Anna Rotkirkh. 2002. "Sovetskie Gendernye Kontrakty I Ikh Transformatsia v Sovremennoi Rossii [Soviet Gender Contracts and Their Transformation in Contemporary Russia]." *Teoreticheskie Problemy,* No. 11: 4–15.

Terretta, Meredith. 2007. "A Miscarriage of Nation: Cameroonian Women and Revolution, 1949–1971." *Stichproben: Vienna Journal of African Studies* 12. Special issue on Fracturing Binarisms: Gender and Colonialisms in Africa: 61-90.

Thayer, Millie. 2001. "Transnational feminism: Reading Joan Scott in the Brazilian Sertão." *Ethnography* 2, no. 2: 243–271.

"The Beijing Declaration and Platform for Action Turns 20." 2015. UN Women, New York, March. Report of the Secretary-General on the 20-year review and appraisal of the implementation of the Beijing Declaration and Platform for Action and the outcomes of the twenty-third special session of the General Assembly (E/CN.6/2015/3).

"The Impact of Spanish Norm Diffusion on Marriage Equality in Argentina." *Latin American Politics and Society* 54, no. 4: 29–59.

Thomas, Gwynn. 2015. "Reform or Transformation? Assessing the State of Gender and Sexuality Rights in Chile." Paper prepared for the 2015 Latin American Studies Association Meeting, San Juan, Puerto Rico.

Thorin, Emilia. 2015. *The Feminist Spring?: A Narrative Analysis of the Media Discourse of the Swedish Party Feminist Initiative.* Masters, Lund University. https://lup.lub.lu.se/student-papers/search/publication/8053272

Tilly, Charles. 1995. *Popular Contention in Britain, 1758–1834.* Cambridge: Harvard University Press.

Tohidi, Nayereh. 1991. "Gender and Islamic fundamentalism: Feminist politics in Iran." In *Third world women and the politics of feminism*, edited by Chandra Mohanty, Ann Russo, and Lourdes Torres. Bloomington: Indiana University Press.

———. 1995. "The Fourth World Conference of Women in Beijing and the Iranian delegation." *Zanan* (Tehran), no. 25 (September).

———. 1996. "'Fundamentalist' backlash and Muslim women in the Beijing conference." *Canadian Women Studies* 16 (Summer): 3.

———. 2002a. "The international connections of the women's movement in Iran, 1979–2000." In *Iran and the surrounding world: Interaction in culture and cultural politics*, edited by Nikki Keddie and Rudi Matthee, 205–231. Seattle: University of Washington Press.

———. 2003a. "Islamic Feminism: Perils and Promises," in *Middle Eastern Women on the Move*: 134–146. Washington: Woodrow Wilson International Center for Scholars. https://www.academia.edu/359702/_ISLAMIC_FEMINISM_PERILS_AND_PROMISES.

———. 2003b. "Women's rights in the Muslim world: The universal-particular interplay." *Hawwa Journal on Women in the Middle East and Islamic World* 1, no. 2: 152–188.

———. 2004a. "Zanan Magazine." In *Encyclopedia of the modern Middle East and North Africa*, edited by Philip Matter, 4: 2423–2424. 2nd ed. Detroit: Macmillan Reference USA.

———. 2005. "Revolution? What's in it for them? Globalized Iranian American women are nudging their homeland toward democracy." In *The Los Angeles Times* (July 31): http://www.latimes.com/news/opinion/sunday/commentary/la-op-iranwomen 31jul31,0,7192154.story?coll=la-home-sunday-opinion

———. 2006. "'Islamic feminism': Women negotiating modernity and patriarchy in Iran." In *The Blackwell Companion of Contemporary Islamic Thought*, edited by Ibrahim Abu-Rabi, 624–643. Oxford: Blackwell.

———. 2007b. "The women's movement in Iran facing a double blackmail" [Grogan-giri-ye doganeh harekat-e zanan]. August 6. http://www.roozonline.com/archives/2007/08/006680.php.

———. 2008a. "Iran's women's rights activists are being smeared." September 17. http://www.womensenews.org/article.cfm/dyn/aid/3743. Reprinted in http://www .femschool.org/english/ spip.php?article149.

———. 2008b. "Ta'amol mahali-jahani feminism dar jonbesh-e zanan-e Iran" [The local-global intersection of feminism in the women's movement in Iran]. http://feminist schl.net/spip.php ?article1660.

———. 2009. "Women and the presidential elections: Iran's new political culture." http://www.juancole.com/2009/09/tohidi-women-and-presidential-elections .html.

———.2010a. "The Women's Movement and Feminism in Iran: A Glocal Perspective." In Amrita Basu (Ed.), *Women's Movements in the Global Era* (375-414). Boulder, CO: Westview Press.

———. 2010b. "A Critical Assessment of Iranian Women's Movement in the Context of the Green Movement for Democracy," in *Jonbesh Zanan: Tahavolat siyasi ve mobarezat-e domkratik, 2010* [The Women's Movement: Political Developments and Democratic Struggles], edited by Golnaz Amin, Iranian Women's Studies Foundation (Proceedings of the 21st Annual Conference of the IWSF, Paris, July 2010). https://www.facebook.com/note.php?note_id=10150315806087356.

———. 2013. "Iran: A Small Window of Hope," In *OpenDemocracy*, July 1. https:// www.opendemocracy.net/author/nayereh-tohidi.

Toor, Sadia. 1997. "The State Fundamentalism and Civil Society." In *Engendering the Nation-state,* edited by Neelum Hussain, Samiya Mumtaz, and Rubina Saigol. Vol. 1. Lahore: Simorgh.

Trading Economics. n.d. "GINI Index in South Africa." http://www.tradingeconomics. com/south-africa/gini-index-wb-data.html.

Tripp, Aili Mari. 2000. *Women and Politics in Uganda.* Madison: University of Wisconsin Press. Oxford: James Currey and Kampala: Fountain Publishers.

———. 2006. "The Evolution of Transnational Feminisms." In *Global Feminism: Transnational Women's Activism, Organizing, and Human Rights,* 51–75. New York: New York University Press.

———. 2015. *Women and Power in Postconflict Africa.* New York: Cambridge University Press.

Tsang, Amie. 2013. "Women of the World's Central Banks." *Financial Times*, October 19.

Tsentr sotsial'no-trudovykh prav (Center for Social Labor Rights). n.d. "Glavnaia [Main Page]." Center for Social Labor Rights.

Tsentr sotsial'no-trudovykh prav. 2011. "Young Mothers of Moscow Fight for Allowance" ['Molodye mamy Moskvy boriutsia za posobiia']. October 4. http://trudprava. ru/news/gendernews/813.

Tsikata, Edzodzinam. 1989. "Women's Political Organisations 1951–1987." In *The State, Development and Politics in Ghana,* edited by Emmanuel Hanson and Kwame Ninsin. Oxford: African Books Collective.

Tsutsui, Kiyoteru. 2006. "Redressing past human rights violations: Global dimensions of contemporary social movements." *Social Forces* 85, no. 1 (September).

"Tunisie législatives 2014: Liste des femmes élues." 2014.

"UN Women Summary Report: The Beijing Declaration and Platform for Action turns 20." 2015. Publishing Entities: United Nations Entity for Gender Equality and the Empowerment of Women (UN Women). http://www.unwomen.org/en/digital -library/publications/2015/02/beijing-synthesis-report#sthash.hUy3273p.dpuf.

Usher, Graham. 1997. "What kind of nation? The rise of Hamas in the Occupied Territories." In *Political Islam: Essays from Middle East report,* edited by Joel Beinin and Joe Stork. Berkeley and Los Angeles: University of California Press.

UNTC. 2016. *Treaties.Un.Org.*

United States. 2016. *Guttmacher Institute.*

Vahdati, Soheila. 2007. "Stop Stoning in Iran, But Don't Confuse the Issue." *Women's eNews* .http://womensenews.org/2007/01/stop-stonings-iran-dont-confuse-the-issue/

Vaid, et al. 2013. "What's Next for the LGBT Movement?" *The Nation.* June 27. https://www.thenation.com/article/whats-next-lgbt-movement/.

Valiente, C. 2003. "The Feminist Movement and the Reconfigured State in Spain (1970s–2000)," in *Women's Movements Facing the Reconfigured State,* Ed. L. A. Banaszak, K. Beckwith and D. Rucht, 30–47.Cambridge: Cambridge University Press.

———. 2008. "Spain at the Vanguard in European Gender Equality Policies," in *Gender Politics in the Expanding European Union. Mobilization, Inclusion, Exclusion.* Ed. Silke Roth, 101–117. Oxford/New York: Berghahn Books: 101–117.

———. 2015. "Age and Feminist Activism: The Feminist Protest Within the Catholic Church in Franco's Spain." *Social Movement Studies* 14, no.4: 473–492.

Van Allen, Judith. 1976. "'Aba Riots' or Igbo Women's War? Ideology, Stratification and the Invisibility of Women." In *Women in Africa: Studies in Social and Economic Change,* edited by Nancy Hafkin Hafkin and Edna Bay. Stanford, California: Stanford University Press.

———. "'Sitting on a Man': Colonialism and the Lost Political Institutions of Igbo Women." *Canadian Journal of African Studies* 6, no. 2 (1972): 165–82.

Vannoy, Dana, Natalia Rimashevskaya, Lisa Cubbins, Marina Malysheva, Elena Meshterkina, and Marina Pisklakova. 1999. *Marriages in Russia: Couples during the economic transition.* Westport, CT: Praeger.

Vargas, Virginia. 1992. "The feminist movement in Latin America: Between hope and disenchantment." *Development and Change* 23, no. 3: 195–214.

———. 2003. "Feminism, globalization, and the global justice and solidarity movement." *Cultural Studies* 17, no. 6: 905–920.

Vasmaghi, Sedigheh. 2015. *Hatman Rahi Hast (There Must be a Way).* Germany: Khavaran Publishing Inc. http://www.makaremi.com/khabr-moearfi-ketab-vasmaghi-fa/.

Villarroel, Gratzia. 2011. "Bolivian Women." *ReVista: Harvard Review of Latin America.* http://revista.drclas.harvard.edu/book/bolivian-women (Accessed April 12, 2016).

Villela, Wilza Vieira. 2001. "Expanding women's access to abortion: The Brazilian experience." In *Advocating for abortion access: Eleven country studies,* edited by B. Klugman and D. Budlender, 87–108. Johannesburg: University of Witwatersrand.

Volga, Vasanth Kannabiran, and Kalpana Kannabiran. 2001. *Mahilavaranam/Womanscape.* Secunderabad, India: Asmita.

———. 2005a. "Peace and irresponsibility." *Economic and Political Weekly,* March 26, 1310–1312.

———. 2005b. "Reflections on the peace process in Andhra Pradesh." *Economic and Political Weekly,* February 12, 610–612.

Wahl, A. v. 2008. "The EU and Enlargement: Conceptualizing Beyond 'East' and West," in *Gender Politics in the Expanding European Union: Mobilization, Inclusion , Exclusion.* Ed. Silke Roth, 19–36. Oxford/New York:Berghahn Books.

Waites, M. 2009. "Lesbian, Gay and Bisexual NGOs in Britain: Past, Present and Future," in *NGOs in Contemporary Britain. Non-state Actors in Society and Politics Since 1945.* Ed. N. Crowson, M. Hilton and J. McKay. Basingstoke, Palgrave Macmillan: 95–112.

Walby, Sylvia. 2004. "The European Union and Gender Equality: Emergent Varieties of Gender Regime." Social Politics: International Studies in Gender, State & Society 11(1): 4-29.

Wang, Vibeke. 2013. "Women's Substantive Representation in Uganda's Legislature." University of Bergen.

Wang Zheng. 1999. *Women in the Chinese Enlightenment: Oral and Textual Histories*. Berkeley: University of California Press.

———. 2016. *Finding Women in the State: A Socialist Feminist Revolution in the People's Republic of China, 1949–1964*. Berkeley: University of California Press.

Wang Zheng and Ying Zhang, "Global Concepts, Local Practices: Chinese Feminism since the Fourth UN Conference on Women," *Feminist Studies*, Vol. 36, Nov. 1, Spring 2010, pp. 40–79.

Waters, Elizabeth. 1993. "The emergence of a women's movement." In *Gender politics and post-communism: Reflections from Eastern Europe and the former Soviet Union,* edited by Nanette Funk and Carol McClurg Mueller, 287–302. New York: Routledge.

Waters, Elizabeth, and Anastasia Posadskaya. 1995. "Democracy without women is no democracy: Women's struggles in post-communist Russia." In *The challenge of local feminisms: Women's movements in global perspective*, edited by Amrita Basu. Boulder: Westview Press.

Watson, Joy. 2014. "The Cost of Justice in South Africa – Tracking Expenditure on Gender Base Violence in the Department of Justice and Constitutional Development," Parliament of the RSA, Research Unit.

WAVE (2016). Women Against Violence Europe. https://www.wave-network.org last accessed September 22, 2016.

Waylen, Georgina. 1994. "Women and democratization: Conceptualizing gender relations in transition politics." *World Politics* 46, no. 3: 327–354.

———. 1996. *Gender in third world politics*. Buckingham: Open University Press.

Weldon, Laural and Mala Htun. 2012. "The Civic Origins of Progressive Policy Change: Combating Violence against Women in Global Perspectives 1975-2005," American Political Science Review, 106, no. 3 (August 2012).

White House, 2015. *Gender Pay Gap: Recent Trends And Explanations*. Council of Economic Advisers Issue Brief.

White, Jenny. 2002. *Islamist mobilisation in Turkey: A study in vernacular politics*. Seattle: University of Washington Press.

Whittier, Nancy. 2011. *The Politics of Child Sexual Abuse: Emotion, Social Movements and the State*. New York: Oxford University Press.

WIDE (2016). WIDE+ and EWL International Conference "Women, Borders Rights? Feminist perspectives on global issues in Europe" 24-25 October, 2016, Brussels. http://wideplus.org accessed September 22, 2016.

Williams, Joan. 2010. *Reshaping the Work-Family Debate: Why Men and Class Matter* Cambridge, MA: Harvard University Press.

Wilson, Ara. 2007. "Feminism in the Space of the World Social Forum," *Journal of International Women's Studies*, Volume 8, Issue 3, April.

Wilson, F. and M. Ramphele. 1989. *Uprooting Poverty: The South African Challenge*. Cape Town: David Philip.

Wipper, Audrey. 1975. "The Maendeleo ya Wanawake Movement: Some Paradoxes and Contradictions." *African Studies Review* 18, no. 3: 99–120.

WLP. 2011. "News from May 2011 Rabat Convening on Women and the Political Transitions in the MENA Region, and a Call for Action". May 25. http://www.learning

partnership.org/lib/news-may-2011-rabat-convening-women-and-political-transitions-mena-region-and-call-action.

WLP. 2014. "Press Release" Morocco's Springtime for Dignity Coalition Decries Prime Minister's Speech on women's 'Role'" June 25.

Wolpe, H. 1972. "Capitalism and Cheap Labour Power in South Africa: From Segregation to Apartheid" in *Economy and Society* 1 (4) 1972.

Women's Budget Group. 2015. "The impact of women of July budget 2015. A budget that undermines women's security." from http://wbg.org.uk/wp-content/uploads/2015/04/July-budget-briefing-2015-WBG.pdf.

"Women In Parliaments: World Classification." 2016. *Ipu.Org.* http://www.ipu.org/wmn-e/classif.htm.

Women's Coalition. 2001. *The Women's Charter: Shortened version.* Harare: Bardwell.

Women Living Under Muslim Laws. 2015. "Iran's Women's Affairs Chief Feels Powerless to Act": http://www.wluml.org/news/irans-womens-affairs-chief-feels-powerless-act

Woodward, Alison E., Mercè Renom, Jean-Michel Bonvin. eds. 2013.*Transforming Gendered Well-Being in Europe: The Impact of Social Movements.* Ashgate Publishing, Ltd.

Working conditions of women working as dancers in dance bars, a study conducted by Research Center for Women's Studies, SNDT Women's University, and Forum against Oppression of Women (FAOW), Mumbai 2005.

World Bank. 2014. "Adolescent Fertility Rate." http://data.worldbank.org/indicator/SP.ADO.TFRT (Accessed April 15, 2016).

World Economic Forum. 2014. "Global Gender Gap Report, 2014."

World Economic Forum, 2015. "Global Gender Gap Report, 2015."

World Values Survey. (2011). *World Values Survey Wave 6 (2010-2014) Results.* Retrieved from http://www.worldvaluessurvey.org/WVSDocumentationWV6.jsp.

"Women in Parliaments: World Classification". 2016.

Xi Jinping. 2013. "Jianchi nannü pingdeng jiben guoce, fahui woguo funü weida zuoyong" [Upholding the fundamental state policy of equality between men and women, exerting women's great role in our country], Xinhua net, October 31. http://news.xinhuanet.com/politics/2013-10/31/c_117956150.htm.

Xin Zhongguo liushinian jiaoyu chengjiu zhan [A display of the accomplishments of education in the sixty-years of the new China]. http://www.stats.edu.cn/.

Xing Zheng. 2015. "Geti siying jinji cheng xina jiuye 'xushuichi'" [Private enterprises have become the "reservoir" for absorbing labor]. http://www.saic.gov.cn/ywdt/gsyw/mtjj/201510/t20151029_163348.html.

Yeatman, Anna. 1990. *Bureaucrats, technocrats, femocrats: Essays on the contemporary Australian state.* Sydney: Allen and Unwin.

Za svobodnoe materinstvo. n.d. *About the campaign (O kampanii).* Retrieved from https://sites.google.com/site/protivabortov2011/.

Zabelina, Tatiana. 2002. *Rossiia: Nasilie v sem'e—nasilie v obshchestve* [Russia: Violence in the family—violence in society]. Moscow: UNIFEM, UNFPA.

Zeyyad [Islamic Khalas Party]. 2000. Interview with Islah Jad, Gaza, October 3.

Zetkin, Klara. 1934. *Lenin on the woman question.* New York: International Publishers.

Zhang Lin and Cai Yunqi. 2012. "Guanzhu daxuesheng xingbiebi: dushu nüsheng youxiu gongzuo nan lingdao duo" [Pay attention to the sex ratio of college students: more excellent female students in school but more male leaders in work place], September 12, *Yangzi wanbao* (Yangzi Evening News).

Zhang, Naihua and Ping-Chun Hsiung. 2010. "The Chinese Women's Movement in the Context of Globalization," in *Women's Movements in the Global Era: the Power of Local Feminisms*, edited by Amrita Basu, Boulder: Westview Press, pp. 157–192.

Zheng, Yefu. 1994. "Nannü pingdeng de shehuixue sikao" [Sociological thinking on equality between men and women], *Shehuixue yanjiu (Sociological Studies)* 2 (1994), 110.

Zhongguo renquan nianjian [The annals of human rights in China]. 2007. Edited by the Association of Human Rights in China, Beijing: Tuanjie chubanshe.

———. 2009b. "The Reinvention of Feminism in Pakistan," *Feminist Review*, South Asian Feminisms: Negotiating New Terrains, No. 91: 29–46

Zippel, K. 2008. "Violence at Work? Framing Sexual Harassment in the European Union," in *Gender Politics in the Expanding European Union. Mobilization, Inclusion, Exclusion,* Ed. Silke Roth, 60–80, Oxford/New York: Berghahn Books.

Zychowicz, Jessica. 2011. "Two Bad Words: FEMEN & Feminism in Independent Ukraine." *Anthropology of East Europe Review* 29, no.2: 215–27.

About the Contributors

Amrita Basu is the Paino Professor of Political Science and Sexuality, Women's and Gender Studies at Amherst College. She is the author of *Two Faces of Protest: Contrasting Modes of Women's Activism in India* and *Violent Conjunctures in Democratic India*. She is the editor or coeditor of *Appropriating Gender: Women's Activism and Politicized Religion in South Asia, Beyond Exceptionalism: Violence and Democracy in India, The Challenge of Local Feminisms: Women's Movements in Global Perspective, Community Conflicts and the State in India*, and *Localizing Knowledge in a Globalizing World*. She has received research awards from the National Endowment for the Humanities, Social Science Research Council, John D. and Catherine T. MacArthur Foundation, and American Institute of Indian Studies.

Ana Alice A. Costa held a Ph.D. in Political Sociology from UNAM, the Autonomous University of Mexico, in Mexico City. She was active in the Brazilian and Mexican feminist movements beginning in the late 1970s. A member of the Faculty of Philosophy and Human Sciences of the Federal University of Bahia (UFBA) in Salvador, Bahia, Brazil, since 1982, she was one of the founders of UFBA's Nucleus of Interdisciplinary Studies on Women (NEIM/UFBA), and director from 1999 to 2004. She was coordinator of the M.A. and Ph.D. Programs on Interdisciplinary Studies on Women, Gender, and Feminism at NEIM/UFBA. She published several articles and books on feminist studies in Brazil. Ana Alice passed away in December 2014, and is deeply missed by her family, friends, colleagues, and students. She has been honored with a Congressional Medal for her achievements as a scholar and as a feminist activist.

Elisabeth Jay Friedman is Chair and Professor of Politics and Professor of Latin American Studies at the University of San Francisco (USF). She is also a coordinator of the USF Global Women's Rights Forum. Her books include *Unfinished Transitions: Women and the Gendered Development of Democracy in Venezuela, 1936–1996* (Penn State Press, 2000) *and Interpreting the Internet: Feminist and Queer Counterpublics in Latin America* (UC Press, forthcoming). She has published articles on women's organizing in Latin America and globally in the *International Feminist Journal of Politics*; *Latin American Politics & Society*; *Signs*; *Politics & Gender*; and *Women's Studies International Quarterly*. Her current research focuses on the impact of the Latin American left on women's and LGBT rights and movements.

Islah Jad (Hossneya Gad) has been an associate professor at the International Affairs Department of Qatar University since 2014. Jad is a lecturer on gender issues and politics at the Women's Studies Institute and Cultural Studies Institute of Birzeit University, where she was the director from 2008-2013. She is a founding member of Birzeit University's women's studies MA program. She has written books and papers on the role of women in politics, Palestinian women and the relationships among them, Islam, and NGOs. Dr. Jad is also a consultant on gender issues for the United Nations Development Programme and is co-author of the UN's Arab Development Report on Women's Empowerment and author of two books. Dr. Jad received her Ph.D. from the School of Oriental and African Studies in London in 2004.

Valentine M. Moghadam is Professor of Sociology and Director of the International Affairs Program at Northeastern University, Boston. Born in Tehran, Iran, Professor Moghadam received her higher education in Canada and the U.S. Her areas of research include globalization, transnational social movements and feminist networks, economic citizenship, and gender and development in the Middle East and North Africa. Among her many publications, Professor Moghadam is author of *Modernizing Women: Gender and Social Change in the Middle East* (first published 1993; second edition 2003; revised and updated third edition Fall 2013); *Globalizing Women: Transnational Feminist Networks* (2005), which won the American Political Science Association's Victoria Schuck award for best book on women and politics for 2005; and *Globalization and Social Movements: Islamism, Feminism, and the Global Justice Movement* (2009, 2013). She has edited seven books, including *Making Globalization Work for Women: The Role of Social Rights and Trade Union Leadership* (2011, with Suzanne Franzway and Mary Margaret Fonow). A co-authored paper with Professor Massoud Karshenas is "Social Policy after the Arab Spring: States and Social Rights in the Middle East and North Africa," published in Fall 2014 in *World Development*.

Poulomi Pal is currently a Fulbright-Nehru post-doctoral researcher affiliated with Amherst College. Her research analyzes models of one-stop crisis centers for survivors of gender-based violence in the U.S., which are currently being proposed as a national policy in India. Previously she worked with Canada's International Development Research Centre as program and research advisor at their Asia Regional Office in New Delhi. She earned her PhD in political science from Jawaharlal Nehru University in Delhi in 2010. Over the years she has worked on gender rights and gender-based violence with the Centre for Women's Development Studies; Women's Studies Centre, Jawaharlal Nehru University; Partners for Law in Development; WomenPower-

Connect; Programme on Women's Economic, Social, Cultural Rights; UN Women India, Bhutan, Maldives, and Sri Lanka; and the Ministry of Women and Child Development, Government of India.

Benita Roth is a professor of sociology, history, and women's studies at Binghamton University. She is the author of *Separate Roads to Feminism: Black, Chicana, and White Feminist Movements in America's Second Wave* (Cambridge University Press 2004), which won the American Sociological Association's Sex and Gender Section's "Distinguished Book Award." Her second book, *The Life and Death of ACT UP/LA: Anti-AIDS Activism in Los Angeles from the 1980s to the 2000s*, also with Cambridge, is in press. She has been an associate editor on *The Journal of Women's History*, where she co-edited a special issue on "Human Rights, Global Congresses, and the Making of Postwar Transnational Feminisms" (24:4, December 2012). Her work is linked by her concerns, as an intersectional feminist scholar, with the dynamics of mutually reinforcing inequalities in social protest.

Silke Roth is Associate Professor of Sociology in the Department of Sociology, Social Policy and Criminology at the University of Southampton (UK). Her areas of research include the participation in and the impact of voluntary organizations, social movements, and non-governmental organizations. Her publications include the books *The Paradoxes of Aid Work: Passionate Professionals* (Routledge 2015), *Gender Politics in the Expanding European Union* (Berghahn 2008) and *Building Movement Bridges: The Coalition of Labor Union Women* (Greenwood 2003), journal articles in *Social Politics, Gender & Society, Third World Quarterly, Sociological Research Online*, and the *Journal for Risk Research*, as well as numerous book chapters.

Elaine Salo was associate professor in the Departments of Political Science and International Relations, and Women's and Gender Studies at the University of Delaware. Prior to that she was the director of the Institute for Women's and Gender Studies at the University of Pretoria South Africa. She has been widely published in the fields of gender studies and sexuality. Her recent publications have included *Gender and African Water Policies* (2015) and "Caster Semenya: The ancients would have called her god. The international re-imagining and re-making of sex and the art of silence" in Sandy Montanõla and Aurelie Olivesi's *Gender Testing in Sport: Ethics, Cases and Controversies* (2016).

Cecilia M. B. Sardenberg is a Brazilian feminist who holds a Ph.D. in Anthropology from Boston University. She has been a member of the Faculty of Philosophy and Human Sciences of the Federal University of Bahia (UFBA) in Salvador, Bahia, Brazil, since 1982, and now holds the position of Professor of Anthropology. She was one of the "founding mothers" of UFBA's Nucleus of Interdisciplinary Studies on Women (NEIM/UFBA), and currently teaches feminist theory at the Master's and Ph.D. Programs on Interdisciplinary Studies on Women, Gender, and Feminism at NEIM/UFBA. She has worked in the area of gender and development in Brazil, both as a practitioner and as a researcher, and has published several articles in Brazil and abroad on feminist and gender studies. She is the convener for the Latin American Hub in the Pathways of Women's Empowerment Research Program Consortium.

Farida Shaheed, a sociologist and human rights activist, is the Executive Director of Shirkat Gah–Women's Resource Centre (Lahore, Pakistan) and served as the first Independent Expert and Special Rapporteur in the field of Cultural Rights for the United Nations Human Rights Council (2009–2015). Decades of combining women-focused research, policy advocacy, and grassroots work have led her to focus both her writings and her activism on the complex forces at play in the interface of women, culture, identity, and governance and state in South Asian and Muslim contexts, particularly in Pakistan. She is a founding member of the Women's Action Forum, the platform that led the movement for women's rights during the 1977–1988 military dictatorship of General Zia-ul-Haq. Awards include the Second Annual Award for Women's Human Rights (1997) and the Prime Minister's Award (1989) for her coauthored *book Two Steps Forward, One Step Back? Women of Pakistan*.

Lisa McIntosh Sundstrom is an associate professor of political science at the University of British Columbia who teaches courses in international relations and comparative politics, often with a focus on civil society and nongovernmental organizations. Her regional area of expertise is Russia and the former Soviet Union, and her major research interests include democratization, human rights, women's rights, the politics of international democracy assistance, and NGO activism in both domestic and transnational politics. She is currently working on a book manuscript with Valerie Sperling on gender discrimination cases at the European Court of Human Rights. She has published in scholarly journals including *International Organization, Global Environmental Politics, Communist and Post-Communist Studies, Europe-Asia Studies, Problems of Post-Communism*, and *Human Rights Quarterly*. Her book publications include *Funding Civil Society: Foreign Assistance and NGO Development in Russia* (Stanford University Press, 2006), *Russian Civil Society: A Critical Assessment* (ME Sharpe, 2005, co-edited with Alfred B. Evans, Jr. and Laura A. Henry), and *Global Commons, Domestic Decisions: The Comparative Politics of Climate Change* (MIT Press, 2010, co-edited with Kathryn Harrison).

Nayereh Tohidi is professor and former chair of the Gender & Women Studies Department and the founding and current director of the Middle Eastern and Islamic Studies at California State University, Northridge. She is also a research associate at the Center for Near Eastern Studies at UCLA, where she has been coordinating the Bilingual Lecture Series on Iran since 2003. A native of Iran, Tohidi earned her BS (with Honors) from the University of Tehran in Psychology and Sociology and her MA and Ph.D. from the University of Illinois at Urbana-Champaign. Her teaching and research expertise include gender and development, women's movements, feminism and Islam, and gender and ethnic issues in MENA, with a focus on Iran and the Azerbaijan Republic. She is the recipient of several grants, fellowships, and research awards, and has held visiting positions at Universities of Iowa, Minnesota, Harvard, UCLA, and USC. Her extensive publications include many book chapters, peer-reviewed articles, and the editorship or authorship of three books: *Globalization, Gender and Religion: The Politics of Women's Rights in Catholic and Muslim Contexts*; *Women in Muslim Societies: Diversity within Unity*; and *Feminism, Democracy and Islamism in Iran*. Tohidi has also served as a consultant to the United Nations (UNICEF and UNDP) on projects concerning gender and development, and women and civil society building in the Middle East and post-Soviet Eurasia. She represented women NGOs at both the third and fourth World Conferences on Women in Nairobi and Beijing sponsored by the United Nations.

Aili Mari Tripp is Professor of Political Science and Gender & Women's Studies and Evjue Bascom Professorship in Gender and Women's Studies at the University of Wisconsin-Madison. Tripp's research has focused on women and politics in Africa, women's movements in Africa, transnational feminism, African politics (with particular reference to Uganda and Tanzania), and on the informal economy in Africa. Her most recent book is *Women and Power in Post-Conflict Africa* (2015). She is author of several award-winning books, including *African Women's Movements: Transforming Political Landscapes* (2009) with Isabel Casimiro, Joy Kwesiga, and Alice Mungwa, and *Women and Politics in Uganda* (2000). She has edited *Sub-Saharan Africa: The Greenwood Encyclopedia of Women's Issues Worldwide* (2003), and co-edited (with Myra Marx Ferree and Christina Ewig) *Gender, Violence, and Human Security: Critical Feminist Perspectives* (2013), (with Myra Marx Ferree) *Global Feminism: Transnational Women's Activism* (2006), and (with Joy Kwesiga) *The Women's Movement in Uganda: History, Challenges and Prospects* (2002).

Wang Zheng is professor of women's studies and history and research scientist of the Institute for Research on Women and Gender at the University of Michigan. She is the author of *Finding Women in the State: A Socialist Feminist Revolution in the People's Republic of China, 1949-1964* (2016), and *Women in the Chinese Enlightenment: Oral and Textual Histories* (1999); and co-editor of *From the Soil: The Foundations of Chinese Society, Translating Feminisms in China*, and *Some of Us: Chinese Women Growing Up in the Mao Era*. A long-term academic activist promoting gender studies in China, she is the founder and co-director of the UM-Fudan Joint Institute for Gender Studies at Fudan University, Shanghai. She has authored two books and co-edited nine volumes on feminism and gender studies in Chinese.

Index

sexual violence, 11, 54
  in India, 139–148
  laws against, 28, 61–62, 141, 349
  rates, 28–29
  sexual exploitation during conflict with,
    61–62
  See also rape
sexuality
  female genital mutilation and, 53, 61,
    257–258
  power with control over, 407–408
  Roman Catholic Church and, 20
  sexual and gender identity rights, 293–295
  social media and, 402
  See also gender and sexuality, Latin America
Shagari, Shehu, 40
Shanghai Women's Federation, 163
Sharif, Nawaz, 114
Sherkat, Shahla, 409, 410, 411
Shramik Sangathana, 131
Shukumisa Campaign, 84, 89, 90
Sierra Leone, 46, 52
Sikkink, Kathryn, 312
Skalli, Nouzha, 339, 351
Slaughter, Anne-Marie, 244
"SlutWalks," 151, 300, 315
social class
  associationalism and, 242, 249, 251, 255–256
  dalit or untouchables, 28, 133, 140, 143, 150
  elimination of, 160
  elite, 50, 51, 133, 157, 286, 398, 399
  middle class, 250
  poverty and, 24–25
  US with associational feminist effort based
    on, 249–252
  working class, Brazil, 311
social media, 244
  Arab Spring and, 32
  BLM and, 254–255
  role of, 122, 175, 177, 178, 351, 398, 436
  sexuality and, 402
social welfare, 25, 79–80, 136, 250–251
socialist states
  China with feminist transformative
    practices, 159–167
  Europe, 196
societal changes, post-Islamist reform era
    (1990s–2005)
  activism and, 414–415
  in context, 413–414
  parliamentary elections and feminist
    intervention, 418–421
  political participation, 415–416
  presidential elections and, 413, 416–418
Sociological Studies (academic journal), 164

sodomy laws, 71, 81
Somalia, 45, 48, 58
Sori, Soni, 140
SOS Women in Distress, 338, 344 (table),
  347
Sotoudeh, Nasrin, 433
South Africa (1950–2014), 30, 55
  anti-apartheid (1900–1994), 71–78
  citizenship rights in, 67, 69–70
  in context, 65–68, 90–91
  economy in, 85–86
  with feminism, definitions of, 68–69
  femocrats and gender-sensitive legislation,
    81–87
  gender-based violence and right to physical
    security, 87–90
  politics in, 65, 79–81
  presidential administration in democratic
    era, 79–81
  state femocrats, feminist alliances, and rural
    patriarchs, 78–81
  white nationalism, segregation, and
    apartheid, 69–71
Soviet Union. *See* Russia
Spain, 191, 192, 208
Special Cells initiative, 136–137
Sperling, Valerie, 221
Squires, J., 209
Stacey, Judith, 246–247
Stalin, Joseph, 216
Starovoitova, Galina, 218
state
  Brazil and dialogues with, 307–310
  censorship, 179
  Economic Community of West African
    States, 47
  with economic justice and neo-liberalism,
    25–26
  feminist responses to rise of Islamist,
    406–408
  feminist state-society relations, 282–286
  femocrats, 3, 22–23, 78–81
  in national context, 18
  Pakistan with protests focused on, 100–108
  political representation and, 23–25
  socialist, 159–167, 196
  women's movements and, 21–26
  with world-system and mobilization,
    Maghreb, 335–340
state feminism, 188, 300, 309
  Brazil, 312–314
  China with transformative practices and
    socialist, 159–167
  participatory, 301, 302, 305, 327
  state femocrats and, 3, 22–23, 78–81